A Hero to His Fighting Men

A Hero to His Fighting Men

Nelson A. Miles, 1839–1925

Peter R. DeMontravel

THE KENT STATE UNIVERSITY PRESS
Kent, Ohio, and London, England

Library of Congress Catalog Card Number 97-35947
ISBN 0-87338-594-2
Manufactured in the United States of America

05 04 03 02 01 00 99 98 5 4 3 2 1

LIBRARY OF CONGRESS CATALOGING-IN-PUBLICATION DATA

DeMontravel, Peter R., 1933–
A hero to his fighting men : Nelson A. Miles, 1839–1925 / Peter R. DeMontravel.
p. cm.
Includes bibliographical references (p.) and index.
ISBN 0-87338-594-2 (cloth : alk. paper) ∞
1. Miles, Nelson Appleton, 1839–1925. 2. Generals—United States—Biography. 3. United States. Army—Biography. 4. United States—History, Military—to 1900. I. Title.
E181.M53D45 1998 97-35947
355'.0092—dc21 CIP

British Library Cataloging-in-Publication data are available.

This book is dedicated to my wife,

Barbara,

with all my love.

Contents

Acknowledgments

IT IS WITH PLEASURE that I acknowledge the contributions of a number of people who have helped to make this biography of Nelson A. Miles possible. First and foremost is my wife, Barbara, without whose collaboration this book could not have been written. Dr. John T. Hubbell, director of The Kent State University Press, made a dream come true when he accepted my manuscript for publication. He and Managing Editor Joanna Hildebrand Craig made invaluable suggestions and many corrections when they reviewed and prepared the manuscript for publication. My three adult children—Christine, Peter, and Patricia Alexander, and her husband, Joseph—all encouraged me in my endeavor and excused my absence when, although I was physically present, my mind had wandered back to the nineteenth century. Chris also helped in the search for sources and the preparation of maps and was invaluable in transferring my manuscript onto a computer disk. I am also pleased that my two delightful granddaughters, Danielle and Carolyn Alexander, made me smile during difficult moments. I am particularly indebted to two librarians at the Larchmont Public Library, Larchmont, New York: Jacquelyn Anderson and Priscilla Dibble opened archives around the nation for my use, through interlibrary loans. Librarians at the library at the College of New Rochelle, New York, also were helpful in my search for sources.

At Fordham University's college, Dr. Robert V. Remini, now a professor at the University of Illinois at Chicago, ignited my love of history. At Fordham University's graduate school, the late Father Harry H. Sievers, S. J., directed that enthusiasm toward an appreciation of biography. At St. John's University, Jamaica, New York, Dr. Richard Harmon's guidance sustained me in my quest for a doctoral degree. Special thanks are due to Robert M.

Utley, author of *Frontier Regulars: The United States Army and the Indians, 1866–1890.* In this work he blazed a trail that guided me through the complexities of the Indian Wars. I would also like to thank Harwood P. Hinton and Bruce J. Dinges, formerly editors of *Arizona and the West: A Quarterly Journal of History,* for publishing my first article, "General Nelson A. Miles and the Wounded Knee Controversy." Patricia Knapp, former acquisitions editor of the University of Nebraska Press, encouraged me to continue working on a biography of Miles.

Finally, among the innumerable curators, archivists, and librarians who extended themselves on my behalf and deserve special mention are: at the National Archives, Washington, D.C., Michael Knapp, Mr. William Lind, and Bob Richardson; at the Manuscript Division, Library of Congress, Washington, D.C., James H. Hutson, Fred Bauman, and Jeffrey Flannery; at the U.S. Army Military History Institute, Army War College, Carlisle, Pennsylvania, Michael J. Winey, Richard J. Sommers, and David Keough; at the Westminster Historical Society, Westminster, Massachusetts, Betsy Hannola, Curator; and at the United States Military Academy Library, West Point, Deborah McKeon-Pogue, Technician for Special Collections.

Introduction

As a war between the states loomed over the nation, a group of foresighted Bostonians decided to hire a former French colonel to groom them for anticipated service as army officers. Eventually, upwards of three thousand men took advantage of the military training supervised by the veteran from France. Following the shelling of Fort Sumter, many of the colonel's students went on to win commissions in the army, but only one, a crockery clerk, advanced to the rank of major general of volunteers. After Appomattox, the former clerk, Nelson Appleton Miles, continued to serve the Republic as an army officer.

When Miles elected to remain in the army, he turned his back on the offer of a wealthy uncle who hoped that the young veteran would join him in business. The decision, which offended his childless relative, cost Miles financially; when the uncle died, he left his nephew only "a small sum" from an estate estimated to be well over a million dollars. After Miles spurned his chance at fortune, he earned fleeting fame on the frontier. Today, few realize that, in turn, he defeated dissident bands of Kiowa-Comanches, Sioux, Nez Perces, and renegade Apaches led by Geronimo, and then skillfully managed the Messiah outbreak of 1890. The climax of his career came in 1895 with his appointment as commanding general of the army.

Although the details of Miles's career have become more familiar to us, the present picture that we have of Miles is flawed. The driving ambition, courage, and self-confidence that were responsible for his military successes and advancement also made him a controversial officer. During the Indian Wars, and again in the Spanish-American War, as Miles compiled a flawless record of military feats, he also begot a legion of enemies. Because the judgments of his critics have influenced the way history has viewed Miles, there is reason to reexamine the career of the officer who was appreciated in his day as "the idol of the Indian fighters."[1]

Unfortunately, Miles's two autobiographies, *Personal Recollections and Observations of General Nelson A. Miles* (1896), and *Serving the Republic* (1911), fail to address many of the controversies in which he was embroiled. The first full-length biography of Miles, Virginia Johnson's *The Unregimented General* (1962), is invaluable for unearthing and making public revealing letters written by Miles to his wife, Mary; however, except for the letters, Johnson cast little additional light on Miles's clashes with his colleagues.

As this biography of Miles was being written, a spate of new biographies appeared. *Nelson A. Miles: A Documentary Biography of His Military Career, 1861–1903,* edited by Brian C. Pohanka (1985), proved useful during the final rewrite, as was Robert M. Utley's "Nelson A. Miles," in *Soldiers West: Biographies from the Military Frontier* (1987), edited by Paul Andrew Hutton. Jerome A. Greene's comprehensive *Yellowstone Command: Colonel Nelson A. Miles and the Great Sioux War, 1876–1877* (1991) and Robert Wooster's scholarly *Nelson A. Miles and the Twilight of the Frontier Army* (1993) are the most recent biographies of Miles.[2]

Although all of these biographers consulted conventional sources of military history, this study also considers the results of a painstaking search for both manuscript collections and nineteenth-century press accounts of Miles's unflinching stand against opponents. This evidence, much of which has not been introduced in earlier evaluations of Miles's career, restores him to a degree of prominence.

– CHAPTER 1 –

A Boy Grows Up To Become a Soldier

Nelson Appleton Miles was born August 8, 1839, in an ordinary one-and-a-half-story farmhouse built by his father, Daniel Miles, in the northeastern Massachusetts town of Westminster. Nelson, the youngest of four children, later recalled how growing up in a small (1840 population, 1,645), rural, New England town helped to prepare him for a life of campaigning. He attributed both his hardy constitution and his mastery of outdoor skills to boyhood fun and games in the woods surrounding the family farm. While still a boy, Nelson began to dream about becoming a professional soldier. He listened, with fascination, to fireside conversations as relatives and neighbors discussed the exploits of earlier generations in battles with Indians or the British. Naturally, tales about his own forbearers had the greatest impact on the mind of the impressionable youth.[1]

The family's martial tradition began with John Myles, the first member of the family to settle in the New World. Born in Wales in 1621, Myles became a Baptist clergyman after attending Oxford University. Because of religious persecution, he led his congregation from Swansea, Wales, to Swansea, Massachusetts, in 1662. Following an attack by the Wampanoag Indians on this village in 1675, Myles became a "Fighting parson," and his stoutly constructed home served as a garrison house for the duration of King Philip's War (1675–78).[2]

John's son Samuel followed his father's religious calling but deserted his father's Baptist faith. After Samuel graduated from Harvard in 1684, he went to England, where he earned a Master of Arts degree from Oxford. Upon his return to Boston in 1689, Samuel became the rector of King's Chapel, an Episcopalian church. After twenty-nine years of service in this parish, Samuel moved first to Connecticut and then to what is now

Petersham, Massachusetts. From his home on the frontier, the former rector had to contend with raiding Indians.

The third and fourth generations of the family brought new battle honors to the Miles family name. During the American Revolution, Nelson's great-grandfather, Daniel Miles, and his grandfather, Joab Miles, joined the patriot cause in time to help defeat the Hessians sent to gather supplies around Bennington, in the present state of Vermont. This victory helped to prepare the way for General John Burgoyne's surrender at Saratoga, on October 17, 1777. Daniel and Joab continued fighting with the American army until the end of the war.

Nelson's mother, Mary Curtis Miles, came from a family devoid of military achievements, but he took pride in the first member of her family to settle in America, William Curtis. In 1632 the *Lyon* sailed into Boston harbor with Curtis aboard. Since Curtis had settled in Massachusetts Bay Colony before 1657, his descendants, including Miles, were welcomed into the Founders and Patriots of America. Miles relished attending meetings of this very exclusive organization. When he spoke at the society's 1899 annual dinner, he proudly referred to his dining companions as "bluebloods."[3]

Miles, like many in his generation who achieved prominence, did so without the benefit of a college education. After Nelson celebrated his sixteenth birthday, he left Westminster for a clerk's job in Boston. In his memoirs, Miles admitted that working in John Collomare's crockery store was not "wholly congenial to my taste or consonant with my ambition." Since he did not tell his readers why he remained at an unattractive position, rather than attend a college in order to prepare himself for a more fulfilling career, one can only speculate. Many of Nelson's contemporaries were raised by families who could not afford to send a son to college and did not know a congressman well enough to seek a West Point appointment. In Nelson's case, however, humble origins did not block his path to the military academy or college. His family supported him financially, and his father surely made some political connections while he served on Westminster's Board of Selectmen. Thus, Nelson probably cut his education short because he lost interest in school. As a childhood friend later recalled, the subject in which Nelson "seemed to take most delight was fighting."[4]

Miles recalled the "feverish excitement" that swept through Boston, initially ignited by the passage of the Kansas-Nebraska Act in 1854, then fanned by a series of inflammatory events, and culminating with John Brown's raid in 1859. Realizing "that we were being threatened by a political hurricane which was sure to break upon us sooner or later," Miles intended to be ready to serve as an officer when the storm broke. Besides reading every book and manual that he could get his hands on, to broaden his grasp of military matters the future general enlisted in an informal officers training program conducted by a retired French colonel.[5]

Despite Miles's combative nature, he did not volunteer for service in the Civil War until he saw that he had a chance to serve as an officer. Prior to the passage of the Army Bill on July 22, 1861, most commissions went to Mexican War veterans, West Point graduates, and militia officers. This limited pool could not begin to fill the countless vacancies in the officer corps created when the July 22 bill authorized the formation of a volunteer army of half a million men. Miles then decided to volunteer. Besides the prospect of satisfying a boyhood dream, Miles later explained that he had reacted to "the dissolution of his government, which . . . he had been taught to cherish and reverently consider precious as life itself."[6]

On September 3, 1861, he began recruiting men in the town of Roxbury, now part of Boston, and in less than a week signed seventy men into Company E, 22d Massachusetts infantry, then took them to Camp Schouler, Lynnfield, Massachusetts, on September 7, 1861. Roxbury had started a fund to be used to pay each volunteer a bonus. Because the townsfolk were slow in contributing, Miles donated enough money to ensure that all of the recruits would receive the expected bounty. To do this, he had to use all of his savings plus a thousand dollars given to him by his father. He even had to borrow an additional twenty-five hundred dollars in order to fulfill the promise made by the citizens of Roxbury. The men of Company E rewarded Miles's generosity by electing him their captain.[7]

The governor of Massachusetts, John A. Andrew, soon punctured Miles's pride in being chosen the captain of his company. On the eve of the regiment's departure for Virginia, the governor sent his adjutant general to Camp Schouler with a letter for Miles in which Andrew explained that because he believed that Miles was too young to serve as a captain, he ordered him to exchange his commission for that of a first lieutenant. In Miles's recollections, he challenged Andrew's explanation. Obviously still rankled thirty-five years after the demotion, Miles argued that the governor had succumbed to political pressure when he gave William L. Coggswell command of Company E.[8]

On October 8, 1861, a dejected Lieutenant Miles boarded a train at Lynnfield Station, bound for Virginia. He was heartened by the rousing welcome the regiment received, first in Boston, then in New York.

The 22d Massachusetts Infantry settled into a camp near Falls Church, where it spent a quiet winter. Miles realized that his prospects for a promotion were dim in the 22d and followed the suggestion of a fellow officer to seek a transfer. A temporary assignment on the staff of Brig. Gen. Silas Casey brought Miles to the attention of Brig. Gen. Oliver Otis Howard, commanding a brigade stationed at Camp California, Bladensburg, Maryland. Howard soon had Miles permanently assigned to his staff as an aide-de-camp.

Miles's outlook brightened in his new assignment. As he explained to his uncle, he had "not been to the 22nd Regt. lately and I think I shall not go again soon for I like where I am so much better. The General lets me do just as I like." Despite Howard's loose reins, his newly installed aide appears to have been fettered by his many duties, which he listed in the note to his uncle. Besides taking part in brigade formations such as guard mounts, inspections, drills, and parades, he wrote reports, supervised the brigade's ordinance section, and assisted Howard during field exercises.

The maneuvers and the realization that weather would curtail any hopes for an immediate campaign irritated Miles. He complained to his uncle that "we are not here to play soldier. All our men dislike the idea of going into winter quarters." On a brighter note, he bragged about his horse, Excelsior, whom he described as "the finest horse on the grounds; he is a perfect beauty." The rider matched his mount in attracting favorable attention.

One of the recruits in Howard's brigade, Charles A. Fuller of the 61st New York Infantry, remembered his first meeting with Miles, a "fine looking young man on the staff of General Howard." Indeed, Miles looked more soldierly than many of his brother officers because he kept his brown hair conservatively cut and his flowing mustache neatly trimmed. Miles's blue-gray eyes did not reveal the steely determination and unflinching courage that would make his name, as one admirer put it, "the pride of the volunteer soldiers of the Union." Writing in *McClure's Magazine* in 1895, George E. Pond marveled that at fifty-six, Miles still looked as fit as a lieutenant and observed that "his nose was the 'conquering beak' of the soldier; that the steadfast blue-gray eyes consorted well with the firm lines of his mouth and chin to denote fixity of purpose and a resolute will."[9]

Throughout his life, Miles's commanding appearance inspired confidence and drew favorable comment. After the artist Frederic Remington met Miles, he recorded, "I felt his presence before conscious of his identity, a good style of man. His personal looks I shall never forget." The fine impression made by Miles was further enhanced by his height. After attending a presidential reception in January 1899, Ellen Maury Slayden, a congressman's wife, jotted down in her journal that Miles "towered like Saul a head and shoulders above his fellows and was always surrounded by admiring ladies." After a luncheon eighteen years later, Mrs. Slayden noted a charming aspect of the seventy-eight-year-old retired general that a journalist might have overlooked. She found that he had "a delightful voice and is a more than an usually graceful talker with some quaint old-fashioned pronunciations in places, like 'men*ace*.'" Unfortunately, Miles began to take such an interest in his appearance that the public eventually became aware of his vanity. Even Mrs. Slayden, who apparently admired Miles, could not resist copying into her diary the *Washington Post*'s observation during the hectic preparations for war with Spain in 1898 that, "When in doubt, Miles has his photograph taken."[10]

During Gen. George B. McClellan's 1862 advance up Virginia's James Peninsula toward Richmond, Miles gained recognition for qualities other than his handsome features. On March 8, 1862, just prior to being transported to the James Peninsula, the Army of the Potomac had been divided into five corps. Howard's brigade, one of three in Brig. Gen. Israel B. Richardson's division, served in Maj. Gen. Edwin V. Sumner's Second Corps. Sumner thought Miles so daring that he said the young staff officer would either get "promoted or get killed." Col. Francis C. Barlow, commander of the 61st New York Volunteers, one of the four regiments that made up Howard's brigade, also noticed Miles. On May 1, Barlow wrote to Edwin D. Morgan, governor of New York, requesting that Miles fill the vacancy in his regiment caused by the dismissal of Col. Spencer W. Cone. Barlow asked for Miles because the "officers and men know, respect, and obey him."[11]

Before the governor had a chance to reply to Barlow's note, the young officer had several chances to demonstrate his worth as a combat leader. On

May 31, the Confederates launched a surprise attack against two corps, separated from the rest of the Army of the Potomac by the rain-swollen Chickahominy River. Late that afternoon, General Sumner received orders to move his corps from its position in reserve, to help check the attack. When the corps reached the Chickahominy, Howard's brigade had to cross the raging river on a dangerously swaying bridge, and, as the sun went down, his men bivouacked near Fair Oaks Station.[12]

At first light on the morning of June 1, fighting broke out between Howard's advance guard and enemy pickets. When the Confederates attempted to outflank Howard's line, the general noticed soldiers from the 81st Pennsylvania Volunteers carrying the lifeless body of their regimental commander, Col. James Miller, to the rear. Howard realized that one wing of the 81st was now without a field officer and called for Miles. The general directed his aide to regroup the wing, already straying from the rest of the regiment. Miles quickly restored order among the disorganized companies, then fought with them the rest of the day. After Howard left the battlefield with a wound that would cost him his right arm, Miles led the 81st in two brigade bayonet attacks that swept the enemy from the field.[13]

Although Miles received a slight wound during his stint with the 81st, when a bullet glanced off a spur before hitting his foot, the injury did not keep him from his duties as a staff officer. Now referred to as a captain in reports, although his service record does not indicate such a promotion, Miles served as acting assistant adjutant general for Howard's replacement, Brig. Gen. John C. Caldwell.[14]

In response to Lee's offensive in the Seven Days' battles, which began on June 26, 1862, McClellan retreated from the Chickahominy River to a new base on the James River. Lee unsuccessfully tried to intercept the retreating Union army at Savage's Station on June 29. Before Caldwell's brigade fell back on Savage's Station, his troops were held in reserve at Allen's Farm, one mile from Fair Oaks. Rather than simply remain at ease until called to action, Miles gathered together a party of axmen from the assembled regiments. The rough road cleared by these woodcutters enabled three batteries to escape from Confederate hands when the Union forces withdrew from Allen's Farm.

During Lee's final attempts to shatter McClellan's army, Miles made himself especially useful to Barlow's 61st New York, probably because he realized he would soon serve with it. The regiment found itself without any support as it faced the enemy across one of the fields at Frayser's Farm, and on the following evening, the 61st came under heavy fire in the final stage of fighting at Malvern Hill. When Miles discovered the predicament of the 61st at Frayser's Farm, he personally guided the 81st Pennsylvania across a bullet-swept field to reinforce the isolated unit. At Malvern Hill, Miles helped a struggling gun crew drag an artillery piece into position to suppress the deadly Confederate rifle fire aimed at the 61st. Barlow realized the value of Miles's timely assistance, and reported that his men were "indebted" to the resourceful staff officer. Caldwell, impressed by Miles's "incessant activity," reported that he could not "speak in terms of sufficient praise" of his "invaluable" services.[15]

Although Miles's commission as lieutenant colonel of the 61st New York was dated May 31, 1862, he did not transfer from Caldwell's staff until the Peninsula campaign ended. He did not try to hide his delight when he reminisced about this promotion in his memoirs. "My tastes were entirely with the fighting force of the army, I preferred command of troops to any staff position." Miles would serve only a brief apprenticeship learning the trade of field officer, but his training would be supervised by an outstanding master. Bruce Catton judged that "one of the best men in the Army of the Potomac was the amazing warlike Manhattan lawyer, Colonel Francis Barlow."[16] The chronicler of the 61st, Charles Fuller, described Barlow thus: "He was not at first sight an impressive looking officer. He was of medium height, of slight build, with a pallid countenance, and a weakish drawling voice. In his movements there was an appearance of loose jointedness and an absence of prim stiffness."

The soldiers of Barlow's regiment soon learned not to judge their colonel by his appearance. Fuller noted that at first he was virtually hated because of "his exacting requirements and severity." However, when the troops came to realize that he would insure that his infantrymen "had what the regulations prescribed, and, that when danger was at hand, he was at the head LEADING them, this animosity was turned into confidence and admiration." Miles came to win the same respect from the regiment that Barlow had earlier earned. Fuller reflected that both officers "were men of doubtless courage and rare military judgment, who LED their men into battle."[17]

Following the withdrawal to Harrison's Landing, most of McClellan's army was ordered to reinforce Maj. Gen. John Pope's Army of Virginia. In late August, these troops sailed to Washington. Lee took advantage of this movement to defeat Pope in the second Battle of Bull Run, after which the Army of Northern Virginia crossed the Potomac north of the capital. The defeat cost Pope his army, which President Lincoln placed under the command of McClellan on September 2. The spirit of the restructured Army of the Potomac soared as it marched in pursuit of Lee through the lovely Maryland countryside in the pleasant weather of early September. Miles recalled that "were it not for the presence of an occasional wounded man or the distant roar of artillery we could have at times imagined ourselves going to a festival instead of a tragic drama."[18]

On Monday, September 15, 1862, Miles led the advance party of the first regiment in the Union column through Boonsboro to Antietam Creek, in search of the enemy. At one point, his men were so close to the Confederates that they saw the last element of a Southern unit pass over the top of the hill ahead of them. Shortly after midnight on the sixteenth, Miles returned to Antietam Creek with a patrol that dared to cross over the stream and advance a short distance beyond the far bank. Fuller, a member of this scouting party, experienced relief when they finally withdrew back behind Union lines.[19]

Lee had considered returning to the Potomac and crossing back into Virginia, but when he received word of Maj. Gen. Stonewall Jackson's victory at Harper's Ferry, he decided to make a stand at Sharpsburg, on Antietam Creek. By the morning of the sixteenth, the two armies faced each other from opposite banks of the stream. In one of the frequent artillery duels that took place after midday, a shell fragment pierced Miles's horse, Excelsior, wounding the animal so badly that it had to be destroyed.[20]

Three major battles took place at Antietam the following day, September 17, 1862. The first occurred in the East Woods by the Dunker Church; second came a series of assaults at the Confederate center; and finally, the Union attempted to cross the Burnside Bridge. The 61st New York, now combined with the 64th New York, attacked the enemy at one of the most fiercely contested strong points along the center of the Confederate line.

Caldwell's brigade, including Barlow's regiment, marched behind Brig. Gen. Thomas F. Meagher's Irish Brigade, as Richardson's division advanced toward the enemy. Confederate Brig. Gens. Robert E. Rodes and George B. Anderson's brigades watched Richardson's division make its approach. The Southern infantrymen, from regiments raised in Alabama and North Carolina, were entrenched in a road running about four feet below the level of the surrounding ground. The Rebel troops had reason to feel confident. Brig. Gen. William H. French's division of Sumner's corps had already been severely battered trying to take their position.[21]

Miles waited beside Barlow as the Irish Brigade moved across fields toward the sunken road. Fuller, from his vantage point with the reserve brigade, saw Meagher's troops take a terrible beating. "They were in our plain sight and we could see them drop and their line thin out. The flags would go down but be caught up, and down again they would go. This we saw repeated in each regiment a number of times." At last, Meagher found his position so desperate that he called out to Barlow, "Colonel! For God's sake come and help me."[22]

Barlow refused to commit his combined regiments until at last he received orders to advance. Then his men charged forward, rushing past the stalled and decimated Irish Brigade. Barlow solved the problem of the sunken road when, within yards of the Confederate line, he abruptly halted his troops and ordered a volley. According to Fuller, "We were so near the enemy, that, when they showed their heads to fire, they were liable to be knocked over." No longer easy targets, the Union infantrymen positioned themselves so that they could fire down the length of the sunken road.

The tide of battle quickly turned against the Confederate troops once their position had been enfiladed. Fuller related how "we were shooting them like sheep in a pen. If a bullet missed the mark at first it was to strike the further bank, and take them secondarily, so to speak." Within minutes, survivors of this slaughter began to wave any scrap of white cloth that they could find. Following the cease fire, more than two hundred Southerners hurried to the rear, under guard, eager to be able to escape from what Fuller called the "pit of destruction."

The chronicler of the 61st climbed down into the natural trench, which would come to be called Bloody Lane, and was appalled by the carnage. The road "was a good many rods long, and, for most of the way, there were enough dead and badly wounded to touch one another as they lay side by side. As we found them in some cases, they were two and three deep." The victors paused for a time to untangle the living from the dead, then shared their canteens with the victims of their assault. Barlow's regiments then crossed a cornfield on Piper's Farm, where they again came into contact with the enemy. Two Confederate batteries began to fire at the approaching Union infantrymen. When the artillerymen momentarily ranged in on their target, one ball of grapes hit Barlow in the groin, and a shell fragment struck him in the face. As Barlow was hurried, unconscious, to the rear, command of the combined New York regiments fell to Miles.

After the barrage that had wounded Barlow ended, the New York infantrymen held their ground until the Confederate troops broke and fled. Because his command had advanced farther than adjoining regiments, Miles received orders to fall back. Miles left skirmishers in place, then withdrew to add his strength to a line already formed by the 53d Pennsylvania. Here the New Yorkers remained unengaged as they patiently stood in line across a field of trampled corn stalks from about 1:00 P.M. until they were relieved by a fresh regiment at about 5:00 P.M.[23]

The tranquil afternoon at Piper's Farm reflected the state of affairs on all of Sumner's fronts. The sixty-five-year-old corps commander held back from using his available reserves for the one last thrust needed to shatter Lee's battered line, and the ever-cautious McClellan did not spur him to action. Miles ruefully reminisced about this lost opportunity, which he believed "would have resulted in the complete routing, if not the annihilation of the Confederate army." Sumner, disheartened by the slaughter of so many of his men in the morning, lost the resolve needed to press forward that afternoon.[24]

One of those who fell was Miles's division commander. Gen. Israel Richardson had been wounded by cannon fire and would later die because his slight wound became infected. Brig. Gen. Winfield Scott Hancock, a West Point graduate who had served in the Mexican War, received command of Richardson's division too late in the day to lead it into action. On October 9, 1862, General Sumner took a leave of absence. His replacement, Maj. Gen. Darius N. Couch, had earned a fine reputation commanding a division of the Fourth Corps during the Peninsula campaign. On November 7, 1862, Maj. Gen. Ambrose E. Burnside replaced General McClellan as commander of the Army of the Potomac, much to the displeasure of the troops in the ranks. To calm his division, Hancock reminded everyone that "we are serving our country, and not any man."[25]

As for Miles, he replaced Barlow as colonel of the 61st New York, officially receiving his new rank on September 30, 1862. He had earned this promotion by performing well at Antietam. Caldwell reported that Miles had "added to the laurels he has acquired on every battle-field where he has been present." The brigade commander noted that when Miles replaced Barlow, "he managed his two regiments in a masterly manner." Barlow wrote his report from a military hospital, where he was recuperating from his nearly fatal wounds. In a terse account, Barlow took the time to cite Miles's "courage, his quickness, his skill in seeing favorable positions, and the power of his determined spirit in leading on and inspiring men."[26]

In 1897 a letter appeared in the *New York Sun* that attempted to tarnish the feat of the combined 61st and 64th at Bloody Lane. According to Fuller, one veteran of the Irish Brigade took exception to a *Sun* article written by a former captain of the 61st, which described his regiment's victory at Antietam. The captain's critic complained that the "flags 'captured' there by Barlow had already been marched over, with a lot of dead rebels by the Eighty-eighth New York, who were too busy fighting to pick them up. Miles was always a glorious fellow."[27]

The official report of Lt. Col. Patrick Kelly of the 88th New York, written after the battle, does not support the contention of the Irish Brigade veteran. Kelly's regiment received orders to "charge and take the enemy's colors if possible." After the regiment advanced about twenty-five paces, however, Kelly realized that he had no support. When efforts to bring up the 63d New York failed, the attack of the 88th seems to have come to a standstill. No mention is made in the report about successfully capturing Confederate battle flags. Thus, the *Sun* letter seems to have resulted from bad feelings toward Barlow and his regiment rather than from an effort to set the record straight.[28]

In fact, the letter definitely indicates that ill feeling existed between Barlow and the Irish Brigade. The final sentence declared that "Barlow did not like us, and once, under a mistake joyfully exclaimed that d——d Irish Brigade has broken at last." When one recalls Barlow's refusal to come to the aid of the Irish Brigade until officially ordered to do so, it appears that there was a basis for the grudge that the veterans of General Meagher's brigade held toward Barlow and his regiment.[29]

Following Antietam, the Second Corps enjoyed an extended period of rest and recuperation at Boliver Heights, near Harper's Ferry. Finally, on October 30, 1862, it led the Army of the Potomac into Virginia. After General Burnside took command on November 7, he decided that the army should move eastward, seizing Fredericksburg, Virginia, located on the southwest bank of the lower Rappahannock, and then break through to Richmond. The city seemed an easy conquest when the Second Corps reached Falmouth on November 17. Unfortunately for the Union troops, there was a delay in obtaining pontoons needed to bridge the river. The pause gave Lee more than enough time to deploy his troops into natural defensive positions along a line of low ridges a mile or so behind the town of Fredericksburg.[30]

Burnside prepared for the attack by dividing the Army of the Potomac into three grand divisions of two corps each. The Left Grand Division would cross the Rappahannock three miles below the town and the Center Grand Division would be held in reserve. The Right Grand Division, composed of the Second and Ninth Corps and commanded by Sumner, would face an almost impossible task.

First, pontoon bridges would have to be constructed across the Rappahannock in full view of those in Fredericksburg, a town filled with Confederate sharpshooters. Then Union infantrymen would have to cross an open plain that stretched from the town to the ridge line, where Lee's army lay in wait, entrenched behind stone walls.[31]

Miles did not participate in the effort on December 11 to complete two bridges leading into Fredericksburg, but he sympathized with the engineers, who could only complete their work after assault groups rowed across the river to clear the far shore of snipers. As soon as dawn broke on the twelfth, Sumner shepherded the bulk of his division across the bridges and into the captured town. Once in Fredericksburg, Miles led the 27 officers and 408 enlisted men of the combined 61st and 64th New York to the lower end of town, where they settled in for the day. While Burnside spent the twelfth wavering from one plan of attack to another, many Union soldiers ransacked abandoned buildings. With relish, Fuller recalled the meal that he shared with a looter from his company, who found fresh lard in a jar; it tasted delicious when spread on hardtack. Burnside finally made up his mind and on December 13 instructed Sumner to "push a column of a division or more along the plank and telegraph roads, with a view to seizing the heights in the rear of town."[32]

In preparation for the attack by the Second Corps against Marye's Heights, Miles led his men to the last street in town, where they formed a temporary picket line, but artillery fire forced him to move the regiment back one block. The bombardment quickened when the Second Corps began its attack, and troops began to fall even before they left the cover of buildings in town. As Fuller moved out, he appreciated the suicidal nature of the mission facing his regiment and confessed that, "I never exerted more will power to make my legs move in the right direction than just here as I viewed the intrenched position of the Confederates, I said to myself, 'We will fail to carry those heights.'"[33]

Miles had no problem as his troops quick-timed their way out of town along Hanover Street until they reached a bridge with its floor planks torn out by the enemy. They had to make their way slowly across the support beams, alarmed as Confederate artillerymen began to concentrate on this choke point. Finally, the combined regiment approached a three-to-four-foot-high stone wall at the foot of Marye's Hill, where Miles formed his troops into a line of battle.[34]

Caldwell's brigade encountered furious resistance as it advanced. The general reported that the "fire here was terrific . . . the hottest I have ever seen. The men fell by the hundreds." The deadliest spot on his front was at "the confluence of two roads, down which the enemy was firing incessantly. Here I met Colonel Miles, who wanted to charge up the road." Caldwell denied Miles permission to attack because "with the small force at my disposal, it seemed to me a wanton loss of brave men."[35]

Possibly the suggested charge up the road would not have been the foolhardy scheme that Caldwell anticipated. The 24th North Carolina of Brig. Gen. Robert Ransom, Jr.'s division and Brig. Gen. Thomas Cobb's brigade fought from behind the stone wall, standing in the natural trench of a sunken road. The situation may have reminded Miles of Barlow's well-placed attack that succeeded at Antietam. In a report written the day after the battle, Miles explained what he had in mind. He saw that the Confederates "were firing from behind a stone wall and rifle pit. We were then within 40 yards of the enemy, and it only needed a spirited charge with the bayonet to close with him, and carry the works." In his report, Miles could not resist including the thought that "I only regret I did not make the attempt alone to carry the hill, relying upon the fragments of regiments then lying upon the ground to follow and support me."[36]

After Caldwell denied Miles permission to lead an attack up the bullet-swept road, he instructed the 61st to protect the right flank of the brigade. On this flank, the New Yorkers became embroiled with a Confederate battery firing grape and shell, supported by infantrymen in rifle pits. Miles's regiment managed to gain an advantage over the battery because the men of the 64th were armed with Austrian rifles, probably the Austrian Lorenz, noted for its long range. Soon the crews of two sections of a battery, situated on an exposed bluff, had to abandon their weapons because of this sharpshooting. Unfortunately for Miles, at this point in the battle a minié ball cut him along the side of his throat.[37]

Fuller, aware of Miles's desire to attack the enemy line, wrote with relief that "an accommodating rebel bullet cut his throat letting out a liberal quantity of fresh, bright blood. This so put him *hors de combat* that he had to leave the field, somewhat to the longevity account of the Sixty-firsters there present." Before Miles allowed himself to be carried from the battlefield, he demanded to see his former brigade commander, O. O. Howard, then in command of a division of the Second Corps. Howard recalled that Miles, "on a stretcher and holding the lips of the wound together, . . . pluckily had himself brought to me to show where he thought I could put my troops into action to advantage so as to make some impression on the enemy's line." Apparently, and despite Caldwell's argument, Miles still believed that the Confederates could be routed from the sunken road.[38]

After dark, the surviving Union troops were ordered to return to Fredericksburg, where they remained until Burnside withdrew his army back across the Rappahannock on December 15, thus ending the battle. The Union casualties in this battle were 1,284 dead, 9,600 wounded, and 1,769 captured or missing, compared to Confederate losses of 608 dead, 4,116 wounded, and 653 captured or missing. Of the 27 officers in Miles's command, only 3 were wounded, but 105 of his 408 enlisted men were casualties.[39]

Hancock appeared to have been impressed by both Miles and his infantrymen in this action. He reported that Miles "conducted himself in the most admirable and chivalrous manner. His battalion behaved with steadiness unsurpassed by any troops." Caldwell, who had an even better opportunity than did Hancock to observe Miles under fire, commended him for displaying "the highest qualities of an officer—coolness, judgment, and intrepidity."[40]

After a short recuperation Miles returned to the Army of the Potomac's winter quarters in the valley of the Rappahannock. He could look back at the campaigns of 1862 with personal satisfaction; he had matured from an ambitious staff officer to a battle-tested regimental commander. In every battle from Fair Oaks to Fredericksburg, Miles revealed both unflinching courage and a natural ability to lead men in battle. He could look with confidence in himself and his regiment to new campaigns in 1863.

Following Fredericksburg, there were a few changes of personnel that would be meaningful to Miles. On January 25, 1863, Maj. Gen. Joseph Hooker replaced Burnside as commander of the Army of the Potomac. General Sumner died at the age of sixty-six while on his way to take command of the Department of the Missouri. General Howard received a promotion to head the largely German-speaking Eleventh Corps. Barlow, his health restored, had received a promotion to brigadier general and now led a brigade in Howard's corps.[41]

— CHAPTER 2 —

Gallantry Recognized from Chancellorsville to Appomattox

Miles enthusiastically anticipated Hooker's spring campaign. His spirits had been raised by Hooker's reorganization and rehabilitation of the Army of the Potomac. The revitalized army still faced the same problem that had led to Burnside's bloody fiasco in 1862, that is, to make an opposed river crossing and then confront a prepared enemy that dominated the battlefield. Miles believed, however, that "one of the best strategic maneuvers of the war was enacted" when Hooker put his army into motion on April 27, 1863.[1]

One corps marched a few miles down the Rappahannock to give the impression that a crossing might be made below Fredericksburg. Meanwhile, Hooker marched a much larger force twenty-five miles up the Rappahannock, trusting that forests, fog, and curtailment of civilian traffic would delay the detection of this movement. After his troops crossed the Rappahannock and its tributary, the Rapidan, they moved back toward Fredericksburg. By April 30, Hooker's three corps had reached Chancellorsville, only twelve miles from Fredericksburg, without encountering opposition. At this point, only one Confederate division of approximately eighty-five hundred men stood between Hooker's fifty-thousand-man army and the unfortified rear approaches to Lee's positions around Fredericksburg.[2]

The next day, May 1, Union troops began moving out of the tangled thickets of a scrub forest known as the Wilderness and onto the relatively open ground beyond Chancellorsville, when their advance guards encountered Southern skirmishers. Lee, now alerted to Hooker's threat, advanced with the greater part of the Army of Northern Virginia up the Fredericksburg Turnpike to meet the challenge. When the two armies collided, the 61st New York, now independent of the 64th, was near the head of the Army of the Potomac. Miles became aware of the clash when he came upon a rapidly retreating brigade of the Twelfth Corps, closely pursued by Confederate infantry, later identified as Brig. Gen. Carnot Posey's Mississippi brigade. Despite the hasty departure of the leading Union brigade, Miles's New Yorkers stoutly held their ground for about half an hour, when one of Caldwell's aides informed the colonel that Hancock's division was about to pull back. The 61st would serve as the division's rear guard. During the withdrawal, the 61st slowly gave ground, pressed by the strongest Confederate skirmish line that Miles ever encountered. Finally, the New Yorkers were able to pass through the Third Corps, which was waiting to replace the 61st as rear guard for the Army of the Potomac.[3] Historians have credited the 61st, as well as the 52d New York, for filling a gap created by the pullout of the Twelfth Corps. Their efforts prevented the Confederates from cutting off Hancock's division, strung out on the road leading back to Chancellorsville.[4]

Miles later criticized Hooker, believing that he "did not appreciate the advantageous position he had gained, for, instead of continuing the aggressive move, he halted his troops and then ordered them to march back a distance and make preparations for fighting a defensive battle."[5]

Early in the evening of May 1, Miles received orders to deploy skirmishers in front of Hancock's main battle line. He selected a position within sight of the Chancellor House, and put his troops to work digging entrenchments on either side of the road that connected Chancellorsville with Fredericksburg. He later described how he tried to use the terrain to his advantage by choosing "commanding ground with some timber and a stream winding through marshy ground in the front. This position I strengthened in every way possible by having the troops slash the timber and construct strong rifle pits for shelter." They worked through the night, hoping to improve their chances of surviving the assaults that they knew could begin anytime after daybreak.[6]

It is fortunate that Miles's skirmishers took such care in preparing their defenses because they were vigorously tested by Southern troops from the divisions of Maj. Gens. Lafayette McLaws and Richard Anderson on May 2. At about 3:00 P.M., after hours of hard fighting, columns of Confederate infantry charged along level ground on either side of the turnpike, in an aggressive attempt to break through Miles's line. Miles later noted that, "In fact, their forces reached within a few yards of our entrenchments, and one colonel jumped his horse over the embankment, and both horse and rider fell dead within our lines." Immediately after the battle, Miles had reported that at the conclusion of this hour-long fight, the Confederates "were hurled back with fearful loss, and made no further demonstrations." Caldwell praised his young colonel because "with a single line of skirmishers, deployed at three paces (he) repelled a determined attack of the enemy made in column, a feat rarely paralleled."[7]

Union observers of Miles's stand could not know that the Confederates had exceeded their orders when they made a full-scale attempt to breach the skirmish line that afternoon. Lee had instructed Anderson and McLaws not to seriously engage the enemy on their front until after Stonewall Jackson launched a surprise attack against the right flank of Hooker's army, defended by Howard's Eleventh Corps. According to plan, approximately seventeen thousand of Lee's troops immobilized at least three times as many Union soldiers, while Jackson started out at sunrise along the Furnace Road. Jackson used a circuitous route to avoid being detected as he marched his three divisions of about twenty-six thousand troops around the Army of the Potomac. As Jackson had hoped, when his troops burst from the woods at 5:00 P.M., they caught Howard's men completely off guard.[8]

Fuller faulted the soldiers of the Eleventh Corps because they "lounged about," neglecting to take elementary precautions. A pictorial history of the Civil War published in 1868 compared Howard's camp to "a militia regiment at the close of a holiday muster rather than an army in the presence of an enemy." In a conversation with Miles some three months after Chancellorsville, Hooker blamed Brig. Gen. Charles Devens, Jr., for the Union defeat. Although the newly assigned commander of the First Division of the Eleventh Corps may have cavalierly dismissed sightings of Confederate troops on his front, the Army of the Potomac should have been able to survive the rout of a division. Miles should have clarified this point when he informed his uncle that the commanding general charged that Devens "lost the important ground and the key position which it was impossible to regain." The immediate effect of Devens's heedlessness, however, cannot be denied.

Startled by an unexpected attack, many Northerners fled for their lives. They began their flight at that point in the Union formation farthest from the Second Corps, but in no time at all, according to Fuller, "'the stampedees' if I may use the word, came across the country and struck our line. They were entirely in favor of continuing on, but we protested against it, and told them they would run right into rebel lines." Fuller recalled that some of these panic-stricken troops refused to stop until "the argument of the bayonet converted them to our idea, and they camped down in our rear."[9]

At the conclusion of the Chancellorsville campaign, Hancock summed up the fighting by his corps on May 2 as a "sharp contest" in which "the enemy was never able to reach my principal line of battle, so stoutly and successfully did Colonel Miles contest the ground." After dark on the second, and again the following morning, Hancock replaced battle-weary regiments in the line with fresh units, "believing from the experience of the previous day and the well-known ability and gallantry of Colonel Miles, that it could be held." Miles took some satisfaction in what he perceived to be Hancock's confidence in him when he recalled that the general, "during these attacks, had sent reinforcements, but he was careful to send regiments whose colonels were junior to me, which left me in command and increased my force to something more than a brigade."[10]

On the third, the defense of the skirmish line played a vital part in the Union plan of battle. When Walker wrote about this action, he explained that "so closely is Hancock's main line drawn into Chancellorsville, that it is deemed to be of great moment that the Confederates be not allowed to reach it except in the last struggle." Southerners also concentrated on the line. The divisions of McLaws and Anderson began a series of continuous attacks at daybreak as Lee maneuvered to reunite the two wings of his army.[11]

Bruce Catton related how Miles responded to these repeated attacks by riding "his horse up and down the line immediately behind the men, holding them to their work. It was an effective stunt—the men liked to know that a ranking officer was up in front with them, taking what they had to take." At some point during Miles's defense of the line, Hancock became so stirred by what he saw that he ordered, "Captain Parker, ride down and tell Colonel Miles he is worth his weight in gold." Miles also impressed his corps commander, General Couch, who confided to his division commanders that "I shall not be surprised to find myself, some day, serving under that young man."[12]

As Confederate troops began to mass before the section of the line manned by the 66th New York, Miles galloped toward Col. Orlando H. Morris, commanding this regiment. Before the two officers had a chance to converse, a bullet pierced Miles's belt buckle with a stunning impact. In his memoirs, Miles recalled that he felt "an instant deathly sickening sensation; my sword dropped from my right hand, my scabbard and belt dropped to the left; I was completely paralyzed below the waist." Without a sign from Miles, almost instinctively, his horse carried him off the battlefield.[13]

Still mounted, Miles reached the Chancellor House, where Capt. Calvin P. Fisher, a military surgeon with the 148th Pennsylvania, had the wounded officer stretch out on a table. The surgeon found that a musket ball had penetrated Miles's abdomen, slightly below his navel. Although the doctor dressed the wound, he did not extract the bullet because he believed that Miles did not have long to live. When the Chancellor House burst into flames after being hit by shell fire, Miles began an ordeal that must have drained all of his strength. The desperately wounded young officer later told how he was "carried five miles on a stretcher, rested in the woods that night, and the next day was carried in an ambulance over a rough corduroy road twelve miles to a field hospital." From the hospital, Miles continued on to Washington, where his brother Daniel cared for him on the last leg of the journey to their home in Massachusetts.[14]

In 1895 Miles told a reporter that when he returned home from Chancellorsville, "I could not move for weeks from my waist downward, and everyone thought I would die." Miles, however, surprised these prophets of doom by surviving; he even managed to move his right foot, which led his doctors to believe the bullet must be on the left side of his body. When the doctors operated to remove the bullet, they "probed for it, laying the bone of my hip bare. They found the bone broken and took out nine pieces, leaving one which they failed to find. They found the bullet several inches further down than these pieces of broken bone."[15] Although one would expect such a wound to cripple Miles, no mention is ever made of his walking with a limp in later life.

Miles's conspicuous display of courage while in command of the skirmish line did not go unmentioned. Hancock praised the youthful veteran for "performing brilliant services," while Caldwell declared that he knew "of no term of praise too exaggerated to characterize his masterly ability. If ever a soldier earned promotion, Colonel Miles has done so." In late June, Hancock, now commander of the Second Corps, offered some additional observations about Miles. He was "one of the bravest men in the army, a soldier by nature. Had we all such men in command of our troops, we could never suffer disaster." Hancock added that, "He is one of that class of commanders who seeks the enemy and fights him—never hides his troops when the cannon sounds in his ears." The officers and men of the 61st apparently missed their commander as much as Hancock did. Surgeon H. C. Vogelle wrote the convalescing colonel that, "We miss you in the Regt. We want your cheerful countenance and humor to relieve the camp of its tedious monotony, as well as your cool and deliberate council and direction in keeping things well balanced."[16]

In recognition of their heroism on Civil War battlefields, many officers received honorary promotions known as brevets. Although Congress virtually eliminated the duties and privileges accorded to holders of brevet rank in 1869 and 1870, officers still enjoyed the social prestige bestowed upon them by their brevet. On March 2, 1867, Miles received the brevet of brigadier general, U.S. Army (regular service), "for gallant and meritorious services in the battle of Chancellorsville, Virginia."[17]

Miles also received the Congressional Medal of Honor for "distinguished gallantry at the battle of Chancellorsville, Virginia, May 3, 1863." A number of Civil War veterans had applied for the nation's highest military decoration after the establishment of a Medal of Honor Legion in 1890. Among the many petitions submitted at this time was one on behalf of Miles. Albert A. Pope, manufacturer of the famous Columbia bicycle, suggested in a letter to Secretary of War Stephen B. Elkins on June 13, 1892, that Miles's performance at Chancellorsville should earn him the medal. To substantiate this claim, Pope included reports from the *Official Records,* extracts from Francis Walker's *History of the Second Army Corps,* and a letter from Couch. After recapping Miles's heroics on the battlefield, he concluded "that Miles is well worthy of receiving from Congress its honors for conspicuous bravery displayed at Chancellorsville." On July 23, 1892, the adjutant general of the United States Army notified Miles that he had been awarded the medal. Of some fifteen hundred Civil War servicemen who received the nation's highest military honor, Miles was among the more than eight hundred veterans who were awarded the medal in the 1890s.[18]

In 1911 Miles recalled the gloom that settled over the North after Hooker's defeat. At a memorial dinner in honor of Maj. Gen. George G. Meade, Miles must have been thinking of his own experiences when he related how "it was almost impossible for a Union officer to go through these northern cities back to his home after being wounded at Chancellorsville, without being almost insulted." Couch resigned on June 10 as commander of the Second Corps. Hancock replaced Couch, who on went to serve as commander of the Department of the Susquehanna, newly created in response to Lee's threat of invasion of the North. On June 28, several days after the Army of Northern Virginia crossed the Potomac for the first time since Antietam, Meade replaced Hooker as commander of the Army of the Potomac.[19]

In the campaigns after Chancellorsville, Lee would be handicapped by the loss of Stonewall Jackson, one of his most trusted generals. After Jackson's successful attack on May 2, he rode forward, after dark with his staff, to study the terrain upon which he would fight the next day. As his party returned through Confederate lines, riflemen from a North Carolina regiment mistook the mounted officers for Union cavalrymen and mortally wounded the general when they fired at the horsemen.[20]

Before Miles had fully recuperated from his wound, Meade and Lee fought the battle of Gettysburg. Aware of the impending encounter, Miles recalled in 1911 how he left his home in Massachusetts, "scarcely able to walk with a crutch, and tried to return to the field of duty, but found it impossible." Rather than give up completely, he volunteered his services to General Couch, now responsible for defending Pennsylvania with the state's militia. Couch gladly entrusted the disabled colonel with a militia brigade training at Camp Huntington, and Miles so excelled at this assignment that Couch repeated Caldwell's recommendation that he be promoted to brigadier general.

Miles had distinguished himself in Pennsylvania despite his unhealed hip, which must have severely handicapped him. As he told his brother Daniel, even two weeks after the Confederates had retreated from Pennsylvania "my wound troubles me very much. The piece of bone which Dr. [Alfred] Hitchcock [of Fitchburg, Massachusetts] thought would grow down, will have to come out either by discharging it as it decays or be removed by an operation." Miles explained that "it still discharges and I may have to have the bone scraped before it will become sound. At times it pains me considerably."[21]

Fortune had smiled on Miles when he had not healed in time to fight with his regiment at Gettysburg. Those who served with the 61st on July 2, when the New Yorkers rushed forward to fill a gap in that part of the Union line called the Wheatfield, faced grim odds that they would soon fall. Of the ninety-three troops in the regiment who entered the field that day, sixty-two were either killed or wounded, including Fuller, who lost both an arm and a leg.[22]

While Miles was still confined to his bed, Barlow made plans for his friend to return to duty as a brigade commander in his division. Barlow eagerly promised Miles that to insure the appointment, he would "go to Washington in person and lay the matter before the President." Gettysburg interrupted Barlow's campaign on behalf of Miles and almost cost the division commander his life. Barlow fell trying to rally his men when Howard's corps broke during the Confederate advance toward the town of Gettysburg on July 1. A minié ball that passed through his body, exiting near the spine, left him temporarily paralyzed.

In late July, Miles rejoined the Second Corps as it camped near the Rappahannock River. Maj. Gen. Gouverneur K. Warren would serve as corps commander until the following spring, when Hancock finally recovered from his wound, received while directing the defense that repulsed Maj. Gen. George Picket's charge on July 3. Miles received command of the First Brigade of Caldwell's division, replacing Col. Edward Cross, who was killed at Gettysburg. Cpl. Robert L. Stewart, 140th Pennsylvania, remembered that when his regiment heard that it would be transferred, the news that it would be into Miles's brigade made the change palatable: "the transfer, for this reason mainly, was enthusiastically endorsed by the rank and file, as well as the officers of the regiment."[23]

Miles dismissed the importance of his campaigning in the fall of 1863. A brief clash at Bristoe Station in October, however, gave Caldwell another chance to recommend a promotion for both Miles and John R. Brooke, who, like Miles, would join the regular army after the war. Barlow, still recuperating from his wound, joined Caldwell in lobbying on behalf of Miles. On November 28, Barlow wrote to Miles that he had discussed the matter with Senator Henry Wilson of Massachusetts, chairman of the Senate Military Committee. Barlow enclosed a copy of the letter that he sent in response to Wilson's request for a written résumé of Miles's qualifications. Barlow's reply sketches a rare picture of Miles as a Civil War combat officer, even though the view is colored by friendship.[24]

According to Barlow, Miles had a "remarkable talent for fighting battles. It is not only that he is very brave (for most officers are that) but he has that perfect coolness and self-propulsion in danger which is much more uncommon. The sound of battle clears his head and strengthens his nerves."

Barlow also noted Miles's ability, "his quickness of perception and skill in taking up positions and availing himself of advantages of ground in action I have not seen equaled." Barlow added that he also had "in an unusual degree the faculty of attracting men to him and arousing their pride and enthusiasm without relaxing discipline." Barlow concluded, "Had I known or had any influence with the President or Secretary of War I would have long ago seen them and urged this promotion." Barlow's and Caldwell's efforts came to a successful conclusion on May 16, 1864, when General Meade requested that Miles be appointed a brigadier general of volunteers "for distinguished gallantry on several occasions in the face of the enemy."[25]

The winter months of 1863–64 were spent refitting the Army of the Potomac. When the army was reorganized on March 23, 1864, by consolidating five corps into three, Barlow had returned to Hancock's Second Corps to command the first division. On March 9, 1864, Lt. Gen. Ulysses S. Grant became general in chief of the Armies of the United States, and shortly thereafter, he established his headquarters with the Army of the Potomac, still commanded by Meade. On May 4 this army opened its 1864 campaign when it crossed the Rapidan.[26]

The opposing armies clashed on May 5 and 6 in the Wilderness, near the old Chancellorsville battleground. This time, Miles's brigade played only a supporting role in the battle that saw Grant's forces mauled by the Confederates. Unlike his predecessor, Grant did not withdraw across the Rapidan after suffering a setback. Instead, after only a single day's rest, the Army of the Potomac moved south and east, hoping to beat the Confederates to an important road junction at Spotsylvania. Lee won the race, and his army formed a protective semicircle around the strategically located town.

The Second Corps probed the left flank of this semicircle on May 10. Barlow's division, including Miles's brigade, crossed the Po River on three bridges that Hancock had just ordered constructed the previous day. On the southern side of the river, Barlow's expedition ran into a strong force of Confederates spoiling for a fight. Hancock later reported that because Meade wanted to avoid having to battle on the southern bank of the Po, he ordered Hancock to withdraw Barlow's division from the shore.[27]

Miles's brigade received the ticklish job of covering the river crossing for the rest of the division, then destroying the two bridges still in place. The operation went very smoothly, although the Confederates attacked with vigor when they realized that they were opposed by only a few regiments. Miles's rear guard easily repulsed the Southerners, however, with the assistance of artillery fire from the heights on the north side of the river. Then they destroyed the first pontoon bridge and pulled up the pontoons of the second bridge as they retreated across it.

The following day, May 11, Miles's brigade was ordered out on a reconnaissance while the rest of Hancock's corps rested. They patrolled along the Spotsylvania Road as far as Todd's Tavern, where they skirmished with pickets before returning to their bivouac area. Here the tired infantrymen were ordered to join the tail of Hancock's column, as the corps marched out of camp to move into position for an assault against the Confederate line scheduled for 4:00 A.M. the next day.[28]

The objective of Hancock's attack was the "Mule Shoe," a mile deep, half-mile-wide salient projecting out from the Confederate line. By coincidence, Robert E. Rodes's and Anderson's divisions of Lt. Gen. Richard S. Ewell's corps defended this bulge; units from these two divisions had also opposed the Second Corps at Antietam's Bloody Lane. When the Second Corps neared its jump-off point, Hancock formed Barlow's First Division into a column of regiments, with Miles's and Brooke's brigades side by side in the first line and the other two brigades in the second line. Hancock's Third Division, commanded by Maj. Gen. David B. Birney, would assault the salient from another approach.[29]

After being delayed by heavy ground fog until 4:35 A.M., the attackers surged forward through the predawn mist. Each man had fixed his bayonet to his loaded but uncapped rifle. The massed troops swarmed over the enemy pickets and then reached the earthworks, protected by a barrier of sharpened stakes. In a letter to Barlow, Miles recalled how "with one bold determined rush, and a loyal shout that made the forest ring, the Union lines quickly tore away the strong *chevaux-de-frise* and brushed aside the rebel bayonets that were bristling over the works."[30]

After the human wave of advancing troops tore apart the obstacles, Miles saw bayonets used for the first time during the Civil War. The melee soon ended in a Union victory. General Ewell confirmed, in his report, that poor visibility masked the approach of the Union infantrymen toward the salient. Once upon his works, "their numbers and want of artillery enabled them to break through our lines, capturing Maj. Gen. Edward Johnson, Brig. Gen. G[eorge] H. Stuart, about 2,000 men, and 20 pieces of artillery."[31]

When Hancock's tired men failed to punch through a second line of entrenchments about half a mile behind the captured outworks, they fell back to the salient, where they repulsed repeated counterattacks. Although neither side could gain any further advantage after Barlow's and Birney's divisions penetrated into the Mule Shoe, some of the fiercest fighting of the war took place on this disputed ground.

One in Birney's division, John W. Haley of the 17th Maine, recorded the intensity of the fighting at the salient. "Confederates sprang over the works and fought with the bayonet and clubbed musket till they were pinned to the earth. Federals hurled themselves over and pushed the lines back a few rods, but were soon swallowed up by the rebound." Haley's impression of the punishment suffered by the combatants indicates why the Mule Shoe came to be called the Bloody Angle. "Lines didn't give way, they melted away. The dead lay in heaps and others took protection behind them. Pandemonium swept right and left, and the earth was literally drenched in blood."[32]

Although Grant's forces had not struck a mortal blow against the Army of Northern Virginia, the Bloody Angle had weakened Lee's forces. Walker estimated Confederate "losses on the 12th of May, in killed, wounded, and prisoners, at between nine and ten thousand making a hideous gap in his army." Douglas Southall Freeman reflected that "in its agonizing demands upon [Lee] the day of the Bloody Angle was second only to the final day of Gettysburg." Miles received credit as one of those responsible for this Union victory. On March 2, 1867, he earned his second brevet, this time that of a major general, United States Army, "for gallantry and meritorious services in the battle of Spotsylvania, Virginia."[33]

When Grant realized that the Confederate lines around Spotsylvania could not be penetrated, the Army of the Potomac marched south and east in another attempt to outflank the Army of Northern Virginia. In anticipation of this maneuver, Lee prepared such impressive defenses on the far side of the North Anna River that after testing them on May 23 and 24, Grant refrained from challenging the Confederates here in a major battle.

Despite being frustrated at North Anna, Grant persisted in trying to outflank Lee, which resulted in a race between the two armies for the crossroads at Cold Harbor. After a grueling overnight march, the Second Corps tramped into Cold Harbor on June 2, before the Confederates had a chance to entrench themselves in a defensive line. Any advantage Hancock may have gained, however, was nullified when Grant consented to postpone an attack scheduled for 5:00 P.M. to 4:30 A.M. on the third. The general in chief had taken into consideration the condition of Hancock's exhausted troops. For example, Miles's brigade started out at 10 P.M. and marched through a hot and humid night, choking on clouds of dust kicked up by the units ahead of them. His men finally struggled into Cold Harbor the following day at noon, after having been on the road for fourteen hours.[34]

Unfortunately for the men of the Second, Sixth, and Eighteenth Corps, when Grant postponed his attack, Lee had time to strengthen the weak spots in his line. The task of the Union troops was compounded by the lack of planning that went into the assault. As in so many earlier battles, they were expected to make another primitive frontal attack along the entire length of the line.

As at Spotsylvania, Miles's and Brooke's brigades spearheaded the assault column into which Barlow had formed his division. Just as the two brigades poured into the fortified sunken road used by the Confederates as their outer works, Brooke fell, badly wounded. After taking the road, Miles sent back thirty prisoners to join the two hundred troops and three guns captured by Barlow's division. After the division's initial successes, however, the Southerners regained every foot of ground taken from them. Murderous fire from well-situated batteries prevented a second line from reinforcing the victors, and, in Miles's case, his men were forced to abandon the outer works when gunners began to concentrate on both flanks of the road. Despite this setback, Miles refused to retreat to the Union lines; instead, he had his men dig in behind a nearby rise in the ground, where they remained a thorn in the side of the enemy until June 12.[35]

When the Second Corps marched southward, away from Cold Harbor, Miles left behind close friends. He later recalled how he spent the evening of June 2 with three youthful colonels, "with whom I had served from the time they were lieutenants, bivouacked that night together and slept under the same blanket; they were laughing and speculating as to the results of the morrow. When dawn came they all gallantly led their regiments and were all dead in fifteen minutes." By the end of the day's fighting, the North had suffered about seven thousand casualties, compared to about fifteen hundred for the South. Miles believed that among the Union dead at Cold Harbor were "many of the best men in the army." The bravest officers and men took more chances, and as a result, paid a higher price with their lives than did their more cautious comrades.[36]

Many survivors of the June 3 battle had lost their trust in Grant. Lt. Lewis P. Caldwell, 1st Massachusetts Artillery, wrote that he still liked "old Grant, although he is too much of a butcher and has too little regard for human life." Haley, reacting to the rumor that Hancock's corps lost three thousand men here in ten minutes, claimed that many troops "expressed freely their scorn of Grant's alleged generalship, which consists of launching men against breastworks." Miles took a contrary view and, in a letter to his uncle, cited Maj. Gens. Benjamin F. Butler, Quincy A. Gillmore, William F. Smith, Ambrose E. Burnside, and George G. Meade for the failure. He charged that "if they had taken pains to find out the enemies weak points and massed a heavy force upon them instead [of] attacking along the whole line with light columns, our loss would have been much less and our success greater." Dispirited by senseless sacrifice, the Army of the Potomac marched south from Cold Harbor on its way to attack Petersburg, twenty miles from Richmond.[37]

All but one of the rail lines that linked Richmond to the rest of the Confederacy passed through Petersburg, but this strategic city was protected by only a few thousand Southern troops. Unfortunately for the Union cause, a series of follies delayed the Second Corps from reaching the city until the Confederates had time to bring up reinforcements. After the chance for a quick victory at Petersburg had slipped out of Grant's hands, the Army of the Potomac settled down for a siege of the city.

Miles's enthusiasm for soldiering began to sag as the spring offensive sputtered. He confided to his aunt that he did "not think there ever was a campaign which tried men's power of endurance like the present one. It is only the strong that remain with us and they [are] very much worn down. It is many night marches and building field fortifications which has worn us down." Miles unburdened himself on the very day that he accepted his commission as a brigadier general of volunteers. His joyless mood on a memorable day becomes understandable with the additional comment that he had "lost many friends during the last campaign and it seems as if I was about the last of the officers that were in this Division in '62."

Just a day after Miles noted the heavy casualty count among Second Corps officers, he told his uncle about a near miss of his own from a potentially lethal fragment. He wrote that while he was in the Union line in front of Petersburg, a "bullet struck the shield of my sword, splitting it in two, a small piece struck my neck on the side only burning it a little. Another piece melted into the handle." Almost as an afterthought, he mentioned that, after a year, his hip wound still bothered him.

On July 26, while Miles's men prepared for a night march intended to focus the enemy's attention at Deep Bottom, he took a moment to dash off a note to his brother Daniel. After remarking that he missed a chance to meet General Butler's family, Miles evidently was back in high spirits when he joked that he "would not mind taking a sneeze at B's daughter." On a more serious note, Miles advised his brother not to volunteer for duty as an officer with the Second Corps. Although he could anticipate serving as a lieutenant on Miles's staff, if anything happened to the young general, Miles warned, Daniel would be reassigned to a frontline regiment. Miles attempted to dissuade his brother from risking such a fate by reminding him about the numerous times that he himself had been exposed to rifle and artillery fire in combat. He reflected that "it has been the prayers of friends at home which has spared me and how thoughtful ought I be to our Heavenly Father for his protection."[38]

The feint by the Second Corps at Deep Bottom was designed to aid a Ninth Corps attack in Petersburg, scheduled for July 30. Soldiers from Burnside's corps had constructed a tunnel in order to place four tons of powder under a fort in Lee's line. This powder would be detonated just before the attack. The diversionary movement began on the night of July 26, when Hancock's corps, supported by two divisions of Maj. Gen. Philip H. Sheridan's cavalry, used pontoon bridges to cross to the north bank of the James River. Troops from the Tenth Corps garrisoned this bridgehead, known as Deep Bottom, located ten miles below Richmond.

Almost as soon as the Second Corps settled in at Deep Bottom, Miles received orders to command a skirmish line directed against Confederate works opposing the Union foothold. Walker described Miles's response to the problem as "one of the most dashing operations of the war." He explained that, "so skillfully were the dispositions made, so rapid and impetuous was the advance of the skirmish line, that without a regiment of reserves showing itself, [Maj. Gen. Joseph B.] Kershaw's works were carried at the first rush and his line was driven back through the woods." The Northern skirmishers triumphantly returned with four twenty-pound artillery pieces abandoned by Southern gunners during their precipitous retreat.[39]

The movement to reinforce Deep Bottom achieved its primary objective of drawing Confederate troops away from Petersburg; it also gave Miles a fresh opportunity to demonstrate his skill as a battlefield leader. On the eve of the scheduled attack, as Southern troops began to mass on the north bank of the James, Hancock's entire command withdrew from Deep Bottom. His men arrived at Petersburg on July 30, in time to see the explosion, which created a huge crater; but the attack that followed the explosion fizzled. Miles served from July 31 to August 9 on a board of inquiry convened to determine the reasons for the attack's failure. On August 9, the board reported that Maj. Gen. Ambrose E. Burnside, commander of the Ninth Corps, and three of his division commanders "appear from the evidence to be 'answerable for the want of success' which should have resulted."[40]

Just five days after completing his duties on the court of inquiry, Miles returned with the rest of the Second Corps to Deep Bottom. Grant believed that there was a chance for success in this sector because he had received information that some of the Confederate defenders had been withdrawn to campaign in the Shenandoah Valley. Hancock's corps, along with the Tenth Corps, was unsuccessful in a series of attempts to flank the enemy positions, which were not as undermanned as Grant had been led to believe.[41]

In one such probe Miles again showed his ability in a critical situation. On August 16, his brigade supported Brig. Gen. David Gregg's division of cavalry in an advance that brought them to a point only seven miles from Richmond. Here the Confederates counterattacked, and the Union task force had to withdraw. Infantry and cavalry formed two lines of battle. After the first line fended off an enemy advance, it would retreat about half a mile, where the second line waited its turn to block the approaching Confederates. Col. Charles Morgan, Hancock's chief of staff, commented that the conduct of this operation "was cool and soldierly. No dead or wounded of ours were left on the field, the cavalry bringing in their dead either strapped across the lead horses or in front of troopers."[42]

Although Grant realized that the Confederates on the north bank of the James were stronger than he had been led to believe, he kept Hancock's corps at Deep Bottom to divert the enemy from a movement by the Fifth Corps against the Weldon Railroad, which ran due south from Petersburg to Wilmington, North Carolina. Gregg's cavalry joined the Second and Tenth Corps, now commanded by Birney, in futile attempts to budge entrenched Southerners who were barring the way to Richmond.

The continuous series of assaults drained Barlow, who became so ill on August 17 that he had to leave the battlefield for the army hospital at City Point. Walker described Barlow just before his departure as "more like a dead than a living man." Walker, then assistant adjutant general of Hancock's corps, attributed Barlow's condition to "disease and the effects of his ghastly wounds, received at Antietam and Gettysburg." But a more devastating setback than physical illness or wounds must have been the loss of Barlow's wife, Arabella, a nurse, who died of typhoid on July 28. Although Barlow did not look fit for duty, the dedicated general returned to his division on August 23.[43]

During Barlow's absence, Miles led the First Division back to Petersburg, and from there on an operation against the Weldon Railroad. The Fifth Corps, commanded by Major General Warren, had already struck the railroad four miles below Petersburg, at Globe Tavern. While Warren consolidated his hard-won foothold on the railroad, two of Hancock's divisions, again accompanied by Gregg's cavalry, began to move south from Globe Tavern, tearing up track. By the evening of the twenty-third, Hancock's eight thousand men had reached Reams' Station, four miles below the Fifth Corps. The next morning, after less than a day with his division, Barlow became so ill that he had to be carried from the field by stretcher. Thus, on August 24, just two weeks after Miles turned twenty-five, and on the eve of a battle, he became a division commander.[44]

Lee could not ignore the Union attempt to destroy one of the few railroads connecting his army with the rest of the Confederacy. If Hancock's troops succeeded in tearing up twelve miles of track, Southern teamsters would be forced to load their wagons at Stony Creek Depot for a thirty-mile trek back to Petersburg. To prevent such a disruption to his supply line, Lee ordered a powerful force commanded by Lt. Gen. Ambrose P. Hill to "move down the railroad, . . . and do all in your power to punish the enemy."[45]

On the evening of August 24, Hancock received a wire from Brig. Gen. Andrew A. Humphreys, Meade's chief of staff. The message warned that between eight and ten thousand enemy troops were moving south from Petersburg, with the Second Corps as their likely target. Walker later questioned Meade's failure to react to this threat to an isolated force. "If Meade did not intend to fight, Hancock should have been withdrawn. If he did intend to fight, Hancock should have been powerfully reinforced."[46]

The defensive works at Reams' Station had been hastily thrown up by another corps on an earlier expedition against the railroad. Expediency forced Hancock to use this position, which would be difficult to defend. On the twenty-fifth, instead of using both his divisions to strengthen these works, Hancock sent Brig. Gen. John Gibbon's division into the field to continue tearing up rails. However, Miles's division took full advantage of their respite from track work to prepare for battle. His pioneer corps slashed much of the timber around the station but did not have time to clear the dense brush in front of the Union lines. Behind entrenchments reinforced by railroad ties, fifty axmen cleared roads leading to the rear. When Confederate troops reached the abatis protecting the breastworks, they found that the closely packed rows of sharpened stakes were laced with wire to make them even harder to penetrate.[47]

Despite improvements, basic flaws in the layout of the perimeter would work against the defenders. The short, seven-hundred-yard western front could hold only two batteries and a few battalions. In battle, these troops would be cut off from the rest of the command by the open track area, forcing supply parties and reinforcements to dash across an exposed embankment, unprotected from enemy fire. Furthermore, the entrenchments north and south of the station were too close to one another, allowing Confederate batteries facing one front to shell defenders manning the opposite line.[48]

While the First Division worked at improving the defenses, Gibbon intended to continue the work of destroying track at Malone's Crossing, some three miles below the station, where Miles had left off the night before. On the road, the Second Division encountered a squadron of Union cavalry pursued by a strong Confederate force. Gibbon's men quickly formed a skirmish line to cover the retreat of the mounted patrol; then they followed Hancock's order recalling them to the station. Here they took up positions along the southern half of the perimeter, while Miles's division manned the northern front. At 1:00 P.M. Miles's division easily repulsed an attack made by two brigades, but in a second attempt a short time later, some Southerners almost reached the Union lines before being driven off. Hancock now anticipated a full-scale attack before sunset.[49]

During the afternoon, Confederate snipers concealed in the treetops killed 134 artillery horses, immobilizing many of the Union batteries. A Second Corps veteran recalled the slaughter of the horses, held together in teams of six. "A peculiar dull thud indicated that the bullet had penetrated some fleshy part of the animal, sounding much like a pebble does when thrown into the mud." He added, "The result of such wounds was to make a horse start for a moment or so, but finally he would settle down as if it was something to be endured, without making a fuss, and thus he would remain until struck again." Then, at about 5:00 P.M., a fierce artillery barrage presaged the expected attack. When the guns fell silent, most of the Northerners emerged from their rifle pits unscathed, but the intense bombardment had demoralized many of the raw recruits recently inducted into the Second Corps. The replacements must have been further shaken as a double assault column raced from the woods toward Miles's division, emitting their eerie yell.[50]

The attack force, North Carolina regiments from the divisions of Maj. Gens. Henry Heth and Cadmus Wilcox, received support from Lt. Col. William J. Pegram's artillery and Maj. Gen. Wade Hampton's cavalry. Although the North Carolinians charged with vigor, it appeared that they would be beaten back until Heth rallied the infantrymen. Heth intended to use the flag of the 26th North Carolina to rouse the thinning ranks of attackers, but the color bearer, Thomas Minton, refused to part with it. Since both men were determined to hold the flag aloft, each grasped the staff as they mounted the Union works, where the general cheered on his troops. Further down the line, a captain from the 28th North Carolina also breached the barricade. Alone, facing the enemy, the officer shouted, "Yanks, if you know what is best for you, you had better make a blue streak toward sunset." Because so many bluecoats followed this suggestion, the 28th joked after the battle that "Grant would have to send Hancock back north to recruit his command." Thus, the Southern attack carried into Miles's position.[51]

Miles reported that at the very climax of the battle, when victory seemed certain, men from three New York regiments, the 7th, 39th, and 52d, broke. He felt that the situation was still under control and ordered troops from another brigade to fill the gap. Instead of following orders, these troops panicked and either ran to the rear or dropped to the ground where they had been standing. From this point on, Miles received mixed results from his men as he attempted to stem the breakthrough into his position.[52]

Fortunately, Miles's Fourth Brigade responded to his encouragement and moved forward to hold the rifle pits. Then he had the 12th New York Artillery support their efforts by firing canister at the oncoming enemy, until Southern infantrymen swarmed into the battery's gunpits. The gunners could not save their weapons because their horses had been targets of the snipers. When the Confederates turned one of the guns around and began to fire at the fleeing troops, the 152d New York was in position to drive the Southerners from their prize. The 152d's halting reaction to a vulnerable enemy must have infuriated Miles. He noted that the inspector of his division, "a very cool and reliable officer, reports that not a shot was fired at it [the 152d], but the men broke from the ranks and fled in a disgraceful manner, only two men in the regiment discharging their pieces."

Miles found himself in the midst of a deteriorating situation. "The panic had become somewhat general, and it was with the greatest difficulty that any line could be formed." Refusing to concede the field to the Confederates, Miles saw his former regiment, the 61st New York, stoutly standing up to the enemy. Using this regiment as an anchor, he formed a new line, and "ordering the firing to cease I directed it to advance with a cheer. It swept the enemy from a major portion of the north face of the work, recapturing three guns of the Twelfth New York Battery, and driving the enemy into the railroad cut."

Miles's successful counterattack heartened Hancock, who admitted that his prospects "at this juncture were in critical condition and but for the bravery and obstinacy of a part of the First Division and the fine conduct of their commander (General Miles) would have ended still more disastrously." Besides seeing the Confederates break into Miles's position, Hancock had been having troubles with his Second Division. He reported that after one brigade of this division fell back, allowing two batteries to be captured, he ordered a counterattack. Although the Confederates were so few in number that they could barely respond to this threat, the Union troops quickly returned to the protection of their works.[53]

While the men of the Second Division were scurrying to safety, Miles sent a force of about two hundred infantry across the railroad tracks to hit the Confederate rear. Hancock realized that the raiding party did not have enough men to be effective, but he could not rouse any of the troops from the Second Division to add their weight to the thrust. This division further disappointed Hancock when it failed to respond forcibly to a "feeble" attack made by dismounted Confederate cavalrymen. Hampton's men enjoyed an "easy success" until they were outflanked by General Gregg's troopers, also fighting as infantry. Gregg, with whom Miles had worked so well at Deep Bottom, managed to check the enemy until Gibbon's men completed a new line. Hancock then instructed Miles to use his division and the 1st New Jersey Artillery to maintain control over the road that led to friendly lines. As soon as night fell, Hancock ordered withdrawal from the station along this road, with Miles in command of the rear guard.

Just before abandoning his position, Miles rode forward to inspect the battlefield. He said that from between the lines, where some of the wounded lay, still unattended, "I could hear the enemy's men calling out their regiments, and I felt confident his loss was greater than ours, that his confusion was equal, and that I could retake all of my lines." The situation was not as promising as Miles thought, however. Although Union dead and wounded numbered 610, compared to 720 of the enemy, the 1,752 missing Northern troops left Hancock outnumbered in an untenable position; he was fortunate that he still had the option to retreat.[54]

The Confederates made no attempt to engage the bluecoats as they tramped away from Reams' Station in the dark, but the following morning cavalry patrols were sent out to round up stragglers. When Lee wired Confederate Secretary of War James A. Seddon news of Hill's victory, he listed as spoils of war "seven stand of colors, 2,000 prisoners, and nine pieces of artillery."[55]

In Hancock's report, he discussed "the bad conduct of some of my troops." He attributed part of their poor performance to their "great fatigue" and to "their enormous losses during the campaign, especially in officers." Furthermore, the regiments that broke at the height of the Confederate attack were newly recruited. Hancock complained that some of the officers in these regiments could not speak English.[56]

Humphreys, Meade's chief of staff during the battle, conceded that the "injurious effect of the large number of raw recruits recently received had not been anticipated, or reinforcements would have been sent to General Hancock." Meade had not only closed his eyes to the large number of recruits recently inducted into the Second Corps but also failed to take into consideration the character of these men. As *Harper's History* pointed out, many of those who meekly marched into captivity without firing a shot were "the scum of the army who had been brought in by the enormous bounties which had been paid for recruits and substitutes."[57]

After Hancock repeatedly saw his men fail to stand up to the enemy, he confided to a staff officer, "Colonel, I do not care to die, but I pray God I may never leave this field." With faith in his corps shaken and his Gettysburg wound bothering him, Hancock probably welcomed the respite from combat when Secretary of War Edwin M. Stanton summoned him to Washington. Stanton proposed that Hancock travel through the North to recruit veterans into a new corps. In accordance with this plan, Hancock relinquished command of the Second Corps to Maj. Gen. Andrew A. Humphreys on November 26, 1864. An 1831 graduate of West Point, Humphreys had become a recognized authority on the hydraulics of rivers after the publication in 1861 of his studies of the Mississippi River for the Corps of Topographical Engineers. During the Civil War, he left McClellan's staff to lead a division. At Gettysburg Meade so appreciated Humphreys' ability that he promoted him to major general and appointed him as chief of staff of the Army of the Potomac.[58]

Although Humphreys's appointment as corps commander necessitated some changes, Miles remained in command of the First Division as Grant's army settled down for a fall and winter siege of Petersburg. The past summer's fighting earned him his third brevet, that of major general of volunteers, "for highly meritorious and distinguished conduct throughout the campaign and particularly for gallantry and valuable services in the battle of Reams' Station, Virginia." During the final quarter of 1864, as Union victories on other fronts made news, it became apparent on both sides that the war would soon be over. The resulting drop in Southern morale became obvious. Miles noted that almost nightly through the winter of 1864–65, Confederate soldiers "crept through their picket lines, dropped their arms, and came to us as individuals or in squads, amounting in the aggregate to thousands."[59]

From February 15 to February 25, 1865, Miles served as corps commander while Humphreys enjoyed a leave of absence. This brief exercise of power allowed Miles proudly, and frequently, to boast that he commanded "the Second Army Corps at the age of twenty-five, when it numbered upward of twenty-six thousand men, and was actively engaged against the Army of Northern Virginia." Actually, as winter gave way to spring, nothing of moment occurred until March 25, when Lee launched a surprise attack against Fort Stedman, on the right of the Union line. Lee ordered this assault to improve the chances of the Army of Northern Virginia to slip away from contact with the Army of the Potomac and join Joseph E. Johnston's forces in North Carolina.[60]

While the Southerners achieved their initial objective at Stedman, only to see attempts to exploit the victory fail, Humphreys probed for weak spots along his line. The Second Corps swept up the entire opposing picket line, but then resistance stiffened and none of the Confederates' main works fell into Union hands. During this limited offensive Miles's men had achieved nothing out of the ordinary, but the manner in which they performed indicated that they were in fine form for the coming campaign. He reported that they had fought with "an unusual spirit of determination and enthusiasm; they fought in line of battle, without works, in a perfect order as if upon drill; scarcely a skulker or coward was noticed in the rear of the line of battle."[61]

On March 29, only four days after Lee's attack at Fort Stedman, the long-awaited Union spring offensive began. The Second Corps and Warren's

Fifth Corps moved westward with the intention of turning Lee's right flank. For the first two days of this operation, Miles led his division through swamps and dense woods made almost impassable by heavy rains. On March 31, Southerners attacked the Fifth Corps just as Warren's men were about to seize control of the White Oak Road. If this Union attempt had succeeded, Confederate troops at Five Forks would have been cut off from the rest of Lee's army.[62]

When Humphreys ordered Miles to go to the assistance of the Fifth Corps, the division commander found himself in the perfect position to do so. Confederate troops were so intent on pursuing Warren's men that they did not notice Miles's division as it made a left half-wheel in order to strike their left flank. This maneuver caught the Confederates off guard and netted Miles's division several hundred prisoners. With this threat to the Fifth Corps eliminated, Warren's men recovered from their early reverses and, with the assistance of Sheridan's cavalry, won an important victory at Five Forks on April 11. During this battle, Miles's division held White Oaks Road to prevent Southern troops from using it to surprise the Fifth Corps.[63]

At 9:00 A.M. on April 2, the Confederates abandoned their positions facing Miles's division along White Oak Road. His division immediately pushed forward and pursued the Southerners toward Sutherland Station. General Heth, who had helped turn the tide of battle against Hancock's corps at Reams' Station, prepared a blocking force of four brigades for another fight with Miles's First Division. After Heth positioned the rear guard along the top of a ridge line, he hurried to Petersburg to assume command of Gen. A. P. Hill's corps. Hill had been killed in a chance encounter with Union troops who had penetrated his lines. As Miles surveyed the enemy in their hastily constructed works, Humphreys met with him to discuss the situation. After Miles assured Humphreys that his division could capture the position without help, the corps commander rode off to rejoin his other two divisions.[64]

Only after seeing his first attack fail did Miles concede that the Confederates had chosen a strong defensive position. His division artillery arrived in time to support a second attack, but this also failed because of timely Southern responses at critical moments. At 2:45 P.M., Miles tried again. He sent a diversionary force against the right flank while a brigade assembled, unnoticed, in woods on the opposite side of the ridge. Effective artillery fire paved the way for the concealed infantry, who gave their customary cheer as they emerged from the woods and swept into the Confederate works. The spoils from this spirited attack included two artillery pieces and six hundred prisoners.[65]

The following morning, April 3, Miles sent out search parties to round up stragglers who had escaped when their position had been overrun. The Union patrols returned empty-handed because the fleeing Southerners had found a ford across the supposedly impassable Appomattox River. That same morning, Grant found that Lee had abandoned Petersburg and Richmond. For three days the Army of the Potomac and the Army of Northern Virginia raced westward, as Lee sought to outflank Grant in order to join Johnston in North Carolina. Walker penned a description of the unique situation in which the two armies found themselves on April 6. "Union forces were marching in lines parallel to those taken by the Confederates, never at a great distance, often in plain sight, each column so intent upon reaching its goal as to be unwilling to lose the briefest time in collisions which could not affect the grand result."[66]

The Second Corps, marching at full speed, came upon a wagon train guarded by a column of infantry near Amelia Court House. For about sixteen miles a running battle ensued as the wagon train raced toward Deatonsville, with Miles's division at the head of the pursuit. The Confederate infantry found it virtually impossible to make a stand in order to enable their wagon train to pull away to safety. At sunset, as the fleeing column attempted to ford Sailor's Creek, the First Division caught up with the harried teamsters and their escorts; the Southern infantry took cover along a ridge from which they hoped they could protect the wagons as they crossed the stream. Miles ordered his First Brigade to attack the gallant rear guard, and the results were spectacular. His men easily overwhelmed the outnumbered enemy, and he reported that they captured "2 guns, 4 colors, his entire train of about 250 wagons, ambulances, etc., together with mules, horses, and all appurtenances, and a large number of prisoners."[67]

The Second Corps resumed the chase at first light on the morning of April 7. The troops followed the enemy by using the roads closest to the rain-swollen Appomattox River. The units at the head of the column sprang into action when they approached a pair of bridges still standing over the unfordable river. A group of pioneers braved enemy bullets as they followed

Col. Thomas L. Livermore of Humphreys' staff in a dash to the far side of the High Bridge. This railroad bridge, supported by sixty-foot-high brick piers, had already been torched by the rear guard, but the Northerners extinguished the blaze in time to save all but four spans from the fire. While Livermore worked to save the High Bridge, Barlow, who had just returned to duty with the Second Corps, rushed forward to take the wagon bridge that ran under and alongside the railroad bridge. The men in his new command, the Second Division, came upon the small squad of Confederates left behind to destroy the bridge so aggressively that the Southerners had no time to burn it in their haste to escape.[68]

Confederate Maj. Gen. William Mahone realized the importance of destroying the bridges in order to enable Lee to pull away from his pursuers. To accomplish this, he ordered a strong counterattack, which caught the Second Division with only some of its units on the north side of the Appomattox.

Miles reached the scene as Barlow's outnumbered troops were being driven back toward the bridge. He immediately ordered his infantry to form along the southern riverbank in an attempt to support the Second Division, but the enemy withdrew only after his division artillery joined in the action. The Second Corps encountered no further resistance as it crossed over the wagon bridge. On the north bank, Humphreys had Barlow follow the Confederates along the railroad line while Miles led the First and Third Divisions on a road toward Farmville. These two divisions were abruptly halted by artillery fire before they reached the town.[69]

From carefully prepared entrenchments, Confederate infantry and sixteen artillery pieces dominated the two roads leading to Lee's intended destination, Lynchburg. Humphreys took the initiative and maneuvered his two divisions in an attempt to outflank the enemy. While the Third Division maintained pressure along the line, Miles formed three regiments into an extended skirmish line that attempted to envelop the enemy. Miles reported that this advance failed because of the "difficult nature of the ground, which was broken by numerous small and sharp ravines, over which the men were unable to move in order." After Miles's bloodied regiments beat back a counterattack, fighting subsided as darkness settled over the battlefield.[70]

Reflecting on the day's events, Humphreys took satisfaction from the performance of his corps at both the High Bridge and outside Farmville, even though he had suffered 571 casualties (424 from Miles's division). He praised the "spirit and promptness" of his corps, and in a footnote, commended all of his commanding officers because they "were at the head of their commands, literally leading them, as they should in a pursuit." He argued that when he confronted the enemy at Farmville, he significantly tied down the Confederate forces until nightfall. This pause made it possible for Sheridan's cavalry, along with the Fifth and Twenty-fourth Corps, to block Lee's progress at Appomattox Court House.[71]

On the morning of April 8, the Second Corps resumed their pursuit of the enemy, who had slipped away from the battlefield in the middle of the night. After marching from 6:00 A.M. to 4:00 P.M., the exhausted foot soldiers were allowed to rest, but at 9:00 P.M. they were ordered back on the road to continue the march for another five miles. The troops endured the rigors of the march with the knowledge that the war might end at any moment. After marching for only six miles on the morning of the ninth, the Second Corps came to a sudden halt when the Confederates raised a flag of truce over their lines. The patient troops spent most of the day waiting for the formal surrender to be made. Miles recalled that once the agreements were signed, "officers galloped in different directions to notify the great cordon of troops then surrounding the army of Lee. . . . All the bands immediately struck up the national airs, such as 'Hail Columbia,' 'The Star Spangled Banner,' etc." A wave of emotion swept through the ranks. "The air was filled with hats, canteens, haversacks, and everything that could be displayed as an expression of great rejoicing. The grim warriors embraced each other and rolled over on the turf with tears of joy coursing down their bronzed faces."[72]

Miles emerged from the Civil War as a tested combat commander. In almost every battle fought by the Army of the Potomac his men were used as shock troops, effectively carrying out the most dangerous and disagreeable assignments. His troops led the army to Antietam Creek and toward Lee at Chancellorsville. His troops were the leading brigade in attacks at Spotsylvania and Cold Harbor. They fought rear-guard actions at the Po River bridgehead and at Reams' Station. Miles also displayed great skill in defending skirmish lines at Chancellorsville and Deep Bottom. For some reason, during battles in which things were at their worst for the Union cause, Miles enjoyed his best moments.

The First Division of the Second Corps, in which Miles rose from regimental executive officer to division commander, has been credited by William Fox, in his analysis of Union casualties, as the division that saw "the hardest fighting," and the division "in which more men were killed and wounded than in any other Division in the Union Army, East or West." He substantiated this claim by citing the more than fourteen thousand casualties it suffered during the course of the war, although it never mustered more than eight thousand men. Miles was among those in the First Division who received multiple wounds. Besides shedding blood at Fair Oaks, Fredericksburg, and Chancellorsville, he was wounded when a fragment pierced his shoulder after a bullet hit his upraised sword during the siege at Petersburg. Instead of becoming gun-shy because of these wounds, Miles tended to disregard the risks of exposing himself to Confederate fire.

Miles's fearless response to danger may have contributed to the two setbacks he experienced during the decisive Appomattox campaign. At both Sutherland Station and on the heights outside Farmville, he impetuously and unwisely attacked the enemy. At Sutherland Station Miles should have waited until his division artillery came up before mounting his first attack, and at Farmville, a brief reconnaissance would have better prepared him to fight on a difficult terrain. Although these two reversals merit critical comment, Miles developed into an extremely able officer. Those who aided him in his rise through the ranks had no reason to regret their assistance. The Civil War governor of New York, Edwin D. Morgan, who had appointed Miles as a field-grade officer in the 61st New York, later wrote: "It was an unusual proceeding to take a lieutenant from another state and thus promote him over the officers of the regiment, but my action was more justified by the brilliant career of Colonel Miles."[73]

Although Miles always held fast to his ambitions, he did not neglect the soldiers who served under him. For example, during the opening of the Appomattox campaign, his infantry must have been thoroughly miserable as they struggled through swamps and thick woods in a drenching rain. To revive their spirits, Miles arranged to issue them a ration of whiskey on the evening of March 30. The significance of this action should not be dismissed too lightly. Miles placed the morale of his men over the teachings of his father, who had tried to stop the traffic in liquor during his tenure as selectman back home in Westminster. To make the respite even more festive, Miles felt that no harm could be done by also sending up the division band since the Confederates knew exactly where his men had bivouacked for the night.[74]

Less than two months after Lee surrendered at Appomattox Court House, Miles received orders to report to Fort Monroe, located at the tip of Virginia's James Peninsula. On May 22, the eve of the Army of the Potomac's Grand Review before the president and his guests in Washington, D.C., Miles took a steamer from Baltimore to Fort Monroe. Here he received command of the Military District of Fort Monroe, where Jefferson Davis, the fallen president of the Confederate States of America, would be imprisoned.[75]

– CHAPTER 3 –

After the Civil War

From Fort Monroe, Virginia, to Fort Hays, Kansas

On May 22, 1865, a detachment of cavalrymen accompanied Miles as he sailed aboard a tug to the steamer *William P. Clyde,* at anchor in Hampton Roads. Promptly at 1:00 P.M., Jefferson Davis and Clement C. Clay, who had been a Confederate commissioner in Canada until he voluntarily surrendered, transferred from the ship to the tug for the short trip to their prison at Fort Monroe. Davis had been charged with complicity in the assassination of President Abraham Lincoln, and Clay was suspected of plotting in Canada against Lincoln's life.[1]

Assistant Secretary of War Charles A. Dana telegraphed Stanton as soon as both prisoners were incarcerated. He reported that "Davis bore himself with a haughty attitude. His face was somewhat flushed, but his features were composed and his step firm." Dana, who had no reason to dissemble about Davis's appearance, added that his "hair and beard are not so gray as has been represented, and he seems very much less worn and broken by anxiety and labor than Mr. [Francis P.] Blair reported when he returned from Richmond last winter."[2]

Davis and Clay were confined separately, in outside cells of double-chambered artillery compartments, with their view of either Hampton Roads or Old Point Comfort partially blocked by heavy iron bars secured across the gun ports. A continuous watch would be maintained over each prisoner by posting a sentry inside his cell, thus assuring the safekeeping of Davis and Clay but completely stripping them of any privacy. An officer and two guards would always be available in the adjoining room of the compartment in case the sentry needed assistance. Throughout the night a lamp would permit the duty officer to look in on his charge every fifteen minutes, as prescribed by regulations, although the light would obviously interfere with the inmates' sleep. A hospital bed, table, chair, and portable commode were the only furnishings allowed in each cell, and initially Davis and Clay were only allowed to read their Bibles.

The strict regulations for the confinement of the prisoners had been signed by Maj. Gen. Henry W. Halleck, who had been assigned commander of the Department of Virginia and Army of the James on April 16, 1865, by Secretary of War Edwin Stanton. These arrangements were judged "almost unbearable" by Hudson Strode, a distant relative and biographer of Davis.[3] There is an explanation for Stanton's treatment of the former president of the Confederacy. Quartermaster Gen. Montgomery C. Meigs, who knew the secretary of war well, observed that Stanton was obsessed by thoughts of "the starvation of 100,000 men at Andersonville under the order of Jeff Davis."[4]

On top of the humiliation of having to use a portable commode in plain sight of his sentries, Davis, on May 23, had to endure being chained. Dana had authorized Miles to "place manacles and fetters upon the hands and feet of Jefferson Davis and Clement C. Clay, whenever he may think it advisable in order to render their imprisonment more secure." In 1895, during one of the periodic revivals of interest in this incident, Dana explained that Stanton had suggested allowing Miles to use such a measure so that Davis would be "prevented from doing violence to himself, or from forcing the guard within the casemate to do violence to him."[5]

In 1905, when the story again made news, Miles disclosed that he took advantage of Dana's authorization during the five days that it took to replace the wooden door of Davis's cell with one made of iron bars. He ordered "light anklets" fitted on Davis "to prevent the possibility of his attempting to jump past the guard or commit any act of violence." Miles justified his concern by reminding his readers that in a similar situation,"a prison doctor and other employees had conspired to help Louis Napoleon escape from captivity."[6]

The prospect of being placed in chains truly upset Davis. When he saw a blacksmith enter his cell with leg irons, he tried to resist, but four soldiers held him down while the shackles were attached and locked. When the guards released their hold on Davis, he sat up on his cot and wept. The sight moved the officer in charge of this detail, Capt. Jerome Titlow, 3d Pennsylvania Artillery, who later admitted to his son "that it was anything but a pleasant sight to see a man like Jefferson Davis shedding tears, but not one word had he to say." After the chains were removed, Davis confided to Doctor Craven that he believed "that the object was to offer an indignity both to myself and the cause I represented—not the less sacred to me because [it was] covered with the pall of a military disaster."[7]

By May 25, the *Philadelphia Telegraph* had full details of what had transpired at Fort Monroe, and the *New York Tribune* reprinted this story on May 27. The article showed little pity for Davis, crowing that "never before was so proud a spirit, so strong a will, so completely subdued." The article speculated that once Davis regained his composure, he might spend some time "thinking perhaps of the many poor soldiers who suffered and were starved in his rebel bastilles on his account, and by his order and permission. Possibly he came to a realizing sense that their comfort and their lives were just as good and valuable as his own."[8]

Detractors of Miles were as emphatic in their condemnation of Davis's jailer. For example, in 1869 the *Raleigh* (North Carolina) *Daily Sentinel* predicted that "history would remember Miles as the man who persecuted and fettered the noble spirit of a man who was a prisoner and, therefore, entitled his commiseration rather than his petty persecutions." More recently, Shelby Foote insisted that Miles sought to satisfy his superiors and, in this case, believed that they wanted Davis in irons. The shackling of the fallen president so disturbed Foote that he made the odious comparison that Davis suffered "in the granite bowels of Fort Monroe—where Miles, acting on Stanton's orders, martyred him about as effectively as Booth had martyred Lincoln."[9]

When Miles ordered Davis fettered he was in tune with the temper of the times, but a more compassionate solution would have enhanced his reputation. Those who have attempted to use this incident to tarnish Miles's record would have been disarmed if he had transferred Davis to new quarters in Fort Monroe's Carroll Hall in May instead of September 1865. One must remember, however, that at the time of his capture Davis had wild thoughts of an impossible escape, and during his captivity he contemplated suicide. Miles avoided both of these mischances when he took advantage of his authorization to place Davis in irons, thus insuring the safekeeping of an important state prisoner.[10]

Throughout the winter of 1865 and spring of 1866, Miles sent weekly reports to the adjutant general's office in Washington on the physical condition of Davis and Clay. Although both of the prisoners remained essentially healthy, they began to show signs of strain due to their strict confinement. On May 9, 1866, along with his own findings, Miles forwarded a report written by Dr. George Cooper, who had replaced Dr. Craven as Davis's physician. Cooper's report appears largely to be an attempt to use confusing medical jargon to describe simple nervous disorders. For instance, the doctor noted that following Davis's meals "dyspeptic symptoms promptly make their appearance, soon followed by vertigo, severe facial and cranial neuralgia, and erysipelatous inflammation of the posterior scalp and right side of nose, which quickly affects the right eye (the only sound one of his) and extends through the nasal duct into the interior nose."[11]

Although the doctor found nothing seriously wrong with Davis, he concluded his evaluation of the patient with the alarming opinion that his "vital condition is low and he has but little recuperative force. Should he be attacked by any of the severe forms of disease to which the Tidewater region of Virginia is subject, I, with reason, fear for the result." When newspapers became aware of Dr. Cooper's concern over Davis's condition, some of them began to abuse Miles. For example, a reporter for the *Richmond Times* lamented that except for "the 'Chronicles of the Inquisition' there are few reports like those of Doctor Cooper now extant." The *New York World* used the doctor's diagnosis to condemn those "who have prostituted their official position . . . by the wanton and wicked torture of an invalid lying a helpless prisoner in the strongest fortress of the Union."[12]

Such stories provoked Miles to protest to Asst. Adj. Gen. Edward D. Townsend that they had defamed "my humanity as a man and my honor and character as an officer." He insisted that Dr. Cooper had no grounds for arousing concern about Davis's physical condition. Miles explained that he routinely evaluated his prisoner's health during their daily walks, and he had detected no deterioration. Furthermore, Davis's "fare has been as good or better than officers in the fort. His quarters have been second to none save the bars and bolts." Finally, we can deduce that Davis had not been reduced to a broken-spirited prisoner, but retained an air of command and expected deference, from Miles's notation that: "It is true I have not made him my associate and confidant or toadied to his fancy."[13]

In a confidential follow-up, Miles questioned the objectivity of Dr. Cooper, whom he believed to be "under the influence" of Davis and his young wife, Varina. Although Miles did not accuse the doctor of disloyalty, he disapproved of his being "exceedingly attentive" to Mrs. Davis and of his meetings with her husband's lawyers. The doctor may have fallen under the sway of the Davises due to the influence of Varina, identified by Miles as "a secessionist and one of the F.F.V.'s [First Families of Virginia] of this state." With some insight, Miles believed that the controversy might be attributed to Mrs. Davis, who desired that since her husband "could not be [a] hero to make a martyr of him."[14]

Maj. Gen. Joseph Barnes, the surgeon general of the U.S. Army, examined Davis on June 5, and reported to Stanton that his "present condition is remarkably good." Barnes also informed the secretary of war that Davis had assured him that "his health is and has been much better than has been represented, and he expressed great annoyance at the reports of his condition which had reached the public." Long before Cooper's report, Miles had done much to ease the condition of Davis's confinement. As a result of these efforts, Davis admitted to the surgeon general that "if the sentinel could be removed from such close proximity to his sleeping room and the light at night dispensed with he could be quite as comfortable as it was possible for anyone under duress to be."[15]

Early in his tenure as warden of Fort Monroe, Miles had sought permission to modify the strict regulations established by Stanton. Because of his petitions, the prisoners were allowed to use tobacco, have access to newspapers and books other than the Bible, take daily walks, and, according to Dr. Craven, enjoy "the best of food and stimulants." Perhaps the most significant improvement for Davis occurred when Stanton approved Miles's request to transfer the inmates from artillery casemates within the fort to cells converted from officers' quarters in Carroll Hall. In September 1865, Miles suggested this move to protect the health of Davis and Clay, once he realized how damp the cells were becoming as fall approached.[16]

Despite Davis's appreciation of the changes wrought by Miles, and his statement to the surgeon general that helped to vindicate him, he had no affection for his jailer. He only once publicly revealed his feelings about Miles; in an article about Andersonville, he characterized the young general as a "heartless vulgarian." During his imprisonment, Davis could not always suppress the animosity aroused by being subject to his jailer. After Miles ordered a long length of tape found in Davis's second-floor cell confiscated because it might be used in an escape attempt, the prisoner called Miles a "damned ass." One suspects that Miles acted properly in this case, however, since Davis's story that he needed the tape to secure mosquito netting is weakened by the fact that the incident occurred in December.[17]

As excitement over Davis's health waned, Miles began to wonder about his own future. Stanton responded to his inquiry about a new assignment with the encouraging reply that he would try to post him to "one of the new regiments as a just acknowledgment of your distinguished service and gallantry." As the summer of 1866 neared its end, Miles became concerned when, instead of a regiment, he received President Andrew Johnson's order that would have him mustered out of the service on September 1. Miles suggested to Stanton that the president may have been influenced in this decision by the "base slanders and foulest accusations which the disloyal press have heaped on me." Because of the damaging stories, Miles accepted the possibility that he might be denied an assignment in the reorganized army; in that case, he requested that Stanton allow him to remain at Fort Monroe until October 5. In a note to General Oliver Otis Howard, Miles explained he hoped to retain command of Fort Monroe until after Davis left the post for his trial, expected to begin on the first Tuesday in October. By remaining at Monroe until after Davis departed, Miles could deny any claim "by the Copperhead Party that I was removed at their request."[18]

Obviously Miles had reached a crossroads. From his correspondence with Howard and Stanton, one would suspect that the possibility of being discharged from the army distressed him. Actually, months before the storm over Dr. Cooper's report had clouded his future, Miles had apparently decided to resign from the army. On January 16, 1866, General Halleck acknowledged Miles's note, "in which you say that you expect soon to leave the service and return to civil life." Thus, it appears that damage to his reputation rather than to his professional plans is what upset Miles during the summer of 1866.[19]

Further clarification of Miles's intentions is found in an 1887 editorial reviewing his career. In Tucson the *Arizona Daily Star* reprinted the *Boston Herald*'s disclosure that after the Civil War, Miles intended to return to Westminster, where he would run for Congress. Although he lacked the financial resources needed to cover campaign expenses and had few political connections, the *Herald* explained that he "had great success during the

Rebellion and possessed faith enough in his star to believe that the same good fortune awaited him in the field of political preferment." According to this report, before Miles had a chance to resign, brother officers convinced him to remain in the army. As a result of their persuasion, after Miles mustered out of the volunteer service on September 1, 1866, on September 6 he accepted a regular commission as a colonel in the 40th Infantry, dated July 28, 1866.[20]

On July 28, 1866, President Andrew Johnson signed the law that reorganized the regular army for peacetime service. The strength of the postwar army reached a high point of 56,815 in September 1867, but by 1874, a series of annual appropriation acts had gradually reduced the number of officers and enlisted men to 27,000. Most of the officers who elected to remain in the army after the 1866 contraction had to accept a lower rank than the one that they had earned during the Civil War. For example, among the West Pointers who became major generals with the Army of the Potomac yet received only a lieutenant colonel's commission in 1866 were George Crook, George A. Custer, and Wesley Merritt.[21]

Since Miles had been granted a colonel's commission when many of his contemporaries had to settle for less, his tenure as jailer for Jefferson Davis apparently did not negatively affect his military career. As for the critics who charged that his prisoner's health had deteriorated while under Miles's care, he answered that the former president of the Confederacy "lived for twenty-four years after he was first imprisoned, and died of old age at the age of 81."[22]

With the unrewarding duty of caring for Davis behind him, Miles reported to North Carolina, where he served as an assistant commissioner of the Bureau of Refugees, Freedmen and Abandoned Lands. This agency, commonly called the Freedmen's Bureau, was headed by General Howard, who established his headquarters in Washington, D.C., on May 15, 1865. The bureau functioned as an administrative branch of the War Department, and an army officer responsible to Howard served as an assistant commissioner in each of the unreconstructed states. The bureau was a temporary agency designed to care for the freedmen and abandoned lands in the South. The tasks confronting Howard's assistant commissioners seemed insurmountable. Miles recalled that his "first orders were to re-establish civil control as far as possible, restore confidence, security, and peace, to conciliate the disaffected element, to remove the existing prejudice between the two races, to promote industry, and to encourage new industry."[23]

Even before Miles received his appointment as the assistant commissioner for North Carolina, he had shown an interest in helping the former slaves. While in command at Fort Monroe, Miles became concerned about those who had fled from their former masters and now lived in the vicinity of nearby Hampton, Virginia.

In contrast with most officers, who routinely tried to convince freed people to return to their home plantations, Miles encouraged former slaves to start new lives.[24] He sought Howard's help, explaining that there had been "a large meeting of colored people in Hampton today, with a view of going to Florida and taking up government lands under the Homestead Act. But as they have been deceived so many times, it is hard to make them believe it is for their best interest to go." Miles hoped that Howard would write a letter encouraging this resettlement plan because the thousands of unemployed freedmen in Hampton trusted and would listen to him.[25]

Although Miles did not record the outcome of the proposed Florida venture, his efforts showed more ingenuity than most in trying to solve one of the problems of the period. The difficulties in trying to create a fair and workable labor system led John A. Carpenter to declare that the "alleged re-enslavement of the Negro was the great issue which prevented the Reconstruction of the South from being a relatively peaceful, harmonious period in American history."[26]

Miles devised one method for satisfying the needs of both workers and planters that attracted attention outside of North Carolina. The *New York Times* reprinted a circular issued by Miles that provided for the registration of laborers in the Tar Heel State. The register would be open to applications from both skilled and unskilled men and women of either race. Every ten days the information regarding those who were still without work was sent from local offices to Miles's headquarters, where the list of applicants was matched with a list of positions to be filled, which had already been forwarded to Raleigh.[27]

Miles also looked to relocation as a solution to the plight of destitute war widows and their children. Besides trying to attract charity from Northern cities to aid those unfortunate people, Miles sought to find employment for them in the manufacturing cities of New England. He suggested to his superiors in Washington that "if employment could be guaranteed them in any part of the country, this Bureau would furnish them with transportation and they would gladly leave these scenes of want and sorrow." As with the Florida venture for former slaves, there is no record of how this relocation plan for aiding the families of North Carolina's war dead worked out.[28]

Miles's most enthusiastic efforts were in the field of education. In reviewing the accomplishments of the bureau in North Carolina, Miles boasted that the "educational branch of the bureau would in itself be a sufficient claim for its [the bureau's] continuance." In his memoirs he noted that after just one year of work by the bureau, 8,529 pupils were enrolled in 101 new schools that were staffed by 145 teachers.[29]

Efforts to educate the freed people were not appreciated by some North Carolinians. The *Daily Sentinel* of Raleigh protested that the schools attracted too many workers from the labor pool. The author of this piece made a significant observation regarding conditions in the North, however, when he asked, "Are all the Northern white children kept at school and taught to make a living by education at the schools? Are they taught not to work?"[30]

Such criticism concerned Miles, who believed that former slaves had little hope for a bright future without the bureau. When he reviewed his accomplishments for Howard's benefit, Miles deplored the fact that "the colored people in this state [North Carolina] scarcely own land enough to stand upon. Occupying still the little slave huts under the shadow of former masters' mansions by sufferance, and without the protecting arm of the Government, they are almost as much within the grasp of their old owners as in the days of slavery."[31]

Besides his duties with the Freedmen's Bureau, Miles also served as commander of the 40th Infantry, a black regiment headquartered at Raleigh. In the summer of 1867, the Reconstruction Act of March 2, 1867, "gave the Army its greatest headache." The act, which divided the South into five military districts, also required each state to adopt a new constitution that provided for black suffrage. Difficulties for the military arose as the army began to register eligible voters who would select delegates to state constitutional conventions.[32]

Miles found out how sensitive this duty could be after he issued a circular insisting that all officials who came in contact with freedmen should encourage them to register and vote in the election for delegates to meet in 1868 to establish a new constitution. He had hoped to avoid criticism by directing that these officials should behave in an impartial manner. Despite his caution, Miles offended some whites because he ordered authorities to be on guard against persons who might try to interfere with the registration process. He explained in the order that "it is known that threats of violence and gross misrepresentations have been used."[33]

The editor of the *Daily Sentinel* immediately replied that, "surely no responsible white man has been guilty of such conduct. Such conversation is seriously reprehensible, but we have heard nothing like it." The editor's argument is weakened, however, by the tone of other statements in the very same editorial. He asserted, for instance, that freedmen "understand equality and union to mean nothing short of eating at a white man's table and sleeping in a white man's bed."[34]

Despite the carpings of the local press, registration officials enjoyed a moderate success in North Carolina. Although approximately 10 percent of the eligible white voters were disfranchised because of previous office holding or wartime service, 106,721 whites and 72,932 blacks were registered. (In 1870 the population of North Carolina was 1,071,361.) In the election of November 19 and 20, some 93,000 voted "for convention," approving a constitutional convention, and 32,961 against.[35]

Miles explained to Howard that many of the white voters either voted against the convention or boycotted the election so that they "might obstruct the work of reconstruction. . . . This opposition is controlled and led by men who have been notoriously antagonistic to the Government for years." The *Sentinel* conceded that many voters in North Carolina used the election to show their displeasure with the proposed convention. The editor, however, accused Miles of doing them a "gross injustice" when he charged that they were "trying to obstruct justice." He argued that those who had opposed the convention did so because they were against "the principles of Radical Reconstruction, because they believed them utterly destructive to the future peace and prosperity of the State."[36]

Despite the hostility of many North Carolinians, the convention took place in Raleigh from January 14 to March 17, 1868. An 1880 account of the proceedings portrayed the Conservative Democrats as a "hopeless minority" who "sat in helpless astonishment as the Northern members of the

Convention uprooted one by one so many of the ancient landmarks of the State." Although the Constitution of 1868 may have seemed tradition-shattering to the Conservative Democrats, it contained many necessary and progressive features. Besides the acceptance of universal manhood suffrage for both races, it provided for the elimination of property and religious qualifications for office holding and voting. It also established a public school system open to all of the children in the state.[37]

Following the framing of the new constitution, elections were held from April 21 through April 25, 1868, to consider the work of the convention and to elect county and state officials and representatives to Congress. Republicans enjoyed an outstanding success, gaining control of the state legislature and all but one congressional seat, winning approval of the constitution, and placing their candidate, William H. Holden, a political journalist, into the governor's mansion. Holden impressed some as opportunistic because he had been an unsuccessful contender for the Democratic nomination for governor before the war, then switched parties afterwards. Horace Roper, Holden's biographer, agreed that because of instances of such behavior in North Carolina, "it became fashionable practice to denounce Holden, personally and politically." In his dissertation Roper offered his evaluation of Holden's place in history. Although unwilling to rehabilitate the governor's reputation completely, the biographer decided that Holden's "program had been one of reform, and a majority of his recommendations, considered so dangerous and radical at the time, were later adopted as matters of common practice in North Carolina."[38]

After North Carolina's readmission as a state, the army assumed a new role. Instead of supervising civil affairs, troops would respond to requests for assistance in enforcing civil law and to maintain order during elections. Civil authorities, however, would soon find out how cautious the commander of the Department of the South, Maj. Gen. George G. Meade, would be in permitting troops to assist them. For example, Holden requested authorization for Miles to use his troops "to aid the civil power in bringing offenders to justice and enforcing the law." Meade's assistant adjutant general, Richard C. Drum, denied the request until "any actual resistance to law which you cannot suppress occurs." As one study explained, Meade "would tolerate nothing that smacked of using troops as a police guard for an unpopular governor."[39]

Both Holden and Miles attempted to budge Meade from his course. Drum acknowledged the receipt of a letter sent by Miles on September 25, 1868, "enclosing the affidavit of a citizen affirming there are a large number of arms secreted at a political clubroom, at Wilmington, N.C." Drum denied Miles permission to seize the weapons because he had not furnished any evidence that the rifles would be used improperly; furthermore, civilian authorities had ignored the situation. Drum then instructed Miles that only after "the proper prosecuting officer . . . is resisted and reports his inability to carry out either the United States or State law, and then and not till then will the commanding officer consider himself justified in interfering."[40]

Miles then forwarded copies of an exchange of his correspondence with the governor to Meade's headquarters in Atlanta. On October 7 Holden had requested troops transferred within the state for "the greatest aid practicable to the civil authorities in maintaining the peace." Miles responded with his view of conditions in North Carolina. The stockpiling of Enfield rifles and "several hundreds of Henry and Spencer rifles (many of them sixteen shooters)" by groups such as "K.K.K.'s" reminded Miles of the South in 1861, when "professions of intense loyalty to the Constitution and laws went hand in hand with concealed preparations for war." Although an "appeal to arms" should be "inexplicable" after the disastrous experience of the past war, Miles warned that "any attempt to excite disturbances by any parties under any pretense whatever are alike foolhardy and criminal."[41]

Miles's persistence ignited Meade's fiery temper. The department commander brought his differences with Miles to Grant's attention just one month before the commanding general would face the voters in his bid for the presidency. Meade felt compelled to involve Grant, however, to ensure "not only that obedience should be given on the part of subordinates, but that there should be harmony of judgment as well." The final line of this letter, a copy of which had been forwarded to Miles, must have stunned the young colonel. Obviously believing that obedience and harmony were missing from his official relationship with Miles, Meade bluntly asked Grant for "a decision in the issue raised, and that the officer whose judgment is not approved—whether it be myself or General Miles, be relieved from further command in this Department."[42]

Happily, the controversy was resolved without any drastic action by Grant, and it left no lasting scars. Meade may even have taken the initiative to heal the breach. Shortly after a conference with Meade, Miles wrote him what can only be considered a letter of apology, protesting that he did not have "the slightest intention to raise any issue with the Commanding General whose orders and instructions will always be cheerfully observed and enforced to the best of my ability." Like so many warriors throughout history, Miles would find that prowess in combat has little bearing on one's ability to avoid the pitfalls of peacetime.[43]

In the fall of 1868, as excitement built up in North Carolina over the approaching presidential election, Miles's flawless performance redeemed his earlier blundering into an avoidable confrontation with Meade. In September Meade ordered troops deployed throughout the states in his department in order to enforce the 1865 law authorizing the army to maintain order at the polls. Still cautious, the department commander required "all intervention of the troops to be subordinate to, and in aid of and cooperation with, the civil authorities."[44]

In accordance with his instructions and after he conferred with Holden, Miles notified Drum of the eight cities in North Carolina where his troops would be stationed. He explained these cities were either on rail or water routes that could be used to transport the troops to troubled areas. Miles also kept in mind the political situation in the state when he made his dispositions. Thus, he concentrated his forces in the central section of the state, "where it is known that the most hostile feelings exist and where disorder and infringements of law and order are to be apprehended." He ended with a pledge that his troops would not interfere with the election.[45]

Miles kept his promise by issuing a special order to his men, reminding them that "under no circumstances will officers or soldiers fraternize with political parties, or in any manner interfere with the peaceful exercise, by all citizens, of their rights and privileges as such." On November 2, the day before the election, Miles's local adversary, the *Daily Sentinel*, printed his general order with the compliment that "it breathes the proper spirit."[46]

After the polls closed, Miles telegraphed headquarters in Atlanta that the "election has passed quietly. No disturbances reported in this state thus far." By the end of the week, the Sentinel had received enough information to announce that "from every section of the state the news is that the late election was one of the most quiet we have had." Rather than credit the presence of the 40th Infantry for the lack of incidents on November 3, the editor praised "the peaceable disposition of our people, and the purposes of the Democrats and Conservatives to avoid all cause of collision."[47]

The election returns showed that in North Carolina 96,449 voters cast their ballots for Grant, while the Democratic candidate, Horatio Seymour, former governor of New York, received 83,559 votes. In the congressional races, after some confusion and delay, the Republicans were given six of the seven seats. On Friday, November 6, the Republicans in Raleigh celebrated their victory from dawn until late into the night. In a public speech, Miles revealed his deep feelings about the election when he spoke of Grant's victory as "a triumph of loyalty over treason, a triumph of patriotism over rebellion and secession." On a higher tone, Miles looked to North Carolina's future and saw that "nothing now remains to be done but for her people to turn their attention to internal improvements, and to the development of the resources of the State. Education, the corner-stone of liberty, must be liberally and warmly sustained."[48]

The editor of the *Sentinel* must have been rankled at the sight of his opponents celebrating the defeat of the Democratic party. He definitely took exception to the courtesies that Miles and Holden exchanged to mark their victory. After Holden sent a telegram to Grant that complimented Miles, and later the same day Miles honored Holden with a fifteen-gun salute, the newspaperman belittled the gestures as a case of "Tickle Me and I'll Tickle You."[49]

In 1868, Miles had more to raise his spirits than just an election victory. A year earlier, while visiting Senator John Sherman's home, the dashing young colonel met Mary Sherman, a niece of Sherman's. In accordance with the formal rituals of a proper Victorian courtship, Mary's family in Cleveland felt free to question Republican senator Charles Sumner of Massachusetts about the young officer who had apparently captured their daughter's heart. Sumner informed Mary's father, Judge Charles T. Sherman, that he found Miles, who had visited his house several times during the winter of 1867–68, to be "intelligent, pleasant and of agreeable manners. He seemed to be a favorite with the ladies." The senator, who described Miles as a "self-made" man, added, however, that "he has not the advantage of a liberal or University education."

The young couple's relationship survived this frank assessment, and Miles took the next step and himself wrote a letter to the judge. "I confess I have felt less trepidation in meeting our enemy than I do in addressing you on the subject when your answer involves my life interest and future happiness." Miles then worked up the courage to ask for Mary's hand.

During the evening of June 30, 1868, in Cleveland's Holy Trinity Church, the twenty-nine-year-old colonel married Mary Hoyt Sherman, at twenty-six the eldest daughter of Judge Sherman of the Northern Judicial District of Ohio. The city's fashionable set had already noted the wedding date on their social calendars, but excitement mounted with the news that Lt. Gen. William T. Sherman and Maj. Gen. Philip H. Sheridan were to be members of the bridal party. Following the ceremony, the guests, including Maj. (Bvt. Brig. Gen.) James W. Forsyth, who would serve under Miles at Wounded Knee in 1890, were "elegantly entertained" at Judge Sherman's home.[50]

Not only did this marriage give Miles access to Mary's uncles, Senator John Sherman and General Sherman, but also, at a later date, to Senator J. Donald Cameron. In 1878 Mary's sister Elizabeth married the senator, who inherited the Pennsylvania political machine put together by his father, Simon Cameron.

Miles probably joyfully envisioned a helping hand from above after Sherman succeeded Grant as commander of the army on March 4, 1869. The ambitious colonel would soon find, however, that marriage to the commanding general's niece would be more of a handicap than a spur to his military career. When Sherman refused to make Miles a department commander after the colonel had put together a string of Indian war victories in 1879, Mary explained to her Uncle John that his brother objected because of "his peculiar sensitiveness about doing any thing for a relation. If General Miles were a stranger he would do this in a moment and listen to the petitions of the people." Happily, as Mary's influence with the general, whom she affectionately called Uncle Cump, waned, her marriage flourished.[51]

Miles's bride developed into a paragon of an officer's wife. Mary had spent most of her youth outdoors and had become an excellent rider. Thus, she felt quite comfortable about accompanying her husband on his assignments to desolate posts on the frontier, even when danger threatened. According to the *New York Times,* "she had been near enough to her husband in some of his Indian fights to hear the shots on both sides." In a 1902 article advising soldiers' wives to keep busy while their husbands served overseas, Mary admitted "what a horror life became during those [Indian] outbreaks." However, what disturbed her during these campaigns was how "thought itself becomes a terror; to sleep, and waken with the dull pain at my heart, and the ever present question uppermost: 'Will today bring the news that he has been killed?'"[52]

When a promotion brought the family out of the wilderness, Miles received postings to San Francisco, Chicago, and New York before finally settling in Washington, D.C. When the couple welcomed visitors into their elegant home at 1734 N Street NW, Mary must have been an invaluable aid guiding her husband away from false steps in the drawing room. Her background as a member of Cleveland's young social set helped her to make the dizzying transition from receiving guests at military outposts to hosting cosmopolitan gatherings. The *New York Times* complimented her as "an active leader in Washington society and one of the most-popular matrons who ever entertained there." The *New York Herald* concurred, adding that "in Washington she was greatly beloved by all who knew her, and her entertainments made her a conspicuous leader of society at the National Capital." According to the *New York Tribune,* at the time of her death in 1904, a number of her guests had been misled by her youthful looks and would find it "hard to believe that she could be the mother of a grown girl and a son entering manhood."[53]

Even before the *Army and Navy Journal* wished the newlyweds "very many years of connubial felicity," it reminded its readers that Miles had "gained an enviable reputation during the war as a brave soldier and rose to be a Major General of Volunteers entirely by reason of his merits." Even when Meade complained to Grant about his determined subordinate, he felt obliged to mention that "no one has higher respect personally for General Miles than myself and that no one appreciates more fully, the distinguished reputation acquired by him for deeds of gallantry enacted during the war." Too young at twenty-nine to rest on his laurels, Miles sought new fields to conquer. He undoubtedly prompted Mary to seek a position for him on General Sherman's staff. Uncle Cump vetoed her suggestion, however, because he believed that Washington "is the very worst place for an officer. Once stationed there, he sinks into the condition of a clerk and loses all taste for military form and ambitions."[54]

After Miles himself made two similar appeals for a staff job, the commanding general abruptly wired him that "in consolidation [of the army] I may have to put you in the Fifth Infantry in Kansas." Two days later, the Colonel received official confirmation that he would command the regiment. In Miles's memoirs he admitted that he "was glad to leave the South at the opening of its new era for new and untried fields of the Far West—different scenes, different conditions, and quite different duties."[55]

Miles and his wife traveled by train to Fort Leavenworth, Kansas, the frontier headquarters established on the west bank of the Missouri River. This important supply depot evoked so many pleasant memories that Miles paused in his description of his westward journey to recall how units looked forward to crowding into the fort as winter approached, abandoning strenuous field duty for the comforts of civilization. From Leavenworth the young couple had to travel about 450 miles farther west to reach Fort Hays, Kansas, home of the 5th Infantry. For the final leg of their journey, which crossed sixty miles of unsettled land, they had to board a work train. Miles vividly described their passage through a landscape covered with buffalo grass and wildflowers and where shrubs and stands of timber flourished by the streams. Miles seemed fascinated by the wildlife that abounded in this rich setting—the herds of buffalo that were still plentiful, along with elk, antelope, and deer.[56]

At Fort Hays, built to protect workers building the transcontinental railroad from Indian raids, Miles found true contentment. It was "a pleasure to be relieved of the anxieties and responsibilities of civil affairs, to hear nothing of the controversies incident to race prejudice, and to be once more engaged in strictly military duties, a profession to which I was devoted." Miles also developed a lasting attachment to the 5th Infantry. He boasted to General Sherman, "I might possibly have the best regiment in the service. I am therefore well satisfied with my present position." As the years passed, Miles advanced to more important commands, but he never forgot his first regiment on the frontier. In 1898 Frederic Remington observed that "soldiers retain this affection for their old regiments, although they may be long out of them. General Miles won't go anywhere without the Fifth Infantry." During an inspection tour of the Philippines, taken less than a year before his retirement, Miles addressed the 5th Infantry. He told the men that he had "spent the best years of my life with the regiment, and, since leaving it, have kept closely in touch with its work. . . . Colonels may come and colonels may go, but the regiment goes on forever." Although no regiment, including Miles's first combat command, the 61st New York, would enjoy as close a relationship with him as the 5th Infantry, Miles acknowledged a rarely noted appreciation of his service with the 40th Infantry, which he had left behind in North Carolina. In 1899 Miles responded to a letter from Theophilius Stewart, a chaplin of a black unit, the 25th Infantry, who was then writing *Colored Regulars in the United States Army.* Miles stated that "the first regiment which I commanded on entering the Regular Army of the United States at the close of the war was made up of colored troops. That regiment—the 40th Infantry—achieved a reputation for military conduct which forms a record that may be favorably compared with the best regiments in the service.[57]

In the fall of 1870, Miles moved his headquarters to Fort Leavenworth, and Mary returned to her family's home in Cleveland, where she gave birth to their first child, a daughter named Cecilia. With Mary away, Miles turned his full attention to his command, which would earn an outstanding reputation in the coming campaigns. His concern for training the troops was evident when he informed Sherman that the "Department Commander Brigadier General [Brevet Major General] John Pope has recommended the concentration of my regiment at some point on the Kansas Pacific Railroad; if his plan is adopted it will give me a fine opportunity for drill and instruction."[58]

– CHAPTER 4 –

Campaign against the Cheyenne, Kiowa, and Comanche

When the southern Plains Indians rose up in 1874, Miles finally had a chance to lead his regiment in battle. The Indian Territory campaign, designated the Red River War in some histories, officially began on July 20, 1874. On that date General Sherman telegraphed permission for Lt. Gen. Philip H. Sheridan to suppress the Kiowas, Comanches, and Cheyennes, who had slipped away from their reservations. Among their reasons for leaving was hunger because they had not received sufficient provisions from Indian agents, and they were also angry at the hardships resulting from the slaughter of the buffalo herds. After twenty-eight buffalo hunters held off hundreds of attacking warriors at Adobe Walls in the Texas Panhandle on June 27, 1874, many tribesmen gave vent to their frustrations by striking out in raiding parties that ranged from Texas north to Colorado and as far east as Kansas.[1]

The army's response to these raids was the responsibility of Sheridan, who commanded the Division of the Missouri from his headquarters in Chicago. Sheridan's division included all of the West up to the boundary with the Division of the Pacific at the continental divide. This huge land mass was divided into four departments: Department of Dakota, Department of the Platte, Department of the Missouri, and Department of Texas.

While Sheridan devised the strategy to be followed in the campaign, actual supervision of the troops in the field was left to Brig. Gen. (Bvt. Maj. Gen.) Christopher C. Augur, commander of the Department of Texas, and Brigadier General John Pope, commander of the Department of the Missouri. Augur and Pope ordered out five columns of troops with instructions to converge in the Texas Panhandle, where they would subdue the rebellious Indians and force them to return to their agencies.

From his headquarters at Fort Leavenworth, General Pope arranged for Miles to move south from Fort Dodge into the Panhandle. At the same time, Maj. (Bvt. Col.) William R. Price would lead four companies of the Eighth Cavalry from Fort Bascom, New Mexico, along the Canadian River as it flowed from New Mexico into Texas. Meanwhile General Augur sent two columns northward from central Texas, one commanded by Lt. Col. (Bvt. Brig. Gen.) George P. Buell, 11th Infantry, and the other by Col. (Bvt. Brig. Gen.) Ranald S. Mackenzie, Fourth Cavalry. Finally, Lt. Col. (Bvt. Maj. Gen.) John W. Davidson, Tenth Cavalry, a black regiment, would leave Fort Sill in Indian territory and close in on the Panhandle from the east.[2]

The 744 men in Miles's command were divided into three battalions. Two of these were made up of four companies of the Sixth Cavalry, while four companies of the 5th Infantry were formed into the third battalion. A few men were detached from this unit to service a ten-pound Parrott and the two Gatling guns in the small artillery battery commanded by 2d Lt. James W. Pope, 5th Infantry. First Lt. Frank D. Baldwin, 5th Infantry, served as chief of scouts for the twenty Delaware Indians, from a reservation near Coffeyville, Kansas, and led by Chief Falling Leaf, and the nineteen frontiersmen who had been hired as guides. A train of sixty wagons and five ambulances, driven by well-armed civilian teamsters, would carry the column's ammunition and supplies.[3]

Before Lieutenant Baldwin set out with a scouting party directly for the Red River country, Miles had the plainsmen demonstrate their marksmanship. Miles and his staff were impressed when the guides used open-sighted army rifles to shred a target placed one thousand yards from the firing line. This shooting match helped the scouts establish their qualifications for the job, and Miles already had complete confidence in their chief, whom he considered one of his "coolest and ablest officers." Like his regimental commander, Baldwin would become a general officer without the benefit of a West Point education. During the Civil War, he won a Medal of Honor while fighting as a captain with the 19th Michigan Infantry at the Battle of Peach Tree Creek, Georgia, on July 20, 1864.[4]

Miles facilitated the ninety-seven-mile march south from Fort Dodge to Camp Supply, his last stop before the wilderness, by having his battalions move out independently. On August 7, Maj. (Bvt. Lt. Col.) Henry B. Bristol, 5th Infantry, left with the foot soldiers, followed on August 10 by the wagon train escorted by Capt. (Bvt. Maj.) Wyllys Lyman, 5th Infantry. Finally, on the thirteenth, the rest of the column began a five-day trek to the supply depot.[5]

After the troops spent a day refitting at the frontier outpost, located in the northwestern corner of the Indian territory, the campaign began in earnest. The troops suffered as the temperature soared above one hundred degrees day after day. The land that they moved across had been stripped of much of its greenery by a locust plague, and a severe drought made drinking water scarce. According to a correspondent traveling with the expedition, "only at long intervals were found holes of stagnant water, impregnated with gypsum and of the consistency of syrup. Men rushed in frenzy and drank, only to find their thirst increased rather than slacked. Even coffee boiled in it was found so bitter that it could not be drank."[6]

In the evening of August 26, Baldwin's scouts rejoined the main command with information that Indians had recently camped on Sweetwater Creek, south of the Washita River. They found the campsite, nestled in a pleasant valley, littered with abandoned equipment indicating a hasty departure. On the twenty-eighth, encouraged by signs that he was closing on his quarry, Miles left the wagon train guarded by two companies of infantry commanded by Captain Bristol. No longer encumbered by the supply train, the rest of the command, including five ammunition wagons and two ambulances, covered sixty-five miles in two days. At 4:00 A.M. on the morning of August 30, the chase began again, with the scouts riding about two miles in front of the main column.[7]

Baldwin's men rode across a broad plain and, at about 8:00 A.M., approached the sharp slopes at the edge of a high plateau known as the Staked Plains. About 250 Cheyenne warriors, who had been waiting in ambush, swooped down upon the scouts as they entered the hills. Miles noted in his report that in their attack, "the dash and courage usual in savage warfare were exhibited," but the advance party refused to give way. Instead, the scouts dismounted and took cover.[8]

The Cheyenne must have been startled by the main party's quick response to the attempted ambush. The *New York Herald* reporter noted that, "Upon hearing the first volley the column fairly flew to the spot, led by the gallant commander, who deployed into line on the gallop and charged the bluffs without halting, cavalry on the right and left, infantry center." Lieutenant Pope sited his three artillery pieces on high ground in order to support the advance. Watching the "rapidity and precision" of the maneuvers before him, the correspondent credited "the extreme coolness and capacity of the commander under the most exciting circumstances and the good effect of years of discipline and drill on the part of the troops."

The attack seemed doomed to failure as Miles's command approached an estimated four to six hundred warriors looking down upon them from the top of the ridges. The journalist told his readers that the fighting men, despite their disadvantage, "sprang unflinchingly to the work, scaled the heights in the teeth of heavy fire and drove the enemy pell mell into the canyons beyond." He explained that, "The hills are so steep and ragged that the troopers were compelled to advance picking their way in a zigzag course to the top, yet at the moment of the onslaught every man was in his place, enthusiastically bent on driving or exterminating the savages concealed at the top." During the confusion of battle, the reporter managed to pick out Miles, mounted on Virginia, the striking mare that had been his warhorse since the final year of the Civil War. The observer kept his eyes on him as he "galloped along the lines, attending personally to the minutest details of the attack and subsequent movement of the troops, ably assisted by his adjutant, Lieutenant [George W.] Baird, and Aide, Lieutenant [William B.] Wetmore, who carried his orders to the right and left wings respectively."

When the Cheyennes, possibly supported by some Comanches and Kiowas, realized that they could not make an effective stand, "they turned, completely routed, flying in all directions." The cavalry steadily pursued, first beyond the Red River, then through their burning tepees, and finally onto the Staked Plains, the tableland in the part of the Great Plains that lies along the border of Texas and New Mexico.[9]

Miles called a halt to the pursuit after the Indians pulled away from his command. He explained in his report that, "My supplies were so far exhausted as not to have warranted my crossing of the Staked Plains, even if I had had means of carrying water, and it became necessary to return to replenish."[10]

Although August 30 had been a day of vigorous combat, neither side suffered many casualties. While there is no doubt that the pursuing forces only saw a sergeant and two men wounded, records vary as to the number of their enemy who fell in battle. Eyewitness accounts, however, dispute the Indians' claims that they only lost a Comanche guide named Mule Smoking. In Miles's report, written two days after the battle, he noted that three bodies were found after the battle, but others on the scene were less conservative in their count. Thompson McFadden, a scout, noted in his diary that the bodies of eleven warriors were found on the field; simultaneously the *Herald*'s correspondent reported that on August 31, on the trail of the tribesmen, "the bodies of seventeen dead Indians, together with abandoned property of all sorts, were passed, which fact not only proved their great loss and severe punishment the day previous but indicated as well their complete rout and demoralization." He explained to his readers that, "Unless pushed to the death, an Indian never permits a dead body to fall into the hands of an enemy."[11]

Miles camped by the Red River while waiting for the wagon train escorted by Captain Lyman's company and a small mounted detachment that he had sent back to Camp Supply for provisions. During the pause, he had a chance to unburden himself in a letter to his wife. He complained that he "had every obstacle but intense cold to contend with—heat, dust, sand, canyons, ravines, mountains, bluffs, and a scarcity of water. Added to that, I find altogether too many incompetent and inefficient officers who have no interest in their duties." To complicate his mission further, although Miles did not know it at the time, about 250 Kiowa and Comanche warriors had left the Wichita Agency at Anadarko with their families. As they moved west to join the main body who had already taken refuge on the Staked Plains, they disrupted Miles's supply lines.[12]

The Indians from the Wichita Agency came upon the wagon train on its way back to the bivouac on the Red River, where Lyman knew supplies would be exhausted by September 13. They also encountered two small parties carrying dispatches. In each case scouts and troops succeeded in fighting off their attackers, but at the cost of two soldiers and a teamster killed and six men wounded. The stout resistance the Indians met in these engagements apparently disheartened some of them. While one group continued on toward the Staked Plains, some turned themselves in at the Fort Sill reservation, while others turned back and on October 3 surrendered at the Cheyenne Agency on the Canadian River.[13]

Miles became so concerned about the failure of the wagon train to arrive when expected that he had his men march to meet it. Detachments were left behind to set up camps on Sweetwater Creek, the Washita River, and the Canadian River. Because supplies were short, the troops enjoyed a respite from hard campaigning that was made even more pleasant after heavy rainstorms on September 7 broke both the drought and the heat wave that accompanied it. Finally, on September 14, Capt. (Bvt. Maj.) Adna R. Chaffee, Sixth Cavalry, destined to become a lieutenant general and chief of staff of the Army in 1904, scouting in advance of the main column, came upon the wagon train at the Washita. Although a relief party from Camp Supply had reached the train just after the Indians had broken off a siege that had lasted for three days and nights, the train had been forced to stop a second time. Twenty-two mules had been killed during the fight, and after a fierce twenty-four-hour storm turned the prairie into a quagmire, the surviving animals were unable to pull the wagons through the mud.[14]

Earlier, on September 7, Miles dispatched his aide to bring Major Price back to camp after learning that the Eighth Cavalry column was now only five miles from him. When the major arrived, Miles, concerned because he had received no word from his train or couriers, instructed Price to search for them. After five days of riding, the major found his path blocked by warriors who intended to fight a delaying action from defensive positions until their families could ride to safety. At first the braves "were very bold," but after they had bought enough time for the noncombatants to flee, they were content alternately to fall back and then resume fighting. After almost three hours of holding back the cavalry, the Indians broke away from the troops and dispersed. No soldiers were hit in this action, but a week later two buried warriors were found in the vicinity of the chase, probably killed by Price's cavalrymen.

Price started back to camp on the thirteenth, the day after his encounter, because he had run out of food except for some unsalted buffalo meat. While on the wagon road, someone in Price's column noticed a scout trying to get their attention. The scout, William Dixon, led a party, including a doctor, back to four wounded survivors of the "Buffalo Wallow" fight in which one private died. After the doctor did what he could for the couriers, Price sent a lieutenant to fetch an ambulance from Miles's camp. Then the Eighth Cavalry rode off, leaving the forlorn messengers alone to wait for the arrival of the ambulance. Price reported hearing gunfire later that same night, but rather than ride to the sound, he decided to continue along the road, hoping to find the wagon train. Since the shots were fired by Lyman's men to alert troops to their location, the major admitted that "there was some feeling expressed because we did not come immediately to their relief." On the fourteenth, Price met up with his own train, which had been traveling independently, and the following day the column from New Mexico entered Miles's camp on the Washita.[15]

Miles assumed temporary command over the Eighth Cavalry until September 20, when "the Department Commander directed that it become part of my command." He reorganized the personnel of the Sixth Cavalry so that the troopers with the most worn-out mounts could be sent back to Camp Supply. In reducing the Sixth Cavalry by half, Miles hoped to lessen the burden of keeping his command supplied. Reducing his column also gave him an opportunity to weed out some of his most "worthless" and "disagreeable" officers. Throughout his career, Miles would habitually confide to his wife about the shortcomings of his officers. For instance, after the drought broke in September, he complained that some of his officers "are worse than useless. They had rather gamble and drink at a post than serve in the field. During good weather they do well, but in the first rain, they curl up like wet hens and do nothing but growl and whine."[16]

Such correspondence has helped give Miles a reputation for being difficult to please, and, in truth, he was never toleratant of incompetents, no matter what their position. While his private letters indicate his impatience with those who did not live up to his standards, his public reports reveal not only a demanding taskmaster but also a fair man who more than appreciated those that he could count on to do their jobs. For instance, at the conclusion of the Indian Territory campaign, Miles recommended that sixteen of his officers be breveted for "especially gallant and valuable services." Among those that he wanted to honor were his aide, Lieutenant Wetmore, and his adjutant, Lieutenant Baldwin; Lieutenant Pope, who, according to the *Herald* observer, "performed splendid service with his 'battery' during the charge [at the Battle of Red River], throwing percussion shells from his Parrotts and balls from the Gatlings at knots of Indians gathered here and there on the bluffs, scattering them at every shot"; Captain Lyman, in command during the wagon train fight; Captain Chaffee, who fired up his cavalrymen as they rushed with drawn pistols toward the enemy by shouting, "Forward! If any man is killed I'll make him a corporal"; and Maj. [Bvt. Lt. Col.] Charles E.

Compton, Sixth Cavalry, who led a charge on August 30 that was described by the *Herald* as "a magnificent spectacle."[17]

Miles's troop reduction, designed to enhance his ability to remain in the field, fit perfectly with Sheridan's plans. Just before the Battle of Red River, he strongly recommended to General Pope that Miles and Price should continue campaigning until the end of the Indian troubles. Sheridan believed that Camp Supply should be stocked to the rafters to enable it to handle the needs of an extended operation. He wrote optimistically that he had "strong hopes that the troubles will be over before winter especially as the Indians have their families with them and are correspondingly encumbered." He made it very clear, however, that "it is the intention of these headquarters to have the Indian question in the Southwest settled before the troops return to their proper station."[18]

Miles realized that the key to an extended campaign was to have enough wagons to carry ammunition, equipment, rations, and forage from Camp Supply to his units in the field. Even as early as the day after the Battle of Red River, Miles reported to General Pope that, "As we are 193 miles from our base of supplies, I would request that additional transportation be sent to Camp Supply to keep us supplied." His adjutant, George Baird, described the logistics problem that Miles encountered in the Southwest: "In too many cases expeditions against Indians had been like dogs fastened by a chain: within the length of chain, irrestible, beyond it, powerless. The chain was its wagon train and supplies."[19]

Miles believed he had begun his campaign at a disadvantage because he had been allotted only sixty wagons, and he complained to his wife that, "Custer, who went no further from his base than we did, was given four hundred." Furthermore, Miles did not expect the shortage to be rectified. He explained that the commanding officer at Camp Supply, Lt. Col. William H. Lewis, 19th Infantry, had shown him a letter from department headquarters stating that Miles could not be furnished with any extra wagons. He fumed, "It was another case of one man thinking he knows more five hundred miles away than one who is on the ground."[20]

After Colonel Lewis realized that shortages had brought a halt to field operations in September, he took extraordinary measures to try to satisfy Miles's needs. On one occasion, although he lacked authorization, he hired fourteen ox-drawn wagons to increase the capacity of a government wagon train bound for the Panhandle. Rather than continue to rely on makeshift solutions, however, Miles suggested that a supply depot be established on the Canadian River, which would be much more accessible to his command. Once this cantonment went up, additional soldiers were detailed by Pope to guard the route from Camp Supply used by civilian wagon trains now contracted to end their trip at the depot on the Canadian.

Despite the construction of a depot and two satellite camps, logistical problems continued to crop up, especially in winter, when trains were sometimes stalled by bad weather. Shortages of feed also had a very disruptive effect on the campaign. Once in October, and again on November 8, Miles attributed forced halts to "the non-arrival of grain." He also found himself in serious straits on December 2, when he wrote his wife that because forage had run out, the animals in his column were "actually starved nearly to death." To ward off a similar breakdown of horses in a future campaign, Miles suggested to his superiors that two cavalry troops with adequate amounts of fodder be employed, rather than eight poorly supplied companies. In the same report, he proposed replacing civilian mule trains with government-owned ox trains to maintain a forty-to-sixty-day store of supplies at depots in the field.[21]

The distance between Pope's headquarters and Miles's command not only obscured the transportation problem; it also caused lapses in the transmission of military intelligence. In 1871 a Kiowa war chief named Satanta had been imprisoned after he boasted to Sherman that he had participated in the massacre of teamsters from a wagon train and had then threatened the general with a pistol. Following his release from prison in October 1873, the chief returned to a Kiowa-Comanche reservation in Indian Territory operated by the Society of Friends. In a note to Sherman on September 27, 1874, Miles referred to the attacks on his couriers and wagon train by warriors who had left this agency. In his letter he asserted that he could have eliminated the problem "with your old friend 'Satanta's' party, fresh from Quaker influences, had I been informed that they were loose. I should have received it by the 5th inst. but the first account of it I read in the *New York Herald*." To improve communication in the field, Miles suggested the use of carrier pigeons and the development of rockets that would produce a thick, colored cloud, which could be seen from a distance throughout the day. He also recommended that all army posts be linked by telegraph lines.[22]

Miles had already won the approval of his division commander, General Sheridan, who sent Pope's adjutant general, Lt. Col. Robert Williams, a letter with the evaluation: "Col. Miles's conduct throughout the campaign, so far, meets my decided approval, and all things considered, he has exceeded my expectations not alone in his successful engagement with the Indians, but in the cheerful manner in which his troops have borne the hardships of the campaign." Sheridan added that "so far all is going well, and I have no instructions to give. I will be satisfied with the action of Col. Miles and do not even wish to embarrass him with suggestions. His action in returning for supplies is perfectly satisfactory."[23]

On October 10, Major Compton left camp with two troops of cavalry and an infantry company as the next phase of Miles's campaign began. Other columns had already clashed with the hostiles, causing them serious logistical problems. Mackenzie's Fourth Cavalry had inflicted a grievous blow to the dissidents' mobility when he captured fourteen hundred ponies at Palo Duro Canyon on September 28. On October 11, Lieutenant Colonel Buell's men began a two-day spree, burning 550 abandoned lodges. This loss in matérial, combined with the supplies destroyed by Mackenzie after his fight, left the Indians with a meager larder as winter approached.[24]

After Miles received a report from Major Compton indicating that his quarry had again sought refuge on the Staked Plains, he devised a plan to flush them from their sanctuary. He positioned a force to the west that would push the Indians toward the east, where Major Price with one infantry company and three troops of cavalry would be on guard near the Washita. On October 13, at the end of Miles's first day in the field, a number of Indians were detected in the distance. At first light the next morning, a pursuit force commanded by Chaffee tried unsuccessfully to catch them; his soldiers did destroy everything that the Indians, identified as Kiowas led by Red Otter, had abandoned in their camp. Because of the close pursuit, the *Cheyenne* (Wyoming) *Daily Leader* reported the Kiowa "are greatly demoralized, and are fleeing in a southeasterly direction, toward their agency, in the southwest part of the Indian territory, about five hundred miles distant from Fort Sill."[25]

On November 8, Miles's command unexpectedly achieved a great coup when scouts riding ahead of an empty wagon train returning to the Washita came upon Grey Beard's camp of Cheyennes. Lieutenant Baldwin, who commanded the escort, sent word to Miles that he intended to attack 110 lodges, located on McClellan Creek, a head stream of one of the branches of the Red River. Miles hoped in vain that the cavalry troop commanded by Major Compton, which he immediately ordered forward, could cover eight miles rapidly enough to support Baldwin.

Baldwin's 98 men climbed into the twenty-three wagons, each drawn by a team of six mules, which were formed in a column of twos. Then his cavalry formed up on either side of the column of wagons. On signal, the teamsters and cavalrymen directed their animals toward the 450 unsuspecting Cheyennes in the village. The warriors made a stand as their families fled; then they fought a rear-guard action, fending off the attackers during a twelve-mile chase. Finally, the Army horses broke down, weakened because they had gone without grain for the previous four days, forcing the cavalry to watch as Grey Beard's band disappeared across the Staked Plains.[26]

The troopers returned to the camp, where they destroyed everything that could be used by the Indians. As the soldiers went about their business, they made a discovery that gladdened their hearts. Two sisters, Julia and Adelaide German, only five and seven years old, were found under a buffalo robe. The two girls had left their home in Fannin County, Georgia, on April 10, 1870, with their parents, four other sisters, and a brother. As the family slowly crossed the country, they stopped for extended periods of time to earn money. On the morning of September 11, 1874, the family prepared to set out from a fork of the Smoky River for their next stop, Fort Wallace, Kansas, about sixteen miles to the west. Just as their wagon began to roll, they were set upon by a band of seventeen Indian warriors and two Indian women. In moments the parents, brother, and two of the sisters were killed and scalped by their attackers. The four surviving sisters were dragged off as captives. The two older girls, Catherine, seventeen, and Sophia, twelve, remained with their captors, but about September 25, when the Indians were just one step ahead of the army, Julia and Adelaide were deemed a handicap and left alone on the prairie. The two little girls miraculously survived by eating refuse found at former army campsites and nibbling on edible vegetation until they wandered back into the hands of Grey Beard's band on November 7.[27]

Miles, with four troops of cavalry, caught up with Baldwin's force just after they discontinued the chase. He recalled that when they returned to

Grey Beard's camp and first saw the two children, he thought that "they were the most emaciated mortals I have ever seen. Their little hands were like bird-claws." After McFadden saw the girls, he noted in his diary that they were in an "almost naked and starved condition, sunburned almost past recognition." A doctor serving with Miles brought the pitiful-looking sisters by ambulance back to Fort Leavenworth, where they were nursed back to good health. When the doctor returned to the expedition, he gave Miles a photograph that showed how rapidly the two sisters had improved in the six weeks since they had been found.[28]

After Baldwin drove the Indians from their camp, they headed toward Price's command. Miles reported that the sound of gunfire must have been heard by some in the major's camp, and a few of his outlying scouts actually fired after the fleeing warriors. Yet, as Miles added in his report, "For some reason not yet satisfactorily explained this force [Price's] did not participate in the engagement, as from its position was imminently fitting, and from its orders . . . was an imperative duty." Almost in wonderment, he explained that while Baldwin pursued the warriors, Price allowed the animals in his battalion to graze for a few hours before moving away from the scene of the action.[29]

Miles raised such a storm over Price's missed opportunity and possible dereliction of duty that Sheridan could not ignore the matter. The division commander took a broad view of Price's conduct, however, and confided to Pope that, "it does not interest the public service sufficiently to warrant the trouble and expense of a trial. It seems to be one of those muddles which will sometimes occur in the best regulated families and is not of sufficient importance to warrant an investigation." Sheridan then suggested to Pope, "if you are of the same opinion, I wish you would take such steps as will settle the trouble amicably, if you can."[30]

Miles found it impossible to let the matter drop, even after he revealed in a letter to Sherman that Pope warned him that both Sheridan and Sherman wanted "the affair of Major Price" settled quietly. In an apparently successful attempt to change Sherman's mind, Miles argued that Price "has done everything in his power to embarrass my movements and committing gross military offenses that ought not to be overlooked." A court-martial, convened at Fort Lyon, Colorado, on July 2, 1875, found that because Price had neglected his duty on November 8, 1874, he would be lowered from seventh to the twenty-seventh slot on the cavalry's list of majors. However, on January 10, 1877, President Grant followed the recommendation of the judge advocate general and ordered that Price be returned to his former standing on the list. Just as Miles persisted in hounding Meade about the danger of weapons in North Carolina, this episode confirms his determination to see his will prevail.[31]

The positive side of Miles's determination can be seen, however, in his efforts to free Sophia and Catherine, the two older German sisters, from their captors. Thoughts of their plight so disturbed Miles that he admitted to his wife, "Last night I could not sleep thinking about their sufferings." Miles's nightmares sprang from what little Julia and Adelaide had told him about life in Grey Beard's camp before the little girls had been abandoned: how "a scene is enacted in their camp every night that would chill the blood of the sternest soldier of my command." Finally, on December 5, Miles had a definite lead to act upon. A patrol returned to camp with information supplied by Mexican hunters that two white girls, believed to be the older sisters, were being held by Cheyennes in the Pecos Valley of New Mexico.[32]

Although blizzards and frigid temperatures usually forced the army to curtail midwinter campaigns in the Panhandle, Miles bridled at the idea of leaving the plains until the Indians promised to free Sophia and Catherine. He declared to Mary Nelson that "any man who gives the order to withdraw troops under these circumstances and leaves those innocent sufferers to their fate damns his name to eternal infamy for all time."[33]

As 1874 came to an end, Miles refused to give up, although his command dwindled to the size of a battalion. On December 28, as planned at the start of the campaign, the Eighth Cavalry began its march back to New Mexico. This loss, combined with Miles's practice of returning units to Camp Supply and Fort Dodge as his manpower needs decreased, left him with three troops of cavalry and four infantry companies. Since some of these units were detailed to begin construction of a winter cantonment south of the Washita, Miles began a reconnaissance on December 28 with only two infantry companies and a troop of cavalry.

Of the five columns originally sent into the Panhandle, only Miles's remained in the field as the new year approached. In a series of sweeps that ended on February 3, his men scouted the area around the head of the Red

River, then searched for trails on their return eastward, back to Fort Sill. In January a band of dissidents were followed so aggressively to the fort that they complained, to a correspondent at Sill, that they had "been run so hard by the soldiers that they have had no chance to kill any meat for their families." Miles praised the endurance of his men, who sometimes marched in temperatures that dropped to twenty-five degrees below zero, and suffered in "northers" that never seemed to let up. Despite the impossible weather, the campaigners showed remarkable spirit, singing "Marching through Georgia" as they tramped across snow-swept, frozen plains.[34]

Miles realized that the Cheyennes who held the sisters were struggling to survive through a harsh winter in desolate haunts and with inadequate supplies. He recalled that he "was convinced that the Indians were so reduced that they would surrender if an opportunity was granted them." Acting on this belief, he selected a small party of friendly Indians to carry a letter to Stone Calf's camp of Cheyennes, said to be situated on a fork of the Pecos River in New Mexico. When Stone Calf received this note, dated January 15, Fort Sill, he had Catherine German read it aloud. The chief had to be relieved when he heard Miles's offer to accept his surrender on condition that the sisters be released to the military, and Catherine had even more reason for thanksgiving because Miles included the news that Julia and Adelaide had been rescued.[35]

A few days later, another party of Kiowa runners arrived in camp bearing gifts meant to persuade the rebellious Indians to return to Fort Sill with the girls. Before carrying word of Stone Calf's acceptance back to Miles, one of those messengers found a chance to slip Catherine a package that contained the picture of her two little sisters taken at Fort Leavenworth. On the back of the picture, Miles pasted a note dated January 21, 1875, Fort Sill: "Your little sisters are well and in the hands of friends. Do not be discouraged. Every effort is being made for your welfare."[36]

When the freezing and half-starved Cheyennes finally agreed to surrender, they ignored Stone Calf's advice to give up at Fort Sill. Grey Beard, who had sought refuge for his band with Stone Calf, convinced them that they would receive more presents for the release of the girls at their own Cheyenne-Arapaho Agency at Darlington, in the Indian Territory. On February 25, 1875, Stone Calf, riding ahead of the main body of his people, reported to Lt. Col. (Bvt. Brig. Gen.) Thomas H. Neill at this reservation.

Neill immediately wired Pope the good news that, "Stone Calf has come in here to surrender himself and the whole Cheyenne tribe, about 1,600 in number with the two white women, Germans." Since the Cheyennes were still three days' travel from the agency, Neill sent ambulances to carry the sisters back to freedom. Finally, at dusk on March 1, with tears streaming down their cheeks, Catherine and Sophia rode past wildly cheering soldiers lined up along the last half mile of the road leading to Darlington.[37]

On March 6, Stone Calf carried a white flag as he led 240 warriors and 580 women and children onto the reservation. The braves placed their weapons in a row on the ground, then all sat down, indicating that they had returned to government supervision. Except for a small number of Cheyennes, who managed to join tribesmen who were allied with the Sioux on the northern plains, the few bands still off the reservations surrendered before summer. When the rebellious Indians gave up what they called the "wrinkle-hand chase," it marked the beginning of a permanent peace on the southern plains.[38]

Much to Miles's credit, he took steps to insure the financial security of the four German sisters. Miles suggested, and Pope endorsed the idea, that money for the girls' expenses and educations should be taken from the annuity fund established by the federal government for the Cheyennes. In 1874 Congress appropriated twenty-five hundred dollars each for Julia and Adelaide, and in response to Miles's prodding, the two older girls finally received the same aid in 1879. Miles cared so much about the welfare of the girls that he had himself appointed guardian of the three youngest sisters until he received orders to leave Leavenworth in 1876. A blacksmith who had taken care of Julia and Adelaide immediately after their rescue then replaced Miles as their guardian.[39]

When Catherine German read Miles's January 15 note aloud to Stone Calf, she had judiciously skipped over his statement, "I hope to see the guilty persons punished." Others, looking forward to a successful conclusion to the campaign, shared Miles's sentiment. On December 18, 1874, Sheridan ordered the establishment of a military commission to try any Indians "who have committed murders, stolen animals, attacked or killed troops of the United States." Although the attorney general set aside this directive, President Grant determined that any Indian implicated in a crime should be imprisoned in the East. When the defeated Cheyennes were paraded past Catherine and Sophia in order to identify guilty warriors, they were only able to pick out three of those who had attacked their family. These three, along with approximately seventy-two others, many of whom had been randomly selected, were sent by train on April 28, 1875, to a former Spanish fortress, renamed Fort Marion, in Saint Augustine, Florida. En route a guard killed Grey Beard during an escape attempt in Georgia.[40]

The final episode of the Red River War began at Darlington prior to transporting the Indian prisoners to Florida. On April 6, 1875, when a warrior bolted to avoid being shackled, soldiers aiming at the Indian fired into a Cheyenne camp, scattering its inhabitants. Second Lt. Austin Henely, rode from Fort Wallace, Kansas, to join in the search for a band still on the loose. Henely, an Irish-born officer who had worked his way up from private to first sergeant during the Civil War, and in 1868 entered West Point, may have accidentally dispensed crude justice in the last fight of the campaign. When he encountered the defiant party at Sappa Creek, Kansas, on April 23, 1875, Henely lost two men while killing nineteen braves and eight women and children. Possibly to dissipate sympathy aroused by the death of noncombatants, whom some accused the army of massacring, Pope claimed that the band attacked by Henely "contained most of the men who were concerned in the massacre of the German family and the abduction and abuse of four girls of the family."[41]

At the conclusion of the Indian Territory campaign, General Pope officially commended Miles and his command for "active, energetic and most efficient service," but Pope's biographer has written that "Pope did not appreciate Miles' attitude," and that "Miles appeared at times more concerned with winning victories to enhance his reputation than with terminating the Indian War." Whatever his motive, Miles's insistence on being properly supplied, his ability to inspire men, and his plain stubbornness resulted in a major roundup of rebellious Indians at a minimal cost in lives for either side. Bitter feelings, however, did arise between Pope and Miles because the colonel would not remain silent about a mismanaged campaign.[42]

Even as peace descended over the southern plains, tempers began to flare in army circles. Colonel McKenzie, victor at Palo Duro Canyon, fretted, in a letter to General Sheridan, that Miles seemed intent on encroaching upon his authority in the Indian Territory. Actually, it was Pope who had originated a plan to have Miles command Camp Supply and the newly constructed cantonment that would become Fort Elliot. Moreover, Miles resisted the idea and complained to Sherman, "in going to the remote region I would sacrifice all personal comfort and gain little or nothing." Instead of serving in the Indian Territory, Miles was sent to Cimarron, New Mexico, in the autumn of 1875.[43]

Miles traveled without his regiment, but upon his arrival in New Mexico, he took command of the troops already on the scene. Rather than immediately order a campaign against defiant Jicarilla Apaches and Muache Utes, Miles had a friendly Indian carry his offer to negotiate to their camp, hidden in the mountains. The rebellious chief took advantage of the proferred truce. During the resulting conference he convinced Miles that contractors had furnished his people with grossly substandard provisions. The Indians returned to their agency on the strength of Miles's promise that their agent, who had absconded, would be replaced by an army officer who would insure that the injustices would be corrected. With peace restored in New Mexico, Miles returned to Fort Leavenworth, where he spent a pleasant interlude with his family until called once again to action following Custer's defeat.[44]

– CHAPTER 5 –

Campaign against the Sioux

TROUBLE WITH THE Sioux on the northern plains became inevitable after the government relaxed enforcement of its obligation to prevent trespassing on lands ceded to the Indians, particularly the Black Hills. Congress had debated the problem early in 1876, but Senator John Sherman admitted to Miles that "it seemed to be beyond solution by Congress." The situation concerned Sherman because "General Sheridan seems to be bent on a war while the feeling here is entirely against it, and but for the interminable delays, incident to Congressional proceedings, some measure would be adopted to prevent it."[1]

Unfortunately, before the politicians could resolve the matter, the army received a request from the Indian Bureau to force rebellious bands of Sioux back onto the reservations. Sheridan hoped to duplicate his success on the southern plains by employing converging columns in the Sioux hunting grounds along the Yellowstone and its tributaries. Following Sitting Bull's stunning victory against Custer on June 25, 1876, the campaign came to an abrupt halt while reinforcements were transferred into the region.[2]

Miles, with six companies of the 5th Infantry, sailed up the Missouri River with orders to report to Brig. Gen. (Bvt. Maj. Gen.) Alfred H. Terry's "Dakota column," camped at the mouth of the Rosebud. When his steamboat stopped at Fort Buford, North Dakota, built on the Missouri just below its confluence with the Yellowstone, Miles noted that the garrison exhibited "the same condition of gloom that had marked the atmosphere of the other places we had passed on the river below." While the morale of much of the army sagged in the wake of Custer's defeat, Miles and the 5th Infantry confidently prepared to enter Indian country.[3]

For Miles, "going to meet the enemies of civilization and protect the defenseless settlements was a delightful enterprise." He conceded that confidence in his regiment helped to inspire his optimism. A correspondent in the field shared his appreciation of the regiment, judging that, "The Fifth Infantry under General Miles, and the Fifth Cavalry under General [Wesley] Merritt, [are] the two finest regiments in the service." Miles had honed the Fifth Infantry into fighting trim at a "military gymnasium" he had established at Fort Leavenworth during the winter of 1873–74. Here his men built up their endurance through calisthenics, improved their marksmanship on rifle ranges, and polished their military skill during demanding field exercises. The trainees being molded into infantry were of an unusually high caliber, according to Miles, because the Panic of 1873, accompanied by high unemployment, had made it possible to recruit "a class of young men into the army who for physical perfection, strength, courage, and intelligence has rarely, if ever, been equaled."[4]

The training program continued even as the regiment steamed up the Missouri. Miles had the troops drilled three times a day, either ashore or aboard ship, and had officers' school held daily in one of the vessel's cabins. On August 2, when the three hundred men of the Fifth disembarked on the Yellowstone, they were reported to be "in excellent condition." The same could not be said for the veterans in the "Dakota column." Just as it had affected garrisons along the Missouri River, Custer's disaster had cast its pall over Terry's camp on the Rosebud. Perhaps time had clouded Miles's memories of Reams' Station when he confided to Mary Miles that he had never seen "a command so completely stampeded as this, either in the volunteer or regular service, and I believe entirely without reason." Miles added that Terry, who had won the thanks of Congress for his 1865 capture of Fort Fisher, North Carolina, and who later became the first volunteer officer in the postwar regular army to wear a general's star, did not "seem very enthusiastic or to have much heart in the enterprise."[5]

Miles had heard enough talk in camp to predict that Terry would withdraw from the field by October, after completing one last "walk-around," but Miles hoped for permission to conduct a winter campaign. On August 8 the Dakota column broke camp and marched up the Rosebud on what proved to be its last operation of the year. Two days later, Terry's and Brig. Gen. (Bvt. Maj. Gen.) George Crook's columns were surprised when they approached one another in the river valley. At an impromptu planning session, the generals approved Miles's suggestion that his regiment be given an independent mission. Such an assignment would not only free Miles from serving under Terry's infantry commander, Col. John Gibbon, it would also, as Miles saw it, free a "fine command in perfect condition and fully equipped" from having "nothing to do but creep along with the expedition." The Fifth Infantry was assigned to patrol along the Yellowstone from the Tongue River to the Powder, in an attempt to block any Sioux bands from fleeing north. Since fresh trails indicated that Indians might already be heading toward fords across the Yellowstone, the regiment hastened north on what one newspaper called "one of the most difficult and remarkable marches ever made by infantry troops."[6]

When Miles received orders to backtrack to the Yellowstone, his men had just completed a sixteen-mile march with Terry's column. At 1:00 P.M. the next day, the regiment reached its objective without detecting any Sioux but after having covered a total of forty-three miles in twenty-four hours. Since the infantrymen had crossed rough country at night, choking on clouds of dust while trying to remain alert against possible attack, a reporter considered their march equal to a sixty-mile march across open terrain. Much in the tradition of Stonewall Jackson's famed "foot cavalry," impressive marches under extreme weather conditions had become a hallmark of the Fifth Infantry since the 1874 Indian Territory campaign.

The late summer sweep into Montana reaped a meager harvest. After Terry's troops completed a fruitless search, they were withdrawn on September 5. Crook had better luck, which helped to compensate for the hardships endured by his hungry troops as they slogged across a rain-sodden prairie on the notorious "Horsemeat March." On September 9, as Captain Anson Mills's squadron rode ahead of the main body to obtain supplies, they cornered a band of Sioux led by American Horse. The Indian survivors of this battle surrendered when Crook's column reached the battlefield, named Slim Buttes after richly colored, eroded hills that rose abruptly from the ground. From a distance they appeared to form unscalable walls protecting a cluster of Norman castles. After the victors drove off a large war party trying to aid their tribesmen, the summer campaign of 1876 came to an end.[7]

While the rest of the army withdrew to winter quarters, Miles remained in the wilderness in command of the District of the Yellowstone, which had been created for him. Custer's defeat had prompted a stingy Congress to open its purse strings and authorize the construction of forts that had been advocated by Sheridan for the past year. Miles constructed a cantonment on the north bank of the Yellowstone, near the mouth of the Tongue River, while Col. George P. Buell built a post overlooking the confluence of the Bighorn River with the Little Bighorn. In 1877 Buell's installation received its official designation, Fort Custer, and a year later, a permanent post, Fort Keogh—named after Capt. Myles W. Keogh, Seventh Cavalry, who had fallen on Last Stand Hill with Custer—replaced Miles's cantonment. A third installation took shape in October 1876, when Colonel Mackenzie ordered a supply depot constructed near the remains of Fort Reno, Wyoming. Indians had burned the original fort after the army abandoned it in compliance with terms in the Treaty of Fort Laramie, signed in 1868. After discovering that the new supply depot had been built on an unhealthy site, a new one named after 1st Lt. John A. McKinney, Fourth Cavalry, killed in battle in November 1876, went up at Clear Creek, a tributary of the Powder River.[8]

The new forts would allow the army to dominate Sioux hunting grounds, making it difficult for large bands to survive away from their reservations. When the hungry Indians returned to their agencies, instead of being greeted by their former agents, they would be met by army officers with orders to confiscate all their weapons and horses. Sheridan expected active campaigning to convince even the most recalcitrant warriors to seek a sanctuary from the troops hounding after them, thus ending the Sioux War.[9]

Even before Custer's defeat forced the generals to reevaluate their strategy, Miles had questioned the effectiveness of conducting a "magnificent scout." In a letter to Sherman, he suggested that as an alternative, a well-trained command, at least half of whom were infantry, should be used to pursue the hostiles. No doubt he hoped that his regiment would be selected to repeat the tactic that had worked so well on the southern plains. Once a mixed force of infantry and cavalry crossed a Sioux trail, they should make it "so uncomfortable for them and giving them no rest [that] they would be compelled to sue for peace."[10]

After being transferred to Montana, Miles immediately recruited a company of scouts. In 1874, during the Red River War, he had seen the ineffectiveness of scouting solely with troops, admitting that "little is accomplished by it." Instead, he recommended, "friendly Indians or daring scouts can be more economically employed to discover the hostile camps, trails or movements of Indians and the Cavalry saved for the direct march, resistless dash and rapid pursuit for which that arm of the service is so well adapted." Besides trailing the enemy, Miles's irregulars were often used as agents in a "system of espionage" or as intermediaries sent into hostile camps with messages.[11]

The scouts recruited by Miles included William F. Cody, better known as "Buffalo Bill," and Luther S. Kelly, who preferred to be called "Yellowstone Kelly." Billy Dixon and Amos Chapman came north from the southern plains to join other colorfully named scouts such as "Liver-eating Johnson," and "Billy the half-breed," who, along with Johnnie Bruguier, could serve as interpreters. These men would serve as the first line of defense for the few infantry companies stationed along the Yellowstone. Miles had six companies of his own regiment at Tongue River, plus two companies of the Twenty-second; the closest supporting units were at Glendive Creek, one hundred miles to the east. Here Lt. Col. (Bvt. Maj. Gen.) Elwell S. Otis, with four companies from his own regiment, the Twenty-second, plus two from the Seventeenth, operated a supply depot. As the campaign progressed, the *Herald* wondered about decisions made in Washington to reinforce "other commands 400 and 500 miles distant from the real seat of war; they would not be doing amiss by giving a little stronger support to this active and efficient command."[12]

On October 16, as the cantonment began to take shape, Miles took a few minutes to jot a brief note to Sherman. The colonel seemed uneasy because a supply train from Glendive had not arrived on schedule. He casually remarked, "I shall start down to meet it tomorrow morning." When Miles met the train on the eighteenth, he found that it had been forced back to Glendive after being attacked by a large number of warriors. When the train started back down the Yellowstone with an additional escort, the Sioux again attacked it, angered that Lieutenant Colonel Otis had ignored a message written by an interpreter and signed "Sitting Bull." The letter, attached to a stick that had been driven into the trail, demanded that the train turn back so that it would not disturb the buffalo. It also ordered that the cargo should be left behind, specifying "all the rations you have got and some powder." Almost humorously, Sitting Bull concluded with the request: "Wish you would write as soon as you can." Any smiles among Miles's men were wiped away when they found that Otis had lost one man and three were wounded in the second attack. As for the Sioux, at least seven braves fell in the attack.[13]

After Otis told his story, Miles determined to capture Sitting Bull. Otis's party continued on its way, reinforced by fifty of Miles's men, who were detailed to complete the construction once they reached the cantonment at Tongue River. Miles himself led 398 infantry north, along Cedar Creek. On October 20, eight miles north of the creek, two Indians appeared on the brow of a hill, waving a white flag. Identified as chiefs from the Standing Rock Agency in North Dakota, they invited Miles to parley with Sitting Bull. Miles's acting adjutant second lieutenant, Hobart K. Bailey, volunteered to ride into the midst of the hostile force to make arrangements for the talks. He negotiated with Sitting Bull's white interpreter, Johnnie Bruguier, who had sought refuge with the medicine man to avoid a warrant for murder. Bruguier would later switch allegiances and work for Miles, who promised to help him with his legal problems. Although Bruguier could not persuade Bailey to have the Rodman gun removed from its position overlooking the conference site, they agreed that leading men from both camps would meet between the lines. When Miles rode out with his staff, infantry companies occupied the tops of two hills flanking the scene, and skirmishers surrounded the wagon train, drawn up in the rear, out of harm's way.[14]

A group of armed braves on horseback stopped about thirty yards from the officers, as approximately a dozen unarmed tribal leaders marched forward in perfect order to complete a circle started by Miles's party. According to a correspondent with the troops, Pretty Bear, a chief in council, rather than Sitting Bull, spoke for the Indians. Miles took advantage of this unlikely meeting to study Sitting Bull carefully. Miles shared his impressions with his wife in a few lines written just days after the parley, describing a man much like himself. Each was a natural leader, with the ability to sway followers. Miles towered over the five-foot-eight-inch-tall medicine man, but both war leaders attracted attention because of their striking appearances, highlighted by firm, distinctive features. At thirty-seven, however, Miles had been described as being in the "full flush of manhood," while his opponent appeared to be about ten years older. Miles also judged that Sitting Bull seemed to feel "that his strength is somewhat exhausted and he appeared much depressed, suffering from nervous excitement and the loss of power."

While onlookers shivered in the cold, both parties slowly narrowed their positions to a single demand. Miles insisted that the Sioux return to government control, either by reporting to some agency or by camping on the Yellowstone near his cantonment, while the Indians were just as insistent that they remain free to hunt buffalo. Having reached an impasse, the parties suspended their talks until the following day, and both sides agreed to retire to their camps.[15]

Early on the twenty-first, as the 5th Infantry moved back up Cedar Creek, some noticed movement in the distance. Miles's infantrymen formed a line of battle and steadily closed in upon approximately eight hundred Indians, until the sight of a white flag held aloft from high ground brought them to a halt. Soldiers and Indians faced one another from ridges rising from the prairie, separated by broken ground. When the *Herald*'s reporter reached the army's vantage point, "a scene of wild, savage pageantry burst upon the vision such as seldom falls to the lot of men to behold, and which made every Fifth Infantry heart thrill with the feeling expressed in Custer's cry, 'Custer's luck.' Here was the biggest village I ever saw." Since "Custer's luck" had run out within view of a similar village, the journalist had good reason to fear that he would share Custer's fate, although Miles had almost double the 216 men who fought with Custer on Last Stand Hill.[16]

Despite the provocation of armed warriors galloping toward them in mock attacks, the troops respected the truce, and Miles suggested that the talks be resumed on a small elevation between the lines. To ensure that neither side enjoyed a numerical advantage at the site, as each soldier approached the hill, an Indian would also ride to the top. These talks lasted even longer than the day before, with movement within both camps revealing the anxiety of those not involved in the discussions. Some of the chiefs finally appeared willing to accept Miles's demand that they return to their agencies when Sitting Bull abruptly ended the parley. The negotiators returned to their respective camps, and it appeared that the Sioux waited for the army to make the first move.

Miles gave the command "Forward," and, in the words of trumpeter Edwin Brown, "the opera commenced." Lyman and Pope, veterans of the

Indian Territory campaign, kept pace with their men moving up the ridges, as did the other company commanders, including Capt. Simon Snyder, 1st Lt. Mason Carter, 1st Lt. Robert McDonald, and Capt. James Casey, all of whom would earn recognition fighting in Montana. As the Indians gave way to the advancing troops, with neither side firing at the other, the *Herald* reporter noticed that the braves moved to high ground flanking the infantrymen. He worried that they would be in position to pounce on Miles's men as their formations lost cohesion passing through ravines or crossing broken ground; however, a company on each flank scattered the warriors gathering together on the hilltops. Surprisingly, neither side appeared anxious to break the truce by firing first, so for about fifteen minutes the belligerents sparred with mounting tension, alert for the sign to attack. The reporter believed that an Indian hidden in a ravine fired the first shot, but both a contributor to the *Army and Navy Journal* and Miles admit that when the colonel noticed a brave setting fire to prairie grass, he ordered a scout to stop the Indian from spreading the blaze. The scout fired at the warrior, who toppled onto the burning grass, and the battle began in earnest.[17]

As wildfire swept across their path, Lt. David Q. Rousseau, brother of Union Maj. Gen. Lovell Rousseau, led his company in an assault up the battlefield's dominant hill. According to the *Army and Navy Journal,* the "movement was beautifully performed, the little company looking like a slender thread as it fearlessly pressed up the almost perpendicular height—while the Indians poured a rapid but harmless fire over their heads, and the key to the field was soon won." The Rodman gun had supported the attack, and as in virtually every fight with Indians, no matter how inaccurate the artillery might be, the Rodman's fire demoralized the enemy.

During the battle individual warriors displayed great skill on horseback, expertly guiding their ponies in brave dashes against the infantry, only to waste their effort because of poor marksmanship. Taking advantage of this weakness, the troops were able to drive the Indians back across their campsite and watch them retreat toward the Yellowstone. Miles credited the success of his men to their discipline and long-range markmanship, which kept all but the most gallant braves at a distance. The *Herald* gave Miles his due as the author of victory, explaining that he "displayed that superb handling of troops that so distinguished him during the war and on the Southern plains. The Indians were so completely baffled by the rapidity of his movements as to be unable to make any formidable opposition." Thus, as a result of the troops' skills with weapons and Miles's generalship, only two soldiers were wounded in battle. At least five Sioux were killed, and all accounts mention seeing braves carrying other bodies from the field. The Indians also suffered the critical loss of several tons of dried meat and a great deal of equipment, which had to be left behind in the hastily abandoned camp. The Sioux were on the verge of facing a winter as bleak as that which the Southern Cheyenne had suffered through in 1874–75.

On the twenty-second, the Fifth quickly picked up the trail of the Sioux leading toward the Yellowstone. Although warriors tried to delay their pursuers with rear-guard skirmishing and by starting prairie fires, the troops pressed forward. The soldiers were encouraged by camp equipage that littered their path and the sight of loose ponies roaming nearby, both of which were taken as signs of a disorganized retreat. After a forty-two-mile chase that lasted two days, they finally reached the Yellowstone, where they were greeted by the sight of Indians on the southern shore under a white flag.

In the resulting negotiations, Miles must have been sorely disappointed when the Sioux spokesman confirmed that before reaching the river, Sitting Bull had separated from the main body. He intended to lead about thirty lodges from his own tribe, the Hunkpapa Sioux, toward Fort Peck. Left behind were members of the Miniconjou and Sans Arcs, who agreed to an unusual settlement. Miles informed General Terry about the agreement in a note written on October 27. Four chiefs and one head warrior were being sent to Terry's headquarters at Saint Paul, Minnesota, under military escort. These headmen would serve as hostages to ensure that their tribespeople would turn themselves in at the Cheyenne River Agency, South Dakota, by December 2.[18]

Miles admitted in his note that he preferred to set out after Sitting Bull rather than guard the surrendered Sioux on a three-hundred-mile march back to government control. He fully believed that the Indians were in no condition to offer further resistance. As a matter of fact, he worried because "they are really starving for food, and I recommended that, as they gave themselves up, if they cannot be fed by the Interior Department, that they be fed as prisoners of war."[19]

Rather than glory in his victory over the Sioux, Miles wrote Terry that "we have fought and routed these people and driven them from their ancient homes. I cannot but feel regret that they are compelled to submit to starvation, for I fear they will be reduced to that condition as were the southern Indians in 1874." In order to try to prevent a repetition of the inadequate provisioning of surrendered Indians, as had happened at the end of the Indian Territory campaign, Miles turned to the most powerful person he knew, General Sherman. He asked the commanding general to "see that they have fair treatment as I know they are satisfied we can whip them every time, and if their people are assured of anything but starvation, they will all surrender."[20]

On November 15 the War Department released Sheridan's report describing Miles's success in obtaining the surrender of four hundred Sioux lodges. The announcement also included Sherman's official reaction, praising Miles, who had "displayed his usual earnestness and energy, and I hope he will crown his success by capturing or killing Sitting Bull and his remnants of outlaws." The congratulations were premature; only about forty lodges surrendered at the Cheyenne River Agency on November 30.[21]

When Miles chose to pursue Sitting Bull rather than escort the defeated Indians back to their agency, one critic compared him to a "dog who dropped the bone he had in his mouth in favor of the larger one he thought he saw in his reflection in the water below." Actually, Miles sacrificed a chance to reap the glory of leading about two thousand rebellious Indians back onto their agency, in order to help end the war. On the southern plains he saw that the army's victory came by applying constant pressure against rebellious Indians rather than actually capturing them. If Miles had retired from the field to insure the surrender of those who had already shown a faint heart, it would have provided a breathing spell for Sitting Bull and his followers, the hard core of the rebellion. Furthermore, following the battles of Slim Buttes and Cedar Creek, the tide of good fortune began to run out for the warring Sioux. No matter how many families huddled in rebel camps, because of the army's relentless pursuit, they were beginning to be seen as hunted fugitives rather than as feared warriors.[22]

Following the completion of the surrender negotiations, Miles brought his men back to the cantonment on Tongue River for a refitting. During his march to camp, Miles informed Terry of his intentions to return after Sitting Bull's Hunkpapas. He described this tribe as "the wildest on the continent."[23]

On November 6, as all but two companies at the cantonment made last-minute preparations for the coming expedition, Miles dashed off a note to Terry. He admitted that he really did not expect to catch many dissidents, but "if I can keep them moving, and make this country untenable for them, I shall at least have accomplished a part of my object." With this goal in mind, the infantry tramped northward for about 155 miles, until they reached Fort Peck on November 15.[24]

Fort Peck, a private trading post, had long been considered a source of ammunition and other supplies for rebellious Indians. The *Herald* reporter covering the Sioux War wondered about both the administration of the Fort Peck Agency and the shortage of troops assigned to that reservation. Although one company of the Sixth Infantry had garrisoned the agency since the fall of 1876, the correspondent felt that more were needed. Furthermore, Thomas J. Mitchell, the civilian agent who still remained in control here, had accepted a Sioux offer of a winter truce. The journalist could not explain "the mystery that surrounds the policy of the government toward these hostile hordes that feed and fatten at Fort Peck during the winter and scalp and mangle the soldierly of the Little Big Horn in the summer."[25]

Miles confirmed that the Sioux who had confronted his regiment at Cedar Creek had found refuge at the Fort Peck Agency. In frustration, he reported that his hands were tied because he had "no authority over these Agency Indians." Thus, he could merely list the names of several of the chiefs and braves that he or his officers recognized and then turn the list over to the agent. Miles considered that his duty had ended when the dissidents had returned to their reservations.[26]

Because Miles had received conflicting reports at Fort Peck about the location of Sitting Bull's camp, he divided his command in order to check the most likely rumors. Battalion-sized scouting parties fruitlessly searched for the hostiles along the Missouri and some of its tributaries, especially the Musselshell River and Big Dry, favorite hunting grounds of the Sioux. One company detoured to Fort Carroll, a private trading post suspected of selling hostiles ammunition; they had orders to put an end to illegal sales. Before leaving Fort Peck on November 17, Miles had a chance to speak to Johnnie Bruguier for the first time. Bruguier told Miles that despite his problems with the law, he had slipped away from Sitting Bull's camp about

November 1, after becoming disenchanted with life on the run. He then volunteered to try to persuade Sitting Bull to surrender at Tongue River, and Miles readily accepted.[27]

Four days after the November sweep began, a messenger reached Miles with a report that Sitting Bull intended to cross to the north side of the Missouri River, some miles to the east of Fort Peck. Miles immediately ordered three companies commanded by Lieutenant Baldwin, already en route to Fort Buford, to act upon the information, which is believed to have come from Bruguier. The colonel instructed his able lieutenant that, "if you do no more than keep them moving you will do well." Baldwin did better than well. When Sitting Bull became aware of troops moving in his direction, he crossed back to the southern shore of the Missouri, at Wolf Point. Then, on December 18, the Sioux discovered Baldwin's 120 men only one mile away from their village at Red Water Creek. Some three hundred warriors, encumbered by their families, fled from the camp toward the Yellowstone River, abandoning supplies meant to see them through the winter. The soldiers paused to burn down tepees containing robes, a large amount of buffalo meat, sugar, and coffee. Then they captured sixty horses before returning to the cantonment. The three companies marched the final seventy-three miles of a five-hundred-mile expedition in forty-eight hours.[28]

Baldwin's troops were probably propelled back to Tongue River by the extreme cold; on December 20, three days before their return, the temperature at the cantonment fell to thirty-six degrees below zero. Troops in the field survived because they had been fitted with protective cold-weather outfits. The government had provided thick woolen socks and the basic uniform, but Miles and his men designed the rest of the gear themselves. Buffalo robes supplemented overcoats, and Miles wore a fur-trimmed greatcoat, which caused the Sioux to name him "Bear Coat." Soldiers made their own overshoes and heavy gloves and used grain sacks as binding to help keep their feet and legs warm. Mufflers were made into masks that covered the entire face, except for small holes for breathing and seeing, leading one commentator to compare the appearance of men using the scarves to that of Klan members.[29]

When Miles had his command improvise cold-weather outfits, he assumed a function that should have been performed by the War Department. Even before he had rectified Washington's oversight in failing to develop such gear, Miles complained to Mary Miles that her uncle William did not pay enough attention to the support services of the army. In his opinion, "Sherman unfortunately does not take that interest or positive action in the organization of the army that it sadly needs. Such matters as clothing, shoes, horse equipment and ordinance are left to worthless staff officers or obscure clerks."[30]

While Miles harried the Sioux in late November and early December, Colonel Mackenzie had even more success against the Cheyenne. On November 25, 1876, MacKenzie's expedition surprised Dull Knife's and Little Wolf's village in the Big Horn Mountains. Mackenzie reported losing an officer and five men, while killing twenty-five Indians in an attack that devastated the Cheyennes. Besides destroying a village of 173 lodges and leaving the survivors destitute, the soldiers captured five hundred ponies. During the first night of their flight toward Crazy Horse's camp of Oglala Sioux in the Wolf Mountains, lightly clad families mourned the death of eleven infants who could not survive in the subzero weather.[31]

The refugees from Mackenzie's attack, along with some of the Sioux who had reneged on their promise to report to the agencies, were dismayed at conditions in Crazy Horse's camp. Other Indians were afraid of further attacks. As a result, on December 16, some of the dissidents decided to negotiate for peace. A party of five chiefs, followed in the distance by twenty-six Sioux warriors, rode toward the Tongue River cantonment carrying a white flag. Some of Miles's Crow scouts approached the peace party in a friendly manner but suddenly attacked their traditional enemy, killing five of them. The Crows were so swift that the Sioux warriors could not save the peace party. Then, at the sound of a trumpet call, they raced from sight, uncertain about the intentions of the troops. As soon as shots were fired, a trumpeter sounded the call to arms, assembling the infantry, who double-timed to the Crow camp. Here the officers and men looked in horror at the murdered Sioux, already scalped and mutilated, who lay beside their truce flag, now soaked with blood. Meanwhile, the guilty Crow scouts had already escaped from the cantonment in order to avoid being punished.[32]

Miles had the sad duty of reporting the ambush to Terry. He lamented that it "was most unfortunate as their coming in would have secured the surrender of at least a thousand fighting men," and later reproached the

Crow agent because his charges had committed "as brutal and cowardly an act as I have ever known." He then demanded that the agent arrest the guilty braves if they reported back to his agency.[33]

In an attempt to retain the trust of the peace-seeking faction within Crazy Horse's camp, Miles sent twelve Crow ponies and a letter of explanation that included an apology to the Sioux. The scouts entrusted with the mission returned without reaching the hostile camp, so the good-will gesture went for nought. Within days of trying to extend an olive branch to his opponents, Miles decided to resort to the sword. Prodded by a raid against the cantonment's cattle herd, Miles organized a midwinter expedition, hoping to follow the rustlers to the hostile camp.[34]

The colonel commandeered an ox train unloading supplies at the post and sent it out on December 26, ahead of the main column. With scouts already well in advance, the ox train rolled smoothly along well-worn paths, escorted by two companies of the Twenty-second and one of the Fifth. Four companies of the Fifth, led by Miles, left the cantonment three days later. Miles recalled that he commanded 436 men in this operation, but a reporter at the cantonment estimated that only about 300 infantry marched out against the enemy. In either case, the Indians would not be overwhelmed by superior numbers, but the soldiers apparently had no qualms about their prospects. As a bystander watched a column of troops swing out along the Tongue River, he turned to Miles and remarked, "Your men seem to think they can whip any number of Indians."[35]

When Miles's battalion overtook the ox train, he abandoned the wagons but took the oxen along to pull his own train through difficult passages. Part of this train consisted of two artillery pieces concealed under canvas, designed to make them look like wagons. As the column progressed south along the river, scouts saw fresh pony tracks and caught the odor of Indian tobacco in the air, indicating that the expedition was being shadowed. It is possible that the Indians were trying to lure Miles into a trap or draw his force so close to their village that those who had hoped for peace would be forced to take up arms to defend their families.[36]

For an ambush to succeed, however, the Indians would first have to contend with Miles's extremely formidable outriders. Yellowstone Kelly identified his fellow scouts as three Johnsons; Tom LaFarge, who served as an interpreter for the Crows; three Crow braves; and a Bannock warrior,

Buffalo Horn, whom he praised as "one of the bravest Indians I have ever had anything to do with." Miles held Kelly in equally high esteem, comparing him with legendary frontiersmen such as Daniel Boone and Kit Carson. Kelly, born in the Finger Lakes region of New York, had lied about his age to join a regular infantry regiment that saw little action during the Civil War. In search of adventure, he explored the Yellowstone area in 1868 and remained in the region because of its natural beauty. When a reporter interviewing another of the colorful scouts had inquired about "Liver-eating" Johnson's nickname, the scout explained that after killing a Sioux bent on murder, Johnson had been so close to starvation that, in order to survive, he roasted the brave's liver. The correspondent found the story hard to believe as Johnson was "quiet, reserved, [and] gentlemanly in his manners, and in no sense rough or violent. One can hardly believe so mild and modest appearing a man could have a history full of perils and desperate adventures on the plains."[37]

Even when Miles's small band of outriders were literally caught napping one drowsy afternoon, they responded so ably that a hostile war party lost its initial advantage and had to retreat. Two soldiers who wandered off while helping to round up oxen one morning were less fortunate. Their bodies were buried on the trail so that tramping feet would erase all traces of their graves. On January 7, the scouts captured a small group of Cheyenne women and children, to whom Miles extended every courtesy. When the hostile camp discovered that four women with four children, apparently from an important family, were being held by Miles, a group of warriors were moved to free the captives. Shortly before dark, the outriders came upon more than one hundred braves gathered together for a rescue attempt. The scouts were so deadly with their rifles that they held back the Indians until an artillery burst and the sight of approaching infantry caused them to scatter. The beleaguered advance guard escaped unscathed, and the skirmish put Miles on guard against the growing number of rebellious braves menacing his path toward their camp.[38]

As the sun set, the command settled into a camp established on the right bank of the Tongue River, surrounded by the Wolf Mountains, about 115 miles south of the cantonment. Troops worked the three-inch Rodman gun to the top of a twenty-five-foot-high plateau overlooking the camp while the twelve-pound bronze Napoleon remained in the valley. The infantrymen had already been tested by passage across increasingly difficult terrain and worsening weather, which had progressed from chilling rain to blinding snow storms. It appeared to most that at daybreak they would endure the decisive challenge of combat.[39]

After dark on January 7, pickets tensed at the sound of braves along the perimeter of the camp, trying to call to the prisoners. A blind exchange of fire quickly died down, as each side realized the futility of trying to pick off targets during a snowstorm. The next morning's reveille sounded at 4:00 a.m., half an hour earlier than usual. By 7:00 A.M. the troops had eaten and were preparing to move out when pickets ran in, shouting that a large number of Indians were approaching the camp. With his field glasses, Miles viewed what appeared to be an endless column of warriors emerging from a canyon and advancing on foot down the valley toward his skirmish line. He estimated that his command faced upwards on one thousand Sioux and Cheyenne and that he was outnumbered two or three to one.[40]

When the skirmish line refused to budge and artillery fire began to range in on the attackers, the braves broke off their attack and swerved toward the high ground flanking the valley. Miles stood beside the Rodman gun, issuing orders from a vantage point on the bluff. Kelly, who had stationed himself near the colonel, called Miles's attention to a group of warriors heading toward a commanding ridge. Miles immediately ordered Captains Edmond Butler and Casey to employ their companies in an attempt to dislodge the enemy from the hill now named Battle Butte. Both officers would later receive brevet promotions and Medals of Honor for the inspired charge against such a formidable position. As the infantry struggled through three feet of newly fallen snow, Big Crow, a Cheyenne warrior, fearlessly danced in full regalia on the high ground facing the troops. Yellowstone Kelly explained that "if the magic of his charm worked he could not be killed, and supported by this demonstration his confederates would carry everything before them." While the Cheyenne dancer defied the soldiers, Lieutenant Baldwin encouraged the advancing skirmishers by riding along their front, waving his hat while cheering the men on, as exposed to fire as was his Indian counterpart.

Encumbered by their cold-weather wear and distracted by hostile rifle fire that wounded two men, the troops nevertheless clambered toward the crest of the ridge. As they came within range of the taunting dancer, they blazed away at the elusive target, until he finally toppled from view, mortally wounded. When Big Crow fell, the warriors on the ridge appeared to lose heart for further combat, and as the first wave of troops struggled over the crest, they abandoned the high ground. Although Miles liked to believe that the enemy had been routed, a heavy snowstorm at noon interrupted the fighting before a decisive blow had been struck.

At 5:00 P.M., as darkness descended over the battlefield, the soldiers withdrew to a natural fort on the plateau protected by the Rodman gun. Here eight seriously wounded men were cared for; but despite the attendants' best efforts, a private died the next day, raising the death toll to two. Since the hostiles had followed their customary practice of removing casualties from the field, a count of Indian dead and wounded was not possible. Baldwin, however, noticed so many blood-smeared patches of snow that he assumed that a number of warriors had fallen. A heavy rain that lasted through the night following the battle dampened spirits that were not revived by a fruitless pursuit that started after daybreak. On the tenth, Miles decided to return to the cantonment because his supplies were running low and his animals were broken down. At noon on January 18, after a total march of 242 miles, the veteran infantrymen straightened their ranks, picked up cadence, and marched with pride as they heard the first faint notes of the regimental band welcoming them home by playing "Marching through Georgia."[41]

During the midwinter pause before renewing operations in the spring, Miles looked to the welfare of his men. He had a large canvas-covered music hall constructed in the cantonment where the regimental band and amateur talent drawn from the troops could perform. On a more practical note, Miles petitioned the secretary of war for an extra issue of clothing for his men. His major argument was that his troops "have made continuous and extraordinary marches, and have actually worn out on an unusual amount of clothing." Unfortunately, there is no record of a response to this request.[42]

Although Miles never directly attacked Crazy Horse's camp, his expedition had helped to convince the dissidents to disperse. Some believe that Sitting Bull made his way to the concentration of Indians in the Tongue River camp about one week after the battle and convinced his Hunkpapa tribesmen to return with him to a refuge in Canada. The huge camp, however, did break up before the end of January, and its inhabitants scattered in different directions. Many of the Oglalas and Cheyennes moved to a valley by the Big Horn Mountains. Meanwhile, the Sans Arcs and Miniconjous drifted to an area north of the Black Hills, and small numbers of rebellious Indians began to turn themselves in at their agencies.[43]

As shortened days had signaled the passing of the hectic summer of 1876, harried warriors reassured one another, "When the snow flies the soldiers will go to the forts and then we will have rest." Instead, troops appeared to be everywhere, and the *Herald* believed that "a mortal fear seized on the warriors and they saw they must surrender or perish. The old men, the women, and children could not run about as in summer, and, above all, the ponies could not be kept alive if they had to travel in deep snow." Following the Battle of Wolf Mountain, Miles reported that, "The Indians appear to have plenty of arms and ammunition, but are otherwise in a destitute condition; some of the prisoners now in our hands were captured with frozen limbs and were living on horsemeat."[44]

Miles believed that the poor condition of the prisoners indicated that the time was right to persuade the dissidents to negotiate. On February 1, 1877, he sent Bruguier with one of the women captives to the camp in the Big Horn Mountains. Once inside the village, after the released captive told about Miles's kindness to the prisoners, the impoverished fugitives listened to Big Leggins (their name for Bruguier) as he explained Bear Coat's offer. They also had a chance to hear a counterproposal carried by messengers from Crook, known to the Sioux as Three Stars. It appeared to Big Leggins that the question was not whether the hostiles were willing to come in but rather to whom they would surrender.[45]

Bruguier returned to Tongue River on February 19 with a group of warriors and chiefs who were interested in listening to the terms. Miles refused to budge from a demand for an unconditional return to government control, plus the loss of arms and war ponies. Despite such an uncompromising stand, he believed that from the discussions "a feeling of confidence and good will was engendered."[46]

Upon returning to the camps, the Indians sent our criers who announced that the war was over. As those who decided to give up rode toward the cantonment at Tongue River, they met runners sent out by the Brule chieftain Spotted Tail and the Cheyenne River agencies, all under the jurisdiction of Crook. Miles reported that Spotted Tail's messengers led the hostiles to believe that at the southern agencies they would receive "more liberal terms, including the right to retain their arms and ponies and to procure ammunition."

The main body camped near a fork of the Powder River and invited Miles to a grand council, hoping to obtain similar terms. When Miles met with them on March 18, he refused to match Spotted Tail's offer but agreed to give them the option of surrendering at either the southern agencies or at Tongue River. Despite his stricter terms, Miles informed Sherman that the leaders indicated that they would come in to his camp because "they believe the power that can whip them can take care of them and it is nearer the buffalo in that they were nearly starved to death at their agencies."[47]

As it turned out, Miles misjudged the intentions of those coming in. On April 22 only about three hundred marched into camp on the Tongue River, while over two thousand, led by Crazy Horse, eventually reported to either the Red Cloud or Spotted Tail agencies. Although Miles must have been disappointed by the small number who surrendered at the cantonment, he correctly pointed out to his wife that "it makes very little difference where they surrender, it will be the result of our efforts during the winter, and not of those troops who turned back on account of the 'inhospitable country.'" The *New York Herald* shared this view, specifying that Miles's operation against Sitting Bull "was the real breaking of the backbone of the Sioux War on the Yellowstone." General Terry also appreciated the value of Miles's work. Following the battle of Wolf Mountain, he called Sheridan's attention "to the great vigor and zeal which have been displayed by General Miles and his officers and men, with extremely limited means and under the most disadvantageous circumstances he has persistently pursued and harassed the hostile Indians."[48]

Miles displayed patience and kindness as he accepted the surrender of Hump's band, primarily Cheyennes, on April 22. Hump, the chief, and his nephew rode into the cantonment ten miles in advance of the main body, who were driving in more than six hundred loaded ponies. Hump, whom the *Herald* journalist described as "Tall, straight as an arrow, and handsome in face and form, he seemed the perfect Indian," turned his Sharp rifle over to Miles in a private ceremony. The colonel tried taking the sting away from the disarmament by telling an aide to "put Hump's name on the belt and gun and put them away for him. Tell him I don't want the ponies now." When the main body finally approached the parade ground, they glanced apprehensively at the flag and soldiers gathered about, while equally nervous ponies began to break away. As young boys ran to round up the ponies, Miles ordered the band to play. Curiosity won out over fear, and intrigued Indians wandered about, examining instruments as the brass band played away. After the braves were disarmed, Hump observed Miles personally caring for his people while they were being fed.[49]

Hump, whose name indicated that he had fine qualities since the most prized portion of buffalo meat comes from its hump, had strong opinions that he willingly shared; he claimed that "Crazy Horse was a fool and Sitting Bull a big coward." When Miles asked if all the rebellious Indians had come in, the chief told him that twenty-four lodges were still out. "I ordered them in, but they have disobeyed me and defied my authority." After a pause, Hump added, "These people are rebels, General, and I want you to send your soldiers and destroy them; I will show the soldiers where to find them."[50]

On May 1, after supplies and reinforcements arrived at the cantonment, Miles started out after the wayward band led by a Miniconjou chief named Lame Deer. The colonel hoped to forestall a violent encounter by sending two of Hump's braves to warn the renegades that if they did not come in, soldiers would come after them. Apparently Miles did not have full faith in this effort because he also sent a lieutenant to the Crow Agency to enlist seventy-five scouts in the expedition. Besides the irregulars, Miles's force consisted of four companies of the Second Cavalry that had reported to Tongue River only a week earlier, on April 23, plus two companies of his own regiment and four from the Twenty-second Infantry. He also included an undesignated detachment of twenty-five mounted infantrymen culled from the two infantry regiments at Tongue River. They were commanded by 2d Lt. Edward W. Casey, Twenty-second Infantry, who was the son of Union Maj. Gen. Silas Casey, breveted for his conduct at the Battle of Fair Oaks in 1862. Hump, and two other warriors who had come in on the twenty-second, joined the expedition's band of scouts.[51]

When the Indian scouts found Lame Deer's camp, they exercised great care to insure that the troops took advantage of all of the natural cover available. They stealthily advanced toward the enemy camp, located near the mouth of Muddy Creek, a tributary of the Rosebud. From dark until midnight, the attackers slowly made their final approach to Lame Deer's village and then waited until 4:00 A.M. on the morning of May 7 to take action. After covering sixty-three miles, Miles had reduced his force to about 225 by leaving behind the wagon train, guarded by two companies of his regiment and one from the Twenty-second.

Miles tried to insure that the slaughter of innocents, which too often occurred during such attacks, did not take place at Lame Deer's camp. Not only did he give "explicit instructions to prevent firing upon women and children," he also had some of his scouts ride through the village, calling out that those who surrendered would have their lives spared. Meanwhile, Casey's detachment charged toward the camp's herd, supported by 2d Lt. Lovel H. Jerome's company of the Second Cavalry. Some of Jerome's brother officers believed that the young lieutenant hoped to earn recognition in battle as a means of stepping out of his father's shadow. Leonard W. Jerome would earn and lose several fortunes as a financier, then be remembered in history as Winston Churchill's grandfather.[52]

While Casey's mounted infantrymen and Jerome's troopers rode off with the camp's herd of almost five hundred ponies, Capt. Edward Ball's battalion of the Second Cavalry, with Miles leading the way, rode into the village. Unfortunately, Miles's precautions did not prevent a confrontation between the soldiers and a group of warriors who had been trapped in the camp. The braves, led by Lame Deer, approached the cavalrymen, and Miles reached out to grasp the chief's hand. At that moment, a scout thoughtlessly leveled his rifle so that it pointed toward Lame Deer, who reacted by firing his rifle as he pulled away from Miles; Miles instinctively jerked his horse's reins, forcing the horse to rear and taking him out of the path of the bullet, which hit the soldier behind the colonel. Capt. James N. Wheelen, Second Cavalry, then shot and killed Lame Deer, setting off a battle. Some of the warriors caught in camp managed to flee into a nearby pine forest to join those who had escaped earlier.

Three companies of the Twenty-second Infantry hiked into Lame Deer's deserted camp, and the cavalrymen were already riding through nearby hills hoping to round up fleeing Indians. At the end of the day's fighting, of the approximately one hundred warriors who had opposed the troops, fourteen were found dead on the field. The army's casualties were all from the

Second Cavalry: four troopers killed, six cavalrymen and an officer wounded. Of the soldiers killed, one in particular, troubled Miles. A cavalryman had been killed after three members of his detail ran off, leaving him as the sole guard for two pack mules. After killing the trooper, Indians rode off with the pack animals, loaded down with four thousand rounds of ammunition. Except for this rich haul, the band, now led by Lame Deer's son, were fugitives left only with the clothes on their backs and their rifles in hand.[53]

The troops spent the eighth burning down the village along with all the supplies found in the lodges. The sturdiest ponies in the captured herd were selected for use by the infantrymen, who entertained the cavalrymen as they tried to manage their new mounts. Captain Ball remained in the field with the cavalry battalion until June 4, but following the destruction of the village, Miles led the infantrymen with their ponies back to Tongue River. At 11:00 A.M. on May 14, the contingent reached the cantonment after marching 209 miles in thirteen days. The battle at Muddy Creek proved to be the final engagement of the Sioux War of 1876–77. Throughout the summer of 1877, patrols from Miles's command harried the survivors of the renegade band, inducing the last of them to surrender on September 10 at Spotted Tail's agency.[54]

Even before the Battle of Muddy Creek, Miles had been aware of critical statements in newspapers made by fellow officers. He mentioned this practice to Mary Miles, assuming that she had already noticed "all the mean little squibs thrown out to the papers from Crook's department and from Agency officers." One such attempt to discredit Miles after the May 7 battle occurred when Crook paid a social call at the offices of the *Cheyenne* (Wyoming) *Daily Leader.* According to the editor, Crook casually mentioned that Lame Deer and his followers had met with Spotted Tail and agreed to surrender, "but after traveling a day or two with 'Old Spot,' decided to turn back for the purpose of having one more hunt in the buffalo country."[55]

This attempt to detract from Miles's most recent campaign by suggesting that Lame Deer had been killed after he had already agreed to surrender attracted little sympathy from the editor. In his judgment, Lame Deer had "been brave, cunning and treacherous to a degree only paralleled by Sitting Bull, and the announcement of his sudden taking off causes a thrill of joy in every border man's heart. His band has scattered to the four winds and will harry the whites no more."

Apparently, Miles was not the only victim of Crook's barbs. General Sheridan, however, was in a better position than the colonel to set the commander of the Department of the Platte straight. In January 1877, after reading uncomplimentary articles about himself, which he attributed to Crook's command, the short-tempered division commander ordered his department commander to stop making "ignorant criticisms of superiors in the newspapers."[56]

Unfortunately for Miles's peace of mind, others besides Crook did not accept his accomplishments with good grace. Aware that a rift had developed between himself and some in the army's officer corps, Miles complained to General Sherman that "I not only have to contend against the same Indians with limited means, but against all the envy and jealousy of the old army and those who do not appear to be doing very much themselves." The commanding general could not do a thing about such a vague charge, but the *Herald* correspondent at Tongue River came to the defense of Miles's "brave and untiring little command." He trusted that his stories of the recent campaign upheld "it and its commander against the envious and belittling criticism from hostile sources. The difficulties encountered and overcome by it cannot be overstated or appreciated by anyone who has not known thoroughly the experience."[57]

Others besides the reporter applauded the efforts of Miles and his regiment. During the same week that Miles organized his expedition against Lame Deer, John Sherman took a moment from his position in the new administration to congratulate his niece's husband. Sherman, who as a senator helped shape financial legislation, had been rewarded by President Rutherford B. Hayes with an appointment as his treasury secretary. Sherman, definitely in a position to know, informed Miles that "Your toilsome march and winter trials have secured you the esteem of all your fellow officers and great popularity with the people." Newspapers serving areas in the region threatened by the Sioux outbreak were especially enthusiastic supporters of Miles. In the spring of 1877, the *Cheyenne* (Wyoming) *Daily Leader* began to petition the "powers that be" to enlarge Miles's district to include all of the areas around the Yellowstone favored by the Sioux. The editor argued that the colonel had "proven by his indomitable energy and splendid management of affairs in that section last fall and winter that even under the most adverse circumstances he could master the situation and could lay the foundation for an early termination of the war by a vigorous spring campaign."[58]

When Miles reflected in his memoirs on the Sioux War, he arrived at some observations as to why his command had won victories while sustaining so few casualties. He pointed out that Indians were skilled riflemen when targets came within two hundred yards, a range that they rarely exceeded during a hunt. They were inexperienced, however, in the techniques needed for accurate, long-distance shooting. Meanwhile, Miles's infantrymen were thoroughly trained in methods for estimating windage and range so that they could properly adjust their rifle sights. Furthermore, Miles took advantage of his insight into the psychology of the Indian warrior to demoralize and drive him from the field. He believed that if a warrior "thinks it is a good day for scalps and plunder he is very daring, but if he thinks the signs are not favorable and he and his companions are receiving serious injury, he can withdraw, with no loss of caste or reputation with his fellows."[59]

In the Sioux War, as in the Indian Territory campaign, Miles's knack for inspiring his men to soldier to the limits of their ability both explained his successes and set him apart from all but a handful of postwar commanders. The series of grueling marches made by companies under his command, while other units remained in their winter quarters, aptly demonstrated this talent. These exhibitions of endurance aroused conflicting opinions. Some, like General Sherman, praised the colonel for his "earnestness and energy," while others, such as Maj. Alfred L. Hough, Twenty-second Infantry, believed "Miles is working his men to death." The major, left in command of the cantonment when Miles set forth on the Wolf Mountain expedition, viewed the departure of the infantrymen with disapproval. On January 11, unaware of Miles's victory three days earlier, he wrote that, "His men are tired and worn and all men and officers seem dissatisfied. His animals are nearly dead. I am afraid he is overdoing the matter: that is, the results do not compensate for the criticism."[60]

Not all of those who served in the field with Miles during such demanding movements shared Major Hough's concerns. Although one veteran of the Battle of Muddy Creek admitted that Miles had again pushed his men to the brink of exhaustion, he added that the colonel, "with that rare faculty he possesses of 'getting more out' of men and animals without hurting them, than is generally deemed possible, and of stopping just at the right moment, gave his weary troops an opportunity to lie down and rest until 2 o'clock next morning." We can make further assumptions about the nature of Miles's leadership from John Finerty's impressions of the colonel during an expedition in 1879. Finerty, then a reporter for the *Chicago Times,* had enough military experience himself, first fighting as a rebel in Ireland and then as a loyalist in the Civil War, to make meaningful observations. He judged Miles to be "a splendid field soldier, prompt, bold, and magnetic. He was always in high spirits which is a good thing in a commanding officer." The man revealed by Finerty does not appear to be a demanding martinet who drove his troops, but rather a leader who could arouse his men to perform at the peak of their ability.[61]

Despite Miles's successes in Montana, capped by the Battle of Muddy Creek, the *Cheyenne Daily Leader* sensed that he was not yet ready to rest on his laurels. The newspaper, very much an advocate of the colonel, printed its opinion, saying that he "wants to get his hands on Mr. Sitting Bull by hook or by crook is certain, and he probably feels that it will be a fitting capstone to his fame as an Indian fighter." Between late May and early June of 1877, new units streamed into the cantonment at Tongue River, all hoping to bring an end to the medicine man's military career. The Twenty-second had been ordered to Chicago, where the infantrymen would maintain order during the 1877 railroad strike, but the cantonment now held more men than ever before. Eleven companies of the Seventh Cavalry and four companies of the First Infantry remained with Miles, while the infantrymen in two companies of the Eleventh barely paused to catch their breath before they resumed their march westward.[62]

The men of the Eleventh were to construct a fort at the juncture of the Little Bighorn and the Bighorn, aptly named Fort Custer. Work also began on the second fort authorized by Congress, following Sitting Bull's stunning victory in 1876. This post, named Fort Keogh, went up within hailing distance of the original Tongue River cantonment. From his headquarters Miles not only supervised his growing army but also cared for the nearby camp of Cheyennes, who had surrendered to him in April. On the plains to the west of the military community, industrious and acquisitive civilians had put together a collection of tawdry buildings. Miles probably felt in no way honored that the growing town, consisting primarily of dance halls, saloons, and gambling dens, had been named Miles City in his honor.[63]

As the Yellowstone Valley hummed with activity, Fort Keogh began to take shape. In addition to the actual fort, quarters were constructed for some of the families of married men in Miles's command. Mary Sherman Miles must have been pleased when she read her husband's letter in which he anticipated her arrival at the new fort aboard one of the first boats scheduled to sail up the Yellowstone after the spring thaw. Miles told his wife that a kitchen and a small dining room had been added on to a sturdy four-room log cabin that they would share. Mary Miles, along with their daughter Cecelia and her sister Elizabeth, finally arrived at the new home on July 11, only to learn that her husband was en route to Glendive. General Sherman intended to stop off at the cantonment as he traveled across the West by boat and wagon on a trip to the Pacific coast. The colonel wanted to be on hand to greet Sherman's party when the commanding general's steamer arrived at the supply depot, rather than wait for him to reach Tongue River. Mary Miles must have been disappointed that her husband had put business before pleasure.[64]

Sherman's visit coincided with one of Montana's loveliest summers. Heavy spring rains had watered the territory's hills and valleys, nourishing fresh growth that bloomed across the landscape. The greenery must have enhanced the appearance of her new quarters, although they surely must have been too cramped for the occasion when Mary Miles entertained her uncle and his guests as they mingled with Fort Keogh's officers. At this reception, Miles had a chance to suggest that the general present the Medals of Honor that some thirty soldiers had been awarded by Congress for their exploits during the Sioux War. On Sherman's last evening at the post, the commanding general personally pinned each medal on the uniforms of the men honored, then the entire garrison passed in review. Four companies of the Fifth Infantry, now facetiously called the "Eleventh Cavalry," rode past Sherman on Indian ponies captured in Lame Deer's camp. Since no objections from Sherman followed this display, Miles's sensible idea of mounting his infantrymen apparently received the commanding general's tacit approval.[65]

Miles had not allowed preparations for Sherman's visit to distract his attention from Sitting Bull, who had found refuge in a camp near Woody Mountain in Canada. On July 4, Miles ordered a column to scout the area between the Yellowstone and Missouri Rivers to prevent a linkup between survivors of Lame Deer's band and the medicine man's camp. Shortly after the sweep, the military hierarchy perceived no further threat from the Sioux in Canada, and Miles received orders to limit his operations to the Yellowstone Valley. General Terry switched the colonel's mission from guarding against raids from Canada to preventing Indians fleeing their agency from reaching Sitting Bull's camp. General Sherman had declared that "I now regard the Sioux Indian problem as a war question, as solved by the operations of General Miles last winter and by the establishment of the two new posts on the Yellowstone now assured this summer."[66]

– CHAPTER 6 –

Miles and the Nez Perce

LATE IN THE SUMMER OF 1877, Colonel Miles became aware of another Indian problem that might involve his command. Primarily from reading newspapers, he kept track of Chief Joseph as his band of Nez Perce managed to keep one step ahead of pursuing troops. Miles had no compunction about fighting this tribe even though he sympathized with their plight. When the Nez Perce reluctantly agreed to give up their home in the Wallowa Valley of eastern Oregon, Miles believed that a new "Indian war, or more strictly speaking, another cruel injustice was to be enacted." He added that the tribe's efforts to resist the encroachment on their land were doomed to failure because "the greed and pressure of the white race were all-powerful."

Following some killings of settlers by resentful Nez Perce, Chief Joseph hoped his people could escape to buffalo country before a war erupted. This Wallowa band probably impressed Miles more than any other tribe that he had encountered. After he came to know these Indians, Miles judged that they "were naturally a strong, intelligent, mountain race, and peaceably disposed." As for the leader of the band, Joseph, who had replaced his father, Old Joseph, as chief in 1871, Miles found him to be "the highest type of the Indian I have ever known, very handsome, kind, and brave. He was quite an orator and the idol of his tribe."[1]

Brig. Gen. Oliver O. Howard, commander of the Department of the Columbia since 1874, had to decide what the army's response should be to the murder of settlers by Nez Perce Indians. When Howard ordered Joseph's camp at White Bird Canyon to be attacked on June 17, any possibility of settling the situation peacefully disappeared. After the Indians fought off the attack and started eastward, other dissidents joined Joseph's party. At a council of chiefs held on July 15, Joseph, who had thoughts of surrendering, watched passively as the council agreed that Looking Glass should lead some eight hundred men, women, and children to buffalo country in Montana. During the pursuit, the army caught up with the Indians in their camps on the Clearwater River in Idaho and in the valley of the Big Hole River in Montana. In each instance the Nez Perce fought the troops to a standstill before continuing on their way and even dared to attack Howard's camp at Camas Meadows in Idaho. Because General Howard habitually lagged two days behind the Nez Perce during the campaign, they named him "General Day After Tomorrow."[2]

On August 3, Miles took his first step toward trying to intercept the Nez Perce as they fled toward Montana. He dispatched 1st Lt. Gustavus C. Doane, Second Cavalry, with a force of Crow scouts escorted by a troop of the Seventh Cavalry to Judith Gap. Doane was to "intercept, capture, or destroy the Nez Perces" if he discovered them at this natural passage between the Yellowstone and Canada. Seven days later Miles ordered Col. (Bvt. Maj. Gen.) Samuel D. Sturgis, Seventh Cavalry, with six troops of his regiment, to the same area with instructions to assume command over Doane's force, but the mission remained the same. Rumors, probably based on fact, began to spread through the ranks of the Seventh Cavalry that their commander resented serving under Miles, "a younger officer." Sturgis, West Point class of 1846, had been stationed at Saint Louis to supervise the mounted recruit service when his son, 2d Lt. James G. Sturgis, was among those killed with Custer. The old campaigner probably thought about settling accounts with Sitting Bull when Miles mentioned that his band of Sioux might move south from Canada, but such reports also raised the alarming possibility that the Sioux might unite with the Nez Perce.[3]

Early in the evening of September 17, a dispatch rider reached Miles with a note written by Howard five days earlier. The Nez Perce had tricked Sturgis into leaving one of the natural exits of Yellowstone Park unguarded and were now crossing Montana. Howard requested Miles "to make every effort in your power to prevent the escape of the hostile band, and at least hold them in check until I can overtake them."[4]

Miles and his men labored through the night preparing and packing equipment for the coming campaign. The colonel only paused long enough to dispatch couriers to Fort Peck and Fort Buford to make arrangements for a steamer to be sent up the Missouri River. This vessel would insure that Miles's command would be resupplied and also take care of the anticipated needs of Sturgis and Howard. At the onset of his march, Miles's command consisted of two troops of the Seventh Cavalry, four companies of his mounted infantry, and two companies of his regiment on foot assigned to escort the wagon train. Two artillery pieces, a twelve-pound Napoleon and a breech-loading Hotchkiss gun, were also taken along. As usual, Miles had a detachment of both civilian and Indian scouts riding ahead of the column, commanded by Lt. Marion P. Maus, First Infantry. Miles overtook three troops of the Second Cavalry, along with one from the Seventh Cavalry, on their way to General Terry, and after he pressed these cavalrymen into his column, he commanded about 360 men.[5]

Miles conducted another of the grueling marches that had made it possible in the past for him to surprise his enemies. With scouts leading the way, the main body came within six miles of the Missouri River on September 23, after covering the last leg, fifty-two miles, in twenty-four hours. After the Second Cavalry had been ferried across the river by a steamer, he released the ship on the assumption that the Nez Perce were still south of the river. Shortly after the vessel sailed out of sight on September 25, a couple of settlers in a small boat reached Miles with the news that the Indians had already crossed the river at Cow Island, about seventy miles farther to the west. Miles immediately recalled the steamer by firing the twelve pounder, anticipating that the sound of the explosion would carry to the ship and attract attention.[6]

After the entire command had crossed the Missouri, the wagon train, with its escort of forty foot soldiers, began to fall behind the rest of the column. The wisdom of mounting infantrymen had been confirmed as they kept pace with the cavalry units in a dash toward a gap between the Bear Paw Mountain to the west and the Little Rocky Mountains to the east. After breaking camp at 4:00 A.M. on the morning of September 30, the mounted units rode across rolling prairies and worked their way north around the edge of the Bear Paw Mountains. At about 7:00 A.M., a scout selected because he had the freshest horse, raced back to the column with word that a recently abandoned Nez Perce camp had been found only a few miles farther up the trail. Despite the fact that the temperature had fallen low enough to freeze the ground and form ice on streams, warriors stripped for battle, wearing little except loincloths and war paint. The 319 mounted troops began to move at a trot, then at a gallop, toward their objective. In Miles's memoirs, he pictured his men in fine fettle as they neared the end of their ten-day, 267-mile chase from Fort Keogh. He recalled that as they galloped toward the village, "some men were joking and one even singing 'What Shall the Harvest Be?' the melody of the tune timed to the foot falls of his charger."[7]

Looking Glass had felt no urgency when the Nez Perce reached an attractive campsite on a low, six-acre terrace on the eastern side of Snake Creek. Thus, on September 29, he recommended that his people set up camp rather than push into Canada, only forty miles to the north. Yellow Wolf, a Nez Perce warrior who later narrated his experiences to a biographer, explained that their herd of horses suffered from tender feet, and the area abounded with grass for grazing. Furthermore, the sense of security felt by most of the Nez Perce seemed well founded. According to Yellow Wolf, they "knew General Howard was more than two suns back on our trail. It was nothing hard to keep ahead of him."[8]

Actually, General Howard had purposely slowed the pace of his pursuit in response to Sturgis's suggestion that, "We must not move too fast, lest we flush the game." The assertion that Howard and Sturgis purposely held back is substantiated by a news story written on September 22 by a correspondent in the field with Howard. He stated that with regard to the Nez Perce, the two commanders "do not push them much, hoping to give General Miles a chance to get ahead of them on the Missouri River: then to attack them simultaneously."[9]

However, the Nez Perce did not allow their lack of concern about Howard to lull them into neglecting camp security. Following Col. John Gibbon's surprise attack against their camp at Big Hole, the Nez Perce constructed elaborate defensive positions whenever they stopped for any period of time. Yellow Wolf mentioned that as a further precaution, some young warriors were stationed on elevated formations to serve as lookouts. The first alarm, however, probably did not come from these sentinels. Two horsemen herding some of the camp's ponies were startled, and fired upon, by Lieutenant Maus's small party of scouts. The two herdsmen may have been the two riders Yellow Wolf recalled dashing into the camp from the south shouting, "Stampeding buffaloes! Soldiers! Soldiers!"[10]

According to Yellow Wolf, Looking Glass rode about telling his people, "Do not hurry! Go slow! Plenty, plenty time. Let children eat all wanted!" The warrior believed that the chief's attempt to calm his people unfortunately insured the eventual capture of many of them. Some, however, did not follow the advice of Looking Glass and took advantage of the warning to stow their belongings on pack animals. These Indians were in a fortunate position to escape when, about an hour after the original warning, the Nez Perce saw one of their scouts riding at a furious pace to the top of the highest bluff in sight, where he used a blanket to signal, "Enemies right on us! Soon the attack!"[11]

As the soldiers advanced at a trot, word passed through the ranks that they were about three miles from the Indian camp; as excitement mounted, the pace quickened to a gallop. Unfortunately, the distance had been misjudged, and the riders and their mounts must have been fatigued after an eight-mile gallop to a high ridge, where they reined to a halt. From this point, soldiers could pick out the Nez Perce herd and guess that undulating ridges blocked the camp from view. Miles believed that his command had reached this crest without being discovered by the Nez Perce. Thus he did not pause to reconnoiter his objective, wishing to maintain the advantage of surprise that he believed he enjoyed.[12]

Charles K. Bucknam from Fort Benton, Montana, and a former Confederate soldier, G. H. Snow, helped to guide the column to a point where the Nez Perce herd could be seen. A *Herald* correspondent managed to scoop most of the press corps after he interviewed both men separately on October 6. Their information, combined with the reporter's own impressions, blended together as words were used to paint a picture of Miles poised to attack the camp. The reporter considered the colonel, who now weighed nearly two hundred pounds, to be a "rough, tough, and ready" commander, impressive looking mounted on his black charger. Given Miles's age (thirty-eight), one would expect to notice the few gray hairs that stood out against the brown hair of his mustache and sideburns; however, the journalist failed to mention a pronounced widow's peak revealed in a photograph taken in 1877, hinting that Miles's hair was prematurely thinning.[13]

Miles wore a soft hat with a broad brim, trimmed with a blue band so that its ends would trail from the back of the hat. He had a hip-length buckskin jacket favored by so many officers because they admired the way the fringes streamed in the breeze as they galloped about. He wore the same uniform pants issued to the enlisted men, light blue trousers with a black stripe sewn along the outside seams. The pants were tucked into coarse boots, and a frontier shirt adorned with a black tie completed his outfit, although he also had a red blanket for protection against sudden drops in temperature. Thus attired, Miles took his place at the head of the column about 9:00 A.M., September 30, and bellowed, "Charge them! Damn them!"[14]

The Second Cavalry led the way, charging toward the left of the village to cut off the Nez Perce herd grazing on the far side of the Snake Creek. As the cavalry raced toward the some eight hundred head of livestock, about one hundred women and children led fully packed ponies northward, guarded by some fifty to seventy warriors. While two troops of the Second Cavalry rounded up the Indians' animals, the third attempted to pursue the fleeing Indians. These troopers were stopped in their tracks during the chase when escorting warriors abruptly switched to the offensive and actually seemed intent on retrieving the captured animals. Joseph had been with this group of braves and helped his teenage daughter join those who were escaping. He explained that he did not ride away with his daughter, who succeeded in reaching Canada, because the rest of his family was trapped, "and I resolved to go to them or die." Although bullet holes through Joseph's clothing testify to how close he came to dying, he reached his wife unscathed. As she handed him his rifle, she said, "Here's your gun. Fight."[15]

Joseph apparently joined the warriors who had elected to defend the southern flank of their camp. These braves remained firm in the face of an intimidating charge by the Seventh Cavalry. Ravines on either side of the southern approach to the village channeled the cavalrymen toward a bluff too steep for horses to climb; thus, Companies A and D, the left and center companies, found themselves in a deadly cul-de-sac. The Indians had patiently waited on top of the bluff until their targets were less than two hundred yards away before they opened fire.[16]

The warriors were extremely effective, and many in the Seventh were hit. Miles, who rode into battle at the head of this regiment, ordered the troopers in the two stalled companies to dismount and assist Company K. When Capt. Owen Hale, Company K's commander, saw the predicament of the two companies to his left, he swerved to the right and led his men onto a spit of high land separating two ravines. The Indians quickly surrounded his troopers, who in some instances defended themselves in hand-to-hand combat. The braves withdrew as the men from A and D companies raced to the rescue, but the mesa provided little cover for the cavalrymen as warriors peppered the bluff. The toll quickly mounted until Lt. Edwin P. Erickson reported back to Miles with the chilling news that "I'm the only damned man of the Seventh Cavalry wearing shoulder straps who's alive."[17]

Actually, Captain Hale and 2d Lt. Jonathan W. Biddle were the only officers in the Seventh who were killed; however, Erickson was the only officer from the regiment on the battlefield because wounds forced the other two company commanders to seek medical attention. The Nez Perce had shown military sophistication in their choice of targets, concentrating their fire on those men giving commands. Furthermore, Miles reported that these warriors were "the best marksmen I have ever met and understand the use of improved sights and the measurement of distances." As a result of this talent, before sundown the Seventh saw killed in action, besides Captain Hale and his adjutant, Lieutenant Biddle, its three first sergeants, four sergeants, and nine privates. In addition, two captains and thirty enlisted men were wounded during the day's action. Of the 115 men in the regiment who spurred their mounts toward the Nez Perce village on September 30, 50 were casualties by nightfall.[18]

Although the survivors of the charge of the Seventh Cavalry were in a perilous situation, they were in a position to dislodge the warriors defending the southern approach to the Nez Perce camp. When Miles ordered the mounted infantry into action, they did not have to charge into the wall of fire that had disrupted the first attack. The men of the Fifth also profited from the experience of the preceding wave and halted approximately one hundred yards from the bluffs before which the Seventh had milled about in confusion. Despite these advantages, men and horses were hit before the troops sprang from their ponies to fight as infantrymen. On the ground they fired a volley before diving for cover to escape the warrior's response. The second volley from their long range rifles scattered the braves who had been sniping at the Seventh Cavalry, allowing the exposed troopers to improve their positions. Deadly fire from Nez Perce marksmen, however, discouraged the foot soldiers from trying to advance beyond the natural ramparts provided by the walls of the bluff.[19]

The soldiers should have taken heed after Miles's acting assistant adjutant general, 1st Lt. George W. Baird, rode into the open and an explosive bullet shattered his right arm and another ripped off most of one ear. Instead, as a sergeant and one of his men cautiously raised their heads to peer over the edge of the rifle pit, a bullet parted the sergeant's hair while another took his companion's life. Later that afternoon, Yellowstone Kelly watched in fascination as Hump slowly slithered across the ground until he reached a position where he could take a shot at the most lethal of the Nez Perce riflemen. After the scout signaled a hit with a triumphant war cry, he pressed his luck by continuing the hunt, only to fall victim to an equally skilled opponent, who shot the scout in the shoulder. Hump painfully pulled himself out of the line of fire; then a tribesman assisted him to the busy field hospital, set up on a ridge behind the line defended by the infantry.[20]

As in the Civil War, Miles rose to the occasion when things went badly for his cause. Henry Remsen Tilton, surgeon for the Seventh Cavalry, noticed Miles "here, there, everywhere. When the first horse is blown a fresh one is mounted, and off again. Three horses are ridden down during the day; their rider never appears to tire." Two scouts who rode into Fort Benton told very much the same story. They were amazed that the colonel escaped without a scratch. One remarked that, "He was the damndest devil I ever saw at the head of such a column on the field in an Indian scrimmage. He was everywhere, and everyone of the boys seemed to know him, and when they heard him call out they jumped, you bet." When necessary, Miles exhorted his men to action, shouting "go for them boys," and "There, light on those sons of b——s." At other times, he looked out for their welfare, asking, "Hello! Are you hit? Take care of them!" and, "There, boys, look out for that damned crowd."[21]

The Nez Perce had been immobilized by the loss of their horses and were now surrounded in their camp. Although groups of warriors would still be able to slip away to freedom, the women, children, wounded, and aged had no hope of outdistancing mounted troops. Thus, the main body of the Nez Perce could avoid capture only by destroying the military effectiveness of the attacking force as they had done at Big Hole, or if Sitting Bull succeeded in coming to their rescue. Since the encircled Indians seemed incapable of raising the siege with their own resources, Miles reported that he made "preparations to meet the reinforcements from the north that the

Nez Perces evidently expected." Thus, fear that Sitting Bull's warriors might reach the Bear Paw battlefield before Howard's or Sturgis's troops arrived may well have inspired Miles to risk one last chance at winning an immediate victory.[22]

With the Second Cavalry occupying the Nez Perce at the north end of their camp, and the Seventh Cavalry positioned along the eastern perimeter, Miles planned to test the western flank of the village. He hoped that an attack, planned for 3:00 P.M., would drive the warriors into the open. Miles selected the southernmost group of lodges as the objective of a two-pronged assault, one led by Lt. Mason Carter, the other by Capt. Henry Romeyn.[23]

Romeyn's assault force consisted of the two companies of the Seventh Cavalry without officers, A and D, plus his own company of the Fifth Infantry. His men were expected to push toward the camp from the east, driving back the warriors they encountered. Unfortunately, as soon as Romeyn rose to wave his hat as a signal to move out, a shot through his lungs knocked him out of the battle. Too few noncommissioned officers had been available for this mission, and with the only officer in the task force wounded, no one pressed the men forward.

After Lieutenant Carter, assisted by Lt. Thomas Woodruff, began their attack, they believed that they were a forlorn hope. They had charged with twenty-seven infantrymen over the top of the bluff that had protected them, onto a quiet battleground. Unaware that Romeyn's attack had already stalled, Woodruff attributed lack of support to the inability of messengers to get through with word of the 3:00 P.M. assault. The infantrymen, left to their own devices, crossed a ravine, then raced along Snake Creek until they reached the village, where they moved in among the teepees. Chief Joseph, one of those who resisted this advance, said, "We fought at close range, not more than twenty steps apart, and drove the soldiers back upon their main line, leaving their dead in our hands." Eight of Carter's men were wounded, two of whom later died. Romeyn recalled that when the infantrymen withdrew to a ravine, they left some of their wounded behind in the village, who were humanely treated by the Nez Perce.[24]

Yellowstone Kelly, along with the rest of Lieutenant Maus's scouts, reached the battlefield after the fight had evolved into a siege. They had been delayed waiting for the column to reach them, until Kelly finally realized that

Miles must have followed a different trail to reach the enemy camp. When the small group of riders reached high ground overlooking the contested area, the scout caught a glimpse of the Nez Perce position. "Looking down into the hollow I could see nothing but a few skin lodges. The women and children were safely secreted in underground excavations, while the warriors held a number of well-placed rock rifle pits, from whose shelter they picked off any who showed their heads." An occasional exchange of shots between snipers, and an infrequent eruption from the steel Hotchkiss gun, signaled that the battle had not yet ended. The breech loader, undergoing a more thorough field test than the ordinance department ever expected, soon ceased firing, however, because it could not be lowered enough to range in on the campsite. To complicate matters, as the gunners tried to solve the problem, they were exposed to enemy rifle fire. When Kelly reached the bluffs at the southern approach to the camp, he noticed blankets covering the bodies of those who had fallen earlier, now arranged in a row behind the firing line.[25]

Miles recalled that as he galloped along the perimeter that hemmed in the hostiles, he made the grim discovery that "a great part of the line encircling camp was dotted with dead and wounded soldiers and horses." Although the colonel obviously realized that he had lost men in battle, he only mentioned his wounded when he wrote the first dispatch to be sent from the battlefield. This message, written at 5:30 P.M. on the thirtieth, announced that he had "surprised the hostile Nez Perce in their camp and have had a sharp fight. I have several officers and men wounded (about 30). About 25 Indians are still in their camp which is well protected." When Miles woefully underestimated the number of his foe, he did not have the heart to admit publicly that such a small group of warriors could defeat his troops. Ever since his assignment as jailer for Jefferson Davis, Miles had been sensitive about newspaper coverage. Since he relished a good press, he apparently did not want to release the bad news of his casualties until they could be balanced by some good news, preferably a victory announcement.[26]

The troops paid a heavy price when they invested their enemy and captured some six hundred of the Nez Perce animals: two officers and twenty-two men were killed, while four officers and thirty-eight troops were wounded. The colonel also listed Hump and another Indian ally with those wounded. When Miles finally notified Terry of these casualties on October 3, he had a better grasp of the situation and realized that he enjoyed the upper hand. He had learned that during the fighting on September 30, both sides had inflicted almost identical losses on each other. Although the warriors were encumbered by their families, during the battle most of the noncombatants were sheltered out of harm's way. Assured of the safety of their relatives, the braves were free to exploit their greatest advantage, meeting an attack from a prepared position. Miles informed Terry that in the clash that followed, the Nez Perce had fought "with more desperation than any Indians I ever met." The desperate nature of their resistance, however, indicated a sense of hopelessness that encouraged Miles to report that he expected to "wear them out and eventually compel them to give up."[27]

Before nightfall on the thirtieth, Miles made a first attempt to open talks with the Nez Perce. They refused, challenging, "Come and take our hair." Despite the brave response, unless they received help from the Sioux, their future looked bleak. Yellow Wolf recalled that as night darkened the campsite, he looked about and saw his people "burying their dead. A wounded young warrior lay on a buffalo robe dying without complaint. Children crying with cold. No fire. There could be no light. Everywhere the crying, the death wail." When Miles reported his casualties on the third, he also had enough information to add that, "The Indians lost seventeen killed, including Looking Glass and Joseph's brother (Ollokot) and three other chiefs and forty wounded."[28]

Conditions were not much better in the army camp. Snow began to fall on the night of the thirtieth; then it either rained or snowed intermittently until October fourth. Since no trees grew near the battlefield, the pickets and wounded were at first forced to huddle miserably in their blankets because they had no wood for campfires. Life became more bearable when the wagon train arrived late in the afternoon of October 1. Tents could now be set up for the wounded, and the train's escort of forty infantrymen freed enough men from picket duty so that details could be sent to look for firewood.[29]

With the arrival of extra supplies, equipment, men, and the twelve pounder, the balance of power at Bear Paw tipped in Miles's favor. Despite a shortage of shells, the gunners found a way to set up the Napoleon to harass the enemy by placing the tail of the weapon in a ditch, its barrel pointed into the sky. With a reduced powder charge, the twelve-pounder could lob shells into the Indian camp like a trench mortar. The cannon shattered the Indians' sense of security, and about noon on October 5 an explosion collapsed the walls of a dugout. Sadly, only noncombatants were victims of this hit. A twelve-year-old girl and her grandmother were so deeply buried in the rubble that would-be rescuers gave up trying to find them.[30]

As the ring around the surrounded Indians grew tighter, their only hope lay in warriors from Sitting Bull's camp in Canada riding to join them in the fight. The war chiefs in this camp were already in council when they heard that the Nez Perce were battling soldiers less than one hundred miles to the south. Virtually everyone in the village argued in favor of aiding fellow Indians.[31]

Fortunately for the hard-pressed soldiers at Bear Paw, Maj. James M. Walsh, superintendent of the North-West Mounted Police, also heard about the plight of the Nez Perce and the intentions of the Sioux. He rushed to Sitting Bull's camp, where he found hundreds of braves streaked with war paint before the council of chiefs, and in a grave voice warned that any warrior "who crosses the boundary line from this camp is, from the moment he puts foot on United States soil, our enemy. Henceforth we shall be to him, if he returns, what he says United States soldiers are to him today—wolves seeking his blood."[32]

When Walsh finished explaining the consequences of Sioux involvement in the Nez Perce War, he retired to a nearby strong point established by his police detachment south of the Indian camp. Late the following day, the chiefs who argued in favor of preserving their sanctuary in Canada prevailed, and peacemakers calmed the excited braves and discouraged them from riding to the Montana battlefield. The tense confrontation between Superintendent Walsh and the Sioux chiefs went unnoticed south of the Canadian border. Thus, few in the United States realized how much credit the Canadian lawman deserved for restraining the Sioux and saving Miles.[33]

On October 1, although the Nez Perce still had reason to hope that help would come from the north, they responded to a call for a truce. After preliminary negotiations were completed, Chief Joseph entered Miles's camp, accompanied by two braves. The troops were intrigued at this rare chance to glimpse a chief as prominent as Joseph. He definitely impressed the surgeon, who found him to be "a man of splendid physique, dignified bearing and handsome features. His usual expression was serious, but occasionally a smile would light up his face, which impressed us, very favorably." Trooper Mulford, who judged Joseph to be about five feet ten, and thirty-five years old, found his black eyes to be "as piercing as an eagle's." He paid particular attention to the way Joseph arranged his black hair, which "is gathered in a loose braid at the back of his head, his scalp lock is ornamented with a cluster of feathers, and long braids hang in front of his ears." When Miles shared his impression with Mary Miles, he seemed captivated by his opponent, whom he regarded as "a very superior Indian, far above any others I have met in intelligence and ability, and a fine looking, mild-mannered man."[34]

At the parlay between Miles and Chief Joseph, the two parties had difficulty communicating. A Nez Perce brave and one of the army's Indian scouts each understood a few words of Chinook, but misunderstandings were bound to crop up due to the limitations of the two translators. The confusion resulting from this makeshift attempt to negotiate is confirmed by the lack of agreement in accounts left by witnesses to the meeting.

Although Captain Romeyn's wound must have kept him from the talks, he received enough information to gain the impression that Chief Joseph's "first proposition was to be allowed to march out armed and mounted, abandoning only the position to his foe." After the chief revealed the losses inflicted on his people by the troops on September 30, Romeyn believed that these casualties explained why Joseph consented to meet with Miles. The chief hoped that they could agree on a way for the noncombatants to leave the battlefield. Although Miles sympathized with the plight of the innocent, when he would not permit any of the enemy to escape, the captain noted that "the Nez Perce went back to renew the battle." On the other hand, Lieutenant Jerome, a witness to the discussion, believed that when the talks ended, the Nez Perce agreed "to bring out all of their guns and move out of their trenches."[35]

Jerome, who had known Joseph before the outbreak, entered the Indian camp to help convince the chief to negotiate with Miles. At that time, he also persuaded him to bring some weapons to lay before Miles; thus, he realized that this gesture had been an expression of good faith rather than an agreement to surrender. When eleven weapons were presented to Miles, however, the colonel misinterpreted the act as a token of surrender, and he later complained, "They pretended to do so [surrender] and brought up a few [rifles], which amounted to nothing; but hesitated greatly about surrendering the remainder."[36]

Jerome, who knew the significance of the eleven rifles, behaved at the conclusion of the negotiations as though he believed that an agreement had been reached with the Nez Perce. If, fifty-three years after the memorable occasion, Jerome correctly set the scene, relations between the two leaders were cordial enough to mislead a young lieutenant. As the Nez Perce party prepared to return to their lines, Miles suggested to Joseph, "you stay here and we will have some coffee." When the colonel then instructed Jerome to "go in and see that they don't cache their guns," the lieutenant had no compunction about entering the Indian camp.[37]

In his annual report, Miles makes a slight distinction: rather than ordering the lieutenant into the camp, he told him "to ascertain what was being done in the Indian village." Almost twenty years later, the colonel added that he simply wanted the lieutenant to study the enemy camp from a nearby bluff. The imprecise order resulted in Jerome being held by the Indians while Joseph remained in army hands. Although the Indians did not mistreat the lieutenant, White Bird, a truculent chief, warned Jerome that if "Joseph no come back; Miles hurt Joseph, me kill you! Savvy?" The Second Cavalry officer felt assured that such a deadly exchange would not take place because he "knew that Miles would protect—not hurt—Chief Joseph."[38]

Although Miles intended no harm to the chief, his reasons for holding Joseph, thus violating a truce, are not clear. He openly admitted his intentions, without revealing his purpose, when he confided to Mary Miles that he "had Chief Joseph in my camp one night and I believe he was acting in good faith, but unfortunately Jerome got detained in their camp; White Bird was disposed to fight it out, and Joseph had to be exchanged for Jerome." Miles apparently believed that if he had more time with Joseph, he would have been able to convince him to encourage his people to surrender. It is unlikely that Miles intended to hold Joseph, the spokesman for peace, as a hostage. Such a provocation would only have aroused the Indians to take a more determined stand.

On October 2, the day Jerome and Joseph were exchanged, a messenger dispatched by Miles prior to engaging the Indians reached General Howard at Carroll. The general reacted to the news that Miles had caught up with the Nez Perce by sailing aboard the *Benton,* with part of his command, to Cow Island. At this ford across the Missouri River, he left his infantry and artillery behind, and accompanied only by his two aides and seventeen scouts, set out to join Miles. Among his scouts were two Nez Perce who had daughters with Joseph's band, and an interpreter, Arthur Chapman. Some of the Nez Perce reputedly did not respect Chapman, a white man who had married a member of the Umatilla tribe from Oregon, but he could speak their language.[40]

Howard explained that he rode ahead of his troops in order to "communicate with Colonel Miles, if possible, in a personal interview." In 1936, Charles Erskine Scott Wood, one of Howard's two aides in 1877, added that the general "began to worry about Miles, fearing he had been surrounded as [at Big Hole, John] Gibbon had been." It would take more than the small party with Howard, however, to extricate the troops at Bear Paw if they were in trouble. Accompanied by one of Miles's dispatch riders, Howard's party traveled seventy-six miles to reach the battlefield on the evening of October 4. Alerted to Howard's approach by his scouts, Miles rode out with a small escort to greet the general's party. With the sound of gunfire in the background, Miles explained that, "We have the Indians corralled down yonder in the direction of the firing."[41]

The arrival of Howard's scouts solved a dilemma facing some of the Nez Perce. After Joseph had returned to his camp, the Indians discussed their options. Although able-bodied adults could still escape to the north, they hesitated about leaving their wounded behind because, as Joseph wrote, they "had never heard of a wounded Indian recovering while in the hands of the white man." Those inclined to surrender held back from doing so because the language barrier made them uncertain of the terms offered by the army. Their impasse ended on the morning of October 5, when Joseph found out that Arthur Chapman, whom he considered a friend, had arrived in Miles's camp with Howard the night before. Joseph stressed the importance of the interpreter's presence, stating, "We could now talk understandingly."[42]

The dismal weather that had dampened the spirits of everyone at Bear Paw since the beginning of the battle finally broke on October 5. At 11:00 A.M., on a sparkling clear day, the two Nez Perce with Howard, George and

Captain John, entered the camp of their tribesmen carrying a truce flag. Joseph agreed to meet with Miles and Howard at a point midway between the two camps. Miles conducted the negotiations with the chief, who gave no sign of bitterness at being held in the army camp on the night of October 1. The chief recalled that the colonel promised: "If you will come out and give up your arms, I will spare your lives and send you to your reservation." Joseph, moved by the suffering of his wounded, and bolstered by the promise that the Nez Perce would be returned to their homes, agreed to the terms. He later explained, "I believed General Miles, or I never would have surrendered." The chief's willingness to entrust his people to Miles's care indicates that the truce violation did not cause him to lose faith in the colonel. Thus, although what happened on October 1 cannot be condoned, what actually happened that day may have been misinterpreted and therefore not as significant as some have claimed.[43]

Miles confirmed that he had promised Joseph that his people would be returned to Idaho, after first detaining them at his post on the Tongue River for the winter. Both he and Howard were convinced that they were following official policy when they offered these terms. When Howard wrote about his Indian war experiences, he pointed out that the commander of the Military Division of the Pacific, Maj. Gen. Irvin McDowell, had advised him that the dissident Nez Perce should be returned to the Department of the Columbia. As for Miles, he complained that no one had responded to his request, made during the campaign, for instructions to guide his actions. As a result, when Joseph capitulated, Miles based his proposal to the chief "on what I supposed was the original design of the Government to place these Indians on their own Reservation, and so informed them."[44]

At about 4:00 P.M., four or five warriors walked alongside their mounted chief as Joseph entered the army camp and approached Howard for the formal surrender. When Joseph offered his rifle to the general, Howard indicated that Miles should receive it. Howard later explained that he declined to accept the rifle "in accordance with my own belief of the courtesy due from a commanding officer to his subordinate, . . . especially when the junior belongs, as Col. Miles did, to a separate department of the one I commanded." Miles recalled that as Joseph handed him the rifle, he looked in the direction of the sun and said, "From where the sun now stands, I will fight no more against the white man." Thus, Miles concluded another successful campaign, but at a higher cost in the lives of his troops than in any of his other Indian war battles.

Those who were wounded at Bear Paw, and later wrote about their experiences, revealed no resentment at the price they paid to help make victory possible. For instance, hospital steward J. B. Gallenne had a leg amputated, and cavalryman Ami Mulford became partially paralyzed after his horse fell on him. While recuperating in the hospital at Fort Rice, North Dakota, they "acclaimed General Custer and General Miles as our ideals of what commanders sent out to end an Indian uprising should be." Romeyn, who suffered from a severe lung wound, thought that he had fought in a battle "of the most brilliant character, 'short, sharp and decisive.'" An explosive bullet fractured the ulna bone of Baird's left arm, and another tore away most of his left ear. Miles's adjutant looked beyond his wounds, and those of the others, to reproach the public for their indifference to the troops who sacrificed their lives in battle. Baird lamented that they are now buried in "a soldier's grave on the field where they fought shoulder to shoulder; like so many other brave men who fell in the 'Battle of Civilization,' they are unknown or forgotten by those who profited by their victories."[45]

Following the surrender, Indians began to trickle into the army camp. Mulford noticed that when warriors reached Miles's headquarters, the rifles that they gave up were "the very best that American inventors were able to produce." After each group was disarmed, Yellow Wolf admitted that, "Miles was good to the surrendered Indians with food. The little boys and girls loved him for that. They could now have hot food and fires to warm by." Drawing on information supplied by his charges, Miles reported that twenty-five Nez Perce were killed and forty-six wounded during the battle.[46]

As daylight slipped away, the intermittent stream of incoming Indians came to a halt. Throughout the night sentries remained on guard around the perimeter of the still-inhabited Indian camp. Despite this precaution, sometime after dark on October 5, White Bird, with a number of his followers, managed to slip unnoticed past the pickets and dash to Canada. On October 12, Major Walsh reported that about fifty warriors, forty women, and a large group of children had escaped from the Snake Creek battlefield and succeeded in reaching Sitting Bull's camp. Since this is the only report of Nez Perce refugees made by the major, White Bird's band and those who escaped on September 30 apparently joined together before entering Canada.

Those who had elected to remain in Montana came out of their camp the following morning to complete the surrender process. Romeyn noted that a total of 87 men, 184 women, and 147 children turned themselves into the troops of Bear Paw.[47]

On October 7, after the wounded had been cared for and the dead buried, a colorful procession left the battlefield. Under a bright sky, as clouds cast their shadows against the distant pine-clad, snow-topped mountains, strikingly dressed Nez Perce led the column toward the Missouri River. A pack train and a prancing pony herd, followed by the mounted troops, were next in the line of march. At the tail of the column, eye-catching travois and ordinary-looking wagons carried the wounded. The hard bottoms of the wagons had been softened by boughs covered with a layer of grass. Unfortunately, however, as they jounced across rough country, Romeyn recalled that "every jolt of the wagon seemed to open up fresh wounds." The only ambulance to accompany the campaigners to Bear Paw carried two severely wounded enlisted men from the battlefield.[48]

On October 12 the column approached the Missouri River, where two steamers were waiting to take aboard the wounded. Infantry would be carried by one of the river boats to the army hospital at Fort Buford, while some cavalry were brought by the second ship to Fort Rice and the rest went to Fort Lincoln, North Dakota. The agonizing ordeal of the wounded became more bearable aboard the smooth sailing steamers, which were furnished with bunks for those who needed them the most. For the able-bodied soldiers, the entire journey back to Fort Keogh remained a lark. The better marksmen brought in an abundance of game, enabling all in what Miles termed his "caravan" to enjoy a nightly feast.[49]

The jaunt came to a triumphant end on October 23. On a day as lovely as the one that marked the beginning of the adventure, Miles and Joseph, followed by their lieutenants, led the column along a road leading down from a plateau to the Yellowstone River. Across the river the garrison snapped to attention as their flag unfurled in the breeze. In honor of Joseph, the band played "Hail to the Chief," then struck a lighter tone with "Not for Joe, oh no, no, not for Joseph," before returning to the original tune.[50]

When Miles brought the Nez Perce to Fort Keogh, he expected them to remain there through the winter, in accordance with his instructions from Howard dated October 7. These orders also specified that the following spring, "unless you receive instructions from higher authority, you are hereby directed to have them sent to my department, where I will take charge of them, and carry out the instructions I have already received."[51]

Unfortunately, the promises made by Howard and Miles to return Chief Joseph and his people to their reservations were countermanded by General Sherman. In November Sherman instructed Miles to move his captives to either Fort Lincoln or Fort Riley, explaining that such a move would cut down on the cost of supplying the Indians with food. When Miles reluctantly carried out this order, he told Joseph, "You must not blame me. I have endeavored to keep my word, but the chief who is over me has given the order, and I must obey it or resign. That would do you no good. Some other officer would carry out the order."[52]

On November 20, only four days after the Nez Perce arrived at Fort Lincoln, Nebraska, Sherman ordered them to be transferred to Fort Leavenworth. When the 431 captives arrived at Leavenworth on November 27, the commandant of the fort made a very unwise choice for their campsite. Joseph later complained about the low Missouri River bottomland selected for his people, explaining it had "no water except river-water to drink and cook with. We had always lived in a healthy country, where the mountains were high and the water was cold and clear. Many of my people sickened and died, and we buried them in this strange land."[53]

In July 1878 the 410 Nez Perce who had survived their malaria-ridden stay at Fort Leavenworth were transferred to the Indian Territory as charges of the Bureau of Indian Affairs. Conditions did not markedly improve, even after the chief moved his people to the west of the Osage reservation and onto the most favorable land that he could find in the territory. In an 1879 article, Joseph informed his readers that even though he had made the best choice possible, the site "is not a healthy land. There are no mountains and rivers. The water is warm. It is not a good country for stock."[54]

When the public remained unmoved by Joseph's plea to "let me have a home in some country where my people will not die so fast," he appealed to General Howard for help. On June 30, 1880, Joseph dictated a letter containing the sad announcement that he had "lost 153 of my people since I was brought to Fort Leavenworth up to [the] present time." After professing his friendship for Howard and announcing his intention to become a Christian, Joseph sought satisfaction from the general: "you told me at the time of [the] surrender that I could go back to my country, Idaho. So I say as you have disappointed me, do something for me now."[55]

Howard responded from his headquarters in the Department of the Columbia, protesting to Joseph that, "You still think I promised to send you back to this Department." In an explanation that may have befuddled the chief, the general explained: "I did not *promise* but I wrote an order to General Miles to take all prisoners to My Department in the spring, which followed [your] surrender. I wrote this order because my Division General, at San Francisco, had told me to dispose of all the prisoners somewhere *within* my Department."

After blaming the officials in Washington for the plight of the Nez Perce, Howard admitted that "I was not at any time in favor of the Indians, who had been at war returning to Camas Prairies [Idaho] or to that neighborhood." He explained that he took this position "because the outrages, committed at the outbreak of hostilities, were so terrible that I knew that the whites and your Indians would have new troubles, and nothing could prevent them." He added that, "In fact, many have been pointed out by name as murderers, and they would have had to stand trial in the courts." Howard informed Joseph that if the Nez Perce had succeeded in being returned to the Department of Columbia, "I should have tried to put you all at some place far removed from Mount Idaho and Lewiston." Relieved that the problem did not materialize, the general encouraged the chief to make the best of it in his new home. He urged him to persuade his people to "make a garden of the land which the government has assigned you, and [if you can get] the children to go to school, and grow up contented and happy and industrious, you Joseph, will show yourself a truly great man, and your people can never be blotted out."[56]

In contrast to the Christian general, Miles did not abandon the helpless prisoners. Instead, he persisted in advancing the cause of the Nez Perce until they were returned to their homes. Initially, he made a strong statement on behalf of the tribe in his 1877 annual report, in which he argued that until they had been forced from their ancestral homeland, they had been loyal to the United States. He reminded his readers that once they went to war, they did not wantonly take lives or destroy property. He added that since the Nez Perce had "been grossly wronged in years past, have lost most of their warriors, their homes, property and everything except a small amount of clothing; I have the honor to recommend that ample provision be made for their civilization, and to enable them to become self-sustaining."[57]

Although Miles had stated the case for fair treatment of the Nez Perce, he had little chance of changing Sherman's mind regarding their exile. Less than a week after their surrender, Sherman confided to his adjutant general that in treating the prisoners, "there should be extreme severity, else other tribes alike situated may imitate their example." In December he reiterated this position when he informed Howard that the Nez Perce "went to war, and must now submit to whatever fate is allowed them, thankful that their lives are spared."[58]

Sheridan, like Sherman, had little sympathy for Joseph's people. Miles had recommended that all of the Nez Perce in Canada, except for three warriors who had indictments issued against them in Idaho, should be allowed to return to their homes. He reasoned that "the trouble with this hitherto loyal tribe resulted from the avarice of their white neighbors, from frauds of their agent and from bad management and misunderstanding by the party having control of their affairs" (the Bureau of Indian Affairs). When this report reached Sheridan's desk, he ignored Miles's plea and ruled that "these Indians should be allowed to sleep in the bed they have made for themselves."[59]

The Nez Perce held in the Indian Territory did not suffer in silence. Their chief went to Washington to plead his case before a congressional committee and Department of Interior officials. Many who spoke with him argued to help his people, but the lot of the Indians remained unchanged. The promise that Miles made at Bear Paw continued to prey on Joseph's mind. In his article he wondered "how the Government sends out a man to fight us, as it did General Miles, and then breaks his word. Such a Government has something wrong with it."[60]

Miles continued his fight to rectify what both he and Joseph considered to be an act of injustice. On January 19, 1881, the colonel appealed by letter to President Hayes, with a copy furnished to Secretary of the Interior Carl Schurz. When Miles reviewed the events of the Nez Perce War, he pointed out that "for the first time in Indian warfare the skill and bravery of the Indians was equaled by their humanity." He then asked the president to consider the grim fact that 180 Nez Perce had died since the surrender.

Although births had offset some of the deaths, only 358 of Joseph's people were alive by the end of 1880.

Miles tried to sway the president's mind by refuting the arguments of those who believed that the Nez Perce should remain in exile. Although some of the warriors would face indictments issued in Idaho, Miles believed that many of those accused of crimes had already died, and the rest were willing to stand trial. Almost as an afterthought, he mentioned that Hayes might feel that some of the braves charged with breaking the law had already suffered so much in captivity that they warranted a presidential pardon.

Miles also addressed the objection to allowing Joseph's people back to Idaho because other tribes might be tempted to follow their example upon seeing the Nez Perce return unpunished to their homes. The colonel discounted this possibility, explaining that if they were returned to their reservation it would be a sign to other tribes that they could expect justice from Washington. He explained that the Indians would realize that "the Government, though all powerful, does not design to punish a whole village for the acts of a few individuals." Miles mentioned, as an added inducement, that the Nez Perce would pay the expenses incurred in returning them to their homeland.[61]

After Schurz studied Miles's letter, he returned it to Hayes with his comments. Unlike the War Department, which had seemed bent on punishing the Indians by keeping them in exile, Shurz claimed that in the past the Interior Department had recommended that they remain in the Indian Territory for their own good. Besides the legal difficulties the Nez Perce faced in Idaho, Schurz informed the president, "it was reported on good authority that if they were returned private vengeance would be likely to be visited upon them without any process of law, and that therefore their return would be apt to result in the destruction of a large portion of that tribe, and in further grave difficulties."

A new development, however, caused Schurz to change his mind and conditionally approve a plan to allow Joseph and his people to return to their homeland. Miles had just been assigned command of the Department of the Columbia and, thus, would soon be in a position to oversee the Nez Perce in Idaho. Schurz recommended that after Miles assumed command, and could protect the Indians who had put their trust in him, they could be returned to the reservation that had been set aside for them.[62]

At last the wheels of bureaucracy began to turn slowly in favor of the Nez Perce, but it took the efforts of many besides Miles to persuade Congress to pass the necessary legislation. Finally, on July 4, 1884, a bill was signed giving the new Secretary of the Interior, Henry L. Dawes, the power to resettle the Nez Perce. On May 22, 1885, under a provision of this law, 268 survivors of the ordeals at Fort Leavenworth and the Indian Territory boarded a train that would take them back to the Pacific Northwest.[63] A foreign observer, distinguished military historian John Keegan, noted that Miles was one of the army officers who "came to feel an increasing distaste for the corruption that raged in the Indian Bureau, for the greed of cattle barons and mining kings, for the racialism of settler politicians, for the expedient readiness of the Federal government to abrogate its treaty obligations to native Americans." Keegan especially appreciated that Miles's "advocacy of the cause of Chief Joseph of the Nez Perces resulted in the survivors of the tribe being allowed to return from Canada, where they had taken refuge with Sitting Bull, and settle near their tribal homes in the Northwest."

While most newspaper accounts ignored the plight of the Nez Perce, they focused on criticisms of Howard's handling of his campaign rather than on Miles's triumph. Unfortunately for Miles's reputation, Howard's poor press had been attributed to Miles's unwillingness to share credit with a brother officer. For example, although a major historian of the Indian wars cited Miles as the only military commander who distinguished himself in the war, he added that "his honors were tarnished by his treacherous seizure of Chief Joseph in violation of a truce flag and by his selfish grab for all the glory."[64]

Miles contributed to his image as a glory-hunting Indian fighter when he sat down on October 5 to write the first announcement of his victory at Bear Paw. This dispatch began with the vainglorious pronouncement, "We have had our usual success." Besides being boastful, the message made no mention of Howard's presence when Joseph surrendered. Such statements were important to an officer's image; when they were released, newspapers eagerly printed them, without changing a word, as bulletins from the battlefield.[65]

Notwithstanding his self-serving October 5 dispatch from Bear Paw, Miles cannot be faulted for his post-campaign conduct. His congratulatory order, written on October 7, dwelt on the accomplishments of the troops and gracefully noted that "General O. O. Howard, who has so persistently waged war against these hostile Nez Perces and driven then from the slope of the Pacific to this remote country, was present to witness the completion of his arduous and thankless undertaking." A week after issuing the order, Miles privately confided to his wife that he had been "very glad" that the general had been with him when Joseph surrendered because "he has been so badly abused that I am willing to give him any help or share any credit with him."[66]

But from this promising start the relationship between the two officers soon deteriorated. The break occurred after some newspapers that printed Miles's congratulatory order omitted the paragraph mentioning Howard. When Howard complained, he added that he wished Miles's friends would stop attacking him. Miles responded that the "congratulatory order was garbled before given to the press"; and as for criticisms made by his friends, "I will say that as far as I know, they have no desire to." Unfortunately, Miles then drove the wedge between the two men even deeper when, in the letter, he vented his own resentment at some of the general's reports and statements to the press.[67]

Miles believed that Howard's quotes, such as "you gave the 'cue' which enabled me to capture the Nez Perce" and "you informed me 'when and where' I would strike the Indians," were "unfair and unjust to me." Three weeks later, although Miles still maintained that some of Howard's "representations" were "not considered in accordance with well known facts," he attempted to placate the general who gave him an opportunity to display his martial talents in the Civil War. He informed Howard that when he realized that some newspapers had not printed the complete order, he had an officer send a copy of it to the *Army and Navy Journal.* He enclosed a clipping of the order in its proper form, taken from the December 8 issue of the journal. Miles suggested to Howard that a troublemaker might have distributed a doctored version of the bulletin to the press, adding that, "If this garbling of official documents has been done by one officer to the prejudice of another, it has been done without my knowledge and outside of my command, and in my opinion is a dishonorable act."[68]

Miles's remarks about Howard's "representations" rankled the general, who replied that "I am astonished at your accusations." Much more damaging to Howard's reputation than any omission in Miles's congratulatory order, however, were newspaper comments about the general's conduct of the Nez Perce campaign. Howard may have read one such article in the October 19 *Chicago Tribune* while aboard the steamer *Benton* carrying casualties back to North Dakota. Although the general had intended to travel directly from Bismarck to Omaha, he altered his itinerary for a trip to Chicago after reading some Chicago newspapers.[69]

Criticism followed criticism in the October 19 *Tribune,* as a reporter recapitulated the trials and errors that occurred during Howard's cross-country pursuit of the Nez Perce. The paper charged that Howard "failed to catch Joseph for the simple reason that he began the pursuit with an inadequate force, a part of which was totally unprovided with the necessary equipment for the projected campaign." For example, the author pointed out that there were not enough fresh mounts to enable the cavalry to keep pace with the Indians.

The article raised the thought-provoking point that "had General Howard appreciated the situation at the beginning, and been more conversant with the Indian nature, there might have been no Nez Perce campaign at all, for Joseph and his band would have surrendered in Oregon had the terms dictated been less harsh and imperative." The proposal made by Howard that most offended the reporter was the "sinister promise" that if Joseph surrendered he would be tried by a military commission.

Howard's critic insisted that one of the sins committed by the general, sometimes called "Bible Chief" by the Indians because of his sincere religious convictions, was that "he omitted on one or two occasions to summon his troops to that extra exertion which might have enabled them, by night marches, to surprise and overcome their foe." As a result of Howard's desultory efforts, Joseph had little respect for the general and displayed his disdain at the surrender ceremonies. The chief entered Miles's camp "in surly silence paying no heed to the presence of the 'Bible Chief' and walked up deliberately to the spot where General Miles was standing. When he found himself in front of General Miles, the wily Chieftain drew himself up haughtily and said: 'I want to surrender to you.'"[70]

As a result of such stories, Howard went down the Missouri River from Fort Lincoln to Bismarck, where he spoke to a reporter from the *New York Herald* before continuing on to Chicago. This correspondent noted that the general "keenly feels the newspaper criticisms and slurs that have been heaped upon him" and that the general "did all that any man could do and had been for a month before the surrender cooperating with General Sturgis and Miles. He did everything in his power to help Sturgis to catch Joseph, and Sturgis failing he gave Miles the cue and information which wrought the result."[71]

At Chicago Howard again unburdened himself, this time to a *Chicago Times* reporter. What seemed to irk the general more than anything else was the widespread report, almost certainly incorrect, that Joseph had snubbed the "Bible Chief" at the surrender. Howard maintained that Joseph had approached him with a smile and then tried to give him his rifle. Howard also denied stories that "a cordial feeling did not exist between himself and General Miles. That was simply a lie, and was unjust to both equally." The reporter added that the general and the colonel "had bunked together on the battlefield, and they had parted as friends."

As the general spoke, he lost his composure and became emotional. With tears in his eyes, Howard began to ramble. "I have had much to aggrieve me, the government has seen fit to rob me of a large sum of money, and I have been too poor to prosecute my claims; and my countrymen have seen fit to heap nothing but abuse upon me." After denying that he had ever written about himself in a boastful manner, Howard wondered "why I should be so abused and maligned, but I suppose it will be kept up until I am dead."[72]

Rather than eliciting sympathy for Howard, the interview became the occasion for some newspapers to mock the "Bible Chief." The *Chicago Times,* which had obtained exclusive permission from Howard to question him, repaid the general by reprinting a tasteless story from the *Springfield Republican.* Titled "Oh! Oh! Howard!" the article declared that, "The trouble with O. O. Howard is that he is an ass. He turns up now in Chicago complaining, and actually boohooing over what the newspapers say about him, and protesting that his countrymen heap nothing but abuse upon him." The author of this commentary criticized the general for repeatedly bragging during the campaign that he would soon have Joseph in his hands. "If he simply had kept his mouth shut and done the best he could to capture Chief Joseph the past season nobody would have thought of pitching into him for failing in a difficult undertaking."[73]

After a reporter from the *Louisville Courier Journal* had a chance to talk with a Nez Perce warrior during the march to Fort Keogh, Howard's reputation took another beating. In halting English, the Indian told the correspondent that General Howard was "no good—no fight—big squaw. General Miles heap good—heap fight—heap shoot long time—no run-away." Interestingly, although the reporter managed to speak to a captive held by Miles, he did not print anything about the colonel himself, which indicates that Miles had not made himself available for interviews.[74]

During the height of the press coverage of the Nez Perce War, Miles found himself safely tucked away at Fort Keogh and out of range of all but the most intrepid reporters. When he finally emerged from the wilderness in late November, he stopped off in Chicago on his way to Cleveland. A *Chicago Tribune* reporter met with him in the Palmer House, and found the colonel to be "modest, and not anxious for notoriety. He is a genial gentleman, pleasant in manners, and a most interesting conversationalist. He is of fine and noble physique and looks every inch a soldier." The article mentioned that Miles "resembles General Grant somewhat, in that he is an inveterate smoker, and evidently a judge of good cigars."

During their chat Miles answered some questions about the battle, but added that, "I dislike exceedingly to say anything of myself in regard to the recent campaign against the Nez Perces. Last fall and winter's campaign against Sitting Bull and the Sioux was a great deal harder, but it was lost sight of in the heat and excitement of the Presidential campaign." As for the Battle of Bear Paw, the colonel limited himself to making a short statement on behalf of his men, who "were compelled to undergo untold exposure, who fought most manfully and bravely, who cheerfully laid down their lives in that far-off land." He wanted it recognized that "their movement under my command was an independent one, planned by myself, accomplished by them through hard marching and desperate struggles and fighting and all the successful results may be attributed to them and their prowess and fortitude throughout the battle."[75]

Miles and his men received the congratulations of General Sheridan and Secretary of War George W. McCrary, but these messages did not dwell on their accomplishments. Sheridan's motives for restraint appeared to be a desire not to offend any of the other commanders who fought in the Nez Perce War. He revealed a diplomatic touch when he told reporters that he "would like to see Generals Howard, Gibbon, Miles and Sturgis share the credit of the campaign in proportion that is due each for honest service performed." As for Sherman, he let it be known that he thought "the victory of General Miles over Joseph will do more to conciliate the Indians than a hundred treaties." The secretary of war simply had Adjutant General Townsend send his congratulations to Miles and Terry.[76]

The warmest thanks extended to Miles came from his department commander, General Terry. He admitted that at the start of Miles's race to catch the hostiles, "there was scarcely any probability that the Nez Perce would be intercepted, and nothing but good judgement, amounting almost to intuitive knowledge, coupled with the most persistent efforts, could have brought the column to the Nez Perce camp before it crossed the frontier." Miles must also have been pleased with the published remarks made by an unidentified army officer. This fellow professional, who may have reflected the view from the ranks, suggested that "Howard and Sturgis [should] have their full measure of credit"; but added that Miles "should have the lion's share of the glory for his achievements." The officer also put his finger on the secret of Miles's success when he mentioned that the colonel "and his fresh ponies were not reckoned in the race at all." Without the innovation of mounting four companies of infantry, who were thus able to keep up with the cavalry, Miles would have confronted the Nez Perce with too small a force to be effective.[77]

While most of the generals had carefully husbanded their praise of Miles, many newspapers elevated him into the first rank of Indian fighters. The *Cheyenne Daily Leader* proclaimed that he had "taken the place of the lamented Custer as an Indian fighter," while the *Chicago Times* judged Miles as second only to Crook as "the greatest Indian fighter living." The charge that Miles had sought this prominence does not stand up. Except for the October 5 victory announcement, no evidence has been presented to substantiate that he exceeded the bounds of propriety in his few statements to the press.[78]

Francis Barlow, who fought beside both Miles and Howard in the Civil War, followed their progress in the Nez Perce War by reading New York newspapers. Annoyed by the criticisms the press heaped on Howard, Barlow wrote him an encouraging letter. He tried to bolster his former corps commander's sagging spirits by telling him such attacks were part of public life. Furthermore, Barlow argued that anyone with military experience would have recognized that Howard had skillfully driven the hostiles into Miles's arms. Tactfully, Barlow praised Howard while indicating that Miles behaved correctly at the conclusion of the campaign; he wrote that he "would not detract in the least from Miles' honors, but I could see that this affair was the consummation of your plans, and I am glad to see that he recognized it in his orders."[79]

– CHAPTER 7 –

Strained Relations between Sherman and Miles, 1878–1885

Following the Nez Perce War, Miles turned his attention back to Sitting Bull, safely ensconced in Canada. When Miles prepared his 1877 annual report, he made no attempt to conceal the antagonism he felt toward the medicine man and his followers. Of all the Indians he had encountered, these were the "wildest and most hostile, led by a man who is not a hereditary chief but who holds his present prominent position through superstition and by his persistent, bitter hostility to the white race, and his determination to maintain Indian supremacy in this section." He believed that such a defiant band would attract like-minded Indians to their camp and thus pose a danger to Montana Territory.[1]

A disagreement between Miles and Sherman over the policy to be followed regarding the Sioux widened when Miles tried to take advantage of his wife's kinship with Sherman to gain preference in promotions and assignments. Sherman cautioned Miles, "You construe your office to be to manage all the Sioux Indians both to the north and south—whereas your post is only one of many." As part of the strategy being implemented within the Department of Dakota, posts along the Yellowstone, such as Fort Keogh, were constructed to force the Sioux out of the area. The displaced Indians would be pushed north to their agencies along the Missouri River, where they would be easier to supervise and cheaper to provision.

Under the current arrangement, Terry had control over the reservations while Miles's main task would be to keep the Rosebud and Powder River valleys clear of any Indians. Sherman believed that within a year the problem would be resolved because the Sioux would be hemmed into their reservations by new settlements. After complaining about the haphazard approach of Congress to the Indian problem, and the difficulties in adhering to established policies because of obstructionism from the Indian Bureau, Sherman wished that, at least, everyone in the army would pull together. He also hoped that Miles might be more content in the future, and urged him not to fret so about the errors of others, or keep yearning for a promotion.[2]

A month later, Sherman used a much sterner tone when he responded to Miles's answer to his first letter. Miles had ignored the proper channels of command by discussing official matters directly with him, rather than going through Generals Terry and Sheridan. Admonished Sherman, "Were I either of those I would resent such acts on the part of others, and will not be guilty of it myself." Besides insisting that Miles follow proper procedure on official matters in the future, Sherman declared that he could not make him a brigadier general or recommend that a new department be created for him. Finally, he turned his attention to Miles's proposals about the Indians north of the Missouri River: "to do nothing rash, but leave time to accomplish much that you now think can be done by you exclusively." Sherman specifically warned Miles that if he went after Sitting Bull's band in their northern sanctuary "without the positive orders of the government here in Washington, . . . on the theory that the Canadian authorities are not acting in good faith, you would endanger the high reputation you now possess."[3]

The very day that the governor general of Canada agreed to accept liability for damages caused in the United States by marauding Sioux living north of the boundary, Sherman sent Miles a copy of the agreement. He expressed a belief that the Canadian authorities were sincere and would do all in their power to restrain Indians who had sought refuge within their land. Not only had diplomacy virtually eliminated the reason for an Indian war in Montana, but, as Sherman explained to Miles, political maneuvering had crippled the army's ability to fight such a war. Democrats in Congress accused the army of trying to start such wars to prevent Congress from reducing the number of troops in service. These congressmen declared that even if a new war erupted, they would insist on limiting the army to twenty thousand men, which meant that five thousand troops were in danger of being cut from the service. Since the army already had its hands full suppressing troubles in Texas, New Mexico, Colorado, and Idaho, Sherman urged Miles to "keep your men well in hand and don't venture out too far—encourage settlers all along the valley, and in time we will give the Sioux north of the Missouri all the fighting they want."[4]

In August 1878, with no sign of trouble in his district, Miles made use of the unusual period of leisure to invite a small group of civilians, including three children, to accompany his family on a tour of Yellowstone Park. Ten officers and one hundred soldiers escorted Miles and his guests until their passage through the spectacular countryside of the upper Yellowstone had to be abruptly halted. Miles had been alerted that hostile Bannocks were following the same trail used by Nez Perce a year earlier. About twenty-five troops were detached to protect the civilian party as it scurried to safety at Fort Ellis, Montana. Freed of his responsibility for caring for noncombatants, Miles could now turn his attention to the belligerants.[5]

The Bannocks had left their agency at Fort Hall and the Lemhi Reservation, both in Idaho, for a variety of reasons, including their antagonism toward the agent at Fort Hall and competition with settlers over land granted to the Indians by treaty. The most pressing reason for taking up arms, however, was hunger. The government had not increased their rations even though growing numbers of settlers had depleted much of the game from their hunting grounds. Furthermore, their primary crop, the camas root, had become scarce after the Camas Prairie had been opened to settlers in violation of an 1868 treaty. In 1877, after General Crook visited their reservation, he predicted a war because "starvation is staring them in the face, and if they wait much longer, they will not be able to fight."[6]

When this war broke out in the summer of 1878, most of the fighting took place in the northwest; but scattered bands went their separate ways, and one approached Miles's district on its way to seek refuge with Sitting Bull in Canada. In his desire to subdue a hostile force, Miles faced the same problem Sturgis had in 1877: how to guard the two natural eastern exits from Yellowstone Park. Rather than risk being embarrassed, as Sturgis had been, Miles decided to divide his small force. He sent his adjutant, Lieutenant Bailey, who had bravely entered Sitting Bull's camp in the fall of 1876, to Boulder Pass with forty men. The thirty-five men left in the command would ride with Miles to Clark's Fork Pass, one hundred and fifteen miles away. When this small force neared a Crow agency, the colonel sent a scout ahead to enlist some warriors to fight with his men. The Crows were eager to join until they saw how few troops were about to face the Bannocks.

After the Crows withdrew their services, Miles continued the march undaunted, but he and his men must have been heartened as a few Crow at a time changed their minds and raced to join them.[7]

When the column reached Clark's Fork Pass, they concealed themselves in a valley just to the side of the pass. The next day, lookouts observed the Indians carefully make their way down the pass, then ride off to a campsite about five miles from the hiding spot of the pursuit force. Well after dark Miles sent two Crow warriors ahead to scout the enemy camp while the rest of his force awkwardly stumbled toward their objective in a downpour. The scouts reported that they had managed to enter the Bannock position by wrapping themselves in blankets. While pretending to tend the herd of horses, they surveyed the layout of the camp and believed that the Bannocks held such a strong position that an attacking force would be beaten back. Miles intended to nullify the advantage enjoyed by the defenders with a surprise attack.

Before sunup on September 4, the Crows and mounted infantry formed as a line of skirmishers along the outside perimeter of the campsite. The attackers carefully picked their way through the enemy pony herd without being detected, then, with rifles blazing and bugles blaring, rudely awakened the Bannocks. While the soldiers quickly overcame the camp's defenders and rounded up most of the survivors, the Crows slipped back to the enemy herd. Within minutes, the Crows and the 250 horses belonging to the Bannocks vanished, as Miles's Indian allies raced their promised booty back to their agency.[8]

The victory came at a very low price to the attack force: only Capt. Andrew S. Bennett, Fifth Infantry, and two Crows, fell in the assault. Miles's troops had captured at least thirty-four Indians, and in his memoirs he claimed that fourteen others had been killed. This count almost coincided with the one printed in the *Cheyenne Daily Ledger*, which reported that thirteen Bannocks had been killed by the soldiers. Some of the Bannocks had eluded the troops after the September 4 attack, and when they were later captured, they claimed that twenty-eight of their band had been killed on September 4.[9]

The casualty count provided by Indian survivors of the predawn raid may well be the correct one since Miles made no mention of taking precautions similar to those he ordered trying to save Indian lives in the attack on

Lame Deer's camp. Both the lack of an interpreter familiar with the Bannock tongue and fear that his small force might not be able to overcome a prepared enemy could have influenced Miles not to try to warn the Bannocks to surrender. Following the short but decisive action, Miles dispatched his prisoners to Fort Custer. After a rider fetched his guests back from Fort Ellis, the reunited party completed their planned tour of Yellowstone Park.[10]

When Miles returned from his interrupted sightseeing tour, he had the Bannocks transferred to Fort Keogh. When he questioned them about the reasons for their rebellion, the Indians invariably answered that they had been cheated and starved by their agent at Fort Hall. Despite their past mistreatment in Idaho, when the Bannocks were allowed to return to their home agency less than a year after they broke out, they enjoyed a kinder fate than that meted out to Joseph's people.[11]

The year 1878 came to a close with the troops stationed at Fort Keogh patrolling the Yellowstone area and putting the finishing touches on a six-hundred-mile telegraph line. The new year opened with an increased number of incidents blamed on the Sioux and the Nez Perce who had found refuge in Sitting Bull's camp. Indian agents from Forts Peck and Belknap along the Missouri River alerted the commissioner of Indian affairs about their fears. Although the incursions below the line had to that point been limited to hunting and horse stealing, in May the agent at Fort Belknap warned that he had "no doubt that we are on the eve of an Indian war."[12]

In response to the growing alarm of his agents, the commissioner of Indian affairs, with the approval of the secretary of the interior, requested that the army move against the marauding Indians. In a response dated June 5, 1879, Miles received orders from General Terry to remove any hostiles found north of the Missouri River. The first contingent assigned to this task left Fort Keogh on July 3, followed by the remainder of the command two days later. The pursuit force consisted of seven companies of the Second Cavalry and a like number from the Fifth Infantry, at least some of whom were still mounted on Indian ponies, plus an artillery detachment and the usual entourage of scouts and friendly Indians, including Hump.[13]

When the command reached Fort Peck on July 9, after a march of about 150 miles, ninety-eight recruits earmarked for the Fifth Infantry joined the column. John Finerty, a reporter for the *Chicago Times* who had first observed Miles in 1876, also met the campaigners at the agency. The reporter renewed his acquaintance with Miles on the steamer *Sherman* as it ferried troops to the north bank of the Missouri. The correspondent noted the signs of wear that the Sioux War had inflicted on the colonel. Although the Indian fighter appeared as fit as ever, exposure to extremes in weather had left his face creased, and flecks of gray could be found through his closely cropped hair.[14]

The two men discussed the current situation, with Finerty directing the conversation toward criticism of British supervision over the Indians who had found refuge in Canada but raided south of the boundary line. Miles suggested that if his troops gained the upper hand in battle, the beaten warriors would more than likely slip back into Canada. When asked if his men would cross over the line after them, Miles replied, "I can hardly give a specific answer at this stage of the proceedings."[15]

Miles also found fault with the ease with which the Sioux obtained weapons in Canada. When they escaped from the United States they were inadequately armed, he asserted, but "Now they have fine arms and plenty of powder and lead. They could only have procured such supplies in the British possessions." Despite the replenished arsenal of the Sioux, Finerty believed that the American troops would triumph over the Indians if they met in battle because they were "well put together and ably commanded." One of Miles's strengths as a leader was his confidence. When an Assiniboin warrior warned him that the hostiles north of the Missouri River were everywhere, like the grass, the colonel replied, "like the grass we will burn them up."[16]

As in earlier campaigns, Miles took advantage of new developments in equipment. This time he established a heliostat system, with six stations, in the field. Unfortunately, the effectiveness of this signaling device, in which mirrors reflected the sun, revealed a major flaw: the mirrors were inoperable when it rained—which it did nonstop from July 13 until the column reached the Canadian line eight days later.[17]

Only two days after starting out from Fort Peck, scouts riding ahead of the main body encountered about four hundred Sioux along Beaver Creek, south of the Milk River. In a running flight, the trail of the hostiles led toward the boundary line, beyond which lay the land called "Europe" by the troops. When Miles ordered his men to pursue the Indians this far north, he exceeded his authority. Just a week earlier, on July 13, he wrote

Mary Miles that Sherman had wired him "that the object of my movement was to defend our friendly Indians, not to move north of the Milk River and to protect the navigation of the Missouri (a river that has been free for twenty years)."[18]

When some Eastern newspapers reported that Miles's border operations had been criticized by authorities in Washington, Mary Miles rushed to her husband's defense, possibly at his prompting. She wrote to her uncle, John Sherman, still the secretary of the treasury, with a plea that he explain Miles's position to President Hayes. She mentioned that she had heard that although the president and the secretary of war had complimented her husband's military ability, they both feared that he might be too "rash." Mary denied these charges, claiming that her husband had been reluctant to participate in what she claimed he termed an "ill advised campaign." If anyone should be censured for the operation, she felt that it should be the author of the campaign rather than Miles. Tactfully, she did not specify whether she meant that Terry, Sheridan, or Sherman should shoulder the blame. Since her husband could not bring critical opinions of his superiors to the president's attention, Mary asked her uncle to do so.[19]

Others besides the president and the secretary of war wondered if Miles might be proceeding too rashly along the Canadian boundary line. On July 19 General Sherman warned Sheridan to "watch out and see that General Miles does not precipitate trouble near our northern boundary. That will come soon enough, but it is not his office to hasten the time." The commanding general explained that such a movement might result in the need to build a string of forts north of the Missouri, and the army simply did not have enough money to construct them at the moment.[20]

Three months before the current campaign had even been mounted, Sherman had raised another financial reason for not trying to force Sitting Bull's band back into the United States. He felt that the American people already had enough Indians to care for, and it was up to Canada to feed and control the Sioux who had sought refuge in their land.[21]

By August 14, after John Sherman had returned to the capital from a New England vacation, he told Mary that her husband was no longer in official disfavor. Both the president and the War Department now claimed that they were "highly pleased" with the way Miles had waged his campaign along the boundary. Their earlier negative comments were "simply a word of caution to avoid a serious engagement with a superior force." Sherman went on to say that he thought that "Miles has greatly raised himself by the admirable manner in which he has conducted this campaign."[22]

The operation had virtually ended within days of Sherman's complaint to Sheridan about Miles. On July 28, Major Walsh of the North-West Mounted Police, accompanied by four of his Mounties and two hostile Sioux, rode into the army camp. One of the warriors, a Hunkpapa named Long Dog, spoke as a representative of all the people in Sitting Bull's camp. When Miles asked Long Dog on "which side of the boundary they intended to remain," the brave pointed to Walsh and answered, "We intended to remain with him." The major added that the Sioux promised that if they were allowed to stay in Canada, they would respect the boundary line in the future. A month later, in his annual report, Miles stated that when Walsh guaranteed the Sioux pledge, he had achieved as much as could be expected from his campaign. Although the truce had been in place for only a short period, Miles felt heartened by the fact that the assurances "given have been rigidly adhered to."[23]

Once negotiations with Walsh and the Sioux had been concluded, the troops began their march back to the Missouri River. As they passed through the Fort Peck Reservation, they arrested 829 "Red River half-breeds" found living on government land. Miles had no sympathy for these descendants of French or Scottish traders who had taken Indian wives; he believed that they supplied and sheltered Sioux war parties. He attempted to put an end to such aid by dispersing those who had been taken into custody. Those of mixed blood known to have migrated from Canada were returned to their homeland, and 158 others were permitted to establish a permanent settlement in the Judith Basin. A last group, sent to Fort Buford, were soon released, causing Miles to complain that their "camp will become again the nucleus for the roaming and disaffected bands, as well as a place of refuge for the lawless."[24]

After his prisoners had been dispatched, Miles supervised the dispersal of his command. After the other units began the movement back to their home posts, only the Fifth Infantry remained to patrol the Missouri River. At this time, word reached Miles that a band of Indians had escaped from the Brule Agency and were heading toward Canada. Miles immediately ordered Lt. Col. Joseph N. Whistler to take five companies of mounted infantry and a Hotchkiss gun to guard the Missouri River from Wolf Point to Popular Creek.

Friendly Indians warned Whistler that the Sioux, led by Lame Deer's son, Fast Bull, were approaching a river crossing near Popular Creek. The colonel ordered a forced march on August 10, and his men arrived just in time to intercept the band as the Indians reached the north bank of the river. Fast Bull's entire party, numbering fifty-seven men, women, and children, surrendered without loss of life and were transported by steamer to Fort Lincoln.[25]

Miles's successful campaign, ending on the high note of the August 10 bloodless victory, muted criticism of his march to the Canadian boundary. General Terry made it clear that Miles had followed orders during this movement. The colonel understood his objective, "and conforming in all respects to the instructions which he had received, by a most happy union of enterprise and audacity, prudence and foresight, succeeded in obtaining these results without the loss of a single soldier."[26]

Sheridan likewise commended Miles, and even Sherman admitted that the colonel's campaign had "accomplished all that was designed and resulted in the withdrawal north of the boundary of all hostile Indians, and a better understanding with the Dominion authorities who have charge of the Canadian Indians."[27]

Miles's campaign helped to keep northern Montana pacified until famine forced the Sioux to abandon their sanctuary in Canada. Once the hunting grounds in the Dominion were cleared of game, bands of hungry Indians began to cross the line into the United States, where they voluntarily surrendered. The exile of the Sioux formally ended on July 19, 1881, when Sitting Bull led 185 Indians into Fort Buford, where he indicated that now the last of his people had returned to government control.[28]

Although Sherman grudgingly praised Miles in 1878, ill feelings between the two officers must have lingered from a dispute a year earlier. In June of 1878, the commanding general provoked a traumatic blowup within his own family, which left him less tolerant at a time when Miles tried his patience. Sherman's son Tom had startled him with the news that he intended to study to become a Catholic priest. In a frank letter to Sheridan, Sherman complained that Tom's decision had nullified all that he had done, after Tom declined to go to West Point, to insure that his son might prosper as a lawyer. He had invested in a blue-chip education, sending Tom, who would turn twenty-two in the fall of 1878, through Georgetown, Yale, and the University of Saint Louis Law School.[29]

Sherman unsuccessfully tried to persuade John Cardinal McCloskey of New York City to intercede before Tom sailed to England to begin his novitiate. Then, at a meeting arranged by Tom with his father in Washington, the general attempted to sway his son with the plea that he had counted on his financial assistance during his retirement years. None of the general's tactics succeeded, and with his son already at sea, he confided to Sheridan that his failure to change Tom's mind "has distressed me more than I can venture to write." Frustrated by this defeat, Sherman undiplomatically told Sheridan, a Catholic, that he thought of his son "as a deserter and feel bitterly against the Catholic Church which has insidiously decoyed away my son for their uses." Sadly, as a result of arguments over their son's decision to become a priest, Sherman's wife, Ellen, a Catholic, decided to live apart from her husband.[30]

Eventually, Sherman's negative attitude toward the Catholic Church must have been communicated to Miles, who had already been exposed to Barlow's disdain for the Irish Brigade at Antietam, a unit composed primarily of Catholics. Thus, the seeds of Miles's anti-Catholicism, which would bloom after he left the army, might be traced back to the influence of Barlow and Sherman.

The emotional storm that had battered the commanding general left him in no mood to entertain impositions by his subordinates, including Miles. He indicated this in a candid note to Sheridan, in which he resolved "to fulfill my office to the best advantage, but my heart is sad and weary." Unfortunately, during this depressed period in Sherman's life, Miles blundered into a confrontation with the commanding general similar to his run-in with Meade ten years earlier. The trouble began when Miles proposed that he be given command of a new department by joining Montana and Dakota into the Department of the Northwest. Sherman informed Sheridan that he opposed this suggestion on the principle that only brigadier generals should command departments because if a colonel were put in charge of a department "there will be no peace and harmony." When Sheridan replied, he obviously saw the matter from another viewpoint.[31]

Sheridan reminded Sherman that two departments were already commanded by colonels. He agreed, however, that it would be unwise to establish a new department for Miles because it "would be difficult geographically, would lead to a large additional expense, and probably a conflict as to rank, which should be avoided." While denying Miles a more important command, Sheridan took this as an opportunity to "freely acknowledge the valuable services of Colonel Miles and his great energy and force of character, and a good way to acknowledge this would be to give him a promotion when his time comes." Sheridan added that if a department suddenly became available and Miles received it, "there is no one who would be more gratified than myself."[32]

After Sherman vetoed Miles's suggestion, he enclosed a copy of Sheridan's note in a letter to Miles, to contradict Miles's claim that Sheridan had favored such a reorganization. Sherman also discounted the colonel's belief that the president and secretary of war would support his plan; they would have nothing to do with it "if they know the storm it would raise about their ears." Furthermore, Col. Jefferson C. Davis had earned the right to be appointed to the next vacant department.

After having dashed Miles's hopes for a higher command, Sherman extended, possibly as a peace offering, the news that Miles would receive a temporary appointment in Washington. He had been assigned to a board that would decide the merits of new equipment proposed for adoption by the army. Mary Sherman Miles had already been informed of her husband's transfer so that she could make arrangements to leave Cleveland for the capital.[33]

During Miles's interlude in Washington, an unfortunate misunderstanding occurred that provoked Sherman to lash out against the colonel with words that have stained his reputation to this day. The suggestion that Miles be made a department commander had not been shelved despite Sherman's disapproval of the idea. For example, in September 1878, delegates of the Montana Territorial Convention recommended that Miles receive the position because of their "confidence in his ability." This measure came before the cabinet in 1879, where it received a favorable reception until Sherman convinced them to abandon the plan.[34]

Mary Miles attempted to have the veto overridden by seeking the assistance of John Sherman. She attributed the commanding general's rebuff of her husband to "his peculiar sensitiveness about doing anything for a relation." She believed that if Miles "were a stranger he would do this in a moment and listen to the petitions of the people, but he seems to regard this as a favor to be refused because he happens to be connected with his family." Miles had been so hurt that he refused to discuss the matter any further, "and he does not know that I am appealing to you," Mary Miles wrote. She hoped that her uncle would be able either to change his brother's mind or to persuade the president to create a department for Miles. After reading the note, John Sherman jotted on the back, "Mr. President: Please read this letter which explains itself."[35]

Hayes responded by discussing the reorganization plan with General Sherman for a second time, on March 8, 1879. The next day, the commanding general sat down and wrote to Sheridan about the interview and its heated aftermath. Unaware that his niece's note had prompted the president to reconsider the matter, Sherman confided that "I have no doubt that Miles complained to the President and represented that we were oppressing him."

Although Hayes may have favored the creation of a new department at the start of the meeting, he was convinced to abandon the idea by reading arguments against it from Sheridan's letter of November 9, 1878. Somehow, the general also convinced the president that the assignment of Col. Thomas H. Ruger to Montana did not put Miles at a disadvantage, even if three colonels now outranked him in the Department of the Dakota.

After Sherman won over the president to his position, he met with Miles, whom he considered responsible for the session. In his letter to Sheridan, he wrote that he told Miles "plainly that he is ungrateful for past favors and opportunities and that I know no way to satisfy his ambitions but to surrender to him absolute power over the whole Army, with President and Congress thrown in."[36]

Sherman, who claimed to have done so much for Miles, would actually do more harm with his intemperate outburst than could be offset by any earlier favoritism. There are only a handful of instances where the commanding general may have had a major influence on Miles's career once marriage drew him into the Sherman family circle. He probably had a hand in appointing Miles to the Fifth Infantry, then ordered him to lead his regiment in both the Indian Territory campaign and the Sioux War. Although these decisions brought Miles into the limelight, Sherman had been more than repaid by a performance that had enhanced the army's reputation. In return, Sherman's impulsive letter, which Miles probably never knew existed, has negatively influenced most Indian War historians when they characterized the colonel.

A flurry of letters between Miles and Sherman did nothing to reduce the strained feelings between the two men. At Sherman's suggestions, Miles initiated the correspondence by presenting his side of the argument. Basically, Miles still resented both being denied a department and the need to contend with yet another senior colonel. He felt that he deserved better because of his successful encounters with the Indians. Sherman countered by pointing out that the War Department had decided against the reorganization, and added that he had tried to reward Miles by offering to put him on recruiting duty in 1878. Although Miles did not belittle the gesture, even the *New York Times* saw the folly of sending the colonel of the Fifth Infantry on such an assignment. The newspaper commented that Miles's "retirement from active service might possibly be acceptable to Sitting Bull and his warriors, but most assuredly not to the people generally."[37]

Miles correctly refused to believe Sherman's excuse that Secretary of War George W. McCrary and the War Department should be held responsible for vetoing the proposed Department of the Northwest. Since the president and his cabinet had originally approved the measure, "I cannot but regard your unfavorable decision and action the severest injury that has been done me by any official or friend." Sherman responded by claiming to remain Miles's friend, but he warned him not to make a "fatal mistake," presumably by going too far in stating his grievances. Miles brought an end to this series of letters by backing down. He asserted that the people of Montana, not he, had suggested the idea of a new department to the president. He then declared that he had "never said one word to the President on this subject or he to me." Miles then conceded that he had "no rights or claims beyond those of a soldier, who has endeavored to do his whole duty." He added that he hoped to leave Washington that very night, March 11, 1879, and, as had Sherman, included an expression of friendship in his letter.[38]

Although both men had paid lip service to their friendship, Sherman continued to rail against Miles and would actively seek to do him a disservice when he was considered for promotion in 1880. After Miles yielded in the face of Sherman's displeasure, he stopped over in a Cleveland hospital for an operation to correct a service-related medical problem. When the colonel returned to Montana in time for the 1879 summer campaign, Sherman apparently had not yet forgiven him for the recent commotion that had been raised in Washington.[39]

In a letter to Sheridan, Sherman accused Miles of being "too apt to mistake the dictates of his personal ambition for wisdom—and, I am sorry to say that his is not just and fair to his commands and superiors. He will absorb all power to himself and ignore his immediate commanders if not supervised and checked." He had spoken openly about Miles to prevent Sheridan from thinking that he had encouraged the strivings of his niece's husband. This would be an unlikely belief for Sheridan to entertain in the light of their recent correspondence on the creation of a new department. Actually, the commanding general still seemed nettled by the flare-up in March, especially when he protested that he had done Miles "a hundred of favors, but because I withheld one he forgets all else."[40]

It is worth recalling that during the same year that Sherman had so many negative things to say about Miles, Grant had remarked that if he were asked to "name the five best officers in our army, now living, I should name Sherman and Sheridan, ranking them alike, Schofield, Miles, Mackenzie. The two younger men have not yet had a chance to show all that's in them and may belong higher than I put them."[41]

Miles still hoped for the star of a brigadier general, and those who had fought with him during the Civil War supported him in this quest. Theodore Lyman, a Harvard graduate who had served on General Meade's staff, wrote that Miles "is a born soldier—one who has the military instinct. He has the very uncommon power of thinking—and thinking to a purpose—in the midst of extreme excitement and peril." Lyman, a naturalist who served as the Massachusetts commissioner of inland fisheries when he wrote this letter in 1878, added that Miles "has courage enough for himself and his men, besides."[42]

Besides such testimonials, Miles enjoyed the support of the secretary of the treasury, John Sherman. After his highly placed ally presented Miles's case to the president, he passed along to the anxious colonel the encouraging news that Hayes intended to act on the matter before he left office.

Furthermore, he saw no complications because "there is not a member of the Cabinet but what appreciates your services and believes you deserving of promotion, and would be glad to aid you to get it."[43]

Miles was so determined to become a general that when the chief signal officer of the army died, he sought that position as a way up the ladder, rather than wait for a vacancy in the regular line. Although Sheridan agreed to recommend Miles for the position, John Sherman had his doubts about the wisdom of such a move. He argued that the Signal Office "depends entirely upon legislation and may be changed and, in case of a Democratic Administration, probably would be changed and you might thus be legislated out of office, and lose your present rank."[44]

Despite the treasury secretary's reservations about such a move, Miles swayed him to lobby for the position. On September 27 Sherman informed Miles that although no appointments would be made until Hayes returned from the West Coast, he had already written the president "rather a strong private letter" pushing Miles for the Signal Office, where he would be in charge of army communications.[45]

On November 19 the *New York Times* prematurely reported that Miles had been appointed as the chief signal officer. For the benefit of its readers the newspaper reminded them of his past services, praising Miles for his "skill and bravery" in both the Civil War and his Indian campaigns. Although six infantry colonels outranked Miles, only William B. Hazen, fifth on the list, had also actively sought the position. The article revealed that although Miles "would prefer active service to the duties of the Signal Office," he sought the assignment for the promotion that went with it.[46]

Hazen also apparently sought the position in order to earn the star that went with it, since there is little in his background to suggest an interest in communications. After graduating from West Point in 1855, he fought on the frontier, then rose to the rank of major general of volunteers with the Army of the Tennessee before accepting a commission as an infantry colonel in the postwar army. Here he risked official displeasure when, in 1872, he revealed abuses by traders at Indian posts to his boyhood friend, Ohio congressman James A. Garfield, who would be elected president in 1880. These allegations, corroborated by the testimony of others, eventually led to a House investigation, which prompted Secretary of War William W. Belknap to resign on March 2, 1876.

Fortunately for Miles, he did not have to compromise his goals to gain a star. On December 15 the president announced that Hazen would receive the appointment as chief signal officer. On the same day, however, Hayes also proposed that Miles be promoted to brigadier general. The two promotions did not please General Sherman, who objected to Sheridan that he "was not consulted and wash my hands of the whole thing." On January 14, 1881, Hayes noted in his diary that he had, "for the present lost the friendship of Gen. Sherman." Hayes believed that the break was attributable to three of the changes he had ordered in December. First was the recommendation for Grant's promotion to captain generalcy; second, Sherman had objected when the president forced Brig. Gen. Edward O. C. Ord to retire; and finally Hayes had "promoted Gens. Hazen and Miles against his [Sherman's] wish."[47]

When a reporter from the *New York Herald* interviewed Sherman on December 21, 1880, the general explained his objections to the president's actions. The proposed captain generalcy "is a rank unknown anywhere except in Spain, for even in Cuba the office has certain civil functions attached to it besides military duties. The rank of general has certainly been the highest thus far known to our country—you know there have only been three generals—General Washington, General Grant and myself." As to the forced retirement of [Brigadier General] Ord, he believed "that if any one had to be retired [Major] General [Irvin] McDowell was the one; for while General Ord has always been successful, General McDowell has not been so. General McDowell is the better office general, but General Ord is the better fighting general." After a pause, Sherman added, "and it is in the field—that's where we want our soldiers."

When Sherman discussed the case of Miles, who had certainly made his mark in the field, he confirmed his niece's accusation that he had a "peculiar sensitiveness about doing anything for a relation." He admitted that he felt "compromised by his [Ord's] retirement because General Miles, who married my niece, was appointed in his place." Sherman explained that "Miles is a very worthy officer, but I did not want every soldier to think, 'Ah, Sherman did that because he wanted to make room for the man who married his niece.'"[48]

The promotion, which Miles accepted on December 18, gave him command of the Department of Columbia. Miles believed that he had truly earned his brigadier general's star. When he recalled the promotion, however, his remarks are devoid of any sense of celebration. "I had been colonel fourteen years, eleven of which I was in command of the Fifth United States Infantry, one of the oldest and best regiments in the army. I parted with them with great regret." From 1881 to 1885, he spent a relatively quiet period in his life overseeing his department, which consisted of Alaska, Washington, Oregon, and Idaho. When faced with the only threat of an Indian war during his tenure, he managed to defuse the situation by listening to the grievances of the tribesmen. He then sent a delegation of chiefs to Washington, where they successfully argued their case.[49]

During Miles's Far Western service, his second child, a son, was born in 1882. The parents named the baby Sherman, probably for Gen. William T. Sherman, who would soon return to civilian life. In November 1883, Sherman retired from the army and Sheridan replaced him as commanding general. Following Sherman's retirement, he and Miles slowly repaired their relationship through a series of increasingly friendly letters.[50]

After spending almost five years in the relative obscurity of the Department of Columbia, Miles sought a more active command and also began to think about a promotion to major general. On June 26, 1885, he reminded Secretary of War William C. Endicott that command of the Department of the Missouri would become vacant July 10. Miles hoped that when the resulting shakeup of commands occurred, he might be assigned either to that department or to the Department of the Dakota, or remain in his present position. Endicott, a Harvard graduate who had practiced law and tried his hand in Massachusetts politics, first as a Whig and then as a Democrat, assigned Miles to the Department of the Missouri.[51]

When Miles thanked President Grover Cleveland for his transfer to the more desirable department, he also discussed the troubled conditions within his new command. Although he believed that "mismanagement and a defective system of controlling Indian affairs" had aroused the Cheyennes, he considered them a "turbulent tribe." He enclosed a copy of an article he had written titled "The Indian Problem," originally published in the March 1879 issue of the *North American Review.* Here Miles advocated that peaceful tribes should remain under the jurisdiction of the Interior Department, but that unruly ones should be managed by army officers under the supervision of the War Department. Miles also advocated the progressive step of making it possible for "civilized and educated" Indians to "have the same rights of citizenship that all other men enjoy."[52]

In July 1885, Miles accompanied General Sheridan on a peacekeeping mission to the disaffected tribes in the Indian Territory. While Miles made preparations for military intervention in case negotiations failed, Sheridan successfully settled the problems that had aroused the tribesmen. Miles then continued on to Fort Leavenworth to assume command of his new department. In December 1885 Miles became excited about a possible promotion to major general; there was an expectation that Maj. Gen. John Pope would soon retire, and in fact Pope resigned from the army on March 16, 1886. The prospects for advancement became even more promising when Miles's former corps commander, Maj. Gen. Winfield S. Hancock, died on February 9, 1886. Now two of the three major general slots were open. Furthermore, Miles had been identified as a "strong" Democrat, which could be an advantage during Cleveland's administration.[53]

Unfortunately for Miles, Cleveland followed the rule of seniority, which seemed the most politic way to fill the vacancies. Howard replaced Pope as commander of the Division of the Pacific, and Terry became commander of the Division of the Missouri. John Sherman, now serving as senator from Ohio, tried to cheer up the disappointed brigadier with the encouraging news that these appointments cleared the way for his promotion when the next vacancy occurred.[54]

– CHAPTER 8 –

The Geronimo Campaign, 1886

WHILE MILES ENJOYED A relatively tranquil tenure, first as commander of the Department of the Columbia from 1881 to July 1885, then as commander of the Department of the Missouri, Indian troubles intermittently plagued the Department of Arizona. In 1882, Brig. Gen. George Crook received command of that department for a second time. During his first tour there, Crook's Tonto Basin campaign, conducted during the winter of 1872–73, followed by his firm rule over the Apaches and Yavapais, brought peace to the area. Only after Crook left Arizona in 1875 to take command of the Department of the Platte, did relations with the Indians begin to deteriorate.

When Crook returned to Arizona in 1882, the region had been unnerved by sporadic Apache uprisings. The general once again displayed his skill in convincing the Indians to return to their reservations. In 1883, again assisted by Indian scouts recruited from the tribes he was fighting, Crook penetrated the Apache refuge in Mexico's Sierra Madre Mountains. This campaign persuaded more than three hundred Indians to return with him to San Carlos, and ultimately resulted in Geronimo and his band surrendering the following spring. For Geronimo peace was a temporary condition, and on May 17, 1885, he rode back into Mexico with forty-two braves and ninety-two women and children. After Crook, named "Gray Fox" by the Indians, again captured the Apaches in their Mexico lair, with the invaluable assistance of his Indian scouts, it appeared that the Geronimo campaign had come to a successful conclusion.

In January 1886, when Crook's efforts to capture Geronimo's band seemed to be fruitless, rumors began to reach the press that President Cleveland might order Miles to relieve him. The *New York Times* could not obtain an official statement about these reports but believed that Secretary of War Endicott and General Sherman opposed the move because it would be unfair to Crook. The newspaper believed, however, that Cleveland would heed the growing number of congressmen and others who called for Crook's removal despite the expected protests of the general's supporters.[1]

Crook's friends insisted that the story of criticism originated from Indian contractors who had seen him interfere with their schemes to defraud the government. Those who profited from trade with the Indians or the army, either on the frontier or in Washington, were commonly referred to as being part of the Indian Ring. It is evident that a loose association of businessmen, bureaucrats, and politicians saw their fortunes or careers advance during times of turmoil on the frontier, profiting at the expense of settlers. Giving voice to the feelings of the times, the *Arizona Star* complained that when Apaches went on the warpath, "the Indian Ring can be growing rich, and enjoying life in and about Washington on the bloody harvest."[2]

The *Times*' source also intimated that Miles may have maneuvered for command of the Department of Arizona, suggesting that Crook's "displacement by General Miles would not have been contemplated if he had spent more time in intriguing in Washington than in fighting Indians in the Southwest."[3] Actually, as one astute observer, General Sherman, saw it, replacing Crook would be an unenviable assignment; as soon as the former commanding general, who had retired in 1883, became aware of the rumored change of command, he advised Miles against the move.

Arizona was "a miserably poor country, and peopled with the refuse of the world. It is not susceptible of settlement like Kansas, but a few herders, miners and prospectors who wander about, utterly defenseless, who can be killed by half a dozen Apaches, as dirty as mud, and as undiscoverable as lizards."

Sherman expected the army to prevail over the Apaches, but warned Miles that success would come only after a number of generals saw their reputations tarnished. He even questioned why the army should be so employed. The weekly homicide toll in Saint Louis equaled the number of murders in the entire state of Arizona; therefore, a sheriff's posse or the people of Arizona should track down the few Apaches who had gone on a rampage. Sherman closed his letter by again advising Miles "not to go there unless positively ordered."[4]

Miles answered almost immediately with an outright statement that he had "made no effort to be assigned to the command of the Department of Arizona. I know the character of that country, the kind of natives and the difficulties to be overcome. I fully appreciate the thankless task before anyone assigned them." He made the decision official on March 23 when he informed Secretary of War Endicott that, "in view of the possible changes in military commands—if it is agreeable to the authorities I would prefer to remain in command of this Department.[5]

In March 1886 Crook negotiated a settlement with the Apaches, but unfortunately the peace was short lived. On March 30 Crook had to inform Sheridan that some of his captives, including Geronimo, had escaped. Sheridan reacted to the bad news with a suggestion that Crook abandon his reliance on Apache scouts and change his tactics. On April 1 Crook replied that because he might be "too much wedded to my own views in this matter, and as I have spent eight years of the hardest work of my life in this department, I respectfully request that I may now be relieved from its command." The following day, Sheridan took advantage of Crook's request and reassigned him to command the Department of the Platte, recently vacated by General Howard.[6]

On the same day that Crook received his new assignments, April 2, Miles received orders giving him command of the Department of the Arizona. His immediate commanding officer would be Major General Howard, recently appointed commander of the Division of the Pacific.

On April 11 eleven salutes from a six-pounder announced the arrival of Miles at Crook's field headquarters at Fort Bowie, in southern Arizona. Miles, who now weighed approximately 210 pounds, had some difficulty getting through the narrow door of the mule-drawn ambulance that had carried him to the station. The added pounds, however, had not detracted from his appearance. A reporter at the scene noted that he was "a tall straight, fine looking man." He added that the forty-six-year-old officer "had a well-modeled head, high brow, strong eye, clean-cut aquiline nose, and firm mouth. It is an imposing and soldierly figure, all around." As Miles limbered his legs to relieve cramps, Crook strode out of his office to greet him. After taking into account Crook's eleven extra years, onlookers who watched the two generals shake hands must have been struck by how two quite different-looking men each projected an aura of authority.[7]

During the 1876 Sioux campaign, when a correspondent intending to ride with the cavalry first met Crook, then forty-seven years old, he observed that the six-foot-tall general was "a spare but athletic man. . . , with fair hair, clipped close, and a blonde beard which seemed to part naturally at the point of the chin. His nose was long and aquiline, and his blue-gray eyes were bright and piercing." In the reporter's eyes, "He looked, in fact, every inch a soldier, except that he wore no uniform." Indeed, like many officers at the time, Crook enjoyed a reputation for wearing whatever struck his fancy while in the field.[8]

When asked to characterize Crook, Howard remembered him as "a sturdy, self-contained, and usually reticent chap, but he made many loyal friends." Howard, who graduated from West Point fourth in the class of 1854, two years after Crook, recalled that the upperclassman "was not very quick at learning; in fact, he graduated 38 in a class of 43, but he was persistent, and what he learned stuck to him." Although Crook may not have shone academically, Howard recognized that the farm boy from Dayton, Ohio, had acquired the practical skills that would lead to success in fighting Indians. "When Crook first went out West he made a splendid record in the Indian troubles, and gained the esteem of the whites and the hearty awe of the redskins. He was a natural frontiersman, and could follow a trail as well as any Indian." Moreover, Crook "was a mighty hunter, and a good shot."[9]

After Crook and Miles enjoyed a midday meal, they closeted themselves in Crook's office, then met again the following morning. That afternoon Miles wrote his wife that at these briefings, Crook appeared to be "very much worried and disappointed, and the troops are somewhat disheartened as they all hoped to go home."[10]

Shortly after 1:00 P.M. on the twelfth, Crook departed from Fort Bowie for Omaha, where he would take command of the Department of the Platte. Despite Sherman's reservations about his conduct of the Geronimo campaign, Crook would maintain his reputation as one of the nation's outstanding Indian fighters. For example, John Finerty, the *Chicago Times* reporter who observed both Crook and Miles in action, noted that Crook did more "in his quiet, steady way, . . . to settle the Indian difficulty than Custer and all the other dashing cavaliers of the American army put together."[11]

By the time of Crook's death on March 21, 1890, he had earned recognition for more than his battlefield exploits. Civil War veterans from Crook's home state praised his impressive record in the war that bound them together; but they looked beyond his exploits with the Union army, where he had become a major general of volunteers with a brevet major general in the regular army. They observed that in the postwar army, while Crook had been an "inveterate foe of the Indian upon the war-path, he was his staunchest friend upon the Reservation. Teaching the Indians to respect the power of the government, he counseled the government to respect the oft-violated rights of the Indian." In this memorial tribute, after the authors applauded Crook's battle honors, they suggested that he deserved even "greater honor for his justice and mercy to a despised race, whose enemies are many, and whose friends are few."[12]

Reduced to an infantry lieutenant colonel after the war, Crook successfully fought rebellious Indians in both the Pacific Northwest and Arizona. In 1873 President Ulysses S. Grant rewarded him for his victories with a double promotion, from lieutenant colonel to brigadier general, much to the chagrin of every colonel in the service. In 1882, when rumors began to circulate that Brigadier General Crook might be made a major general, a letter signed "eighty six officers of the Army" reminded President Chester A. Arthur that Crook "was advanced to his present rank from the grade of Lt. Col., to the prejudice of every Colonel of the line."[13]

The officers, who apologized for remaining nameless because of regulations, hoped that "the serious nature of our subject may lead you to pardon this breach of decorum." They then attributed Crook's promotion in 1873 to Grant's belief that "articles which were constantly appearing in different journals of the country to the credit of Genl. Crook were reliable." Without citing any specific example, they charged that "those puffs were penned by a staff officer of Genl. Crook, and that they contained statements which were wholly untrue, and which were contrary to the opinion and knowledge of every officer of the Army." Unfortunately, by overstating their claim and withholding evidence, Crook's critics weakened their chances of convincing anyone that the general had manipulated the press.

In fact, Capt. John G. Bourke, Third Cavalry, who developed into an author talented enough to have both his historical and ethnological studies published, promoted Crook's image in his writings. Although he was only sixteen years old in 1862, Bourke managed to enlist in the Fifteenth Pennsylvania Cavalry, where he served as a private for the duration of the Civil

War. He fought with such distinction at Stone River, Tennessee, that in 1887 Congress belatedly awarded him a Medal of Honor. Following demobilization, the young veteran received an appointment to West Point, from which he graduated eleventh in his class in 1869.

The combat-hardened lieutenant reported for duty in the Southwest, where he became a member of Crook's staff. Except for a six-month leave of absence in 1883, during which he honeymooned in Europe, Bourke campaigned alongside Crook until March 1886. As Crook's Geronimo campaign appeared to be coming to a successful conclusion, Bourke left Arizona for special duty at the War Department. He remained in Washington until April 1891, in order to prepare both his observations on Indian life and his Indian war experiences for publication. Recent scholarship indicates that when Bourke described his adventures on the frontier, he "omitted the bad and exaggerated the good in General Crook."[14]

Besides complaining about self-serving dispatches issued from Crook's headquarters, the authors of the letter to the president were also critical of the general's performance in the Sioux War. They railed against "the imbecility he exhibited" during this campaign, but failed to substantiate their claim.[15]

Actually, Crook enjoyed few successes in 1876, and even suffered a rare setback in a battle against an alliance of Sioux and Cheyenne warriors near Rosebud Creek, Montana, on June 17 of that year. Finerty, an eyewitness to this action, noted that Crook "was dissatisfied with the encounter because the Indians had clearly accomplished the main object of their offensive movement—the safe retreat of their village." Sherman shared Crook's displeasure with the outcome of this fight in an off-the-record comment to Sheridan. The commanding general had more on his mind than the escape of a band of hostiles. He confided to Sheridan his belief that had Crook's command of about one thousand men maintained pressure against the large number of braves led by Crazy Horse, these Indians would have been unable to join the growing camp on the Little Big Horn. Although Sherman did not believe that Crook should be censured, he reflected that if he had maintained contact with this war party, "the Custer Massacre was an impossibility."[16]

The rumors that had provoked the eighty-six officers to fire their ill-advised and ineffectual broadside proved to be false. On October 26, 1882, John Pope received the promotion made available by the retirement of Maj.

Gen. Irvin McDowell. In 1886 Terry and Howard would be the next two brigadier generals to advance. Crook's turn would come in 1888, after a disability forced Terry to retire from command of the Division of the Missouri on April 5, 1888. Miles also had his eye on this vacancy, but Senator Sherman explained to him that when President Cleveland "was approached it was manifest that he had made up his mind to promote Crook as the ranking Brigadier General."[17]

In the spring of 1886, as Crook traveled back to the Department of the Platte, which he had commanded from 1875 to 1882, Miles reviewed his new situation. He had inherited a formidable command, consisting of forty troops of cavalry and forty-six companies of infantry. After receiving reinforcements, he could deploy five thousand troops against Geronimo's band of twenty warriors, now slightly slowed by their concern for the thirteen women who rode with them. Although overwhelmingly outnumbered, the Apaches, skilled in eluding their pursuers, would demonstrate that reliance on troop strength alone would not rein them in. Natchez, the son of Cochise, the hereditary chief of the Chiricahuas, served as Geronimo's lieutenant. On April 20 Miles issued a field order outlining how he intended to comply with Sheridan's instructions for the campaign. These orders were contained in the commanding general's April 3 order which sent Miles to the Department of Arizona.

Sheridan assigned Miles the dual mission of preserving peace among the Apaches on the reservations while striving to bring about "the destruction or capture of the hostile Apaches." His only specific instructions were that Miles should establish his headquarters within hailing distance of the Southern Pacific Railway and make "active and prominent use of the regular troops" in his department. The commanding general explained that he kept his directives to a minimum because he did not wish to "embarrass" Miles with advice from War Department offices located far from the scene of the action.[18]

Miles divided Arizona and New Mexico into twenty-seven observation districts, which were linked by twenty-seven heliograph stations, similar to the six that he had experimented with in Montana in 1879. Miles intended that at the first sign of a hostile intrusion, a warning would be flashed from station to station, alerting units as far as four hundred miles away within two hours. The signal stations would coordinate a relay system allowing fresh cavalry troops to relieve commands that had joined in the chase earlier.[19]

Troop leaders were instructed to respond to the alarm with their "lightest and best riders," who were expected to be able to keep after their quarry for forty-eight hours, covering up to two hundred miles. While the cavalry would act as a pursuit force, most of the infantry were scattered throughout the department, guarding virtually every strategic location or installation in the Southwest. Although Miles departed from Crook's practice of using Apache scouts as a combat force, he intended to use them as trackers.[20]

Miles's immediate superior, Major General Howard, commander of the Division of the Pacific, applauded his former aide's opening moves. From his headquarters in San Francisco, he wrote Sherman that Miles had started the campaign "with his usual vigor. Crook has had various troubles the past year. A few Apaches have wondrously avoided his troops, and self-constituted volunteers have been paralyzed by their boldness. By playing back and forth from Mexico across the mountains they succeed. Miles' liveliness may surprise them."[21]

Before Miles had the time to establish his communications network, Geronimo's band tested the new department commander. Only one station had been set up when the Apaches rode out of Mexico into Arizona's Santa Cruz Valley on April 27. They seemed intent on replenishing their mounts but did not hesitate to kill anyone who crossed their path. Thirteen civilians, including a mother and her child, were murdered by the raiders, who had split into several small parties at the start of their raid. Incidents such as these that occurred during the outbreak might lead someone who read Miles's report to conclude that Apaches lived "Jekyll and Hyde" lives. Miles observed that "their docility and meekness while peaceable was only excelled by their ferocity and cruelty when at war."[22]

Twenty-five units pressed the intruders, clashing with them in five separate skirmishes. When Capt. Thomas C. Lebo's troop of "Buffalo soldiers" of the Tenth Cavalry cornered one party in Mexico, after a two-hundred-mile chase, 2d Lt. Powhatan H. Clarke ignored intense fire to carry a wounded black trooper to safety. Miles commented that when a "youth" rescues a "veteran," an exploit that would win the 1884 West Point graduate a Medal of Honor, "it indicated that the days of chivalry have not passed."[23]

Miles also honored two Fourth Cavalry officers for their tenacious pursuit of Geronimo's band into Mexico. Capt. Charles A. P. Hatfield, an 1872

West Point graduate, earned a major's brevet for surprising the hostiles outside of Santa Cruz in northern Mexico, and 2d Lt. Robert D. Walsh, West Point 1883, received a brevet promotion to first lieutenant for intercepting a band of Apaches in Mexico's Patagonia Mountains. Walsh was the officer who responded to an alert that Indians had been sighted by the signal detachment at Antelope Springs, which then flashed the information to Fort Bowie and Fort Huachuca.[24]

Following these skirmishes, the Apaches managed to slip away, although they had to leave livestock and supplies behind to escape. They were grand masters at this form of cat-and-mouse guerrilla warfare. Miles analyzed their success and found that they invariably chose the most difficult routes across the mountains. When their horses gave out, they simply stole new mounts in the next valley. Since no such replacements were available to the cavalry, their animals were kept fresh by leading them around the more punishing heights, while the troopers were forced to follow the trail on foot. Geronimo's band also avoided supply problems by their ability to live off the land or steal whatever they needed, while the troops were invariably beset by shortages, particularly grain for the horses, since the cavalry often operated in areas that were devoid of suitable grass for forage.[25]

After the engagement outside of Santa Cruz on May 15, at least one group of Indians turned north, toward Arizona, perhaps hoping to receive assistance from their tribesmen at the San Carlos Agency. But Miles had already taken steps to quarantine the reservations when, on May 3, he had met with Lt. Col. James F. Wade, Tenth Cavalry, the commander at Fort Apache, and Capt. Francis E. Pierce, Eighth Infantry, who commanded the San Carlos Agency. In this conference, held at Fort Thomas, Arizona, Miles instructed both officers to increase their control over the Chiricahua and Warm Springs Apaches.[26]

Following their fight with Walsh on June 6, the frustrated and exhausted renegades withdrew deep into Mexico. On June 11 the *Arizona Daily Star* editorialized that Miles had "done everything in his power to protect the settlers and punish the red fiends, and no doubt many lives have been saved through the rapid movement of his troops." Looking to the future, the newspaper suggested that "five more weeks of campaign like unto the past five will make the hostiles tired; add to this General Miles' acquired knowledge of the topography of the country which he was a total stranger to six weeks ago, improves the complexion of the campaign very much."[27]

Shortly after Miles settled into his new command, he began to organize a small expeditionary force that would carry the search for Geronimo into Mexico. He handpicked Capt. Henry W. Lawton, Fourth Cavalry, whom he described as "a giant in stature [Lawton was six feet four inches tall], and a man of great energy and endurance" to command what he claimed to be "one hundred of the strongest and best soldiers that could be found, all excellent riflemen." In fact, Lawton, destined to rise to major general of volunteers during the Spanish American War before being killed in the Philippines in 1899, formed his flying column from just two companies. Thus, the selection of enlisted personnel was not as selective as Miles wished his readers to believe.[28]

Lawton, aided by six young lieutenants and guided by twenty Indian scouts, led a force of thirty-five men from Troop B, his own command, and twenty men from Company D of the Eighth Infantry, as well as packers to handle two pack trains. Miles personally selected Leonard Wood, a twenty-five-year-old Harvard-trained surgeon, to accompany Lawton into Mexico. Wood subsequently took advantage of opportunities created by the Spanish American War to leave the medical department as a captain and to take command of the First U.S. Volunteer Cavalry, better known as the Rough Riders. Wood's first step up the ladder toward eventual military and political prominence took place after Miles assigned him to Lawton's force. After serving as a physician to both Presidents Grover Cleveland and William McKinley, Wood was promoted to major general in 1903; in 1910 he was named army chief-of-staff.[29]

On May 5 Lawton's force proudly marched out of Fort Huachuca as the band played "The Girl I Left Behind Me." Initially, his men stalked the Apaches along the boundary, with the intention of driving any Indians flushed from cover toward troops positioned to block their getaway. One of Lawton's patrols, commanded by Lieutenant Walsh, took advantage of a sighting by a signal detachment to surprise a party of Apaches at twilight on June 6. Following this engagement, Geronimo's entire band withdrew into Mexico's Sierra Madre Mountains.[30]

The Mexican government, with its hands full fighting a war with the Yaqui Indians, allowed American troops to cross the border in pursuit of the Apaches. To support an expeditionary force, a supply camp had been established about 150 miles south of Arizona, at Oposura. On June 29 Lawton's campaigners gratefully entered this camp to refit, having already traveled 1,395 miles in pursuit of their elusive enemy. On July 6 they renewed the hunt, leaving behind some Indian scouts whose term of service had come to an end.

All the troops shared hardships as they campaigned in terrain described by Lawton as "indescribably rough and the weather swelteringly hot, with heavy rains every day or night." In such an inhospitable region, he noted, "The endurance of the men was tried to the utmost limit. Disabilities resulting from fatigue reduced the infantry to 14 men, and they were worn out and without shoes." When Wood, who had remained with the command from the start, foresaw the end of their nearly-two-thousand-mile journey, he noted in his diary that we were "all feeling cheerful as we realized that one of the longest, if not the longest march after hostiles in the history of our army was at an end, or nearly so."[31]

While Lawton's men combed through Mexico's rugged Sierra Madres, Miles turned his attention to another front. Early in June, 1st Lt. James Parker, West Point 1876, who would eventually earn a brigadier general's star, rode to the top of El Moro Mountain with Miles to introduce him to the terrain around Fort Huachuca. Parker recalled suggesting to Miles, as they surveyed the countryside, that a false alarm be sounded, announcing a hostile raid. During such outbreaks, the reservation Apaches customarily assembled in an enclosed area of Fort Apache, where they could be accounted for, thus avoiding suspicion that they had assisted the renegades. Parker proposed that at this time the penned-in Indians could easily "be surrounded by the troops, disarmed, taken to the railroad and shipped east as prisoners of war." Miles replied, "Why that would be treachery, I could never do that."[32]

Although the method suggested by Parker may have originally disturbed Miles, after a month of pondering, he came to accept the idea of removing about five hundred Apaches from Fort Apache. On July 5 he confided to his wife that these Indians were "to some extent in sympathy with the hostiles and liable to go out at any time. It requires a large force to keep them in check and I am anxious to move them to some other part of the country." Miles may have been influenced in his change of heart by his increased familiarity with the Apache way of war during Geronimo's raid.[33]

On June 18 he reported to Howard that the Apaches had "been constantly pursued and harassed, and whipped out of their mountain strongholds, and finally driven back into Old Mexico. Miles then complained that they were "not carrying on war on any principle of civilized warfare." In contrast to the empathy that he had developed for every other tribe that he fought, Miles held his current foe in contempt. In the past, he had battled Indians who had been provoked to take to the warpath, whereas he viewed Geronimo's raiders as "simply a band of outlaws, murderers and assassins, and are worse than wild beasts for they kill for the love of killing. That, surely, is not a trait common to wild beasts in general; even the feline species may torture their prey; yet they kill for food."[34]

To substantiate this harsh judgment, Miles argued that the "inhuman Apaches lie in wait for some poor unarmed Mexican or American settler, kill defenseless women and brain innocent children, and gratify their savage nature by practicing the cruellest of tortures." Such deeds branded them as "criminals," who deserved to face methods used by police to apprehend fugitives. For instance, he believed that a reward might be posted for the capture of Geronimo along with the other members of his war party. Miles also thought that dogs could be used to help track down the Apaches, citing a precedent established in the Seminole War.[35]

Rather than resort to unconventional tactics, however, Miles decided to isolate Geronimo by removing other Apaches from Arizona, while at the same time attempting to induce him to surrender. Just two days after he broached the idea of transferring Indians out of Arizona in his letter to Mary Miles, he repeated the suggestion to Howard. He believed that the 198 Warm Springs and 236 Chiricahua Apaches of Fort Apache, whom he considered to be "nominally prisoners of war," should be removed to the Indian Territory, where they would be easier to control. Miles predicted that as long as they remained among the vulnerable settlements of Arizona, they would not change their ways because their "traditions perpetuate the spirit of war."[36]

To sway opinion in Washington to his view, Miles accompanied Lucius Lamar, Jr., an agent of the Interior Department, then headed by Lamar's father, on an inspection of the reservation. He later recalled that the Indians at Fort Apache "were having their drunken orgies every night, and it was perfect pandemonium. It was dangerous to go near them as they were constantly discharging pistols and rifles." Following this tour, Miles enjoyed the support of the Secretary of the Interior, suggesting the wisdom of inviting his son to Fort Apache.[37]

With Lamar won over, Miles next turned his attention to the reservation Indians. He hoped that they could be persuaded to accept a move onto a section of the Kiowa, Comanche, and Apache Reservation in the Indian Territory. To do this, he gained Sheridan's approval to send a delegation of their leaders to the capital. Thirteen Apaches escorted by Capt. Joseph H. Dorst (West Point 1873, Fourth Cavalry) arrived in Washington on July 17, where they were contacted by Capt. John Bourke, who had recently been assigned to special duty at the War Department. The *Arizona Daily Star* angrily charged that General Crook's former aide intended "to influence the Indians against General Miles and his plans."[38]

According to the newspaper, Bourke "attempted to run the delegation himself, but this not being permitted by Captain Dorst, he worked on individual members of the party." The *Star* reported that Bourke gave most of his attention to Chato, who was notorious for leading a raid through the Southwest in 1883 that took the lives of at least eleven Americans, but who later redeemed himself by serving as a scout for Crook. Indignantly, the reporter wrote that Bourke "even went so far as to dine with Chato and present him with a certificate of merit—for what is unknown, unless it was for being the greatest murderer in the lot."[39]

Following Bourke's intrusion, Sheridan entered into the negotiations with a revision that would drastically alter Miles's plan. Miles complained to Mary Miles that Sheridan (at the request of President Cleveland) had asked about moving the Apaches to Florida rather than to the Indian Territory. Miles objected that this "would be bad faith, condemned by all of the eastern press." On August 2, when Miles responded to Sheridan's query about Florida, he argued that "the Indians would consider it an act of bad faith." After a rambling review of the proposal, he declared, "There must be some safe place where the Government can locate these wards away from the cannons and mountains of Arizona, that would be agreeable to them." Miles hoped to sway the commanding general back to the original plan by pointing out that in the Indian Territory the Apaches "would see how other Indians prosper, and I believe the effect would be good."[40]

While officials in Washington pondered the issue, the Apache delegation left Washington empty-handed on August 3. Since no promises had been made, all they had to show for the trip were the mementos given to Chato. The Indians were uncertain about the outcome of their visit, and on August 14 Captain Dorst wired the War Department from Fort Leavenworth about their "uneasiness." He reported, however, that Chato had received the impression in Washington that his people would be allowed to remain at Fort Apache. Although he had nothing in writing to substantiate his belief, "the present of a medal from Secretary Interior, the possession of an unimportant certificate from Captain Bourke and Secretary of War, and the fact that he had not been told he would have to move seemed to satisfy him." After Dorst's party reached Leavenworth, where they were detained, the Indians told the captain that they expected their families to meet them at the fort. In a quandary, Dorst requested instructions from the adjutant general as to what to tell the delegation about their future. Miles immediately summoned Dorst to Arizona for a conference, where it was decided to give the Apaches a choice. They could elect to "be considered friendly treaty Indians," which meant that they would have to "conform to the wishes and directions of the government and consent to the peaceable removal of all of their people from Arizona." Alternatively, they would "be considered as individuals, responsible for the crimes they had committed."[41]

Miles informed the War Department of his instructions to Dorst on August 20, then added that Lieutenant Colonel Wade had completed all of the preparations necessary for moving the Indians from Fort Apache. Five days later, the Secretary of the Interior added his endorsement to the recommendation already approved by Cleveland, Endicott, and Sheridan that the reservation Indians be moved to Fort Marion, Florida. On the twenty-eighth Howard's headquarters informed Miles that President Cleveland did "not think the Apache Indians should be treated otherwise than as prisoners of war, as it is quite certain they will not agree with the Government as to their location, which I am satisfied should be Fort Marion."[42]

Miles attributed the unfavorable decision to his "enemies at Washington," who had "done so much to embarrass and oppose my efforts that they are quite likely to spoil the whole thing." Although he admitted that if the Indians got wind of Sheridan's order, his department would be thrown into chaos by an uprising of angry Indians on the reservation, Miles also had the Apaches' best interests in mind. In his opinion, the move to Florida would be "very bad policy and unjust, particularly to the women and children. One of Geronimo's children had already died since he was sent there. This campaign is like many others, the annoyances in the rear are greater than those in the front."[43]

Miles left the actual direction of removing the Chiricahua and Warm Springs Apache Indians out of Arizona to Civil War veteran Lt. Col. James F. Wade, the son of Senator Benjamin F. Wade of Ohio. To help ensure the success of the operation, four additional troops of cavalry were ordered to Fort Apache to reinforce the three already there, supported by two infantry companies. The assembled troops expected fanatical resistance when they attempted to take control of the reservation, but Miles had unwittingly defused an explosive situation by arranging for the chiefs, who would have inspired the warriors to battle, to visit Washington.

On August 29 Wade had the assembled warriors disarmed at the conclusion of a Sunday muster. When Lieutenant Parker originally suggested this plan, Miles had replied, "Why that would be treachery"; but in his recollections he justified the betrayal of the Apaches to prevent an Indian war, "for there was a very large hostile element in the camp. It would have resulted in the sacrifice of many innocent lives, as well as serious censure upon the management of the affair."[44]

The Apaches began their march into captivity on September 7, and on the twentieth, 103 children and 278 adults, some of them former scouts, arrived at Fort Marion. On August 31, the *Arizona Daily Star* applauded the round-up of the Apaches and praised Wade, for "it was a work requiring great courage and greater tact, as the slightest mistake would have stampeded the entire tribe to the mountains, and cost the lives of many settlers."[45]

Although Miles had favored removing the San Carlos Indians from Arizona, he could not prevent them from being sent to what he termed "sickly Florida." Later Miles's enemies would attempt to discredit him because he had persisted in trying to persuade his superiors to choose a more suitable reservation for the Indians. For instance, on August 30, the acting secretary of war, Brig. Gen. Richard C. Drum, advised Cleveland that Miles suggested sending them to Fort Union, New Mexico. Miles had recommended Fort

Union because the Apache children could be sent to schools, while the adults "would acquire habits of industry, until such time as the government should provide them permanent residence and means of self support. By this means they will be completely under control. They would be satisfied and the public would be rid of their presence without loss of life." The *Star* explained to its readers that the expected move to Fort Union would leave Geronimo's party "without any city of refuge and cuts off his supply of recruits and squaws, leaving him out in the wilds of Mexico, wounded, worn out and discouraged making it a question of a very short time, when he will have to surrender."[46]

Less than a month after Lawton's expeditionary force crossed into Mexico, Miles began to think about trying to induce Geronimo's band to surrender. On July 1 he had questioned a warrior who had returned to the reservation following the fight with Hatfield outside of Santa Cruz, in Sonora. The Indian convinced the general that the hostiles were exhausted from the constant pursuit, leading Miles to believe that they would listen to his terms. Two of Geronimo's fellow Chiricahuas, Martine and Kayitah, agreed to seek out the Apaches in Mexico.[47]

On July 13, 1886, 1st Lt. Charles B. Gatewood, Sixth Cavalry, received orders from Miles to join the two Indians, with instructions to tell Geronimo, "Surrender, and you will be sent with your families to Florida, there to await the decision of the President as to your final disposition." Gatewood had been selected for this mission because he had gotten to know the Apache leader at the White Mountain Reservation.[48]

Lieutenant Gatewood had earned the respect of the tribesmen during his long service in the Southwest, which began almost immediately after his graduation from West Point in 1877. His assignments as commander of scouts and acting agent for the White Mountain Apaches gave the Indians a chance to judge his character. Gatewood's son, West Point 1906, who followed in his father's footsteps as an army officer, pointed out that the lieutenant's "acquaintance with individuals of the different tribes was extensive; and his reputation among them became widespread from the Mescaleros of New Mexico to the Yumas of the Colorado River."[49]

After some difficulties, Gatewood's small party, which included an interpreter, a packer, and a courier, joined Lawton's command in Mexico. The linkup proved to be especially helpful because, as Gatewood explained, Lawton's "system of gathering information was almost perfect, and valuable time was thus saved." Reports from these agents that the hostiles were near Fronteras, in northern Sonora, drew troops toward the town. With two interpreters and an escort of six troopers from the Fourth Cavalry added to his party, Gatewood moved out, with the rest of Lawton's command trailing behind.[50]

On August 24 Martine and Kayitah found, and were invited into, Geronimo's camp, situated in a bend of the Bavispe River. While Kayitah remained in the camp, probably as a hostage, Martine returned to Gatewood. In his annual report, Miles explained that Martine brought back word that they "wanted to 'talk peace' and that if I would meet them for that purpose there would be no harm done me." Miles reported that the following morning the lieutenant "rode boldly into their presence, at the risk of his life, and repeated the demand for their surrender."[51]

At the very start of the parley, Gatewood advised Geronimo's band that if they surrendered they would "be sent with your families to Florida, there to await the decision of the President as to your final disposition. Accept these terms or fight it out to the bitter end." Twenty-one warriors, including Natchez and Geronimo, discussed Miles's proposal for the rest of the day. Gatewood had time the next day to jot down a brief note to his wife, before a courier left for Fort Huachuca. He told her that on the twenty-fifth the Apaches argued against going to Florida, but that they were "tired of fighting & want to be united with their families once more. They were all cheerful, feeling sure that since Gen. M. sent me all the way from [Fort] Stanton [New Mexico] to meet them, he must have a good heart."[52]

After nightfall forced the two sides to recess their talks, Gatewood found that Lawton had established a camp in the area. The following morning, Gatewood greeted Geronimo and a few accompanying braves as they approached this site. The Apaches left their weapons with their tethered ponies before entering the camp with the lieutenant. Gatewood informed his wife that at this time Geronimo agreed to "go with me anywhere as I had never harmed him, but always helped him along when he was at [Fort] Apache. He wanted to meet Capt. L., so they had a hugging match before the whole command."[53]

On October 15, in a report that he prepared for Miles, Gatewood gave a fuller version of the agreement reached among the Apaches on the twenty-fifth. Geronimo told Gatewood that they had agreed that "if you will give your word that we can meet General Miles, with safety, without arrest or attack by Americans, we will go to meet him and accept his terms. We will throw ourselves on his mercy—something we have never done before." When Gatewood later wrote an article about this episode, he added that at a critical moment in the negotiations on the twenty-fifth, he mentioned that the San Carlos Indians would soon be removed to Florida. The lieutenant pointed out to them that this meant that if they returned to Arizona, "It would mean living among their enemies, the other Apaches. This piece of news was an unexpected blow."[54]

The Apaches must have realized the bleak fate that faced them if they did not come to terms. Now that their traditional refuge in the mountains of Mexico had been penetrated, Gatewood reported, "they knew it was only a question of time as to their annihilation. The prospect of surrender under the circumstances was welcome. Pursued so that they had no rest they looked with favor upon a chance to lay down their arms with a hope of having their lives spared."[55]

Leonard Wood confirmed the sense of defeat the Apaches felt. Geronimo had told him, "We have not slept for six months and are worn out." He also "stated that he and his party were tired out and anxious to join their relatives in Florida. All they seemed to dread especially was falling into the hands of the civil authorities in Arizona."[56]

On August 28 the Apaches, who retained their weapons, began the ride north toward Skeleton Canyon for a proposed rendezvous with Miles. Gatewood, accompanied by an interpreter, remained with Geronimo at the latter's request, while Lawton's troops served as a buffer, ready to fend off any threat to the Indians. Two days later, as the tense riders approached the border, Lawton went ahead to use the heliograph at San Bernardino Ranch to contact Miles. The day before the general received Lawton's message he had written Mary Miles that he would not negotiate "unless I am pretty sure they are sure to surrender. Geronimo and Natchez pretend they want to surrender, but they are very unreliable."[57]

Because Miles had little faith in the intentions of his enemy, he proposed two options in the third, and last, of a series of heliograph messages to Lawton on August 31: "If the Indians give you any guarantee or hostage that they will surrender to me I will go down." However, if the Apaches should become defiant, Miles instructed, "you can use any other means you think advisable, you will be justified in using any measures." But Miles made it clear that Lawton should take action only as a last resort, concluding, "If they surrender they will not be killed but rightly treated. I am ready to start but not unless I am sure that it will do good."[58]

Miles's determination to preserve the lives of the Indians if they came to terms ran counter to the prevailing attitude of his superiors in Washington. A week earlier, President Cleveland had advised Miles that "nothing will be done with Geronimo which will prevent our treating him as a prisoner of war, if we cannot hang him, which I would much prefer." In September, when asked about Geronimo, General Sheridan replied to a reporter, "There is no doubt what should be done with him. He is entitled to no mercy."[59]

For the moment, Geronimo forestalled bloodshed when he consented to send one of his warriors, a cousin named Perico, to Fort Bowie as a hostage. On September 2 Miles responded to this gesture by setting out with a troop of cavalrymen on a sixty-five-mile ride from the fort to Skeleton Canyon. Shortly after the general's column rode into Lawton's camp late in the afternoon of the third, Geronimo made his appearance.[60]

Miles was immediately struck by both Geronimo's commanding eyes and manner. He compared the Apache's sharp, clear, black eyes with those "of General Sherman when he was at the prime of life and just at the close of the great war." At fifty-seven, the Chiricahua warrior had lost none of the vigor that had made him such a formidable adversary. When Geronimo spoke, Miles received the impression that each of his gestures "indicated power, energy and determination."[61]

After Geronimo explained his reasons for taking to the warpath, he put his faith in the advice that Gatewood had given him in Mexico: "Trust General Miles and surrender to him." Within hours of his return to Fort Bowie, while impressions of what had transpired at Skeleton Canyon were still fresh in his mind, Miles notified Howard of the terms accepted by the Apache leader. The hostiles were allowed to surrender as prisoners of war, assured only "that it was not the way of officers of the Army to kill their enemies who laid down their arms." When Miles added that his captives "expect banishment" from Arizona, he tried yet one more time to save the

San Carlos Indians from exile in Florida. This time Miles tried to interest Howard in relocating the Apaches at Forts Riley and Leavenworth in Kansas. He argued that these two installations "would be suitable places for confinement, and the worst of the men and boys could be placed within Fort Leavenworth Military Prison."[62]

After Geronimo reached an agreement with Miles on the third, he grinned and in his native tongue said to Gatewood, "Good, you told the truth." The following day, the Apache leader convinced the actual chief of the tribe, Natchez, to come in with the rest of the war party. Miles described the son of Cochise as a "slender, lithe fellow, six feet two, straight as an arrow, and, I judge, was of about the age of thirty or thirty-five years, suspicious, watchful and dignified in every movement." As on the day before, Miles negotiated in such a manner that despite a language barrier, he managed to win the confidence of an opponent. Gatewood judged that Natchez "was as much pleased with General Miles as was Geronimo."[63]

Less than a month after the parleys along the border, Brig. Gen. David S. Stanley, commander of the Department of Texas, questioned both Natchez and Geronimo about the agreement that they had reached with Miles. The two Apaches responded, independently, that the general had promised them, "Lay down your arms and come with me to Fort Bowie, and in five days you will see your families, now in Florida with Chihuahua [the Apaches sent from Arizona to Florida on August 29, 1886], and no harm will be done to you." In Miles's annual report, he explained that he offered these terms because "I did not suppose that the Indians who surrendered or were captured would in any marked degree be considered different from those hostile Indians who had in the past surrendered to others and myself in other parts of the country."[64]

On September 5 Miles and the cavalrymen from Bowie escorted an ambulance carrying Geronimo, Natchez, three warriors, and an Indian woman back to the fort. As the ambulance rolled past the mountains that had so recently sheltered his band, Geronimo commented to Miles, "This is the fourth time I have surrendered." Miles tartly snapped back, "And I think it is the last time you will ever have occasion to surrender." Just after nightfall, Miles's party rode into Bowie, completing the sixty-five mile trip in eleven hours.[65]

Only after the Apaches climbed down from the ambulance were they disarmed, but Miles immediately took steps to protect his now-defenseless captives. Miles later recalled that "in order not to be disturbed by civil authorities, or have any contest with them, I put a strong guard around the reservation, which was quite an extensive tract of land." Actually, as Miles reported to the War Department, he did not want the local officials to get their hands on his prisoners because the outcome "would be simply a mockery of justice."[66]

While Miles's party advanced toward Fort Bowie, alternating between a trot and a gallop, those left behind at Skeleton Canyon traveled at a much more leisurely pace, arriving early on September 8. After the Indians who came in with Lawton had a chance to select the clothing they would need, all of the former hostiles, as well as Martine and Kayitah, were hustled under guard from the fort to Bowie Station, where a train awaited them. Miles appreciated the irony as bandsmen from the Fourth Cavalry sent them off to the tune of "Auld Lang Syne." When the general boarded the three-car train just before it pulled out at 1:30, he anticipated a bright future. Just the day before, he wrote to Mary Miles that with preparations completed to send the Indians out of Arizona, "It is a brilliant ending of a difficult problem." Unfortunately, Miles was premature in thinking his problems were behind him.[67]

– CHAPTER 9 –

Brigadier General Nelson A. Miles and the Aftermath of the Geronimo Campaign

FOLLOWING THE EMBARKATION by train of Geronimo and his band from Fort Bowie, Miles became embroiled in a series of encounters with his superiors that turned attention away from his accomplishments in Arizona. These disputes tarnished Miles's reputation and have contributed to misjudgments about the honors awarded after the campaign and the surrender terms Miles offered to Geronimo.

Close behind the congratulatory telegrams came wires questioning both the terms that brought Geronimo's war party in and details of Miles's fight to move the Indians out of Arizona. When President Cleveland and Secretary of War Endicott considered these two issues, their discussion was hampered because they were away from Washington for most of the critical month of September.

On August 30 Cleveland left Saranac Inn, New York, to hunt and fish in the remote upper-lake region of the Adirondack Mountains, while Endicott escaped Washington's summer heat by vacationing in New England. To complicate matters further, the adjutant general, Brig. Gen. Richard C. Drum, had been appointed acting secretary of war, much to the displeasure of Sheridan, who reportedly objected because "he was thus required to serve under and report to his inferior in rank." Sheridan also did not enjoy the best relationship with Endicott. According to the *New York Herald,* "both are reasonable men as individuals, but as public officers it is notorious in army circles that they are not getting along harmoniously."[1]

On September 8, General Howard had sent a telegram to Miles's headquarters stating that both Cleveland and Sheridan wanted the war party kept at Bowie. Prior to this message, however, Miles had notified Sheridan that since the prisoners could not be securely held at Bowie, they should be moved "out of this mountain country, at least as far as Fort Bliss, Union, or Fort Marion, Fla., for safety. Any disposition can be made of them hereafter as the Government may direct." When Sheridan consulted Cleveland about the problem, the president authorized that the Apaches be "sent to the nearest fort or prison where they can be securely confined. The most important thing now is to guard against all chances of escape." Unfortunately, the War Department unintentionally irked Howard when it neglected to send him a copy of the wire notifying Miles of the decision. Furthermore, the fact that Cleveland's authorization enabled Miles to ignore Howard's order to hold the Apaches in Arizona infuriated Howard.[2]

When Howard found out that Geronimo's band had left Fort Bowie the day before, he dashed off two heated telegrams to the War Department. In the first wire, he directed his anger toward Miles "for not complying with orders." In the second dispatch, he again found fault with Miles, then complained to the adjutant general because the president's decision had been sent directly to his subordinate, rather than through division headquarters.[3]

Howard requested that all future orders to Miles be sent through his office, in order to "be able to enforce obedience." As an example of Miles's disobedience he cited the movement of "Geronimo and his band to San Antonio, Tex., en route to Fort Marion, Fla., which is certainly not a compliance with the President's orders to send them to the nearest fort or military prison." Howard insured that he would get attention by requesting "that this dispatch may be laid before the President."

When Howard officially reprimanded Miles for not holding the Apaches at Bowie, the indignant brigadier responded that he "left Fort Bowie with the captured Indians on the morning of September 8. The dispatch was received there at 4:05 P.M. of September 8." Miles later complained privately to the territorial governor of New Mexico, Edmund G. Ross, that "It is remarkable that the only order I am charged with disregarding was one I never saw for a month after it was sent, and it is fortunate that I did not as . . . we might not now have the Apaches in Florida."[4]

Miles did not realize it at the time, but it appears that his acting assistant adjutant general, Capt. William A. Thompson, had made it possible for the Indians to be whisked out of Arizona. As the Apaches were being carried by wagon from the fort to the station, Captain Thompson, his tongue loosened by a few drinks before noon, shared a confidence with his friend,

Leonard Wood. Pointing to his pocket, the captain told Wood, "I have got something here which would stop this movement, but I am not going to let the old man [Miles] see it until you are gone; then I will report it to him." Wood assumed that Thompson had secreted "orders from Washington not to permit the Indians to leave Arizona, but knew that if he acted on this no end of confusion would result."[5]

By delaying the delivery of the wire, Thompson made it possible for his commander to conclude the campaign with honor. President Cleveland had signified his determination that Geronimo's war party "should be very safely kept as prisoners until they can be tried for their crimes or otherwise disposed of." Howard realized that the president's wishes conflicted with the pledge given by Miles to Geronimo, "that it was not the way of officers of the Army to kill their enemies who laid down their arms." This assurance, and the information that Geronimo's band "expect banishment from this country," was contained in the report that Miles sent to Howard on September 6.[6]

Instead of trying to reconcile the differences between the president and one of his generals, however, Howard added to the confusion by wiring Washington a severely abbreviated paraphrase of Miles's report. He misled the authorities when he advised that the Apaches were "prisoners of war; surrender unconditional." Two days later, Howard partially rectified the record when he notified the War Department that Miles had just telegraphed him with the reminder that "There is an erroneous impression regarding Indian prisoners of war. They surrendered with the understanding that they would be sent out of the country." Despite this clarification, speculation remained about the actual terms reached by the two parties at Skeleton Canyon.[7]

Because Miles had proposed a humane settlement of the Geronimo campaign, he fell into official disfavor. The president returned to Washington on the evening of September 22, and met with Drum the following morning. Drum notified Endicott that at this conference, Cleveland "appeared most displeased at General Miles' evident departure from orders and directed me to call for a report of the capture to be forwarded by telegraph, which I have done."[8]

In response to Drum's demand, Howard finally sent the War Department an unabridged copy of Miles's September 6 report, accompanied by

Howard's explanation for terming the surrender unconditional. He wrote that he based his choice of words on the "general tenor" of Miles's telegram, which stated that after all of the conditions proposed by Geronimo had been turned down, the Apaches agreed to surrender as prisoners of war. Furthermore, "the use of the words 'wholly submissive,' and the absence of any specified terms, led me to the use of the words 'surrendered unconditionally.'" When the War Department received a copy of Miles's original report almost a month after it had been sent to Howard's headquarters, however, it was apparent that Geronimo had been assured "that it was not the way of officers of the army to kill their enemies who laid down their arms" and "the Apache prisoners expect banishment from this country."[9]

Miles, who had been Howard's aide during the 1862 Peninsula campaign, wrote to him about the mishandling of the September 6 report. Miles not only questioned why the report had been pigeonholed at division headquarters but also why the "brief dispatch" sent East by Howard "was of quite a different character" from the original report. Most galling of all to Miles, however, was that it was upon Howard's version of the surrender "that the Lieutenant-General's [Sheridan's] order to hold the Apaches at Bowie was based, the order itself being predicated upon a condition that did not exist." Howard's justification for his treatment of Miles's report was that "it was so exceeding lengthy that I deemed it better that the text should go by mail with my report and save the cost of telegraphing."[10]

When the public became aware of the president's displeasure with Miles, many of the territorial newspapers came to the support of the department commander. For example, the *Daily Star* of Tucson spoke for the people of the Southwest who did not "care whether it was conditional or unconditional surrender as long as the fiends were unable to harass them further. It is not blood in revenge our people are seeking. It is simply protection from the government's wars." The *Star* indicated that although the settlers applauded the outcome of the campaign, it "is said to be a sad blow to a certain class of whites upon both sides of the line, men who made merchandise out of the misfortune of the settlers." These profiteers "secured valuable mining and ranch property for a fraction of their value in consequence of terror inspired by the savages, and who would have supplied the latter with the means to carry on the murderous work indefinitely."[11]

Even more important to Miles's self-esteem, the *Army and Navy Journal*, read by virtually every officer in the service, came to his defense. The weekly chronicle of military affairs pointed out that Miles may "have departed from the letter of his instructions, but it does not follow that he has exceeded the reasonable discretion allowed him." After the *Journal* reminded its readers that Miles had received orders for "the destruction or capture" of Geronimo's band, it revealed that the authorities in Washington now argued that "a surrender is not a capture in any sense of the word." The editor did not support the distinction made by the War Department, reasoning that "What the country wants is peace in Arizona; not an opportunity to banish a few Indian scalps."[12]

Miles did not waver from his conviction that he had brought the campaign to a proper conclusion. On October 14 he wrote to Mary Miles that the Apaches had "placed themselves entirely at our mercy, and we were in honor bound not to give them up to a mob or the mockery of a justice where they could never have received an impartial trial." He added that "After one of the most vigorous campaigns they surrendered like brave men to brave men, and placed themselves at the mercy of the government." Although, as the newly appointed commander of the Department of Arizona, Miles had denounced Apache warriors for their cruelty, it appears that his opinion had gradually been tempered by his appreciation of their courage.[13]

While the generals sought to resolve their fate, the Apache prisoners languished at San Antonio. In response to Howard's objection to the movement of Geronimo's band out of Arizona, on September 10 Drum ordered Brig. Gen. David S. Stanley, commander of the Department of Texas, to stop their train. After a prolonged period of investigation and indecision, the president finally acted on the assurance that Miles had given Geronimo, that he and his followers would be treated as prisoners of war. On October 19 the secretary of war, in accordance with Cleveland's decision, had the warriors sent to Fort Pickens, Florida, separated from their families, who would be held at Fort Marion.[14]

Thus began the almost permanent exile of the Chiricahuas from Arizona. In 1887 the men held at Fort Pickens were joined by their families, while the rest of the Apaches in Florida were transferred to Mount Vernon Barracks near Mobile, Alabama. The following year, the Fort Pickens prisoners were finally reunited with their kinsmen in Alabama. In 1894 all of the San Carlos Indians were moved to Fort Sill, Oklahoma, which would be home for Geronimo until he died of pneumonia in 1909. The exodus finally ended for 187 Chiricahuas in 1913, when they were allowed to return to the Southwest and settle on the Mescalero Reservation in New Mexico.[15]

As the authorities pondered the fate of Geronimo's band, the *Army and Navy Journal* noted Miles's fall from grace, then characterized Arizona as "the graveyard of military reputations." After discussing the efforts of both Crook and Miles in the Southwest, the editor concluded that: "All signs fail in a dry time, and neither success nor failure seem to protect the soldier in desert Arizona."[16]

The secretary of war publicly chastised Miles in his annual report, declaring that when the general stated that Geronimo's party was on its way to Florida, his "order was in direct opposition to the President's order." This attack annoyed General Sherman, who pointed to the military bureaucracy as the cause of Miles's troubles: "There never was or will be much sympathy with the fighting Army in Washington, because it is so much more easy to fight on paper than in the field. After a thing has been done, any of these belligerent noncombatants could have done it much better."[17]

After maligning Miles's reputation, Endicott went one step further. On October 9, Miles asked the secretary of war to return him to his previous assignment as commander of the Department of the Missouri. When word leaked out that Miles would not be returned to this desirable assignment, a *New York Times* editorial found it "almost incredible that General Miles's ability and skill, thus called into play to render a great public service in relieving the Southwest frontier of a great scourge, should be made a personal detriment to him, and that his very success should be turned to his disadvantage." The editor, who reported that Miles had "the strongest claim" for the department, felt that Miles had been slighted because of the complaint in his 1886 annual report about the poor quality of the shoes made in the military prison at Fort Leavenworth.

Apparently the criticism touched a sore point since Drum's report had recently praised the institution and its products. The newspaper correctly observed that if Miles had ignored mention of the shoddy shoes worn by his men in Mexico, "he would have been guilty of dereliction of duty. Yet he has been accused of 'needlessly making trouble' for the military prison in a way that should prevent his assignment to the department whose headquarters are at Fort Leavenworth." The editor concluded, "it is very evident that General Miles has not been justly dealt with." The rumors that Miles would be denied the Department of the Missouri proved to be correct: he remained commander of the Department of Arizona until Maj. Gen. Alfred H. Terry retired from command of the Division of the Missouri in 1889.[18]

Rather than extend an olive branch to his enemies, Miles added fuel to his feud with the War Department. According to the *Army and Navy Journal,* "the independent spirit shown by him since the surrender has tended to deprive him of the glory which he would otherwise have received from this end of the line." The editor conceded, however, that Drum "is not particularly friendly toward him and that he has not troubled himself to present Gen. Miles's case in the best possible light."[19]

In September, after Miles received notice that a request for leave to visit his family in Washington had been denied, he had yet another public squabble with the adjutant general. Miles blamed Drum for the rejection of his request for leave, and asked his wife's brother-in-law, Senator Don Cameron, to go over the adjutant-general's head in order to have the leave approved. After Cameron saw Cleveland about what was thought to be Drum's meddling, he wired: "Miles—the fellow you are kicking about is the President himself. You have better let up." Cleveland, who had already turned down an official request made by Miles on September 26 to report to him in person about Geronimo's surrender, seemed determined to avoid even a chance meeting with the general in the capital.[20]

Much more detrimental to Miles's interests than Drum's actions were those emanating from Howard's headquarters. By October 4, Miles realized and complained to Mary Miles "that General Howard or someone at his headquarters suppressed my full account of the surrender of Geronimo, and sent a short dispatch of his own saying that they had surrendered unconditionally." The complications caused by this distortion of the record naturally rankled Miles, who nevertheless managed to contain his anger until after he read the published correspondence concerning Geronimo's surrender.[21]

Seething at what he had read in the government document, Miles reminded Howard that, according to War Department regulations, he had the authority to send his "telegraphic report announcing the capture of the hostile Apaches, direct to Washington, and had I done so I believe I would have been relieved of the annoyance and misrepresentations by which I have been harassed for the last eight months." Miles accused Howard of keeping the report "pigeon-holed at Division Headquarters for nearly a month notwithstanding that I was being denounced, meanwhile, from one end of the country to the other for not reporting the fact of the surrender."

In some bewilderment, Miles continued: "You not only failed to set me right when it was within your power so to do, but you seem to have gone out of your way in the opposite direction." He specifically cited the wire sent by Howard to the War Department on September 9, 1886, because, as he pointed out, it contained "a statement which you asked to have laid before the President, charging me with disregarding and 'asking three times to be relieved from carrying out the President's orders.'" Miles fretted because "Of course that statement created a prejudice against me in the mind of the Chief Executive, and the fact of that report being laid before the Senate of the United States gives the charge publicity."[22]

A little less than a month earlier, Miles had first brought this telegram, which included what he now termed "the unjust accusation," to Howard's attention. At that time, Miles explained that although he sought to have the Apaches "sent to a healthful location, there was not an hour's unnecessary delay in carrying out the President's orders, neither did I ask to be 'relieved' from executing these orders."[23]

Miles readily admitted the obvious, that he "respectfully and in most earnest language remonstrated against sending 400 people from the mountains of Arizona to a narrow prison pen in the fever strickened [*sic*] districts of Florida." Events also made it impossible to dismiss the grim prediction that Miles had made just six months earlier. He had the dubious satisfaction of being able to remind Howard that his "opposition to sending those Indians to Florida, was in part due to the fact that I anticipated just what has already occurred, namely: sickness, a cry of distress, strong sympathy and an effort to return the Indians to the Southwestern territories, . . . where they have been a terror for generations."[24]

The most blatant mischief discovered by Miles was carried out by Howard's adjutant general, Col. Chauncey McKeever. McKeever had sent an article clipped from an Arizona newspaper to Drum. He attributed the story, which criticized Endicott, to a staff officer in Miles's Department of

Arizona. After Miles found out what had happened, he confronted Howard in a personal note, objecting that McKeever's action resulted in "prejudicing in the eyes of the Secretary of War, that officer, and indirectly, myself."[25]

Miles added that the attack "was done by secret correspondence unbeknown to the officer concerned or myself, and is a matter which in my judgment should receive the condemnation of all honorable men." The fact that these intrigues emanated from Howard's office was especially unpardonable since "Three times in your life you had been seriously embarrassed and in need of the help of your friends and three times I had gone to your relief—once on the ground of friendship—twice through a sense of justice."

When a month passed without a response from Howard, Miles referred McKeever's false allegation to the War Department. In an official letter, routed through the headquarters of the Division of the Pacific, he complained that such conduct was a very "mischievous method of personal attack upon the reputation and standing of one officer by another." He explained that he brought the matter to official attention because he believed that it was "injurious to the welfare of the service."[26]

Although both Howard and Drum penned innocuous endorsements to Miles's accusation, Sheridan considered McKeever's ploy "subversive of discipline and likely to do injustice to a brother officer." The commanding general, however, also criticized Miles, suggesting that if he had "felt aggrieved by any action of Col. McKeever he should, if he deemed it necessary, have preferred charges in the regular manner, but not take it upon himself to administer censure."[27]

The *Army and Navy Journal* reprinted two paragraphs from the *Washington Critic* informing the military establishment of some of the reasons behind the efforts to detract from Miles's accomplishments. Predictably, the article mentioned that he had not attended West Point, and then it revealed that "his politics are too Democratic to be popular at the War Department." Finally, the *Critic*'s columnist dropped a bombshell when he wrote "but the real influence at work to rob him of the prestige of the Apache campaign and involve him in unpleasant complications are of another sort, and not of the masculine gender." Further speculation about "unpleasant complications" withered from a dearth of information, although

Miles must have been involved in some relationship, no matter how innocent, for the *Army and Navy Journal* to take such a rumor seriously. But Miles soon had more to contend with than rumors.[28]

Miles finally managed to arrange a reunion with his family late in November for what he hoped would be an extended stay in Washington. Within a week of his arrival, according to the *New York Herald's* capital correspondent, "a distinguished army officer on duty here privately informed the general that it would be well for him to leave for the West at once." The newspaperman found that, "Upon making further inquiry Gen. Miles was told that his enemies at the department, who were jealous of the fame he had wrested from Gen. Crook, would make trouble for him if he remained." Miles temporarily left Washington for Chicago, but then returned to the capital, where he remained through December.[29]

Miles's quarrels with his fellow officers, unseemly as they may have been, paled in comparison to his feud with Crook. During the Sioux campaign of 1876–77, when they first faced a common enemy, Miles privately expressed doubts about Crook's generalship. After returning from an eighty-four-mile march following the Battle of Wolf Mountain, Miles wrote his wife that his men had trekked "almost into the back door of Crook's command. I am surprised to learn that he turned his back on that very large Indian camp; it must have been within forty miles of his camp, and had been there for weeks."

He also found fault with Crook's 1876 annual report because the general had magnified the power of the Sioux, who had acquired repeating rifles. He derided Crook's concerns, telling his wife that if he "believed the Indian such a formidable enemy, I would not risk myself in this country a week. 'Ten thousand times more formidable' than when armed with the bow and arrow! What chance has a command against those Indian monsters! Such statements only intimidate a command."[30]

Their second fight against a common opponent took place in Arizona during the Geronimo campaign. When Miles replaced Crook as commander of the Department of Arizona, he enjoyed a rare opportunity to advance his reputation at his rival's expense. With their professional standing at stake, each brigadier kept a sharp eye on the other.

In June, after the Apaches slipped away into Mexico, Miles became touchy about criticism. He complained to Mary Miles that newspapers were printing "absurd reports and false statements about the Indians" and about "the statements thrown out by Crook." Miles found Crook's remarks especially unwarranted since, in his view, "He made a dead failure of this, as he has of every other campaign."[31]

What probably aroused Miles was his predecessor's comments in the June 19 issue of the *Army and Navy Journal.* In an interview first published by the *Lincoln* (Nebraska) *Journal,* Crook infringed upon his replacement's domain when he discussed the situation in the Department of Arizona.

Crook argued that if the Apaches "could be made to believe confidently that they would be sent to join their friends in Florida, I think they would come in and peace be restored." To proceed otherwise "means an endless war. Those 20 men will last twenty years." In a tone reminiscent of his 1876 annual report, Crook concluded that the Apaches "must have the concession I have indicated, or its equivalent in terms to suit them, or they must be hunted down—a thing next to the absolutely impossible and sure to ruin a large section of country, and at a fearful cost to the Army."[32]

In December Crook's prestige received a blow when Cleveland finally credited Miles for success in Arizona. In his annual message to Congress, after referring to the eighteen-month uproar caused by Geronimo's warriors, the president announced that "General Miles . . . succeeded better than Crook in the management and direction of their pursuit." Less than a week later, Miles received a tangible reward for his triumph along with a vindication of his decision to send the former war party to Florida.[33]

In accordance with Cleveland's wishes, on December 15 Endicott signed an order adding southern California to the Department of Arizona. Headquarters for this enlarged command would be moved to Los Angeles from Prescott, Arizona. A dispatch from Washington to the *Army and Navy Journal* explained the reason behind the reorganization. Shortly after Cleveland's speech to Congress, Secretary of War Endicott complained in his annual report that sending the surrendered Apaches to Florida "was in direct opposition to the President's order." On the same day that the War Department announced changes in the Department of Arizona, a correspondent wired that "The President feels that injustice has been done General Miles, and is doing his best to make up for it."

The newsman, who appeared to enjoy excellent sources within the military bureaucracy, explained that apparently Endicott had been unaware that "When General Crook's terms of agreement with the hostile Apaches were disapproved by the President, instructions were given which authorized the sparing of their lives, but otherwise their surrender was unconditional." Since peace had been brought to the Southwest without exceeding the limit of Cleveland's order to Crook, in "vindication of General Miles' judicious and successful course, and in recognition of the services of his gallant troops, his responsibilities have been increased."[34]

Like his superiors, Sheridan had ambivalent thoughts about Miles. At the end of the campaign, he tendered such faint praise to the department commander that the *Arizona Daily Star* editorialized that the commanding general "evidently don't [*sic*] take well to General Miles, if his annual report to the Secretary of War can be taken as an index of his feelings." The report did state that "Miles went to work with commendable zeal. His troops followed up the hostiles with vigorous energy, broke up their camps by attack four or five times, and gave them no rest until they surrendered on Sept. 4." The statement, however, sprang more from Sheridan's determination to publicize the "active and prominent" role of regular troops in the campaign than his wish to praise Miles.[35]

While Miles may have been disappointed by Sheridan's indifference, Crook seethed at some of Sheridan's remarks. Crook wrote Webb Hayes, a hardware manufacturer and son of President Rutherford B. Hayes, that "during his recent trip East, he [Sheridan] told a reporter that I had disobeyed orders & that Miles didn't, etc. etc. & that I in my Resume report had made an attack on him and Miles." Crook also complained to Hayes that on another occasion Sheridan told a mutual friend that "I had went on the principle of setting a thief to catch a thief while in Arizona but that I had failed there." He added that Sheridan also commented that what had made Crook "so hot [is] that Miles had caught him [Geronimo's band] with white troops" (regular soldiers rather than Apache scouts).

Crook also communicated to Hayes his belief that Miles did not deserve praise from the commanding general. "Now General Sheridan knows that Miles' operations against those Indian [*sic*] had no more to do with securing their surrender than did your killing that '. . . Anaconda Grizzly bear last fall,' but he won't let me publish that report." Some of those who had recently served in Arizona shared Crook's opinion about crediting his replacement with the victory.[36]

Referring to an interview given by veterans of the Geronimo campaign who were enjoying a leave in San Francisco, the *Alta California* reported that "None of them attempted to detract from the glory that has fallen on General Miles, but they adhere to the claim that General Miles found his plan a failure, and only after falling back on the idea of General Crook in employing Indian scouts did he achieve success."[37]

Miles resented such reports, especially those that originated at the War Department. When asked about official claims that detracted from his work in Arizona, he told a reporter that they "emanate from the brains of an unscrupulous and envious person, whose object appears to be to distort the truth with an intention of injuring me regardless of the just praise due the troops for their extraordinary services in achieving a permanent peace in the Southwest." He then added, "Many of the statements are devoid of truth; others are weak arguments and labored theories. The pretense that the surrender of Geronimo and other hostiles was other than a result of the gallant and arduous operations of the troops in the field is simply childish."

Miles ridiculed his detractors, declaring: "One might imagine from reading some of the statements that the red handed Apaches have been all summer trying to get up a cheap-rate excursion to the yellow fever districts of Florida." He questioned how any "intelligent man" could believe that Indians who had "been roaming over the mountainous region for generations, masters of the situation, would have thrown down their arms, sacrificed their property, surrendered their liberty, accepted permanent banishment from their native country, placed themselves and their families at the mercy of the Government, unless they had been subjected by military forces."[38]

Almost as soon as Geronimo climbed aboard the train that would carry him into captivity, a debate that has lasted to this day erupted over the proper allocation of credit among the victors. The paucity of official recognition for some of those involved caused comment in Army circles as well as lingering bitterness in some quarters. In 1929, before an audience of Indian War veterans, Brig. Gen. James Parker related some of his experiences as a lieutenant in Arizona forty-three years earlier. With his military career behind him, Parker could speak both knowledgeably and frankly before his fellow professionals.

Parker believed that "what Lawton and Gatewood accomplished was a remarkable achievement, and both of these officers should be awarded, if possible, posthumously a medal for distinguished service." He then discussed the assistant surgeon who found tramping through Mexico to be a springboard into the company of politicians and generals in Washington. That is where Leonard Wood received the decoration in 1898 that provoked Parker to observe, "Curiously enough the only actor in this drama who received substantial reward was Leonard Wood. He received a Congressional Medal of Honor 'for distinguished gallantry' in this campaign. The award of this medal has been the subject of considerable discussion."

Miles, who had died in 1925, would have been delighted with Parker's appraisal of his work. The former cavalry lieutenant, who first met the general at Fort Huachuca in 1886, declared that "The real credit for the success of this campaign was due to General Miles. He supported Lawton in every way. He deported to Florida the remainder of Geronimo's tribe, and thus deprived Geronimo of a base of operations, and a home." Parker added that, "He discovered that to run down and capture Geronimo's band within a reasonable time was not practicable, that it would be better and save more lives of citizens to treat with him. He sent into Mexico, Gatewood for that purpose."

For Miles to "obtain Geronimo's surrender he promised to protect him from the civil authorities of Arizona and New Mexico who were keen to arrest and hang him." Furthermore, "To carry out this program, in spite of orders from Washington, he shipped Geronimo and his band out of the dangerous territory before the civil authorities had become aware of what was going on." Parker concluded that "For this he received the censure of the President. But he delivered the southwest and northern Mexico from a century old thralldom of murder and ravage."[39]

The only official gesture of recognition to Miles for restoring peace had been to enlarge his department, leading the *New York Times* to comment that his success "brought him little but sneers and snubbings at Washington." In contrast, the people of Arizona gratefully applauded his campaign against Geronimo. In December 1886 the citizens of Pima County decided to contribute toward the purchase of a sword as a gift to their benefactor. By the following April, eight hundred dollars had been collected toward the thousand-dollar cost of a sword to be designed and engraved by Tiffany.[40]

The chairman of the finance committee expected to raise the remaining two hundred dollars by the middle of May, especially since contributions made in the Prescott area had not yet been deposited into the fund's account. Miles was particularly pleased with the nature of the donations because, as he told Sherman, "no one outside of the Territory or in any way connected with the Army, or any corporation, was allowed to contribute."[41]

The presentation of the sword, planned for September 4, 1887, had to be postponed because Miles broke his leg in a carriage accident in Los Angeles on August 31. Two months later, although his leg had not completely healed, he and his wife traveled by train for a week's vacation in Tucson, where the people of Arizona honored him on November 8. From his seat on a grandstand shaded by cottonwoods, Miles felt touched as he looked out over the sea of excited spectators gathered before him on the banks of the Santa Cruz River. He later said that he had never experienced such "heartfelt gratitude, or a more universal demonstration of regard, than was exhibited by those people of all classes, from the highest to the humblest; even the poor Mexicans and Papago Indians have a feeling of relief and security for life and property that they have not experienced heretofore." Local enthusiasm for Miles ran so high in 1887 that the *Arizona Daily Star* suggested that he would be an ideal presidential candidate in 1888.[42]

Most of the key officers in the Geronimo campaign received some trophy to remind them of their victory. Miles had the sword, described in 1887 as "the most artistic weapon ever made in the United States." On September 17, 1886, Henry Lawton was presented with a gold watch and chain at a banquet in Albuquerque; in 1898, Leonard Wood, now the protégé of presidents rather than generals, was awarded a Medal of Honor; and each of these officers would eventually advance in rank. Incredibly, Charles Gatewood, who had been indispensable in obtaining the surrender of Geronimo's band, came away from the campaign empty handed. He received neither a promotion nor a medal for the courage and skill he exhibited in Mexico, and was still a first lieutenant when he died of cancer in 1896 at the age of forty-three.[43]

In 1926 Gatewood's son submitted his father's account of his mission into Mexico to the *Saturday Evening Post* for publication. In his cover letter to the editor, he complained about "what amounted to a theft of credit from the man who caused the surrender of these Indians, and the transfer of that credit to others who played only minor roles in the affair." He then named Miles, Lawton, and Wood as the officers who had enhanced their reputations at his father's expense.[44]

The legend that Miles neglected to commend Gatewood in order to keep all of the glory for himself is so prevalent that it is even found in reference books. For instance, *The Reader's Encyclopedia of the American West* states that "Gatewood did meet Geronimo and arranged negotiations that led to his surrender, but Miles never credited him for this work." This assertion, however, does not take into consideration the record indicating that Miles attempted to see that Gatewood received his due.[45]

In Miles's 1886 annual report, he wrote that after contact had been established with Geronimo's camp, Gatewood "rode boldly into their presence, at the risk of his life, and repeated the demand for their surrender." The *Washington Critic* observed that this portrayal of "Gatewood's heroic nerve" will "add much to the honor that young officer has earned."[46]

Less than two weeks after the Apaches had been dispatched from Arizona, Miles named Gatewood to his staff. Although a fellow Sixth Cavalry officer saw the appointment as a reward from Miles for Gatewood's service in Mexico, the officer's congratulatory letter also expressed the preoccupation with the allocation of glory following the campaign. Gatewood, known to his friends as "Beak" because of his prominent nose, learned from the note that before his appointment as Miles's aide "There had been ugly rumors floating around that credit wasn't being bestowed altogether where it was due, and that while not wishing to disparage any one else's efforts, that C. 'Beak' Gatewood was not getting the encomiums and congratulations that were his."[47]

When Gatewood sought a transfer in December 1886, Miles readily endorsed his application for a position as a staff officer in either the commissary or quartermaster department. The department commander's recommendation contained standard phrases, such as Gatewood "is fully competent to discharge the duties of the staff position he seeks, and his merits being unusual I take great pleasure in commending him to the favorable consideration of the appointing power." But Miles also reminded the adjutant general that his aide's "zeal and courage are of the highest order, and recently in the campaign against Geronimo he bore a very conspicuous part, especially at the close, when his good judgment and heroism aided much in bringing about satisfactory results."[48]

Despite Miles's solid recommendation, Gatewood did not receive the desired appointment and remained an aide for four years. He finally returned to the Sixth Cavalry in 1890, during the military buildup in the Dakotas, where he became ill during winter operations against the Ghost Dancers. Soon after returning to duty after almost a year's recuperation, Gatewood had to go on disability retirement because of wounds suffered in an explosion while he was fighting a fire at his post.[49]

In 1895 a captain from the ailing lieutenant's regiment initiated a request, to which Miles added his recommendation, proposing that Gatewood be awarded a Medal of Honor. They cited him "for gallantry in going alone at the risk of his life into the hostile Apache camp of Geronimo in Sonora, August 24, 1886." Although Leonard Wood would receive this medal in 1898 for his exploits in the same campaign, the acting secretary of war notified Miles "that the terms of the law authorizing the issue of Congressional medals of honor for most distinguished gallantry 'in action' do not permit the recognition by that means, of the bravery of this officer."[50]

From the evidence, Miles truly appreciated Gatewood's accomplishments in Mexico. Shortly before Miles died, he spoke with a retired officer, Col. William C. Brown, about the Geronimo campaign. Brown recalled that Miles "agreed with me that Wood and Lawton were not at all the chief factors, but that Gatewood was the man who took the chief risks."[51]

That the War Department did not bestow upon Gatewood the recognition that he earned is inexcusable, but the mean fate of Martine and Kayitah is even more shameful. The two Apache scouts, who located Geronimo's camp and arranged his parley with Gatewood, were hustled off to Florida with the rest of the Apache prisoners. As Utley has suggested, Martine and Kayitah might well have been desolate living apart from their tribesmen, but living as captives in exile was a sorry reward for their invaluable services. It is to Miles's discredit that he never acknowledged his debt to Gatewood's two scouts.[52]

The lack of recognition of Martine and Kayitah not only satisfied Sheridan's desire to focus attention on the regular troops but also reflected Miles's coolness toward Crook's Apache scouts. Miles had a chance to explain his reservations about the use of these auxiliaries when he testified before the House Committee on Indian Affairs on February 15, 1890. The *New York Sun* informed its readers that Miles "had no confidence in the Indian scouts. If they were true to the military they were false to their own people. He had no use for men who would hire out at the rate of $13 per month to trail their friends and relatives for delivery to their enemy."[53]

Gatewood supported Miles's doubts about the loyalty of the Apache scouts. He informed the editor of the *Army and Navy Register* that "much of the ammunition issued to them went into the belts of the hostiles. As far as my observation went in the earlier part of the campaign, Chatto and the other Chiricahua scouts could scarcely be considered faithful; they hindered rather than aided the operations of the troops." Although some suspect that Miles may have pressured his aide into criticizing the scouts, Gatewood's observations are supported by another officer.[54]

An unidentified officer from the Department of Arizona wrote the editor of the *Army and Navy Journal* about an incident that occurred when some Apache scouts were being discharged at Fort Bowie. He related that just before the Indians left the post they were assembled for an inspection. Bundles supposedly holding personal belongings attracted Miles's attention, and he ordered them opened. "Reluctantly they complied, and no less than 40,000 rounds of ammunition besides a large number of revolvers and other side arms were found secreted in the parcels. The ammunition and arms were at once confiscated, notwithstanding the open murmurs of dissatisfaction on the part of ex-scouts."[55]

At the 1890 House hearings Miles directly challenged Crook's recommendation to transfer the Chiricahuas from Mount Vernon Barracks, near Mobile, Alabama, to Fort Sill, in the Indian Territory. Since Miles had recommended relocating the Apaches onto this reservation in 1886, Crook glibly attributed his change of mind to "anything to beat me." Actually, when Crook offered that explanation, he had already read the reason behind Miles's opposition in the *New York Sun.* Even though the hearing had received limited press coverage, Crook characterized the few newspaper reports as being a product of "Miles' 'Literary Bureau.'"[56]

The *Sun,* which carried its stories of those who testified before the Indian Affairs committee in its back pages, reported that when Miles took the stand on February 15, he "referred to the desperate character of the Apaches, and said if they were sent to Fort Sill there would be practically nothing between them and the mountains of Mexico. He said that if they got back West they would in all probability be mounted in six weeks." Miles, however, continued, as he had in the past, to advocate a healthier home for the Apaches. According to the *Sun,* "He believed that the Indians might be moved to a colder climate, for instance, near the tract where the Cherokee Indians in North Carolina are located, and where they could see how civilized Indians live."[57]

In 1898, four years after all of the Apaches, including Geronimo, had finally been moved to Fort Sill, the Apache leader met Miles at the Trans-Mississippi and International Exposition. At this fair, where Geronimo spoke to Miles for the first time since boarding the prison train in Arizona, he is said to have complained through an interpreter that the general had lied to him at Skeleton Canyon. Indeed, the ultimatum Miles instructed Gatewood to present to Geronimo included the assurance that he would be reunited with his family in Florida, which was not honored until 1887.[58]

In Miles's 1886 annual report, Miles provided a public explanation for his promise to send the Apaches into exile with their families. He wrote that he "did not suppose that the Indians who surrendered or were captured would in any marked degree be considered different from those hostile Indians who had in the past surrendered to others and to myself in other parts of the country." His determination to rush his prisoners out of Arizona indicates that privately he believed that they were in greater jeopardy than other captured tribes. He had informed his wife a little more than a month after Geronimo's band had surrendered that "we were in honor bound not to give them up to a mob or the mockery of a justice where they could never have received an impartial trial."[59]

Initially, his superiors had envisioned a grimmer fate for the Apache prisoners than the one engineered by Miles. General Howard believed that "to save their necks" warriors in Geronimo's band "will turn state's evidence, as was the case with the Modoc murderers." In that instance, after being tried by a military commission for slaying Brig. Gen. Edward R. C. Canby and the Reverend Eleasar Thomas at a peace conference, Captain Jack, who led the attackers, and three of his followers, were hanged.[60]

In a similar vein, less than a week after the Apaches boarded the prison train General Sheridan told a reporter that Geronimo "is entitled to no mercy. If he cannot be dealt with summarily, he will probably be removed east of the Mississippi, to Florida perhaps, the very place where he doesn't want to go. The Dry Tortugas would be a good reservation for him."[61]

As for President Cleveland, he contemplated initiating a new policy for the disposition of marauding Indians by using Geronimo's band as an example. Following a press conference at the War Department on October 4, it was reported that the president intended that the Apache prisoners be brought to "trial by civil courts" and anticipated "their prompt punishment for the crimes they had committed." Thus, Miles found himself out of step with his commanders. Although this caused him to fall temporarily into official disfavor, he fulfilled the pledge that "it was not the way of the officers of the Army to kill their enemies who laid down their arms."[62]

— CHAPTER 10 —

The "Messiah" Outbreak of 1890

MILES YEARNED FOR the position vacated by Alfred H. Terry in 1888, command of the Division of the Missouri, with its rank of major general, but Senator Sherman warned him not to get his hopes up. Neither he nor Senator Cameron could intercede with President Cleveland on Miles's behalf because, as he explained to his nephew-in-law, "It would be looked upon purely as a family affair and would weaken rather than strengthen you. Indeed, from information received, your case has been somewhat prejudiced by several persons calling on the President in your behalf, which, with him, creates a prejudice against you rather than for you." Although Sherman had made arrangements for some important Democrats to lobby for Miles, he had little hope of success because Crook enjoyed such seniority over Miles. Less than two weeks later Sherman informed Miles, "When the President was approached it was manifest that he had made up his mind to promote Crook as the ranking Brigadier General." Perhaps as a gesture of consolation, Miles received command of the Division of the Pacific, with headquarters in San Francisco. But since a major general's stars did not come with this appointment, Miles still had little tangible evidence of the War Department's appreciation of his conduct of the Geronimo campaign.[1]

On March 21, 1890, General Crook died of heart failure while exercising with dumbbells. An unidentified spokesman for Miles told a reporter "that while Gen. Miles and Gen. Crook were not, for obvious reasons, on good terms since the late Indian troubles, he had great respect for Crook, and was very much shocked by his death." Following Crook's death, Miles became concerned about the hostile clique that had formed against him. He feared that his enemies might try to use their influence to bar him from replacing Crook as commander of the Division of the Missouri.

With his goal of promotion to major general in possible jeopardy, Miles sought the assistance of Senator Henry L. Dawes of Massachusetts. The general confided to the senator that "every man has some enemies and mine appear to be all in Washington and the War Department." He also saw a threat from another quarter, worrying that he might encounter hostility from "the Catholics in order to advance one of their own class [John Gibbon] who is next on the list."[2]

Senator John Sherman confirmed Miles's worst fears, warning his niece's husband that President Benjamin Harrison had strong misgivings about naming Miles to the position formerly held by Crook. The senator explained that Harrison thought that Miles was "if not disobedient, at least a troublesome man to get along with." As an example, the president cited Miles's opposition to the plan, endorsed by his administration, to transfer the Apaches to Fort Sill.[3]

Miles took advantage of the senator's warning about Harrison's apprehensions. He rushed by train from New York to the nation's capital, where he undertook to persuade the president to promote him. Harrison, who had commanded the 70th Indiana Volunteers through the Atlanta campaign, graciously consented to see Miles. The five-feet-six-inch-tall president, who had been fondly called "Little Ben" by the men in his regiment, must have been favorably impressed by the well-groomed brigadier general as he strode into the executive office.[4]

On April 5 Miles sent Mary Miles, who had remained at home in San Francisco, details of his White House visit. Private audiences with Harrison could be chilling affairs; after such sessions, some spoke of the president as a "human iceberg." Miles, who had stood up to Jefferson Davis, faced down Sitting Bull, and won the confidence of Chief Joseph and Geronimo, added another coup to his string of victories in personal encounters. He told his wife that although Harrison greeted him warmly enough, he received the impression that the president had decided against him; however, after a "half an hour we were on good terms and at the end of an hour I am satisfied he had made up his mind to appoint me." Miles was correct, and the Senate immediately confirmed Harrison's choice. Miles savored his victory, confiding to his wife that "The top round of the ladder gives me more pleasure I think than any of the others."[5]

The future looked bright for Miles, who took command of the Division of the Missouri on September 15. When Oliver O. Howard reached his legal retirement age on November 8, 1894, and John M. Schofield on September 29, 1895, Miles would become the senior major general in the army. In building his impressive military record, however, Miles had created a legion of enemies. One of his foes (identified only as "a prominent army officer") attempted to discredit Miles, shortly after he assumed command of the Division of the Missouri, by floating a rumor that the general had presidential ambitions. The *New York Times* eventually defended Miles, saying that his hat had been thrown into the presidential ring "by one of his worst enemies in Washington, without the authority or knowledge of General Miles, and for the purpose of doing him an injury." The purpose of the rumor, the newspaper stated, was to arouse "the petty enmity and jealousy of some Republicans and hostility of some Democrats, especially those who are acquainted with his purposes and character." Although embarrassed by the incident, Miles "considered it unbecoming to take any notice or make any answer to the unjust and unwarranted statements."[6]

The anonymous officer who had given the false information to newspapers also attributed an alarm about conditions at the Sioux agencies to Miles's desire "to create a scare and pose as the savior of the country." Miles protested privately to Schofield, commanding general of the army. When an officer "can falsely state through the public press that such disposition of troops is the result of a selfish and unworthy motive, then such action is an undoubted military crime." Miles demanded that the officer "be placed in arrest, and brought before a military tribunal for his offense," but Schofield apparently downplayed the matter and pigeonholed the complaint.[7]

The allegation that Miles had misrepresented conditions in his division was unjustified. By 1890 conditions on the Sioux reservation were deteriorating. Miles blamed the Indian discontent on hunger and the government's failure to keep the promises made by the Sioux Commission in 1889. The disappearance of buffalo and game, a drought and crop failure in 1889 and 1890, and insufficient rations at the agencies had placed the Sioux in desperate straits.[8]

On October 22 a correspondent for the *Black Hills Daily Times* (South Dakota) reported that the Messiah religious movement had reached the Standing Rock Agency in North Dakota, home of Sitting Bull's band of Hunkpapa Sioux. James McLaughlin, the local agent, had recently learned from One Bull, an Indian policeman and nephew of Sitting Bull, that a group of young Indians had persuaded Kicking Bear, the inspired apostle of the 'Messiah'" at the Cheyenne River Reservation, to come to Standing Rock and describe his mystical experience.[9]

Kicking Bear claimed to have traveled to a remote and uninhabited region at the edge of the continent, where he met a long-haired man with crucifixion wounds. Together they climbed a ladder through the clouds to a higher world presided over by the "Father of the Son." The deity told Kicking Bear that he knew "about the suffering of my red children at the hands of the white men," and announced that he was "going to make a change in the affairs of the world." He promised to bury the white race under thirty feet of fresh earth, together with those Indians who had taken up the white man's ways. By extensive dancing, the nonprogressive (unassimilated) Indians could "stamp the new soil under their feet and so climb to the top" (a practice known as the Ghost Dance). The "father and the son" pledged to provide the surviving Indians with money, buffalo, and light wagons. Those few whites who escaped burial, he concluded, "will not be able to make powder strong enough to send a bullet through my red children's skin . . . and my red children shall all live happily as they were 400 years ago."[10]

Government officials at each Sioux agency noted that the situation became volatile when hungry Indians were introduced to the new religion. Special Indian agent E. B. Reynolds, for example, advised the Indian Bureau in Washington, D.C., that the Brules at Rosebud boasted that they would rather "die fighting" than starve. As the new religion promised "their return to earth at the coming millennium, they have no great fear of death." The Indians were preparing for a holy war, and were selling everything they owned in order to buy weapons and ammunition. Agent Daniel F. Royer blamed the local messianic movement on the breakdown of law and order at Pine Ridge. Whenever Indians violated the law, "the first thing they do is join the Ghost Dance, and then they feel safe to defy the police, the law, and the agent."[11]

Acting Commissioner of Indian Affairs R. V. Belt heeded the warnings, and on November 13, 1890, he recommended that the Army take steps to avert an outbreak at the affected agencies. Four days later, General Miles ordered Brig. Gen. John R. Brooke, commanding the Department of the Platte at Omaha, to protect lives and property at Rosebud and Pine Ridge. Miles served with Brooke during the Civil War and admired him as a scrappy fighter. In the peacetime military, Brooke had few opportunities to demonstrate his ability and, like many men of action, he lacked enthusiasm for handling routine matters.[12]

Miles's primary objective was to prevent the Ghost Dancers from uniting in one large band. As an initial step, he instructed Brooke to arrest the Indian leaders and separate them from their followers. In these delicate operations, he repeatedly warned against a confrontation. Shortly before Brooke took to the field, Miles advised, "One thing should be impressed upon all officers, never to allow their commands to be mixed up with the Indians, or taken at disadvantage." On November 23, three days after Brooke reached Pine Ridge, Miles again cautioned him to keep his command apart from the Indians: "Hold them all at a safe distance from your command. Guard against surprise or treachery." On December 7 Miles repeated his warning for a third time.[13]

Meanwhile, Miles attempted to defuse the discontent on the Sioux reservations. In late November he traveled to Washington, D.C., and obtained money from army appropriations to purchase extra food for the Indians and persuaded the secretary of the interior to raise the level of rations to that specified by treaty. He also attended a White House conference with President Harrison and Secretary of War Redfield Proctor. Proctor was a shrewd Vermont businessman and politician with a reputation for remaining unruffled in tight situations. Appointed secretary of war in March 1889, Proctor fit comfortably into Harrison's official family, sometimes known as the "Businessmen's Cabinet."[14]

During the White House visit, Harrison and Proctor outlined administration policy for handling the unrest at the Sioux reservations. The president urged Miles "to take every possible precaution to prevent an Indian outbreak, and to suppress it promptly if it occurs. He gave the general a free hand to transfer troops and equipment into his division, but at the same time cautioned against arresting Sitting Bull. His warning was in response to a letter from Agent McLaughlin, insisting that the Interior Department cancel a proposed plan to have William F. "Buffalo Bill" Cody talk the Sioux medicine man into surrendering. The prohibition, however, was only temporary. "When, in your opinion," Proctor informed Miles, "adequate preparations are complete, and you think arrests should be made, he [Harrison] will not interfere, feeling that your judgement of these matters would be better than his." To avoid any misunderstandings, the secretary repeated the president's instructions in a note sent to Miles at the Ebbitt House Hotel.[15]

At a press conference held in Chicago on December 4, Miles explained his plan for ending the Indian hostilities. First, he would try to persuade as many Ghost Dancers as possible to return to their homes. Army units would then encircle those who remained defiant. On a map Miles indicated how his soldiers would move into positions on three sides of the Ghost Dance camp, which was located on an easily defended plateau in the Badlands, seventeen miles north of the Pine Ridge Agency. At the same time, soldiers would be placed between the Indians and the white settlements. The southern section of the cordon remained open, to encourage the Ghost Dancers to move in that direction, toward Pine Ridge. His officers, Miles once again stressed, had been instructed to keep their troops from direct contact with the Indians.[16]

Miles had taken steps to arrest hostile leaders, including Sitting Bull, whom he feared would again attempt to clear settlers from his former domain. The arrest of the Sioux medicine man, the general argued unconvincingly, would prevent "a threatened uprising of colossal proportions, extending over a far greater territory than did the confederation inaugurated by the Prophet and led by Tecumseh, or the conspiracy of Pontiac."[17]

On December 6, two days after the press conference, Miles sent a confidential telegram to Schofield in Washington. The seizure of Sitting Bull, which Miles had authorized before his White House visit, had been aborted. As instructed, Buffalo Bill had set out to bring in Sitting Bull (the star of his 1885 Wild West show) without using force. But soon after the showman left on his mission, a military courier overtook him with the president's order to turn back. Miles worried that the extensive press coverage given Buffalo Bill's mission might cause Sitting Bull to flee to Canada, and suggested that the Sioux leader be taken into custody at once.[18]

Schofield did not share Miles's fears and advised against arresting individual Indians. He also suggested that Miles should concentrate on convincing the Ghost Dancers to return to their agencies. Once the Indians were back on their reservations, "it will matter little what becomes of Sitting Bull or any other Indian who is not an actual military leader." In fact, the arrest of individuals "might deter the warriors from voluntary surrender." Schofield acknowledged, however, that the president had left the final decision up to Miles.[19]

On December 10 Miles ordered Brig. Gen. Thomas H. Ruger, commanding the Department of Dakota, to arrest Sitting Bull. Two days later, Ruger instructed Lt. Col. William F. Drum at Fort Yates, the military headquarters for the Standing Rock Agency, to seize the Sioux leader. Drum was to ask Agent McLaughlin at Pine Ridge to cooperate in the endeavor. Accordingly, Drum and McLaughlin drafted a plan for Indian police, supported by a detachment of soldiers, to arrest the medicine man.[20]

Before daybreak on December 15, thirty-nine experienced Indian policemen and four volunteers surrounded two cabins belonging to Sitting Bull. Eight uniformed Indians rushed into one of the huts, while ten others stormed the second. The Sioux leader meekly surrendered and followed the instructions of his captors until he reached the door of his cabin. Seeing a large crowd of tribesmen milling about outside, he suddenly shouted, "I am not going. Do with me what you like. I am not going. Come on! Take action! Let's go!" Galvanized by this call to arms, several Sioux in the crowd opened fire, killing four Indian policemen and wounding three others, two mortally. Eight tribesmen, including Sitting Bull and his seventeen-year-old son, were also killed. The surviving Indian law officers held off the attackers for about two hours, until a column of cavalry arrived.[21]

The bungled arrest generated mixed feelings. President Harrison made no public comment, but Cody later claimed that the president, while in Indianapolis, confided "that he had allowed himself to be persuaded against my mission." Harrison was sorry that he had not allowed Cody to handle the arrest. Miles, however, had no regrets about the operation, and dismissed the death of Sitting Bull as "the tragic end of a tragic life." With a measure of respect and relief he reflected on the passing of the slain medicine man: "Since the days of Pontiac, Tecumseh, and Red Jacket, no Indian has had the power of drawing to him so large a following of his race, and holding and wielding it against the authority of the United States, or of inspiring it with greater animosity against the white race and civilization."[22]

On December 17 Miles arrived at Rapid City, South Dakota, and there established his field headquarters. Three days later, he wrote to his wife that, despite fears that Sitting Bull's death might provoke an uprising, an uneasy peace still prevailed. So far he had managed the tense situation without the death of a single soldier or settler, but he did not know how long his good fortune would last. Privately, Miles blamed President Harrison and the Republicans for the precarious state of affairs. More than a year had passed and the politicians had not yet ratified the 1889 treaty with the Sioux. The hungry Indians viewed the delay as yet another broken promise. Miles was appalled that the government "should disregard promises and get the Indians into such a condition, and then order the military to prevent an Indian War."[23]

Miles sent a similar, but more diplomatic, message to General Schofield. The Indian problem, he stated, "cannot be solved permanently at this end of the line." Congress must fulfill the treaty obligations "in which the Indians were entreated or coerced into signing." The tribes had signed away "a valuable portion of their reservation, and it is now occupied by white people, for which they [the Indians] have received nothing."[24]

Following the death of Sitting Bull, Capt. Ezra P. Ewers and Lt. Harry C. Hale, with authority from Miles, induced Hump, the Sioux leader who had fought with the army at Bear Paw against the Nez Perce, to surrender peacefully, along with most of his people. A small number, however, refused to give up and joined another band of Ghost Dancers under Big Foot. On December 23, Miles ordered Lt. Col. Edwin V. Sumner, who was encamped near Big Foot's village, to arrest the dissidents. The order came too late, for on the night of the twenty-second the entire band had started south. Maj. Samuel M. Whitside and a detachment of Seventh Cavalry immediately set out in pursuit, and on December 28 overtook the runaways. As the cavalry approached, a brave raised a white flag and the Indians surrendered unconditionally. Whitside escorted the Sioux captives to Wounded Knee Creek, where Col. James W. Forsyth arrived later that night with reinforcements. As senior officer, Forsyth assumed command of the troops and the prisoners.[25]

In accordance with instructions from General Brooke, the following morning, December 29, Forsyth detailed two companies to disarm Big Foot's band. Contrary to Miles's repeated warnings, as the troopers began a personal search for weapons they became mixed in with the Indians. When a soldier attempted to inspect a young Indian's blanket, a battle erupted. A medicine man threw dirt into the air and blew on a crude whistle, whereupon a hot-headed Sioux youth fired a rifle, which he had concealed beneath his robe. At this juncture, warriors rushed to retrieve weapons taken from them by the troops.[26]

Upon receiving the first fragmentary reports of the fight, Schofield wired Miles and praised "the brave 7th Cavalry for their splendid conduct." Miles, however, had doubts about Colonel Forsyth's conduct at Wounded Knee, and on January 1 bluntly advised Schofield that "the action of the colonel commanding" should be "a subject of investigation." Schofield immediately retracted his congratulations. In a second telegram, he passed along a message from Secretary of War Proctor that "the President has heard with great regret of the failure of your efforts to secure the settlement of the Sioux difficulties without bloodshed." Proctor added, "The President hopes that the report of the killing of women and children in the affair at Wounded Knee is unfounded, and directs that you cause an immediate inquiry to be made and report the result to the Department." "If there was any unsoldierly conduct," the secretary concluded, "you will relieve the responsible officer and so use the troops there as to avoid its repetition."[27]

The fight at Wounded Knee infuriated Miles. His anger and disappointment were apparent in a letter to Mary Miles: "Two nights ago I thought I had the whole difficulty in my hand, and without the loss of a single life. But all my efforts to prevent a war appear to have been destroyed by the action of Lieutenant Colonel Sumner [who had allowed Big Foot's band to escape] and Colonel Forsyth." On January 3 Miles arrived at Pine Ridge. The following day, he relieved Forsyth from command of the Seventh Cavalry, and ordered a court of inquiry to investigate the colonel's conduct in disarming the Sioux. Composed of Maj. J. Ford Kent and Capt. Frank D. Baldwin, both from Miles's staff, the board was to determine "whether dispositions of the troops was [*sic*] judicious," and to ascertain "whether any noncombatants were unnecessarily injured or destroyed."[28]

In a letter to his wife, Miles blamed the Wounded Knee tragedy on either "blind stupidity or criminal indifference." Forsyth's actions, he charged, were "about the worst I have ever known. I doubt if there is a second lieutenant who could not have made better disposition of 433 white soldiers and 40 Indian scouts, or who could not have disarmed 118 Indians encumbered with 250 women and children."[29]

Meanwhile, Forsyth's suspension from command had angered the officer corps. Responding to pressure, the Harrison administration made a partial about-face. General Schofield notified Miles that the president had not intended "at this time in the midst of a campaign any further inquiry than you yourself could make without the necessity of a court, the purpose being simply to determine whether any officer had been so derelict in duty as to make it necessary to relieve him from command." As Miles read Schofield's wire, he doubtless realized that Harrison hoped for a tidy solution to the Forsyth case. The board of inquiry obliged on January 13, when it criticized the colonel's troop dispositions but absolved him of having disobeyed orders.[30]

Rather than placate his brother officers and the president by allowing the matter to die a natural death, Miles revived the controversy when he reconvened the board to hear General Brooke's testimony. On January 18, after questioning Brooke, the board amended its findings. Forsyth had disobeyed Miles's order on November 23 to hold the Indians "at safe distance" and "guard against surprise or treachery." In his defense, Forsyth testified that General Brooke, in his presence, had admitted to Miles that as the dispatch had been marked "confidential" he had not passed the order to Forsyth! Nevertheless, the board concluded that Miles's November 23 directive had also been "embodied" in a general order issued to all units of Brooke's command at Pine Ridge Agency, which included "Colonel James W. Forsyth, 7th Cavalry." Major Kent and Captain Baldwin, undoubtedly urged on by Miles, thus stretched their interpretation of the general order to censure Forsyth for disobedience.[31]

On the sensitive issue of the death of noncombatants, Kent and Baldwin agreed that "the fact that several women and children were killed and wounded could be ascribed only to the fault of the Indians themselves, and force of unavoidable and unfortunate circumstances." However, more than just "several" unarmed Indians fell at Wounded Knee. On the night of December 29, agency Indians carried some casualties from the battlefield, making an exact count of the dead and wounded Sioux impossible. A civilian contractor collected 146 frozen corpses at the site of the fighting and billed the government $292 for burial of the bodies. He identified the victims as eighty-four men and boys, forty-four women, and eighteen children. In addition, fifty-one wounded Indians were brought into the hospital at Pine Ridge, seven of whom later died. The death toll continued to mount. Three weeks after the tragic event, Miles noted, "Every day we hear of poor women, little girls and boys and children found dead and frozen to the ground, or crawling over the prairie, for a distance of one hundred miles north and south." Army casualties included one officer and twenty-four troops killed, with four officers and thirty-three enlisted men wounded; two civilians were wounded as well.[32]

Miles's attempt to censure Forsyth for the bloodletting was widely condemned in army circles. Leading New York newspapers noted that the criticism seemed "to be directed against the policy of relieving an officer during the progress of a campaign instead of waiting until the troubles are settled." Miles's action reminded one officer of the early years of the Civil War, "When every officer with an independent command had not only an enemy in front of him, but a court-martial behind him." Forsyth's removal from command, another officer observed, held up "a warning finger to every colonel in the little army around Pine Ridge, to tell them that the death of each Sioux must be explained." A correspondent with the troops at the Sioux agency confirmed, "The announcement of the suspension of Colonel Forsyth came like a flash and created amazement in some minds. Official mouths are closed to all inquiries on the subject."[33]

Miles wrote to his wife that "my enemies have taken up his [Forsyth's] case and propose to attack me on that score. If they wish to support the most abominable criminal military blunder and a horrible massacre of women and children I am ready to meet them on that ground." Miles's enemies were not alone in supporting Forsyth. On January 7, 1891, less than two months before his death, General Sherman wrote his niece, Mary Miles, to urge her husband "to so act that never again will the Sioux dare to disturb the progress of this country. The more he kills now, the less he will have to do later." If Forsyth had been relieved "because some squaws were killed, somebody had made a mistake, for squaws have been killed in every Indian war . . . in a fight the coolest man cannot distinguish female from male."[34]

Elaine Goodale, supervisor of education at the Pine Ridge Agency, challenged the proposition that the troops were unable to distinguish noncombatants from hostiles at Wounded Knee. After talking with survivors of the fight, she told the Deadwood *Times,* "There is no doubt that the majority of women and children had no thought of anything but flight. They were pursued up the ravines and shot down indiscriminately by the soldiers." Although Goodale conceded that some of the killing had been unavoidable, she nonetheless believed that in many instances the soldiers had intentionally shot down women and children. She found it particularly disturbing that the "irresponsible action of one hot-headed [Indian] youth" should have triggered "a general and indiscriminate slaughter of the unarmed and helpless."[35]

Eyewitness accounts given long after the event stressed that many of the deaths at Wounded Knee had occurred not during the confusion of battle but after shooting from the Indian side had died down. Once opposition had ceased, Forsyth should have ordered an immediate cease-fire and made his officers and noncommissioned officers restrain their men.[36]

In fact the undisciplined behavior of the soldiers partly reflected the low regard in which the general public held Indians. As details of the fight became known, for example, the Deadwood *Times* gloated over the Indian dead: "Among the 'good Indians' was Big Foot himself, dead as a smelt." The reporter urged the troops to "give no quarter, but kill all prisoners." "Why," he asked, ". . . should we spare even a semblance of an Indian? Wipe them from the face of the earth."[37]

In the same spirit, few soldiers or civilians supported Miles's efforts to censure Forsyth. After reviewing the findings of the board of inquiry and other reports, General Schofield advised Secretary of War Proctor on February 4, 1891, "The conduct of the Seventh Cavalry, under very trying circumstances, was characterized by excellent discipline, and in many cases, by great forbearance." Eight days later the secretary endorsed Schofield's recommendation with the notation: "Colonel Forsyth will resume command." Later that month Proctor privately expressed the hope that the "little family disturbance" growing out of Wounded Knee would soon subside.[38]

Secretary Proctor's decision to exonerate Forsyth may have been based more on expediency than on the merits of the case. The *New York Times* revealed that the secretary had become very annoyed when both Miles's and Forsyth's reports on Wounded Knee appeared in the newspapers. He had been "particularly anxious" to keep the documents from the public, "lest they might lead to criticism of his department and the management of the Indian campaign." When questioned about the leak, Col. Chauncey McKeever admitted that he had allowed a reporter to see the dispatches. Newspapers later identified McKeever as the officer who had earlier floated the groundless rumors about Miles's presidential ambitions.[39]

Since McKeever had intrigued against Miles in 1886 and again in 1890, it is not surprising that the *New York Times* portrayed the two officers as "bitter enemies," but the source of their enmity is not known. McKeever's motive in another scheme that backfired is readily apparent. As the Wounded Knee controversy attracted attention, McKeever tried to arrange the forced retirement of Brig. Gen. John C. Kelton, who had been seriously ill, so that he might replace him as adjutant general of the army. On Kelton's very first day back on duty, he had McKeever's desk moved into an office already crowded with clerks, assigned him trivial tasks, and appointed another assistant adjutant general to take his place.[40]

Meanwhile, from his field headquarters at Pine Ridge, Miles tried to restore confidence among the agency Indians and bring in the remaining dissidents. His task became easier as adequate food supplies reached the reservation and army officers known and trusted by the Sioux replaced some of the civilian agents. Miles also sent out runners with his promise that Indians who returned to their agencies would be treated fairly. Sioux leaders who had surrendered to Miles after earlier outbreaks knew that he kept his word.[41]

At the same time, Miles employed his troops effectively to impress upon the dissidents the futility of further resistance. "Instead of concentrating the troops in a huddled mass in the center of the camp as Gen. Brooks [*sic*] had them," a correspondent of the *Washington Evening Star* reported, Miles "has thrown them out into permanent picket lines upon the top of that ridge that encircles the agency valley." Miles thus increased the visible presence of his troops, who dominated the reservation below. Troops under General Brooke and Col. Eugene A. Carr cautiously pushed the Ghost

Dancers back to Pine Ridge, and messengers warned that "they must decide whether the military should be their friend or their enemy."[42]

The policy of persuasion backed by force proved successful. On January 11 Miles notified the War Department that the Indians were on the first leg of their trek back to the Pine Ridge Agency. Four days later, approximately four thousand Sioux passed along White Clay Creek to a campsite less than a half mile from the agency. Cavalry and infantry guarded the path as a two-mile column of Indians passed. Many of the Indians were on foot or rode in wagons; others used travois, while some of the mounted braves drove the huge Sioux pony herd into the camp. From the crest of a hill just to the north of the agency, artillerymen stood by their guns, ready to bring them to bear on the village below.[43]

On the fourteenth, Miles arranged the details of the surrender with a delegation of chiefs who came in to parley. The following day, he told a *New York Herald* correspondent that the Sioux leaders had agreed "to have the different bands gather up their arms and turn them in, which they are now doing." Kicking Bear, whom Miles considered the leader of the Ghost Dancers, was the first to surrender his rifle on the morning of the fifteenth. Miles predicted that "others of the same character will follow."

Unlike at Wounded Knee, the responsibility for collecting weapons rested with the chiefs, who were expected to control their followers and arrest anyone who broke the peace. Clerks recorded the name of each Indian who turned in a weapon, so that he would be reimbursed when the pistol or rifle was sold. As a good-will gesture, Miles delivered to the Sioux hundreds of pounds of sugar and coffee, plus several thousand pounds of flour. Allowing the chiefs to disarm their young men precluded a confrontation with the military, but it may also have encouraged some dissidents to conceal their arms. Miles admitted to the *Herald* reporter, "Of course many of the young men will hold back and some may cache their guns, but I believe the disarming will be complete." Miles later reported that the four thousand Sioux had given up fewer than two hundred rifles.[44]

A correspondent for *Harper's Weekly* who remained at Pine Ridge after the surrender stated that at one point Miles had considered the Ghost Dance religion "merely a cloak for the plot which was to have burst when the grass got green"; at that time the lives of hundreds of settlers living in isolated areas could easily have been "snuffed out." However, the issue of a spring uprising was mere conjecture, and in any event the Sioux Ghost Dance had thrown into bold relief the plight of the hungry Indians at the agencies. Miles's skill in suppressing the outbreak certainly prevented the tragedy at Wounded Knee from erupting into a full-scale war. Col. George B. Sanford, an eyewitness to the surrender of the Sioux, later stated that Miles was "the most ambitious officer" that he had encountered in the army. He quickly added, however, that Miles's "cool and judicious conduct" had saved untold lives during the Messiah outbreak.[45]

As the situation around Pine Ridge became more relaxed, the Deadwood *Times,* which less than a month before had advocated a policy of extermination, praised Miles "for his humane treatment of these poor, outraged and misled savages." The Indians had been driven "into a revolt against the authority of the government through the miserable action of an Indian policy, the thieving propensities of government contractors, and the troublesome conduct of self-interested squaw men." Obviously, the editor considered the Sioux troubles a thing of the past.[46]

On January 21, 1891, the thirty-five hundred troops who had participated in the Wounded Knee campaign paraded in a grand review at the Pine Ridge Agency. Miles, mounted on a pitch-black horse, surveyed the display from atop a small elevation. In place of an army overcoat he wore a fur-trimmed greatcoat—perhaps the same garment first noticed by the Sioux in 1876 when they named him "Bear Coat." An admiring correspondent described Miles as "the idol of the Indian fighters." If the reporter correctly gauged the feelings of the troops, it was a fitting climax to the campaign.

Miles long remembered the parade at the Pine Ridge Agency. "The scene was weird and in some respects desolate," he recalled twenty years later, "yet it was fascinating to me—possibly on account of the jubilant spirit occasioned by the reflection that one more Indian war had been closed." At first he watched the maneuvers quietly. But he began to stir when Col. Eugene A. Carr, one of the few field-grade officers who may have surpassed even Miles's demanding standards, passed at the head of the Sixth Cavalry. Carr had earned the Medal of Honor during the Civil War, and three state legislatures had bestowed votes of thanks upon him in the Indian wars. Nine years older than Miles, and a West Point graduate, the colonel apparently had found his niche in life commanding a regiment.[47]

Miles showed even greater interest when Maj. Guy V. Henry and the Ninth Cavalry approached. The black troopers had distinguished themselves the day following the fighting at Wounded Knee Creek. After an overnight march of eighty-five miles, highlighted by an Indian attack on his wagon train, Henry received word that the Sioux had trapped the Seventh Cavalry in a valley about six miles distant. Rousing his exhausted cavalrymen in the afternoon, Henry galloped to the scene and drove the Indians from the high ground, enabling Col. James Forsyth to withdraw from his vulnerable position. In a note to Forsyth, Henry deprecated his part in the so-called Drexel Mission fight, but later he candidly admitted to General Schofield that the Ninth had "assisted in getting the 7th out of a bad place."[48]

As the black troops marched from the field, the lively strains of "Garry Owen" announced the Seventh Cavalry. With Forsyth temporarily relieved of command, Maj. Samuel M. Whitside led the regiment. When Whitside waved toward Miles, the general could barely contain his enthusiasm. His displeasure with its commander had not lessened his fondness for the Seventh, which dated back to 1869, when he and Mary Miles were close friends of George and Elizabeth Custer at Fort Hays.[49]

This massive exhibition, conducted in the middle of nowhere, attracted a large audience. Indians from Pine Ridge viewed the display from the hills surrounding the agency; they had pulled hoods over their heads to protect them from frigid winds. The hills funneled icy gusts into the valley, kicking up dust clouds that occasionally obscured the marching units. After a long wagon train and the ambulance corps had rumbled past the commanding general, and the last soldier passed in review, an awesome quiet settled over the field. Although the curtain had fallen on the final act of the Indian wars, some in the audience could not tear themselves away from the suddenly empty, windswept stage. Glancing up, a reporter noted that "the sullen and suspicious Brules were still standing like statues on the crests of the hills."[50]

Although General Miles had brought the Ghost Dance campaign to a successful conclusion, he found little pleasure in his victory. Instead of praise he faced discord and grumbling in the officer corps for removing Forsyth from command. But Miles remained steadfast in his belief that Forsyth should be censured. Writing to his wife on January 15, 1891, he pronounced the colonel's action a "most abominable, criminal military blunder and a horrible massacre of women and children." Twenty-six years later he still maintained this view. In a letter written on behalf of the Sioux survivors, Miles described Forsyth's conduct as "most reprehensible" and "the whole affair as most unjustifiable and worthy of the severest condemnation."[51]

In the eyes of the officer corps, Miles paid a high price for his action against Forsyth. According to the *Army and Navy Journal,* he had violated what had been the unwritten "rule of exemption." The rule specified that no matter what the enterprise "no blasting of reputations honestly and previously established, would follow a gallant and faithful discharge of duty, even though mistakes might be made." Miles had challenged this self-serving "rule," and his brother officers gave him no quarter. Instead of censure, the *Journal* urged that commendations be extended to Forsyth and the Seventh Cavalry for their "sound thrashing" of the "bloody Sioux." This statement suggests that Miles was out of step with the reactionary thinking of his contemporaries, and that he had dared to propose new ways of treating the Indians. It also suggests that students of the Indian wars who simply attribute Miles's unpopularity in the army during this period to "unattractive personality traits" should consider a broader view of the break of the controversial commander with his brother officers during the Wounded Knee campaign.[52]

Although Miles had to contend with a hostile clique within the army, many others admired him, especially the enlisted men. In 1894, when he took command of the Military Department of the East, with headquarters at Governors Island, the *New York Times* reviewed his career. The reporter noted that "Miles had the personal equipment of the commander, as well as the mental attributes, for he was tall and graceful, and with a manner that would have compelled obedience had it not been a willing subject of his personal magnetism." The author of this biographical sketch added that the general "was popular with the soldier, and he is revered today by members of his old commands as an officer who was just and fearless." At odds with current belief, the newspaper also declared that his "promotion was not an example of personal favoritism. It came after brave deeds and daring performances in actual battle."[53]

The general public also held Miles in high regard. In 1896 funds were raised by popular subscription to present Miles with an impressive home at 1734 N Street in northwest Washington, D.C. During that same year, Harvard University showed its appreciation of Miles by awarding him college honors, as did Brown University in 1901. Although the public apparently held Miles in high regard, except for these gestures of appreciation, little evidence of this esteem for him can actually be documented.[54]

– CHAPTER 11 –

From Command in Chicago to Commanding General of the Army

FOLLOWING THE SURRENDER of the Ghost Dancers on January 15, 1891, Miles enjoyed a tranquil year as commanding general of the Department of the Missouri until he was roused by a false alarm. War fever began to smolder after Chilean seamen killed an American sailor from the cruiser *Baltimore* during a barroom brawl in Valparaiso. In December, as relations between the two nations remained heated, Miles received orders to report to Washington.[1]

After questioning a "prominent" officer at Jefferson Barracks in Saint Louis, a reporter warned that the call for Miles indicated that the administration was preparing for a war with Chile. His source explained that after Miles received his first Western assignment, "it is fact that he has never been summoned to Washington unless it was to be given a command of which fighting was expected."[2] Although the furor ended after Chile agreed to pay reparations, the public's perception of Miles as a man of action received a boost from the press coverage.

In 1894 Miles received a call to arms that would again blazon his name in headlines. Pullman workers, recently supported by the American Railway Union, had been on strike in Chicago since May 11. On July 2, while on leave in New York, Miles received orders to return to his headquarters in Chicago.

Instead, Miles rushed to the capital, and on the evening of July 2 he hurried to a White House conference attended by the president, Secretary of State Walter Gresham, Secretary of War Daniel S. Lamont, Attorney General Richard Olney, and John M. Schofield, the commanding general. All withheld judgment after Miles suggested that conditions in Chicago did not yet warrant the use of federal troops.[3]

Miles had silent allies in Gresham and Lamont, both of whom privately agreed with the general's position. Cleveland had not yet made up his mind about calling out the regulars, hesitating because he believed that the press had exaggerated the seriousness of the situation. Those who opposed Miles's view included Schofield and Olney. The attorney general, who as a lawyer in Massachusetts had represented a number of railroads, hoped to persuade the president to use federal troops to restrain the strikers.[4]

By July 2 the strikers had demonstrated their strength by stripping trains of their crews, thus bringing railroad traffic in Chicago to a virtual standstill for the second day in a row. The city, however, remained quiet. Furthermore, if trouble did develop, John P. Altgeld, the governor of Illinois, could order units of the state militia into Chicago. The state troops had already proven their effectiveness in breaking up demonstrations at Cairo, Danville, and Decatur.[5]

Following the White House conference, which ended at midnight, Miles returned to the Shoreham Hotel for his mail before retiring for the night at Senator John Sherman's home. The next morning he met with Olney and Lamont at the attorney general's office. Here Olney instructed Miles about the federal injunction authorized by the president, at his insistence, just the day before. This court order was characterized in the press as a "veritable dragnet" because a broad interpretation of its provisions would permit the arrest of any striker.[6]

After the injunction had been served, strikers who refused to obey it would be arrested by marshals or their deputies. Miles would be responsible for the protection of government officials carrying out this provocative duty. To ensure their safety, the general received authorization to order his troops into Chicago as soon as he believed that they were needed.[7]

After Miles left Olney's office, in time to catch the 11:30 A.M. train to Chicago, the attorney general received a telegram from Federal Marshal John W. Arnold that accelerated the pace of federal intervention. Arnold informed Olney that on the day before, the second, he futilely tried to disperse a mob that had used railroad cars to block tracks at Blue Island, a town outside the city limits of Chicago. Unaccountably, although the disturbances did not continue on the third, the marshal used the Blue Island incident to request United States troops "in the city." He contended that only the regulars would be able to "procure the passage of mail trains" and to "enforce the orders of the court."[8]

As Miles's train clattered toward Chicago, Olney, armed with the marshal's telegram, convinced the president to call out the troops. Accordingly, at 4:00 P.M. Schofield wired instructions for Col. Robert E. A. Crofton's 15th Infantry, garrisoned at nearby Fort Sheridan, to move into the city. Crofton's force, augmented by neighboring units, was "to execute the orders and processes of the United States Court to prevent the obstruction of the United States mails, and generally to enforce the faithful execution of the laws of the United States."[9]

Miles arrived in Chicago at 11:30 A.M. on the fourth, less than two hours after Colonel Crofton had completed his troop dispositions. These did not please Schofield, who wanted the regulars concentrated at Chicago's Lake Front Park, rather than scattered about the city as Crofton had done. Unfortunately, Schofield barely alluded to his intention in his preliminary movement order. Only in Schofield's autobiography did he point out that by remaining at the park, the regulars "could most readily have protected the sub-treasury, custom-house, post-office, and other United States property, and also have acted in a formidable body at any other point where their services might properly have been required."[10]

The first gathering of unruly crowds occurred shortly after federal troops were posted within the city. For example, the presence of two companies of infantry supported by artillery and cavalry in the stockyards attracted more than five thousand men, women, and children. According to the *Chicago Daily News,* because they so "resent the interference of United States troops" crowds blocked a Swift and Company meat train. It took a bloodless bayonet charge by 190 infantrymen to free the train from strike sympathizers, but it could not leave the yard because of a locked gate.[11]

Despite the stockyard incident, Miles optimistically told a reporter that he thought "the backbone of the strike is broken." "Who can stand against the United States?" he reasoned. "The strikers will soon realize their position and the trouble will be over. Five companies are now on their way here to assist in maintaining order." The newspaperman indicated, however, that the men from Fort Sheridan had not intimidated the bystanders when he asked, "Will the soldiers respond with bayonets or bullets to a repetition of the taunts, jeers and curses heaped on them yesterday?" Miles answered that his men were "too well disciplined" to "pay attention to such things."[12]

Schofield had similar confidence in the regulars. Aware of the bayonet attack in the stockyards, he declared, "Our boys are showing remarkably good judgment. They are coolheaded and do not intend to shed blood without cause. I think the battle from now on will be fought out in the courts." Although Schofield would not be disappointed in his faith in the regulars, he was wrong about the battleground.[13]

At virtually the same time that Miles gave assurances that there would be no more disorder, a crowd in the stockyards began to overturn railroad cars and burn switches. The situation became so threatening that in the evening Miles anxiously wired the War Department that "unless the mobs are dispersed by the action of the police, or they are fired upon by United States troops, more trouble may be expected as the mob is increasing and becoming more defiant." The harried general then came to the crux of the matter: "Shall I give the order for troops to fire on mob obstructing trains?"[14]

Schofield reminded Miles that "The mere preservation of peace and good order in the city is, of course, the province of the city and state authorities." When he brought up the ill-advised deployment of the troops from Fort Sheridan, Miles responded that Colonel Crofton had acceded to the wishes of the U.S. marshal. Miles added that as the situation worsened on the fifth, he unwittingly anticipated Schofield's order as he began, with a few exceptions, to reassemble his command in the park. Infantry from Fort Brady, Michigan, and Fort Leavenworth, Kansas, had already reinforced the armed camp now forming on the shores of Lake Michigan.[15]

On July 6 early-morning strollers along Chicago's Columbus Drive gathered to peer at the cantonment that had sprung up overnight. Just south of the imposing statue of Columbus, sentries patrolled the perimeter of a tent city in which stacks of polished carbines glistened in the sun. In an adjacent field about one hundred corralled horses ignored the growing crowd of excited spectators. Colonel Crofton established his headquarters almost within the shadow of the statue while a telegraph wire strung into a nearby tent identified his communications center.[16]

On the seventh, the regulars assigned to the stockyards welcomed a large contingent of infantry and cavalry who would share their duties, while a new tent city blossomed on the grounds of the federal building facing Clark

Street. This outpost made it unlikely that the $15 million in coin stored in the subtreasury building would be scooped up by looters. Miles, whose command would peak at 1,936 United States troops on July 10, established his headquarters in the Pullman Building. A telegraph wire running into a fourth-floor window kept him in touch with the units in the field.

Although Miles's command would grow rapidly, he admitted to a reporter that his men were limited by their orders. They could only take action "with the United States marshals, and their endeavors to enforce the peace." The reporter observed that when asked a sensitive question, Miles "doesn't sit still and look out of the window. . . . Straightway he fires off an answer of some kind or other as nonchalantly as if he were touching off a little six-pound cannon." This comment confirms a transformation in Miles's relationship with the press. Following all of his frontier campaigns, through the capture of Geronimo's band, Miles spoke only to a handful of reporters; but by the winter of 1890–91, as he sought to round up the Ghost Dancers, the general began to speak freely to correspondents on the scene.[17]

Frederick Remington, the noted correspondent and artist, pointed out a drawback in employing regulars on strike duty. While covering events in Chicago for *Harper's Weekly*, he argued, "Our statesmen fail to understand that soldiers are not police, and that police work deteriorates troops. Soldiers only know their trade—that's fighting." Unlike the police, soldiers "never study law or how to be diplomatically nice on occasion. They should never be made to associate with a mob except after their manner, which is to get strategically near enough and then shoot."[18]

When the attorney general read newspaper accounts of the situation in Chicago, he could not restrain himself. Indignantly, Olney blurted out that "if Miles would do less talking to newspapers and more shooting at strikers he would come nearer to fulfilling his mission on earth and earning his pay."[19]

It appeared Miles might fulfill the attorney general's desire for bloodshed on July 6, as authorities in Chicago faced the two most trying days of the strike. Throughout the entire period of lawlessness, damage to railroad property would never exceed $4,000 in a single day, except on the sixth, when the bill came to $340,000. The first report of civilian casualties also occurred on the sixth, when a railroad detective shot four men as a mob overturned freight cars on the Illinois Central line. The following day, twenty-six civilians were reported killed or injured. From the eighth to the fourteenth, a total of ten civilians would be listed as casualties, but this did not include fourteen railroad employees who were counted in a separate category.[20]

The dramatic decrease in violence may be partially attributed to Chicago's mayor, John P. Hopkins, who gave orders on July 6 for the city's police force to crush the mobs. When reports later surfaced that Miles had pressured the mayor to take this action, the general set the record straight in a letter of clarification requested by Hopkins. As rioting in Chicago intensified without what the general believed to be an adequate response by local officials, he admitted only that he reminded the mayor that "the authorities in Washington expected that the municipal and state governments would, to the extent of their power, preserve the public peace and order in the city."[21]

As the police force struck out more aggressively against rioters, they were heartened by the presence of six regiments of militia ordered into the city by Governor Altgeld on July 6. Although pleased that the governor had taken action, Miles faulted the operations of the militia because he had not been "apprised even of their location or any of their movements." During the course of their stay in Chicago, the five thousand militiamen were responsible for killing five people and wounding sixteen.[22]

Miles had a hand in quelling the disorders by throwing the shadow of the regulars across the path of the rioters. Since the railroads in Chicago bore virtually the entire brunt of the mobs' wrath, the eight companies of infantry Miles placed in the city's six major depots on July 7 would now be within striking distance of the most likely trouble spots. Furthermore, while their original mission to assist marshals remained unchanged, he finally instructed his command: "If any acts of hostility are committed, such as firing into a train or trains, assaulting them with rocks or pieces of iron, or throwing stones, the assault shall be repelled by the use of firearms." The *Chicago Daily News* warned its readers to heed the threat since the 15th Infantry "is a regiment of Indian fighters and when they shoot, they aim their rifles in the direction of a man's anatomy where his breast is located. The men are good shots and generally come pretty close to the mark they have in view."[23]

According to Miles's plan, the infantry who were detailed to the depots would board special trains along with U.S. deputy marshals and track crews. Although these troops were never tested within the city, Miles intended that when trouble brewed, his men would "fight their way out and back, thus clearing the lines of communication of rioters and obstructions and opening the blockade of the entire railway system."[24]

Even the president played a role in dispersing the Chicago mobs when he stripped away the excuse of being just curious bystanders. On July 8 Cleveland issued a proclamation condemning those in "unlawful obstructions, combinations and assemblages" as "public enemies." Because of "the stern necessities that confront" troops operating against mobs, the president advised all Chicagoans "to abide at their homes, or at least not to be found in the neighborhood of riotous assemblages."[25]

Miles commented to reporters that Cleveland's "proclamation is a warning to those people who have been composing the mobs of the past ten days that they must cease their disturbances and let the property of the railroads alone." He warned, "The time for temporizing is past. That is what the President means and the people at large should understand it."[26]

The resolve shown by the combination of forces arrayed against the strikers caused them to waver, then scatter. Trouble subsided so quickly that by July 12 Miles could tell a reporter, "We have had no demand for troops and have moved none up to this hour. Our report shows trains are beginning to move with more regularity and without interference by lawless persons." After another newsman visited Miles's headquarters that day, he compared the atmosphere of the Pullman Building with "the quietude of a country church."[27]

Railroad traffic in Chicago had so returned to normal by July 19 that all the federal troops were withdrawn from the city. With the exception of the 9th Infantry, which returned to its garrison on Lake Ontario, at Sackett's Harbor, New York, the regulars began a twenty-four-mile march, under a blazing sun, north to Fort Sheridan. At Sheridan they were able to participate in uncommon but invaluable large-scale fall maneuvers while waiting in vain for a resurgence of labor unrest in Chicago.[28]

Labor leaders had naturally protested the use of the United States army in Chicago. In a letter to President Cleveland, Patrick J. Dalton, Chicago's master craftsman of the Knights of Labor, called for the removal of the troops from the city because when they were ordered in, "there was neither foreign enemies or domestic insurrection against the constituted authority of the government, at a time when the local civic forces were able to keep the peace, and even the state militia was not needed nor called into action." Although the regulars had been unwanted by labor, uninvited by the local authorities, and unauthorized to do little more than protect federal property, they arose above those trying circumstances to perform with distinction. Miles may have gone too far when he claimed that these troops "saved this country from a serious rebellion," but, as one newspaper observed, "It is impossible not to admire the discipline of the troops of the Regular Army, who seem to succeed in moving the delayed trains without either using or suffering violence."[29]

Unfortunately, an incident in Hammond, Indiana, just across the state line from Chicago, bloodied the outstanding record of the Department of the Missouri. On Saturday night, July 7, some residents of Hammond attacked the rail yards. They roughed up a train crew and a yardman, tore up tracks, upended from twenty-five to thirty boxcars, and only the prompt response of the fire department saved a Pullman car that they had set afire. The following morning, a special train commanded by Capt. (Bvt. Maj.) Wilson T. Hartz, carrying thirty-five men from Company D, 15th Infantry, arrived in time to rescue a train that had just fallen into the hands of a mob.[30]

The *Lake Country News,* published each Thursday in Hammond, printed a detailed account of what happened on July 8, although it understandably favored the locals in their confrontation with the federal troops. For instance, when a reporter mentioned Hammond, he deprecated the lawlessness that occurred there on the seventh by remarking that it was a "naughty, naughty city." The newspaper probably hit the mark, however, when it reported that "the citizens were indignant at the arrival of U.S. troops."

When the military train pulled into the railroad yard, Hammond's mayor, Patrick Reilley, tried to convince Captain Hartz that his troops were not needed. Since a crowd could plainly be seen swarming over a train stalled nearby, the captain ignored the mayor's plea to withdraw and ordered his men "to 'shoot to kill' any person who might offer to molest or interfere." The mob prudently withdrew, allowing the train to continue on its way, and no further confrontations took place until 4:30 P.M.

A crowd had gathered around a partially burnt Pullman car left standing in a distant part of the yard. All eyes were focused on the detached

Pullman car, being rocked back and forth with ropes in an effort to overturn it, when the special troop train rounded a curve and crept toward the mob. Without warning, shots were fired from the approaching train, scattering the bystanders. When the train reached the Pullman car, three soldiers climbed down from the engine and, according to the *Lake County News,* "fired deliberately into the crowd of spectators."

The soldiers mortally wounded Charles Fleischer, a packing-house carpenter, who had entered the crowd to find his child. They also shot a twenty-three-year-old cannery worker in the left leg and slightly wounded a few others. The *News* protested that "The worst features of the shooting was that every person was an innocent spectator. . . . At the first shots the crowd ran pell-mell and there was no excuse for the additional shots fired."[31]

The *News* neglected to provide details of the aftermath of the fatal confrontation, merely commenting that if "there had been arms at hand a bloody riot would have followed." In fact, according to another local paper, the *Crown Point Register* of Lake County, Indiana, the rioters "soon rallied and would probably have annihilated the little band had not reinforcements arrived from Chicago." The *Chicago Daily News* confirmed that following shouts from the crowd of "Get your guns boys," the soldiers were forced to defend themselves inside a passenger coach until three companies of regulars came to their relief.[32]

Distraught because of the lethal tactics of Captain Hartz's soldiers, two prominent townsmen feverishly composed a telegram informing Indiana's governor, Claude E. Matthews, that "Troops shooting down people promiscuously without provocation. . . . Please act quickly and use your own discretion." The governor responded by ordering sixteen companies of state militia, totaling eight hundred men, to Hammond. He also sought to bring the townsfolk to their senses, warning them that "Lawlessness and riot must be suppressed. Citizens obeying the law have nothing to fear. Resistance to national or state authority must be punished."[33]

Shortly after midnight on July 9, the War Department received Miles's initial report of disturbances in Hammond, in which he overestimated the number of civilian casualties. Officials in Washington, who had kept abreast of developments in Indiana from a steady flow of news dispatches, referred to the press reports in order to downplay the seriousness of the incident. At the same time, they used the engagement to serve as a reminder of the new rules for the use of weapons announced by Miles the day before. After a conference at the War Department, a Chicago reporter explained that the "action of the troops at Hammond marks another phase of the exercise of military power—namely, the dispersal of mobs that obstruct the free passage of interstate and mail trains."[34]

Just two days after the Hammond incident, rumors of the administration's displeasure with Miles's generalship were so prevalent that Schofield took notice of them. He told correspondents that his maligned subordinate "has conducted himself in a manner entirely satisfactory. I do not tolerate any criticism of his course, and the President feels just as I do in this matter." This faint praise given on the eve of Miles's victory would be the only commendation he would receive for helping to restore order in Chicago.[35]

The Pullman strike naturally influenced Miles's thinking about disputes between employers and their employees. During Miles's brief stay in Washington, prior to his departure for Chicago, Matilda Gresham told her husband, the secretary of state, that "In his heart General Miles has a contempt for George M. Pullman, and his sympathies are with the masses." With the strike behind him, Miles lost his enthusiasm for the masses in general, but retained an appreciation for "the man who labors in any honest and honorable occupation." He advocated that to avoid "too much concentration in the cities," the working man should move to the countryside, on land made available through extensive irrigation projects.[36]

Mob violence in Chicago had soured Miles on the masses, especially those among the proletariat who were foreign born. Remington had reinforced the popular perception that most of those who were running rampant through the streets were immigrants when he described the rioters as a "malodorous crowd of anarchist foreign trash." Like the artist, the general publicly embraced xenophobia, advising workers to lobby for the closing of U.S. borders to "the vast hordes of cheap and degraded labor" flooding into the United States from Europe.[37]

Almost before railroad traffic had returned to normal in Chicago, the August issue of the *North American Review* publicized Miles's thoughts about labor disputes. It was in this article that he revealed his opinion of policies to reduce labor tensions in the future. The general also suggested how future strikes might be handled. Miles expected each level of government from local to national to utilize their "strong army" in order to insure "perfect security in life and property." Beyond this, he urged "American manhood to exert its principles." His countrymen should rally "Under the shadow and folds of 'Old Glory,'" willing to preserve law and order, rather than support "anarchy, secret conclaves, unwritten law, mob violence, and universal chaos under the red or white flag of socialism."[38]

A few months after Chicago had been swept clear of radicals, the retirement of Oliver O. Howard cleared the way for Miles to be named to the second highest office in the military hierarchy. On November 20, 1894, Miles assumed command of the Department of the East, and the next day, accompanied by his wife and two aides, Capts. Francis Michler and Marion Maus, he boarded a ferry at the Battery in order to inspect his new headquarters, located on Governors Island.

The *New York Times* applauded Miles's promotion, citing both "his intrepidity in the Civil War and his daring valor on the frontier." The general "was popular with the soldiers, and he is revered today by members of his old commands as an officer who was just and fearless."[39]

The late-fall weather cast a pall over Miles's moment of glory. He reflected the somber mood that washes over New York when a cold drizzle and a lowering sky dampen both body and soul. Rain prevented Fort Jay's garrison from honoring their new commander with a review, but as the fort's cannon saluted his arrival, Miles mentioned to a reporter, "It is very sad to me! The last time I was here I shook the hand of General Hancock, and I have not been here since."[40]

In this comment one glimpses the man shielded behind a New Englander's habitual reserve. Eight years had passed since Hancock's death, yet the sincerity of Miles' regard for his former corps commander is evident. Although Miles had difficulty expressing the bonds of loyalty that drew him toward officers who had earned their reputations on the battlefield, he could be found in their corner when they were targets of the military bureaucracy.

On July 19, 1892, for example, Col. Eugene A. Carr received a promotion to brigadier general, only to find that his achievement was tainted. When Schofield elevated Carr, he intended that he be retired before President Harrison left office in 1893. When Schofield informed Carr of the nature of his advancement, during a visit by the latter to the War Department on August 1, the new brigadier protested that "had I known of any such condition touching my promotion, I would not have accepted it."[41]

In January 1893 Schofield formally requested that Harrison retire Carr one year before he reached mandatory retirement age, by utilizing the provisions of an 1862 law. Schofield acknowledged that he wanted this done so that his friend, Col. William P. Carlin, could "be appointed Brigadier General and at once retired from active service." Miles unsuccessfully tried to check this plan by providing Carr with a recommendation, for any use "you can make." He wrote that from their shared experiences, "I know that you are physically and mentally qualified to command a Department or a large body of troops, and are one of the most competent Generals in the Army."[42]

The same year that Carr unwillingly left the service, the chief medical officer sought to deny Col. William R. Shafter command of a department because of his poor physical condition. Again Miles came to the aid of a battle-tested officer who had earned a Medal of Honor during the Civil War. Miles reminded the War Department that Shafter "has been tried under fire, and *not found wanting.*" He acknowledged what appeared to be the most significant complaint, that Shafter "has varicose veins," adding that "[I] am also aware that hundreds of other officers are similarly affected." Miles went on to cite Shafter's accomplishments despite his ailment, including service against the Sioux in 1890–91, when "he voluntarily went with his regiment and endured the hardships and exposure of the rigorous winter campaign in that climate." Although disappointed in this 1893 effort to support Shafter, Miles congratulated the colonel in 1896, when he received command of the Department of California."[43]

Although Miles spent less than a year in New York, he considered his time there "the pleasantest in my military life." Besides the attractions of the city itself, the general enjoyed the company of prominent men. Miles soon found himself caught up in the city's social whirl; he joined the Lafayette Post of the Grand Army of the Republic, spoke at the Waldorf to members of the Grant Banquet Association, and appreciated the welcome given him by metropolitan-area army and navy officers at a reception in his honor at the United Service Club.[44]

In the spring of 1895, Miles inspected the major military installations in his department. One of his most satisfying moments came at Fort

McPherson, outside of Atlanta, where he enjoyed a visit with the relocated 5th Infantry. The tour provided grist for his annual report, in which Miles called for the modernization of the nation's coast defense installations.[45]

When Schofield retired on September 29, 1895, Miles fretted until October 2, when President Cleveland officially notified him that he now commanded the army. This office offered little satisfaction. After General Sherman assumed command, he had complained to his brother that his "office has been by law stripped of all the influence and prestige it possessed under Grant, and even in matters of discipline and army control I am neglected, overlooked, or snubbed."[46]

When Schofield succeeded Sheridan as commanding general, he recalled that the "condition of the War Department at that time was deplorable," which he attributed to Sheridan's poor health. His predecessor had been so ill with heart trouble that he had been unable to exercise any control over the department. After Schofield made administrative changes, he found that "things went much better, but it was at best only an armed truce, with everybody on board."[47]

The power of the general of the army had been stripped away by President Ulysses S. Grant's orders of March 26, 1869, and July 15, 1870. When the president asserted his authority to issue all orders regarding military matters, which he did through the secretary of war and adjutant general, the commanding general became a figurehead. If the senior officer of the army hoped to have any influence at all as an adviser to the president and secretary of war, he would need a diplomat's skill, which Miles lacked.[48]

The plain-spoken general found himself almost victimized by enemies within the capital even before he reached Washington. The *Army and Navy Journal* revealed that "It is undoubtedly the fact that a determined effort was made to prevent the assignment of Gen. Miles, for we know who were concerned in this attempt and, to some extent, the arguments used by them to accomplish this purpose." Unfortunately, the article left its readers in the dark about who was actually involved in the unsuccessful attempt to deny Miles the commanding general's office.[49]

Newspapers, which did not enjoy the *Journal*'s sources within the military sphere, could only speculate about why Miles had been slighted by the administration. The *New York Herald* disagreed with widespread stories that attributed the War Department's three-day delay "as a punishment to General Miles for publicly stating that he had been selected for this duty in advance of the official announcement." Although the *Herald*'s Washington correspondent insisted that the orders had been held up only until the commanding general's staff had been selected, Miles had released the news of his selection one week earlier, after hearing it from Lamont. Thus, the *Journal* claimed to have inside information about a clique opposed to Miles, but it also appears that the president had reason to reprove the general.[50]

After the formal publication of Miles's order, the administration received the applause of the *Army and Navy Journal.* The unofficial arbiter of the military profession ruled that the only basis for blackballing Miles would be for "incapacity," which "was impossible to truthfully urge in this instance." The *Times* believed that the stir would have no effect on Miles's tenure in office and predicted that he should "find his new duties entirely congenial. Gen. Miles has many friends in Washington, who are glad to know that he is now to occupy the lofty place which has been filled by so many officers, who, like himself, won distinction in the field."[51]

Following the snub from the administration, the secretary of war directly affronted Miles when Congress considered a bill to elevate him to lieutenant general. The *Herald* incorrectly assumed that he would receive this promotion in 1896, believing that even though Miles was a Republican, Cleveland, a Democrat, "would undoubtedly approve such a resolution in recognition of the gallant service the general has rendered in behalf of the United States." Miles, who had been identified as a Democrat in 1886, had apparently switched party allegiances in time to work for Senator John Sherman's nomination as the Republican candidate for president in 1892.[52]

In 1895, when the lieutenant general bill came before Congress, the House Military Committee had favorably reported the measure, and the *New York Times* explained that congressmen from both parties supported the measure because they considered "Gen. Miles as a representative of the volunteer soldier of the rebellion, and they wish to reward him accordingly. But Secretary of War Daniel S. Lamont convinced the Senate Military Committee to pigeonhole the proposal. According to the *Times,* Lamont argued that such a promotion should "be conferred only upon men who had rendered distinguished service like Grant, Sheridan, and Sherman; that whatever were Gen. Miles's services, they did not exceed in value those of many other officers equally distinguished, and that it was inadvisable, therefore, to single him out for such an honor." The secretary of war neglected to add that Grant, Sherman, and Sheridan each received further promotion from lieutenant general to the rank of four-star general of the army. President Cleveland, who had differences with Miles about both Geronimo and the pullman strike, overcame opposition from the Grand Army of the Republic and a majority of the House when he saw the Senate committee shelve the bill.[53]

Miles did not dwell on his inauspicious initiation as the commanding general, but almost immediately he began to lobby for a modern army. In 1896 he unsuccessfully urged Congress to increase the 25,000-man army to a minimum strength of one soldier for every 2,000 citizens. (For example, in 1890 the population of the United States was 62,947,714; this would justify an army of approximately 31,500 men.) He believed that the army, as one of the "pillars of the government," should grow as the nation grew. The following year, in his annual report, Miles again failed to shatter what he called the "crystallized" notion that the army should remain at the 25,000 limit.[54]

Miles met with more success in alerting Congress to the need for improving the nation's coastal defenses. As he later explained, he could only succeed after he convinced Congress that stone-and-brick fortifications that had cost millions during the Civil War could be devastated by modern guns; furthermore, the weapons in the forts, designed to repel wooden ships, had become obsolete.[55]

Miles had first campaigned for improvements in coastal defenses as commander of the Department of the Columbia in 1884. He continued the fight in 1890, when he commanded the Division of the Pacific, and again in 1895, when he took charge of the Department of the East. Now, as commanding general, he found himself in the perfect position to advance his cause once more. In order to make meaningful recommendations, Miles undertook an inspection of military installations in the Northeast that summer, then visited the Far West and Pacific Coast in the fall of 1896.[56]

While in the West, Miles went out of his way to visit posts scheduled to be closed, to assure himself that they had outlived their usefulness. The Harrison administration had begun a policy, continued by Cleveland's, of closing small outposts scattered about the West. The War Department found it more efficient to mobilize regiments stationed near cities, taking advantage of their excellent railroad facilities, rather than the time-consuming operation of calling in isolated units. The *New York Times* also cited the example of the military intervention in Chicago's railroad strike as a further benefit of this policy. Miles, however, felt compelled to dissociate the policy of concentrating units near cities from the advantage of a military presence during strikes. In his 1896 annual report, he protested against the "unwise argument" that found fault with establishing garrisons near urban areas "as a danger and menace to the laboring classes." Rather, he pointed out a particular benefit of basing troops in urban areas, that "in fact, the destruction of our great commercial and manufacturing cities would be a national disaster far more serious and appalling to the great masses of the laboring population than it would be to any other class of our people."[57]

In 1896, the Werner Company of Chicago published an unwieldly titled book, *Personal Recollections and Observations of General Nelson A. Miles, Embracing a Brief View of the Civil War; or, From New England to the Golden Gate, and the Story of His Indian Campaigns, with Comments on the Exploration, Development and Progress of Our Great Western Empire.* When the *Army and Navy Journal* reviewed this unique book, it explained that it was not "the purpose of the author to write his memoirs or a history, but to present rather a series of sketches suggested by his wide and varied experiences." Even a casual reader who browses through this book, with sketches by Frederick Remington, would realize that it was too ambitious, being part anthropological study, part autobiography, part history, and part travelogue. And a reviewer for the *New York Times* pointed out another flaw, one that is common in all of Miles's writings; he exhibits "a soldierly reticence that makes the reader wish for more details."[58]

Following Miles's tour, he put new life into the coast defense program, which had been initiated by Congress in response to an 1885 report issued by a board headed by Secretary of War William C. Endicott. The program began with good intentions, but in 1896 Miles regretfully pointed out that from 1888 to 1895, "the appropriations for both guns and fortifications were so limited as to practically paralyze the work for the construction of high- power guns and fortifications for the protection of our coast." By the following year, he could list a number of fortifications that had been modernized but were still inoperative because no troops were available to man the installations.

On the eve of war with Spain, Miles startled Congress with the news that three forts protecting Washington were "useless." Some lawmakers were wrong, however, in doubting the commanding general's claim that the army had no funds to purchase ammunition for Forts Monroe, Foote, and Washington. According to the *New York Times,* these congressmen thought that he "was over zealous to secure the adoption by Congress of his recommendations for increased appropriations for fortifications." Miles had, in fact, complained to Secretary of War Russell A. Alger about the lack of ammunition for seacoast batteries on January 20, 1898. The chief of ordnance, Brig. Gen. Daniel W. Webster, explained to the secretary that because of the small supply of available ammunition, "it has been the policy of the Department to retain the major portion of this ammunition at the arsenals, in order that it may be sent to any threatened point." In accordance with this ridiculous policy, "Within twenty four hours after the receipt of instructions at an arsenal, ammunition could be placed upon the cars and forwarded to any point desirable."[59]

In 1897 Miles availed himself of a wonderful opportunity to broaden his professional background when the War Department ordered him to observe the war between Greece and Turkey (a war in which Greece would be unsuccessful in its support of an uprising in Crete). He sailed on May 5 aboard the *Saint Paul,* which would arrive in Constantinople on May 19.[60]

The commanding general received a cordial welcome from the sultan, who gave his visitor permission to tour the front. But Miles's stay in Turkey was cut short by orders from the War Department to report to London by June 15, in order to attend Queen Victoria's Diamond Jubilee, commemorating her sixty-year reign. He left for Athens on the twenty-fifth in order to compare what he had seen of the Turkish army with the Greek forces. He found little worth mentioning after inspecting the Greek army and, under a truce flag, the battleground; however, following his visit, he relished the chance to visit Europe's armories.

Outside of Naples, Miles found the Armstrong cannon factory producing a field gun that he admired; and in Vienna, he heard that the Austrian government was about to produce a superior rifle that would replace the remarkably durable Mannlicher rifle. After arriving in London on June 15, and being very favorably impressed by every aspect of the jubilee, Miles visited the weapons factory at Enfield, which had already produced 717,000

Lee-Metford rifles for the empire's forces. Before leaving for the Continent, he also had a chance to tour the Maxim factory at Eynsford.[61]

Miles had shown an interest in developments in ordinance at least since the Nez Perce campaign, when he field-tested a steel Hotchkiss gun. At times his fascination with artillery brought him into slight risk. While Miles observed the test firing of a pneumatic high-explosive gun at Glen Cove, Long Island, in 1896, a premature detonation seriously injured a nearby onlooker.[62]

True to form, between studying the Waterloo battleground and troops in Russia, Germany, and France, Miles visited arms works at Spandau, the Krupp works at Essen, the Gruson works at Magdeburg, and the navy yards at Kiel. He returned to England, where he toured the Vickers works at Sheffield and Armstrong's at Newcastle upon Tyne, before boarding the *Saint Louis* on October 2, bound for New York.

In Europe, Miles had observed impressive military displays: a parade of 6,000 men in Rome, a naval review of 108 vessels manned by 38,000 sailors at Spithead, an encampment of 60,000 troops outside of Saint Petersburg, 120,000 soldiers conducting maneuvers near Frankfurt, and finally, a review of the entire 75,000 men in the French army at Saint-Quentin.

When Miles later reflected about this tour, he estimated that Europe had about four million men under arms, which he considered "a colossal burden upon the people." As an advocate of preparedness, however, he warned against "the danger of going to the other extreme, and by overconfidence, apathy, or indifference reach a degree of weakness that would tempt the ambitions or avarice of foreign powers." When Miles wrote those words in 1911, he could also have cited the chaotic experience in 1898, when an unprepared nation rushed into war with Spain.[63]

Miles as a young man, age twenty (1859). With limited formal education and no military training, Miles left his position as a clerk to enter the Union army as a lieutenant in 1861. He rose to general in chief of the army in 1895, and on June 6, 1900, Congress approved his promotion to lieutenant general. Courtesy of Chicago Historical Society.

Nelson Miles, age ten (1849). Elementary school classmate Patrick Brosnahan later recalled in an interview with the *Boston Sunday Post,* March 19, 1899, that "the study in which [Miles] seemed to take the most delight was fighting." Courtesy of the Chicago Historical Society.

Miles fought with the Second Corps. He was commissioned brigadier general of volunteers on June 9, 1864; on August 25, 1864, he was breveted major general of volunteers. Courtesy of the Bowdoin College Library.

Mary Miles. The marriage of Miles to Mary Hoyt Sherman on June 30, 1868, gave the young colonel access to Mary's uncles, Senator John Sherman and Gen. William Tecumseh Sherman. Courtesy of the Westminster, Massachusetts, Historical Society.

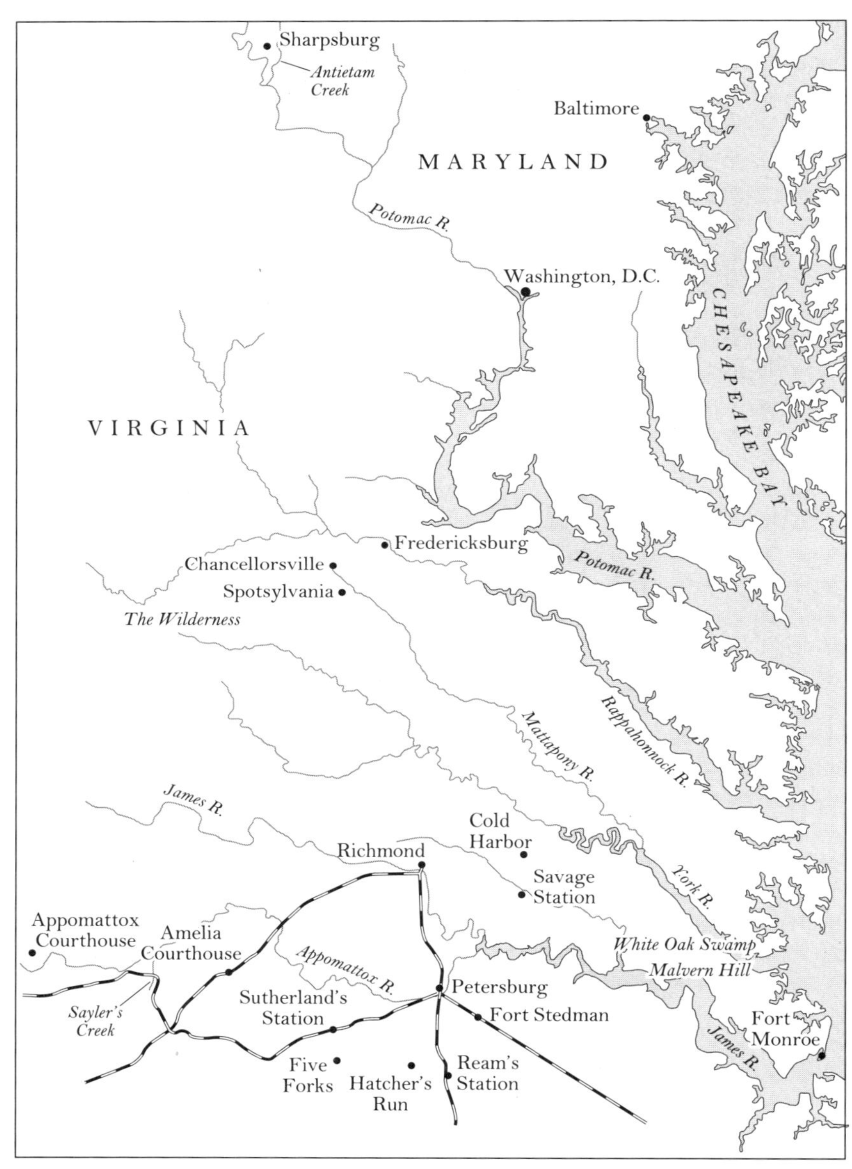

The Eastern Theater of the Civil War.
Miles fought in every major battle of the Army of the Potomac except Gettysburg.

Carroll Hall, Fort Monroe, Virginia (ca. 1885), where Miles served as jailer of Jefferson Davis, fallen president of the Confederate States of America. Courtesy of the Casement Museum, Fort Monroe, Virginia.

Chief Joseph of the Nez Percé Indians. Courtesy of the Washington State Historical Society.

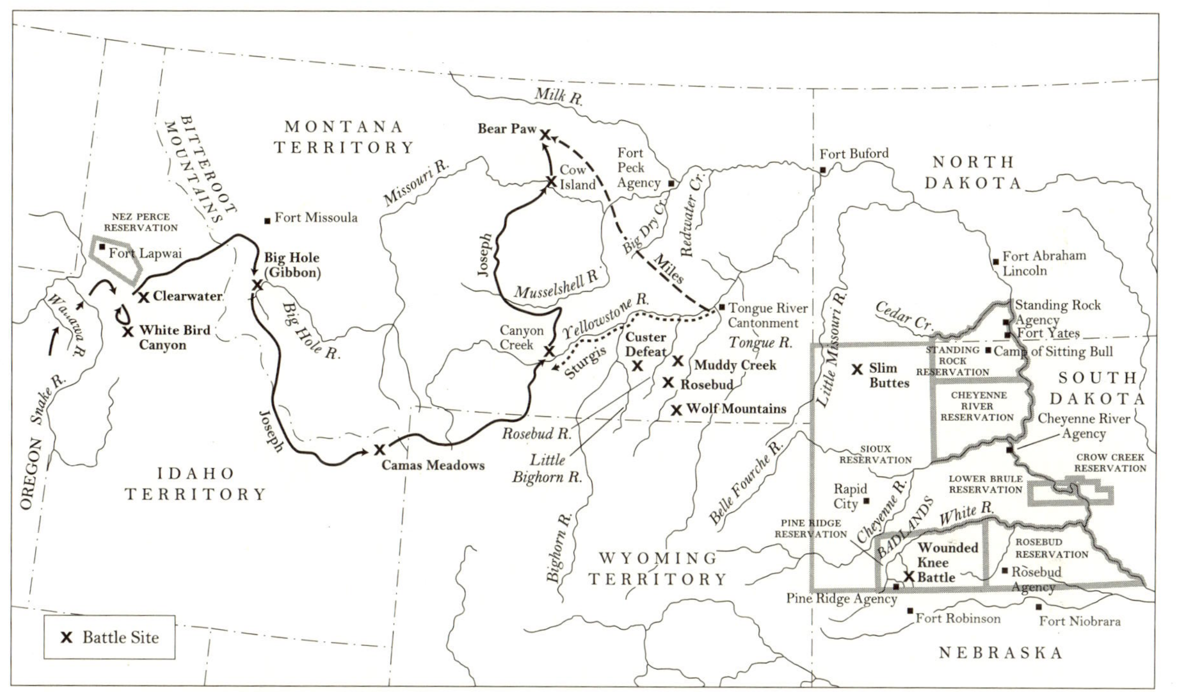

The Northern Plains.
Miles's Sioux and Nez Perce campaigns (1876–77) and the "Messiah" outbreak of 1890.

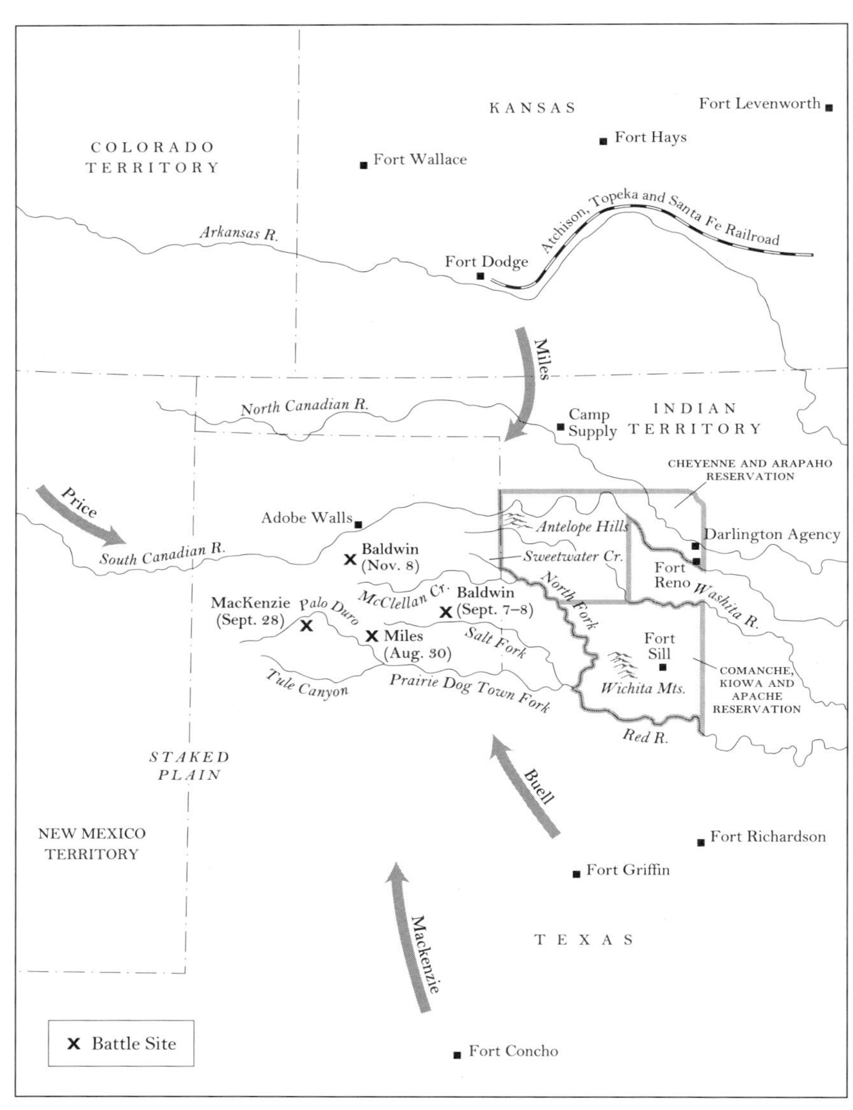

The Southern Plains.
Miles's campaign against the Cheyenne, Kiowa, and Commanche, 1874–75.

Miles wrote that Sitting Bull, the great chief of the Lakota Sioux, "was a man of powerful physique, with a large, broad head, strong features, and a few words which were uttered with great deliberation; a man evidently of decision and positive convictions." Nelson A. Miles, *Serving the Republic,* 149. Courtesy of the National Archives.

Chauncey McKeever, while in the adjutant general's department, maneuvered against Miles. Later, McKeever was reduced to the assistant adjutant generalship of the army because he tried to arrange the forced retirement of the adjutant general, who had been ill. Courtesy of the U.S. Military Academy, West Point.

Nelson A. Miles, brevet major general, commanding the District of the Yellowstone, Montana, 1876–79. Courtesy of the Montana Historical Society.

"General Miles charging the Indian Camp—the Dash into the ravine." From *Frank Leslie's Illustrated Newspaper,* November 3, 1877. Courtesy of the New-York Historical Society.

Geronimo, a war shaman of the Chiricahua Apaches, 1884. On rushing Geronimo and his band into exile, Miles wrote, "We were in honor bound not to give them up to a mob or the mockery of justice where they could never have received an impartial trial." Virginia Johnson, *Unregimented General,* 253. Courtesy of the National Archives.

Miles, standing, at the sword-presentation ceremony in Tucson on November 8, 1887, honoring him for the capture of Geronimo. Courtesy of the Arizona Historical Society.

Miles and William F. (Buffalo Bill) Cody at Pine Ridge, North Dakota, January 16, 1891. Miles wrote his wife that the Wounded Knee tragedy was an "abominable, criminal military blunder and a horrible massacre of women and children." Virginia Johnson, *Unregimented General,* 294. Courtesy of the U.S. Army Military History Institute.

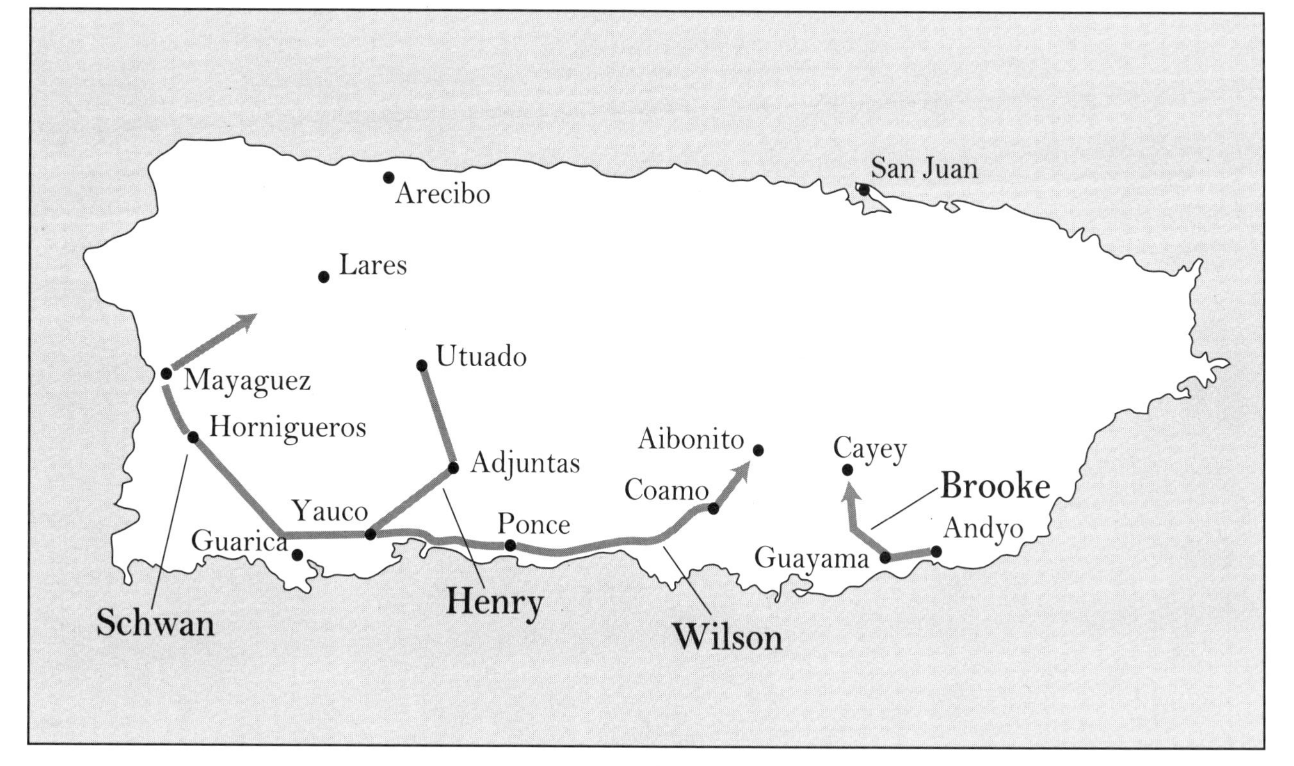

The Puerto Rico Campaign, July 25–August 12, 1898. Miles's expeditionary force was divided into four commands, each of which would cross the island, converging on San Juan.

A meeting of the generals to arrange the surrender of Santiago, July 13–14, 1898. At the right are two Spanish officers, one of whom is Gen. José Torol. The American generals, from left to right, are Miles, William R. Shafter, and Joseph Wheeler. The generals met in a valley between opposing lines around Santiago, Cuba, under the branches of a tropical tree that would later be called the Tree of Peace. Courtesy of the National Archives.

Russell Alexander Alger was President William McKinley's secretary of war from 1897 to 1899. Later he served as a U.S. senator from Michigan. Courtesy of the National Archives and Records Administration.

Elihu Root served as President Theodore Roosevelt's secretary of war from 1899 to 1904. He later served Roosevelt as secretary of state from 1905 to 1909 and then as a U.S. senator from New York. Courtesy of the National Archives and Records Administration.

This portrait of Nelson A. Miles shows him in the full uniform of his newly assumed rank of lieutenant general, 1900. Courtesy of the Chicago Historical Society.

Theodore Roosevelt during his speaking tour in 1910. During this tour, the former president gave a speech before the Colorado legislature that provoked Miles to tell a reporter that "in condemning the decisions of the Supreme Court of the United States and its venerable bench Theodore Roosevelt is guilty of treason." *New York Times,* August 30, 1910. Courtesy of the National Archives and Records Administration.

This cartoon appeared in the *Washington Evening Star* on May 2, 1903. Because Miles was off the mark in his 1903 Philippines report, he not only missed an opportunity to preserve the honor of the army, but, according to the *Army and Navy Journal* of May 9, one of his last official acts as commanding general left "the patriotic citizen 'posed, puzzled and perplexed.'"

General Nelson A. Miles's funeral procession, May 19, 1925. Courtesy of the National Archives.

— CHAPTER 12 —

The Spanish-American War

Girding for Battle

IN NOVEMBER 1896 Miles predicted that if a war with Spain should occur, "it would be a naval conflict at the start, and for some time. Our navy is considered to be of greater efficiency than that of Spain." He then focused attention on the weapons of war, admitting that "We easily could get volunteers for our army, but we lack high power guns with which fighting is now done. It takes a year to make a high power gun, and almost as long to prepare the tools and machinery for making them."[1]

Following the sinking of the *Maine* in Havana harbor on February 15, 1898, Miles commented further. Sadly for the men who would suffer, the McKinley administration paid little heed to his sage observations. Miles was forced to watch as the army he led in name only became hobbled by misguided command decisions, the effects of which he had foreseen but could not forestall.

For instance, early in April, Miles proposed that the regular army should be increased to 62,597 men, who would do the actual fighting while the National Guard manned the coast defenses. At first, 50,000 volunteers would be required to garrison the coastal fortifications, with a later call for an additional 40,000 men to reinforce those units and to serve as a reserve. Finally, 10,000 volunteers (designated "immunes" because they had recently recovered from yellow fever and were believed to be immune from the disease) would be enlisted, bringing a total of 162,597 troops into service.[2]

Political pressure from the National Guard convinced President McKinley to approve a revision of the bill proposed by Miles. The revised bill authorized state formations to enter the service as intact units, commanded by their own officers, and with an expectation that the War Department would allow them to win their fair share of glory overseas. The new measure, which became a law on April 22, held the regulars to about 65,000 men, while no limits were set on the number of volunteers that could be called by the president. Under the provisions of this law, about 275,000 men served in the army during the war, 59,000 of whom were regulars.[3]

In his autobiography Miles complained about the burden of quartering, training, and equipping a hundred thousand more volunteers than were originally requested. He quoted the Duke of Wellington, who, in a similar predicament in Spain, remarked, "An army well equipped, disciplined, officered and instructed is far more effective than a larger one without these essential conditions." In an article in the *North American Review,* written within a year after the war, Miles pointed out that since only fifty-two thousand troops were overseas at the time of the Spanish surrender, "peace could have been secured without requiring a single volunteer to leave the country, and thus the necessity of the enormous volunteer army, and the expense and inconvenience incident to its organization and maintenance, could have been avoided."[4]

After the National Guard ensured a prominent role for itself in the war, Miles faced the task of molding the state troops into fighting trim. They were, he judged, "as a rule, inefficient, and, as a body, could practically be disregarded." Most of these outfits had been saddled with obsolete equipment, and Miles was concerned about the professional ability of the replacements for many officers who chose to remain home rather than accompany their units into active duty.[5]

Miles unsuccessfully suggested that the volunteers should remain in local camps until they were equipped and trained. While the recruits were being transformed into soldiers, noncommissioned officers and company-grade officers would have an opportunity to be schooled in the art of leadership. Meanwhile, higher commands could be assembled before troops were concentrated at the large camps being prepared for them.[6]

When the War Department ignored Miles's advice, and ordered the volunteers sent directly into the large camps, chaos resulted. For example, Capt. James Rockwell, Jr., chief of ordnance of the Department of the South, admitted to a reporter that as of May 18, his long-depleted stock of weapons and ammunition had not yet been replaced by shipments that he had expected some time earlier.

Thus, 550 men of the First Ohio Cavalry "came here with one carbine for the entire command. They have nothing in the way of cavalry, not even horses." If the volunteers had been held at local camps until they had been outfitted for field service, Camp Thomas could have properly performed its role as an assembly area from which troops could be deployed overseas.[7]

In his 1898 annual report, Miles faulted the decision to concentrate recruits in camps such as George H. Thomas, hastily thrown up near Chattanooga, Tennessee. By early June, sixty thousand men were stationed at this sprawling camp, located on the 8,190-acre Chickamauga and Chattanooga Military Park, established in 1890 as a site for military exercises.[8]

In Miles's judgment, the scarcity of essential supplies in such camps "was to a great extent the cause . . . of the debilitating effect upon the health and strength of the men, who were otherwise in good physical condition." As an example, he could have cited the 425 troops who had died at Camp Thomas by the end of September, as the price paid for swamping the camp's staff with more men than they could possibly oversee.[9]

Following years of financial neglect by Congress, the Ordnance Department had been unable to stockpile either modern infantry weapons or smokeless ammunition. As the nation girded for war, Miles sought to insure that his men would not go into battle with flawed equipment. For instance, on April 18, 1898, Miles wrote the secretary of war recommending the replacement of both the .45 caliber Springfield rifle and the 30 caliber Krag-Jorgensen rifle, a Norwegian-designed, Danish military model.[10]

Brig. Gen. Daniel W. Flager, the chief of ordnance, did not attempt to answer Miles's criticism that many of the single-shot Springfields would be inaccurate because they had worn grooves caused by extensive use. Instead, he defended the Krag-Jorgensen, commonly known as either the Army Magazine Rifle or the Krag, a five-round magazine rifle used by the regulars in place of the Springfield. Flager pointed out that the Krag had been recommended by a board of officers on August 19, 1892, after the rifles of fifty-three manufacturers were tested over a period of two years. Because American gunsmiths complained about the decision to adopt a foreign-made weapon, a second board tested fourteen American-made magazine rifles. This board found, Flager reported to the secretary of war, "that the gun now known as the Army Magazine Rifle was better adapted for the military service than any other that had been presented to it, including the Lee Rifle [Straight Pull Caliber .30], one of the rifles recommended by Miles."[11]

Miles had decided to recommend other rifles because he had received unfavorable reports about the Krag-Jorgensen, and because no other leading military power used the weapon. Besides the Lee .30 caliber, Miles also suggested for possible adoption the .23 caliber used by the navy or the .30 caliber Winchester model 1895. The Ordnance Department immediately tested the .23 caliber navy rifle and found "that it is not an arm suitable for Army use." General Flager explained that "The caliber is too small and the bullet too light, weighing only 113 grains as compared with 220 grains for the Army rifle bullet. It was found to be materially less accurate than the Army rifle, the light bullet being readily deviated by wind."[12]

The secretary of war decided to give the .30 caliber Winchester model 1895 repeating rifle a more thorough trial than any of the other weapons recommended by Miles. On May 2, 1898, Secretary of War Russell Alger instructed the chief of ordnance to purchase ten thousand Winchesters for field tests. The rifles, which were delivered in early January 1899, were issued to both infantry and cavalry regiments. After studying the results of these tests, a board of officers deemed the Winchester "not a suitable arm for the United States military service."[13]

General Flager apparently resented Miles's intrusion into his bureau's affairs. In his initial response to Miles's recommendations, he officially reported, "It cannot be conceived that General Miles has such knowledge on the subject as would warrant anyone in taking his advice in the matter."[14]

Flager had misjudged both Miles's appreciation of weapons and the soundness of the 1890–92 board's recommendation favoring the Krag-Jorgensen. When the *Army and Navy Journal* evaluated this weapon following the Spanish-American War, it informed its readers that the board had favored the Krag because "it was believed to be the best single loader in existence." The officers who conducted the tests deemed this to be a significant advantage, according to the *Journal,* because "of the danger of the waste of ammunition by the raw troops upon whom we should have to depend in case of war." American troops realized that their magazine rifle had been chosen for an inappropriate feature when they encountered the .30 caliber Belgian Mauser repeating magazine rifle used by Spanish troops in Cuba. The *Journal* explained that "the result of our experience there was to give our officers and men a great respect for the Mauser, not as a superior arm, but as embodying the magazine system of loading, the very feature to which the Board objected." The article admitted that it sounded reasonable when the Ordnance Department faulted the Mauser because its clip of five bullets made it difficult to fire individual rounds; but on the battlefield, "We found then that we had the wrong end of the argument, not that we want to pump out shot by the clip full all the time, but because in some situations the ability to do so may become a critical advantage."

The *Journal* suggested that the United States follow the example of Great Britain, then in the process of converting the single-loader Lee-Metford into the same type of rapid-fire magazine rifle used by all the other major European powers. The change to clip loading would enable a "soldier to load five shots about as quickly as the Krag-Jorgensen can load one."[15]

Even the discredited .45 caliber Springfield, foisted by necessity on many volunteer units, outperformed the .30 caliber Krag in some respects. The Springfield not only appeared to be more trouble-free than the Army Magazine Rifle but also to be a more deadly weapon. The adjutant general, Brig. Gen. Henry C. Corbin, expressed his preference for the Springfield over the Krag, especially for use in the Philippines, because "in the firing likely to occur in country thickly wooded or with dense undergrowth, as in the neighborhood of Manila, the Springfield rifle, with the smokeless cartridge, is the more efficient weapon."[16]

Although a 1960 study of the Krag-Jorgensen judged that the rifle "ranked among the finest of military shoulder arms during the decade it was in use as a regular army issue," the author conceded that "There were times it jammed, and wouldn't fire because the bolt handle wasn't fully seated." He also admitted, "some experts thought it was uncomfortable to carry; some thought it was slower to load than clip loaders; some thought that the rattle of cartridges being loaded and the snap of the magazine closing was too noisy."[17]

The 1960 study considered the sights of the Krag, used by all of the regulars and some volunteer units during the Spanish- American War, to be "an abomination." An 1898 article in *Scientific American* found that the sight did not permit "adjustment to overcome the drift of the bullet or deflection produced by the wind, and the absence of such feature has been a source of much complaint on the part of the troops." The flawed sight had been so obvious that soon after the war ended, General Flager proposed that it be redesigned.[18]

Perhaps the issue of gravest consequence raised by Miles prior to the Cuban invasion was his objection to a landing during the summer, which he termed the "'rainy' or 'sickly' season." Following the war, statistics compiled by a Spanish military journal identified by month the fluctuating risk of dying from yellow fever in Cuba. The study reviewed the experience of the Spanish army of some two hundred thousand troops, including volunteers, serving on the island in 1896. Of the 23,580 yellow fever cases admitted to hospitals, 7,309 patients died of the disease. The study found that "The mortality, very light during March, April, February, May and January, when it did not reach 200 deaths per month, rose regularly in June, July and August, diminished in September, and reached the maximum, 1336 deaths, in November, to descend abruptly in December to 750 deaths."

Although Miles did not have the medical statistics to fortify his argument, he reinforced his case by forwarding a letter from Brig. Gen. George M. Sternberg, the army's surgeon general, to the secretary of war. Sternberg, who had achieved recognition for his research in both bacteriology and epidemiology, supported Miles's concern about the spread of disease if the troops landed in Cuba during the summer. To clinch his point, Miles cited a similar recommendation by Dr. James Guiteras, whom he referred to as "a well-known authority on yellow fever." In his letter of April 18, Miles did not limit himself to advising against a summer campaign because American troops "would undoubtedly be decimated by the deadly disease." Surprising because of our experience with interservice rivalries, the commanding general looked forward to the American navy gaining "superiority" over Spain's, which could "compel the surrender on the island of Cuba with very little loss of life and possibly avoid the spread of yellow fever over our own country." This is an unexpected argument from the general reputed to be a seeker after glory.[19]

In May, when it appeared that Miles's advice might be heeded, the support services heaved a sigh of relief. The commissary general, Charles Patrick Eagan, admitted that despite his best efforts, he had procured only half the rations needed to sustain a Cuban expeditionary force. Likewise, the quartermaster general, Marshall I. Ludington, found it impossible to satisfy the demands on his department. For instance, he obtained only 50 percent of the canvas needed by the army, although the government had already purchased all of the canvas available in the United States.[20]

When Miles advised against a summer campaign, he had as an ally Lt. Col. Arthur L. Wagner, then chief of the Military Information Division. After Wagner graduated from West Point in 1875, he fought as a second lieutenant in the 6th Infantry against both the Sioux and Nez Perce in the campaigns of 1876 and 1877, then against the Utes in 1880–81. Promoted to first lieutenant in 1882, he made a significant contribution to the army following his appointment to the Infantry and Cavalry School at Fort Leavenworth, Kansas. Here, Wagner worked to transform the school into the General Service and Staff College, and is credited as being one of the prime movers behind the establishment of the Army War College.

Two of Wagner's works were used as textbooks at both West Point and the General Service and Staff College, others were reprinted abroad, and one received a gold medal from the Military Service Institution. Leonard Wood's biographer, Herman Hagedorn, considered Wagner "an inspired teacher" who "set his mark upon a whole generation."[21]

In February 1898 Wagner was promoted to lieutenant colonel, and one month later he was chosen to head the Military Information Division. This division, a unit of the adjutant general's office, had been established primarily as an intelligence-gathering agency by Adj. Gen. Richard C. Drum during Grover Cleveland's first term as president.[22]

Almost before Wagner had a chance to settle into his new office, he joined in the debate on the timing of a Cuban invasion. On April 11 he sent the War Department a memorandum refuting the arguments of those who pressed for a summer landing; Miles kept a copy of this report in his files. Wagner said that complaints that the war cost the nation millions of dollars for each day it continued gave America the appearance of a "nation of 'dollar chasers,'" willing to sacrifice the lives of servicemen to save money.

Further, according to Wagner, some proponents of a summer campaign maintained that "The eyes of the world are upon us: our system is upon trial: our honor is attacked: we claim to be a strong nation; and we cannot afford to be resisted with success even for a few months by their [Spain's] weak kingdom." He reminded his readers that "the eyes of the world were upon us at Bull Run also." To avoid such an inauspicious start to the Spanish-

American War, he urged a "brief delay demanded by the most ordinary precautions."

Wagner cautioned, "It requires doubtless some moral courage to resist a popular demand for immediate action, but it is the part of wisdom and patriotism to be sure that we are ready before we begin any aggressive movement." He added that Americans should "not allow the efforts of our nation to be sacrificed to an invisible foe in the shape of disease when after a brief period of preparation and waiting we could easily overcome visible foes in Spanish uniforms."

Perhaps the most convincing argument put forth by Wagner's opponents concerned the effects that a delay would have on the Cuban families forced into concentration camps. In 1896 Spanish general Valeriano Weyler began to build concentration camps in which even women and children were held in his attempt to suppress a Cuban revolution against Spanish rule. By postponing a landing until the fall, when the rainy season ended, the planned naval blockade of Cuba would be prolonged. It would be the *reconcentrados,* rather than the Spanish troops, who would be the first to face starvation as the blockade took hold. Wagner coolly calculated, however, that the "deplorable" deaths of the *reconcentrados* would be "less disastrous" than the likelihood of a yellow fever epidemic along the eastern seaboard. He believed that a quarantine would not prevent the spread of the disease to U.S. shores.[23]

As plans for the conduct of the war were being debated, some observers criticized mismanagement in the War Department. In the June 5 Sunday supplement of the *New York Herald,* Poultney Bigelow, then employed by the *London Times,* attacked "major generals of recent creation, and amateur soldiers generally, who are playing havoc with the health and welfare of our brave army." In an article titled "Shall Politics and Incompetence Command Our Army?" Bigelow asked, "Who is in command? Today no one knows." The correspondent particularly objected to the "back stairs intrigue against the head of the army."[24]

Early in April, President McKinley had accepted retired Lt. Gen. John M. Schofield's offer of assistance. The ensuing daily meetings at one o'clock between the retired general and the president led Bigelow to ask, "What would we think of a ship with three or four captains aboard? Yet our little army has been distracted for the last month with half a dozen commanders in chief."[25]

Although Bigelow had named Schofield as the one who had undermined Miles's authority, the retired general's experiences within the administration reveal that he shared Miles's impotence in shaping command decisions. Both generals had proposed invading Puerto Rico first, while delaying a landing in Cuba until winter. Schofield had even hoped, as had Miles, that the destruction of the enemy fleet would force a surrender of the Spanish army in Cuba.

When Schofield penciled a private, thirty-nine-page memoir of his wartime experiences with the McKinley administration, he provided an inside look into the operations of the War Department prior to the Cuban invasion. He only became fully aware of what had actually happened within the department after he informed the president in May of his intention to leave Washington in the wake of the decision to land on Cuba in July.

At that time, the president made a last, seemingly innocuous request for Schofield to leave a message with Secretary of War Russell A. Alger. When the retired general sought to avoid the errand, he recalled that "for the first time [I] spoke of my unsatisfactory relations with the Secretary of War. I said I had evidently offended the Secretary in some way and his conduct toward me was unpleasant." McKinley retorted that Alger "entertained toward me the kindest and most friendly feeling and manifested the greatest respect for all my opinions and recommendations."

Schofield at last understood what had taken place while he sought to serve McKinley. He now realized that "while the Secretary's conduct toward me had for a long time become more discourteous and even offensive, in most marked contrast with his former cordiality, the President had been made to believe that his former manifestation of friendship and esteem had been continued." Rather than make Alger's misrepresentation a divisive issue on the eve of battle, Schofield left Washington quietly but filled with frustration.

It rankled Schofield that because of Alger's maneuvers when the president initially sought to utilize "all the expert military knowledge and experience within his reach," Alger thwarted this effort. Schofield suggested that Alger succeeded in displacing the generals "by the self-confident assurance . . . that he himself was an all-sufficient master of the art and science of war, who did not hesitate to make plans and issue orders for military operations of momentous consequences without consulting the President." For example, while McKinley still pondered the wisdom of a spring invasion of Cuba, "an order to that effect had already been given by the Secretary of War to the Commanding General of the Army and met his earnest protest."

Schofield lashed out, in his private journal, at Alger's mismanagement. "The unnecessary losses, suffering and privations which the army has endured have been caused by the incompetence and reckless ambition of the Chief of the War Department." Unlike much of the press at the time, Schofield believed that the service departments were "efficient" and their officers "capable and diligent." He attributed the failures of the bureaus to the lack of "a capable head to direct them. This has been sorely wanting. The Secretary had been incapable and the Commanding General has not been permitted to act or exercise control." Schofield also explained that Miles could not serve as McKinley's chief-of-staff because "neither the law nor the Army Regulations or the President's orders require or authorize the General to perform any such duty."[26]

Schofield's account of his service in the McKinley administration is just one of many reports charging that Russell A. Alger did not competently administer the War Department as the army readied itself for battle. Given Alger's background, one would not expect the disappointing performance that he gave directing his department during the war.

Eleven years after Alger's birth in a log cabin in 1836, he displayed determination and loyalty following the death of both of his parents. Despite his limited means, the young boy cared for at least one of his sisters, while not neglecting the studies that prepared him to become a lawyer in 1859. That year he moved from Ohio to Michigan, where he would eventually earn a fortune from investments in timberland.

Although Alger's Civil War record lost some of its luster following a contested charge that in 1864 he was absent without leave, overall he served with distinction. While earning promotions from captain to colonel while fighting with the Fifth Michigan Volunteer Cavalry, Alger received several wounds and won brevet promotions to both brigadier and major general for gallantry.

Alger honed his executive skills after winning a term as Michigan's governor in 1884. In that office he earned a reputation sound enough to have himself endorsed as a "favorite son" candidate at the 1888 Republican national convention. One year later, he demonstrated his popularity on the national level, when Union veterans selected him to command the Grand Army of the Republic.

Only after Alger joined McKinley's cabinet in March 1897 did his limitations begin to show. He did not share Miles's foresight concerning the need to modernize the army. More significantly, following the March 9 passage of what was popularly called the "Fifty Million Dollar Bill," a measure to strengthen the nation's defenses, Alger accepted McKinley's self-imposed restrictions on spending the appropriations. This has led one of his biographers to suggest that if the secretary truly disagreed with the president's interpretation of the bill, he should have had the moral courage to resign from the cabinet.[27]

Following the February 1898 sinking of the *Maine,* public attention turned to the War Department, where decisions regarding mobilization and strategy would be made. With unwarranted self-confidence, Alger succeeded in monopolizing command of the army and attention in the newspaper headlines. Just as Schofield had, Miles saw his effectiveness as an adviser to the president shorn by the secretary of war right before the final invasion plans were made.

Alger sought to eliminate the commanding general as a competitor for the president's ear on May 26, the very day that the initial session to discuss a June landing took place. Even as Alger planned to remove Miles from the scene, he reassured McKinley about his relationship with the commanding general. Following a top-level conference on the twenty-sixth, attended by the secretary of the navy, John D. Long, and Miles, among others, Alger informed the president that he had "said but little this morning thinking possibly the navy official might be led to think there is some difference between General Miles and myself, which there is not. Except I have not approved his plans."[28]

At this most critical time, Alger ordered Miles to make an inspection tour of Camp Thomas and of the troops assembled at Mobile, Alabama, and Tampa, Florida. At the bottom of a copy of this message to the commanding general is written the misleading statement "order not obeyed. Gen. Miles saying he was in the habit of issuing his own orders. He never visited and inspected a camp during the war."[29] In fact, Miles only had time to inspect Tampa before departing overseas, where he remained in the war zone until peace was restored.

For Miles, who had believed that the conflict with Spain could have been solved through arbitration rather than war, seeing the management of that war fall into the hands of amateurs seemed the height of folly. He later observed, "It is sometimes easy for the thoughtless and inexperienced to involve a country in war, but disastrous when they attempt to direct its military."[30]

Four days after receiving Alger's order to inspect Tampa, among other camps, Miles departed by train with his family and staff for that port of embarkation. He had decided to see for himself what conditions were like as troops assembled for the Cuban invasion. After establishing his headquarters in the Tampa Bay Hotel on June 1, he spent the next morning in a conference with the commanders chosen to lead the Cuban expedition: Maj. Gen. William R. Shafter, commanding the Fifth Corps, and Maj. Gen. Joseph Wheeler, a former Confederate officer, now in command of the cavalry branch of the army.[31]

On the afternoon of June 2, accompanied by his staff, Miles informally inspected the military establishment at Tampa and found it wanting. He had "found great confusion and the place was crowded with an indiscriminate accumulation of supplies and war materials. The confusion was occasioned partly by the want of rail facilities and partly by the system of loading and invoicing war material." He added that "The side tracks of the railroads from the port of Tampa to Columbia, South Carolina, were blocked with cars and trains, and this caused great difficulty in properly equipping an expedition for effective war service."[32]

In 1898, despite being able to boast about advances such as electric tram cars, the city of Tampa must have disappointed Miles as much as its military encampment had. An Englishman described the city of twenty-five thousand as being "built on a sandy patch cut, as it were, out of the primeval forest. Tampa is typical of Florida; there is sand, and then sand, and lastly sand." The *Army and Navy Journal* ominously warned against the selection of Tampa as a camp because much "of the surrounding country is low and marshy and a small stagnant brook that makes its way through the lower part of the town is probably responsible, in part at least, for the unsavory reputation which the town enjoys."[33]

By 1895, however, plans submitted to the Naval War College had begun to mention Tampa as an assembly point in case war broke out with Spain. When President McKinley reportedly confirmed this choice in 1898, he had in mind not only its proximity to Cuba and its port but also the opportunity its location would provide to acclimatize Northern troops to subtropical weather. But planners may not have foreseen the problem caused because only a single railroad track and a path connected the port of Tampa with the city, nine miles distant.[34]

Miles immediately took steps to free the docks and the rail system, which had become choked. On June 2 he informed the War Department how he expedited the loading of the nine ships that could be tied up along the port's two double wharves at a time. He divided those detailed to handle the cargo into three shifts, so that stevedoring became a round-the-clock operation.[35]

Miles also responded to a problem caused because no one at the point of origin had identified the contents in the railroad cars sent to Tampa. Because some three hundred boxcars stranded along the east coast of Florida had no description of their contents, officers were forced to search from car to car, hoping to find equipment needed by their commands. Miles recommended to Alger that "rigid orders" be issued to assure that future shipments would be thoroughly identified. He also alerted the secretary that, as a result of the missing documentation, inadequately equipped units reporting to Tampa remained unfit for service. "Several of the volunteer regiments came here without uniforms; several came without arms, and some without blankets, tents or camp equipage. The Thirty-second Michigan, which is among the best, came without arms." To stress the seriousness of the problem, he noted that "[Brig.] Gen. Guy V. Henry reports that five regiments under his command are not fit to go into the field."[36]

Even before Miles had boarded the train bound for Tampa, the press, with Poultney Bigelow among those in the forefront, mounted an offensive against the army's mismanagement. Following the declaration of war against Spain, Bigelow took leave from his avocation of traveling, which provided material for his historical writings, to serve as an American correspondent for the *London Times.* The forty-two-year-old reporter's father, John Bigelow, had teamed with William Cullen Bryant as owner and editor of the *New York Evening Post* until he distinguished himself as consul-general at Paris during the Civil War. The father devoted his later years to writing biographies and history. He gave his son Poultney a first-rate education at Yale and then at Columbia University Law School.[37]

Bigelow's campaign to reform the Army began with a letter published in the *London Times* on May 23; some of his observations were repeated by the *New York Times* on June 4. He informed his readers about the "terrible condition" and "lack of organization" at Tampa. For example, "in a hot and pestiferous climate men are compelled to wear winter clothing, eat winter rations—fat pork and beans, with no fruit or vegetables to cool their super-heated blood—while carloads of fresh fruit and vegetables are going north to the New York and Chicago markets."

In his *Times* article Bigelow attributed the failure to address the troops' needs to "red tapism at Washington or to that military appendage mis-named the staff." The military bureaucracy's lack of foresight particularly perplexed Bigelow since "America must have known a year ago that war was inevitable, [but] her army is not fit to move." Interestingly, he believed that the "American press, with rare exceptions, hushed up the seamy side of the war, partly from ignorance and partly from deliberate purpose."

Bigelow, personable enough to enjoy a long-lasting friendship with Kaiser Wilhelm II, also won the confidence of at least one of McKinley's department heads. Thus, he could reveal that "a member of the Cabinet has confided to me that he is opposed to sending troops to Cuba until in fit condition, but that it is impossible to oppose the popular clamor." The letter ended with a challenge to the president: "If President McKinley would tell the people the facts honestly, he might be defeated in Congress; but he would have the satisfaction of having done his duty."[38]

Just one day after Bigelow's bleak assessment of the army's state of readiness appeared on the front page of the *New York Times,* the same newspaper published his article, "Shall Politics and Incompetence Command Our Army?" Besides protesting attempts to undermine Miles's authority, Bigelow cited instances of poor performance by staff officers at Tampa. Stung by the correspondent's criticism, each of the bureau chiefs reacted to the charges according to his own temperament.

Quartermaster General Marshall I. Ludington took Bigelow's attack in stride. Rather than refute the correspondent's charges of shortages at Tampa, he simply had an aide prepare a list of equipment that had already been sent to Shafter's troops in Florida.

Surgeon General Sternberg tried to make light of Bigelow's criticisms of his department. To the charge that no flooring had been provided for tents, Sternberg answered that "soldiers at Tampa don't want floored tents this time of year. Besides they propose to go to Cuba shortly." He casually dismissed the complaint that the troops lacked bathing facilities as "ridiculous when the ocean beach is right there before him. The government is not supposed to furnish a soldier with cologne for his toilet." To seriously suggest that the troops bathe in saltwater reflected poorly on the surgeon general's interest in the men's welfare. To blunt the attack on his department, Sternberg cited the fact that less than two percent of the troops at Tampa had been infected with any disease.[39]

In his memoirs Bigelow wrote, "We wondered why in this land of much water no man could get a bath—why our tents might not have been pitched by the sea or on the banks of a stream! The answer that came back was the same wearisome one: politics!" The correspondent who would be battle tested in Cuba explained that, "Some patriot had leased certain barrens to his government, and there we were condemned to wilt and grow sick, rather than that a politician be deprived of his profits." As for the restrictions that the troops found had been placed on the use of water, Bigelow explained, "The very water we drank was charged for by the aldermen of Tampa, and no one was allowed more than an amount that would have seemed small on a sea voyage. A sentinel guarded each water-tap as in times of famine."[40]

Commissary General Charles P. Eagan appeared to take the published criticisms personally, telling a reporter, "You may say for me that this man Poultney Bigelow, whoever he is, is a ———, please use that word—he is a ———." Eagan explained that his anger came "not so much in personal resentment as from indignation at the unnecessary alarm that this man is bringing to the fathers and mothers of the men in camp of whom he is writing." Although Eagan would continue to ignore local conditions when he allotted rations, he correctly pointed out that his bureau had provisioned an army that had experienced virtually a tenfold increase in manpower almost overnight.[41]

Two days after Bigelow's article appeared, Miles reprimanded the quartermaster general, commissary general, and the chief of ordnance for their inefficiency in supplying the expeditionary force. From its Washington bureau, the *New York Times* not only revealed the details of Miles's June 7 dispatch but also the response of the rebuked department heads. In a telegram signed by each, the three bureau chiefs explained that they had been compelled by a law, now repealed, to accept bids over a ten-day period before they could fill supply requisitions.[42]

In a "Topics of the Times" column written at the height of Surgeon General Sternberg's pillorying by the press, the newspaper suggested that Sternberg should have followed the example of Miles, Maj. Gen. Wesley Merritt, and Shafter's officers in Cuba. In each instance, a protest that reached the public resulted in steps being taken to rectify a problem. On June 11 the same newspaper editorialized that Miles's criticism of the bureau chiefs "is nothing short of a denunciation of the Secretary of War." The editor explained that "The country will believe that he might with great accuracy have included the Secretary of War in his denunciations. But he could not do so directly without gross insubordination, and he has done so indirectly but none the less effectively."[43]

Even before newspaper speculation rocked an already unsteady relationship, Alger had decided to deny Miles permission to accompany the expedition to Cuba, notwithstanding that the commanding general had been "explicitly informed" by both himself and the president that he "was at liberty to go in command of the Santiago [Cuba] expedition, or to organize the force for the invasion of Puerto Rico."[44]

On June 5 Miles acted on the promise and notified Alger that "This enterprise is so important that I desire to go with this Army corps [the Fifth] or to immediately organize another and go with it to join this, and capture position No. 2 [Puerto Rico]. "Miles did not help his cause with his clumsy wording of an alternative mission, and he played into Alger's hands by not following up on his original request. In Alger's account of the war, he candidly admitted that he pigeonholed Miles's request until June 15. By that time the expedition had already been at sea for one day. As a result of his bent promise, Alger had the satisfaction of writing that "Miles did not command the Santiago expedition, and that he did not was his own mistake or misfortune. He lost the opportunity to command in the greatest land battle of the war."[45]

In Miles's retelling of the matter, written in 1899 for the *North American Review,* rather than dwell on the glory denied him, he simply explained that "most of the regular Army was included in this expedition, and on account of the importance of the enterprise, I desired to go with it, but was directed to return to Washington." Alger's minimum-rate, ten-word telegram of summons to the commanding general instructed, "Important business requires your presence here; report at once. Answer." Miles dutifully replied that he would leave for Washington on the next train north.[46]

As Miles boarded an evening train to the capital, he could reflect on the hectic two weeks he had spent attempting to clear up the confusion in Florida, while also dashing off solutions to problems that might face the Fifth Corps in Cuba. Although a number of his messages were filed in wastebaskets at the War Department, the *New York Times* credited the "sharp words" he aimed at the bureau chiefs for having "had a wonderful effect in removing the congestion of freight in the neighborhood of Tampa." And when Miles looked overseas, unlike some of his contemporaries, he included the Cuban insurgents in his plans, coordinating their operations with those of the Fifth Corps.[47]

Also to his credit, Miles never relented in his intelligence-gathering efforts. Lt. Andrew S. Rowan not only established communication between Miles and Gen. Calixto García, a commander of rebels in the eastern end of Cuba, but also returned to army headquarters in Washington with two of García's staff officers, who were a storehouse of information about conditions in Cuba. Miles also managed to provide Alger with the names and tonnages of all the ships anchored off Santiago de Cuba on April 4, as well as additional information about the harbor, after questioning two former residents of the city.[48]

Miles enjoyed less success when he attempted to influence actual operations. After the invasion fleet returned to Tampa, following the sighting of ships incorrectly thought to be Spanish, Miles proposed that an announcement be made that Shafter's men were now at sea. He hoped that if U.S. warships would then sail along the course that the invasion fleet would follow to Cuba, they might encounter the Spanish fleet, tempted from safe waters by the bait of transports at sea. Alger dismissed this idea with a curt comment on the bottom of the message: "Of course no such announcement was made."[49]

Until the last minute, Miles hoped to persuade the secretary of war to move on Puerto Rico before invading Cuba. On June 6, just two days before the Fifth Corps left port on the aborted cruise, Miles wired "merely as a suggestion. To leave No. 1 [Cuba] safely guarded. This corps, with the combined assistance of the Navy, to take No. 2 [Puerto Rico] first before it can be reinforced."[50]

Miles had offered several arguments to support his belief that Puerto Rico should be secured before Cuba. He pointed out that the Spanish garrison of seventeen thousand troops on Puerto Rico would be a much less formidable enemy that the estimated force of at least eighty thousand men on Cuba. This disparity led him to conclude that "the best policy was following the well-known principle of cutting the enemy's force in two and overpowering the weaker wing first."[51]

Besides the advantage of conserving the lives of American troops by attacking the enemy's weakest link, Miles believed that by capturing Puerto Rico a potential threat to the Fifth Corps in Cuba would be eliminated. Finally, he retained his concern about the "danger of putting an army in Cuba during what is known as the 'rainy' or 'sickly' season," which he first communicated to the president on April 18.[52]

Alger wasted no time in squelching Miles's "suggestion." The same evening that he received Miles's telegram, he bluntly wired back: "The President says no. He urges the utmost haste in departure of No. 1 [Cuba], and also of No. 2 [Puerto Rico], as indicated by you, but that No. 1 must be taken first."[53]

Unbeknownst to the commanding general, it may have been his April 18 letter to Alger that destroyed the president's confidence in him. This is the letter in which Miles, in what clearly seems to be an attempt to avoid the needless loss of life, not only warned against the danger of yellow fever but also proposed postponing the Cuban campaign until the United States established naval superiority over Spain.

According to Adj. Gen. Henry C. Corbin, McKinley read Miles's letter just a few days after he had signed the joint resolution for Cuban intervention. In an emotional outburst, the president declared: "God willing and not failing us, we shall end the war before the General would have us begin operations. He little understands me; no more does he know the temper of our people. I deplore the war, but it must be short and quick to the finish." McKinley concluded, "I had a right to expect better things of General Miles." Corbin believed that after this blow to the president's faith in Miles, he "never sought his advice and never gave it any weight when offered."[54]

Before the invasion fleet's delayed June 14 departure for Cuba, Miles prodded Shafter to take advantage of the pause by preparing for the landing on hostile shores. He instructed Shafter to have his transport officers confirm the location of supplies loaded aboard each ship and asked if "arrangements [had] been made in order that if so many rations of any kind, ammunition, hospital supplies, etc., should be required, that they would know at once where they can be found?" Miles also ordered Shafter to "have one of your transports move out to-day to some beach, made a landing as you would on the coast of Cuba, using your engineer corps and all appliances for the purpose of seeing that everything is in perfect order."[55]

On April 29, Alger and McKinley both approved Miles's recommendation, made that same day, for Shafter to take command of the troops at Tampa, an assignment that would tax him to the limit. On June 7, Shafter admitted to Corbin, in a personal letter, that he knew that "to you in Washington it seems we are awfully slow in getting off, but I have been working night and day since I have been here: I have never worked so in my life and never expect to again."[56]

Despite the long hours Shafter spent readying the Fifth Corps for action, he did not find time to comply with Miles's instructions. Marion P. Maus, who served as both the senior inspector general of volunteers and Miles's aide-de-camp during the war, criticized Shafter's preparations for cargo operations. Maus, whom Miles described in the Nez Perce chapter of his memoirs as "a famous hunter and splendid soldier," charged that the loading at Tampa had been haphazard and that the Fifth Corps lacked an adequate supply of "appliances for landing."[57]

Maus had informed Miles that he had "repeatedly invited the attention of both Generals Shafter and [his chief engineer, Brig. Gen. William] Ludlow" to the problems he had observed but that still had not been addressed. As for Miles's instructions to practice unloading a cargo ship, Maus reported, without further explanation, that "This order was never carried out." He believed that the War Department might be a factor in Shafter's independence. Although Miles was the senior officer in Tampa, "dispatches were constantly sent direct to General Shafter conveying instructions, contrary to military usage."[58]

Alger's discourtesy to Miles may have affected Shafter's relationship with the commanding general. When Maus prepared his observations for Miles, he noted that "There was an apparent disposition to resent your direction or control, which was clearly shown by General Shafter himself." During his stay in Tampa, Miles gave no visible sign of being slighted by both his superiors and subordinates. Frederic Remington recalled that when he approached Miles to complain about cavalrymen being sent to Cuba, where they would fight as infantrymen, he was struck by Miles's "quiet manner, which is habitual with him." The artist, however, did feel that Miles belonged in the field rather than at a headquarters. In comparing a colonel whom he admired with Miles, Remington observed that the officer "is soldier all over—he couldn't be anything but a man on a horse. He wouldn't look right in a chair any more than General Miles does."[59]

When Miles arrived in Washington on June 17, the *New York Times* commented that he "looked hale and hearty, despite the three weeks of incessant work of bringing order out of chaos in the hurriedly concentrated army." When a reporter asked the commanding general about plans for future operations, Miles cautiously answered that such expeditions "will be equipped and sent. That almost goes without saying, for when we entered upon war an aggressive campaign was formulated and approved, which contemplated the sending of expeditions and their cooperation toward the successful prosecution of the war." Miles, however, refused to give any specific information about contemplated movements.[60]

Newspapers were less discreet than the general about discussing future plans. The *New York Herald* informed its readers, in a story written the day before Miles reached the capital, that when he arrived there President McKinley would order him to prepare an invasion force that would set sail for Puerto Rico within two weeks. The correspondent also revealed that Fernandina, Florida, would serve as the embarkation point, but he did not know exactly when troops would begin to concentrate at that port city north of Jacksonville. The reporter attributed this gap in information on officials at the War Department who "will give no intimation as to when the troops will be sent to that place, but I am assured that it will be within the next few days."[61]

On June 14 the *Herald*'s headlines proclaimed that Miles's army would be "Off to San Juan within ten days"; but just five days later the newspaper had to correct itself. Because of a shortage of steamships, the *Herald* now believed it would be at least three weeks before the expedition could set sail.

The importance of the invasion had suddenly grown in significance after Admiral Manuel de la Cámara's fleet sailed from Cádiz on June 16. Military planners were initially uncertain of the fleet's destination and wanted to deny the Spanish warships a safe harbor at Puerto Rico.[62]

Shortly after the Fifth Corps landed at Daiquirí on June 22, Miles received the long-sought call to action. His orders, dated the twenty-sixth, alerted him to prepare troops "for movement and operations against the enemy in Cuba and Puerto Rico." Miles so appreciated the significance that Cuba was included in his mission that he abstracted the quoted line from his orders, then had it printed in italics in his annual report.[63]

As newspapers reported almost daily changes in the plans for the invasion of Puerto Rico, public attention turned to press speculation about dissension between Alger and Miles, and to the hard reality of the Fifth Corps's drive to capture Santiago de Cuba. The Miles-Alger controversy had been fanned by a *New York Times* editorial concerning a half-hour meeting between the two men on June 17, the day the commanding general had returned to Washington.

The *Times* editor joined the rumormongers guessing about the conversation between the commanding general and the secretary of war. Without any confirmation, he supposed that Miles "was bound to report what he saw [at Tampa], and to accompany his reports with appropriate comments." The *Times,* which early in June had called for Alger to resign because "his administration has been conspicuous only for apathy and inefficiency," now used Miles in its latest attack on the beleaguered secretary. On the presumption that Miles had argued with Alger, as had General Merritt, the editor remarked that for the secretary of war to "be in a position to overrule Gen. Miles and Gen. Merritt on military questions is not only an absurdity in itself, but a danger to the country." The editorial then asked, "Has not the incompetency of Secretary Alger and the bungling and blundering which have marked his conduct of his department yet convinced the President of his unfitness for such a place at such a time?"[64]

In response to continued press allusions to "'friction' in the Army," Alger told a reporter for the *Army and Navy Journal* that "The stories in the sensational papers that there is any trouble between Gen. Miles and myself—or anything of a kindred nature—is utterly unwarranted, is malicious and untrue, and without a shadow of foundation." He explained that "such reports are simply gotten up for the purpose of disorganizing the service and embarrassing every official as much as possible."

In the same issue of the *Journal,* Miles did not directly discuss the stories of discord in the service, but came to Alger's support by defending his bureau chiefs. After he drew attention to "the great burden and labor of equipping an army of 278,000 men," Miles reminded critics that our country "did not have these things on hand and it was absolutely necessary to acquire them in a few weeks' time. Within a comparatively short time the troops have been mobilized, officers appointed, the men drilled, disciplined, and prepared for the serious duties of actual war."

Impressed by the general, the journalist remarked that "Miles may well congratulate himself and the Army on the results of this preparation. One of the most difficult operations of war—the landing of troops on a hostile shore, has been completed without the loss of a man." However, the day after the *Journal* complimented the army for the "auspicious beginning" of the campaign, Shafter wired some disquieting news to Alger. Although the Fifth Corps had Santiago "well invested on the north and east, but with a very thin line," Shafter warned that "Upon approaching this [town] we find it of such character and the defenses so strong it will be impossible to carry it by storm with my present force, and I am seriously considering withdrawing about five miles and taking up a new position on the high ground." The telegram also contained Shafter's grim estimate that, to date, he had suffered a thousand casualties. Among those out of action were Generals Wheeler and Samuel Young, due to illness, and Brig. Gen. Samuel Hawkins, hit in the foot. The corps commander even had to report himself "unable to be out during the heat of the day for four days, but am retaining command."[65]

In his memoirs, Miles identified Shafter's July 3 telegram as the reason behind McKinley's order, which he followed, that he "go to Santiago and give such orders as might be required for the welfare and success of the army." Actually, as Miles noted in his annual report, the decision to send him to Cuba occurred only after Shafter informed Washington on July 4 that in order to take Santiago "I want 15,000 troops speedily, and it is not certain that they can be landed, as it is getting stormy."[66]

The destruction of Admiral Pascual Cervera's squadron off Santiago de Cuba on July 3 raised the possibility, in Miles's mind, of avoiding an assault on Santiago. On July 5 Miles, almost certainly motivated by the commendable goal of keeping loses at a minimum, suggested to Alger that since the army's objective in Cuba had been accomplished with Cervera's defeat, "I deem the present time most favorable for proceeding immediately to Puerto Rico. I consider it of the highest importance that we should take and keep that island, which is the gateway to the Spanish possessions in the Western Hemisphere." The secretary of war later recalled that Miles's "proposition to withdraw our army from the siege of the garrison and city of Santiago was, of course, not approved."[67]

Alger seemed almost as reluctant to allow Miles to go to Cuba as he was to accept Miles's recommendation to make Puerto Rico the prime objective of the war. As early as June 23, Miles personally sought to persuade the president to permit him to take charge of the front-line troops; his wishes were sidetracked, however, by the need to supervise preparations for the Puerto Rico campaign. As late as the evening of July 5, the *Tampa Morning Tribune* reported that the administration had decided against sending Miles to Cuba because "General Miles now sees that General Shafter is competent to conduct the campaign and if Miles should go, it might be a reflection on Shafter's ability."[68]

Even after Miles departed from Washington on the evening of July 7, en route for the cruiser *Yale,* anchored off Charleston, Alger apparently had second thoughts about sending him to Cuba. In Colonel Maus's confidential report, he reminded Miles that when the commanding general's party boarded the steamer on the evening of the eighth, they were told that the ship had been held for them despite the fact that "a telegram, sent after your departure from Washington, had been received, directing the vessel to sail."[69]

The secretary of war's express desire to prevent an injustice to Shafter also influenced him to send a telegram that could have disrupted command of the Fifth Corps, and certainly did humiliate the commanding general. On July 7 the adjutant general wired Shafter that Alger "directs me to inform you that Gen. Miles left here at 10:40 last night for Santiago with instructions not to, in any manner, supersede you as commander of the troops in the field near Santiago, so long as you are able for duty." In fact, few dispute Miles's contention that: *"No such order about superseding was ever give to me"* (emphasis in original). As Miles had suspected in Tampa, the secretary of war tampered with the commanding general's authority in Cuba, but in this case Alger's handiwork would eventually become public knowledge.[70]

Miles left for the front with no regrets at leaving the world of bureaucrats and their intrigues behind him. At Washington's railroad terminal, he told a *Herald* reporter waiting to see him off that "I prefer to be in the company of soldiers rather than '———' and then he paused. 'I love to be among brave men,' he continued. 'I am never so happy as when I am on the battlefield.'"[71]

– CHAPTER 13 –

The Surrender at Santiago and the Puerto Rico Campaign

NEAR MIDNIGHT ON July 8, 1898, Miles sailed from Charleston for the Cuban battlefront aboard the trans-Atlantic steamer *Paris,* which had been converted into a cruiser and renamed the *Yale.* The *Yale* traveled in company with the *Columbia,* another former ocean liner. Now armed and carrying approximately fifteen hundred reinforcements for the Fifth Corps, the two ships reached Santiago de Cuba on the morning of July 11. Just three weeks earlier, on June 22, Shafter's troops had begun to disembark at Daquiri following the discovery of Admiral Pascual de Cervera's fleet of Spanish warships in the Santiago harbor by Commodore Winfield Scott Schley's Flying Squadron on May 28.

A formidable fleet from the navy's North Atlantic Squadron, commanded by Acting Rear Admiral William T. Sampson, joined the Flying Squadron's blockade on June 1. It would have been foolhardy for the U.S. warships, now under Sampson's orders, to risk the minefields and forts shielding the Spanish ships anchored within the harbor. Thus, while the navy bottled up Cervera's fleet in Santiago, the army fought to expose those ships by neutralizing the harbor's defenses. When Cervera's squadron sought to flee from a no-longer-secure sanctuary on July 3, following the capture of El Caney and San Juan Hill by the Fifth Corps two days earlier, every one of his ships was destroyed by navy gunners. The task of capturing the city of Santiago still faced the men of Maj. Gen. William R. Shafter's Fifth Corps, now disconcerted because the first cases of yellow fever had raised the fear of an epidemic.

The *Yale* and *Columbia* approached Santiago during a naval bombardment of the city's defenses. In response to a message from Miles, however, Sampson interrupted his duties aboard his flagship, the *New York,* to meet with the commanding general on the *Yale.* At this conference, Miles proposed to capture Santiago by landing troops first on the west side of the harbor and then on the east side, and he received Sampson's assurance that the fleet's firepower would support the planned invasion. Following this meeting, Miles landed at Siboney, a port in American hands approximately nine miles east of Santiago. Here, he telegraphed Shafter that he would visit him at his headquarters the following day, the twelfth.[1]

The scene at Siboney must have disheartened Miles, in part because he saw the first signs of an epidemic that might endanger the Fifth Corps. His aide, Lt. Col. Marion Maus, noted that the hospital established for yellow fever victims already had several patients, including Brig. Gen. Henry M. Duffield, commander of a brigade of Michigan volunteers, and Adj. Gen. Henry C. Corbin's son. A distressed Maus found the area "dirty and in disorder; tents containing disabled or sick soldiers were scattered about; the grounds had not been policed, and a number of old shacks were still standing, some of which had been infected with yellow fever."

Maus described an incident in his report to Miles that reminded him "of the poor Greeks" whom they had observed in the 1897 war with Turkey. "Wagons were arriving from the front filled with sick, at one time I observed a wagon with a load which had remained for perhaps half an hour without anyone paying any attention to it; by your direction the surgeon was ordered to have the occupants taken into the hospital." Maus added, "The wagons were common escort wagons, without springs." Miles responded by instructing Col. Charles R. Greenleaf, chief surgeon of the army, to correct unsatisfactory conditions at the hospital compound, including the burning of old buildings.[2]

On July 12, Miles's second day on Cuban soil, he and his staff rode some six miles to Shafter's camp, situated along a rain-swollen tributary of the San Juan River. With a critical eye, Maus noted that "The ground upon which the camp was located was muddy and the accommodations very poor. There was little tentage, while it rained most continuously." Miles's aide also expressed concern about Shafter, judging that the general "was evidently not in good physical condition for active service; his foot was swollen and heavily bandaged, while an attendant was continuously rubbing his neck."[3]

At the conclusion of the discussion between the two generals, Miles directed Shafter to invite Spanish general José Toral, commander of the Spanish

Fourth Army Corps occupying Santiago de Cuba, to a meeting between the lines during a cease-fire. (Toral had assumed command of the enemy troops in Santiago when Gen. Arsenio Linares was seriously wounded at San Juan Heights on July 1.) Miles also asked that Toral be informed that the commanding general of the American army had arrived in Cuba with reinforcements. Miles had earlier decided to leave these troops berthed aboard the *Yale* and *Columbia,* delaying his planned invasion in order to give Toral a chance to surrender.[4]

Miles believed the situation in Cuba to be so critical that he cabled Washington for "discretionary authority" to conduct what he later termed an "immediate and decisive action" in case negotiations failed. The reply from Secretary of War Russell Alger authorized Miles to "accept surrender by granting parole to officers and men, the officers retaining their side arms. The officers and men after parole to return to Spain, the United States assisting." If the surrender terms were rejected, Alger ordered Miles to "assault, unless in your judgement an assault would fail. Consult with Sampson and pursue such course as to the assault as you jointly agree upon. Matter should be settled promptly."[5]

If Toral should refuse Miles's terms, Alger sought to ensure the success of an assault by asking Secretary of the Navy Long to "order the fleet off Santiago to at once force its way into the bay, if possible, to aid the army in the capture of Santiago and the Spanish army defending it." Santiago had to be taken as soon as possible because yellow fever had already broken out among the campaigners and heavy rains had eroded supply routes to the battlefield and weakened front-line trenches, "making the holding of our lines almost impossible." The rains were so heavy that during a visit to the battlefield Miles was wildly cheered by men in the 6th Illinois, who preferred going stark naked to the discomfort of working in thoroughly soaked uniforms. Even the officer who saluted the commanding general wore nothing but a gold chain.[6]

With a combined attack from the sea scheduled to be launched against Santiago at noon on July 14 if the Spanish commander remained defiant, Miles felt ready to negotiate from a position of strength despite the Fifth Corps's problems. Earlier talks between Shafter and Toral had floundered when Washington rejected Toral's offer to abandon Santiago if his troops were allowed to retire to Holguín, protected by a promise of safe conduct.

After Toral turned down a counterproposal to surrender unconditionally, the cease-fire ended at 4:00 P.M. on July 10. The fleet then renewed the bombardment of Santiago, which lasted until 1:00 P.M. the next day, when another truce went into effect to permit a new round of talks to begin.[7]

Following Shafter's note of July 12, the two sides met at 9:00 A.M. the following day in a valley between the opposing lines. The negotiators gathered under the spreading branches of a tropical tree, which would later be called the "Tree of Peace." Two staff officers and an interpreter accompanied General Toral, while the larger American contingent included Generals Miles, Shafter, and Wheeler. Even though the new terms approved by McKinley contained the attractive promise of repatriation, the *Times* reported that Toral could not accept them because the United States demanded that his men leave their weapons behind and their fortifications intact. The Spanish general explained through an interpreter that he would be court-martialed and shot if he allowed his men to abandon their arms. When Shafter reminded him that the Fifth Corps had just been reinforced, Toral shrugged and replied, "I am but a subordinate and I obey my Government. If it be necessary, we can die at our posts."[8]

The Spanish general's brave declaration and soldierly bearing impressed the Americans. For example, Maus noticed that Toral "was by no means in good physical condition; his pale, sallow face was much worn and showed the effect of fever, from which he said that he was suffering. He was a very dignified and courtly man, and most courteous in his manner."[9]

Toral spoke candidly of his predicament, admitting in Maus's presence that one of his staff officers had counted fifty-seven ships in the American fleet menacing Santiago. Toral's added knowledge that many of the ships were transporting troops convinced Maus that the Spanish general "was depressed and hopeless as to continuing the resistance." According to the *New York Times,* however, Toral seemed unconcerned about the resumption of the naval bombardment because he claimed that on the tenth and eleventh, gunfire from the warships wounded only six of his soldiers and damaged only four houses. A naval board later determined that forty-six shells had hit the target area, damaging fifty-seven structures, but some of the damage may have been wrought by earlier shellings of the city.[10]

An interpreter aiding the American officers prepared notes of the formal proposals and counterproposals discussed by Shafter and Toral. After Toral explained that he had to obey his government's orders, he suggested lengthening the truce beyond 5:00 A.M. of July 14. With well-chosen words he explained that the delay would "allow me the time to receive an answer from my government. It can do you no harm; it will not weaken your position; it will not strengthen mine. I appeal to your soldierly feelings." In a plea that all military men would understand, he continued: "You see, I am in a very bad plight, and my strong desire, my only wish, is to save the honor of the Spanish army." He concluded with the prayer that he would not have "to submit the forces under my command, and myself, to the insult and humiliation of a surrender, or to the disaster of a stubborn defense, for they deserve better treatment. This is all I ask; this is all I can do."

When Shafter denied the appeal for a delay, Miles requested "permission . . . to say a few words." "Certainly, certainly," responded the commander of the Fifth Corps. Earlier, when Miles had courteously inquired about General Linares's wound, Toral replied that his commanding general would probably have his left arm amputated at the shoulder. When Miles now attempted to convince Toral to surrender, he again exhibited a spirit of concern for a foe, attempting to relieve the burden of duty "at any cost" from his opponent's shoulders.

Miles reminded Toral that before the earlier battles in the Santiago campaign, "you had a fleet in the harbor to protect, and a city and its inhabitants to defend. You were expecting reinforcements, and your way for a retreat was open, but now the circumstances are entirely different." Miles reviewed how the situation had deteriorated. "Your fleet has been destroyed; the majority of the inhabitants have left the city. You are surrounded by overwhelming forces. Your retreat is cut. You expect and perhaps could get no reinforcements." After warning the besieged general that up to fifty thousand American reinforcements were available, Miles suggested that Toral's predicament justified surrender. "'There are occasions in which it is more than a duty—a necessity—for a commanding general to act for himself, independent of his government. And if you have no authority, you ought to have it,' said General Miles, smiling."

Toral responded that he lacked the authority and thus "I can do nothing else than obey the army regulations and do my duty." He then repeated the plea denied by Shafter: "what harm could come to you from granting the delay I ask for? My only wish is to avoid the loss of blood and to save the honor of the Spanish army." Shafter remained unmoved and held firm to the 5:00 A.M. deadline until Miles arranged for a private conversation with Shafter on the far side of the "Tree of Peace."

When the two major generals returned to face their opponents, the interpreter had the impression that Miles "looked worried." He also reported that, "After short parleying, General Shafter said he would allow General Toral until noon of the 14th, and that General Toral would endeavor to reach a decision or to have an answer from his government." Reviewing this episode, even Secretary of War Alger admitted that Miles's "Good judgment on this occasion undoubtedly saved much bloodshed."[11]

Following this concession, the Americans returned to their lines and gathered outside the tent that served as Wheeler's headquarters. The scene impressed a correspondent from the *New York Times,* who described it for his readers. Miles, wearing a blue fatigue uniform distinguished only by his officer's shoulder straps, and a single gold cord around the crown of his campaign hat, "looking the ideal soldier, sat on an empty ammunition box and formed the center of the party." Shafter sat to his right, while Gen. Calixto García, the Cuban insurgent leader, wearing a white uniform spattered with mud, flanked him on the left. The reporter seemed taken by the Cuban revolutionary leader, who "wore a large, weather-worn Panama hat, and at his side was a silver-mounted machete. Gen. Garcia has a strong, swarthy face, with a deep bullet scar in his forehead. In a general way, he is not unlike a Cuban edition of General Miles." Wheeler, "with a grizzled beard, small of stature, and in a brown campaign uniform," faced the three other generals. Beside Wheeler stood Sampson's representative, naval constructor Richmond P. Hobson, who had failed in his brave attempt to block Santiago harbor with the collier *Merrimac.*

Protected from the weather by the tent's awning, the generals and their staff officers referred to maps as they discussed plans to end the campaign. Then, after a meal of hardtack, beans, and coffee, Miles and Shafter, accompanied by their aides, joined García in an inspection of that part of the lines manned by Cuban troops.[12]

The following morning the Spanish defenders watched as the invasion fleet maneuvered into position to land infantrymen under the cover of naval gunfire if negotiations failed. Fortunately for all involved, before the truce expired at noon Shafter received a letter from Toral containing the good news that Captain-General Ramón Blanco y Erenas, the supreme commander of the Spanish forces in Cuba, had authorized Toral to "agree upon capitulation on the basis of returning to Spain.[13]

At noon on the fourteenth the peacemakers again gathered under the branches of the tree in the valley. When this brief conference ended, the American negotiators believed that all that had to be done before the formal surrender was to select commissioners who would draw up the articles of capitulation. The American representatives, Generals Wheeler and Lawton, aided by Lt. John D. Miley, met with their Spanish counterparts later that afternoon. At this session, a potential problem developed when the Spanish commissioners disclosed that they were only empowered to arrange a "preliminary agreement." The nettlesome demand that the surrendered troops be allowed to retain their arms also resurfaced.[14]

When Lawton insisted that an attempt be made to resolve the differences that night, Toral responded by accompanying his commissioners to a 9:30 P.M. meeting. Here he personally asserted that the actual "capitulation" could only take place after the "Government at Madrid wired its approval." In some consternation, Shafter telegraphed Miles, who had returned to Siboney, preparatory to boarding the *Yale* on the fifteenth. Shafter alerted Miles that "The surrender is not, as we thought, settled, and there may be trouble yet over the matter. All sorts of points are being raised—the greater being that capitulation cannot be made without confirmation by the Madrid Government."[15]

This development did not faze Miles, who reassured Shafter that "Surrender was as positive as anything could be and they asked that a commission be appointed to arrange details to carry into effect the terms of surrender." Miles later reported that Toral's "manner was so sincere and the language of General Blanco so positive, that I felt no hesitancy in accepting it in good faith, and stated that he would surrender, under the condition that the Spanish troops should be repatriated by the United States." Miles added that Toral had pleasantly surprised him at the conference by agreeing to surrender all of the Spanish troops in the Department of Santiago, many of whom were safely garrisoned up to one hundred miles from the closest American troops.[16]

On the morning of July 16, the approval from Madrid that Miles had anticipated reached Toral, giving him permission to surrender. The nine articles of capitulation sanctioned by the Spanish government confirmed all of the terms agreed upon during preliminary negotiations. These included the obligation of the Spanish forces to aid in the removal of mines in Santiago harbor and permission from the United States for Toral to return the military records of the Department of Santiago to Spain. The ninth of the Articles of Agreement concerned the potentially divisive question of who would have custody of the Spanish weapons. The commissioners agreed that the defenders of Santiago would be allowed "to march out with all the honors of war, depositing their arms, to be disposed of by the United States in the future, the American Commissioners to recommend to their government that the arms of the soldiers be returned to those 'who so bravely defended them.'"[17]

At 9:00 A.M. on July 17, the American delegation, led by General Shafter and accompanied by General García, received General Toral's formal surrender. Shafter set a chivalrous tone to this meeting by giving Toral the spurs and sword of General Joaquín Vara del Rey, who fell at El Caney. After General Toral announced, "I deliver up the city and province of Santiago de Cuba into the authority of the United States," he reached to surrender his sword, only to be stopped by a motion from Shafter. As the Spanish officers then presented arms, Shafter accepted Santiago "in the name of the Government of the United States." From the *New York,* Miles declared, "I am most gratified over the surrender of Santiago. The terms are just as good as an unconditional surrender."[18]

Although Shafter had behaved impeccably toward a defeated foe during the surrender ceremony, his relations with some of his own comrades in arms took an unpleasant turn. Naval officers in Sampson's squadron felt that he had slighted them because they had not been represented at Toral's capitulation, and, as at Tampa, Shafter again began to ignore Miles. As Maus noted, "With the favorable trend of affairs the manner of General Shafter had greatly changed; he at once became confident, captious and resentful."[19]

Just one day after Toral's formal surrender, Shafter informed Miles of a unique arrangement in the Army's chain of command. Miles became aware of this development shortly after he suggested to Shafter that "if it is thought more advisable to move troops to fresh camp on the foothills or mountain side as surgeons advise, act accordingly." After Shafter acknowledged his willingness to comply because "no one is more anxious than myself to get away from here," he added that: "It seems from the orders given me that you regard my forces as part of your command." He then explained to Miles that "nothing will give me greater pleasure than serving under you, General, and I shall comply with all your requests and directions, but I was told by the Secretary of War that you were not to supersede me in command here."[20]

Miles reacted coolly to this turn of events, informing Shafter that he had "no desire and have carefully avoided any appearance of superseding you." He reminded his subordinate, however, that his "command is a part of the United States Army, which I have the honor to command." He also called Shafter's attention to the July 13 cablegram addressed to Major-General Miles, which confirmed his supremacy when the secretary of war authorized him to decide how the Santiago campaign should be concluded.[21]

Although Miles temporarily dismissed Shafter's challenge to his authority in order to direct his full attention to the Puerto Rican campaign, he would vent his resentment when the war ended. Miles had no regrets as he prepared to leave Cuba; besides Shafter's affront to his prestige as commanding general, he shared the misery of all of those who served on the island during the rainy season. According to the *New York Times,* "rain now falls in sheets every day, drenching the soldiers, washing out the roads, and swelling the streams into torrents." Like Miles, Maus had soldiered under extremes in temperature, but nothing had prepared him for the "hurtful" experience of campaigning while exposed to unrelenting tropical rainstorms. He reported that he had been "exposed to the Arctic cold of Montana or the burning heat of Arizona and New Mexico, and yet, in no case have I ever before felt such enervating and injurious effects [of weather], and I can readily understand the terrible results upon our Army exposed for a much greater length of time."[22]

When Maus considered the suffering of the troops, he complained that the American forces should not have been sent overseas "without necessary supplies, and at the same time without due provision for the wounded, in establishing properly equipped hospitals and ambulances. In the end it would have paid to have delayed for this purpose, or not to have landed the troops until it would have been done properly." Schofield also looked at the Santiago campaign with a professional eye, and saw things much the way Maus had:

"The unnecessary losses, suffering and privations which the army has endured have been caused by the incompetence and reckless ambition of the Chief of the War Department."[23]

The *Army and Navy Journal* reprinted an article from the *London Spectator,* probably the most balanced opinion regarding the difficulties braved by the Fifth Corps. Looking at America's war from foreign shores, the *Spectator* noted that "The United States is learning with indignation the details of what its troops had to endure before Santiago, and is inclined to make a scapegoat of Mr. Alger." The British observer argued that "It is hardly fair to put all the blame on him. The real cause of the misery and muddle was the absurd belief so widely entertained in America that you can make war without preparation. Amateur soldiering, especially amateur transport and commissariat, is cruel work."[24]

The Puerto Rican invasion fleet commanded by Capt. Francis J. Higginson, sailed from Guantánamo Bay, Cuba, on July 21. Five warships, the *Massachusetts, Dixie, Gloucester, Columbia,* and *Yale,* the last two carrying troops, escorted nine transports. The 3,415-man expeditionary force included the 6th Massachusetts and 6th Illinois, plus five regular light batteries of artillery, two companies of engineers, and a signal corps company. These units had originally been ordered to Cuba as reinforcements for Shafter, but with peace at hand Miles kept the troops cooped aboard their transports and isolated from the disease-ridden island. Although he had also been given the authority to enlist units of the Fifth Corps into his command, when Miles declined to do so he explained to Shafter that "First: they have done enough; Second: they might carry the fever."[25]

The troops who sailed with Miles were to be organized into a division to be commanded by Brig. Gen. Guy V. Henry. This landing force would be augmented by the 3,571 troops under Maj. Gen. James H. Wilson's command who had left Charleston for Puerto Rico on July 20. Four days later, 2,896 additional officers and men, led by Brig. Gen. Theodore Schwan, set sail for Puerto Rico from Tampa. On July 28, Maj. Gen. John R. Brooke, who would serve under Miles as commander of the First Corps, sailed from Newport News with another contingent of 5,317 officers and men. According to the adjutant general, when the Puerto Rican expeditionary force reached its peak strength in August, there were 641 officers and 16,332 enlisted men on the island. Following the war, with Spanish records available for study, Miles reported that the enemy garrison on Puerto Rico numbered 8,233 regulars and 9,107 volunteers.[26]

During the second day at sea, Miles surprised Higginson with the news that he intended to land at Guánica, on the southwest shore of Puerto Rico, rather than at Cape Fajardo, on the northeast tip of the island, as originally planned. Over Higginson's objections Miles prevailed with the argument that "so much time has occurred since the movement was decided in that direction [Cape Fajardo] and publicity has been given the enterprise, that the enemy has undoubtedly become apprised of our purpose."[27]

Although many newspapers had indeed announced that Fajardo would be Miles's objective, the *New York Times* anticipated a change in plans, and correctly speculated that the landing would take place at Guánica, fifteen miles west of Ponce. This educated guess followed the July 23 release by the War Department's Bureau of Information of a press statement titled "Military Notes on Puerto Rico." The *Times* assumed that most of the information contained in the release had been gathered by Lt. Henry F. Whitney, who had disguised himself as a deckhand and sailed to Puerto Rico aboard a British cargo vessel. From May 15 to June 5, Whitney risked his life spying along the southern coast of the enemy-held island.[28]

Following the campaign, when a correspondent from the *Army and Navy Journal* asked Miles about his decision not to land at Fajardo, the general pointed out that he had "proceeded from Santiago to the north side of Puerto Rico, where I was to have met steam lighters and tugs from the United States. These did not put in an appearance, and, in fact, not one of them turned up to this day." Miles added, "There is no harbor at Fajardo, and not securing the lighters and tugs, I determined to change my plan and surprise the enemy, at the same time securing a safe landing for my forces." He had avoided a fiasco at Fajardo with his decision to change the fleet's destination. The absence of lighters or barges, used to unload supplies from the convoy, would have critically handicapped an invasion. This is particularly true when one considers that the harbor the invasion force was dependent on was described by the *New York Times* as "poor, being reached by difficult channels, whose greatest depth is 18 feet."

Miles also returned to the argument that had persuaded Captain Higginson to change course for Guánica. The "Spaniards were fully informed as to the plans adopted in Washington. They were given out there in minutest detail long before I was ready to move, and the whole thing was thoroughly exploited before the public and the press of the entire world." If, as Miles believed, the Spanish were concentrated at Fajardo, the Americans would have found themselves at a decided disadvantage. Miles, who later wrote that Fajardo "had been originally selected at the instance of officers of the Navy," used a map to explain to an English reporter that the landing would have been made on a peninsula. "You might get hemmed in in a place like that. It is so small."[29]

The *Army and Navy Journal* applauded Miles's decision to abandon Fajardo in favor of Guánica, citing as reasons that "Ponce, the most important town in Puerto Rico, is but a short distance away—that the majority of the insurgent element is located in the southwest, and lastly, that every step gained from Ponce to San Juan would give him [Miles] control of the only railroad and projected railroads." Thus, by landing at Guánica, Miles also found himself in the perfect position to comply with the secretary of war's July 23 instructions "to have one of your engineer officers make a survey for a railroad which it may be decided to build up towards San Juan." This letter, hand-carried by a lieutenant appointed to Miles's staff, explained that, "If you think that it is best, and if it is built, it should be a good road to be used hereafter for commercial as well as military purposes, and thus have a permanent value; all of which will belong to the United States, of course."[30]

While the press wondered where Miles would strike, the Spanish deployed small craft whose crews searched for telltale smoke on the horizon. To thwart these seaborne scouts, the blacked-out invasion fleet slipped through the Mona Passage toward Guánica at night. Miles recalled, "In the gray shadowed light of the evening and night the fleet presented a picture unlike anything I had ever seen before." In searching for a comparison, the Indian-war veteran wrote, "One familiar with the western plains of a quarter of a century ago might have been reminded of a pack of large gray wolves cautiously and noiselessly moving in the shades of night, or the dim light that ushers in the dawn, upon their prey."[31]

On the morning of the July 25, the sun's first rays struck the oversize flag streaming from the *Gloucester*'s mast as the warship boldly sailed past the bay's rocky headlands into Guánica harbor. J. Pierpont Morgan's yacht the

Corsair had been renamed the *Gloucester,* after being converted for use by the navy. The armed cruiser, commanded by a survivor of the *Maine* and a hero of Santiago, Lt. Cmdr. Richard Wainwright, fired at a blockhouse, then into the hills. The ship's gunners carefully avoided hitting the town to spare civilian lives as they displayed the *Gloucester*'s fire power in an attempt to weaken the enemy's will to fight.

A thirty-man landing party encountered no resistance as a launch carried them to the shore defended by the blockhouse. Spanish infantry opened up on the Americans only after two sailors lowered a Spanish flag flying in front of the fortified building and raised an American flag in its place. The sailors, who had carried a Colt rapid-fire gun ashore with them, answered the Mausers, while the *Gloucester*'s three and six pounders attempted to discourage Spanish cavalry detected riding to the aid of their countrymen.

Seeing his landing party in imminent danger, Wainwright called over to the Associated Press dispatch boat, *Cynthia II,* the *Gloucester*'s sole companion in the harbor, to complain: "They fired on us after their flag was down and ours was up, and after I had spared the town for the sake of the women and children. The next town I strike I will blow up." Back on shore, the landing party had strung barbed wire in front of a hastily dug trench, topped with stones, which they had named Fort Wainwright in honor of their captain.

Some of the Spanish cavalry reached the town's lone street while infantry were still sniping at the Americans. The threat so aroused those aboard the *Gloucester* that even the ship's doctor and paymaster could not be kept from the cruiser's guns. As the gunners began to home in on their targets, the Spanish hastily withdrew from Guánica, abandoning the town to the Americans before 9:45 A.M. The landing party came through the skirmish unscathed, while four Spaniards were found to have been killed.

In response to a semaphore message from shore calling for reinforcements, regular artillerymen from one of the seven transports in the fleet, the *Lampasas,* were the first to disembark, followed by Red Cross nurses. The transports were methodically unloaded as the troops crowded into boats, which were towed to land, four or five at a time, by steam launches. After Miles stepped aboard the *Gloucester* from the launch of the *Massachusetts* to offer his congratulations to Wainwright, he joined his forces who were sorting themselves out on shore. Probably the men of the two volunteer infantry regiments were the most relieved at being on solid ground again, since they had been cramped aboard their transports for more than two weeks. Although most of the disembarked troops were fit, at least thirty men from the 6th Massachusetts had been afflicted with typhoid fever while aboard the *Yale,* from which the only fatality had been buried at sea.[32]

The *New York Times,* which had based its prediction of a landing at Guánica on information supplied by the War Department, used the same source to forecast the strategy of the campaign. After Yauco and Ponce on the southern coast fell, the *Times* expected Miles to advance northeast across the island toward San Juan, seventy miles away. Field artillery batteries should have no difficulty keeping pace with the infantry in this drive since Puerto Rico's two most important cities were connected by what the article called a "splendid fourteen-foot/wide/macadamized road." In contrast, in the northeast, where Miles had refused to land, the first dozen or so miles from Fajardo to San Juan were "nothing but a cart track. In the rainy season it is almost impassable, and in the absence of a vast amount of engineering work, would soon be as difficult as that from Siboney to the front at Santiago."[33]

The 6th Massachusetts and the 6th Illinois had been formed into a brigade commanded by Brig. Gen. George A. Garretson. During the evening of July 25, a company from this brigade, while an outpost duty, detected the enemy. Although two additional companies were dispatched to reinforce the picket line, at about 2:00 A.M. on July 26 the Spanish were willing to challenge the Americans in battle. General Garretson raced to the scene with five additional companies and, in what Miles termed "a spirited and decisive engagement," drove the enemy from the road to Yauco. Richard Harding Davis, the noted correspondent, found humor in the poor discipline shown by green troops shooting at shadows in the night. Apparently, some stray shots hit a transport housing "the Red Cross nurses, who were delighted at being under fire, even if the fire came from the Sixth Illinois."[34]

Although Garretson would receive Miles's commendation for "his courage, skill, and enterprise in winning the first fight on Puerto Rican soil," two other officers felt the commanding general's wrath for their flawed performance in battle. Miles requested and the secretary of war ultimately accepted the resignation of both the regimental commander and the executive officer of the 6th Massachusetts. The colonel of the 6th had first attracted Miles's attention when, as Miles informed Washington, the colonel "feigned sickness" at Santiago, then earned his enmity when he repeated the ploy at Guánica.

In response to an inquiry by the secretary of war, instigated by the governor of Massachusetts, Miles further explained why the examining board that he had convened had accepted the resignation of both officers. After Colonel Greenleaf, the chief surgeon, examined the regimental commander and found him to be malingering, he ordered the colonel off a hospital ship anchored at Guánica. This occurred on the very evening that his regiment would face an enemy for the first time. As for the lieutenant colonel, Miles complained in his letter to Washington that the officer remained in his tent even after "part of his regiment was engaged. He was within sound of the fight and did not even assemble balance of regiment to reenforce part engaged if it should have been necessary." The *New York Times* threw further light on the shortcomings of the regiment's officers when it reported that "white officers refuse to return the salutes of the Negro company" in the 6th Massachusetts.[35]

On July 27 four men from Garretson's command were wounded as the brigade drove the Spanish from Yauco in a fight that cost the enemy three killed and thirteen wounded. Although both the highway and railroad to Ponce now lay open, the navy beat the army to the city. On the same day that Garretson took Yauco, Maj. Gen. James H. Wilson aboard the *Obdam,* and Brig. Gen. Oswald H. Ernst on the *Grande Duchesse,* arrived at Guánica with reinforcements. Rather than allow the troops to disembark, Miles informed Higginson that these men should be landed at La Playa, the port two miles from Ponce. To pave the way for this operation, Cmdr. Charles H. Davis of the auxiliary cruiser *Dixie,* supported by two gunboats, the *Annapolis* and the *Wasp,* tested the harbor's defenses on the afternoon of July 27 and found them to be nonexistent.[36]

Although Commander Davis received official recognition for accepting the surrender of Ponce after his squadron had penetrated the harbor, a youthful ensign from the *Wasp* probably received the honor before the commander had. According to Richard Harding Davis, the ensign, who was the first officer ashore, confronted the captain of the port with an ultimatum that Ponce must surrender or suffer a naval bombardment. When the harbormaster telephoned the military commander of Ponce about the threat, the commander agreed to withdraw his garrison of some three hundred troops from Ponce in order to spare the city. The correspondent added that three officers who had sauntered into Ponce to see the sights, and finally Miles, also received the surrender of the city. The readiness of Ponce to yield seemed to amuse Davis, who chuckled that "for anyone in uniform it was most unsafe to enter the town at any time unless he came prepared to accept its unconditional surrender."[37]

The bloodless transfer of power at La Playa, the port of Ponce, took place at 6:00 A.M. on July 28, as marines raised the American flag over the customhouse. With the exception of the harbormaster, who remained at his post after Captain Davis assured him that he would not be taken prisoner, every Spanish soldier and bureaucrat had withdrawn from Ponce. The commanding officer would later be imprisoned by his government for his unwillingness to resist the Americans; but, as Miles pointed out in his opponent's defense, "it would have been fruitless if not disastrous for him to do so, as he would have been menaced both in front and rear by a superior force."[38]

Miles sailed to La Playa with the convoy carrying General Wilson's command. Wilson came ashore at about 7:30 A.M., aboard the first boat launched from transports, and Miles landed about fifteen minutes later. Richard Harding Davis described the warm welcome that greeted Miles: "the several thousand people who were waiting for General Miles on the wharves and housetops and swamping the small boats in the wake of his gig shouted 'Vivas' and shrieked and cheered." Wilson, the military governor of the city and province of Ponce, made the customhouse his temporary headquarters, then joined Miles on the balcony of the alcalde's palace at Ponce to acknowledge the enthusiastic salutes of the population.

Although both generals were impressive in their dress uniforms, the towns folk who gathered before the palace were apparently disappointed to learn that Miles, rather than Wilson, was the commanding general. Like all of the men on the island except the clergy, Wilson shunned the use of a razor. This led onlookers to whisper that Miles, who only sported a mustache, "should have been an archbishop."[39]

Following the entrance into Ponce, Miles fueled the spirit of goodwill with a proclamation declaring, "The chief object of the American military forces will be to overthrow the armed authority of Spain and to give the people of your beautiful island the largest measure of liberty consistent with the military occupation." This document was probably drawn up at the War Department, since Alger had written Miles on July 23 that he hoped "to have a proclamation in Spanish, signed by you, to be sent in great numbers, by scouting parties, etc., throughout Puerto Rico, telling those people that your coming is not to interfere with their personal and religious rights, but to protect them all."[40]

Miles took seriously the provision that promised the Puerto Rican people that his forces intended "to bring you protection, not only to yourselves but to your property." A regular artilleryman recalled that in Puerto Rico "To steal anything, from a kiss to a cow, was a capital offense; while houses and churches might have been lined with gold and jasper, or infected with smallpox, so stringently were we kept out of them—at least during the hostile period."[41]

The artilleryman correctly noted the good behavior of most of the American troops during the campaign, although breakdowns occurred. For example, on August 12, the very day that military operations were suspended, a private believed to be in the 6th Illinois reportedly enjoyed a meal at a home in Adjuntas after eliciting the dinner invitation with his rifle. The investigation of this offense came to an abrupt halt when the name of the culprit, furnished by division headquarters, did not match any of those on the regiment's roster. Four days later, residents of Utuado complained about the far more serious crimes of highway robbery and rape. Unfortunately, the perpetrators could not be identified, but the division commander attempted to protect the civilian population from further violations by declaring the town off limits to troops after 8:00 P.M.[42]

Those found guilty of misconduct paid a high price for their transgression. A private in the 6th Illinois who paid a restaurant bill with Confederate money, which he probably perceived to be a lark, received a sentence of thirteen months at hard labor. In a more serious incident, a private in the 2d Wisconsin Volunteer Infantry was sentenced to a life term at Leavenworth for killing a regular from the 13th Infantry in a barroom brawl.[43]

The troops had been kept on a tight rein to prevent them from marring the good relations that Miles was determined to establish with the people of Puerto Rico. One of the reasons Miles later gave for landing at Guánica was to take advantage of what he characterized as the "considerable disaffection among the people in the southern portion of the island." The *New York Times* confirmed that the region "of Guanica and Ponce is said to be the section of the island where the opposition to Spanish rule is strongest and where a propaganda in favor of accepting the Americans as deliverers instead of as enemies could be most advantageously begun." The article presumed that Miles intended to win "over the people of the province by as many friendly overtures as possible, having regard to the ultimate benefits of such a policy on the permanent American rule, which it is proposed to establish there."[44]

Almost as soon as Miles landed at Guánica, his expectation of assistance from Puerto Rican revolutionaries came to pass. A courier made his way to Miles with a message from Félix Matos Bernier, the insurgent leader of the province of Ponce. The letter promised that the invading American army could "count on the great masses who are prepared to second your gigantic strength" probably pleased Miles; more important, however, was the hard intelligence that the guerrillas could pass along to his forces. In Bernier's very first communication with the Americans, he warned that at the outskirts of Ponce, "on the roads of Adjuntas and Canas, the Spanish government is actively engaged in constructing several trenches to foolishly obstruct the march of the army of liberty, and they are concealing themselves in the small neighboring hills and difficult passes in the cañons in order to carry out this resistance."[45]

To foster the allegiance of the Puerto Ricans to the United States, Miles went on a flag-raising campaign, asking the War Department to send him all of the American flags that could be spared.[46] The request may actually have been prompted by the people of Ponce, who had spontaneously paraded past Generals Wilson and Miles on July 28. Richard Harding Davis noted that the only thing missing during this review "was an American flag. It was only a detail, but the populace seemed to miss it." The correspondent believed that extra flags were "about the only article with which the expedition was not supplied. Frantic cabling to Washington repaired the loss, and within a week, flags were sent out all over the island and raised upon the roofs of many a city hall."[47]

Miles went beyond merely showing the flag to win over the island's inhabitants to America's cause. He paid for supplies and rented ox-carts and other equipment at Juanica, rather than indulging in the usual military practice of simply appropriating whatever was needed. Miles also had as many laborers as possible hired and paid promptly, not only for the services that they could provide the army but also as a way to provide a living for many of the island's poorer families. Furthermore, at Ponce, when Miles discovered that native foremen were taking a cut from the pay stevedores earned, he instantly put a stop to the extortion. With Miles establishing high standards of conduct, Richard Harding Davis noted that his command "played the conquerors with tact, with power, and like gentlemen."[48]

As a result of Miles's policy of respecting the rights of the people of the island, Maus could comment that "our Army was received as friends and liberators." Davis supported the colonel's view, observing that "Peace came with Porto Rico occupied by our troops and with Porto Ricans blessing our flag." Miles acknowledged this happy state of affairs when he reported that "At least four-fifths of the people hail with great joy the arrival of United States troops, and requests for our national flag to place over public buildings come in from every direction."[49]

As good as relations with the islanders seemed to be, Miles almost overstated the case in one of his reports. A British correspondent broadly smiled when he read this dispatch, which claimed that the welcome at Ponce had been "extremely patriotic." For a moment the general wondered what had prompted the grin, "but after a few seconds his face cleared and he laughed. 'I ought to have used another word,' he said. 'Certainly those people could not have changed into good Americans as quickly as all that. But it will be understood in America.'"[50]

The troops who had entered Ponce to the cheers of the inhabitants soon became restless as they waited to advance on the enemy. General Wilson later complained, with some justification, that in case "our movement into the interior depended upon a prompt advance after our first appearance, it would have been seriously endangered by the failure of the War Department to fill my requisitions, and by its generally inadequate preparation to meet perfectly well-known conditions." Although it took less than a day for the troops to disembark from the transports, more than a week was required to unload their equipment. Wilson blamed the slow operation on the failure of the War Department to satisfy his requests for motorboats and flats.[51]

While the Americans waited to begin the offensive, Puerto Ricans who volunteered for service with the Spanish army began to surrender in droves. On August 2 Miles reported that approximately three hundred volunteers had already turned themselves in, and "reports are received here from different parts of the island that volunteers refuse to march or fight any longer and that in many places they are waiting to surrender and receive their pardons and return to their homes." Invariably, the defecting volunteers, many of whom had served Spain in order to avoid persecution, promptly reported to the U.S. provost marshal's office in Ponce, where they turned in their weapons before being paroled.[52]

Their own countrymen were not as lenient with the volunteers as the Americans had been. A good number were rounded up and hustled to Ponce's plaza by embittered natives, many of whom had been political prisoners. According to the *New York Times,* "Bloodhounds could not have been more savage." The article chastised the "jeering mobs" that "mistook liberty for license and were crazed with a thirst for vengeance." General Wilson received credit for averting a tragedy when he warned the townspeople "that they could not wreak revenge under the protection of our flag, and peremptorily ordered that the arrest of Spanish suspects should cease."[53]

As forces were being assembled for the coming offensive, military analysts looked forward to evaluating the American volunteer regiments that were slated to do most of the fighting. In the Santiago campaign, only two volunteer infantry regiments and one dismounted cavalry regiment took part in the fiercest fighting. In Puerto Rico, fourteen of the seventeen infantry regiments ordered to the island were volunteer units; just one regular cavalry regiment, the Fifth, would serve with three mounted volunteer regiments from Pennsylvania and one each from Brooklyn and New York. Shafter had had to make do in Cuba with no more than five or six light batteries, all regular, on the line at any one time; while Miles would have the support of thirty-six siege guns and sixty field pieces, distributed among six regular and six volunteer light batteries and seven regular heavy batteries.[54]

Miles divided the expeditionary force into four commands, each of which would cross the island to converge on San Juan. Brig. Gen. Theodore Schwan's Independent Brigade, composed solely of regulars until after the fighting ended, would unite with Brig. Gen. Guy V. Henry's Provisional Division as they crossed the western half of Puerto Rico. On the eastern side of the island, Maj. Gen. James H. Wilson's column would move along the main road from Ponce to San Juan, in combination with Maj. Gen. John R. Brooke's command. After speaking to Miles, British correspondent John Black Atkins explained that "Each pair would converge till there were only two armies; and then those two would converge till there was only one army. And that would be when the attack was to be made on San Juan."[55]

Since the two western columns had to cover more ground than the eastern ones in the movement to San Juan, Miles explained to Atkins that the eastern columns "could just be as slow as they liked, I didn't want them to hurry, because, you see, they might have got there too soon." The *Army and Navy Journal* printed a letter applauding Miles's concept of mutually supporting columns, and pointed out that "had the enemy made any resistance he was held in front while his flank was being turned, obliging him to retire."[56]

The expeditionary force camped along the road to San Juan as the troop buildup continued. During the afternoon of July 31, Schwan arrived at Ponce with a force of regulars from Tampa, and that evening the auxiliary cruiser *St. Louis* sailed into the harbor with General Brooke aboard. The next day the *St. Paul,* carrying Brig. Gen. Peter C. Hains and the 4th Ohio, reached the island, and on August 2, the 2d and 4th Pennsylvania came ashore. On August 5, just days before the general offensive began, the 2d and 3d Wisconsin joined the 16th Pennsylvania.[57]

Almost on the eve of battle, as the newly arrived units were being organized into their assigned commands, the volunteers were issued Krag-Jorgensen rifles as replacements for their Springfields. General Wilson later commented, "With any men less intelligent than the American soldier this might have been a costly if not fatal change, but the volunteers readily adapted themselves to the new rifle."[58]

Prior to the major advance, Wilson instructed ten companies of the 16th Pennsylvania to probe along the road to San Juan. On the evening of July 30, the reconnaissance force enjoyed the enthusiastic welcome of the townspeople of Juana Díaz, capping their unopposed ten-mile scout along the island's only true highway. By August 4 the Pennsylvanians had advanced six more miles to the bridge over the Descalabrodo River, with patrols warily continuing toward Coamo.[59]

Wilson expected the enemy to defend Coamo, which he described as "a small and beautiful town in the coffee region some twenty miles inland on the main road." He based his expectation on the town's location, which was "a commanding site of great natural strength, where one determined soldier might well defy a hundred."[60]

Meanwhile, instead of disembarking from the *St. Louis* at Ponce, Brooke received orders to land forty miles farther east at Arroyo. From the third to the fifth of August, units assigned to Brooke's column unloaded their equipment before moving up a side road leading to the highway to San Juan. This spur ran northwest from Arroyo, through Guayama, to Cayey, where it joined the main road. Once at Cayey, Brooke would be in position to cut off the retreat of any Spanish troops from Aibonito, which would be Wilson's objective after taking Coamo.[61]

On August 5 troops in Brooke's column skirmished with the Spanish garrison at Guayama. Two regiments from Brig. Gen. Peter C. Hain's brigade, the 4th Ohio and the 3d Illinois, encountered about five hundred of the enemy. Leading elements of the 4th Ohio exchanged shots with Spanish pickets until five rounds from two dynamite guns convinced the enemy to withdraw into the hills. Three Ohio infantrymen with minor wounds and two Spanish casualties were treated in a temporary hospital; the retreating defenders left behind the body of a comrade killed in the fight. The American liberators were welcomed into what the *New York Times* called "the cleanest and most picturesque" town in Puerto Rico by cheering villagers who had raised a flag in their honor.

Three days later, on August 8, Brooke informed Miles that one officer and five men from the 4th Ohio had been wounded skirmishing with the enemy about three miles north of Guayama. Capt. French Ensor Chadwick, who commanded the *New York* during the Spanish-American War and wrote a history of the war during his retirement, explained that following that skirmish Brooke's "column was not in readiness to advance by reason of the non-arrival of cavalry, artillery, and wagons until August 13."[62]

As preliminary movements were being made along the highway to Ponce, U.S. Marines made unopposed landings along the eastern coast of the island in order to restore service at several lighthouses, including one at Cape San Juan. While the marines were exposing the vulnerability of the eastern coast of Puerto Rico, Miles's chief of engineers, Brig. Gen. Ray Stone, was preparing the way for General Henry to crack open the center of the island."[63]

Miles had the good fortune to have General Stone on his staff. During the Civil War, Stone had been promoted from major with the 1st Pennsylvania Rifles to colonel of the 148th Pennsylvania Volunteer Infantry. He distinguished himself during the Peninsula campaign, then was severely wounded while leading an inspiring charge at Gettysburg, for which he received a brevet of brigadier general. Following the war, the Union College graduate proved his expertise as an engineer by clearing Hell Gate Channel and other obstructions in New York Harbor, then leading the fight for good roads in New Jersey.[64]

Stone proved his worth early in the Puerto Rican campaign by reopening the railroad from Yauco to Ponce. Spanish sympathizers lost no time in producing train-engine parts that they had hidden away after he convinced them that unless they cooperated, they would be imprisoned. He also found and destroyed five mines during an inspection of the tracks running between the two cities. Then, on August 5, Stone undertook his most challenging assignment of the campaign when he began to improve a rough trail that crossed the mountains.[65]

With a mixed force of volunteers, regulars, and Puerto Rican laborers, he began to improve an eighteen-mile track from Adjuntas to Utuado. Upgrading the trail would facilitate General Henry's drive from Ponce, through Utuado, to Arecibo on the northern coast of the island, about thirty-five miles west of San Juan. The terrain in the western mountains was so rugged that the Spanish had left the route unguarded; and although the *New York Times* noted Stone's work, it reported that "a movement there is improbable."[66]

Plans called for Henry's "Provisional Division" to be reinforced by Schwan's Independent Brigade at Arecibo. The Independent Brigade, made up of the 11th Infantry augmented by two companies of the 19th Infantry and supported by a troop of the 5th Cavalry, and a light battery from each the 3d and the 5th Artillery, would sweep westward from Yauco, through Sabana Grande and San Germán, to Mayagüez on the western coast of the island, before swinging to the northeast to take Lares on the way to Arecibo. Schwan's orders were to free western Puerto Rico of all Spanish troops as rapidly as possible, without exposing his command to an ambush.[67]

On Sunday morning, August 7, the anxiously awaited general offensive began. When Miles notified Alger of the movements of each of the columns, he added the encouraging news that the "American flag is floating in nearly all the principal places in Porto Rico." Then he confidently requested "that no more troops or laborers be sent to Porto Rico." As the army moved into the back country in order to invest San Juan from the rear, Miles had misgivings that the navy might attempt to take the capital from the sea.[68]

In a confidential message, he asked Alger to "suspend" any orders authorizing Captain Higginson to move against San Juan until after the army surrounded the capital. Miles explained that a random naval bombardment would "violate" the president's orders because "innocent women and children" might be killed or wounded. He also pointed out that an unsupported fleet action would be "an interference with the work given the Army by the President." Alger replied that he had been assured that there had been no plans for a naval operation against San Juan, "but, for a certainty, positive orders have been issued prohibiting the move you suggest."[69]

Miles's apprehensions about interference from the navy did not distract him from vigorously prosecuting the campaign. Field telegraph and telephone lines, which he later claimed "followed close to the picket and skirmish lines," made it possible for him to maintain contact with each of his columns. The Signal Corps detachment would ultimately string hundreds of miles of communication lines in Puerto Rico.[70]

Brigadier General Schwan, the German-born commander of the Independent Brigade, had immigrated to the United States in 1857. The sixteen-year-old youth immediately joined the 10th Infantry, where he endured the hardships of the Utah Expedition of 1857–58. He fought as a company-grade officer with the Army of the Potomac in the major campaigns of 1863 to 1865, winning a gold Medal of Honor for rescuing a wounded fellow officer from a bullet-swept battlefield at Preble's Farm, Virginia. In 1886, following service on the Western Plains and as an instructor at the Fort Leavenworth School of Application, Schwan became an assistant adjutant general with the rank of major. At the outbreak of the war with Spain, he received a promotion from lieutenant colonel, earned in 1895, to colonel. Now a brigadier general of volunteers, Schwan would lead his regulars on a ninety-two-mile march through Spanish-held territory in a little more than a week.[71]

Schwan's Independent Brigade moved from Ponce to Yauco, where his men spent the day of August 8 preparing for a westward sweep to Mayagüez, their first objective. On the morning of the tenth, the column passed through San Germán. Sick soldiers were left in the town's hospital to free the army ambulances for casualties expected in the battle that appeared to be brewing. Schwan had been informed that the entire garrison of Mayagüez, reported to number 1,362 troops, of whom 252 were volunteers, was advancing along the San Germán road to challenge his column.

As Fifth Cavalrymen scouted ahead of the main body outside the small village of Hormigueros, seven miles south of Mayagüez, they were warned of the enemy's presence by poorly aimed shots. Schwan decided to attack even though the Spanish troops had a commanding view of his approach route from two lines of trenches they had constructed across a series of low hills. Schwan posted his artillery on high ground to the left, facing the enemy, while elements of the advance guard positioned Gatlings on a hillock to the right of the dug-in Spanish troops. As the infantry began to advance toward the center of the enemy's line behind a screen of artillery fire, the Gatlings opened up and the troop of cavalry maneuvered around to the left, threatening to outflank the defense line. The Spanish troops felt so menaced by the combination of forces arrayed against them that they broke from the trenches and retreated in some disorder. The Americans found a wounded lieutenant left behind in a trench by his men, and the fleeing troops did not attempt to make a stand at Mayagüez, even though defensive works had been prepared for them in the seaport.

The Independent Brigade camped where it had fought and tended to the fifteen Americans wounded in the battle, one of whom was Schwan's aide, who had been shot in the foot. Two soldiers had been killed, and although the victors could only estimate that the enemy had lost fifteen men, with thirty-five more wounded, Schwan felt justified in reporting that he had "inflicted heavy loss" upon the enemy. The next day, after the advance guard combed through Mayagüez, Schwan met with the mayor, who promised to obey the brigadier general's orders. Schwan then rode at the head of his command, as the regulars paraded through the town to the accompaniment of their band and the cheers of many of the twenty-two thousand inhabitants. The column continued less than two miles beyond the city, and then the entire command bivouacked on the road, except for cavalrymen assigned to monitor the enemy's withdrawal.

The following morning, August 12, a pursuit force led by Lt. Col. Daniel W. Burke set out toward Lares with orders to slow the Spanish retreat. Schwan had not ordered a full-scale advance because drenching rains had made the roads impassable and many of his men were in no shape to challenge the steep slopes leading into the central mountains. The infantry had marched along difficult roads first enervated by August's oppressive heat and then made miserable by tropical downpours. Furthermore, following the Battle of Hormigueros, the worn-out foot soldiers had spent long hours on picket duty to guard against a surprise attack.[72]

Burke's task force consisted of six companies of the 11th Infantry, supported by both a cavalry and an artillery platoon. The regulars struggled along rough roads made worse by the rains, muscling field guns up precipitous inclines. At sunset the exhausted troops gratefully settled in for the night along the Las Marías Road. At 5:10 on the morning of the thirteenth, the troops resumed their difficult climb along the steep road until they reached Las Marías, where they were told about a number of Spanish troops who were trapped nearby.

An enemy force, reported to number seven hundred men, had been cut off on the wrong side of the Río Prieto, now swollen by the recent rains. As the Americans descended the mountainside toward the river, shots were exchanged across the valley floor; but rather than stand and fight, most of the Spanish troops escaped into the hills. In the brief skirmish, five of the enemy were known to have been killed, and some of those who had made a desperate attempt to escape by swimming across the turbulent river were believed to have drowned. Among the fifty-six prisoners taken were fourteen wounded men, along with their battalion commander, who had been too ill to lead his troops to safety. Two Spanish medical officers had risked falling into American hands in order to remain behind to care for the colonel, found confined to bed in a nearby cottage.

Material discarded along the roadside suggested that the Spanish troops had become demoralized by the persistent pursuit, but part of the brigade's breakdown could also be attributed to their colonel's illness. But even the victors had been so thoroughly exhausted by the physical demands of keeping pace with the Spanish withdrawal that they did not try to round up stragglers. Instead, Burke's men spent the remainder of August 13 recuperating, with plans to continue after the enemy the next day.[73]

John Black Atkins, who had arrived on the island too late to observe any of the combat, depicted Schwan's arduous drive as "capturing villages as you might pick berries along a hedge." The British correspondent then explained how General Henry had worked in tandem with Schwan, following a route that would block the escape of any of the enemy fleeing from the Independent Brigade. When Atkins wrote that Henry's Provisional Division had crossed a "mountain track," he probably did not realize that the march had been a grueling trek.

The Provisional Division included not only Garretson's brigade of the 6th Massachusetts and the 6th Illinois but also a battalion of the 19th Infantry and a troop of the Second Cavalry. The *Times* reported that a battery of the 7th Regiment sent to support the Provisional Division had to turn back, after six horses and the gun they were pulling slipped over the edge of the mountain road.[74] On August 8, Miles reported that "General Henry, with Garretson's brigade, is moving across, via Adjuntas and Guayaho and Cayes."

Henry reached Utuado with three infantry battalions, screened by a small cavalry detachment, on the thirteenth. He expected Garretson to come up with the rest of the brigade in time to join him in an attack on Arecibo the next day. General Henry, a career officer who had graduated from West Point in 1861, undoubtedly anticipated that he would prove his worth in combat in this war, as he had in both the Civil War and the Indian wars. He had won a Medal of Honor for bravery at Cold Harbor, where two horses had been shot from under him, and he received a brevet brigadier general's star after being severely wounded while riding to the rescue of comrades on the Rosebud in 1876.

Unfortunately for Henry, the pace of his current command's advance failed to match the rapid movement of the Ninth Cavalry in 1890, when he led the regiment on an overnight march of eighty-five miles to reinforce Miles at Wounded Knee. Henry officially attributed his slow progress from Adjuntas to Utuado on "the inability of the inexperienced and unseasoned troops of Garretson's brigade to perform the work which I expected from them." He conceded, however, that his men had been handicapped by "the dependence upon the ox-cart transportation over roads whose grades will only admit of packs."[75]

Miles took pride in work done to improve the route from Adjuntas to Utuado, boasting to Atkins that he had "just heard that the first wagon has passed over it." The track may not have been as serviceable as the commanding general represented it to be, thereby undervaluing the labor of the men in the 6th Illinois and 6th Massachusetts. The trail had been so rugged that the shoes of the volunteers had been torn to pieces during the march, leaving them barefoot at the end of the campaign. Furthermore, the *New York Times* confirmed how impenetrable even the improved path proved to be when it revealed that Henry's men were in dire need of supplies. The newspaper explained that the garrison at Ponce "says it is impossible to transport supplies over the mountain trail, and it has been arranged to send them to Arecibo, an open port."[76]

While Henry's volunteers trudged across the mountains running east and west across the south-central part of the island, James H. Wilson's command advanced along the main road toward San Juan. Wilson, a seasoned campaigner and trained engineer, had graduated sixth in the West Point class of 1860. Transferred from Grant's staff in 1863, where he had served primarily as a topographical engineer, to the cavalry, Wilson would receive the brevet rank of major general in October 1864, when he was appointed as chief of cavalry for the Military Division of the Mississippi. After five years of postwar service as a lieutenant colonel, Wilson resigned from the army to combine careers as a businessman, engineer, and author.[77] In 1898, Wilson, who had not yet reached the army's retirement age, volunteered for the Spanish-American war.

Wilson would go on to serve under Maj. Gen. Adna R. Chaffee in China during the Boxer Rebellion. He now commanded a column that included Brig. Gen. Oswald H. Ernst's brigade of volunteers. Ernst, who had graduated from West Point in 1864, served as an engineer both in the field and in the classroom; he taught at the military academy before becoming superintendent of that institution in 1893. Two of Ernst's regiments, the 2d and 3d Wisconsin, had landed in Puerto Rico only two days before the offensive began, but the 16th Pennsylvania had gone through a rehearsal for battle in the bloodless capture of Juana Díaz.[78]

On August 7, the first day of the offensive, Wilson moved his headquarters from Ponce to Juana Díaz in preparation for an assault on Coamo, fourteen miles farther up the road. Wilson estimated that approximately 250 Spanish soldiers defended the town, which dominated both the main route to Ponce and a fork of that road that ran to Santa Isabel on the southern coast of the island. Two miles below Coamo, along the way to Santa Isabel, a blockhouse had been built that could bring fire to bear on both of the roads.

Miles accompanied Wilson to the front, where he approved the former cavalry commander's plan to lock up Coamo's garrison with the 16th Pennsylvania Infantry, commanded by Col. Willis J. Hulings. The regiment would stealthily move out at night, using a mountain trail to bypass the town. Richard Harding Davis related how Huling's infantrymen had to climb along a path "which would have broken the hearts of any less enthusiastic soldiers; and on the following morning the rest of the command, horse, foot, and artillery, acted as 'beaters' for it, and swept the Spaniards back into the waiting arms of the Pennsylvanians."[79]

At 6:00 A.M. on the ninth, General Ernst led the 2d and 3d Wisconsin toward Coamo, supported by both light artillery batteries and Troop C of the New York Volunteer Cavalry. Four guns from the batteries were brought to bear on the blockhouse, which they succeeded in setting on fire at about 8:00 A.M. As the few Spanish defenders abandoned their untenable positions, the sound of gunfire came from the far side of Coamo, indicating that the 16th Pennsylvania had just shut the back door, trapping the enemy troops between them and the advancing Wisconsin infantry.[80]

Wilson later recalled the sights and sounds of the developing battle, which he had viewed from the top of an elevation, accompanied by his staff and a signal corps unit. He noted that "by eight o'clock in the morning the narrow valley both above and below the town, and the surrounding heights, were reverberating with the field artillery and the tearing rattle of our Krag-Jorgensens." Wilson added that "An outlying blockhouse on the road to Los Baños held by the enemy's pickets, was set afire by our shells and the whole beautiful landscape was soon covered by the smoke and made horrid by the noise and confusion of battle."[81]

The anvil and hammer operation conceived by Wilson had succeeded despite the poor execution of his plans, which called for an attack on both fronts of Coamo to commence at 7:00 A.M. The 16th Pennsylvania only established its blocking position at the rear of the two at 8:00 A.M. because Miles's chief engineer, Lt. Col. John Biddle, acting as the regiment's guide, strayed from the correct trail during the night march. As for the Wisonsin infantrymen, once they passed the smoldering blockhouse at 8:00 A.M., the only obstacle they encountered was a destroyed bridge that stymied one battalion's progress. Still, they apparently had so much ground to cover during their advance that they entered Coamo at 9:40 A.M., too late to join the battle.

As the 16th Pennsylvania began to ford the Coamo River, after having struggled down from the heights overlooking the valley, they heard the sounds of a battle starting up. Three and a half miles to the rear artillery had just begun firing on the blockhouse. As a result of Lieutenant Colonel Biddle's unfamiliarity with the terrain, Colonel Huling's men found themselves farther away from the main road than had been intended. Spurred on by sounds of gunfire, however, the Pennsylvanians rapidly advanced to a plateau overlooking the road, from which they were separated by the Cuyon River. It appears that the 16th had caught the Spanish troops on the highway as they were withdrawing to Aibonito. Wilson conceded that between seventy and eighty support troops managed to escape before Huling's men closed the road.

One company's attempt to seize the road was beaten back by Spanish troops fighting from ditches and behind trees. Following that both sides spent about an hour exchanging shots. Finally, a battalion maneuvered into a position where fire from the infantry could sweep the length of the road. The Spanish troops immediately began waving anything white to signal a surrender. Under a truce flag 5 officers and 162 men relinquished their weapons before becoming prisoners of the 16th. The victory cost the Pennsylvanians 6 wounded, only 1 of them seriously. The Spanish lost 4 privates as well as their 2 commanding officers, a colonel and a captain, "who behaved with most exceptional and reckless bravery," according to Richard Harding Davis.[82]

Troop C of the New York Volunteer Cavalry, commanded by Capt. Bertram T. Clayton, who had graduated from West Point in 1886, arose at 4:00 A.M. on the ninth to prepare for a long day in the saddle. After riding south for six miles along the Santa Isabel Road, to insure that both it and an outpost at Los Baños were clear of enemy soldiers, the troop returned to Coamo, entering the town at 9:30 A.M., ten minutes ahead of the two Wisconsin regiments. Anthony Fiala, one of the New York troopers, remembered that as he rode through the village he noticed "the natives looking at us in a sort of dazed fashion, and calling out that they were 'Porto Rico Americanos.'"

After trotting through the town, the troop rode past cheering Pennsylvanians who were escorting their prisoners back to the same campsite that they had used before starting off on their night march. The cavalrymen were sobered when they came upon the scene of the battle, described by one trooper as strewn with "dying horses, broken equipments, hundreds of Mauser cartridges, rifles, pieces of uniforms, saddles and packs, while bright red stains in different places bore silent witness to life poured out." A mile from Coamo the troop took a fifteen-minute break, after which Captain Clayton received the approval of two staff officers to continue after the enemy. The retreating Spanish sought to destroy the bridges they crossed in order to slow their pursuers, but in most instances, Troop C reached the bridges in time to save them. Spanish engineers were able to detonate charges that severely damaged one bridge four miles from Coamo. When troops raced forward to investigate the blast, they found a single cross beam left intact, connecting the two sides of a canyon. The New Yorkers managed to reach the far side of the bridge by having one man at a time lead his horse across the beam. As they pondered the situation, Wilson rode up in the company of a few staff officers. He decided that a squad of cavalrymen should remain behind to repair the span while the rest of the troop contented itself by taking one last bridge that could be seen farther up the mountainside. Wilson's final instructions to Clayton's men were that if they came upon the enemy, they should "lick h—— out of them."[83]

Wilson was concerned about taking his next objective, Aibonito, five miles from Coamo. As he noted in his memoirs, the city "was a place near the top of the mountains, not only so strong of itself but so covered by fortifications and guns on the craglike and lofty ridges of El Peñon and Asomanti, that it was impossible to reach them by a front approach." He explained that one of his options for a frontal attack would be to advance across the countryside, which "although as beautiful as the Vale of Cashmir, was so broken and tumbled into ravines and impassable ridges that regular operations through it were impracticable." Wilson's only other alternative, he noted in his memoirs, would be to use the military highway as it twisted up the mountainside, exposing his men to "the enfilading, plungings, and cross fire of the batteries above." He concluded that "the enemy's position on the summits beyond was impregnable by direct attack."

Wilson had no intention of launching a frontal attack against such a strongly defended position; instead, his West Point–trained engineers, guided by area residents, found a route that bypassed Aibonito. While these scouting parties climbed along rough mountain trails, the rest of the command spent two days in a camp described by Wilson as located next to a "steam flowing with crystal water, amidst mountain air which was filled with balm and pleasant odors." The peaceful interlude ended at 1:25 P.M. on August 12, when Wilson's artillery opened up on the Spanish batteries dug in on El Peñón and Asomante.

Wilson not only intended to divert attention from Ernst's men, who were preparing to slip past Aibonito that night, but also to determine the strength of the enemy facing him. Since Wilson later revealed, in his autobiography, that at about this time "Rumors of peace had already begun to reach us at the front," the ensuing battle could have been avoided.[84]

An artillery duel began as soon as light battery F, 3d U.S. Artillery, unlimbered its four guns in a meadow to the left of the main road, about two thousand yards from the Spanish positions at the crest of the mountain. Richard Harding Davis believed that this combat "was one of the most exciting fights of the war. Not only could the artillerymen see each other's guns plainly without the aid of a glass, but they could see the men who served them as well, and they answered shell with shell and with the speed of a ball volleyed across a tennis net."[85]

Although the Spanish howitzers were firing too high to disturb the American artillerymen, they ranged in on the 3d Wisconsin, holding a hill to the right of the road. Here Davis saw one shell explode almost at the feet of a British naval attaché to Washington, Capt. Alfred Paget. Five infantrymen were knocked to the ground by this blast, and the correspondent wrote that for a moment he lost sight of the attaché "in a cloud of dust and smoke, from which no one expected to see him reappear alive, but he strode out of it untouched, remarking in a tone of extreme annoyance, 'There was a shell in the Soudan once did exactly the same thing to me.'"

Paget paused briefly under a tree to rest and collect himself, until a shell hit it, killing two infantryman and wounding several others. As the attaché, again untouched, braved enemy fire to assist one of the injured men to safety, Davis thought that this "sight did more to popularize the Anglo-American alliance with the soldiers than could the weightiest argument of ambassadors or statesmen." Miles mentioned the same incident to Atkins, adding that "When the man was safely removed out of danger Captain Paget said, . . . 'I really think they must be finding our range.' 'I think,' General Miles said, 'he is the bravest man I ever saw. I have written to your War office about Captain Paget.'"[86]

After about two hours the American artillerymen appeared to have gained the upper hand, silencing one of the two howitzers opposing them and driving the Spanish infantrymen from their trenches. But as one of battery F's four guns sought to take advantage of the withdrawal by advancing about a quarter mile toward the enemy, Spanish infantrymen returned to their trenches. Their accurate shooting, as well as renewed fire from the howitzers, forced the hasty retreat of the American gun crew. At that moment, a lieutenant who had just raced forward with a second gun fell, wounded by a bullet that traveled through his body from shoulder to hip. Fire slackened on both sides as a horse-drawn ambulance carried the officer from the battlefield. As if by mutual consent, the incident brought an end to the fighting at Asomante.

As the firing ended, Wilson sent one of his staff officers behind enemy lines under a truce flag to ask for a surrender. The following day the Spanish commander responded: "Tell the American General, if he desires to avoid shedding of blood to remain where he is." In this, the last battle in Puerto Rico, Wilson lost two men to the shell burst in the tree, and two infantrymen and an artillery officer were wounded.[87]

At 4:23 P.M. of August 12, the secretary of war notified Miles that "The President directs all military operations against the enemy be suspended. Peace negotiations are nearing completion." Miles immediately communicated this information to his commanders, effectively bringing peace to the island. Wilson returned to Coamo, Schwan to Mayagüez, Henry to Adjuntas, and Brooke to Guayama. For the first time since the *Maine* blew up on February 15, and except for a few clerks, the Army and Navy Departments were closed on Sunday, August 14.[88]

When Miles recapped the Puerto Rican campaign for John Black Atkins's benefit, he took pride in the fact that only three of his men had been killed in action, although a fourth infantryman who died of wounds received on the twelfth should be added to the toll. The British correspondent remarked that any general but Miles, "after capturing a whole island might have obscured the fact [of so few battle deaths] as tasting of bathos. To this man it meant a game well played."[89]

– CHAPTER 14 –

Following the Spanish-American War

Scandals and Military Pettiness

MILES COULD TAKE satisfaction from the favorable responses to a successful campaign. Senator Redfield Proctor of Vermont, who had been secretary of war when Miles strayed from the party line during the Wounded Knee controversy, praised him now because his "work in the Porto Rican expedition and campaign has been excellent in all respects. That has gone smoothly; not a lisp of criticism. I wish that you might have had time to capture the whole island as I believe you would have done with very little loss."[1]

Even Secretary of War Russell Alger noted that success in Puerto Rico was "in part due to the general plan of campaign, for which General Miles should receive full credit. The campaign in Puerto Rico had been well conceived and skillfully executed."[2]

Many who appreciated Miles's efforts contrasted the generalship exhibited at Puerto Rico with that shown during the Santiago campaign. Richard Harding Davis believed that "The reason the Spanish bull gored our men in Cuba and failed to touch them in Porto Rico was entirely due to the fact that Miles was an expert matador and Shafter was not." Richard Harding Davis opined, "it is hardly fair to the commanding general and the gentlemen under him to send the Porto Rico campaign down into history as a picnic."

As Davis wrote admiringly, an army composed primarily of volunteers "advanced with the precision of a set of chessmen; its moves were carefully considered and followed to success." The correspondent concluded that "As an eye-witness of both campaigns one is convinced that the great success of the one in Puerto Rico was not due to climatic advantages and the cooperation of the natives, but to good management and good generalship."

Davis resented the prevailing opinion that the campaign had been "a successful military picnic, a sort of comic-opera war, a magnified field day at Van Cortland Park" because "it was hardly fair, either to the army in Porto Rico or to the people at home. It cheated the latter of their just right to feel proud." He conceded, however, that the campaign had been a "picnic because the commanding generals would not permit the enemy to make it otherwise. The Spaniards were willing to make it another nightmare—they were just as ready to kill in Porto Rico as in Cuba—but our commanding general in Porto Rico was able to prevent their doing so."[3]

James H. Wilson believed, although Cuba and Puerto Rico were equally "difficult" and "sickly," that apart from the spread of typhoid fever, which had its inception in stateside training camps, and intestinal disorders caused by local produce, those serving in Puerto Rico "were free from epidemics and any unusual sickness. The records showed but few deaths and at no time over twenty-three per cent from all causes unfit for duty, the larger part of which were light cases, mostly developed after the campaign had ended." In comparison, Wilson pointed out that American officers in Cuba had to resort to a "round robin" letter to determine the dangerous spread of yellow fever, which expedited the evacuation of the Fifth Army Corps to Camp Wikoff at Montauk Point, Long Island.

Wilson, certainly overstating the matter, concluded that "the campaign and occupation of Porto Rico in July and August were managed so well that the officers and men . . . regarded it as a continuous gala *fiesta*"; in contrast, he continued, "the campaign and capture of Santiago at practically the same time of year were characterized by sickness, disorder, and general mismanagement, which came uncomfortably near to national disaster and disgrace."[4]

Nicholas Senn, an early advocate of antiseptic surgery and a professor of surgery at some of Chicago's leading medical schools, confirmed Wilson's assertions about the origin of typhoid fever in Puerto Rico. The Swiss-born Senn, whose interest in military medicine led him to form the Association of Military Surgeons of the United States in 1891, served as a surgeon with the rank of lieutenant colonel in Cuba and Puerto Rico. While there he examined the case histories of troops ill with typhoid fever on Puerto Rico.[5]

Senn informed Col. Charles R. Greenleaf, chief surgeon of the army, that "careful study of 200 cases, of which I have reliable information, shows disease in every instance was contracted before leaving the United States. By far largest number contracted in Camp George H. Thomas, . . . Camp Alger comes next; fewest cases from Tampa." Greenleaf added an endorsement to this report before Miles forwarded it to Washington, recommending "that all fever-infected camps in the United States be abandoned. Every possible precaution has been taken here to prevent its spread."[6]

In a public letter, Senn charged that "There was no difficulty in tracing the disease [yellow fever] to a total lack of precaution on the part of the General in command. Col. Greenleaf had given his advice and directions before the army left Tampa, but they were not heeded." However, he explained, "Owing to want of co-operation on the part of Gen. Shafter, the medical officers were powerless in preventing and combating the dreaded disease."

Senn then contrasted what he believed to be Maj. Gen. William R. Shafter's disregard for his men with the leadership shown by Miles, who "laid his plans wisely and with special reference to gain the desired object with as little suffering and loss of life as possible." The doctor judged that "Every movement of the campaign was made with this view in regard for the welfare and success of our troops rather than a desire for personal gain and aggrandizement, which characterized the Cuban campaign as every one knows." The letter concluded with Dr. Senn's observation that Miles relied upon and cooperated with his medical officers to safeguard the health of his troops.[7]

Despite the favorable outcome of the Puerto Rico campaign, General Guy V. Henry found a lesson to be gained from his march across the island. In any future such operation, he advised, both a cavalry regiment and a Hotchkiss battery should be part of the expeditionary force. If such units had been part of his command in Puerto Rico, "operating over the line traversed by me, and in conjunction with Schwan's command, [I] could have captured or dispersed every Spanish command and opened every seaside town in the Western portion of the island between Ponce and Arecibo, if not to Dorado by the 13th instant." Henry then disclosed that "it is understood that their use was recommended by the Commanding General and it is to be regretted that they were not given an opportunity to demonstrate their ability and absolute necessity in this theater of operations."[8]

With the coming of peace, Miles looked forward to a family reunion on the island that he had just secured for the United States. His fifteen-year-old son, Sherman, was already with him, serving as a volunteer aide after having wisely, considering his age, declined the governor of Massachusetts's offer of a second lieutenant's commission in a regiment from that state. From New York City, Mary Miles and their twenty-nine-year-old daughter, Cecilia, traveled to Charleston, South Carolina, from which they sailed to Puerto Rico on August 18. While aboard the *Obdam,* Cecilia met a very bright signal corps officer, thirty-four-year-old Captain of Volunteers Samuel Reber, who had been commissioned in the cavalry following his graduation from West Point in 1886. Captain Reber, who had studied electrical engineering at Johns Hopkins University, was on his way to Puerto Rico, and later Cuba, where he would be in charge of telegraph and telephone service.

A shipboard romance blossomed between the couple, fueled by Reber's memories of ten-year-old Cecilia playing in pinafores when he himself was a teenager. He admitted to a youthful attraction to William Tecumseh Sherman's grandniece when the distantly related pair met at a family gathering (Samuel was the general's grandnephew). In a reprint of a story from the *New England Home Magazine,* the *Army and Navy Journal* revealed that during the voyage "Miss Miles congratulated him upon his record in the Cuban campaign. . . . 'Thank you' he said. 'I hope for a promotion in the Regular Army next year, and when it comes ———' The sentence was left unfinished unless the blush that deepened Miss Miles' cheek might be called its completion." Apparently, he implied that he had a marriage proposal in mind. In fact, their marriage on January 10, 1900, at Saint John's Church in Washington, D.C., preceded his promotion to captain on July 1 of the same year.[9]

Just three days before peace would be celebrated in Puerto Rico, Miles insured that he would not enjoy a postwar honeymoon with Secretary of War Alger or Adj. Gen. Henry C. Corbin. On that date, August 10, a correspondent for the *Kansas City* (Missouri) *Star* received the impression that Miles responded "with considerable suppressed feeling" during an interview in Ponce. What evidently spurred Miles's intemperate remarks was lingering resentment of the message sent by Corbin on July 7, assuring Shafter that he would not be superseded by Miles when the commanding general arrived in Cuba. The fact that a copy of this dispatch had not been sent to Miles, although it had been released to the press after he had sailed, added to the humiliation done to him by the War Department. Miles complained privately in a letter written on August 15 to Emily W. Heintzelman, widow of Capt. Charles S. Heintzelman, who had died of tuberculosis on February 27, 1881, that she "would be surprised if you knew the low intrigue that has been resorted to, but so far it has failed."

The *Star* reported Miles's position that the War Department's scheme for Shafter to remain in charge in Cuba "was based on an impossibility." The situation in Cuba had been similar to one in which a colonel arrives with the rest of a regiment to a place held by a captain with his company; "the colonel would not supersede the captain; he would simply take command of the entire force, as I did at Santiago."

To prove his point, Miles said that after he arrived at Cuba, all of the messages from the War Department concerning the surrender were sent to him rather than to Shafter. The public did not realize this because the dispatches "were very much mutilated and garbled" before being released, while "several very important ones which would have thrown a clearer light upon the situation were entirely suppressed."

Miles gave as an example of an unreleased cablegram the one he sent to Alger on July 21 alerting him that "There is not a single regiment of regulars or volunteers with General Shafter's command that is not infected with yellow fever." In this message, sent by Miles just before he sailed to Puerto Rico, he explained to Alger that "general directions were given General Shafter to be executed under his orders and supervision" for relocating camps as high as possible up the mountains. Miles added that if this did not stop the spread of yellow fever, he believed that the troops should be evacuated from Cuba to a temperate region of the United States such as New England.

The *Star* reporter commented that this cable "was suppressed by the Secretary in Washington and no attention was paid to the recommendations of General Miles, which outline the plan now followed by the War Department, but for which others are claiming credit." The newspaperman also charged, after seeing a copy of the dispatch in Miles's headquarters, that "it was Shafter's disobedience of orders and Secretary Alger's disregard of General Miles' recommendations that was responsible for the terrible condition of the Santiago army as revealed by the appeal of the commanding officers [in the "round robin" letter] at that point made public August 4, fourteen days after Miles' telegram."[10]

On August 25 the *Star* noted that "Miles's talk stirs things. The East is aroused at the disclosures made in the *Star*'s interview." As an example of a disapproving reaction to Miles's remarks, the *Star* reprinted an editorial, "General Miles Is Fluent," published by the *Washington Post* on August 24. The *Post* editor believed that the interview made "General Miles speak in a spirit of rankest folly and insubordination. It makes him ascribe to Secretary Alger and Adjutant General Corbin the meanest and most odious actions." The story "pictures him as misrepresenting the situation during his sojourn at Santiago and criticizing the government in very much the tone that would be adopted by an indignant schoolmaster trouncing a recalcitrant pupil."

After the editor dismissed as "strange accusations" Miles's charges of being the victim of suppressed or garbled cables, he asked a key question about the July 21 cable alerting Washington about yellow fever in Cuba: "If General Miles knew this, and was in command why did he not execute the reforms of which he speaks? Certainly he had the authority to do so if he was actually the general-in-chief." In fact, the editor suppressed that portion of the interview in which Miles explained why he delegated responsibility to Shafter. He had been "extremely anxious" to sail to Puerto Rico because during discussions in Washington "it was agreed that the necessity of securing a foothold upon Spanish soil was very great. In accordance with this idea I left Santiago as soon as the surrender was complete."[11]

The *Post* editorial concluded by condemning Miles, charging that "never before in the history of civilized nations has a military officer as savagely accused his government of imbecility and bad faith." The editor judged that "It is well nigh impossible to reconcile such a flagrant offense against propriety with the possession, on General Miles's part, of the merest scrap of self-respect and common sense."[12]

On the other hand, the *New York Times* used the occasion to censure the secretary of war and concluded that Miles's account "places directly upon the Secretary the responsibility for the unnecessary retention of the army before Santiago. The delay in the removal of that army was the cause of hundreds of deaths and thousands of ruined lives." The editor considered both "the protest of all the commanding officers" and the gist of Miles's interview "pretty clearly insubordinate. But it is safe to say that nobody will be brought to trial for either. Each was a 'commendable indiscretion.' The two taken together fix the responsibility for avoidable sickness and death unescapably upon the Secretary of War."[13]

Later in the week the *Times* renewed its editorial attack against Alger, basing its new indictment on his secret dispatch to General Shafter. The secretary of war's departure from custom led the writer to conclude that he "was fomenting a conflict of authority between the General in Chief and the General in immediate command at the very time when it was most important, for the country that the two should work together. And this he did by a message to the subordinate not communicated to the superior." This omission led the editor to announce that "We cannot express the contempt which every decent man must feel for this piece of 'politics' more strongly than by saying that it was entirely characteristic of Secretary Alger."[14]

The *New York World,* which supported Miles, reminded its audience "that Gen. Miles told Gen. Shafter to stand firm and demand the surrender of Santiago when the latter telegraphed to Washington on an eventful Sunday that he was afraid that it would be necessary to fall back." The *World* also mentioned that "It was common gossip that Gen. Miles was held back at the beginning of the war, and that it was only when he earnestly solicited the President to send him to the front that he was permitted to take an active part." The correspondent pointed out that "The day before Gen. Miles left for Cuba, Secretary Alger said with emphasis to inquirers that Miles was not going to Santiago and would not be permitted to go there. The next day it was announced that he was going to Santiago."[15]

The *Army and Navy Journal* reminded its professional audience that traditionally there has been a struggle for power because "for our Army no head is provided; or rather it has three heads—the Secretary of War, the Adjutant General, and the ranking officer of the Army." Adjutant General Corbin had emerged as the most influential of the reigning triumvirate because he had "virtually made himself the Commander-in-Chief, thus supplying the missing link between the President and the Army." It could not "be expected that the Major General Commanding would submit patiently to be set aside or deprived in a measure of his prerogative of command, as he was when he was met in Cuba with the dispatch we published last week virtually depriving him of authority over a subordinate." The *Journal* reduced the fight in the War Department, however to a competition among three officials, each of whom had "sought to fill a vacant place and it is natural that there should be some crowding, but it calls for no harsh words. What we want is a Lieutenant General or a General who shall command the Army."[16]

According to the *New York Times,* a proposal that would have satisfied the wishes of the *Journal,* by promoting Miles to lieutenant general, would be opposed, as would a bill to advance Corbin to major general. The introduction of these measures would result in a "collision" between supporters of Miles and those of Corbin. The *Times* assumed that "Opposition to the promotion will be forced so hard, it is said, that the only possible way of getting promotion for Miles will be by consenting that promotion shall also be given to Corbin." The article concluded by saying that the charge that "efforts to 'queer' Miles at Tampa and at Santiago were part of a programme to discredit him in the eyes of the country, is repudiated by friends of Gen. Corbin, as they should be. But that does not fully reassure the friends of Gen. Miles."[17]

The Washington correspondent for the *New York Evening Post* sent a column to the *Star* that may explain why the War Department took no official notice of Miles's interview with the *Star.* The newsman believed "that Secretary Alger shares with Miles the latter's suspicions against Adjutant General Corbin, and for this reason it is doubtful whether Miles's enemies—among the most active of whom has been and is General Corbin—will be able to draw official rebuke upon Miles."[18]

In a profile of Corbin on the occasion of his retirement, the *Army and Navy Life* explained that Presidents Hayes, Garfield, Arthur, McKinley, and Grant had all befriended the adjutant general, because "he excited the jealousy of smaller fry and ambitious rivals and has come in for the share of abuse and mud-slinging which seem to fall to the lot of successful men." Corbin's portrait in the *Dictionary of American Biography* also refers to his "enemies," explaining that they "called him 'pushing, ambitious, and showy,' but they conceded that he had the interests of the army at heart."

Until the Spanish-American War placed Miles and Corbin in opposing camps, they had kept private any differences between them. Corbin, like Miles and many other officers who had jockeyed for positions at the top of the post–Civil War army, began his military career as a volunteer officer. He was only nineteen years old when he received a second lieutenant's commission in 1862 in the 83d Ohio Infantry, before transferring to the 79th

Ohio. From 1863 until the reorganization of the army in 1866, Corbin served with the United States 14th [Negro] Infantry, where he rose from major to colonel and brevet brigadier general. His gallantry at Nashville, Tennessee, and Decatur, Alabama, earned him two brevets, which had been recommended by Maj. Gen. George H. Thomas.

Following the war, Corbin considered a career in law until Grant—who, like Corbin, grew up in Clermont County, Ohio—convinced him to remain in the regular army. After a two-month stint as a second lieutenant in the 17th Infantry, the former colonel became a captain in the 38th Infantry. For ten years he commanded a company, sharing the hardships and dangers of the frontier.

While on recruiting duty in Ohio in 1876, Corbin renewed his wartime friendship with the governor of Ohio, former Bvt. Maj. Gen. Rutherford B. Hayes. Following Hayes's inauguration as president in 1877, Corbin became his military aide; in 1880 Hayes appointed him assistant adjutant general with the rank of major. Corbin steadily climbed up the bureaucratic ladder until, on February 25, 1898, he received command of the adjutant general's department with the single star of a brigadier general.[19]

Following the outbreak of the Spanish-American War, his dispute with Miles became so well publicized that Corbin could not ignore the stories it inspired. Unfortunately, his treatment of the break may not have been completely frank: "The facts are that there never was any personal controversy between us. That General Miles tried to discredit and destroy me is true." Corbin explained, "This was not by reason of any personal difference, but because of my friendly relations with the Secretary of War and the President. He was hostile to both of them, particularly so toward the Secretary of War."

Corbin also dismissed Miles's efforts in Puerto Rico, insisting that the surrender of Santiago "made that of the Spanish troops in Puerto Rico only a question of the presence of an authorized agent of our government to receive it." He went on to say that "happily no campaign was necessary, and the surrender took place after the most trifling opposition to the landing of our forces."[20]

Secretary of War Alger naturally shared Corbin's displeasure at Miles's public revelations. According to the *New York Times,* Alger's friends believed that he was "deeply angered and troubled by the attack made upon him by the General commanding the army. If he could crush Gen. Miles and afterward stifle public criticism there is no doubt he would exercise the power." The secretary of war exercised restraint, however, because "he is most anxious that the entire matter be smoothed over with the least publicity and with as much avoidance as possible of inquiry into collateral matters involving the War Department in censure for general mismanagement."[21]

On September 2, the *Times* reported that "the Secretary of War now makes it known that he does not intend to make a fuss about Gen. Miles, that there is to be no court of inquiry or court-martial." Although Alger had hoped that the uproar over the *Star* interview would become yesterday's news, reporters would not let a good story die.[22]

Miles and his staff joined the 2d Wisconsin aboard the *Obdam,* while the *Chester* would carry the 40th Pennsylvania, as well as Generals Schwan and Haines, to New York. After the two transports sailed from Ponce on September 1, the War Department announced that upon their return to the United States the troops would not be allowed a parade. General Wilson later wrote that "While no explanation of this unusual course was ever made, I have always supposed that it was due partly to politics and partly to the controversy which was soon on in full between Miles and the Administration in regard to the food supply of the army."[23]

On September 7, when Miles alerted Alger that he had arrived in New York Harbor, he requested permission to camp for a few days at either Governors Island or David's Island off New Rochelle. He explained that his men had "not been paid nor had clothing issued them since leaving Chickamauga, and both pay and clothing much needed." The financially embarrassed and ragged troops were as yet unaware of the War Department's indifference to their needs as they lined the rails of the *Obdam* as it sailed into New York Harbor.[24]

The volunteers from Wisconsin received a heartwarming but unofficial welcome home early in the morning of September 7, when the warships that had destroyed Admiral Pascual de Cervera's squadron formed a passage in New York Harbor through which the transport sailed. The returning troops were greeted first by the *Indiana,* then by the *Brooklyn,* the *Texas* and *Prairie,* and the *Panther* last in line. The band aboard the *Prairie* added a bit of pomp to the occasion by playing "Hail to the Chief." Not authorized to fire a salute, each ship dipped its flag as the palm-and-flag-bedecked *Obdam* sailed by, exciting a lusty exchange of cheers between the seaborne soldiers and sailors. Above the din someone called, "Miles, old man, you took care of your boys and you don't have to square yourself with the widows and orphans."[25]

The *Obdam* tied up at Pier H in Weehawken after it was determined that all of the soldiers aboard the transport were fit. Although most of the troops may have been strapped for funds, they eagerly disembarked to sample the pleasures of Weehawken and forget their disappointment at docking on the wrong side of the Hudson River. A *New York Times* reporter caught up with one private from Company C, 2d Wisconsin, who admitted that he "expected a rousing reception, and ovation to Gen. Miles, a grand parade, with all the New York volunteers and a lot of the regulars to receive us."

The private had enjoyed the fleet's welcome in the harbor, commenting on the "grand reception, floating flags, waving banners, rousing cheers, leading us further in our delusion, then we are poked over here in a little out-of-the-way 'Dutch' settlement, Weehaugen—that none of us ever heard of and we don't even get to go to New York." The disappointed soldier blamed this state of affairs on "Politics," and related that one of his buddies told him about "an internal war, or something like that, and that Gen. Miles was a Democrat, and they were going to give him the worst of it—didn't want him to have any popular parade, that it was on the schedule to give him the cold strike and not the warm reception." Unperturbed by the War Department's snub, the soldier predicted, "Gen. Miles will beat them all out, for he is as wise, fine, and noble a man as ever had shoulder straps on. Every man of us worship that man. He's all right. Look how he has treated us—not a man sick."

While the troops prepared to entertain themselves until seven o'clock, when they would depart by train for Wisconsin, Miles boarded the *General Meigs*. Accompanied by his son, Sherman, and an aide, he made the short trip across the Hudson on the Quartermaster Department boat. From New York's Twenty-second Street pier, a carriage brought the small party to the Waldorf Astoria Hotel, where a *New York Times* reporter recognized the fatigue-clad general.

After giving him time to settle in his suite, the newsman requested an interview and Miles graciously agreed to answer questions. He apparently had taken the official cold shoulder in stride, telling the man from the *Times* that he "never had any particular plans for a parade." He acknowledged, however, that he had expected his men to be allowed to set up a temporary camp in the metropolitan area, which would have entailed a parade of sorts. Miles admitted as much when he continued, "If they had marched through the streets to such a camp I think it would have done no harm. There has been so much talk of the horrors of this war that I would like to have the public see soldiers who, though volunteers, came back in good condition." Miles credited Assistant Surgeon General Charles R. Greenleaf for the faultless medical care received by the Puerto Rican expeditionary force. This led the reporter to question "why it was that so many soldiers had been stricken with fever in Cuba and sent home mere living skeletons, while conditions in Puerto Rico were so different."

After hesitating for a moment, Miles replied: "I do not care to go into that question now. I do not desire to criticize the conduct of any officer, engaged in the war. There has already been too much beating up of the dust behind our armies." This thought led him to add, "Too much criticism, complaint, and condemnation already, and the public has lost sight of the success and glory attending the efforts of our soldiers."

Since this assertion did not jibe with Miles's remarks in the *Star* interview, the reporter wondered about the authenticity of that story. Miles immediately answered this question, explaining "that he read it in the *Kansas City Star* and that the article contained only some slight errors of minor importance. The statements, he said, were substantially correct." Offered an opportunity to clarify any of his observations, Miles declined to do so, and when the newswriter continued to dwell on the topic, Miles suggested that they drop "the gloomy and profitless subjects."

Earlier in the day, Miles had dictated a press statement in which he virtually repeated what he had first told the newsman from Kansas City. He now said that the morning press release contained all that he wished to say about the matter. When the reporter asked if Miles thought that he might be "court-martialed for his criticisms of the Secretary of the War, he replied dryly that he had not received his charges yet."

Although Miles had planned to enjoy an evening at the theater before returning to Washington the next day, he never had a chance to leave the hotel. An unending flow of well-wishers blocked his getaway from one of the Waldorf's parlors, obliging him to shake countless hands well into the night. Such informal but heartfelt receptions for Miles so provoked Shafter that when he asked Corbin if Miles was expected in Chicago, he sarcastically wondered "whether or not one of those triumphal arches is to be given to him for his distinguished services in Porto Rico and in the capture of Santiago."[26]

On September 8 Miles and his wife traveled to Washington by train, as planned. Although their arrival had not been announced, a large crowd had gathered at the station to await them. Among those who enthusiastically greeted the couple when their train pulled in was a *New York Times* reporter, who questioned Miles about his remarks of the day before. Miles responded that he had not made "the statements in order that the condition of the army or its conduct might be investigated. . . . I made them to set myself right." Miles explained that he objected to comments made to reporters by those who had made his "position absurd and silly. I was, according to those statements, merely an idle traveler in Tampa and Santiago de Cuba, with no authority whatever." Because of such "misleading" stories, he "felt that my duty to myself, to my family, and to my friends, demanded my true position and relations should be made clear and unmistakable."[27]

On the heels of this explanation as to why Miles had issued a press release, the press revealed that President McKinley would select a commission to investigate the War Department. An unnamed department official believed that Miles had blundered in candidly admitting his motive for publicizing differences with the military bureaucracy. The official, obviously sympathetic to Miles, pointed out that "The public was quite ready to believe that he had made his withering criticism of Secretary Alger and Corbin for the purpose of shielding the army from future abuses by means of a thorough investigation and exposure of the mismanagement of the campaign in Santiago."

Unfortunately for the army, however, Miles had abdicated a chance to "champion the rights of his men when he limited his role in any investigation to simply correct a personal injustice." The chatty bureaucrat, wise in the ways of officialdom, argued that as a result of this decision, the commanding general "can no longer appear in the high role of prosecutor of those, whoever they may be, who have caused the suffering of the soldiers of his country. The inquiry will go ahead without his initiative, without his aid even." Miles would be divorced from the investigation because it had been convened"not upon his charges or representations, for he disclaimed that he wished to force such an inquiry."

The War Department source believed that with Miles declining a role in investigating the conduct of the war, the secretary of war would escape unscathed. Many of those who would be found wanting within the department would draw attention to those who had foisted incompetents onto the nation's payroll. "Alger was but the cat's paw drawing out chestnuts for hungry politicians. He can say to the court that Congressmen, Governors—possibly the President himself—demanded the appointment of certain civilians and beardless youth to posts of great responsibility." The bureaucrat appreciated the "considerable astuteness behind the apparent frank demand for an investigation. It was very clever. Few of the politicians who have clamored for an investigation will be very anxious to have the Secretary pinned to the wall if he himself has to be skewered on the same frogstick."

Miles, always an avid newspaper reader, must have had his eyes opened by the *Times*'s unsettling conclusion that "the investigation will result in nothing." He himself would later draw attention to another reason for discrediting the president's commission as an impotent charade. His friends informed the *New York World* that Miles "strenuously objected" to being called before the commission because "he considers that the absence of any authority in the commission to administer the oath to witnesses is fatal. No power exists to prevent false statements, the ill-effects of which, even if subsequently disproved, cannot be eradicated."[28]

Miles, now openly at odds with the administration, had already found out how opponents could punish him for not being a team player. On September 21 the *New York Times* revealed that his adversaries in the War Department had seriously considered "ousting" him as the commanding general of the army. The newsman intimated, however, that President McKinley would only reluctantly have approved such a blow at Miles's prestige; apparently, the president's regard for Miles had grown "after General Shafter sent his famous telegram that his lines were thin, and he did not think he could hold his position." From then on, according to the correspondent, "General Miles was allowed to push his own plans for the closing campaign." In discussing the attempt to remove Miles from office, the article revealed that Corbin had been his main nemesis during the war. The reporter believed that until McKinley's faith in Shafter had been shaken, the adjutant general had successfully "used his influence with the President to defeat every plan that General Miles has conceived or suggested."[29]

Despite the slights aimed at him by his opponents in the military bureaucracy, Miles exercised restraint when he wrote his 1898 annual report. The *Army and Navy Journal* characterized the report as "of unusual interest and importance, as it gives a general summary of our war history during the last year from the point of view of the headquarters of the Army."[30]

Besides providing a review of the Spanish-American War, Miles used his report to repeat for the thirteenth year his recommendation for completing a coastal defense system. He also reiterated his proposal that Congress should authorize the army to enlist one recruit for every thousand residents in the United States. This would give the army an authorized strength of approximately seventy-six thousand men in 1900.

The third and only original recommendation in Miles's report advanced a plan for policing the nation's newly acquired overseas empire. He suggested raising "an auxiliary force of native troops" with an officer corps composed of U.S. Army officers. He believed that this semi-military organization, similar to what was used in India and Egypt, "would pacify the native elements of the islands, and would be in the interests of economy and good government."[31]

His annual report, which he delayed because of a bout with an unidentified tropical fever, reflected none of the resentment that Miles must have felt toward the military bureaucracy. As in the past, his opponents had appeared determined to deflate his public image, first by denying him a welcoming parade, then by leaking the embarrassing news that his tenure as commanding general had been in jeopardy.[32]

Further slights occurred on October 12, when Miles appeared with the president at Omaha's Trans-Mississippi Peace Jubilee. The *New York World* reported, "Gen. Miles snubbed at Omaha. Not invited to the President's luncheon and given a back seat at the ceremonies. . . . He was quietly but effectively suppressed." Without identifying who might be responsible, the reporter attributed Miles's being maneuvered out of the limelight to either "negligence or studied intent."[33]

At the time of the jubilee, Miles may have dissipated the ill will that some in the administration had felt toward him. On October 7, the *New York Times* mentioned that rather than dwelling on the investigation of past mistakes, Miles had been concentrating on the army's role in the future. It added that "the President it is said, as well as the Secretary of War, has been inclined to give much weight to General Miles." Unfortunately, the respect that Miles may have earned was endangered when he finally reacted against those he believed responsible for his shabby treatment.[34]

On October 23 Shafter alerted Corbin that Miles "was wild with suppressed rage." Shafter explained that as the two generals returned east from Chicago, Miles told him that "there will be the biggest fight you ever saw in Washington." Shafter's advice to Miles was "not to stir up a fight for you will get the worst of it and we can and should stand on the deeds of the Army, and that the Administration of the War Department was none of his business or mine."

Shafter had to admit defeat in this effort, advising Corbin, "but it was no use, he was breathing vengeance on the Department and will do all he can to raise trouble. He talked and acted like an insane man and asked me if I was going to be used (mentioning names which I will not) to help cut his throat." From the tenor of these remarks, it appears that Miles believed that his adversaries had not completed their campaign to deprive him of honors he felt he had earned. Shafter then warned Miles against a fight in which he would be mismatched. "I told him the persons named did not need any help from me as they would take care of themselves." Although Miles must have suspected that Corbin had a role in the affronts to his dignity, Shafter told the adjutant general that "Your name was not mentioned, but he will hurt you if he can." After reviewing the support the president enjoyed, especially in the West, Shafter dismissed Miles as a "man whose disappointed ambition leads him to thrust his little personality into this whirlwind of popular enthusiasm, [he] will be ground between the upper and the nether mill stone."[35]

Despite Shafter's apprehensions, Miles did not lose his composure while testifying before Congress regarding a reorganization of the Army. On December 12 he explained the details of a bill he had himself written as Congress compared it with one sent to the House Committee on Military Affairs by its chair, John A. T. Hull of Iowa, a Republican.

When Miles went before the House committee, he again recommended that there should be one soldier for every thousand persons living in the United States, and one resident auxiliary for every two thousand inhabitants in U.S. overseas possessions. He then explained that cavalry regiments should be reduced to the number of troopers a commander could properly maneuver, that is, one thousand men. Miles also believed that artillery formations would be more effective if they had four guns, rather than the six they had carried into battle during the Spanish war.

Schofield took the stand after Miles to discuss the strained relationship that was traditional between a commanding general and the secretary of war. He explained that the problem arose because the commanding general had virtually no authority or even influence, making the adjutant general the more important of the two officials. To remedy the situation, Schofield suggested that the president be authorized to select his own commanding general, who would be recognized as the president's executive officer, superior to the heads of all the staff bureaus.

Miles returned to the committee hearings to comment on Schofield's observations. He maintained that according to current law he clearly commanded the army, as had his predecessors for the past one hundred years. Miles opposed Schofield's idea that his position should be replaced by an executive staff officer to the president—not "from a personal standpoint," according to the *Times,* "as he was ready to be retired at any time. But he believed in the principle of a rank and authority commensurate with the responsibility." In response to a question, Miles recommended that the secretary of war should be limited to directing the administrative work of his department. The article explained that Miles claimed that "it was manifestly impossible for any man to come in from civil life and at once become familiar with all the appliances of war." The reporter noted, however, that Miles agreed that the president should be able to replace a commanding general "that was not liked," but cautioned that "the selection should not be so far down the list as to amount to favoritism, for that would not be approved by the people."

Miles stressed throughout his testimony that, with one exception, his own situation had not inspired his comments about the army. That exception was his frankly stated expectation that he and Generals Merritt and Brooke would not receive the recognition they deserved for their accomplishments in the Spanish-American War. To rectify that oversight, his reorganization bill provided vacancies for two lieutenant generals, which he hoped would be filled by Merritt and Brooke. A week before it had been reported that Miles's bill created three new positions; besides two slots for lieutenant generals, it also provided for one general of the army, presumably meant for Miles. The article noted that Miles concluded his testimony by referring "to the cruel working of the system by which Meade, Hancock, and Thomas had never received the rank and recognition due them for eminent services, two of them going broken-hearted to their graves." Schofield agreed with Miles on this issue, also advocating that generals should receive their just due for their services to the nation.[36]

Schofield's main concern during the hearings was to convince the president to appoint a general staff. He reminded those in power that the United States had copied England's system of bureaus, which poorly served that country's military in wars in the Crimea, Egypt, and India. As a result, England eliminated the bureaus and copied the practice of its continental neighbors by appointing a chief of staff and a general staff. Miles differed with Schofield only on the tenure of staff officers. While Schofield recommended allowing a competent staff officer to remain on the general staff for an extended period of time, Miles believed in rotating officers between the field and the staff.

Schofield expected his attempt to reform the War Department to fail, as had past efforts, because of the opposition of the bureau chiefs "with their great social and political pull." Schofield noted that the members of the Senate and House military committees "have received from the Secretary of the War and the Adjutant General an immense amount of patronage during the past few months, and this, together with their long personal acquaintance with the bureau chiefs, have caused them to feel most friendly toward them." The *Army and Navy Journal* reported that, furthermore, President McKinley would follow the advice of Alger, who along with Corbin and Congressman Hull were committed to the bureau system.[37]

In a decision influenced by partisan politics, Congress agreed on March 2, 1899, to accept a compromise reorganization plan that maintained the bureau system, in preference to the plans put forth by Miles and Hull. When army reformers, including Elihu Root (secretary of war, first for President McKinley, then Theodore Roosevelt, from 1899 to 1904), again pressed for a general-staff system a few years later, they proposed that a chief of staff to the president should replace the commanding general. Root also recommended a system of rotation from staff to line, bringing to an end the practice of permanent assignments to bureaus in the War Department. Assistant Adjutant General William H. Carter, who played a major role in guiding the bill for a general staff corps through Congress, deprecated the office of commanding general as being "merely an empty title, luring prominent generals to sure disappointments and lifelong grievances."[38]

Although the latter bill provided that Miles would be the first chief of staff, thus maintaining his rank as the foremost general in the army, he campaigned against the measure. In a statement before the Senate Committee on Military Affairs on March 20, 1902, Miles argued against "substituting" the system responsible for victories in previous wars with "one that is more adapted to the monarchies of the Old World." He excused the lapses of the Commissary Department during the Spanish-American War as being "not the fault of the system, but those responsible for its administration." Miles concluded by citing the experience of the Boxer Rebellion, where "the thorough supply and equipment of the American troops excited the envy and admiration of all the allied troops, and especially those of Germany, where they have the imperial staff corps."[39]

The *New York Times,* supportive of Miles in his past jousts with the War Department, differed with him in this instance. In the course of Miles's testimony, according to the newspaper, he threatened to quit the army if he did not have his way. "The reason he gave for the statement is that the bill is utterly subversive of the interests of the military establishment." The *Times* editorially rebuked Miles for his statement: "In spite of Gen. Miles's great services we do not think it discreet in him to challenge a direct issue between himself, and the Secretary of War by threatening to resign if the department bill is enacted." The good will that Miles lost by his ultimatum is evident in the editor's remark, "if we consider that the attitude then taken has been the General's habitual attitude toward the measures of the department we shall be in a position to understand and allow for much irritation on the part of the official head of the department [Elihu Root]." Miles fought a losing battle, but received considerate treatment from the victors. Carter, a colonel at the time of the bill's passage on February 14, 1903, later mentioned that "as salve to the opposition" the bill would go into effect only after Miles retired.[40]

December 1898 was a busy month for Miles; he first testified before the House Committee on Military Affairs, then responded to a summons from the president's commission investigating the conduct of the War Department in the war with Spain. The War Department Investigating Commission came to be popularly referred to as the Dodge Commission because Grenville M. Dodge served as its chairman.

After Miles informed Maj. Stephen C. Mills, the commission's recorder, that "for reasons which I believe to be the best interests of the Army, I have no volunteer testimony to offer," the Dodge Commission formally requested that he testify on December 21. When Miles took the stand he declined to take an oath, possibly to attract attention to his belief that the president had weakened his commission by not authorizing it to require sworn statements. The *New York Times* reported that during his testimony, Miles responded to questions "in a clear, unhesitating way" describing his experiences during both the Santiago and Puerto Rican campaigns.[14]

During his appearance before the commission, Miles described the confusion at Tampa, the insufficiency of tugs and launches at the landing beaches, and the scarcity of medical supplies in Cuba. He cited a message from Shafter to Corbin on August 4, revealing that "four men in the Thirty-third Michigan died in the past week for lack of medicine." When questioned about sick men being exposed to the elements, Miles related how he had once ordered his aide in Cuba "to find the surgeon, and to assist and hurry in any accommodations that could possibly be used to get these men under shelter, as they were then out in the open wagons in a drenching rain and sick with fever."

Miles told the commission that one of the very first telegrams that he sent after landing in Cuba requested that a work force experienced in constructing port facilities be sent to the island as soon as possible. The piers and wharfs that they would build would expedite both the landing of supplies, including badly needed medicines, and the evacuation of sick and wounded troops. In addition, he ordered a regiment off the battle line so that it could assist the medical corps in caring for its patients.

Commission member James A. Sexton of Illinois had earned his rank of colonel in the Illinois National Guard and knew about soldiering from his service in the Civil War. Wounded in the battle of Nashville, Sexton was now commander in chief of the Grand Army of the Republic. He began to direct Miles's testimony toward its explosive climax when he asked about the sufficiency of commissary and quartermaster stores for the Puerto Rican expedition. Miles complained that his request to Alger not to have rations loaded in bulk, but rather broken down so that each command could carry its own, went unheeded. As a result, "large quantities of vegetables—for instance, potatoes and onions, and articles of that kind—would be stored down in the hold of the ship, and no one knew until they opened the hatches what was there." Furthermore, "Very often the vegetables were spoiled by the heat in the steamers during the voyage, so that they had to be thrown overboard and the troops did not get them." The supply problem continued after the landing at Puerto Rico because the first thirty-six steamers to reach the island did not have bills of lading, forcing quartermasters to guess as to their cargoes.[42]

Miles now turned his attention to Sexton's question about the Commissary Department: "You asked about food. In my judgement that was one of the serious causes of so much sickness and distress on the part of the troops." He wondered why the usual practice of slaughtering beef cattle as needed from a herd sent with the troops had not been followed. Colonel Sexton then asked, "Was not the beef sent in refrigerator cars from the United States in better condition than it would have been by sending it on the hoof?"

Replying with a brisk "No sir," Miles gave examples of the common practice of shipping live cattle by ship. Then he added, "in my judgement, there is some serious defect in that refrigerator beef, and also the canned beef that was furnished." He continued, "There was sent to Porto Rico 337 tons of what is known as, or called, refrigerated beef, which you might call embalmed beef," thus casually coining a phrase that would come to be indelibly associated with the Spanish-American War. Miles went on to say "and there was also sent 198,508 pounds of what is known as canned fresh beef, which was condemned as far as I know by nearly every officer whose command used it." To substantiate the last statement, Miles produced extracts of reports about the canned beef. For example, the colonel of the Ninth Infantry wrote that "The meat produced disordered stomachs, was not nutritious, soon became putrid, and in many of the cans was found in course of putrefaction when opened."

When the line of questioning began to stray away from the meat furnished in Cuba and Puerto Rico, ex-governor Urban A. Woodbury of Vermont asked Miles to return to the topic. Miles took this opportunity to introduce a letter addressed to the assistant adjutant general of the army, written by a volunteer surgeon, Maj. William H. Daly from Pennsylvania. Dr. Daly described his experiences with refrigerated beef, which he believed had been kept fresh by adulterating it with chemicals. He first became suspicious when the chief commissary officer at Tampa, Col. John F. Weston, showed him a quarter of beef that had been kept in the open for sixty hours. When neither officer could detect any evidence that the meat had spoiled, Daly concluded that "It is impossible to keep fresh beef so long untainted in the sun in that climate without the use of deleterious preservatives, such as boric acid, salicylic acid, or nitrate potash, injected into it in quantities liable to be hurtful to the health of the consumer."

One of the most graphic passages contained in Daly's report described what happened as he cared for 255 military patients being returned to the United States aboard the transport *Panama*. Although the fresh beef brought aboard at Ponce appeared to be in good condition, it "had an odor similar to that of a dead human body after being injected with preservatives, and it tasted when first cooked like decomposed boric acid, while after standing a day for further inspection it became so bitter, nauseous, and unpalatable as to be quite impossible for use."[43]

When Dodge suggested that the beef used by the army was the same as that used in the United States, Miles replied that "The refrigerated beef, if put into proper cold-storage cars, and then taken out at New York and other places over the country, would be comparatively fresh." But he made the point that "when you take it out of the cold-storage cars and put it on a transport without adequate cold storage it would not keep cool if shipped to the Tropics." Dodge next asked whether Miles believed "the transportation of it there deteriorates it." Miles replied, "I do not think that beef such as was sent to Cuba and Porto Rico would be good in any country, in the stomach of any man."

When Dodge asked Miles whether he preferred live cattle to refrigerated beef, Colonel Sexton, no longer able to contain himself, exclaimed, "He objects to using embalmed beef anywhere." Miles then answered for himself: "If I was furnished for any expedition in this country, or any other, with such stuff, I would prohibit the men from taking it." In the course of another question, when Dodge explained that the commissary general had delayed in sending beef on the hoof to Puerto Rico until an iceplant could be constructed, Miles replied, "Well, I have never known troops moving against a hostile enemy carrying an ice plant and refrigerating plant with them."

Shortly thereafter, commission members began a new line of questioning, asking Miles his opinion about the selection of stateside campsites during the war. Midway through this phase of the hearing, Miles outlined the requirements for preserving the health of troops. He stated that "the most important one is cleanliness, and next to keep the men dry and properly sheltered, with change of clothing etc., and the third, wholesome food; and if you violate any one of these requirements your men are bound to be sick and debilitated."

Of all the sites selected, Miles judged Camp Alger, in northern Virginia, to be "the most objectionable." When asked why, he replied, "On account of its low ground, the known character of the country—it is known to be a country infested with typhoid—and its distance from facilities for bathing." Miles had testified earlier that an officer who reported directly to Secretary of War Alger, through the adjutant general, did not include Camp Alger when he recommended camps to be constructed at three sites in Virginia: Falls Church, Vienna, and Leesburg, which were all on the same railroad line. The commanding general also admitted, "There were twelve regiments there [at Camp Alger] before I knew that had been selected."[44]

When asked about Chickamauga Park, Georgia, Miles replied that "The ground was suitable, but it was overcrowded." Miles also introduced a letter from Dr. Senn, which he had forwarded to Alger in August, regarding Camp Thomas at Chickamauga and typhoid fever among the troops in Puerto Rico. Here, the doctor concluded that because of the "great prevalence of the disease in Camp George H. Thomas, it appears to me Medical Department of the Army should recommend immediate evacuation of the camp."[45]

Miles had better things to say about the camps in Florida. The ground at both Jacksonville and Fernandina was "suitable," and troops stationed at these places could bathe in the ocean. As for Miami, Miles pointed out that "when the yellow fever threatened the garrison at Key West they would move the troops up to Miami. It is on the coast where they have the advantage of seabathing, and it is considered a healthy place." He believed that those who came down with typhoid fever in Miami had either contracted the disease elsewhere, or ignored the precaution of only using water from artesian wells. Miles even agreed that Tampa had been a necessary choice as a port of embarkation because "Nine steamers could be loaded at the same time, and it was much nearer Havana than Mobile, New Orleans, Savannah, or other places along the coast."

Miles's testimony, which the *New York Times* characterized as being "rather brief," concluded with his assertion that none of "the many evils which existed" required the attention of Congress to correct. After the "evils" had been revealed, the War Department underwent a thorough housecleaning, beginning with the Commissary Department and ending with the retirement of the commanding general. As a result of Miles's allegations, there would be further investigations, protestations, and explanations,but he had raised an issue that had caught the public's fancy and would become part of the lore of the Spanish-American War.[46]

When Theodore Roosevelt, then governor of New York, distinguished between four kinds of beef that he had personal knowledge of while serving with the First Volunteer Cavalry, the average American fully realized what had provoked Miles. The former Rough Rider's most precise description of the army's beef ration is found in his written statement to an army court of inquiry appointed by the president to investigate Miles's "allegation" about commissary supplies.

In describing four categories of beef furnished to the Rough Riders, Roosevelt wrote that CORNED CANNED BEEF "was good. There was never any complaint about it. It was eaten with avidity, and was healthy." On the other hand, he completely disapproved of "CANNED ROAST BEEF. This was our ordinary beef ration, and it was thoroughly bad." Unfortunately for his troops, canned roast beef "was the only meat given us on our transport going to Santiago and on the transport returning to Montauk Point, and for the month following the landing it was issued to us about as often as pork was issued."

Roosevelt related that his "eyes were first opened to the quality of the beef" when he noticed one of his men about to throw away his meal of canned roast beef. Roosevelt laughed when the trooper explained that he could not eat the meat, "and ordered him to try. He tried, with the result that he immediately vomited." Roosevelt testified that he "then kept watch and found that very few of the men would eat more than a very small part of the beef; that it tended to make them sick; and they grew weaker on the diet."

Without mincing words, Roosevelt dismissed the controversy over canned roast beef, stating that he did "not regard it as a subject for controversy at all. The canned roast beef issued to the army during the Santiago campaign made a thoroughly poor ration." It was "tasteless at the best, nauseating at the worst, and that when living on it the men speedily weakened and became sick." As for the current investigation, Roosevelt declared, "no matter what the analyses may now show, and no matter whether or not certain cans of this beef prove edible, that as a ration in the Santiago campaign it was poor, and that practically everybody so considered it at the time."

Roosevelt then discussed what he too called "EMBALMED BEEF. While our troop ship the *Yucatan* was in Tampa Harbor, two or three quarters of chemically treated beef were put aboard her and stowed on the forward deck under cover. They speedily became so offensive that I reported the facts and had them condemned and thrown overboard." Without naming his source, Roosevelt went on to say: "I have been informed since my return that these quarters of beef were put on merely as an experiment, without expense to the government."

As for the fourth category, fresh or refrigerated beef, Roosevelt wrote that shortly after the capture of Santiago "we were issued beef brought on ships into the harbor, which we knew as fresh beef. I understand it was refrigerated." He considered this product "good beef and we enjoyed it very much. Once or twice a little of it spoiled, but this was merely owing to delaying in carting it out to the camp." Roosevelt concluded, "It gave all the men diarrhea, especially at first, but we thought this was simply the change of diet and it greatly improved the health and spirits of the man as a whole."[47]

Roosevelt, who would later become one of Miles's most implacable enemies, explained to him on January 14 why he had become involved in the controversy. "When I saw you testifying to what I knew to be the truth about the meat, I felt it my duty to write and aid you." Furthermore, when the Rough Rider saw Miles deserted by the officer corps at the investigation, he admitted that he "was dumbfounded by the report of many of the officers' testimony and am wholly unable to understand it. I have, however, found that very naturally even brave and good officers are most reluctant to testify where their testimony may get them into trouble and may ruin their future careers."

Roosevelt, who had served as assistant secretary of the navy from April 19, 1897, until he resigned to join the Rough Riders on May 6, 1898, did not wish to criticize anybody in the military establishment unfairly. Rather, his wish was "to prevent such troubles arising in the future. The administration of the War Department ought to be as efficient as the administration of the Navy Department." Like Miles, Roosevelt believed "It is folly to pretend that this was the case during the last war, and it will be worse than folly if we fail to realize that such was the case and to try to bring the Army up to the standard it should be brought up to."[48]

Unfortunately for the army, the bureaucrats chose to close ranks and censure their accuser, rather than seize the opportunity to reform the War Department. Adjutant General Corbin, who emerged virtually unscathed from the investigation, would use his autobiography to place the burden of wrongdoing on the shoulders of Miles and Dr. Daly. He charged that "The story . . . of bad food, and particularly of 'embalmed beef,' was no less than a crime by those with whom it originated." In Corbin's opinion, "The 'embalmed beef' of which so much has been written was no more and no less than the refrigerated beef of commerce, a food product that has been and is today of inestimable value to the troops serving in the tropics." Corbin, however, must have turned a deaf ear to the testimony about the various forms of beef rations when he went on to "attribute the good health of the soldiers of my present command more to the abundant supply of this so called 'embalmed beef' than to any other one cause."[49]

Brig. Gen. Charles P. Eagan, the commissary general, risked and lost much more than had Corbin, by using the presidential investigation to make a self-destructive attack against Miles's honor. In 1874 the Irish-born soldier, who had fought as a volunteer infantry officer during the Civil War, transferred from the excitement of service on the plains to the routine of a staff officer. While in Washington, he apparently did not impress Corbin, who described him as being "irascible, erratic and not possessed of superior judgment."[50]

On January 12, 1899, Eagan reappeared before the War Department Investigating Commission, popularly known as the Dodge Commission, to reply to Miles's charges, which, according to Alger, had struck the commissary general "with the suddenness and sharpness of a blow from an assassin's knife out of the dark." Although Eagan had three weeks to prepare a counterthrust, his abusive tirade against the commanding general when he took the stand gives no indication of any forethought. Referring to typed notes, Eagan took particular exception to Miles's testimony about canned roast beef. "General Miles was asked by your committee how tinned fresh beef became part of the army ration." The commissary general then supplied Miles's response: "You had better ask the Secretary of War or the Commissary General. I think they can tell you. I know it was sent as an experiment."

Eagan declared that "when General Miles charges that it was furnished as a 'pretense of experiment' he lies in his throat, he lies in his heart, he lies in every hair of his head and every pore in his body, he lies willfully, deliberately, intentionally, and maliciously." After Eagan went on to say, "I wish to force the lie back into his throat," he added a phrase the *New York Times* refused to print, which was "covered with the contents of a camp latrine."

If Miles could not prove his allegation about the roast canned beef, said Eagan, then "he should be denounced by every honest man, barred from the clubs, barred from the society of decent people, and so ostracized that the street bootblack would not condescend to speak to him." Miles deserved such treatment because "he has fouled his own nest, he has aspersed the honor of a brother officer without a particle of evidence or fact to sustain in any degree his scandalous, libelous, malicious falsehood, viz. That this beef or anything whatever was furnished the army under 'pretense of experiment.'" Eagan eventually came to his point that "this very canned beef we are speaking of has been a part of the army ration since February 8, 1888." He then scolded his superior officer: "Whether General Miles is ignorant of this, I do not pretend to say, but he takes it upon himself when asked who fixed it as part of the army ration to say: 'You will have to ask some one here in Washington.'"[51]

A memorandum contained in Miles's papers addresses the issue raised by the commissary general. According to this critique of Alger's article "The Food of the Army during the Spanish War," the author, presumably Miles, argued that canned fresh beef had only been a part of the army's travel ration. In 1895 regulations prohibited tinned fresh beef from being used as part of the field ration, and neither the president nor the secretary of war had sanctioned a change in this regulation. In comparison to the period from 1895 to 1898, when only 660 pounds of this form of beef had been supplied to American soldiers, 7 million pounds of this product had been accepted by the Army during the war. The memorandum concluded that 7 million pounds of canned fresh beef was "a quantity far in excess of the actual or prospective needs of the military service, and to the detriment rather than the advantage of the public interest."[52]

The *New York Times* appreciated Miles's reaction to Eagan's testimony. An editorial described him as behaving "with much dignity as well as with much intelligence. He has ignored the personal insults of his subordinate. These were matters, as he viewed it, to be dealt with not in his personal interest, but in the interest of the United States Army." Thus, rather than discrediting Miles, Eagan's barbed remarks would cause the commissary general some discomfort.[53]

Eagan could feel a bit abashed in the company of his comrades in arms, realizing that they must be aware of the *Army and Navy Journal*'s judgment that it could "recall no act of any officer of our Army which has ever been received with more universal condemnation in the Army and beyond it than that of General Eagan in turning a flood of indecent and vulgar abuse upon the Major General commanding." Eagan would also pay a price, albeit a small one, for conduct unbecoming an officer and a gentlemen and "obnoxious, in the highest degree, to the discipline and good order of the military establishment."[54]

After a court-martial convened by Secretary of War Alger found Eagan guilty of the above charges and sentenced him to dismissal from the army, President McKinley commuted the sentence "to suspension from rank and duty for six years." Since the president did not include a suspension of pay in the commuted sentence, one officer commented that "Eagan has been retired in disgrace on full pay six years before he would have been retired with honor and on three-fourths pay."[55]

If Eagan had been patient, both the report of the commission investigating the war and testimony heard by the Army beef court, which held its first hearing on February 20, 1899, would have placated him. He would have been especially pleased that the presidential commission praised his department because "wherever the troops were ordered, whether to the various camps in the United States, or in Puerto Rico, Cuba and Manila, the rations prescribed by law were on the transports and at the camps with the soldiers."[56]

As for the commissioners' attitude toward Miles, the *Army and Navy Journal* wrote, "They appear to have a decided prejudice against the General. They may have, or think they have, good reason for this, but the display of it is not becoming in a document which should be severely judicial in its character and tone." For instance, in resolving Miles's charges about "embalmed beef," the commission collected twenty-nine samples of refrigerated beef from both stateside and overseas camps. Chemical examinations of these samples revealed, according to the commissioners' report, no "boric or salicylic acid or other deleterious chemicals found." This reminded the *Journal* of "the case of the Irishman who complained that he was convicted on the testimony of two spalpeens who saw him do it, when he could produce a hundred witnesses who would swear that they did not see him."

In another instance, the commission responded to the numerous complaints about canned roast beef by presenting an 1897 endorsement by Miles of the use of tinned beef in Alaska. The *Journal* pointed out, however, that this letter "has no significance, as it makes no reference to canned roast beef and apparently canned corned beef is what is referred to, for an argument is given to show that salting does not destroy the value of meat as food or tend to produce scurvy. Besides Alaska is not Cuba." The *Journal* also challenged the commissioners' statement that no one in the navy had complained about canned roast beef, reminding its readers that a marine colonel had publicly criticized this product.[57]

One of the sharpest criticisms for Miles in the report concerned his alleged "dereliction of duty" in not alerting the War Department about his "belief or suspicion" about bad beef. Miles had an opportunity to address this issue on February 20, when he appeared before the Army Court of Inquiry, or beef court, established on February 9, 1899, by President McKinley "to investigate certain allegations of the Major General Commanding the Army in respect to the unfitness for issue of certain articles of food furnished by the Subsistence Department to the troops in the field during the recent operations in Cuba and Puerto Rico."[58]

In contrast to the members of the court, presided over by Maj. Gen. James F. Wade, all of whom displayed "scarfs, bullion, and buttons" on their full-dress uniforms, Miles wore his fatigue uniform. One of the first questions concerned some newspaper interviews he had given. Regarding one appearing in the December 23, 1898, *New York Journal,* Miles declared that he did "not recall anything in the interview that had not been given in my testimony or transmitted in my reports. You will observe it contains a number of my declinations to name officers or my authorities, and refuses to answer. It must therefore be incorrect in its representations." As for a sensational interview in which Miles claimed to have new evidence about "embalmed beef," published in the February 1, 1899, *New York Herald,* the commanding general had a letter "from the gentlemen who, I understood, wrote this, in which he says he is willing to swear that I declined to be interviewed, and that, thinking something had to be given out, he had proceeded to write what he knew were the facts."[59]

It appears, however, that on February 1, at least one newspaper would accurately print a statement in which Miles exaggerated the facts about new evidence. On the evening of January 31, Miles told a newsman from the *New York Times* that "What I have said about the 'embalmed beef,' however, is abundantly substantiated by evidence. I have the affidavits of men who have seen the process of embalming beef or treating it chemically for the purpose of preserving it." According to the same newspaper, Miles set the record straight during his appearance before the court. This article revealed that "his only evidence was what was contained in the report of officers, and statements of men who claimed that the beef had the odor of an embalmed body, and they had seen fluid injected into beef, and other indications of chemical treatment."[60]

When asked when he first became aware of the problem of canned roast beef, Miles said that he had heard criticisms about this form of beef at Tampa, but he did not realize it had become part of the field ration. When complaints resurfaced at Santiago, he had been so preoccupied with the campaign that he regarded them as the usual bellyaching of the troops. Miles finally realized the extent of the problem after he returned to New York from Puerto Rico and found that troops stationed at Montauk were too ill to join his men in a parade. The *New York Times* explained that Miles knew "there was no yellow fever at the Point, and he thought the men certainly ought to be over their malaria. He therefore ordered an inquiry into the beef, about which there had been so much complaint." Questioned about whether this had been reported to General Eagan's office, "Gen. Miles leaned forward drawing his brows to a furrow and replied forcefully: 'I am not required, sir, to report to the Commissary General.'"

In response to a query about his reason for delaying to take any "action in the beef matter," Miles said "that he had delayed because he did not want to act until he had secured the very best authority, which was information from the most reliable sources." On September 20 Miles issued an order through the adjutant general's office, requiring regimental commanders to report about the beef supplied to them during the war. The issue of Miles's characterization of canned roast beef as being a "pretense of an experiment" came up next. Miles explained that he presumed that "it was being issued as an experiment" because he did not believe it had been authorized as a field ration.

Eagan's main grievance against Miles would be resolved when the commanding general admitted that he had erred in using the expression "pretense of experiment." Miles testified that, "As far as indicating fraud, I wish to state that no such inference was intended, it was perhaps an unfortunate expression, and had my attention been called to it I might have amended it to say—well, 'on the theory of an experiment.'" Miles stood firm, however, on the point that, "As a matter of fact, it was an experiment, and a very costly one." The final round of cross-examination concentrated on refrigerated beef. Miles related that he first suspected that this beef might have been preserved with additives when officers at Ponce could offer no other explanation for how it could remain fresh for seventy-two hours. Dr. Daly had made the first official report about chemically preserved beef, but since then Miles had received about one hundred letters complaining about this product. Such terms as *embalmed, decomposed, injected, poisoned,* and *spoiled* were used to describe beef believed to have been treated. Miles also presented the court with a list of ships and the amount of condemned refrigerated beef thrown overboard from each of the vessels.[61]

The day after Miles's appearance before the court, veterans of the Santiago campaign were heard from. An infantry colonel testified that when he ate refrigerated beef, he could taste either kerosene or chloroform, and a cavalry lieutenant colonel complained that it had a "musty smell." A commander of a cavalry brigade told the court that his adjutant informed him that two quarters of beef had been carried aboard their transport at Tampa by someone who, according to the *New York Times,* "claimed as the result of treatment [the meat] would keep in the tropics two or three days. The second day it became so offensive that it was thrown overboard."

Almost to a man, the officers corroborated Miles's complaints about canned roast beef, testifying that most of the troops simply discarded this ration, and of the few who tried to eat it, many retched immediately afterwards. They also agreed with Miles that beef on the hoof should have been used to feed their troops. If the campaigners had not been ordered to report about bad beef, however, the *Times* said that they "would have permitted the unsatisfactory ration to pass without further notice as incident to warfare and to the peculiarly trying circumstances with which the army was confronted at the outbreak of war."[62]

Canned roast beef received short shrift from the court of inquiry in its report, approved by the president on May 6, 1899. The members concurred that during the twenty-year period prior to the war the regulars had avoided this ration, using on average twenty-five hundred pounds per year, and during the war "its use as part of the field ration had never been sanctioned by the President or Secretary of War." As for the commissary general, the court believed that his purchase of seven million pounds of this product was "unwarranted and reckless." Although Eagan had been motivated by "the earnest desire to procure the best possible food for the troops," the court judged "this act of the Commissary General of Subsistence a colossal error, for which there is no palliative."

The court disagreed with Miles's protestations that in some instance "embalmed beef" had been furnished to the troops. It declared, "The use of refrigerated beef on shore, after the troops had secured convenient harbors and landing facilities, was wise and desirable. The court believes that there was no better food available or practicable." With that stated, the court had no alternative but to find "that the Major General commanding had no sufficient justification for alleging that the refrigerated beef was embalmed, or was unfit for issue to troops." The court also followed the lead of the war investigation commission, and rebuked Miles for not giving a timely warning about bad beef so that the secretary of war could correct the problem.[63]

Alger had hoped to have Miles punished more severely. On February 1, and again on the second, the secretary of war met with the president. According to the press reports, "on both occasions there were informed persons at the War Department who said that the object of his visit was to bring Gen. Miles to trial for disrespect to the investigating commission and to the President of the United States."

Alger had been furious after Miles spoke to reporters on the evening of January 31. His comments effectively returned the beef scandal to headlines on the very day that Alger had expected the storm stirred up by Miles's earlier testimony to subside. The commissary general had already been found guilty, and the war investigation commission's report, expected to close the book on the controversy, would be released on February 1. It is even believed that after Eagan's court-martial, Alger sought to insure that peace would finally prevail by trying to convince Miles not to revive the beef issue in the future.

On the thirty-first, although Miles apparently intended to limit his remarks and did refuse comment about Eagan's trial, the *New York Times* reported that "he replied to some specific questions with explicit frankness." Besides repeating his charges about "embalmed beef," Miles had something new to say about canned roast beef. He referred to reports about bad beef coming in from regimental commanders and declared, "They cannot be successfully disputed. I don't care what sort of men deny them." Further along in his remarks Miles insured that he would catch the attention of the public when he added: "I now know what the trouble was. There was no life or nourishment in the meat. It had been used to make beef extract, and after the juice was squeezed out of it the pulp was put back in the cans and labeled 'roast beef.'"[64]

Alger's effort to remove Miles from the office of commanding general came to naught because President McKinley wished to avoid a public quarrel. One unnamed officer quoted by the *New York Times* argued that although the bureaus sought to satisfy the needs of the army, "there is also a strong conviction, supported by innumerable reports, that somebody was making money out of the contracts for food and clothing, and that the contractors were more solicitously humored than were the soldiers." This led the officer to conclude, "If they break Miles for doing his level best to prove that the soldiers were not well taken care of, and that the contractors were the objects of chief solicitude of the War Department, the Administration that commits so blundering a crime" would pay a price at the polls.[65]

The very next day, the same newspaper again warned of the price to be paid if Miles were punished when it noted that McKinley had "his ear to the ground . . . and he hears some comments that Alger disdains to heed. Gen. Miles always has been a friend of the soldier. The soldiers know it. They sometimes have thought since April 21, 1898, that all the officers of the army were not their friend." Thus, in deciding whether to discipline Miles, "upon the request of Alger the President knows that the country might be stirred into an undesirable fever of admiration for a man not afraid of criticism when his provocation was in so good a cause as the protection of the private soldier from official imposition." Today most historians suggest that Miles raised the issue of bad beef as a ploy to advance his political fortunes—they also appear satisfied with the court's criticism of him for not promptly reporting his suspicions. In 1899 *The Nation* concluded that the beef court's verdict "lets out everybody who is in any way responsible for sending the foul and uneatable stuff to the soldiers, but leaves Gen. Miles still censorable for calling attention to the fact that it was not sent." Furthermore, it has been pointed out that McKinley emerged unscathed from the controversy. A contribution to a military encyclopedia judged that the president's "creation of a special presidential inquiry had initially deflected and eventually dissipated the public outcry aroused by the sensational revelations of August 1891."[66]

It is also probable that McKinley refrained from doing anything to enhance Miles's popularity because that might encourage the general to challenge him for the presidency. Miles had speculated that he might be a viable candidate for the office and may have already tested the water. In August 1899, Theodore Roosevelt wrote his friend and sponsor, Senator Henry Cabot Lodge, that "Miles unfortunately has the Presidential bee in his bonnet, even to the extent of wishing me to run as Vice-President on the ticket with him."[67]

An undated memorandum found among Miles's papers confirms his conversation with Roosevelt about such a slate, but denies its importance. According to this note, "In the autumn of 1898 a man in Kansas wrote to General Miles saying his ticket was Miles and Roosevelt. On meeting then Colonel Roosevelt in Washington not long after, General Miles mentioned this fact, not considering it of any importance or worthy of any serious consideration." His casual suggestion that they might be running mates bothered Miles enough, however, that when he later met Roosevelt at Pennsylvania Station, "lest the story be repeated or misunderstood, he asked the Colonel to consider it in the strictest confidence, and received the assurance from him that it would be so considered."[68]

In January 1902, when the president of Boston's Commonwealth Club bluntly asked Miles about the truth of a story in a local newspaper naming him as a presidential candidate, the commanding general replied: "I deeply regret these reports. Like many others in the past they are absolutely unauthorized. They do not emanate from myself, nor from my friends, and I trust that the public will not be misled by them." He then made it clear that if he ever had any dreams about capturing the White House, they definitely did not tantalize him now: "I have not been, and am not now, a seeker for Presidential honors."[69]

After Alger lost the battle to court-martial Miles, he continued his campaign to slight the commanding general, while at the same time defending against further revelations of mismanagement. For instance, he insured that staff officers would be kept on a leash too short to permit them to follow the example of Inspector General Joseph C. Breckinridge and his assistant, both of whom actively investigated complaints about beef. On March 23, 1899, the War Department ordered that "hereafter no chief or acting chief of staff corps shall be detailed or ordered to any duty by any authority without the approval of the Secretary of War."[70]

In May rumors found their way into print that Maj. Gen. Wesley Merritt would replace Miles, who would return to the Department of the East. Since Merritt had approved a recommendation that Alger be dismissed from the army in 1864, some doubted that the secretary would elevate the recently returned commander of the Philippine expedition. An unnamed officer assigned to the War Department pointed out, however, that "Merritt is ambitious; he is nearing his retirement [June 1907]; he cannot hope to hold command long; and naturally talks in a way that is agreeable to the Secretary. We all do that. Even the beef board is subject to that feeling." The knowledgeable bureaucrat added that he had been told "that whether the beef court goes light on Miles or hits him heavily, the President will withdraw from him further opportunities as Commanding General, to provoke another row about bad beef." Although those who were skeptical about the reported demotion of Miles would be proven to be correct, the commanding general again saw his name bandied about in public.[71]

Miles could take heart, however, from those who supported his jousts with Alger. For instance, President Charles W. Eliot of Harvard University, where Miles had received an honorary Doctor of Laws degree in 1896, provided a thoughtful insight when he introduced Miles before the Harvard Republican Club on March 23, 1899. Eliot, reflecting on the recent war, concluded, "Cowardice is rare in our race. There is, however, a higher kind of courage which, at the expense of calumny and obloquy, seeks fearlessly to make known the truth. And this is the sort of courage that Gen. Miles has shown during the last four months."[72]

— CHAPTER 15 —

Miles Inspires White House Discipline

JUST AS SECRETARY OF War Russell Alger had wanted to see General Miles cashiered, so President McKinley began to yearn for Alger's resignation. With a presidential election just a year away, McKinley wished to put the issue of a mismanaged War Department to rest; furthermore, developments in the Philippines warranted new leadership in the department. On June 19, 1899, Miles, virtually an outcast in the corridors of power, could only tell a reporter, "I know nothing concerning the story that the War Department is suppressing the news from Manila. But everybody knows that things are very serious here." Within a month, the story that the newsman hoped Miles could confirm hit the headlines. On July 17, a round robin sent by correspondents from Manila complained that the military had censored reports that might alarm Americans because they told of the determined resistance United States troops faced trying to quell Filipino insurgents.[1]

Alger had sealed his fate during the last week of June 1899, when he announced that in 1902 he would be a candidate for the Senate. His removal from the cabinet became imminent after he accepted the support of Michigan's governor Hazen Stuart Pingree, who, although a Republican, had become an irritant to McKinley by challenging him on numerous issues, such as imperialism and the need for antitrust legislation.[2]

McKinley did not have the heart to demand personally that his secretary of war resign immediately, rather than on January 2, 1900, as proposed by Alger. Instead, the president detailed the distasteful job to his ailing vice president, Garret A. Hobart, who would die on November 21 of a heart condition. Alger received the bad news when he and his wife spent a mid-July weekend at the Hobart's house near Long Branch, on the New Jersey shore. Following his traumatic holiday, the secretary of war dawdled on his way back to Washington, D.C. He finally met with the president on Wednesday, July 19, in a meeting described by the *Army and Navy Journal* as "anything but cordial." The resulting resignation would become effective on August 1, but Alger would eventually have the consolation of winning one of Michigan's Senate seats in 1902.[3]

Henry C. Corbin noted in his autobiography some of the happenings in Washington while Alger vacationed at the seashore. During a ride on that fateful weekend, the president told the adjutant general what was happening at Long Branch, New Jersey. Both men "agreed that the best constitutional lawyer within reach should be selected" for the coming vacancy. Corbin explained that the War Department needed a person with such a background to plan how the newly acquired islands would be governed.

The adjutant general is one of a few, including Secretary of State John Hay, who take credit for suggesting Elihu Root as Alger's replacement. Corbin saw Root "as having . . . particularly distinguished himself in the Constitutional Convention of that state [New York, in 1894], and in many ways his character and fitness were pre-eminent over those of any other names that suggested themselves."[4]

McKinley made an inspired choice when he decided upon the talented corporate lawyer Elihu Root to serve as the next secretary of war. According to the *Dictionary of American Biography,* "probably no other American during the first quarter of the 20th century, excepting Theodore Roosevelt and Woodrow Wilson, exercised more influence in projecting the United States toward leadership in world affairs."[5]

Root would leave his mark on the army before going on to win even greater plaudits as a secretary of state under President Theodore Roosevelt and then to serve as a senator from New York. Besides more than adequately fulfilling the task for which he was chosen—that is, devising the legal framework for binding the United States with its new possessions—Root helped to modernize the army.[6]

In his 1938 biography of Root, Philip C. Jessup described conditions at the War Department in the summer of 1899 as "a mess. The war had demonstrated its inefficiency and corruption. Its red tape was proverbial. Personal jealousies and spite crippled the efficiency of the personnel. Officers long entrenched in sinecures in Washington had been successful only in firmly establishing their political position with congressional and senatorial backers." On August 1, following Root's swearing-in ceremony, Alger introduced the new secretary to Miles. If there was a competition to capture the secretary's attention, Miles lost to Corbin that day. The adjutant general, who had briefly met Root at the White House during the evening of July 24, monopolized the evening. After Corbin joined Root for dinner at the Arlington Hotel, where both were staying, the two officials spent three hours driving in the countryside seeking relief from the hot and humid capital city.[7]

But while Corbin quickly won Root's ear, Miles soon regained his prestige as commanding general. Under an order restoring the office of commanding general to its former power, the inspector general's office was placed under the control of both the secretary of war and the commanding general. Just before Alger resigned from the War Department, he deleted the provision giving the commanding general control over the inspector general's office. Root, although reluctant to begin his tenure in office by setting aside an order of the official whom he replaced, was probably swayed by the argument that for the commanding general to carry out his duties effectively, he had to be aware of the army's business. This led the *New York Times* to declare that "A month ago Gen. Miles had no duties to perform, and it was not necessary for him to have any such information. Now it is regarded as a matter of course that he should be placed in possession of it."[8]

When it came time for Miles to review 1899 in his annual report, he had reason to be pleased. The army was in a "transitional state," he reported. After stagnating at 25,000 men for the twenty-four-year period ending in 1898, its authorized strength began to increase in stages until on March 2, 1899, it reached a level of 65,000 men, which met Miles's goal of one soldier for every thousand U.S. inhabitants. Besides the regulars, the army could also field a volunteer force of 35,000 men, which it did, organizing them into twenty-five regiments destined to serve in the Philippines. Miles could also proudly report that as a result of efforts to construct and modernize fortifications along our shores, "it is hoped that in a short time our coasts will be in a proper condition of defense."

Miles praised the many American soldiers who were subjected to frigid winters in American posts, then called on to campaign in the tropics during the summer: "Rarely in any service have troops experienced such unusual changes in climate, yet . . . the utmost loyalty, fortitude, and faithful performance of duty have been manifested," he wrote. Reference to the buildup of troop strength in the Philippine Islands was the only clue in Miles's report that the army did not have the archipelago under control. Besides the 971 officers and 31,344 troops already stationed there, Miles's 1899 report revealed that 546 officers and 16,553 men were on their way to the islands.[9]

On June 6, 1900, when Secretary of War Root issued an order creating the rank of lieutenant general and named Miles to that rank, it crowned his career. Even the fact that Root filled the major general's slot with Corbin could not dull Miles's satisfaction at achieving one of his most cherished goals. The Senate would confirm Miles's appointment on February 2, 1901.[10]

In the summer of 1900, Miles yearned to join the army in the field. He formally requested permission on July 18 to be sent to the Philippines, where "important military changes are to be made," and China, where "not only the lives, but also vast property interests of our citizens, necessitate the immediate presence of a strong military force." On July 20, when Chinese nationalists known as the Boxers, in their attempt to drive foreigners from China, laid siege to the legations in the capital city of Peking, Miles recommended to Root that an expeditionary force of fifteen thousand men be sent from the Philippines to China. On July 26 Miles prepared a list of artillery units that might also be sent for use against the Boxers.[11]

Root did not completely agree with the recommendations. He pointed out to McKinley that if a massive redeployment of troops from the Philippines to China were to be made, Filipinos who had cooperated with American forces would be at the mercy of insurgents, who could also disrupt the government of the underprotected islands. Furthermore, although Miles had made some practical suggestions about which artillery units could be sent to China, Root complained that his "artillery propositions involve from $750,000 to a million dollars and couldn't be filled before next spring or summer."[12]

On August 4, and under a German general, about twenty thousand troops from the six allied nations participating in the International Relief Force began their advance to lift the siege of Peking. Adna R. Chaffee, who enlisted in the Sixth Cavalry of the regular army in 1861 and served with that regiment for twenty-seven years before becoming a field grade officer, led the United States contingent of about two thousand soldiers and marines, designated the China Relief Expedition. To insure that Chaffee, then a colonel in the regular army, would not be glaringly outranked by allied officers, Corbin convinced Root and McKinley that if the Senate confirmed Chaffee's promotion to Major General of Volunteers, it would be legal even though no vacancy existed for that rank. Chaffee had the delicate task of protecting American lives and property from the Boxers while at the same time insuring that the U.S. government would "maintain its relations of friendship with the part of Chinese people and Chinese officials not concerned in outrages on Americans."[13]

On August 15 Chaffee telegraphed the War Department from Peking to say, "legation relieved last night. Purpose of expedition being accomplished, what is the further wish of government as regards the use of troops? . . . Apprehend considerable difficulty supplying large force during winter about Peking." Obviously Miles had overstated the manpower requirements for Chaffee's relief expedition, thus providing the secretary of war with grounds for questioning his advice in the future. However, Miles could not have known the number of troops that other nations would commit to the relief force, and he did not want Chaffee to be at a disadvantage when he met the Boxers in battle.[14]

Root distanced himself even further from Miles when the twenty-five volunteer regiments were being organized. He asked the commanding general to select the regular officers whom he believed to be best qualified for command of the new regiments, but added that he did not want the public to know that promotions were being considered at the War Department in order to keep his office from being overrun with applicants and their sponsors. As he always had before, Miles advocated following the rule of seniority to avoid the suggestion of favoritism, a rule that had proved useful in the past. As Miles wrote in his 1900 annual report, "appointments of officers [would] be made with a due regard for the principle of seniority, and that each case be passed upon by a board of the highest officers of the Army, as was done in the reorganization following the civil war."[15]

Root disagreed that an officer's time in grade should determine whether he would be promoted. He believed that younger men would be more capable field officers than their seniors, who were more likely to be physically limited and set in their ways. Most damaging to the relationship between Root and Miles, however, was that the story reached the newspapers, and Root attributed the leak to Miles. Years later, Philip Jessup wrote that Root told him that this "incident convinced him that Miles would not cooperate and therefore he never trusted him." This situation so annoyed the secretary of war that on September 4, 1901, Root complained to McKinley that the commanding general sought "to promote his own views and undo my plans. It acts on the department very much like mixing seidlitz powder."[16]

Jessup concluded that Root "found that Miles now had illusions of greatness and a presidential bee in his bonnet which made him uncooperative and insubordinate." Miles was a difficult commanding general to work with, but the explanation Jessup offers for Miles's obstinate behavior is debatable. The claim that Miles had a "presidential bee in his bonnet" has the ring of truth in it; however, headlines proclaiming Miles's unstatesmanlike quarrels were not likely to advance a candidate's campaign.[17]

Rather than being politically inspired, Miles's clashes at the War Department appear to be the result of his determination to advance policies that he believed would serve the army best. Although the *New York Times* could correctly declare that in September 1898, Miles had not been "the knight errant for the cause of the Army," by December of that year he had become the champion for the men who served under him. Sadly, Miles's lack of finesse left him ineffective in his duels on their behalf.[18]

Miles rarely verbalized his feelings, but he expressed his attachment to his profession in his 1911 autobiography. Regarding the army he wrote, "I held [it] in the highest regard, and to the service of which I was devoted." Unfortunately for the smooth running of the army, the luster of his own record, and the tranquility of his colleagues in the War Department, the commanding general's unyielding stand occasionally produced such explosive showdowns that reporters could feast on the fallout.[19]

The most lavish of the banquets that were served to the press at Miles's expense occurred during Theodore Roosevelt's first term as president. The relationship between the two headstrong men began on an auspicious note, when the Rough Rider supported Miles during the beef controversy. Roosevelt, then governor of New York, had nothing to gain and much to lose in goodwill from the McKinley administration because of his testimony. During that same year, 1899, in a letter to William Conant Church, editor of the *Army and Navy Journal,* Roosevelt revealed an admiration for what he termed "Miles' military feelings." Roosevelt believed that Miles displayed this quality when he swiftly took the officers of the 6th Massachusetts to task for their deficiencies, while Shafter evidently lacked it for ignoring the fact that officers of the 71st New York Volunteers did not join their men in the attack upon San Juan.[20]

By August 1899, Roosevelt's favorable opinion of Miles began to wane after Miles showed an interest in becoming a competitor for the presidency. In Roosevelt's first mention of Miles's suggestion that they run on the same ticket, he also made his first negative comment about the commanding general. In a letter to Lodge, written just days after Root's appointment as secretary of war, Roosevelt wrote, "I very much fear that he [Root] will find difficulty in getting in with Miles."[21]

In the spring of 1901, Miles spoke at a dinner and had the poor sense to tell the guests that Roosevelt had not been at San Juan Hill. Miles was technically correct, for as Roosevelt felt compelled to explain to one of those who had attended the dinner, "the ridge which we ultimately took was sometimes called San Juan and sometimes not. It was a continuation of the ridge to which we commonly gave the name." Roosevelt and his Rough Riders had in fact overrun a fortified hill flanking San Juan Hill, prosaically named Kettle Hill for the utensils found there used to process sugar cane.[22]

Much as Miles had stewed after learning of the dispatch intended to deprive him of command at Santiago, Roosevelt seethed at having the details of the greatest day of his life questioned. In a letter to George Hinckley Lyman, chair of the Republican State Committee of Massachusetts, he simply described the battleground and substantiated his role in the action. After thinking for four days more about Miles's comments, Roosevelt, now vice president, could no longer contain himself. In a follow-up letter to Lyman, he unleashed his anger at Miles, writing: "What a scoundrelly hypocrite the man is!" He then brought up Miles's proposal: "I told you, did I not, how he came on to see me to ask if I would not go into an agreement with him to run for President with me as Vice-President?"[23]

Roosevelt, who inherited the presidency and the White House following McKinley's death on September 14, 1901, had not told Miles of his displeasure at the general's nit-picking about where the Rough Riders had fought. Therefore, when President Roosevelt invited the commanding general to join him for a ride just weeks after he took the oath of office, Miles must have believed that they were on the best of terms. Meanwhile, the president was simply biding his time, waiting for the occasion to exact retribution.[24]

Roosevelt's opportunity came when Miles made yet another slip of the tongue—this time as he spoke to reporters in Cincinnati on December 16, 1901. A naval court of inquiry had just finished reviewing the performances of Rear Admiral William T. Sampson and Commodore Winfield S. Schley at the Battle of Santiago. Admiral George Dewey, who presided over the court, issued the only dissenting opinion when the rest of the court criticized some of Schley's actions in the battle. Miles broke an army regulation when he remarked to the press, "I am willing to take the judgment of Admiral Dewey in that matter." His concern had been aroused by negative comments made by those hostile to Schley because, as he said, "I have no sympathy with the efforts which have been made to destroy the honor of an officer."[25]

Two days after newspapers printed the interview, Secretary of War Root questioned Miles about the authenticity of the story. Miles must have been taken aback when Root added that if the reports were true, he would be afforded "such opportunity for explanation in writing as you may desire." Miles replied the very next day, the twentieth, with the plea "that my observations . . . were merely my personal views." He must have known better, however, when he claimed that "there was no impropriety in expressing an opinion the same as any other citizen upon a matter of such public interest." Virtually every military officer would have recalled that Rear Admiral Richard Meade had been forced to leave the navy prematurely after he criticized Benjamin Harrison's administration for not taking a stronger stand in the Chilean affair of 1891.[26]

In an attempt to shore up his position, Miles sent a second letter to Root on December 21, in which he clarified why he spoke up for Schley. The commodore had been called a "coward," or even more colorfully a "poltroon," because he opened the blockade line when he sailed away from the Spanish fleet to gain more room to maneuver. Miles wrote that these attempts "to destroy the reputation" of Schley had offended him because he believed that the commodore "like all other officers, regard his honor more sacred than life."[27]

Root had already sent a letter dressing down Miles when the letter of clarification reached him. The secretary of war dismissed this attempt to rectify the situation as not changing "the case. The necessity for repeated explanation but illustrates the importance of the rule which you have violated."[28]

The secretary of war, at the direction of the president, informed Miles that "your explanation of the public statement made by you is not satisfactory." He quoted the first article of the Regulations of the Army, which declared in part that "deliberations or discussions among military men conveying praise or censure, or any mark of approbation, toward others in the military service . . . are prohibited."

Root argued that the commanding general, who should set the example, had instead been "subversive of discipline." To make matters worse, the controversy within the Navy Department which Miles had blundered into was "generally deplored even by the participants, as tending to bring the service into disesteem at home and abroad and to destroy those relations of mutual confidence and friendship between naval officers which the interests of effective service require." Accordingly, said Root, "You had no business in the controversy and no right, holding the office which you did, to express any opinion. Your conduct was in violation of the regulation above cited and of the rules of official propriety; and you are justly liable to censure which I now express."[29]

Roosevelt had earlier disclosed his opinion of the Sampson-Schley case to Henry Cabot Lodge. As McKinley's vice president, he believed "Either the President and Secretary [of the navy, John D. Long] ought to have stood by Schley straight out from the beginning, or if they shared the belief of ninety-five per cent of the navy, including all the best officers, they should have hit him hard at the very beginning." When Roosevelt went on to speculate that Admiral Dewey would be selected to preside over the court of inquiry, he confided that he had "lost every vestige of confidence I once had in Dewey's moral courage in a case like this. He has got the same thirst for notoriety that has helped to ruin Miles, and in his soreness at the result of his own folly, he has become very bitter against the administration."[30]

Miles sought to set himself right with the president at a meeting held in the White House the same day that he received Root's letter, December 21. A Republican congressman from Massachusetts, Samuel Leland Powers, who was waiting to be received by the president, observed and described what took place when the two men met. After a messenger brought Miles's card into the president's second-floor office, Roosevelt stepped into the adjoining reception room. When the president said, "General step this way," Miles joined Roosevelt in a far corner of the room. They spoke so softly that Powers could not overhear their conversation until the president, "in a very loud voice said, 'General, you had no right to do what you did, and I am not inclined to overlook it.' General Miles immediately turned on his heel, and in a distinct voice said, 'Good day, Mr. President,' and stalked out of the room."[31]

The editor of the *New York Times* confided to his good friend Root that his letter of censure to Miles "was brutal. 'It was intended to be,' said Root." Root's biographer wrote that rather than consider Miles's remarks as an unfortunate indiscretion, Root "insisted that it was part of the general conviction reached by the President and himself that Miles was a real difficulty and must eventually be eliminated." A few days after Miles's White House interview, Roosevelt explained his problem concerning the commanding general to Columbia University's professor of dramatic literature, James Brandler Matthews: "As regards Miles, I feel that any man who fails to back me up is either a fellow wholly incapable of reasoning or else a man who had never taken the trouble to reason, or, finally a wrong-headed person."[32]

The humorist Finley Peter Dunne parodied the exchange between the president and the commanding general in an essay titled "White House Discipline." Dunne's creation, Martin Dooley, related that Roosevelt told Miles that he should "know that an officer who criticizes his fellow officers, save in th' reg'lar way, that is to say in a round robin, is guilty iv I dinnaw what . . . I am forced to administer ye a severe reproof."

Dunne, who reminded his readers in this piece that Roosevelt had not been censured after criticizing the War Department in a "round robin," had the rare ability to remain Roosevelt's friend after poking fun at him. In fact, their relationship began after Dunne's Mr. Dooley suggested that Roosevelt's book, *The Rough Riders,* be renamed *Alone in Cuba.* Rather than take offense, Roosevelt, then the governor of New York, reacted with good spirits. After joshing Dunne that "Now I think you owe me one," Roosevelt graciously requested that the next time the Chicago-based humorist came east "you pay me a visit. I have long wanted the chance of making your acquaintance." The White House reprimand did not seem amusing to some observers, however, as it did to Dunne.[33]

The *Army and Navy Journal* expressed its "regret" after it confirmed that "the President openly rebuked the Lieutenant General Commanding in the presence of others during the visit of General Miles to the White House. The Army Regulations, as we have stated, elsewhere, forbid such a showing of disrespect toward even a non-commissioned officer by his superior in rank." Henry Watterson, editor of the *Louisville Courier-Journal,* also supported Miles. In a personal letter, he discussed his editorial treatment of the incident, and pointed out that he "did not write either from partisan interests or personal ill will; although I know the President to be, and during the twenty years of my acquaintance with him to have been, a most ill-judging, inconsiderate person."[34]

Even Henry F. Pringle, who received a Pulitzer Prize for his biography of Theodore Roosevelt, appeared to sympathize with Miles when he wrote, "The distress of Miles was pitiful." Pringle noted that "The *Army and Navy Register* openly defended General Miles. It said, with some truth, that the views expressed on the Sampson-Schley affair had not justified 'the severity—not to say the brutality' of the reprimand imposed." He also noted that the *Register* published "a phrase that must have sent Roosevelt's anger to white heat: General Miles had been entitled to consideration at the hands of 'a man of no military experience, a younger man, as yet hardly trained in the responsibilities and tribulations of his high office.'"[35]

As for Miles, he wasted no time in exiting the scene of his humiliation. He caught the 4:00 P.M. train from the capital and checked into New York's Waldorf Astoria Hotel later that evening. A reporter from the *New York Times* found him in the hotel's lobby reading a newspaper with bold headlines informing readers of his reprimand. When asked about the incident, Miles "smiled and said: 'I have nothing to say about it.'" He again refused to comment after the newsman asked, "Don't you think that perhaps the President and Secretary of War have been a little hasty in their action?"[36]

Almost one month later, Miles came as close as he ever would to publicly commenting on the controversy. On January 18, 1902, he addressed the New York Press Club at its annual banquet. He opened his talk with the comment that, "Unlike the newspaper man, the soldiers may not talk back." A little more than two months after the interview had been given, however, in another letter to Root, Miles denied that he had violated any regulations when he concurred with the published opinion of Admiral Dewey: "There was nothing in anything said by me that in intention or in fact cast reflection upon or criticized any branch of the public service or any private officer." Although bravely stated, this may have been a tenuous defense for Miles's published comments. As the *New York Times* editorialized when the incident first made news, "The President and the Secretary of War are not acting as partisans. They are not taking sides in the controversy. They are merely enforcing regulations made to be obeyed." This episode, however, reveals the hostility of both Root and Roosevelt toward Miles. They used the occasion of a thoughtless lapse by the general to publicly take him to task. Miles, now aware that he had somehow incurred the administration's disfavor, would stiffly strive to maintain his dignity rather than try to rectify the situation.[37]

Just two months after Miles first experienced executive discipline, he again blundered into Roosevelt's wrath. On February 17, Miles met with the president at the White House to gain approval of a plan for the Philippines before he submitted it to Root. To repeat a tactic that had worked well for him in the Indian Wars, he hoped to obtain permission to bring ten men from Cuba and Puerto Rico to the Philippine Islands. These spokesmen "could properly explain to the Filipinos the benefits their people have derived through friendly relations with this country." Then, after Miles had attracted the attention and won the confidence of the insurgents, he would ask permission to bring a delegation of Filipinos to Washington, D.C., "in order that they may see and know the advantages of our civilization and realize the disposition of our government toward them, at the same time affording an opportunity for a full consultation, whereby intelligent and definite action may be taken concerning their future."[38] Unfortunately for Miles's peace of mind, his innocuous proposal was enclosed in a cover letter that thoroughly riled the president.

That afternoon Roosevelt fired off a blistering response to Miles, and the next day provided Root with details of his heated response. The president had fiercely reacted to allegations contained in Miles's cover note. Roosevelt wrote Root that he told Miles that "I do not at all like the clear implication in some of your sentences that brutalities and cruelties had been committed by our troops in the Philippines." The president accounted for the "sporadic cases" that had occurred as "simply another way of stating that there has been war in the Philippines."

The president minimized the charges of misconduct in the Philippines by comparing them with the massacre at Wounded Knee. Miles must have been infuriated when he read Roosevelt's opinion that "after a somewhat careful study of the facts, I am convinced that our troops have been very merciful in the Philippines, much more so than in the old-time Indian warfare on the plains." Then, in a thrust that pinked Miles personally, Roosevelt charged, "In the Wounded Knee fight the troops under your command killed squaws and children, as well as unarmed Indians and armed Indians who had ceased to resist." With his next jab, the president exonerated Miles from responsibility for the massacre while at the same time deprecating the general's military ability, writing that he understood "that you, who were not actually present, could not prevent these outrages, and could not have prevented them had you been present."

In disparaging Miles, Roosevelt made a glaring error. He declared that the outrages in South Dakota "were conducted in the course of the brief and not very difficult campaign, in which you commanded the forces, and that the perpetrators were never brought to justice or punished in any way. My remembrance is that no effort was made to punish them or bring them to justice." Besides being undeserved, this criticism is ironic, for if Miles had had his way with courts-martial in South Dakota, a precedent would have been established for the proper treatment of those held by the army that could have guided the officer corps in the Philippines.

The president argued that "The difficulties encountered by our generals in the Philippines, and the provocations endured by our soldiers were a thousand fold greater than was the case in the Wounded Knee campaign." The Rough Rider concluded, "Yet I question whether we have to regret in the Philippines any incident as bad as the massacre at Wounded Knee."

The president reminded Miles that "thoughtless persons and ill-wishers of the army and government" had attempted to use Wounded Knee to criticize President Harrison's administration as well as "you and your fellow soldiers. Their attitude was bad; but it was not as bad as the attitude of those who, without a hundredth part of their justification, seek today to attack the administration and the army for what has gone on in the Philippines." Roosevelt explained that he had brought all of these facts up "so that you may realize, by comparison with your own experience, how well the army has done in the Philippines and how unsubstantial the grounds for complaint are."

With his intended message to the general sent, the president finally addressed and found fault with all of Miles's proposals. At the morning meeting, Miles suggested that Emilio Aguinaldo, the leader of the Army of Filipino Revolutionaries and a leading advocate of Philippine independence, might be included in the delegation of Filipinos selected to visit the United States. Roosevelt scoffed at this idea, pointing out to the commanding general that "In this campaign of yours against the Sioux, the arch-instigator of the trouble, the Aguinaldo of the period, was Sitting Bull. . . . The Indian police were sent out to arrest him, and when he resisted he was killed. We have behaved more mercifully in the Philippines."

The president also dismissed the idea of bringing any Filipinos to Washington as "more folly." Roosevelt argued that each "really capable Indian campaigner" believed that during the campaigns "one of the chief difficulties to overcome was the tendency of certain sentimentalists and of members of the 'Indian Ring' to pet the hostile Indians, make much of their chiefs, get delegations of them to come on here, and shower attentions upon them, while neglecting the friendly Indians." He pledged not to make a similar mistake in the Philippines. Instead, only after the insurrection was quelled in the islands would the natives be allowed to elect three delegates, who would be sent to Washington.

The president could not restrain himself from lashing out at Miles one more time: "The allegations of cruelty and misconduct on our part in the Philippines to which you refer in your letter are baseless slanders, partly upon the civil government, chiefly upon the Army of which you are the head." Roosevelt concluded with a final insult to his commanding general: "To send you out [to the Philippines] as you suggest could do no good. I am inclined to think that it would do mischief."[39]

Root's public letter of reprimand to Miles, which some thought might be an overreaction to an undeniable provocation, was mild in comparison to the degrading comments made by Roosevelt. He appears to have attempted to humble the general into silence about brutalities in the Philippines simply to avoid political embarrassment. Following this incident, Roosevelt began to consider the idea of forcing Miles to retire from the army.

Before Roosevelt could think of dismissing the commanding general, he recommended that the secretary of war make "a record of certain facts" regarding Miles. In a "private and confidential" letter to Root, he outlined his own problems with the general, beginning with Miles's proposal of February 17. He found this to be "couched in language which amounted to an endorsement by the head of the army of some of the most unfounded slanders which have been put forth on the stump and in Congress by the violent traducers of the army and of the nation."

Roosevelt put it on record that during his months in office he found that Miles "has not the slightest desire to improve or benefit the army," being rather guided by "his selfish ambition, his vanity, or his spite." Roosevelt offered Miles's testimony before the war investigation committee as an example of "the extreme unwisdom of trusting him in any position where he can imagine it to be for his interest to discredit the American government or the American army." The president saw Miles's testimony "not as desire to tell the truth—whoever was affected, but as a championship of himself against Secretary Alger and President McKinley." This charge came from the man who had informed Miles in 1899, that "when I saw you testifying to what I know to be the truth about the meat, I felt it my duty to write and aid you."[40]

The president then recalled Miles's proposal that they become running mates in the 1900 national election. When Miles made this suggestion on February 26, 1899, Roosevelt found his "estimate of the political situation" to be "utterly fatuous." He explained to Root that "the proposition was interesting only because, in the first place, it showed the man's political folly, and, in the second place, it gave me a glimpse of a most unpleasant side of his character as major general commanding the army." Roosevelt based this judgment on Miles's expectation of being able to upset "President McKinley and deprive him of a renomination or re-election upon what he regarded as the probable failure of our arms in the Philippines." In a most damning accusation, Roosevelt said of Miles that "He repeated again and again, obviously with the utmost satisfaction, that disaster would certainly befall our troops and that possibly they might be driven out of the islands, and that this would discredit the administration of President McKinley and further the ambition of any one who was against him."

Roosevelt had dismissed Miles's views as "so foolish" and "so ignorant" that he would "not have thought of the matter again had it not been for the very unpleasant impression which his conduct necessarily made upon me in view of his being the commanding general of the army. I told Senator Lodge of the matter at the time." On August 10, 1899, when Roosevelt first wrote Lodge about Miles's invitation to run, made less than six months earlier, he intimated that he was not sure whether he had mentioned the offer before. In this letter, however, the Rough Rider did not mention Miles's pessimism about the Philippines; he did comment optimistically on the steps that Elihu Root, then newly installed as secretary of war, would take to "smash" the insurrection. Furthermore, less than two weeks after Miles supposedly predicted to Roosevelt that "the disgrace which befell our army would vindicate himself [Miles] and help the opponents of the Administration," the then-governor of New York "very gladly" agreed to Miles's request to testify before the beef commission. Thus, if Miles had revealed any disloyal designs toward the government, which is unlikely, it would appear that Roosevelt agreed to cooperate with him in his sedition.[41]

A column written on March 3 by an individual staying at Washington's New Willard Hotel, the writer identified only as H. W. but who was possibly Henry Watterson, caught the president's attention. The item, which appeared in an unidentified Washington, D.C., newspaper, renewed Miles's campaign to be sent to the Philippines. The columnist supported this effort because the commanding general "has coaxed submission many times of the aborigines when to subdue them by force of arms would have cost too much. He could and would bring order out of chaos, if sent to Manila with adequate power, in a few months. We might then come to a parley." Roosevelt sent the column to Root, commenting that "our amiable friend is at his usual tricks. Now he is letting the fact leak out, for political purposes, that he has asked to be sent to the Philippines." To the casual reader, the point of the leak, if that is how the columnist obtained the information, was to prompt the authorities to send Miles to the Philippines, rather than some vague "political purposes."[42]

Four days after Roosevelt sent Root the newspaper column regarding Miles and the Philippines, he prepared a memorandum for Root to attach to Miles's February 17 proposal. In this statement for the record, the president pointed out that revelations in the press of Miles's plan and the administration's reaction to it could only have come from the commanding general. The president then once again replied to Miles's charge about the "severity" of the methods employed by American troops in the Philippines. He replied, "The warfare in the Philippines has been conducted by our troops with very great leniency; with far greater leniency than was shown by General Miles and his fellow soldiers in their warfare in the old days against the Indians on the plains." With full knowledge that he was writing for the record, the president added, "General Miles' course in endeavoring to discredit the army of which he is head by the publication or endorsement of untruthful attacks upon it is not creditable to him."

The president also recalled that Miles had been in charge of "the small army" responsible for the death of more than sixty women and children at Wounded Knee: "suffice it to say that such a slaughter of women and children has not been even remotely approached in any case in the Philippines." In the aftermath of Wounded Knee, "his [Miles's] failure to act until specifically required to do so by the authorities at Washington caused a delay of some two months, and the regiment had meanwhile been ordered from the district." Roosevelt blamed the fact that no one was punished for the massacre on Miles's inaction and recommendations, and declared, "The mere recital of the facts in this case is enough to show the extreme unwisdom of relying upon General Miles to mitigate the severities of war."[43]

Since the record of what actually took place after the tragic confrontation at Wounded Knee was available at the War Department, it is inexplicable that the president could stray so far from the truth. On January 4, 1891, Miles relieved Col. James W. Forsyth from command of the Seventh Cavalry and ordered a court of inquiry to investigate the colonel's conduct at Wounded Knee. The board tried to provide a tidy solution on January 13, when it criticized Forsyth's troop dispositions but absolved him of disobeying an order intended to prevent a clash between soldiers and Ghost Dancers. Miles reconvened the board to question Brig. Gen. John R. Brooke, and on the basis of his testimony, censured the colonel on January 18 for disobedience. After reviewing the case, the commanding general of the army, John M. Schofield, advised Secretary of War Redfield Proctor on February 4, 1891: "The conduct of the Seventh Cavalry, under very trying circumstances was characterized by excellent discipline, and in many cases, by great forbearance." Eight days later, Proctor endorsed Schofield's recommendation with the notation, "Colonel Forsyth will resume command."[44]

The president next addressed Miles's recommendation during the Boxer Rebellion to transfer fifteen thousand troops from the Philippines to China. Roosevelt pointed out that "The actual result showed that there was not the slightest need in China of these troops; and had they been withdrawn from the islands there would undoubtedly have been an immense impetus given to the insurrection." This led the president to conclude, "In other words, the only important advice that General Miles has given in relation to the Philippines if adopted, would have meant a terrible increase in the loss of life and a corresponding increase in the expenditure of money."[45]

On the issue of the future of the Philippines, as on virtually every matter under discussion, the president and the commanding general did not see eye to eye. In 1900 Roosevelt wrote, "no competent witness who has actually known the facts believes the Filipinos capable of self-government at present." Miles, on the other hand, argued that despite three centuries of Spanish rule, the Filipinos had become a highly civilized nation of "quiet, industrious, polite people. Many of the better class are college bred." He cited as proof of their ability the many government positions currently held by Filipinos and their attempt, as they joined the Americans in the fight against Spain, to form a government with a constitution similar to that of the United States. As proof of their high level of civilization, Miles wrote, "They had treated the thousands of prisoners they had captured so humanely that the Spanish government rewarded Aguinaldo with high honors." He concluded his attempt to persuade his readers about the wisdom of granting self-government for the Philippines with the provocative notion that the United States would "have the glory of having established the first republic in the Orient."[46]

The battle of Miles's February 17 proposal finally ended with a flurry of endorsements to the original letter. On March 24, Miles bravely restated some of his arguments before conceding that since his "measure, as suggested, is not deemed advisable, I do not ask for its further consideration." The following day, the secretary of war responded with familiar rejoinders to each of Miles's points, then expressed regret that Miles had mentioned a letter written on February 7, 1902, by the head of the Philippine commission, William H. Taft. Because Miles had referred to the letter, which contained charges of mistreatment of Filipinos by American troops, it would have to be included among correspondence relating to the Philippines to be sent to the House of Representatives. Although Root more than implies that he would have withheld evidence from Congress, he saw this to be his duty: "Such charges ought not to be published against our countrymen whom we have sent to labor and fight under our flag on the other side of the world before they can be heard in their own defense."[47]

On March 21, 1902, the *New York Times,* among other newspapers, reported the resolution introduced by a congressman from Texas. If the resolution had been passed, Miles's request to be sent to the Philippines and his plan to bring peace to the islands would have been transmitted to Congress. The next day Roosevelt confided to the New York journalist Oswald Garrison Villard that "General Miles' usefulness is at an end and he must go." The president, however, found the task of ridding himself of Miles to be more difficult than he supposed. According to the *New York Times,* his advisers argued against a forced retirement because the commanding general has "more strong friends in the Senate" than "did any other officer, and what makes it more embarrassing is that these friends include many of the most influential of the Republican Senators, and a summary disposition of Gen. Miles's case would be likely to anger men who no Republic Administration has been anxious to fight."

The article also mentioned that "many Senators are disposed to be somewhat touchy over the indications that the President wants to punish him [Miles] for statements made to a Senate committee." This reference is to a hearing on March 20, 1902, regarding the General Staff bill—formally known as the Root Army Reorganization Act of 1901, and sometimes referred to as the Root Bill—at which Miles threatened on March 20, 1902, to resign his commission. He argued that if the general staff plan passed, "it would have the effect of destroying the unity of the army, . . . the necessity of having one head to the army and of controlling authority." William Harding Carter, Root's military guide through the obstacles in the way of reforming the army's command system, looked back at this obstacle in an article that he wrote in 1918 when he was a major general. He explained that a general staff was meant to serve as a replacement for "the office of Commanding General of the Army, which had long been merely an empty title, luring prominent generals to sure disappointment and lifelong advances." Carter explained that Root's 1902 bill planned to create "a chief of staff with power of supervision and coordination of bureaus, as well as of other parts of the military establishment."[48] From a review of the early years of the general staff, it is evident that a chief of staff "would eliminate much of the wasteful red tape and buck-passing and free the secretary of war for most important matters. Assisted by the General Staff, the chief of staff would investigate and recommend solutions to technical questions to the secretary."

Henry Watterson's comments in Washington added to Roosevelt's discomfort: "From the day when he [Miles] refused to become an orderly for the Administration he was marked for punishment." Watterson brought up Miles's interview in Cincinnati to point out that Roosevelt "fairly leaped at the first chance to assail and humiliate Gen. Miles that seemed to offer itself, for he had, as a matter of fact, no authority either under the Constitution of the United States or the articles of war, to reprimand the General except for a single offense." The threat of the forced retirement of Miles was used to chide the Republican Roosevelt. Watterson observed that Miles had been "fighting the battles of his country when our puissant Presidential bronco-buster was fighting the battle of the nursery."[49] Watterson's observations may well have been the final straw as Roosevelt contemplated what to do about his commanding general. In comparing the battle honors earned by the two men, Roosevelt's splendid *day* is put in proper perspective when compared with Miles's splendid *record,* not only in the Civil War and Indian Wars but in Puerto Rico as well. It is fair to say that Roosevelt was likely not be well disposed toward Miles, who could make him feel uncomfortable about San Juan Hill, an achievement that meant so much to the president.

A thoroughly frustrated Roosevelt disclosed to Herman H. Kohlsaat, editor and publisher of the *Chicago Times Herald,* that "Miles is a perfect curse. He has been a detriment to the army for the last eight years. No man of his rank has ever had so purely faked a record as a soldier." As Roosevelt saw the problem, he "did not know whether I am justified in avoiding trouble for myself by keeping in a man who deliberately works damage to the service; and who has not done a stroke of decent work since I have come in."[50]

Roosevelt summoned Kohlsaat to the White House after the editor advised him not to follow his instincts and rid himself of the commanding general. Kohlsaat told his host that he "knew General Miles's irritating qualities, as both Cleveland and McKinley had told me of their dislike for him, but his record as a soldier and Indian fighter was greatly in his favor. I repeated the G.A.R. veterans' admiration for him." Since Miles would reach retirement age in a year, he should "be sent around the world on an inspection tour of the world's armies, and when he returned it would take him some weeks to write his report; then his time would be up and he would drop out automatically." Roosevelt responded, "That's a bully idea. I want you to tell it to Root." When Kohlsaat stopped by Root's home before catching the train for Chicago, he recalled that the secretary of war told him, "Although I do not feel as strongly as the President does over Miles, I think your suggestion a wise one."[51]

Newspaper publisher John C. Shaffer, of the *Chicago Post,* claimed to have given the same advice to the president. Shaffer recalled that after a luncheon, as they stood alone by a window in the White House, Roosevelt said, "Shaffer, Secretary Root and I have concluded to depose General Miles. His recent speech in Cincinnati is an outrage—he is destroying the discipline of the Army, and the only remedy for this is to dismiss him." The publisher warned the president, whom he described as being "very much agitated in his manner," that "if you depose General Miles at this time, you will make him a great hero. The Imperialists of New England and the Democratic Party will take up his cause and give him the nomination of the Democratic Party for President and this is what he is seeking." Roosevelt retorted, "By Jove, I think you are right." Shaffer then proposed that Miles be sent to the Philippines. The president responded, "On the principle of giving the calf enough rope, it would hang itself." After a few moments the president came to a decision, and told the publisher, "I think your suggestion is good and I will confer with Secretary Root at once."[52]

As a result of Roosevelt's gambit, on September 11, 1902, Miles escaped from the bureaucratic battles in Washington. Accompanied by his wife and his aide, Colonel Maus, along with Mrs. Maus, a stenographer, and a messenger, the party set out for the West Coast, where the General inspected the coastal defenses for which he had lobbied so diligently. On November 1 the travelers sailed from San Francisco for Hawaii, where Miles checked on the condition of his troops before continuing on to Guam.[53]

During Miles's inspection of troops and military conditions on Guam, he met with Apolinario Mabini, a spokesman for the Filipino insurgents and author of the new republic's constitution. Root's biographer, Philip

Jessup, characterized Mabini as "a confirmed adherent to the cause of absolute independence" who was his government's "most brilliant figure." Miles described Mabini, now a prisoner under constant guard, as "emaciated, crippled, paralyzed below the waist, yet mentally a giant. He spoke with great feeling of the misfortunes of his country and the oppression of his race." Mabini complained to Miles that he could not understand "why he was kept a prisoner on a remote island; that he could do the United States no harm, and that the tomb was not afar." Mabini had been exiled to Guam by Maj. Gen. of Volunteers Arthur MacArthur, then commander of the Division of the Philippines and military governor of the islands. Mabini had shared the fate of thirty-one other revolutionaries who had also refused to swear allegiance to the United States. After Miles returned to the United States, he managed to secure Mibini's release.[54]

It was in the Philippines, however, that Miles caused the greatest stir. In his autobiography, he stated that he had "received a number of complaints of unauthorized and unwarranted acts of the military toward prisoners in their hands in order to obtain information concerning arms, numbers, and disposition of the Filipino troops, and I issued rigid orders prohibiting such unjustifiable acts." Miles explained that when he issued these orders, he "was prompted by a sense of justice and humanity, to preserve the good name of our army."[55]

After he returned to the United States, Miles submitted to the secretary of war both a report of his inspection of military posts on the islands and a special report detailing instances of mistreatment of Filipinos by American troops. Information about most of the cases in Miles's special report came from Filipinos who spoke directly to him about their abuse by American soldiers. In one instance, a lieutenant had already pleaded guilty to his offense, thereby preventing the full record of his misconduct from being revealed at a hearing. One of three priests mistreated by this officer told Miles that during his ordeal the lieutenant knocked out one of his front teeth and robbed him of three hundred dollars; only the intervention of a major saved the three prisoners from being killed. The lieutenant was sentenced to a suspension from command for three months as well as having fifty dollars a month deducted from his pay for the same period.

Miles had been told of a few instances where troops had killed Filipinos. In one case a sixty-five-year-old man who had been beaten into unconsciousness was left in his burning house. In another, several Filipinos who had been crammed into a small building were reported to have suffocated. Further, seven prisoners who refused to lead a patrol to their camp were said to have been either bayoneted or shot to death; and Miles wrote that two men on Luzon "were whipped to death." He noted that "These facts came to me in a casual way, and many others of similar character have been reported in different parts of the archipelago."

Miles named several generals serving in the islands who would not tolerate the abuse of Filipinos by the men serving under them, but he reported that he "was informed that it was common talk at places where officers congregated that such transactions had been carried on either with the connivance or approval of certain commanding officers." Because Miles "found that with certain officers the impression prevailed that such acts were justifiable," he sent the commander of the Division of the Philippines, Maj. Gen. George Davis, a "letter of instructions," signed by his aide-de-camp, Lt. Col. Marion P. Maus.

Maus informed Davis that in the Philippines "acts have been committed which are not in accordance with the rules of civilized warfare and are detrimental to the honor and discipline of the army." He explained that "such unauthorized and unwarranted acts tends to give the junior officers and soldiers of the army an impression that such acts are justifiable and customary in civilized warfare." To remedy "such a dangerous and injurious impression," Maus advised that any instructions or orders that "suggest, inspire, encourage, or permit any acts of cruelty and unwarranted severity be annulled, cancelled and rescinded, and such acts are hereby prohibited." He then praised Davis for being among those "who effectively conducted their military operations without resorting to any of the methods prohibited by the rules of civilized warfare" and concluded by declaring that "It is the duty of the army to preserve unsullied the high character it has maintained for more than a century."[56]

With the unpleasant duty of correcting lapses in the conduct of the Division of the Philippines behind him, Miles and his party boarded a steamer bound for Hong Kong and then Canton, China. At their next stop, the Russian-held Chinese city of Port Arthur, Miles heard concerns about the possibility of a war with Japan from the Russian admiral commanding eighty thousand soldiers and sailors stationed in the Far East. On December 24 the travelers took advantage of this admiral's invitation, and sailed for Taku aboard a battleship. Two days later, they arrived in Peking, and the next day, the twenty-seventh, during an audience with the imperial family, the empress dowager told Miles that "the success of the American Army was assured under a commander so celebrated."

Miles's entourage left China and headed for Moscow and Saint Petersburg using the Trans-Siberian Railway. The general found the trip to be fascinating; he compared the immense plains that he crossed in the dead of winter with the American West. He later wrote, "It is much greater in extent, better timbered, well watered, with an abundance of natural resources, very little mountainous country, and the zone passed over would compare favorably, as far as climate is concerned, with our own temperate or middle zone." When Miles reached Paris, he also favorably commented on the Russian railroad, saying that he found it to be "in far better condition than I expected. It was very much like the Northern Pacific, Great Northern and other of our trans-continental railways in their early days. Being a new road, of course it is not yet perfectly systemized." Miles hastened to add, however, that "Still, after the sixteen days we were traveling it, we were late only a few hours at Moscow. There are sleeping cars, and one travels with a degree of comfort, and even luxury, that would have astonished Peter the Great, or the Alexanders."[57]

While in Paris, Miles accepted an invitation to visit King Edward in England, whom he regarded "as one of the strongest as well as one of the most gracious sovereigns in the world." The party of tourists returned to Washington on February 17, 1903, where the commanding general commented that "our 20,000 men on duty in the islands are in fine condition." This observation delighted an editor at the *Army and Navy Journal,* who used it to counter "chronic whiners [who] have been protesting for four years that white men could never live in the Philippines, that it was cruel to keep American soldiers there and that after a few months they would wither and die like sheep."[58]

Miles submitted two reports on the Philippines, dated February 19, 1903, to the secretary of war, who initially kept their contents from public knowledge. Jessup admitted that Root did not exhibit a "crusading zeal for righteousness" in bringing an end to the mistreatment of Filipinos by the army, but added that the secretary of war "neither inspired, nor approved, or countenanced the atrocities." The president had been alerted on December 30, 1902, by governor of the Philippines, William Howard Taft, that Miles "has left his trail through the islands in his effort to besmirch his own cloth and I doubt not our anti-imperialists will enjoy a new feast of blood and brutality on his return. He is a curiously constituted man. I don't understand him." The Philippine reports and Taft's letter did nothing to endear Miles to Roosevelt, who confided to his newspaper friend Villard that "Governor Taft has written me in a manner condemnatory in the highest degree of Miles . . . and of the course taken by Miles while in the island—stating that he was obviously trying not to get at the truth but to stir up trouble."[59]

When his Philippine reports were finally released, it appears that Miles received more criticism for their contents than did the administration. Root had decided to make the dispatches public after the Massachusetts Reform Club requested copies of them. The prudent course seemed to be to risk being chided for the disclosures in the reports rather than be assailed for suppressing embarrassing facts. The dispatches were distributed at a press conference on April 27, along with a reply written by the judge advocate general.[60]

When the *Army and Navy Journal* published the documents on May 2, 1903, it rebuked Miles, saying, "To catch up and circulate to the discredit of the Army he commands the gossip he hears in traveling through the enemy's country is hardly the office of the Lieutenant General." Miles, who had risked official wrath to defend Schley's honor, disregarded the reputation of fellow officers in reporting accusations of cruelty made "in a casual way." The rules of conduct demanded that "every officer and man in the military service should be made to feel that his character and his honor are safe in the keeping of his superiors, who will not suffer him to be condemned except upon sworn testimony which shall be accepted by a jury of his peers."[61]

While the *Journal* believed that Miles's report "damaged him in the opinion of all fair-minded men," the public took the disclosures about mistreatment of Filipinos in stride. It has been suggested that military censorship and the party loyalty of many newspaper publishers meant that some of the incidents that occurred in the Philippines were downplayed. Furthermore, as a result of victory in the war with Spain, "the credit of the American soldier was high in the eyes of the American public." Finally, racism lessened the impact of the revelations because both the American people and troops overseas regarded the Filipinos as an inferior race. As one officer put it, regarding the death of Filipinos, "I'd sooner see a hundred niggers killed than one of my men endangered." The lieutenant's casual slur exemplifies the overt racism present in the military at the turn of the century. The five thousand black troops who participated in the Philippines campaign could have been disheartened if they had known that Maj. Gen. Elwell S. Otis, commander of the Department of the Pacific and military commander of the Philippines from August 29, 1898, to May 5, 1900, suggested that orders transferring two black regular regiments to his command be rescinded because he questioned their loyalty. In fact, except for nine cases of desertion, black troops "fought in the war with distinction," according to a history of the campaign.[62]

Harper's Weekly attempted to rationalize the atrocities. While admitting that American troops campaigning in the Philippines "have been guilty of extreme severity and even cruelty," the influential journal contended that, "Unhappily, such incidents are inseparable from war, and especially from war against a treacherous and savage enemy." But this excuse for excesses had been specifically addressed in the order that Miles had issued to the commanding general of the United States Army in the Philippines.[63]

Perhaps a weekly journal of opinion, *The Outlook,* provided the most dispassionate view of the dispute over Miles's report. The president and his officer corps must have been pleased with its declaration that "There is no General [Valeriano] Weyler in the American Army." This referred to the Spanish general who, in 1896, some American newspapers began to call "the Butcher" after he started to build concentration camps. But it is likely that most of the officers would only grudgingly accept its judgment that "it is not so certain that they have all been eager to bring the guilty parties to exposure and punishment. The desire to shield the reputation of the army is natural; but it is always a mistake to attempt to shield an organization by concealing the crimes of individuals who belong to it."

When Miles sought to address a serious lapse in the conduct of a handful of officers in the Philippines, he may have been too cavalier with the reputation of the army he cherished. As *The Outlook* suggested, Miles could have enhanced the army's good name even as he publicized instances of misconduct. "General Miles's report should have made account of the splendid philanthropic work which many army officers have been engaged in—the building of roads, the feeding of the impoverished and the famine-stricken, the establishment of schools, and the active participation in the work of teaching." The news magazine also correctly raised the issue of Miles's grave accusations based on what it termed "hearsay testimony of a very doubtful character." Thus, because Miles's observations were off the mark, he missed an opportunity to write a report as convincing as the situation in the Philippines demanded. In conclusion, Miles raised a critically important issue, but in too casual a manner; however, because he acted to prevent further lapses, he had the satisfaction of being able to note in his memoirs that he had worked in the Philippines "to preserve the good name of the army." When he considered this service to the nation, he stated that he "would rather that any official act of my life might be erased than to have omitted discharging a duty prompted by a sense of justice and humanity."[64]

Miles, who had testified against the general staff plan just before he began his world tour, must have felt outmaneuvered to learn that Congress had passed it during his trip abroad, and President Roosevelt had signed the bill into law on February 14, 1903, just one day before the travelers returned to the United States. Although the *Army and Navy Journal* conceded that Miles's "argument against the bill is a very strong one," in retrospect, it is apparent that the commanding general had closed his eyes to one of the main lessons of the Spanish-American War. William Harding Carter explained that following the war the time was ripe for change because "public opinion was aroused over our shortcomings to a degree that victory could not assuage and still." Although Root's plan set in motion a series of reforms that would modernize the army, the general staff itself had an inauspicious beginning. When Root, who would become Roosevelt's secretary of state in 1905, resigned as secretary of war in 1904, his successor, William Howard Taft, allowed the bureau chiefs to make inroads upon the chief of staff's authority. In fairness to Taft, however, Root's reform bill was subject to misunderstanding. As military historian Russell F. Weigley explained, Root's "approach to the functions of the General Staff" was "apparently confused and certainly imprecise." To illustrate his point, Weigley quoted one officer who recalled that when he reported for duty with those assigned to the General Staff, "None of us had any conception as to its true functions."[65]

Roosevelt, who so far had bullied Miles in virtually every one of their contests, finally issued a presidential challenge that must have delighted the commanding general. In an attempt to winnow out-of-shape officers—many of them Civil War veterans—from the army, Roosevelt ordered all officers to complete a ninety-mile ride within three days. Jumping at the chance to prove his mettle, the commanding general set out from Fort Sill, Oklahoma, at 8:00 A.M. on July 14, wearing his campaign uniform with a white summer helmet to protect him from an unrelenting sun. At 5:10 P.M. on the same day, Miles rode into Fort Reno, Oklahoma, ninety miles away. Nine mounts were needed to complete the ride, but the general still had enough stamina to conduct a mounted review of the six infantry companies stationed at Reno. Then horse and rider dramatically leaped across a gorge to ensure that the general would catch a northbound train at El Reno, about five miles from the fort. Miles told a waiting reporter that he "enjoyed every minute of the trip; there was one time I felt particularly good. That was when I came up to the men who had charge of the pack teams, just south of the Canadian River. They had lunch ready, and I enjoyed it with them."

Miles's feat elicited the praise of the *Army and Navy Journal,* which spoke for the service when it announced, "The Army are proud of the Lieutenant General commanding." The editor added that: "General Miles is a splendid specimen of military manhood and we will back him for physical endurance, as well as other soldierly qualities, against any soldier of his years in any army in the world." As Miles's August 8 birthday approached, bringing him to the mandatory retirement age of sixty-four, his popularity with the public reached a high point, which presented the president with a problem.[66]

In a letter to George B. Cortelyou, secretary of commerce and labor, Roosevelt protested that upon Miles's retirement, "Nothing will hire me to praise him. There has been really a gust of popular anger against me; I am not writing too strongly when I say popular anger." The president admitted that he would have to pay for his adamant stand: "The feeling against me, especially in the Grand Army, is so bitter that certain of my friends in Illinois and Indiana have told me that they believe that if the election were held at present I should lose those states.[67]

The administration's ungallant conduct at Miles's retirement deserved a negative response. Just before the commanding general would be officially separated from the service at noon on the eighth, the secretary of war's private secretary brought to Miles a brief order announcing his retirement; the document contained no mention of Miles's services to the republic. Miles's aide then delivered a note of acknowledgment to Root's office, as the general and the secretary, who had refused to speak to one another for almost a year, remained true to their vows of silence to the bitter end of their official relationship.

To add insult to injury, a breach of protocol occurred when Samuel Baldwin Marks Young, who would succeed Miles, arrived at the War Department wearing the three stars of a lieutenant general one and a half hours before the current lieutenant general would leave office. Most overlooked this impropriety, however, as they fastened their attention on what the *New York Herald* characterized as the "official neglect and discourtesy" of the president and his secretary of war to Miles. The newspaper considered it a "significant fact" that even "high ranking officers of the army who have hitherto differed from General Miles in his criticism of the administration are emphatic in their opinion that an injustice has been done the army and veterans of the Civil War." These military men specifically objected to "the refusal of the administration to give recognition to the indisputable bravery which General Miles showed throughout the Civil War and when fighting the Indians."[68]

On August 29, the *Army and Navy Journal*, which had found fault with Miles for his Philippine reports earlier in the year, spoke up for the general in this instance. The editor found it convenient to quote *Harper's Weekly*, which admitted that the commanding general's "course of action" had been "irritating" to the administration and "harmful" to the army. The magazine then asked, "But was the offence sufficiently aggravated to justify the President in wholly ignoring General Miles' really splendid past, and merely pointing to the door? Would Lincoln have done it? Would Cleveland or McKinley? Would any President?" *Harper's* then answered its own question: "Obviously the country thinks not." The magazine suggested that the "whole people" of the nation—"if the unanimous voice of the press means anything—feel hurt, mortified, and ashamed, not so much on account of the old soldier who has been cheated, or cheated himself maybe, out of his just dues as on account of their President, who had disappointed them and humiliated himself." The *Journal* then added its own opinion: "A word of courtesy toward General Miles . . . would have saved a world of trouble. Now the administration is getting it right and left from the newspapers, and what the newspapers are saying is re-echoed among all classes of people in general conversations."[69]

The issue of the *Army and Navy Journal* that reached its readers on the morning of the eighth, the day of Miles's retirement, was an example of how to put bygones aside to graciously mark the occasion. After enthusiastically commending the commanding general's battlefield performance, the editor explained, "If he has been less successful as an Army administrator, he has failed where other distinguished soldiers have failed before him, and under conditions which made success practically impossible."[70]

Some newspapers, like the *New York Times,* were as unstinting in their praise of Miles as they were unrestrained in their criticism of Roosevelt and his cohorts. The editor asked, "Where in history has the record of a brave and brilliant soldier come to such a contemptuous closing?" The newsman continued, "An impartial world will read with astonishment, and the American people with indignation, the story of the ignoble manner in which the Administration has chosen to record the retirement of Gen. Nelson A. Miles."[71]

Other publications, like the *New York Sun,* were more evenhanded, berating both parties equally. The *Sun* criticized the "disputes and recriminations which cast a cloud on the reputation of Gen. Miles during the closing years of his active service as Commanding General [which] were unfortunate also in revealing in him serious temperamental weaknesses, and we have been compelled to criticize his conduct with severity." Miles was "a cantankerous marplot and his conduct was so distinctively unmilitary as to render him justly liable to a court-martial." But, continued the *Sun,* Miles had reason to be indignant: "Not unnaturally, exhibitations of puerility, vain displays of trifling amateur military performances, theatrical elevation of rather cheap heroes and hustling of military novices to shove themselves into notice ahead of veteran soldiers, in the Spanish war, excited the contempt of Gen. Miles, and oftentimes they deserved it."[72]

In a letter to the secretary of war, the president blamed Miles for the press storm stirred up at his retirement: "I think that Miles must be given credit for more low cunning than we thought. What an inredeemable blackguard and scoundrel he is, and how the jacks and fools do take to him." In a postscript, Roosevelt suggested that Root prepare a "memorandum" for the files about Miles's Philippine reports, "which should make clear . . . as you so well know how well to make it clear, that he has played the part of traitor to the army and therefore to the nation. His intriguing disloyalty should be made manifest so that there can be no mistake about it in the future." The president apparently was not content simply to dishonor Miles at his retirement, but wanted his name sullied through history.[73]

The secretary of war's response disappointed the president. Rather than dwell on the Philippine reports, Root explained that the retirement order did not contain "laudatory expressions" because "I did not see how I could issue an order praising Miles as General Commanding the army without falsehood and hypocrisy; that even as to his Civil War record I could not speak of him as a great General because he had held only subordinate command."

Roosevelt praised Root's letter because it gave him "just exactly what I want, an authoritative statement by you who have been over Miles, using the language that should be used about him." The praise was qualified, however, because the president went on to write that "what I wished was, not a justification of your action . . . I do most emphatically want that there shall be something left on file in the War Department for our justification in future years." Roosevelt lost no time in sending a copy of Root's letter to Lemuel Clarke Davis, the editor of the *Philadelphia Ledger* At this time, the president claimed that he "knew nothing whatever of the case until after public statements had appeared in the press; yet I not only approve of Root's course, but I should have been heartily ashamed of him if, with his knowledge of the facts, he had followed any other."

Miles's return to civilian life under trying circumstances did nothing to diminish his enthusiasm for his former calling. In 1911 he wrote, "To serve such a Republic as ours has been not only a sacred duty but also almost enjoyable life-work." Apparently the passage of eight years had dimmed the memory of unpleasant squabbles with his associates, which were as much a hallmark of his military career as was his outstanding record.[74]

Miles proved to be a difficult man to get along with throughout his life, but his personality defies simple explanation. As William Howard Taft observed after first meeting the general, "He is a curiously constituted man." Throughout his life, Miles followed a self-imposed code of conduct that restrained him from answering or explaining the damaging charges made by his enemies. The record contains so many of these accounts that anyone relying on them could be misled. Unfortunately for a biographer, Miles's own writings provide no insight into what provoked him to mar virtually every professional relationship with his cantankerous behavior.

From the Civil War through the Spanish-American War, Miles was the nation's warrior. Unlike many warriors, however, Miles never became callous about the lives of those he led into battle or indifferent to the fate of his opponents. Victories bought at even minimal cost lost their thrill, and the general developed the instincts of a peacemaker. He used all of his military skill to try to achieve a bloodless victory at Wounded Knee, initially shied from having his troops brought into the Pullman strike, hoped that the Spanish-American War could be averted by arbitration, and regretted the war in the Philippines. Upon reflection, he wrote that he would "rejoice to see the dawning of the day when the war drums shall throb no longer, when useless wars for the gratification of people's avarice and man's selfish ambition shall be no more."[75]

As a commanding officer Miles maintained the morale of his troops by ensuring that they were both properly trained and fully equipped for combat; then he inspired his men to achieve victory in their battles. The sound execution of each one of Miles's campaigns is evidence that his performance matched his ambition.

During the Red River War, the colonel gave the hostiles no rest because of his determination to rescue their girl captives. His pressure convinced the Indians to free their hostages and return to their reservations. Miles did not allow the men in his Yellowstone command to become dispirited by the Custer disaster, but instead led them so aggressively that the Cheyenne and Sioux under Sitting Bull either returned to government control or fled with their Hunkpapa leader into Canada. While many laughed at the army's futile attempt to foil the Nez Perce as they raced for Canada, Miles moved his men so swiftly that ridicule turned into respect for his soldiers, who came out of nowhere to besiege and then capture Chief Joseph with part of his tribe. When Miles parleyed with Geronimo, he displayed the skill of a diplomat as he convinced the Apache leader to surrender with his band. During the winter of 1890–91, Miles, now wearing the second star of a major general, gave a superb performance suppressing the Ghost Dancers, displaying his abilities as both a tactician and a strategist. These abilities were confirmed by his adroit maneuvering of troops both in Chicago and in Puerto Rico. Only upon achieving the position of commanding general did the self-made officer fail to rise to the challenge of his office. Although many of Miles's proposals for fighting the Spanish-American War deserved a hearing, his failure to have them debated bear witness to his ineffectiveness as a spokesman for the army he loved. The dogged determination that served Miles so well on the battlefield crippled him in maneuverings so common in the political arena.

As the siege of Santiago neared a climax, Miles was sent to Cuba in response to an unsettling message from General Shafter. There he proved his worth despite an attempt by the secretary of war to undercut his authority. Miles prevented the unnecessary sacrifice of Fifth Corps troops when he took responsibility for extending a truce. If the Spanish defenders of Santiago had not been given time to receive permission to surrender, their sense of honor would have compelled them to reengage American troops in battle. Then, before sailing for Puerto Rico, Miles initiated measures that he expected Shafter to follow, to deal with yellow fever as it began to spread among the troops of the Fifth Corps.

After landing on Puerto Rico, Miles conducted a triumphant campaign, noteworthy for the small number of American lives lost as the army captured the island. Unfathomably, Miles's well-directed performance received some wretched reviews. For example, when an impressive history of the Spanish-American War considered Miles's accomplishment, the author used the occasion to tarnish the general's reputation. He regarded Miles's order to land at Guánica, rather than at Fajardo, as "entirely consistent with the erratic behavior and suspiciousness that Miles manifested throughout the war. He was too unstable to hold a command of great importance; it is fortunate that the situation he encountered in Puerto Rico did not make undue demands on him."[76]

After doing his best to help win the war with Spain, Miles lost his postwar battle to indict the War Department's commissary department for supplying troops with "embalmed beef." Historians have looked askance at the commanding general for provoking this controversy because, as one wrote, "it left an ineradicable stain upon the prestige of the service." However, the stain may have been an acceptable price to pay, because the investigation emphasized the need to reform the system for feeding the troops. Although not often mentioned in discussions of the beef controversy, the army took advantage of Congress's authorization on July 7, 1901, and immediately began to hire veterinarians to inspect rations to begin what one authority has called "the finest and most effective food inspection service in the world." Unfortunately, Miles's difficulties with the War Department confirmed his long-held belief that the bureaus in Washington were out of touch with the problems of campaigners in the field. Thus, although his opposition to the creation of a general staff proved to be wrong-headed, it is understandable why he resisted a bill for reorganizing the army.[77]

Miles was soundly beaten in his repeated jousts with President McKinley's successor, Theodore Roosevelt, and his secretary of war, Elihu Root. When *Harper's Weekly* scolded each of the principals at the time of Miles's retirement for their public feud, it particularly faulted Miles because he had "been a thorn in the flesh of the administration." The journal explained that Miles had "interfered seriously with the good work of the War Department; he has made accusations over and over again that may or may not have been susceptible of proof, but were certainly unbecoming one in his position." *Harper's* went on to say that "he has been consistently bombastic and condescending and generally a nuisance, apparently playing to the galleries with some ulterior—probably political—purpose in mind."[78]

Although *Harper's Weekly* may have misinterpreted the motive behind Miles's unseemly behavior, it correctly portrayed how cantankerous the commander of the army had become. Since Miles had been an inspiring warrior on the battlefield, the unbecoming transformation requires an explanation. There is little reason to disagree with those who speculate that Miles's perverse conduct when dealing with high administration officials may have masked his discomfort at not being as well educated or sophisticated as they were. Furthermore, Miles readily admitted both his preference for service in the field with his troops and his contempt for the bureaus that he believed poorly served those campaigners. So despite his prominent position, as a result of such an attitude, Miles found himself an outsider at odds with the military bureaucracy. This is supported when one compares Miles's behavior in the corridors of power with his dignified manner while dealing with ordinary citizens. At the time of Miles's death, a reporter from his hometown of Westminster, Massachusetts, remembered him as being "well known to all the towns folk: hail-fellow-well-met with them all, yet with a dignity none thought of overstepping." To illustrate the regard that his neighbors felt in the general's presence, the journalist related that when one person was asked if she had any photos of Miles, the woman replied, "Oh no. . . . He was not the kind of man you would dream of asking to pose for you."[79]

Miles, who Theodore Roosevelt dimissed as a "brave peacock" because of his vanity and love of pomp, deserves a more accurate epitaph. In 1910 a balladier honored Miles, asserting that the general, who was "solid with the ranks," might be a

> little partial to the medals on his chest.
> He's got a darned good right to be;
> he earned 'em in the West.[80]

Epilogue

On August 10, 1903, while some newspapers were still carping about Secretary of War Root's blunt retirement order, others began to report a boom for Miles as the Democratic Party's vice-presidential candidate in 1904. The *New York Herald* believed that he would capture the votes of Civil War veterans, "and the old soldier vote is still a powerful factor in nearly every northern state." The *New York Tribune* explained that Miles would have to be content with the bottom half of the ticket because all of the party's leaders were contending for the top spot.[1]

With the approach of the Democratic Party's national nominating convention, to be held in Saint Louis in July 1904, political maneuvering began to heat up. When Miles returned home from a Western trip in May 1904, although he refused to discuss his candidacy with the *New York Times,* he admitted, "The conditions at this time are the most important of any campaign I have ever known. But I do not wish to go into any statement of my views at this time." When asked again if his recent trip was made for political purposes, he answered, "Gen. Jackson used to tell a story about a man who grew rich by minding his own business. I have been trying to mind my own business, but I have not grown rich." He then explained, "My recent trip was for another purpose. I went to attend the Good Roads Convention at St. Louis, to attend a reunion of veterans at Emporia, Kan., and also to give some attention to a business venture, from which I have some hopes of making a little money."[2]

After Miles tested the water, however, he felt encouraged enough to discuss strategy for capturing the Democratic nomination with a delegate-at-large from Kansas, David Overmyer. Following a promising meeting with the head of the sixty-eight-man Pennsylvania delegation, Miles suggested to Overmyer that "it will be well for you to cultivate him, as you can make him a strong supporter."[3]

Even as Miles actively sought a spot on the Democratic ticket, the Prohibitionist Party eyed him as their candidate for president. Miles's attitude toward liquor, especially for soldiers, had changed since the waning days of the Civil War, when he requested that whiskey be brought to the front lines for his men. Following the February 2, 1901, congressional ban on the sale of intoxicating beverages at army canteens, Miles reported that "it is believed that no injury has resulted thereby and that the law has been beneficial."[4]

Although Miles appreciated the work of the temperance movement, he declined the honor of running as their candidate. In a letter made public by the New York delegation on June 28, Miles explained to the National Prohibition Convention that the nomination would be "an added and greatly valued token of approval and confidence," but it would not "afford that opportunity for efficient and important public service which would be the chief motive for my resuming official life."[5]

On July 9 at the Democratic National Convention, Overmyer nominated Miles for the presidency. Although the speech garnered praise as a "glowing tribute" to Miles, it did not win over many delegates. The *New York Times* reported that when Miles toured Saint Louis hotels seeking to attract votes, a former Republican congressman introduced him to a small party at the Southern Hotel, "and then the Gen. sat down and watched the deserted corridors for a while. 'He's reconnoitering to see where the Indians are,' remarked 'Charley' Edwards of Texas."[6]

Miles's hope of being nominated reveals his political naïveté. It should have been obvious to him that, as Henry Cabot Lodge pointed out to Roosevelt in 1903, Miles "will never run on the Democratic ticket. The South will never nominate or support the man who put Jeff Davis in irons."[7]

Shortly after Miles endured a major public disappointment at not getting on the Democratic ticket, he suffered a tragic private loss. His wife had been at the United States Military Academy visiting their son, Sherman, when she suddenly died on the evening of August 1, 1904. Mary Miles had experienced heart trouble for about a year and a half following a heart attack she suffered as she climbed the stairs to one of New York's elevated railways. Her condition so worsened during the winter of 1903–4 that her family feared that she would not survive. Encouraged by her apparent recovery, she and her husband spent the summer enjoying the pleasant weather at a cottage conveniently located near West Point. She was reported to have been "feeling particularly well and cheerful on Aug. 1." After a day spent making social calls with Sherman and her daughter, Cecelia, she was stricken as she prepared to retire.[8]

Miles received the sad news as he was on his way from Washington to rejoin his family at West Point. Following Mary Miles's funeral at West Point on August 3, her body was taken to Washington, where she was laid to rest in the family mausoleum at Arlington National Cemetery. Miles had selected a site in the cemetery for his family's tomb far from the most popular tourist paths. The *New York Tribune* described the location as "a beautiful plot of ground on the crest of a long sloping hill which rises from the Potomac and overlooks the city of Washington."[9]

Leading officials in Washington paid their respects. President and Mrs. Roosevelt sent a telegram, and Secretary of War Taft attended the burial services. For Miles, however, the most moving expression of sympathy must have been a note signed "The Old Fifth," published in the *Army and Navy Journal.* A veteran of the Indian Wars wrote that "Those who took part in that service and shared the life at the frontier posts recall the peculiarly close friendship which common anxieties, perils and hardships availed to make." Mary Sherman Miles's "life touched and adorned so many social circles, there will not be elsewhere greater and more sincere grief at her death than that felt by the now widely scattered members of the old-time circle of her husband's regiment, the Fifth Infantry." Some thirty-five years after the newlyweds joined the regiment at Fort Hays, the old soldier spoke for his comrades when he wrote that "Upon her grave, with deepest grief, they would lay a wreath woven of rembrance of many joys and perils shared, of steadfast affection and of most sincere respect."[10]

The dual traumas of the loss of his wife and his political dreams within a month did not drive Miles from the public stage, but his role would become far less prominent. After he withdrew from the 1904 presidential race, he did little to aid the futile campaign of the Democratic candidate, Judge Alton B. Parker of New York. His most conspicuous contribution was the inclusion of one of his speeches in the Democratic Party's campaign textbook.

In this speech, originally given before Chicago's Iroquois Club, Miles challenged Theodore Roosevelt's boast that the United States was on its way to becoming a world power. Miles believed that "our boast of being a world power by mere brute force would be justly held in contempt and our existence as a republic would be of short duration. The world is too familiar with the spectacle of a strong power expanding by subjugation. Rome, the strongest of empires based on force, thus wrote her history and wrought her ruin."

According to Miles, the United States paid a heavy price for embracing a policy of imperialism. "To say nothing of the thousands of lives that have been lost or ruined in the conquest of the Philippines, we have expended enough treasure, drawn from the people of this country, to have put water on every quarter section of our arid land, thereby benefitting millions of our home-builders, or to have built a splendid system of good roads over our entire country."[11]

The year ended on a hopeful note for Miles. On December 4, the governor-elect of Massachusetts, William L. Douglas, announced that Miles had agreed to serve on his staff as adjutant general of the state's militia. The Army Appropriation Act of 1904 provided that the secretary of war could assign retired officers to state or territorial militias. About thirty states took advantage of this provision, and at least eight brigadier generals now served as adjutant generals in the National Guard. This appointment would return Miles to a position of some prominence, and also allow him to earn the full pay of a lieutenant general—eleven thousand dollars, plus allowances, which would be paid by the federal government. In addition, Massachusetts would pay him another three thousand dollars for administering the commonwealth's military affairs and for service with the state's six thousand–member National Guard.[12]

But on January 26, 1905, even this bit of good fortune for Miles turned to ashes. When the Senate debated the proposed 1905 annual army appropriations bill, Senator Henry Cabot Lodge opened an attack on the provision dealing with the appointment of retired army officers. The *New York Times* reported that Lodge's attack "was aimed at Gen. Miles" and that Lodge "denounced the provision as needless and unjust." The article confided, however, that Lodge believed that "the pay of a Lt. Gen. which would be received by Miles is large, but if he was to do active duty in the militia, there was no reason why he should not be paid for it."

The attack begun by Lodge gained momentum as other senators spoke out against the provision. Vermont's Senator Redfield Proctor complained "that there was an unseemly scramble on the part of retired officers to obtain active duty in order to secure greater pay." A reporter added that "when the bill came up for consideration, 'unfair' 'unmanly' and 'cowardly' were some of the adjectives used in characterizing that provision."[13]

In February the Senate put the matter to rest by arranging a compromise. Any retired officer above the rank of major would receive his retired pay, rather than full pay, when serving on active duty. When this compromise was initially proposed in January, the *Times* estimated that in addition to his retirement pay, Miles would receive twelve hundred dollars in allowances. The question of Miles's pay became academic in December 1905, when he resigned from active duty with the Massachusetts National Guard.[14]

An event that Miles could finally enjoy whole-heartedly occurred on November 24, 1909, when his son, Sherman, married Davide Yulee Noble at Saint John's Church in Washington, D.C. The *Army and Navy Journal* noted that the bride's "only ornament was a diamond and sapphire pin, the gift of the groom. Her bouquet was the old-fashioned round one of bride roses and white orchids." After the ceremony guests attended a reception at Miles's home on N Street, attractively decorated with asparagus ferns, white chrysanthemums, and white roses.[15]

Two years after his son Sherman's marriage, Miles succeeded in publishing his second autobiography, *Serving the Republic: Memoirs of the Civil and Military Life of Nelson A. Miles, Lieutenant General.* Some of his satisfaction at this accomplishment must have evaporated, however, after he read what the *New York Times* had to say about his work: "He forces us reluctantly to the conclusion that nature, in showering upon him a thousand gifts, denied him that of imagination. He seems to have passed unmoved and unimpressed among scenes the mere description of which would set an ordinary man's pulse leaping." The reviewer took some of the sting out of his criticism when he added, "He does write interestingly of the Indian life and the Indian wars, and he sketches the great war chiefs with a vivid pen."[16]

Less than a month later, in a listing of books that might be given as Christmas presents, the *Times* contradicted its original review. Here the critic judged that "This is one of those commentaries on history without which no national record can be perfect. He has always been a soldier, and the story of his experiences will be found as exciting as any novel and as trustworthy as a studious confirmatory use of official documents can make them."[17]

While the *New York Times* debated with itself over the literary merits of Miles's writing, *The Independent* pointed out the major shortcoming of Miles's memoirs: "Altho his life has been active and useful, he has been singularly unable to add material facts to our knowledge of the events in which he participated." *The Independent* explained that Miles "seems never to have been really in the inner confidence of the authorities at Washington, and when his one great chance came—the Spanish War—he was cheated of his opportunity." Besides being unable to shed much light on the decision-making process in official high circles, Miles refused to air the details of his clashes with those both in and out of the service.[18]

A rare exception to his self-imposed code of silence occurred, however, just a year before the publication of *Serving the Republic.* In a speech before the Colorado legislature on August 29, 1910, former president Theodore Roosevelt cited two Supreme Court cases in which attempts to regulate business abuses were found to be unconstitutional. He went on to complain that "the Supreme Court of the United States possessed and unfortunately exercised the negative power of not permitting the abuse to be rectified." The *New York Times* reported that "it was an extraordinary speech. It will no doubt be accepted throughout the country as a criticism of the Supreme Court of the U.S."[19]

Miles joined those who protested against Roosevelt's remarks, telling a reporter from the *New York Times* that "in condemning and criticizing the decisions of the Supreme Court of the United States and its venerable bench, Theodore Roosevelt is guilty of treason. Look at his political tracks, since he returned from the African wilds. It is a trail of discontent, bombast, disaffection, and even treason."

After denouncing Roosevelt for his attack on the Supreme Court, Miles compared his presidency negatively with that of the current officeholder, William Howard Taft, "which, in my opinion, has been eminently proper and dignified and a great improvement on the Administration that preceded it." Miles continued by complaining about a trip Roosevelt would begin on October 6, which the *New York Herald* described as a "whirlwind tour to preach the doctrine of 'New Nationalism' to the West and South."

The *New York Times* quoted Miles as saying, "this politician starts on a one-man tour, a personal political campaign, haranguing the people, inciting discontent, mixing with malcontents, embarrassing those in authority and power without an excuse or reason for such unprecedented conduct."

Miles undoubtedly based his opinion on Roosevelt's just-completed, three-week whistle-stop jaunt across sixteen Western states. This tour, which began on August 23, so annoyed Miles that he had described it as "disgusting, this constant vulgar exhibition of a former President running loose over the country surrounded by newspaper men, for whose edification he walks, talks, eats, and sleeps." In Miles's view, Roosevelt played up to the press by reveling in "the light of what should be to a sane man undesirable publicity. But that is what he lives for, and the real people are getting wise."[20]

This defamatory interview, so out of character for Miles, was not simply an opportunity for him to vent suppressed anger at his former nemesis. It also revealed his conservative leanings. In his *Times* interview, Miles had clearly allied himself with Taft after Roosevelt had challenged the president's conservative principles. The split between the two has been attributed to a speech delivered by Roosevelt at Osawatomie, Kansas, during his whistle-stop tour of the West. One of Roosevelt's biographers, William H. Harbaugh, considered this speech, given on August 31, 1910, to be "perhaps the most radical speech of his career." Besides criticizing the Supreme Court for its social-legislation decisions, Roosevelt campaigned for his program of social reform, the New Nationalism.[21]

As the end of the winter of 1911–12 approached, Miles entertained his brother, Daniel, who visited him in Washington. Daniel Curtis Miles, born in Westminster, Massachusetts, on June 1, 1827, had always been close to his younger brother, Nelson. When Daniel taught school for sixteen terms, Nelson had been one of his pupils. During the Civil War, Daniel had twice helped his wounded brother return home from the battlefield. In later years, Daniel prospered as a chair manufacturer, banker, and as an investor in real estate in southern California and Montana. During his visit, Daniel collapsed and died on Lafayette Square, opposite the White House, on February 22, 1912. Miles, who was driving along Pennsylvania Avenue at the time, stopped his car when he saw a crowd gather. The retired general must have been shocked when he peered over the shoulders of the onlookers and saw

Daniel's lifeless body on the ground, but he did not hesitate to lift his brother into the car and drive him home.[22]

A year after Daniel's death, Miles announced that he would seek the Republican nomination for the congressional seat made vacant by the death of William Henry Wilder of Gardner, Massachusetts. Some wondered that Miles would seek the Republican nomination since he had been considered a Democrat. Others questioned whether he could be considered a Massachusetts resident. Finally, when the issue arose of whether Miles could hold a seat in Congress while receiving an army pension, the retired general took himself out of the race by not registering as a candidate.[23]

Disappointed in his hope of serving in Congress, Miles turned his attention to the Guardians of Liberty. On June 9, 1911, ex-congressman Charles D. Haines founded this organization in Washington, D.C. According to its "Declaration of Principles," it was a "non-religious, non-partizan [*sic*], non-racial moral force to promote patriotism and a sacred regard for the welfare of our country." Under Haines's leadership, however, the organization had aroused a storm of criticism, especially among Catholics. For example, James Cardinal Gibbons warned that "This order is mainly nothing more than an attempt to revive the bigotry of the A.P.A. [American Protective Association], which was assumed to have died of inanition."[24]

On January 7, 1913, the *New York Times* reported a change in the leadership of the Guardians, as Haines resigned as chief guardian, to be replaced by Miles. The organization's reputation for promoting nativist and anti-Catholic propaganda did not improve under Miles's leadership. In an editorial published on November 19, 1914, the *New York Times* cautioned that "from time to time there sweeps over the country a causeless, reasonless fury of bigotry. . . . It wears different names; Know Nothingism at one time, the A.P.A. at another, the Guardians of Liberty at another."[25]

Even more frustrating for Miles than seeing his efforts to launch a fulfilling retirement career flounder may have been the curious fate of a movie that he helped to make in 1913. The retired general had traveled to Pine Ridge, South Dakota, where William F. Cody's Historical Film Company would shoot a reenactment of the Sioux outbreak of 1890. The War Department agreed to provide the filmmaker with both military equipment for use as props and men of the Twelfth Cavalry, who would portray the soldiers who had compaigned in Sioux country almost a quarter of a century earlier.

Miles, assisted by some of the officers who had served with him in 1890, including Brig. Gens. Frank Baldwin, Jesse M. Lee, and Marion Maus, served as the movie's technical adviser. During preparations to film battles from the past, a reporter from the *Denver Post* observed that "Miles designated each action of the Indians and the soldiers so that it might conform with the original action in the years gone. The great general saw that the picture was historically correct in every detail and that not a feature was forgotten." According to retired general Charles King, credited as the author of the screenplay, Miles considered his parley with a delegation of dissident chiefs on January 14, 1891, to be the climactic scene of the movie. King informed Milwaukee's *Evening Wisconsin* that "it was to reproduce the pictures of that great peace congress, not a battle, that General Miles and the survivors of his staff Generals Lee, Maus, and Baldwin, journeyed to Pine Ridge."[26]

The largest cast ever assembled up to that time had been brought together at Pine Ridge, including Sioux warriors who had challenged the army in 1890, as well as Miles, who would play himself. The *Gardner* (Massachusetts) *Journal* reported that at a news conference, Miles outlined the scenario that the amateur actors hoped to bring to life. The movie "would begin with the Indian dissatisfaction and their starving condition, followed by the arrival of the false Messiah and his subsequent exhortations which led to the revolt." The article continued, "Then it is planned to picture the massing of the troops, the battles, the death of Sitting Bull and finally the surrender."[27]

Inevitably, misunderstandings cropped up in such a massive undertaking. A film historian saw the humor when "The Indians, falling from their horses in the battle scenes, kept forgetting, in their desire to watch the proceedings, to lie down and die." The same authority noted that because of Miles's determination to record everything just as it actually happened, his friendship with Cody ended. Miles insisted that a scene be shot in the Badlands, squelching Cody's objection at the expense and difficulty of filming at such a remote location.[28] It appears, however, that the break may have been caused by more than a simple difference of opinion. Miles sounded quite irritated about Cody's depiction of the military when he complained to Baldwin that "This fraud and outrage on the [reputation of the] army ought not to be encouraged or permitted. Cody always has represented the soldiers and citizens secondary and insignificant to the 'Cow Boys.'"[29]

Three days after Miles penned his letter, Cody telegraphed Baldwin: "OUR ONLY GENERAL DISPLEASED WITH PICTURES LAYING BLAME ON ME ALL PICTURES AND TITLES HAVE BEEN CHANGED ACCORDING TO HIS SUGGESTIONS I HAVE ALWAYS ADMIRED OUR GENERAL AND FOUGHT FOR HIM IN EVERY WAY I AM MUCH DISTRESSED AND AM LEAVING FOR CODY WYOMING TONIGHT."[30]

Government officials, including Secretary of the Interior Franklin K. Lane, apparently thoroughly enjoyed the movie when it opened in Washington, D.C., on February 27, 1914. Despite the movie's warm reception, Kevin Brownlow, a film historian, noted that bureaucrats in Washington limited its release. Furthermore, he believed that when it was rereleased in 1917, there were "veiled remarks about the government's attempts to suppress it." Besides the government's efforts to restrict the film's distribution, exhibitors may have been reluctant to show a movie that would cut into their profits because of its unusually long running time of two and a half hours.

Today only a few clips of the eight-reel film have been located. The search for prints has been complicated because the movie was shown under a number of titles. Cody referred to it as the *Last Indian Wars for Civilization,* but other titles include the *Wars for Civilization in America* and *The Last Indian Battles, or from the Warpath to the Peace Pipe.* Brownlow is confident that if a copy should be found, it "would represent a historical prize of immense value. . . . The search for this extraordinary film should not be abandoned."[31]

Miles managed a trip to Europe before filming at Pine Ridge began on September 26, 1913. He toured the battlefields of the First Balkan War and visited his son, Sherman, a first lieutenant serving as a military attaché to Romania, with accreditation to American legations in Bulgaria, Greece, Montenegro, and Serbia. Miles, never far from the action, even managed to become enmeshed in the Second Balkan War, which began following Bulgaria's attack on Serbia during the night of June 29–30. Although the retired general was briefly held prisoner in Sofia, the capital of Bulgaria, he sympathized with that country. Besides condemning attrocities committed against Bulgarians, he sought to have Great Britain use its influence to force Turkey to surrender the city of Adrianople to Bulgaria. Miles sailed home from London shortly after the Treaty of Bucharest was signed on August 10, 1913.[32]

One year later, Miles voiced his alarm as the nations of Europe were poised at the brink of an even greater war. On August 2, 1914, the day after Germany declared war on Russia, and the day before Germany declared war on France, Miles told a reporter from the *New York Times* that "I am afraid one of the most terrible wars in the history of the world is at hand. Some countries of Europe are war mad." He predicted "it will take one big war, a tremendous sacrifice of lives, and a great loss of money to open their eyes to their folly."

Miles, now a confirmed peacemaker, suggested, "Let representatives of every nation form a peace congress. Give that peace congress full power in all disputes, and have it definitely understood that every nation will abide by its decision." According to Miles's plan, "If one nation disobeys the dictates of the peace congress give that congress power to order the armies and navies of all other nations to drive forcibly the wayward nation into submission." The retired general did not delude himself about the prospects of his plan: "But it will take one great war on the continent before some European countries will see lasting benefit of such a plan."[33]

On August 3 Miles also spoke to a large audience of African-Americans, who had gathered in Harlem to support their brothers who were serving as policemen, firemen, or national guardsmen. The folly of a world stumbling into war preyed on his mind. "Today, nearly twenty millions of young men of Europe are being forced to fight each other and fill untimely graves in a conflict that seems to be as little called for as any that has ever occurred on the face of the globe." He then accurately predicted the nature of the coming war. "In injury and fatalities, it bid fair to be the most destructive war ever waged, in view of the magnitude and importance of the nationalities engaged and their marvelous equipment of the most approved machines and implements of destruction."

Miles then turned his attention to what the *New York Times* termed the "Future of the Black Race." Forgetting about Liberia when he called for the creation of an independent black nation, Miles told his African-American audience that "You might be better off if there were a recognized nation of colored people which they could call their own." He then suggested that "perhaps the intelligence acquired in the past few years by your race may be utilized as a great civilizing force for the great black belt of Africa with its 160,000,000 of inhabitants." Miles then challenged the audience to aid this population, "which need the intelligence of such teachers and missionaries as your race has already raised up in this country."[34]

The sinking of the *Lusitania* by a German submarine on May 7, 1915, with the loss of 128 American lives, spurred the advocates of peace into action. For example, in August 1915, Henry Ford announced that he would use part of his fortune to promote peace.[35]

When Miles visited Ford's headquarters in Detroit shortly after this announcement, the *New York Times* had to admit that "it could not be learned what they spoke about." However, since much of the ensuing article discussed peace proposals, one can speculate that Miles intended to share with Ford his ideas for ending the war.[36]

With hopes for victory replacing dreams of peace after the United States entered the war, Miles still seemed intrigued with what he regarded as President Woodrow Wilson's lost opportunity to end hostilities. Ellen Slayden and her Texas congressman husband James L. Slayden had joined Miles as luncheon guests at retired general Anson Mills's home on December 30, 1917. At this gathering, Miles maintained that after the sinking of the *Lusitania,* the president should have called a conference of neutral nations. At such a conference, "The Kaiser would have welcomed the opportunity to make peace at a time when he would have proved himself the greatest war lord the world had ever seen." Mrs. Slayden admitted that Miles had surprised her, confiding in her diary that he "seemed sincere and sweet natured, not at all the peacocky old militarist I have thought him sometimes when in his panoply of war."[37]

The warrior's trappings that Miles loved to display now adorned a man who shied from militarism. During 1916 congressional hearings, held to determine how the United States should prepare to defend itself, Miles recommended restraint. On January 31 he advocated a standing army of only 150,000 men, which could serve as a skeleton for an army to be expanded to 394,000 in wartime. Argued Miles, "There is nothing to indicate that a larger military force will be required in the near future, if ever." Miles also argued against universal military service because "you can't Germanize the American people."[38]

On February 9, after Miles's second appearance on Capitol Hill, the *New York Times* reported that "Testimony that pleased the pacifist element in the House was furnished to Committees in Military and Naval Affairs today by General Nelson A. Miles, U.S.A., retired." After asserting that the United States could easily drive an invading force from its shores, Miles challenged the idea of resorting to conscription in the United States. He cited an incident during the Civil War, "When draft riots broke out and active troops were withdrawn from Gettysburg to suppress Philadelphia riots because of the unpopularity of the idea."

The reporter added that Miles "advocated expansion of the National Guard rather than the creation of a Continental Army, favored three year enlistments, recommended a regular standing army of 140,000 or 150,000 men, and submitted an army reorganization plan of his own, contemplating recruiting a force of 1,200,000 men by expanding the units of organization."[39]

As the U.S. entry into World War I appeared to be imminent following the release of the Zimmerman Note on March 1, 1917, which contained a proposal by Germany of an alliance with Mexico in case of war between Germany and the United States, and the public uproar when U-boats sank several American merchant ships, Miles volunteered his services to Woodrow Wilson's secretary of war, Newton D. Baker. Perplexed as how to use the seventy-seven-year-old retired general, Baker gracefully replied that he did not see, "at this time, in what way your services could best be utilized in view of your high rank in the army, but it is possible that, in time of emergency, the Government may need the advantage of your great experience and wealth of information on military matters." Fortunately for all concerned, the military situation never deteriorated to the point where a nineteenth-century warrior would be called upon to fight in a modern war.[40]

President Wilson had already called for a special session of Congress when Miles spoke before a convention of the National Guard Association on March 27. Refusing to be caught up in the enthusiasm of the moment, Miles had faith that lasting peace would be achieved in the future, despite his misgivings about the war that the United States would enter on April 6. "I trust that when this war is over there will be intelligence enough, patriotism enough, in the civilized world to ring down the curtain upon that appalling tragedy and make it the closing scene in the terrible drama of war."

The *New York Times* also reported that Miles cautioned about "the plan to centralize all of the military power in Washington. It opened the door, he said, for possible future usurpation or autocracy. He urged that the present system of maintaining army, navy, and National Guard should be perfected, as an alternative."

The retired general could draw from his own battlefield experiences when he advised that "The quickest way to end wars is [an] effective, strong, offensive campaign." He confidently added, "And if this nation in all its power and grandeur once arouses itself and exerts its full power, as I trust it will, I believe it would be possible to end the war inside of twelve months, if not inside of six."[41]

Although Miles had repeatedly advocated an international peacekeeping organization, during the 1920 presidential campaign he bolted from the Democratic Party after it endorsed the League of Nations. The *New York Times* reported that Miles had decided to support the Republican candidates, Warren G. Harding and Calvin Coolidge, because they "believed in the adjudication of international controversy by arbitration and were opposed to the surrender of our national character and sovereignty to a super-government." He praised Harding as "a strong character and a profound statesman, in his experience, disposition and principle the same type as Abraham Lincoln." Miles no doubt had in mind the strong stand taken by Harding's running mate, then governor of Massachusetts, during the Boston police strike in 1919, when he said, "Coolidge is a worthy successor of John Hancock and has demonstrated his reverence for and his ability to maintain a true and legal government of law and order."[42]

The *New York Times* did not take lightly Miles's desertion from Ohio governor James M. Cox's camp because it appeared to furnish the Republicans with "illustrious proof that high class Democrats cannot endure Governor Cox as the Presidential candidate of their party." The editor reminded his readers of Miles's 1913 aborted run for a seat in Congress as a Republican, after having publicly rebuked former president Theodore Roosevelt, also a Republican. The editor then compared Miles's congratulatory telegram to president-elect William McKinley, a Republican, with his "antipathy" to President Grover Cleveland, a fellow Democrat. This checkered history led to the conclusion that although Miles may have been "a gallant soldier," politically "he has never been of value to any party and his skirmishes with public questions have not shown any strategical merit." Although Miles may have strayed from the path followed by orthodox Democrats, his independence did not merit the *New York Times*'s judgment that "As a bolting Democrat the General is a good deal of a joke."[43]

Even as Miles became more politically conservative with age, he remained a remarkably open-minded military thinker. On the eve of his retirement, he wrote Secretary of War Root a note that the *New York Times* described as a "plea for changes." Miles foresaw reforms, some of which would only be implemented by the army as the United States prepared to enter World War I. First, Miles recommended a reduction in the cavalry because "The marvelous development in modern arms—rifles, machine guns, and quick-firing field artillery—renders the cavalry as formerly used on the battlefield, obsolete." In order to incorporate bicycles, motorcycles, and automobiles into the army, "five regiments of cavalry should be discontinued, and a corps of five regiments should be organized, thoroughly trained and constantly employed in the use of these appliances." His second proposal called for a "flying corps or corps of observation." This innovation was called for in a letter written four months before the Wright brothers made the first flight in a powered, heavier-than-air plane on December 17, 1903.

Miles expected that an air corps, with supporting units (the most important of which would evidently have consisted of combat engineers), would "open the way for the advance of the army, to obtain information, to reconnoiter the country, and to repair or build roads and bridges." Officers for this corps would be drawn from all of the branches of the army, for service from two to four years. Placing emphasis on road building, Miles intended that the new corps would be equipped with the latest road-building machines. He recommended that this force should conduct exercises in every region of the country in order to gain road-building experience across every possible terrain. Miles argued that "such a corps would be of more important, practical, and direct benefit to the country in time of peace than all of the rest of the army, and in time of war would be invaluable." Miles expected that the exercises would result in extensive road construction, as a result: "The millions of dollars that are now uselessly expended for one-third of the mounted force could in this way be utilized in bringing about a great improvement in the army, conferring a great benefit upon the country, at the same time training a most important corps for military service."[44]

In 1925 Miles again demonstrated that age had not clouded his strategic vision, when he appeared before a House Select Committee headed by Floran

Lampert of Wisconsin. With Brig. Gen. William (Billy) Mitchell as the star witness, the hearings had been held to investigate the capability of the nation's air power to defend the United States. Miles attached such importance to this sensitive topic that he received permission to testify in executive session. Although he also refused to discuss his appearance before the committee with newsmen, the *New York Times* report of the hearings confirms Miles's grasp of the problems and potential of air power. After warning that the United States had to protect both seacoasts from air attack, Miles "referred to the trials and heartaches of Langley [on December 8, 1903, Samuel P. Langley made an unsuccessful attempt in a power-driven airplane], and the difficulties . . . which stood in the way of those who would have helped Langley if they had been permitted to do so."[45]

The years had been kind to Miles. In the summer of 1918, a resident of Westminster who had never met the retired general accepted the invitation of the pastor of the town's Baptist church to visit Miles. When they arrived at his homestead, located about two miles outside the town, they followed the sound of wood being chopped until they came upon Miles felling a tree. The caller later wrote that the gentlemen farmer "sprang to meet us; a man nearly 80 then, but splendidly set up, still hale and hearty." The visitor added that "He greeted his old friend and minister with a firm clasp and an affectionate hand on the shoulder, then accepted me as a friend of his friend with a warm courtesy that I have never forgotten."[46]

On May 15, 1925, Miles, along with his son Sherman's mother-in-law, escorted their grandchildren to the Friday afternoon performance of Ringling's circus in Washington, D.C. As the small party entered the huge circus tent, Miles stopped to tell John Ringling, "You know I never miss the circus." Miles then led the way to their seats in the third row, two sections away from where Grace Coolidge, the president's wife, was sitting.[47]

During the grand entry, colorfully decorated horses carrying flag bearers trotted past the venerable general. Miles snapped to attention, probably delighted to demonstrate a parade-ground salute to an audience of civilians. As the crowd settled back in their seats at the end of the opening procession, Miles suddenly fell backwards, into the arms of a doctor sitting in the next row, where he died without a murmur. The *Washington Post* reported the cause of death as acute dilation of the heart.[48]

Tributes to Miles filled the newspapers as final funeral arrangements were delayed until the *Leviathan* docked in New York on Sunday, May 17, carrying Miles's son, Sherman, home from Constantinople. The *Washington Post* referred to Miles as "America's grand old fighting man," while headlines in the *New York Times* announced that he was "MOURNED BY INDIANS HE FOUGHT. 'Big Bear' as they called him, feared in warfare, but respected for his fairness—General was a diplomat of the council fires."[49]

Miles would have been gratified with the glowing review of his career in the *Army and Navy Journal,* especially its declaration that "During the War with Spain it was considered very unfortunate and unjust to a great soldier that General Miles was not placed in command of the expedition to Cuba." The article explained that "He was overlooked, however, through the political influence of some persons who disliked him, despite the fact that he was commanding general of the United States Army."[50]

America's noted World War I hero, Gen. John J. Pershing, who had campaigned with Miles in Sioux country before being called to Washington to serve as his aide from 1896 to 1897, had kind words for the general who had become his friend. In a press statement Pershing said, "It was my good fortune to have service under Gen. Miles." After recalling these assignments, Pershing added, "I have always had the greatest admiration for him as an officer and as a high type of citizen. He was an exceptionally splendid soldier, and during the trying days of the frontier campaigns, was the idol of all who were associated with him."[51]

On Tuesday, May 19, Miles's coffin was carried on an artillery caisson from his apartment at the Rochambeau, which had been his primary residence since 1910, to Saint John's Episcopal Church for religious services. The funeral procession that passed from the church and through the heart of official Washington to Arlington National Cemetery was as eye-catching as the cavalcades that often marked the end of one of Miles's Indian campaigns. Six pitch-black horses hitched to the caisson followed at a solemn gait two clergymen in black-and-white vestments. High-ranking officers, their dress uniforms adorned with medals, flanked the coffin, while black-ribboned carriages carrying mourners, including the president, followed the caisson. About three thousand soldiers, sailors, and marines marched, each contingent keeping in step with its own service band. In contrast to the impeccable ranks of able-bodied men currently serving the nation were the veterans, shuffling to keep in step and the more frail among them gamely struggling to keep pace with their comrades. The banners carried at the head of each unit identified which war they had soldiered through with Miles. Civil War veterans marched with the Military Order of the Loyal Legion or the Grand Army of the Republic, although some of these men may have been tempted to march with the Indian War Veterans' Societies, which they had also earned the right to join. Those who fought in the war with Spain or the war in which Miles could only serve in spirit, World War I, marched with the more recent organizations, such as the Spanish War Veterans, the Military Order, Veterans of Foreign Wars, or the American Legion.

The *Washington Post* captured the scene as Miles's "body was borne tenderly amid sounds that at intervals were martial and then funereal—the boom of the minute guns, the mournful strains of Chopin's funeral march, the thud of marching soldiers, the clatter of cavalry and the rumble of artillery." While the military formations in the cortege may have attracted most of the attention, the determination of the veterans to do what they considered to be their duty must have been impressive to see. The same devotion to duty that gave these men the fortitude to endure dangerous and arduous campaigns in the past, now required them to escort the body of a brother-in-arms to the mausoleum where he would join his wife.[52]

Notes

Introduction

1. *Army and Navy Journal,* Apr. 26, 1890, 666; Charles G. Seymour, "The Final Review," *Harper's Weekly,* Feb. 7, 1891, 106.

2. Nelson A. Miles, *Personal Recollections and Observations of General Nelson A. Miles* and *Serving the Republic: Memoirs of the Civil and Military Life of Nelson A. Miles, Lieutenant General;* Virginia Johnson, *The Unregimented General: A Biography of Nelson A. Miles.* More recent biographical material is contained in Brian C. Pohanka, ed., *Nelson A. Miles: A Documentary Biography of His Military Career;* Robert M. Utley, "Nelson A. Miles"; Jerome A. Greene, *Yellowstone Command: Colonel Nelson A. Miles and the Great Sioux War, 1876–1877;* and Robert Wooster, *Nelson A. Miles and the Twilight of the Frontier Army.*

1. A Boy Grows Up to Become a Soldier

1. Miles, *Serving the Republic,* 4–7.

2. Miles family genealogy from Nelson A. Miles obituary, *Fitchburg Sentinel,* May 16, 1925, and Miles, *Serving the Republic,* 6–7; George W. Ellis and John E. Morris, *King Philip's War,* 64.

3. Miles quoted in *New York Times,* Feb. 15, 1899.

4. Miles, *Personal Recollections,* 23. Daniel Miles's biography in William S. Heywood, *History of Westminster, Massachusetts, 1728–1893,* 781; *Boston Post,* Mar. 19, 1899.

5. Miles, *Serving the Republic,* 9–10.

6. Ibid., 14.

7. Organization of Company E in John L. Parker, *History of the 22nd Massachusetts Infantry, 2nd Company Sharpshooters, and 3rd Light Battery in the War of the Rebellion,* 11; source of funds in Miles, *Personal Recollections,* 30.

8. Miles, *Personal Recollections,* 30. Miles is listed as "Capt. 22 Mass., Inf.... 9 Sept. 61" in a memorandum dated Dec. 27, 1901, Washington, D.C., Nelson A. Miles's personal file, Records of the Adjutant General's Office, 1780s–1917 (RAGO), Record Group (RG) 94, National Archives (NA), Washington, D.C. Miles reduced in rank in Special Order 498, William Schouler, adjutant general (AG), to Col. Henry Wilson, commanding officer, 22d Regt., Mass. Vols., Oct. 7, 1861, n.p., in Nelson A. Miles Collection, U.S. Army Military History Institute, Carlisle Barracks, Pennsylvania (hereafter cited as Miles Collection).

9. Parker, *History of 22nd Massachusetts Infantry,* 67. Miles to uncle and aunt, Oct. 15, 1861, Camp Wilson, Halls Hill, Miles Collection; Miles to uncles, Dec. 18, 1861, HQ General Howard's

First Brigade, Miles Collection; Charles A. Fuller, *Personal Recollections of the War of 1861, 61st Regiment, New York Volunteer Infantry,* 11; quote by Francis A. Walker, *History of the Second Army Corps in the Army of the Potomac,* 53; George E. Pond, "Major-General Nelson A. Miles," *McClure's Magazine* 5 (Nov. 1895): 562.

10. Frederic Remington, *The Collected Writings of Frederic Remington,* 601; Ellen Maury Slayden, *Washington Wife: Journal of Ellen Maury Slayden,* 24, 317 17.

11. Sumner quoted in Oliver O. Howard, *Autobiography of Oliver Otis Howard, Major General, United States Army* 1:187; Barlow to Governor Edwin D. Morgan, May 1, 1862, near Yorktown, Va., Miscellaneous Mss., New York Historical Society; Stephen W. Sears, *To the Gates of Richmond: The Peninsula Campaign.*

12. Gilbert E. Govan and James W. Livingood, *A Different Valor: The Story of Joseph E. Johnston, CSA,* 141–57.

13. General Howard's report, June 3, 1862, in *War of the Rebellion: A Compilation of the Official Records of the Union and Confederate Armies,* vol. 11, 1:69–70 (hereafter cited as *OR*); Report of Col. Thomas J. Parker, 64th New York Infantry, June 2, 1862, Fair Oaks Station, in ibid., 770–71.

14. Details of Miles's Civil War wounds in *New York Times,* Oct. 26, 1895. An example of Miles identified as a captain in Brig. Gen. John C. Caldwell's report, July 6, 1862, camp near Harrison's Landing, in *OR,* vol. 11, 2:62.

15. Barlow's report, July 5, 1862, camp near James River, *OR,* vol. 11, 2:68. Caldwell's report, July 6, 1862, camp near Harrison's Landing in ibid. 2:62.

16. Bruce Catton, *Mr. Lincoln's Army,* 203.

17. Fuller, *Personal Recollections,* 7, 107.

18. Miles, *Serving the Republic,* 42.

19. Fuller, *Personal Recollections,* 57.

20. Miles, *Serving the Republic,* 42.

21. Stephen W. Sears, *Landscape Turned Red: The Battle of Antietam,* 236.

22. Details of the 61st in battle reported in Paul Jones, *The Irish Brigade,* and in Robert C. Athearn, *Thomas Francis Meagher: An Irish Revolutionary in America.*

23. Miles's report, Sept. 19, 1862, in *OR,* vol. 19, 1:291; Fuller, *Personal Recollections,* 59.

24. Analysis of Sumner's inaction in Walker, *History of the Second Army Corps,* 117–18; Miles, *Serving the Republic,* 46.

25. Hancock quoted in Francis A. Walker, *General Hancock,* 52.

26. Caldwell's report, Sept. 24, 1862, Bolivar Heights, Harper's Ferry, in *OR,* vol. 19, 1:286; Barlow's report, Sept. 22, 1862, General Hospital, Keedysville, Md., ibid., 290.

27. Undated letter signed "Irish Brigade" in Fuller, *Personal Recollections,* 70.

28. Kelly's report, Oct. 5, 1862, Bolivar Heights, Harper's Ferry, in *OR,* vol. 19, 1:298.

29. Barlow quoted in letter signed "Irish Brigade," in Fuller, *Personal Recollections,* 70.

30. On November 17, Fredericksburg was occupied by a regiment of cavalry, four infantry companies, and a light battery. Walker, *General Hancock,* 58.

31. Douglas Southall Freeman, *R. E. Lee: A Biography* 2:42–44.

32. Miles, *Serving the Republic,* 48; strength of Miles's command in Hancock's report, Dec. 25, 1862, Falmouth, Va., *OR,* vol. 21, 1:230; Fuller, *Personal Recollections,* 78.

33. Fuller, *Personal Recollections,* 79.

34. Ibid.

35. Caldwell's report, Jan. 21, 1863, *OR,* vol. 21, 1:233.

36. Edward J. Stackpole, *Drama on the Rappahannock: The Fredericksburg Campaign,* 206;

Miles's report, Dec. 14, 1862, Fredericksburg, Va., *OR,* vol. 21, 1:237.

37. Miles's report, Dec. 14, 1862, Fredericksburg, Va., *OR,* vol. 21, 1:237. Details of this wound in *New York Times,* Oct. 26, 1895.

38. Fuller, *Personal Recollections,* 81; Howard, *Autobiography* 1:340.

39. Stackpole, *Drama on the Rappahannock,* 276. Losses in Miles's regiment in General Hancock's report, Dec. 25, 1862, Falmouth, Va., *OR,* vol. 21, 1:230.

40. General Hancock's report, Dec. 25, 1862, Falmouth, Va., *OR,* vol. 21, 1:230; General Caldwell's report, Jan. 21, 1863, HQ Caldwell's brigade, ibid., 234.

41. Sumner's death in Miles, *Serving the Republic,* 49. Howard and Barlow's promotion in John A. Carpenter, *Sword and Olive Branch: Oliver Otis Howard,* 45.

2. Gallantry Recognized from Chancellorsville to Appomattox

1. Miles, *Serving the Republic,* 51.

2. Bruce Catton, *Glory Road,* 160–66.

3. Miles's report, May 5, 1863, Lacy House Hospital, Falmouth, Va., *OR,* vol. 25, 1:322.

4. Walker, *History of the Second Army Corps,* 223; Shelby Foote, *The Civil War: A Narrative* 2:278.

5. Miles, *Serving the Republic,* 52; Ernest B. Furgurson, *Chancellorsville 1863: The Souls of the Brave,* 127.

6. Miles, *Serving the Republic,* 53–54.

7. Ibid., 54; Miles's report, May 5, 1863, Lacy House Hospital, Falmouth, Va., *OR,* vol. 25, 1:323; Caldwell's report, May 12, 1863, HQ Caldwell's brigade, ibid., 319.

8. McLaw's report, May 10, 1863, HQ Div., *OR,* vol. 25, 1:825–26.

9. Fuller, *Personal Recollections,* 86; Alfred H. Guernsey and Henry M. Alden, *Harper's Pictorial History of the Civil War,* 492; Miles to uncle, Sept. 12, 1864, HQ First Div., Second Corps, Miles Collection. Mention of "warning reports that Devens chose to treat in so cavalier a fashion" in Edward J. Stackpole, *Chancellorsville, Lee's Greatest Battle,* 227. Also see John Bigelow, Jr., *The Campaign of Chancellorsville,* 287–88; and Furgurson, *Chancellorsville 1863.*

10. Fuller, *Personal Recollections,* 86; Hancock's report, May 19, 1863, near Falmouth, Va., *OR,* vol. 25, 1:313; Miles, *Serving the Republic,* 54.

11. Walker, *History of the Second Army Corps,* 240.

12. Catton, *Glory Road,* 199–200. Both General Couch and General Hancock quoted in Walker, *History of the Second Army Corps,* 231.

13. Col. Orlando H. Morris's report, May 18, 1863, HQ 66th Regt., N.Y. Vols., *OR,* vol. 25, 1:333; Miles, *Serving the Republic,* 55.

14. Dr. Fisher and Miles in Pohanka, *Nelson A. Miles,* 37; Miles, *Serving the Republic,* 55.

15. *New York Times,* Oct. 26, 1895.

16. Hancock's report, May 19, 1863, near Falmouth, Va., and Caldwell's report, May 12, 1863, HQ Caldwell's brigade, *OR,* vol. 25, 1:315, 320–21; Hancock's memorandum, June 24, 1863, and Surgeon H. C. Vogelle to Miles, June 10, 1863, Falmouth, Va., Miles Collection.

17. For a discussion of brevet rank, see Russell F. Weigley, *History of the United States Army,* 110–11; also James B. Fry, *The History and Legal Effect of Brevets in the Armies of Great Britain and the United States from Their Origin in 1692 to the Present Time,* 230 (for the law of Mar. 3, 1869), 231 (for the law of July 15, 1870). Citations of brevet appear in Case of Nelson A. Miles, Major General, U.S.A., and late colonel, 61st New York Vols., Application for Medal of Honor, June 24,

1892, War Department, RG 94, Military Archives, NA (hereafter cited as Case of Nelson A. Miles); 1876 and 1897 guidelines for the medal in Robert E. Wyllie, *Orders, Decorations and Insignia,* 41–42;

18. AG to Miles, July 23, 1892, Washington, D.C.; Albert A. Pope to Secretary of War Stephen B. Elkins, June 13, 1892, Boston, Mass.; Couch to Elkins, May 16, 1892, Norwalk, Conn., all in Case of Nelson A. Miles. John J. Pullen, *A Shower of Stars: The Medal of Honor and the Twenty-Seventh Maine,* 134.

19. Nelson A. Miles, "General Meade Anniversary Banquet," 30.

20. Frank E. Vandiver, *The Mighty Stonewall,* 478–94.

21. Miles, *Serving the Republic,* 61–62; Couch's report, July 23, 1863, HQ Dept. of the Susquehanna, excerpted in Pohanka, *Nelson A. Miles,* 39; Miles to Daniel Miles, July 19, 1863, Huntington, Pa., in Miles Collection.

22. Fuller, *Personal Recollections,* 36.

23. Barlow to Miles, May 26, 1863, HQ First Div., Eleventh Corps, Miles-Cameron Family Papers, Library of Congress (LC), Washington, D.C. An interesting account of Barlow's wound appears in John B. Gordon, *Reminiscences of the Civil War,* 151–52; Miles, "General Meade Anniversary Banquet," 31; Robert L. Stewart, *History of the One Hundred and Fortieth Regiment, Pennsylvania Volunteers,* 154.

24. Caldwell's report, Oct. 28, 1863, camp near Turkey Run Bridge, *OR,* 1, vol. 29, 1:256; Barlow to Miles, Nov. 29, 1863, Boston, plus enclosure, Barlow to Wilson, Nov. 28, 1863, Boston, in Miles-Cameron Family Papers.

25. Meade to Lt. Col. Theodore Bowers, asst. adj. gen., Armies of the U.S., May 16, 1864, HQ Army of the Potomac, in *OR,* vol. 36, 2:812; Miles date of rank in AG office memorandum, Dec. 27, 1901, Washington, D.C., in Nelson A. Miles personnel file, RAGO, RG 94, NA.

26. Andrew A. Humphreys, *The Virginia Campaign of '64 and '65: The Army of the Potomac and the Army of the James,* 3. Barlow replaced General Caldwell, who permanently resigned from the Second Corps. Walker, *History of the Second Army Corps,* 63. The potential for problems that was created when Grant joined Meade in the field was lessened because "Meade chose not to see the awkwardness and observed that Grant's objective in coming here to the headquarters of the Army of the Potomac is to avoid Washington and its entourage." William S. McFeely, *Grant: A Biography,* 156–57.

27. Hancock's report, Sept. 21, 1865, Baltimore, Md., in *OR,* vol. 36, 1:330–31.

28. Miles to Barlow, Jan. 6, 1879, in Francis Barlow, "The Capture of the Salient, May 12, 1864," 256–60. Miles's report, Oct. 30, 1864, HQ First Brig., First Div., Second Army Corps, in *OR,* vol. 36, 1:370–71.

29. Barlow, "The Capture of the Salient," 249. Hancock's report, Sept. 21, 1865, Baltimore, Md., in *OR,* vol. 36, 1:335.

30. Miles to Barlow, Jan. 6, 1879, in Barlow, "The Capture of the Salient," 261.

31. Miles, *Serving the Republic,* 66; Ewell's report, Mar. 20, 1865, Richmond, Va., in *OR,* vol. 36, 1:1072.

32. John W. Haley, *The Rebel Yell and the Yankee Hurrah: The Civil War Journal of a Maine Volunteer,* 156.

33. Walker, *General Hancock,* 202; Freeman, *R. E. Lee* 3:328; brevet citation in Case of Nelson A. Miles.

34. Walker, *History of the Second Army Corps,* 507.

35. Miles's report, Oct. 30, 1864, HQ First Brig., First Div., Second Army Corps, in *OR,* vol. 36, 1:371–72.

36. Miles, *Serving the Republic,* 70. It is uncertain which three colonels Miles bivouacked with, since six colonels were killed at Cold Harbor on June 3, 1864.

37. Lt. Lewis P. Caldwell, 1st Mass. Artillery, June 8, 1864, in camp near Gaines Mills, in Robert G. Carter, *Four Brothers in Blue, or Sunshine and Shadows of the War of Rebellion,* 428; Haley, *The Rebel Yell and the Yankee Hurrah,* 165; Miles to uncle, June 28, 1864, HQ First Brig., First Div., Second Corps, in Miles Collection.

38. The basic reason Hancock did not spur his corps to Petersburg on June 15, according to his report (Sept. 21, 1865, Baltimore,Md., in *OR,* vol. 40, 1:304), was that the dispatches from Grant, "which I received between 5 and 6 P.M. on the 15th, were the first and only intimations I had that Petersburg was to be attacked that day"; Miles to Aunt Mary, June 27, 1864, HQ First Brig., First Div., Second Corps; Miles to uncle, June 28, 1864, and Miles to brother Daniel, July 26, 1864, HQ First Brig., First Div., Second Corps, in Miles Collection.

39. Walker, *General Hancock,* 248.

40. Retirement from Deep Bottom in Hancock's report, Sept. 21, 1865, Baltimore, Md., in *OR,* vol. 40, 1:311. Findings of the board of inquiry, Sept. 9, 1864, HQ Second Corps, in ibid., 128–29. The division commanders cited in the report were James H. Ledlie, Edward Ferrero, and Orlando B. Willcox.

41. Walker, *History of the Second Army Corps,* 575.

42. Col. Charles Morgan, Hancock's chief of staff, quoted in ibid., 576–77.

43. Ibid., 578; death of Barlow's wife in Pohanka, *Nelson A. Miles,* 48.

44. Miles receives command of the First Division in Hancock's report, Sept. 12, 1864, in *OR,* vol. 42, 1:222. Humphreys, *The Virginia Campaign of '64 and '65,* 278–79.

45. Lee to Hampton, Aug. 24, 1864, HQ Army of Northern Virginia, in *OR,* vol. 42, 1:851.

46. Walker, *History of the Second Army Corps,* 585. Hancock's corps was not at full strength because Brig. Gen. Gersham Mott's division remained in the line at Petersburg. The nearest supporting unit was Warren's Fifth Corps, approximately four miles north of Reams' Station.

47. Miles's report, Aug. 30, 1864, HQ First Div., Second Army Corps, in *OR,* vol. 42, 1:252; George C. Underwood, asst. surgeon, 26th North Carolina Regt., in Walter Clark, ed., *Histories of the Several Regiments and Battalions from North Carolina in the Great War, 1861–'65* 2:389.

48. Walker, *History of the Second Army Corps,* 582–83; Hancock's report, Sept. 12, 1864, in *OR,* vol. 42, 1:224, 226.

49. *OR,* vol. 42, 1:223.

50. Stewart, *The One Hundred and Fortieth Regiment,* 234; John D. Billings, *Hardtack and Coffee, or the Unwritten Story of Army Life,* 327. Miles believed that more than 134 horses were killed; in a note to his uncle he estimated that 240 horses had been shot down. Miles to uncle, Sept. 12, 1864, HQ First Div., Second Corps, in Miles Collection.

51. Composition of attack force in Lee to Secretary of War James A. Seddon, Aug. 26, 1864, HQ Army of Northern Virginia, in *OR,* vol. 42, 1:851. Details of General Heth's action in George C. Underwood, "26th Regt. North Carolina Troops" 2:389; captain and men of the 28th North Carolina quoted by Brig. Gen. James H. Lane, "28th North Carolina" 2:480, both in Clark, *Histories of Several Regiments.*

52. Details of Miles's efforts in the Battle of Reams' Station in Miles's report, Aug. 30, 1864, HQ First Div., Second Corps, in *OR,* vol. 42, 1:253.

53. Hancock's observations in Hancock's report, Sept. 12, 1864, n.p., in *OR,* vol. 42, 1:226–27.

54. *Miles's* report, Aug. 30, 1864, HQ First Div., Second Corps, in ibid., 254; Union casualties in Hancock's report, Sept. 12, 1864, ibid., 228; Confederate losses in Humphreys, *The Virginia Campaign of '64 and '65,* 283.

55. Lee to Seddon, Aug. 26, 1864, HQ Army of Northern Virginia, in *OR,* vol. 42, 1:851.

56. Hancock's report, Sept. 12, 1864, *OR,* vol. 42, 1:227.

57. Humphreys, *The Virginia Campaign of '64 and '65,* 283; Guernsey and Alden, *Harper's Pictorial History of the Civil War,* 703. To meet conscription demands first established by the Federal government in 1863, cash bounties were offered to attract volunteers. Since each level of government contributed to the bounty by 1864, a volunteer could earn more than a thousand dollars when he enlisted. See *The American Heritage Pictorial History of the Civil War,* 485.

58. Hancock quoted in Stewart, *The One Hundred and Fortieth Regiment,* 236–37; Hancock replaced by Humphreys in Walker, *History of the Second Corps,* 640; Humphreys, *The Virginia Campaign of '64 and '65,* 307; *Dictionary of American Biography* (*DAB*), s.v. "Humphreys, Andrew A."

59. This citation appears in the Case of Nelson A. Miles. The brevet is dated August 25, 1864. Miles, *Serving the Republic,* 79.

60. Pohanka, *Nelson A. Miles,* 56; Gordon, *Reminiscences,* 403.

61. Miles's report, Mar. 28, 1865, HQ First Div., Second Corps, in *OR,* vol. 46, 1:197.

62. Walker, *History of the Second Corps,* 660.

63. Miles's report, Apr. 20, 1865, HQ First Div., Second Corps, in *OR,* vol. 46, 1:710; Humphreys, *The Virginia Campaign of '64 and '65,* 332.

64. Humphreys, *The Virginia Campaign of '64 and '65,* 368; Miles's report, Apr. 20, 1865, HQ First Div., Second Corps, in *OR,* vol. 46, 1:711.

65. *OR,* vol. 46, 1:711.

66. Escape of Confederates in Guernsey and Alden, *Harper's Pictorial History of the Civil War,* 762; Walker, *History of the Second Corps,* 677.

67. Miles's report, Apr. 20, 1865, HQ First Div., Second Corps, in *OR,* vol. 46, 1:712. The Second Corps suffered 396 casualties. Walker, *History of the Second Army Corps,* 680. Miles and Walker both call the stream Sailor's Creek; Southern historians refer to it as Sayler's Creek. Freeman, *R. E. Lee* 4:83.

68. Walker, *History of the Second Corps,* 681–82; Guernsey and Alden, *Harper's Pictorial History of the Civil War,* 768; Humphreys, *The Virginia Campaign of '64 and '65,* 387. Maj. Gen. William C. Mahone was responsible for destroying the bridges. Freeman wrote that "General Lee exploded when he got word of the blunder. . . . The last hope of the shattered army was being allowed to slip away." Freeman, *R. E. Lee* 4:99.

69. Miles's report, Apr. 20, 1865, HQ First Div., Second Corps, in *OR,* vol. 46, 1:713; Humphreys, *The Virginia Campaign of '64 and '65,* 387.

70. Humphreys, *The Virginia Campaign of '64 and '65,* 389–90. Miles's report, Apr. 20, 1865, HQ First Div., Second Corps, in *OR,* vol. 46, 1:713.

71. Humphreys, *The Virginia Campaign of '64 and '65,* 390–91.

72. Miles, *Serving the Republic,* 91.

73. William Fox, *Regimental Losses in the American Civil War, 1861–65,* 115; Pond, "Major-General Nelson A. Miles," 564, 566; *New York Times,* Oct. 26, 1895.

74. Miles to Lt. Col. Charles A. Whittier, Mar. 30, 1865, HQ First Div., Second Corps, in *OR,* vol. 51, 1:1209. The band was sent to entertain the men, and permission to issue whiskey was

granted. Whittier, asst. adj. gen., Second Corps, Mar. 30, 1865, HQ Second Corps in ibid., vol. 46, 3:296. Daniel Miles's work for prohibition in Heywood, *History of Westminster, Massachusetts,* 781.

75. Special Order No. 243, Edward D. Townsend, asst. adj. gen., HQ of the Army, AG's Office (AGO), to Miles, May 19, 1865, Washington, D.C., in *OR,* ser. 2, vol. 3, 1:560.

3. After the Civil War: From Fort Monroe, Virginia, to Fort Hays, Kansas

1. Charles A. Dana, assistant secretary of war, to Secretary of War Edwin M. Stanton, May 22, 1865, Ft. Monroe, in *OR,* ser. 2, vol. 17, 1:563. Charges leveled against Davis and Clay in President Andrew Johnson's proclamation, May 2, 1865, quoted in Miles, *Serving the Republic,* 99.

2. Dana to Stanton, May 22, 1865, Ft. Monroe, in *OR,* ser. 2, vol. 8, 1:564. This description of Davis is at variance with that given by the army physician who cared for Davis at Fort Monroe. Dr. John J. Craven stated that Davis looked "much wasted and very haggard." John J. Craven, *Prison Life of Jefferson Davis,* 28. Miles argued that Davis "was as strong and agile as other men of his age, 56." To substantiate this statement, he pointed out that Davis claimed "at the time of his capture of his ability, single handed and alone, to tumble a mounted soldier from his horse and then spring into the saddle and escape." Nelson A. Miles, "My Treatment of Jefferson Davis," 415.

3. Dana to Stanton, May 22, 1865, Ft. Monroe, "Regulations," in *OR,* ser. 2, vol. 8, 1:564–65; Hudson Strode, *Jefferson Davis, Tragic Hero* 3:238. A more recent biography agreed that Davis received "inhuman treatment" in prison, and attributed it to "the Malignant Secretary of War, Edwin M. Stanton." Clement Eaton, *Jefferson Davis,* 262.

4. Meigs quoted in Benjamin P. Thomas and Harold M. Hyman, *Stanton: The Life and Times of Lincoln's Secretary of War,* 613.

5. Authorization for chaining Davis in Dana to Miles, May 22, 1865, Ft. Monroe, in *OR,* ser. 2, vol. 8, 1:565; Dana to *New York Sun,* Sept. 3, 1895, in Miles, "My Treatment of Jefferson Davis," 415.

6. Miles, "My Treatment of Jefferson Davis," 415.

7. Captain Titlow to his son, July 4, no year, Roanoke, Va., in Robert McElroy, *Jefferson Davis* 2:527–30; Craven, *Prison Life of Jefferson Davis,* 59.

8. *New York Tribune,* May 27, 1865.

9. *Raleigh* (N.C.) *Daily Sentinel,* Apr. 24, 1869; Foote, *The Civil War* 3:1034, 1049.

10. Miles to Asst. Adj. Gen. Edward D. Townsend, Oct. 2, 1865, Ft. Monroe, Va., in *OR,* ser. 2, vol. 8, 1:761; Craven, *Prison Life of Jefferson Davis,* 40.

11. Dr. Cooper to the AG, U.S. Army, May 9, 1866, Ft. Monroe, Va., enclosed in Miles to AG, U.S. Army, May 10, 1866, Ft. Monroe, in *OR,* ser. 2, vol. 8, 1:908.

12. Extract from *Richmond Times* and *New York World,* May 24, 1866, in Miles to Townsend, May 26, 1866, Ft. Monroe, Va., in *OR,* ser. 2, vol. 8, 1:914–19. Miles also enclosed a story from the *New York Times,* May 24, 1866, and a story about Mrs. Davis from an unidentified newspaper.

13. Miles to Townsend, May 26, 1866, Ft. Monroe, Va., in *OR,* ser. 2, vol. 8, 1:914.

14. Ibid., 919.

15. Barnes to Stanton, June 6, 1866, Washington, D.C., in ibid., 924.

16. Halleck to Miles, May 24, 1865, Richmond, Va., ibid., 570; Stanton to Miles, July 22, 1865, ibid., 710; Craven to Miles, Sept. 1865, Ft. Monroe, Va., ibid., 740.

17. Strode, *Jefferson Davis* 3:501; Bvt. Maj. Charles Muhlenberg to Capt. John McEwan, aide-de-camp and acting asst. adj. gen., Dec. 29, 1865, Ft. Monroe, Va., *OR,* ser. 2, vol. 8, 1:841. Rest of tape incident in Miles to Townsend, Dec. 29, 1865, Ft. Monroe, Va., in ibid., 841.

18. Stanton to Miles, Aug. 2, 1866, Washington, D.C., Miles-Cameron Family Papers; Miles to Stanton, Aug. 24, 1866, Ft. Monroe, Va., *OR*, ser. 2, vol. 8, 1:955; Miles to Howard, Aug. 29, 1866, Washington, D.C., Oliver Otis Howard Papers, Bowdoin College, Brunswick, Maine. The expected trial never took place, and Davis was released on bail from Fort Monroe on May 13, 1867.

19. Halleck to Miles, Jan. 16, 1866, HQ Military Div. of the Pacific, San Francisco, Calif., in Miles-Cameron Family Papers.

20. Editorial in the *Boston Herald* (n.d.), rpt. in (Tucson) *Arizona Daily Star*, Oct. 8, 1887; Miles's date of rank in Miles's personnel file, RAGO, RG 94, NA.

21. Robert M. Utley, *Frontier Regulars: The United States Army and the Indians, 1866–1891*, 10–15.

22. Miles, "My Treatment of Jefferson Davis," 417.

23. Miles, *Serving the Republic*, 102.

24. John R. Kirkland, "Federal Troops in the South Atlantic States during Reconstruction, 1865–1877," 331–32.

25. Miles to Howard, Mar. 8, 1865, Ft. Monroe, Va., in Oliver Otis Howard Papers.

26. Carpenter, *Sword and Olive Branch*, 123.

27. *New York Times*, Aug. 4, 1867.

28. Miles's report to unidentified recipient, Washington, D.C., n.d., quoted in *Raleigh Daily Sentinel*, July 29, 1867.

29. Miles to Howard, Dec. 4, 1867, Raleigh, N.C., *Raleigh Daily Sentinel*, Jan. 4, 1868; and Miles, *Serving the Republic*, 104.

30. *Raleigh Daily Sentinel*, Jan. 4, 1868.

31. Miles to Howard, Dec. 4, 1867, Raleigh, N.C., ibid.

32. James E. Sefton, *The United States Army and Reconstruction, 1867–1877*, 128.

33. Miles's circular no. 13, July 1, 1867, Raleigh, N.C., *Raleigh Daily Sentinel*, July 9, 1867.

34. Ibid.

35. Hugh T. Lefler and Albert R. Newsome, *The History of a Southern State: North Carolina*, 487–89.

36. Miles to Howard, Dec. 4, 1867, Raleigh, N.C., *Raleigh Daily Sentinel*, Jan. 4, 1868.

37. John W. Moore, *History of North Carolina from the Earliest Discoveries to the Present Time*, 325. At the convention there were seventy-eight white native Republicans, sixteen carpetbaggers, thirteen blacks, and thirteen conservatives. Richard L. Zuber, *Jonathan Worth: A Biography of a Southern Unionist*, 281. The 1868 Constitution described in Lefler and Newsome, *History of a Southern State: North Carolina*, 490.

38. Lefler and Newsome, *History of a Southern State: North Carolina*, 484–85. The accomplishments of this legislature are studied in Allan W. Trelease, "Republican Reconstruction in North Carolina: A Roll-Call Analysis of the State House of Representatives, 1868–1870." Holden's detractors discussed in Horace W. Roper, "William Woods Holden: A Political Biography," 284; idem, *William H. Holden: North Carolina's Political Enigma.*

39. Holden to Meade, Sept. 14, 1868, Raleigh, N.C., and Richard Drum, asst. adj. gen., to Holden, Sept. 15, 1868, HQ Dept. of the South, Atlanta, Ga., Letters Sent and Received, Dept. of the South, NA; Kirkland, "Federal Troops in the South Atlantic States," 236.

40. Drum to Miles, Sept. 29, 1868, Atlanta, Ga., and Richard Drum, to Holden, Sept. 15, 1868, HQ Dept. of the South, Atlanta, Ga., Letters Sent and Received, Department of the South, NA.

41. Holden to Miles, Oct. 7, 1868, Raleigh, N.C., and Miles to Holden, Oct. 9, 1868, HQ Dist. of North Carolina, Raleigh; complete copies of both letters in the *Raleigh Daily Sentinel*,

Oct. 10, 1868, and in Miles to Drum, Oct. 9, 1868, Raleigh, N.C., Letters Sent and Received, Dept. of the South, NA.

42. Meade to Grant, Oct. 9, 1868, HQ Dept. of the South, Atlanta, Ga., Letters Sent and Received, Dept. of the South, NA. Col. Theodore Lyman, Meade's aide, recalled that during a wartime outburst of temper, the general's eyeballs "stood out about one inch." Lyman quoted in Freeman Cleaves, *Meade of Gettysburg,* 248.

43. Meade's possible conciliatory gesture was an unsigned telegraph to Miles, Oct. 13, 1868, Goldsboro, N.C., in Letters Sent and Received, Dept. of the South, NA. Miles to Drum, Oct. 22, 1868, Raleigh, N.C., in ibid. Although there is no record of a rapprochement before Meade's death on November 6, 1872, Miles willingly attended Meade's anniversary banquet in 1911 and spoke very highly of him there. Miles, "General Meade Anniversary Banquet," 28–31.

44. Meade's annual report, Oct. 31, 1868, Atlanta, Ga., *Annual Report of the Secretary of War, 1868* 1:81–82, NA (hereafter cited as *SW Annual Report*).

45. Miles to Drum, Sept. 25, 1868, Raleigh, N.C., in Letters Sent and Received, Dept. of the South, NA. Two companies were assigned to Raleigh and Goldsboro; one was located each in Charlotte, Fayetteville, Greensboro, Plymouth, Salisbury, and Weldon.

46. General Orders no. 10, HQ Dist. of North Carolina, Raleigh, Oct. 30, 1868, *Raleigh Daily Sentinel,* Nov. 2, 1868. This order was unusual enough to be mentioned in Sefton, *The United States Army and Reconstruction,* 230.

47. Telegram, Miles to Drum, Nov. 3, 1868, Letters Sent and Received, Dept. of the South, NA; *Raleigh Daily Sentinel,* Nov. 2, 1868. Actually, one incident marred the election: a freedman was killed during a riot at Asheville. Lefler and Newsome, *The History of a Southern State: North Carolina,* 374.

48. Election returns in Lefler and Newsome, *The History of a Southern State: North Carolina,* 374–75; *New York Times,* Nov. 13, 1868.

49. *Raleigh Daily Sentinel,* Nov. 7, 1868.

50. Charles Sumner to Charles Sherman, Aug. 16, 1867, Boston, and Nelson Miles to Charles Sherman, Sept. 6, 1867, Raleigh, N.C., in Johnson, *Unregimented General,* 33–34; *New York Herald,* July 1, 1868.

51. Mary Sherman Miles to John Sherman, Mar. 1879, Washington, D.C.; extensive extract in Johnson, *The Unregimented General,* 215. "Cump" is derived from Sherman's middle name, Tecumpseh.

52. *New York Tribune,* Aug. 3, 1904. Mary Sherman Miles, "What Shall the Soldier's Wife Do?" 1207.

53. A description of the house at 1734 N Street NW, now the headquarters for the General Federation of Women's Clubs, appears in Mildred White Wells, *United in Diversity,* 107–22. *New York Times,* Aug. 3, 1904; *New York Herald,* Aug. 3, 1904; *New York Tribune,* Aug. 3, 1904.

54. *Army and Navy Journal,* July 11, 1868; Meade to Grant, Oct. 9, 1868, HQ Dept. of the South, Atlanta, Ga., Letters Sent and Received, Dept. of the South, NA. General Sherman mentions Mary's letter to him written Oct. 19, 1868, in Sherman to Mary Sherman Miles, Oct. 21, 1868, HQ Military Div. of the Missouri, St. Louis, Miles-Cameron Family Papers.

55. Miles to Sherman, Mar. 12, 1869, Raleigh, N.C., and Sherman to Miles, Mar. 13, 1869, Washington, D.C., both in William T. Sherman Papers, LC; Miles, *Serving the Republic,* 107.

56. Miles, *Serving the Republic,* 108–10. A handbook with detailed information on Fort Leavenworth and all others where Miles served is Robert W. Frazer, *Forts of the West.*

57. Miles, *Serving the Republic,* 111; Miles to Sherman, Nov. 19, 1870, Leavenworth, Kans., William T. Sherman Papers; Frederic Remington, "Colonel Roosevelt's Pride," 321; Miles to

Theophilus Stewart, Aug. 5, 1899, in Theophilus G. Stewart, *Colored Regulars in the United States Army.*

58. Miles to Sherman, Nov. 19, 1879, Leavenworth, Kans., William T. Sherman Papers. In 1900 Cecilia Miles married Capt. Samuel Reber, who had graduated from West Point in 1886. Reber was promoted to colonel in 1916 and was a wireless expert with the Signal Corps until he retired from the army in 1919. He was a vice president of the Radio Corporation of America at the time of his death in 1933. *New York Times,* Apr. 18, 1933.

4. Campaign against the Cheyenne, Kiowa, and Comanche

1. Utley, *Frontier Regulars,* 213–14.

2. *New York Herald,* Sept. 26, 1874 (account written Sept. 5, 1874).

3. Ibid.; Joe F. Taylor, ed., "The Indian Campaign on the Staked Plains, 1874–1875: Military Correspondence from the War Department Adjutant General's Office File 1815–1874," 197; Pohanka, *Nelson A. Miles,* 80; Robert C. Carriker, ed., "Thomas McFadden's Diary of an Indian Campaign, 1874," 200.

4. Carriker, "Thomas McFadden's Diary," 200; Miles, *Serving the Republic,* 124; Alice Blackwood Baldwin, ed., *Memoirs of the Late Frank D. Baldwin, Major General, U.S.A.*

5. *New York Herald,* Sept. 26, 1874.

6. For description and history of Camp Supply, which became Fort Supply in December 1878, see Robert C. Carriker, *Fort Supply, Indian Territory: Frontier Outpost on the Plains. New York Herald,* Sept. 26, 1874.

7. *New York Herald,* Sept. 26, 1874; Carriker, "Thomas McFadden's Diary," 203.

8. *New York Herald,* Sept. 26, 1874;. Miles to asst. adj. gen., Dept. of Mo., Mar. 4, 1875, Ft. Leavenworth, Kans., in Letters Received, AGO, 1780s–1917, RG 94, NA (hereafter cited as Letters Received–AGO).

9. *New York Herald,* Sept. 26, 1874; Baldwin, *Memoirs of the Late Frank D. Baldwin,* 71.

10. Miles to asst. adj. gen., Dept. of Mo., Mar. 4, 1875, Ft. Leavenworth, Kans., Letters Received–AGO.

11. Casualties in *New York Herald,* Sept. 26, 1874, and Carriker, "Thomas McFadden's Diary, 16. Carriker, who edited the diary, noted that the official record listed one soldier and one civilian scout wounded. In all probability, the record should also have included one Delaware scout, who was slightly wounded while fighting. Besides McFadden, the Indian claim of one death appears in James L. Haley, *The Buffalo War,* 137. Miles's report, Sept. 1, 1874, camp on bank of Red River, Tex., in Taylor, "The Indian Campaign on the Staked Plains," 24.

12. Miles to Mary Sherman Miles, Sept. 6, 1874, extract in Johnson, *The Unregimented General,* 54; Miles to asst. adj. gen., Dept. of Mo., Mar. 4, 1875, Ft. Leavenworth, Kans., Letters Received–AGO. Although the rebellious Indians usually sought refuge in the canyons bounding the Staked Plains, Maj. William R. Price believed they also camped "on the Staked Plains adjacent to those streams [two forks on the Main Red River],—if pressed they will go further out on the plains." Taylor, "The Indian Campaign on the Staked Plains," 55. Utley estimated that by the end of August "the enemy consisted of some 1,800 Cheyennes, 2,000 Commanches, and 1,000 Kiowas, mounting in all perhaps 1,200 fighting men. They moved in large encampments along the twisted breaks surrounding the headquarters of the Washita and the various forks of the Red, in the Texas Panhandle." Utley, *Frontier Regulars,* 221–23.

13. Carriker, "Thomas McFadden's Diary," 210–13; Miles to asst. adj. gen., Dept. of Mo., Mar.

4, 1875, Ft. Leavenworth, Kans., Letters Received–AGO.

14. Miles's movements in Miles to asst. adj. gen., Dept. of Mo., Mar. 4, 1875, Ft. Leavenworth, Kans., Letter Received–AGO; Carriker, "Thomas McFadden's Diary," 211–13. The Indians broke off the siege because of the approach of Price's column. Capt. Wyllys Lyman's report of the wagon train fight in Lyman to Baird, Sept. 25, 1874, camp on Dry Fork of Washita River, *Army and Navy Journal,* Oct. 31, 1874, 186–87.

15. Price to Gen. Robert Williams, asst. adj. gen., Dept. of the Mo., Sept. 23, 1874, Canadian River, in Taylor, "The Indian Campaign on the Staked Plains," 46–55.

16. Miles to asst. adj. gen., Dept. of Mo., Mar. 4, 1875, Ft. Leavenworth, Kans., Letters Received–AGO; Miles to Mary Sherman Miles, Sept. 18, 1874, camp on Washita, extract in Johnson, *The Unregimented General,* 55–56.

17. Miles to asst. adj. gen., Dept. of Mo., Mar. 4, 1875, Ft. Leavenworth, Kans., Letters Received–AGO (in this report, Miles misspelled "Henely" as "Hendy"); *New York Herald,* Sept. 26, 1874; Chafee quoted in Maj. George W. Baird, "General Miles' Indian Campaigns," 353.

18. Sheridan to Pope, Aug. 24, 1874, Chicago, in Philip H. Sheridan Papers, LC.

19. Miles to Pope, Aug. 31, 1874, expedition camp on Red River, Tex., entire report printed in *New York Herald,* Sept. 9, 1874; Baird, "General Miles' Indian Campaigns," 351.

20. Miles to Mary, Sept. 14, 1874, camp on Washita, extract from Johnson, *Unregimented General,* 55; Carriker, *Fort Supply, Indian Territory,* 99–103. After being moved from its original position to a point near the Sweetwater Creek, the cantonment was designated Fort Elliot on February 3, 1875. Frazer, *Forts of the West,* 149.

21. Miles to asst. adj. gen., Dept. of Mo., Mar. 4, 1875, Ft. Leavenworth, Kans., Letters Received–AGO, mentions supply problems in October and on November 8; the report also contains Miles's recommendations. Miles to Mary Sherman Miles, Dec. 2, 1874, camp on Washita, extract in Johnson, *Unregimented General,* 66.

22. Details of Satanta's confrontation with Sherman in Utley, *Frontier Regulars,* 210. Miles to Sherman, Sept. 27, 1874, camp on the Canadian, William T. Sherman Papers. Miles to asst. adj. gen., Dept. of Mo., Mar. 4, 1875, Ft. Leavenworth, Kans., Letters Received–AGO.

23. Sheridan to Lt. Col. Robert Williams, asst. adj. gen., Dept. of the Mo., Oct. 6, 1874, Chicago, in Philip H. Sheridan Papers.

24. Utley, *Frontier Regulars,* 226. Details of Mackenzie's victory appear in Sherman to Gen. Edward Townsend, Oct. 14, 1874, St. Louis, Mo., in Taylor, "The Indian Campaign on the Staked Plains," 75. For a biography of Mackenzie, see J'Nell L. Pate, "Ronald S. Mackenzie," in Hutton, *Soldiers West.*

25. Miles to asst. adj. gen., Dept. of Mo., Mar. 4, 1875, Ft. Leavenworth, Kans., Letters Received–AGO; *Cheyenne Daily Leader,* Oct. 24, 1874.

26. Miles to asst. adj. gen., Dept. of Mo., Mar. 4, 1875, Ft. Leavenworth, Kans., Letters Received–AGO; Baldwin, *Memoirs of the Late Frank D. Baldwin,* 71–75.

27. Baldwin, *Memoirs of the Late Frank D. Baldwin,* 76; Mrs. Frank C. Montgomery, "Fort Wallace and Its Relation to the Frontier," 257–61; Grace Meredith, *Girl Captives of the Cheyennes,* 59. Meredith's account should be extremely reliable, since she is a niece of the sisters and used Catherine's notes as the basis for her history.

28. Miles, *Serving the Republic,* 127–28. Miles did not realize that the girls had been left alone on the prairie. He attributed their poor condition to the hardships they endured as their captors sought to escape the army and their consumption of the "coarse food" that sustained the Indians. Carriker, "Thomas McFadden's Diary," 224.

29. Miles to asst. adj. gen., Dept. of Mo., Mar. 4, 1875, Ft. Leavenworth, Kans., in Letters Received–AGO.

30. Sheridan to Pope, Dec. 17, 1874, Chicago, Ill., in Philip H. Sheridan Papers.

31. Miles to Sherman, Dec. 27, 1874, camp near Adobe Walls, William T. Sherman Papers; *New York Herald,* Jan. 11, 1877.

32. Miles to Mary Sherman Miles, Dec. 2, 1874, camp on Washita, extract in Johnson, *Unregimented General,* 66; report of girls in White Bird's camp, Miles to asst. adj. gen., Dept. of Mo., Dec. 5, 1874, camp on Washita River, in Taylor, "The Indian Campaign on the Staked Plains," 128–29; Miles, *Serving the Republic,* 128. Haley, *Buffalo War,* 202–3, wrote that the two older girls had been sexually abused. He based this on a report written by Indian agent John D. Miles immediately after the girls were rescued. At that time, his wife had questioned the two sisters and provided her husband with the details of numerous instances of sexual abuse.

33. Miles to Mary Sherman Miles, Dec. 17, 1874, camp on White Deer Creek, in Johnson, *Unregimented General,* 69.

34. Miles to Mary Sherman Miles, Jan. 11, 1874, camp on Elm Fork, in ibid. Miles to asst. adj. gen., Dept. of Mo., Mar. 4, 1875, Ft. Leavenworth, Kans., in Letters Received–AGO; *Topeka Commonwealth,* Jan. 23, 1875, *Army and Navy Journal,* Feb. 27, 1875, 453–54.

35. Miles, *Serving the Republic,* 128; Meredith, *Girl Captives of the Cheyennes,* 67.

36. Meredith, *Girl Captives of the Cheyennes,* 70. Miles, *Unregimented General,* 129, provides one version of the note; another is Montgomery, "Fort Wallace and Its Relation to the Frontier," 26.

37. Neill to Pope, Feb. 22, 1875, Cheyenne Agency, Indian Territory, via Wichita, Kans., Feb. 25, 1875, and details of the welcome of the German girls in Montgomery, *Fort Wallace,* 264–65.

38. Neill to asst. adj. gen., Dept. of Mo., Mar. 7, 1875, camp near Cheyenne Agency, in Taylor, "The Indian Campaign on the Staked Plains," 190–92. Utley, *Frontier Regulars,* 223, explained that "the Indians, also soaked by the storms, long remembered the next few weeks as 'the wrinkled-hand chase.'" Similarly, Haley, *The Buffalo War,* 188, explained that the rebellious Indians, who were "constantly pounded by the frigid northers with hardly any days to dry out, miserably and aptly named [it] the "wrinkled-hand chase."

39. Montgomery, "Fort Wallace and Its Relation to the Frontier," 267.

40. Miles's note to Stone Calf quoted in ibid., 264. Sheridan quoted in Carl Rister, *Border Command: General Philip Sheridan in the West,* 195–96. Rister says there were seventy-five prisoners, as does Miles, *Serving the Republic,* 130; Utley, *Frontier Regulars,* 233, mentions seventy-four; Paul A. Hutton, *Phil Sheridan and His Army,* 258, mentions seventy-two; Haley, *Buffalo War,* 220, mentions seventy-seven. The girls "pointed out three of the guilty ones." Meredith, *Girl Captives of the Cheyennes,* 108.

41. Mention of the Sappa Creek "massacre" in Haley, *The Buffalo War,* 219; an account of Sappa Creek found in Utley, *Frontier Regulars,* 230. Pope to Townsend, June 12, 1875, Ft. Leavenworth, Kans., in Taylor, "The Indian Campaign on the Staked Plains," 236–37. In an editor's note, Joe Taylor concedes that the battle "has been the source of controversy." Although Taylor cites reports that support Lieutenant Henely's account of the battle, he mentions an article that he says describes the battle as "a massacre of innocent Cheyenne Indians going peaceably north to join their northern kin." Ibid., 221n.

42. Pope to Drum, Apr. 7, 1875, Ft. Leavenworth, Kans., Letters Received–AGO; Richard N. Ellis, *General Pope and U.S. Indian Policy,* 190.

43. Mackenzie to Sheridan, Apr. 17, 1875, quoted in Haley, *The Buffalo War,* 206–7; Miles to

Sherman, Apr. 26, 1875, Ft. Leavenworth, Kans., in William T. Sherman Papers.

44. Miles, *Serving the Republic,* 132–4.

5. CAMPAIGN AGAINST THE SIOUX

1. John Sherman to Miles, Feb. 26, 1876, Wash., D.C., Miles-Cameron Family Papers.

2. Utley, *Frontier Regulars,* 252, 273.

3. Miles, *Serving the Republic,* 143.

4. Ibid.; *New York Herald,* Aug. 27, 1876. The commander of the 5th Cavalry, until his retirement on July 1, 1876, had been Col. (Bvt. Maj. Gen.) William H. Emory.

5. Miles to Mary Sherman Miles, July 29, 1876, Yellowstone River, and Aug. 4, 1876, camp opposite Rosebud, Mont., in Johnson, *Unregimented General,* 89, 93–94; *New York Herald,* Aug. 11, 1876.

6. Miles to Mary Sherman Miles, Aug. 4, 1876, camp opposite Rosebud, Mont., and Aug. 7, 1876, camp at the mouth of Rosebud, in Johnson, *Unregimented General,* 94–95; *New York Herald,* Aug. 19, 1876.

7. John C. Finerty, *War Path and Bivouac, or the Conquest of the Sioux,* chap. 20. American Horse and another warrior, plus three Indian women and a child, were killed. Ibid., 191. Crook lost three men and eight were wounded, including Lt. Adolphus H. von Leuttwitz, 3d Cavalry, who lost his leg. Utley, *Frontier Regulars,* 271.

8. Frazer, *Forts of the West,* 79–80, 82, 183.

9. Sheridan's revised strategy in Hutton, *Phil Sheridan and His Army,* 322.

10. Miles to Sherman, June 15, 1876, Ft. Leavenworth, Kans., in William T. Sherman Papers.

11. Miles to Mary Sherman Miles, Jan. 5, 1875, mouth of the Tule, excerpt in Johnson, *Unregimented General,* 70; Miles to asst. adj. gen., Dept. of Mo., Mar. 4, 1875, Ft. Leavenworth, Kans., Letters Received–AGO. Miles mentions his "system of espionage" in *Serving the Republic,* 126.

12. Miles mentions scouts in *Serving the Republic,* 145. John S. Gray, "What Made Johnnie Bruguier Run?"; Luther S. Kelly, *Memoirs of Luther S. Kelly; New York Herald,* Nov. 30, 1876.

13. Baird, "General Miles's Indian Campaigns," 354; *New York Herald,* Nov. 6, 1876.

14. *New York Herald,* Nov. 6, 1876; Gray, "What Made Johnnie Bruguier Run?" 42–46. The two chiefs from Standing Rock, Long Feather and Bear Face, were on a peace mission trying to induce Sitting Bull to return to the agency. Miles, in *Serving the Republic,* 148, said he had 394 men; the *New York Herald,* Nov. 6, 1876, said he had 398, as did Baird in "General Miles's Indian Campaigns," 355.

15. Baird, "General Miles's Indian Campaigns," 355; Miles, *Serving the Republic,* 148–50; Miles to asst. adj. gen., Dept. of Dakota, Oct. 25, 1876, camp opposite Cabin Creek on the Yellowstone, Letters Sent, Yellowstone Command, Records of U.S. Army Continental Commands, 1821–1920, vol. 5, 1876–77, RG 343 (hereafter cited as Yellowstone Command); Miles to Mary Sherman Miles, Oct. 25, 1876, Camp Fire on the Yellowstone, excerpt in Johnson, *Unregimented General,* 118; Kelly, *Memoirs,* 148–49. Sitting Bull was forty-five. Stanley Vestal, *Sitting Bull, Champion of the Sioux,* 3; Robert M. Utley, *The Lance and the Shield: The Life and Times of Sitting Bull;* and Utley, "Sitting Bull."

16. *New York Herald,* Nov. 6, 1876. Here the reporter refers to "new arms" used by the army, indicating that they may also have been better armed than Custer's command. *Army and Navy Journal,* Feb. 10, 1877, 431.

17. *Army and Navy Journal,* Feb. 10, 1877, 431; *New York Herald,* Nov. 6, 1876; Miles, *Serving the Republic,* 151–52; Edwin M. Brown Diaries, 1876–77, Montana Historical Society, Helena.

18. *Army and Navy Journal,* Feb. 10, 1877, 431; *New York Herald,* Nov. 6, 1876; Miles to asst. adj. gen., Dept. of Dakota, Oct. 27, 1876, Yellowstone Command.

19. Ibid.

20. Miles to asst. adj. gen., Dept. of Dakota, Oct. 27, 1876, Yellowstone Command; Miles to Sherman, Oct. 27, 1876, HQ Fifth Inf., Yellowstone, William T. Sherman Papers.

21. *Cheyenne Daily Leader,* Nov. 16, 1876; Harry H. Anderson, "Nelson A. Miles and the Sioux War of 1876–77," 26.

22. Anderson, "Nelson A. Miles and the Sioux War," 26.

23. Miles to asst. adj. gen., Dept. of Dakota, Oct. 28, 1876, Yellowstone Command.

24. Miles to asst. adj. gen., Dept. of Dakota, Nov. 6, 1876, Yellowstone Command.

25. *New York Herald,* Feb. 19, 1877.

26. Miles to asst. adj. gen., Dept. of Dakota, Nov. 18, 1877, Yellowstone Command.

27. Miles to asst. adj. gen., Dept. of Dakota, Dec. 21, 1876, Yellowstone Command. The story of the Frenchman identified at Beure (probably a phonetic spelling of "Bruguier") in *New York Herald,* Feb. 19, 1877; and Gray, "What Made Johnnie Bruguier Run?" 45.

28. *New York Herald,* Feb. 19, 1877; Miles to Baldwin, Dec. 11, 1876, Yellowstone Command; Edwin M. Brown Diaries.

29. *New York Herald,* Jan. 16, 1877; Miles, *Serving the Republic,* 146–47; Pond, "Major-General Nelson A. Miles," 568–69.

30. Miles to Mary Sherman Miles, July 29, 1876, Yellowstone River, excerpt in Johnson, *Unregimented General,* 146–47. Perhaps Miles should have aimed his criticism at the secretary of war, who assumed the power to run the army. Robert G. Athearn, *William Tecumseh Sherman and the Settlement of the West,* 258.

31. MacKenzie to Crook, commanding Powder River expedition, Nov. 26, 1876, camp on Powder River, in *Army and Navy Journal,* Dec. 16, 1876, 293; Utley, *Frontier Regulars,* 275–76.

32. *New York Herald,* Feb. 19, 1877; Edwin M. Brown Diaries; Harry A. Anderson, "Indian Peace Talkers and the Conclusion of the Sioux War of 1876," 235–37.

33. Miles to L. H. Carpenter, agent of the Crow Indians, Mont., and Miles to Terry, commanding Dept. of Dakota, Dec. 17, 23, 1876, Yellowstone Command.

34. Miles to Terry, Dec. 17, 1876, Yellowstone Command; Kelly, *Memoirs,* 166.

35. *New York Herald,* Feb. 16, 1877; Miles to Mary Sherman Miles, Mar. 15, 1877, HQ Yellowstone Command, quoted in Johnson, *Unregimented General,* 139. Baldwin estimated that Miles had two hundred men. Baldwin, *Memoirs of the Late Frank D. Baldwin,* 79.

36. Miles, *Serving the Republic,* 153; Kelly, *Memoirs,* 167; Anderson, "Nelson A. Miles and the Sioux War," 27.

37. Kelly, *Memoirs,* 167; *New York Herald,* June 4, 1877; Miles, *Serving the Republic,* 145. Kelly identified one of the Johnsons as "liver-eating Jonson"; Jerome A. Greene, *Yellowstone Command,* 164, identified another as George Johnson.

38. Kelly, *Memoirs,* 168–72.

39. Details of the Battle of Wolf Mountain from the following eyewitness accounts: Miles, *Serving the Republic,* 154–56; Baldwin, *Memoirs of the Late Frank D. Baldwin,* 79–89; Kelly, *Memoirs,* 172–75; and Diary of Edwin M. Brown. Also consulted: Don Rickey, Jr., "Battle of Wolf Mountain"; Anderson, "Nelson A. Miles and the Sioux War," 25–27, 32; Mari Sandoz, *Crazy Horse, The Strong Man of the Oglalas,* 352–53.

40. Sheridan to AG, U.S. Army, Feb. 6, 1877, Chicago, Ill., HQ Military Div. of the Missouri, Letters Received–AGO.

41. Details of battle and official casualties in ibid. Here Miles listed three men killed, but in Rickey, "Battle of Wolf Mountain," 52, it is explained that Miles included a herder killed on January 3 in his report. *New York Herald,* Feb. 6, 1877, names four soldiers who were killed during the expedition. If so, Yellowstone Kelly's report that two soldiers were killed while rounding up oxen would be correct, instead of the one reported by Miles. Trumpeter Brown stated that six slightly wounded soldiers were not included in the report. From signs on the battlefield, Brown estimated that fifteen Indians were killed and twenty-five wounded. Diary of Edwin M. Brown. Brown also mentions being welcomed by the band. Number of miles marched in Baldwin, *Memoirs of the Late Frank D. Baldwin,* 86.

42. Baird, "General Miles's Indian Campaigns," 357; Miles to secretary of war, Feb. 20, 1877, Yellowstone Command. The letter was simply addressed to the secretary of war, since the matter would be decided by a new secretary appointed by President-elect Rutherford B. Hayes.

43. Anderson, "Nelson A. Miles and the Sioux War," 32. Anderson contradicts Vestal, *Sitting Bull,* 212, who claims that Sitting Bull could not find Crazy Horse's camp.

44. *New York Herald,* May 31, 1877; Sheridan to AG, U.S. Army, Feb. 6, 1877, Chicago, Ill., HQ Military Div. of the Missouri, Letters Received–AGO.

45. Miles to asst. adj. gen., Dept. of Dakota, Saint Paul, Minn., Dec. 27, 1877, HQ Dist. of the Yellowstone, Fort Keogh, Mont., in Montana Historical Society (hereafter cited as Miles, 1877 Report); Sandoz, *Crazy Horse,* 357–58.

46. Miles, 1877 Report.

47. Ibid.; Miles to Sherman, Apr. 8, 1877, Tongue River, Mont., in William T. Sherman Papers. Further information on Indian efforts to end the Sioux War in Anderson, "Indian Peace-Talkers and the Conclusion of the Sioux War," 233–54.

48. Miles, 1877 Report; Miles to Mary Sherman Miles, Apr. 15, 1877, HQ Yellowstone Command, Mont., in Johnson, *Unregimented General,* 169; *New York Herald,* May 31, 1877; Sheridan to AG, U.S. Army, Feb. 6, 1877, Chicago, Ill., HQ Military Div. of the Mo., Letters Received–AGO.

49. Hump is identified as a Cheyenne chief in both *New York Herald,* June 4, 1877, and *Cheyenne Daily Leader,* June 20, 1877.

50. Cheyenne Daily Leader, June 20, 1877. Hump is identified as a Sioux in *Army and Navy Journal,* June 16, 1877, 723.

51. Lt. Alfred F. Fuller, Second Cavalry, wounded in the Lame Deer Fight, was sent by steamer from Tongue River to Bismarck. Here he told a reporter that twenty-five mounted infantrymen fought in the battle and recounted other details of the fight. *Cheyenne Daily Leader,* May 29, 1877. Other eyewitness accounts: a noncommissioned officer in the Second Cavalry in *New York Herald,* June 11, 1877; Miles, 1877 Report; Miles, *Serving the Republic,* 161–63; Baldwin, *Memoirs of the Late Frank D. Baldwin,* 90–95; and *Army and Navy Journal,* June 16, 1877, 723. A complete summary of the battle plus three contemporary accounts in Gray, "The Lame Deer Fight."

52. "Explicit Instructions" in Miles, 1877 Report. This is supported by an interview with Lieutenant Fuller, who stated that "Gen. Miles had given imperative orders forbidding the harm of women and children, and caused his interpreters to shout as they advanced that all who surrendered would be protected." Quoted in Gray, "The Lame Deer Fight Ends the Sioux War," 19. A brief description of some officers in the Second Cavalry in *New York Herald,* Apr. 25, 1877.

53. Miles, *Serving the Republic,* 162, credited Captain Wheelan with shooting Lame Deer, while the *New York Herald,* June 11, 1877, credits Private Davis, Second Cavalry; but the news-

paper probably attributed the shooting of Lame Deer to the private because it was he who took the chief's war bonnet and gave it to Miles, which could lead spectators to assume that he killed Lame Deer. Story of the pack mules in *Army and Navy Journal,* June 16, 1877, 723. Reported numbers of Indian dead vary. The most reliable count is in Miles, 1877 Report. Although Miles did not include this incident in his annual report, he included it in Miles to asst. adj. gen., Dept. of Dakota, May 16, 1877, cantonment at Tongue River, Mont., in Letters Received–AGO.

54. Number of miles marched in Baldwin, *Memoirs of the Late Frank D. Baldwin,* 94.

55. Miles to Mary Sherman Miles, Apr. 15, 1877, HQ Yellowstone Command, Mont., in Johnson, *Unregimented General,* 169–70; *Cheyenne Daily Leader,* June 1, 1877.

56. Ibid. General Sheridan quoted in Hutton, *Phil Sheridan and His Army,* 327. For a review of Crook's campaign of 1876 and a discussion of his ability, see James T. King, "Needed: A Re-evaluation of General George Crook."

57. Miles to Sherman, Mar. 29, 1877, Tongue River, Mont., in William T. Sherman Papers; *New York Herald,* Apr. 7, 1877.

58. John Sherman to Miles, Apr. 30, 1877, Washington, D.C., in Miles-Cameron Family Papers; *Cheyenne Daily Leader,* Mar. 15, 1877.

59. Miles, *Serving the Republic,* 162.

60. Sherman quoted in *Cheyenne Daily Leader,* Nov. 16, 1876; excerpt of letter, Maj. Alfred L. Hough to his wife, Jan. 11, 1877, cantonment at Tongue River, in Anderson, "Nelson A. Miles and the Sioux War," 25–27, 32.

61. Unnamed Muddy Creek veteran's letter in *Army and Navy Journal,* June 16, 1877, 723. Finerty, *War-Path and Bivouac,* 249–50.

62. *Cheyenne Daily Leader,* June 20, 1871; Miles, 1877 Report, Dec. 27, 1877, Ft. Keogh; Baird, "General Miles's Indian Campaigns," 365.

63. Ami Frank Mulford, *In the Seventh United States Cavalry: Custer's Favorite Regiment,* 95–96.

64. Miles to Mary Sherman Miles, Apr. 5, 1877, HQ Yellowstone Command, in Johnson, *Unregimented General,* 168–69; Baird, "General Miles's Indian Campaigns," 360.

65. Baird, "General Miles's Indian Campaigns," 360.

66. Sherman to Secretary of War George W. McCrary, July 17, 1877, n.p., excerpt in Miles, *Serving the Republic,* 166; General Terry's report, Nov. 12, 1877, HQ Dept. of Dakota, U.S. Sec. of War, Annual Report for 1877, 1:499.

6. Miles and the Nez Perce

1. Miles, *Serving the Republic,* 171, 181.

2. Details of the flight of the Nez Perce in Merrill D. Beal, *"I Will Fight No More Forever": Chief Joseph and the Nez Perce War.* Also see Alvin M. Josephy, *The Nez Perce Indians and the Opening of the Northwest,* and Mark H. Brown, *The Flight of the Nez Perce.* Chief Joseph's account of the war is in Chief Joseph, "An Indian's View of Indian Affairs." Howard's account of the war is in Oliver O. Howard, *Nez Perce Joseph.* A recent account is David Lavender's *Let Me Be Free: The Nez Perce Tragedy.*

Generals Sheridan and Sherman crossed a spot on the Black Tail Deer Creek on August 16, 1877, where the Nez Perce would kill a man and scatter his party a few days later. William Sherman and Philip Henry Sheridan, *Travel Accounts of General William T. Sherman to Spokane Falls, Washington Territory, in the Summers of 1877 and 1883,* 112.

3. Miles, 1877 Report, 12. Rumors of Sturgis's resentment in Mulford, *In the Seventh United States Cavalry,* 83.

4. Howard to Miles, Sept. 12, 1877, Clark's Fort, Mont., in *SW Annual Report for 1877* 1:514.

5. Miles, 1877 Report, 13. Estimate of number of men commanded by Miles was 319 mounted men (*Chicago Times,* Nov. 27, 1877) and 40 foot soldiers (Henry Romeyn, "The Capture of Chief Joseph and the Nez Percé Indians," 286); Lieutenant Maus brings the number to 360.

6. Miles, *Serving the Republic,* 174–75; Miles, 1877 Report, 13.

7. Miles, *Serving the Republic,* 176; Kelly, *Memoirs of Luther S. Kelly,* 191. Numbers in the attack force and ground covered in an interview with Miles; *Chicago Times,* Nov. 27, 1877.

8. Nelson C. Titus, "The Last Stand of the Nez Perces," 148; Lucullus McWhorter, *Yellow Wolf: His Own Story,* 204.

9. Sturgis's note quoted in Howard, *Nez Perce Joseph,* 263. *San Francisco Chronicle,* Oct. 4, 1877; entire article appears in Brown, *The Flight of the Nez Perce,* 366.

10. McWhorter, *Yellow Wolf,* 204–5; Kelly, *Memoirs,* 191–92.

11. McWhorter, *Yellow Wolf,* 205.

12. Miles, *Serving the Republic,* 176–77. Baird, like Miles, believed "The surprise was complete." Baird, "General Miles's Indian Campaigns," 363.

13. *New York Herald,* Oct. 11, 1877. The correspondent interviewed each man separately at Fort Benton, Montana, then checked their accounts with one another and the official report to ensure the accuracy of each story. A picture of Miles taken in 1877 appears in Kelly, *Memoirs,* 176.

14. *New York Herald,* Oct. 11, 1877.

15. Joseph, "An Indian's View of Indian Affairs," 428. Joseph believed seventy warriors escorted the women and children, while Romeyn, in "The Capture of Chief Joseph," 287, believed there were fifty or sixty warriors.

16. Joseph, "An Indian's View of Indian Affairs," 428.

17. Brown, *Flight of the Nez Perce,* 391–96; Josephy, *The Nez Perce Indians and the Opening of the Northwest,* 619.

18. Romeyn, "The Capture of Chief Joseph," 287; Miles to Terry, Oct. 17, 1877, camp on Squaw Creek, Letters Received–AGO. Capt. Myles Moylan, Seventh Cavalry, reported 115 men from his regiment fought the Nez Perce. Brown, *Flight of the Nez Perce,* 380. Brown states that there were 125 men from the Second Cavalry and 90 mounted men, plus 40 men on foot, from the Fifth Infantry.

19. Romeyn, "The Capture of Chief Joseph," 288; Lt. Thomas M. Woodruff to his mother, Oct. 15, 1877, on board steamer *General Meade* near Fort Peck, Mont., in Montana Historical Society (hereafter cited as Woodruff Letter); Miles, *Personal Recollections,* 271; *New York Herald,* Oct. 11, 1877.

20. Henry Tilton [Remson], "After the Nez Perces," 403; Miles, *Personal Recollections,* 273; Kelly, *Memoirs,* 193–95.

21. Tilton, "After the Nez Perces," 403; *New York Herald,* Oct. 11, 1877.

22. Miles, 1877 Report, 15.

23. Ibid.; Woodruff Letter; Romeyn, "The Capture of Chief Joseph, 288–89.

24. Romeyn, "The Capture of Chief Joseph," 288–89. The only exception was when "One sergeant of the cavalry who, remembering Little (Big) Horn, fired on an approaching Indian with his revolver and was killed because he refused to surrender." Carter's force consisted of fifteen men from Company L and ten men from Company F, Fifth Infantry, plus "two or three odd men." Woodruff Letter. One of the "odd" men could have been the sergeant from the Seventh Cavalry. Chief Joseph, "An Indian's View of Indian Affairs," 428.

25. Kelly, *Memoirs,* 192–93; *New York Herald,* Oct. 11, 1877; Romeyn, "The Capture of Chief Joseph," 288.

26. Miles, *Personal Recollections,* 272; Miles to General Howard, General Sturgis, or Maj. David H. Brotherton, Sept. 30, 1877, camp near the Bear Paw Mountains, in *SW Annual Report, 1877* 1:512.

27. Miles to Terry, Oct. 3, 1877, camp near the Bear Paw Mountains, *New York Herald,* Oct. 8, 1877.

28. Tilton, "After the Nez Perces," 403; McWhorter, *Yellow Wolf: His Own Story,* 201; Miles to Terry, Oct. 3, 1877, camp near the Bear Paw Mountains, in *New York Herald,* Oct. 8, 1877. Chief Joseph recalled that eighteen warriors and three women were killed during the first twenty-four hours; "An Indian's View of Indian Affairs," 428.

29. Tilton, "After the Nez Perces," 403. The Nez Perce used buffalo chips for fuel. McWhorter, *Yellow Wolf: His Own Story,* 204.

30. Romeyn, "The Capture of Chief Joseph," 290; Baird, "General Miles's Indian Campaigns," 364; McWhorter, *Yellow Wolf: His Own Story,* 220.

31. Sioux response to news of the Nez Perce battle in John P. Turner, *The North-West Mounted Police, 1873–93* 1:340; *Cheyenne Daily Leader,* Oct. 6, 1877.

32. Turner, *The North-West Mounted Police* 1:341.

33. Ibid.

34. Tilton, "After the Nez Perces," 403; Mulford, *In the Seventh United States Cavalry,* 123; Miles to Mary Sherman Miles, Oct. 14, 1877, HQ Dist. of the Yellowstone, Missouri River, opposite Lynn Creek, entire letter in Johnson, *The Unregimented General,* 207.

35. Miles's scouts could speak "some Chinook." Miles, *Personal Recollections,* 274. Chinook "jargon . . . was not prevalent among the Nez Perces, and only an occasional member of the war party understood it." McWhorter, *Yellow Wolf: His Own Story,* 214. Details of the opening parley in Chief Joseph, "An Indian's View of Indian Affairs," 428–29; Tilton, "After the Nez Perces," 403; and Romeyn, "The Capture of Chief Joseph," 290. Interview of Lovell H. Jerome by Robert Bruce, "Jerome's Own Story," in Chester A. Fee, *Chief Joseph,* app. 2, 338.

36. Fee, *Chief Joseph,* 338; Miles, *Personal Recollections,* 274.

37. Fee, *Chief Joseph,* 338; Miles, 1877 Report, 16.

38. Miles, 1877 Report, 16; Miles, *Personal Recollections,* 274; Fee, *Chief Joseph,* 338.

39. Miles to Mary Sherman Miles, Oct. 3, 1877, camp near Bear Paw Mountains, entire letter in Johnson, *Unregimented General,* 203; Lucullus V. McWhorter, *Hear Me, My Chief! Nez Perce History and Legend,* 489.

40. McWhorter, *Hear Me, My Chief!* 496; Charles E. S. Wood, "The Pursuit and Capture of Chief Joseph," in Fee, *Chief Joseph,* app. 1, 322. Wood and Howard's son, Guy Howard, were the general's two aides. Other details of the march to Miles's camp in Howard's Supplementary Report of the Non-Treaty Nez Perce's Campaign, Dec. 26, 1877, HQ Dept. of the Columbia, in *SW Annual Report, 1877* 1:629 (hereafter cited as Howard's Supplementary Report).

41. Howard's Supplementary Report, 629–30; Wood, "The Pursuit and Capture of Chief Joseph," 322.

42. Joseph, "An Indian's View of Indian Affairs," 429.

43. Ibid.; McWhorter, *Hear Me, My Chief!* 489–90.

44. Oliver O. Howard, *My Life and Experiences among Our Hostile Indians,* 300; Miles, 1877 Report, 16–17.

45. Howard to Col. C. H. Larrabee, Dec. 4, 1877, n.p., in Howard Papers; Miles, *Personal Recollections,* 275; Mulford, *In the Seventh United States Cavalry,* 132; Romeyn, "Capture of Chief Joseph," 291; Baird, "General Miles's Indian Campaigns," 365; Miles's casualties in Miles, 1877 Report, 14–15.

46. Mulford, *In the Seventh United States Cavalry,* 124–25. McWhorter, *Yellow Wolf: His Own Story,* 225; Miles to asst. adj. gen., Dept. of Dakota, St. Paul, Minn., Oct. 6, 1877, camp near Bear Paw Mountains, Letters Received–AGO.

47. *New York Herald,* Oct. 22, 1877; Romeyn, "Capture of Chief Joseph," 291.

48. Tilton, "After the Nez Perces," 403; Romeyn, "The Capture of Chief Joseph," 291. An enlisted man shot through the hips died as he was transferred from the ambulance to the steamer.

49. Romeyn, "The Capture of Chief Joseph," 291, although Romeyn did not mention Fort Rice. Mulford, *The Seventh United States Cavalry,* 131, listed the fort as the destination for some of the cavalrymen. Tilton, "After the Nez Perces," 404; Miles, *Serving the Republic,* 180.

50. Miles, *Serving the Republic,* 180–81.

51. Howard to Miles, Oct. 7, 1877, battlefield at Eagle Creek near Bear Paw, *SW Annual Report, 1877* 1:631.

52. Report to Carl Schurz, secretary of interior to Pres. Rutherford B. Hayes, Feb. 21, 1881, Washington, D.C., in Letters Received–AGO; Chief Joseph, "An Indian's View of Indian Affairs," 430.

53. Joseph, "An Indian's View of Indian Affairs," 430. Romeyn noted that 418 Nez Perce surrendered at Bear Paw; "After the Nez Perce," 291. The increase of thirteen prisoners is not explained but is discussed in McWhorter, *Hear Me, My Chief!* 530.

54. McWhorter, *Hear Me, My Chief!* 530; Chief Joseph, "An Indian's View of Indian Affairs," 431.

55. Reuben James writing for Chief Joseph, June 30, 1880, Oakland Agency, I.T., in Howard Papers.

56. Howard to Chief Joseph, July 20, 1880, n.p., Dept. of the Columbia, in Howard Papers.

57. Miles, 1877 Report, 17.

58. Sherman to General Townsend, Oct. 10, 1877, n.p., quoted in Beal, *"I Will Fight No More Forever,"* 266; Sherman to Howard, Dec. 12, 1877, Washington, D.C., in Howard Papers.

59. Baird to Miles, July 22, 1878, HQ District of Yellowstone, July 27, 1878, Ft. Keogh, Mont., Howard Papers; Sheridan's endorsement, Aug. 18, 1878, HQ Military Div. of the Mo., Chicago, RAGO, NA.

60. Joseph, "An Indian's View of Indian Affairs," 431.

61. Miles to President Hayes, with a copy to Secretary Carl Schurz, Jan. 19, 1881, Washington, D.C., in RAGO, NA.

62. Schurz to President Hayes, Feb. 21, 1881, Washington, D.C., in RAGO, NA.

63. Besides Miles, some others who fought for the Nez Perce included Charles Wood, the Presbyterian Church, and the Indian Rights Association. Beal, *"I Will Fight No More Forever,"* 288–94; John Keegan, *Fields of Battle: The Wars for North America,* 310.

64. Utley, *Frontier Regulars,* 319.

65. Miles to Terry, Oct. 5, 1877, camp on Eagle Creek, Mont., in *SW Annual Report, 1877* 1:515.

66. General Orders No. 3, HQ Dist. of the Yellowstone, Oct. 7, 1877, in the field, camp near Bear Paw Mountains, in *SW Annual Report, 1877* 1:632; Miles to Mary Sherman Miles, Oct. 14, 1877, Missouri River opposite Lynn Creek, in Johnson, *Unregimented General,* 207.

67. Miles reiterated Howard's complaints contained in Howard to Miles, Oct. 25, 1877, Cedar Rapids, Iowa, then answered them in Miles to Howard, Jan. 8, 1878, HQ Dist. of the Yellowstone, Mont., in Howard Papers.

68. Miles to Howard, Jan. 8, 1878, and Miles to Howard, Jan. 31, 1878, HQ Dist. of the Yellowstone, Ft. Keogh, Mont., in Howard Papers.

69. Howard to Miles, Mar. 29, 1878, n.p., in Howard Papers; Wood, "The Pursuit and Capture of Chief Joseph," 333; Howard's Supplementary Report, *SW Annual Report, 1877* 1:633.

70. *Chicago Tribune,* Oct. 19, 1877.

71. *New York Herald,* Oct. 23, 1877.

72. *Chicago Times,* Oct. 26, 1877. His problem with the government was that on March 10, 1874, a court of inquiry began to investigate charges of irregularities in one of the Freedmen's Bureau accounts that had been under his supervision. The case was settled in Howard's favor on March 12, 1879, but he estimated his legal expenses were seven thousand dollars. Carpenter, *Sword and Olive Branch,* 230–35.

73. *Chicago Times,* Nov. 1, 1877.

74. Story carried in *Cheyenne Daily Leader,* Nov. 4, 1877; also in *Chicago Times,* Oct. 31, 1877.

75. *Chicago Tribune,* Nov. 27, 1877.

76. Sheridan to Terry, Oct. 11, 1877, Chicago, contained the thanks of the secretary of war, Sherman, and Sheridan; the entire message in *Cheyenne Daily Leader,* Oct. 12, 1877. *Chicago Times,* Oct. 11, 1877; *Cheyenne Daily Leader,* Oct. 28, 1877.

77. Report of General Terry, Nov. 12, 1877, HQ Dept. of Dakota, St. Paul, Minn., in *SW Annual Report, 1877* 1:516; *Cheyenne Daily Leader,* Oct. 14, 1877.

78. *Cheyenne Daily Leader,* Oct. 19, 1877; *Chicago Times,* Nov. 27, 1877.

79. Barlow to Howard, Oct. 29, 1877, New York, N.Y., in Howard Papers.

7. Strained Relations between Sherman and Miles, 1878–1885

1. Nelson A. Miles to asst. adj. gen., Dept. of Dakota, Dec. 27, 1877, Ft. Keogh, in Operations in the District of the Yellowstone in 1877, pp. 18–19, Montana Historical Society.

2. Sherman to Miles, Jan. 9, 1878, Washington, D.C., in Miles-Cameron Family Papers.

3. Sherman to Miles, Feb. 9, 1878, Washington, D.C., in William T. Sherman Papers.

4. Sherman to Miles, Mar. 30, 1878, Washington, D.C., in Miles-Cameron Family Papers; *Papers Relating to the Foreign Relations of the United States Transmitted to Congress with the Annual Message of the President,* 344–46. Extensive material relating to Sitting Bull and his stay in Canada is found in Public Archives, Ottawa. The Earl of Dufferin (Frederick Blackwood) was governor general from 1872 to 1878.

5. Miles, *Serving the Republic,* 192.

6. *Cheyenne Daily Leader,* May 31, 1878, blamed the Indian agent; Utley, *Frontier Regulars,* 323, blamed hunger. Brigham D. Madsen, *The Bannocks of Idaho,* 227–30.

7. Miles said seventy-five Crows had joined his force; *Serving the Republic,* 192–93. *Cheyenne Daily Leader,* Sept. 13, 1878, reported that thirty-five friendly Crows joined Miles. Additional details in Pond, "Major-General Nelson A. Miles," 571–72, where the leader of the Bannocks is identified as Elk Horn.

8. Miles, *Serving the Republic,* 194–95.

9. Ibid., 195. *Cheyenne Daily Leader,* Sept. 13, 1878; Madsen, *The Bannocks of Idaho,* 224.

10. Miles, *Serving the Republic,* 195.

11. Miles's Annual Report, Sept. 1879, Ft. Keogh, in *SW Annual Report, 1879* 1:74.

12. W. L. Lincoln, Indian agent, Ft. Belknap, Mont., to Ezra A. Hayt, commissioner of Indian affairs, May 22, 1879, Ft. Belknap Agency, Mont., in *SW Annual Report, 1879* 1:69. Included in Miles's report is a letter from W. Bird, Indian agent, Ft. Peck Agency, to Hayt, June 13, 1879, Ft. Peck Indian Agency, Poplar River, Mont., ibid. 1:70.

13. Ibid. 1:71; Finerty, *War-Path and Bivouac,* 260, 262.

14. Finerty, *War-Path and Bivouac,* 244; Miles's Annual Report, Sept. 1879, Ft. Keogh, in *SW Annual Report, 1879* 1:71.

15. Finerty, *War-Path and Bivouac,* 245.

16. Ibid., 245, 249–50.

17. Ibid., 252. In this experiment, the six stations were intended to connect Fort Keogh to Fort Custer. Roger E. Kelly, "Talking Mirrors versus the Indians," 59.

18. Finerty, *War-Path and Bivouac,* 256, 263; Miles to Mary Sherman Miles, July 13, 1879, camp on Rocky Creek, in Johnson, *Unregimented General,* 218.

19. Mary Sherman Miles to John Sherman, n.d. [except 1879], Fort Keogh, in Johnson, *Unregimented General,* 218–19. When Sherman replied to Mary Miles, he mentioned that he was answering her letter of July 28. John Sherman to Mary Sherman Miles, Aug. 14, 1879, Washington, D.C., in Miles-Cameron Family Papers.

20. Sherman to Sheridan, July 19, 1879, Washington, D.C., in Sherman-Sheridan Letters, Philip H. Sheridan Papers.

21. Sherman to Sheridan, Apr. 18, 1879, Washington, D.C., in Philip H. Sheridan Papers.

22. John Sherman to Mary Sherman Miles, Aug. 14, 1879, Washington, D.C., in Miles-Cameron Family Papers.

23. Miles's Annual Report, Sept. 1879, Ft. Keogh, in *SW Annual Report, 1879* 1:72.

24. *SW Annual Report, 1879* 1:72–73; Utley, *Frontier Regulars,* 287; Finerty, *War-Path and Bivouac,* 290–91.

25. Miles's Annual Report, Sept. 1879, Ft. Keogh, in *SW Annual Report, 1879* 1:73.

26. Pohanka, *Nelson A. Miles,* 122–23.

27. Ibid., 123, 124.

28. Utley, *Frontier Regulars,* 288.

29. Sherman to Sheridan, June 5, 1878, Washington, D.C., Sherman-Sheridan Letters, vol. 2, Philip H. Sheridan Papers.

30. Ibid. Ellen Sherman lived in Baltimore with her two youngest daughters during the winter of 1878–79, while Sherman lived in Washington with their two oldest daughters. James M. Merrill, *William Tecumseh Sherman,* 373–74.

31. Sherman to Sheridan, Nov. 4, 1878, Washington, D.C., Sherman-Sheridan Letters, vol. 2, Philip H. Sheridan Papers.

32. Sheridan to Sherman, Nov. 9, 1878, Washington, D.C., in ibid.

33. Sherman to Miles, Nov. 12, 1878, Washington, D.C., in Miles-Cameron Family Papers, LC.

34. *New York Times,* Sept. 20, 1878; Mary Sherman Miles to John Sherman, March, n.d., 1879, Washington, D.C., in Johnson, *Unregimented General,* 214–15.

35. Johnson, *Unregimented General,* 214–15.

36. Sherman to Sheridan, Mar. 9, 1879, HQ U.S. Army, Washington, D.C., in Sherman-Sheridan Letters, vol. 2, Philip H. Sheridan Papers. Besides Ruger, Cols. John Gibbon and

William B. Hazen outranked Miles; all were West Pointers.

37. Miles to Sherman, Mar. 9, 1879, Washington, D.C.; Sherman to Miles, Mar. 10, 1879, Washington, D.C.; and Miles to Sherman, Mar. 11, 1879, Washington, D.C., in William T. Sherman Papers. *New York Times,* May 5, 1878.

38. Miles to Sherman, Mar. 10, 1879, Washington, D.C.; Sherman to Miles, Mar. 10, 1879, Washington, D.C.; and Miles to Sherman, Mar. 11, 1879, Washington, D.C., in William T. Sherman Papers.

39. Johnson, *Unregimented General,* 217.

40. Sherman to Sheridan, July 19, 1879, Washington, D.C., Sherman-Sheridan Letters, vol. 2, Philip H. Sheridan Papers.

41. Johnson, *Unregimented General,* 221.

42. Theodore Lyman to President Rutherford B. Hayes, Dec. 5, 1878, Brookline, Mass., in Miles-Cameron Family Papers.

43. John Sherman to Miles, Aug. 21, 1880, Washington, D.C., in Miles-Cameron Family Papers.

44. Sheridan to Miles, Sept. 13, 1880, n.p., General Correspondence, Sept.–Dec. 1880, box 27, Philip H. Sheridan Papers; John Sherman to Miles, Sept. 13, 1880, Washington, D.C., in Miles-Cameron Family Papers.

45. John Sherman to Miles, Sept. 27, 1880, Washington, D.C., in Miles-Cameron Family Papers.

46. *New York Times,* Nov. 19, 1880; *DAB* s.v. "William Babcock Hazen."

47. General Sherman to Sheridan, Dec. 13, 1880, Washington, D.C., in Sherman-Sheridan Letters, vol. 2, Philip H. Sheridan Papers; and T. Harry T. Williams, ed., *Hayes: The Diary of a President, 1875–1881,* 307.

48. *New York Herald,* Dec. 22, 1880. Sherman attributed the decision to force out Ord instead of McDowell to "politics," explaining that "General McDowell came here to New York to vote for General Garfield in a very ostentatious manner while General Ord did not do that." Ibid. Mary Sherman Miles to John Sherman, n.d., 1879, Washington, D.C., in Johnson, *Unregimented General,* 214–15.

49. Adj. gen. office memorandum, Dec. 27, 1901, in Letters Received-AGO; Miles, *Serving the Republic,* 207, 212–13.

50. Johnson, *Unregimented General,* 225; Merrill, *William Tecumseh Sherman,* 393. Sherman Miles graduated from West Point in 1905. From 1914 to 1916 he was an observer with the Russian army. In 1918 he served as chief of intelligence for the First Corps in France. He was the acting chief of military intelligence in the War Department on December 7, 1941. In January 1942 he was promoted to major general (temporary), and a month later he was assigned to command the First Corps Area with headquarters in Boston, where he remained until he retired in 1945. Sherman Miles died on October 7, 1966. *New York Times,* Oct. 9, 1966; U.S. Army, "Biographical Sketches of General Officers in World War II," typescript, n.d., n.p., Archives, U.S. Military Academy, West Point, N.Y.

51. Miles to Secretary of War William C. Endicott, June 26, 1885, Vancouver Barracks, Washington Territory, in William C. Endicott Papers, Massachusetts Historical Society.

52. Miles to Cleveland, July 20, 1885, in the field, Ft. Reno, I.T., in Grover Cleveland Papers (microfilm), Graduate School, City University of New York (original Cleveland Papers in LC).

53. *Arizona Daily Star,* Apr. 4, 1886.

54. John Sherman to Miles, Mar. 19, 1886, Washington, D.C., in Miles-Cameron Family Papers.

8. The Geronimo Campaign, 1886

1. *New York Times,* Jan. 9, 1886; Robert M. Utley, "Geronimo," and, *Frontier Regulars,* 369–93; Jerome A. Greene, "George Crook," in Hutton, *Soldiers West,* 115–36.

2. Greene, "George Crook," in Hutton, *Soldiers West,* 115–36; idem, *Phil Sheridan and His Army,* 98; Marshall Trimble, *Arizona: A Panoramic History of a Frontier State,* 192; *Arizona Daily Star,* Apr. 21, 1887.

3. *New York Times,* Jan. 9, 1886.

4. William Sherman to Miles, Jan. 5, 1886, St. Louis, in Miles-Cameron Family Papers.

5. Miles to Sherman, Jan. 8, 1886, Ft. Leavenworth, Kans., in William T. Sherman Papers; Miles to Endicott, Mar. 23, 1886, Ft. Leavenworth, Kans., in Endicott Papers.

6. George Crook, *General George Crook: His Autobiography,* 241–66. See also Odie B. Faulk, *The Geronimo Campaign;* Donald E. Worcester, *The Apaches: Eagles of the Southwest;* Dan L. Thrapp, *The Conquest of Apacheria;* and Britton Davis, *The Truth about Geronimo.* For a study of Geronimo, see Angie Debo, *Geronimo: The Man, His Time, His Place.* For the rivalry between Crook and Miles, see Robert M. Utley, "Crook and Miles: Fighting and Feuding on the Indian Frontier."

7. Charles F. Lummis, *Charles Fletcher Lummis Reports on an Apache War,* 66–67, 70.

8. Finerty, *War-Path and Bivouac,* 6.

9. *New York Times,* Mar. 22, 1890. Crook had died on March 21.

10. Miles to Mary Sherman Miles, Apr. 12, 1886, Ft. Bowie, Ariz., Johnson, *Unregimented General,* 231.

11. Finerty, *War-Path and Bivouac,* 317.

12. In memoriam, companion George Crook, Ohio Commander, Military Order of the Loyal Legion of the U.S., in RG 94, Office of the Adjutant General (AGO), Appointment Commission and Personnel Branch Document File (ACPBDF), NA. For further study of Crook see James T. King, "George Crook, Indian Fighter and Humanitarian," *Arizona and the West* 9 (1967): 333–48.

13. Eighty-six officers of the army to the president of the U.S., Mar. 29, 1882, New York, in Maj. Gen. George Crook's File, box 772, RG 94, AGO, ACPBDF, NA. At this time Miles was in command of the Department of the Columbia, with headquarters at Vancouver Barracks, Washington.

14. *DAB,* s.v. "John Gregory Bourke"; King, "Needed: A Re-evaluation of General George Crook," 225. For further details about Bourke, see Lansing B. Bloom, "Bourke on the Southwest" Joseph C. Porter, "John G. Bourke," in Hutton, *Soldiers West,* 137–56.

15. Eighty-six officers of the army to the president of the U.S., Mar. 29, 1882, New York, in Maj. Gen. George Crook's File, RG 94.

16. Finerty, *War-Path and Bivouac,* 93; Sherman to Sheridan, Feb. 17, 1877, Washington, in Sherman-Sheridan Letters, Philip H. Sheridan Papers. Although Crook may not have lived up to expectations at Powder River on March 17, 1876, and at Rosebud Creek on June 17, 1876, his aide earned recognition for his part in these battles. As a result of Bourke's performance in these two actions, he received a brevet as major on February 27, 1890.

17. John Sherman to Miles, Apr. 17, 1888, Washington, Miles-Cameron Family Papers.

18. Copy of Sheridan's order to Miles, Apr. 3, 1886, Washington, D.C., in Miles to AG, Sept. 18, 1886, *SW Annual Report, 1886* 1:165.

19. Miles's Field Order No. 7, Apr. 20, 1886, Ft. Bowie, Ariz., in ibid.; Roger E. Kelly, "Talking Mirrors versus the Indians"; Bruno J. Rolak, "General Miles' Mirrors: The Heliograph in the Geronimo Campaign of 1886."

20. Miles's Field Order No. 7, Apr. 20, 1886, Ft. Bowie, Ariz.,in Miles to A.G., Sept. 18, 1886, *SW Annual Report, 1886* 1:166.

21. Howard to Sherman, Apr. 27, 1886, HQ Div. of the Pacific, Presidio of San Francisco, Calif., in William T. Sherman Papers.

22. Miles, telegram, June 7, Calabasas, Ariz., to the War Department, in *Arizona* (Tucson) *Daily Star,* June 10, 1886. Miles reported the ordeal of the Peck family in Miles to AG, Sept. 18, 1886, *SW Annual Report, 1886* 1:167, 170, noting that fourteen people had been killed; apparently another person died after June 7. Miles, *Serving the Republic,* 220.

23. Miles, telegram, June 7, Calabasas, Ariz., to the War Department, in *Arizona* [Tucson] *Daily Star,* June 10, 1886; Baird, "General Miles's Indian Campaigns," 369; Miles to AG, Sept. 18, 1886, *SW Annual Report, 1886* 1:167. Clark drowned in 1893.

24. *SW Annual Report, 1886* 1:169; Rolak, "General Miles' Mirrors," 151.

25. Miles to AG, Sept. 18, 1886, *SW Annual Report, 1886* 1:169; Utley, *Frontier Regulars,* 49.

26. Miles to AG, Sept. 18, 1886, *SW Annual Report, 1886* 1:168.

27. *Arizona* (Tucson) *Daily Star,* June 11, 1886.

28. Miles, *Serving the Republic,* 224; *DAB,* s.v. "Henry Ware Lawton." Lawton was born March 17, 1843, in Manhattan, near Toledo, Ohio.

29. Lawton to AG, Sept. 9, 1886, en route to Ft. Marion, Fla., *SW Annual Report, 1886,* 1:176. For information about Leonard Wood, see Hermann H. Hagedorn, *Leonard Wood.*

30. Rolak, "General Miles' Mirrors," 149; Miles to Lawton, May 20, 1886, Nogales, Ariz., in Lawton Papers, LC.

31. Lawton to AG, Sept. 9, 1886, *SW Annual Report, 1886* 1:178; Wood's diary, Aug. 28, 1886, in Leonard Wood Papers. For an enlisted man's view of campaigning with Lawton, see Lawrence Vinton, "The Geronimo Campaign: As Told by a Trooper of 'B' Troop of the 4th U.S. Cavalry." Although Lawton reported that his cavalrymen had been left behind at the camp at Oposura, Maj. Harry C. Benson, who had been one of Lawton's lieutenants, convincingly argued in 1909 that the men of Troop B, Fourth Cavalry, "remained with the command from start to finish and had very much the hardest work, but they never became exhausted nor were ordered back." Maj. H. C. Benson, "The Geronimo Campaign." On May 20, 1886, Miles informed Lawton about the location of troops who were "put in position with the hope of intercepting them [Geronimo's war parties] as you *drive.*" Miles to Lawton, May 20, 1886, Nogales, Ariz., in Lawton Papers.

32. James Parker, "The Geronimo Campaign," *Proceedings of the Annual Meeting and Dinner of the Order of the Indian Wars of the United States,* 32 (hereafter cited as *Order of the Indian Wars, 1929*).

33. Miles to Mary Sherman Miles, July 5, 1886, Ft. Apache, Ariz., in Johnson, *Unregimented General,* 240.

34. Miles to Howard, June 18, 1886, Ft. Huachuca, in Howard Papers.

35. Ibid.

36. Miles to Howard, July 7, 1886, Ft. Apache, in U.S. Senate, "Letter from Sec. of War, transmitting correspondence with Miles relative to the surrender of Geronimo," 49th Congress, 2d sess., Feb. 11, 1887, Ex. Doc. No. 117, 50–51.

37. Miles, *Personal Recollections,* 497.

38. Sheridan to Miles, July 13, 1886, Washington, D.C., and Miles to Sheridan, July 15, 1886, Albuquerque, N.M., Ex. Doc. No. 117, 53, 55; *Arizona Daily Star,* Aug. 31, 1886. The delegation included ten men and three women.

39. *Arizona Daily Star,* Aug. 31, 1886.

40. Miles to Mary Sherman Miles, July 31, 1886, Wilcox, Ariz., in Johnson, *The Unregimented General,* 243; Miles to Sheridan, Aug. 2, 1886, Wilcox, Ariz., Ex. Doc. No. 117, 56–57.

41. Dorst to AG, U.S. Army, Aug. 14, 1886, Ft. Leavenworth, Ex. Doc. No. 117, 63; Miles, *Personal Recollections,* 498.

42. Miles to AG, U.S. Army, Aug. 20, 1886, Ex. Doc. No. 117, 63–64; Lamar to Endicott, Aug. 25, 1886, Dept. of the Interior, ibid., 65; 2d Lt. George H. Chase, asst. adj. gen., HQ Div. of the Pacific, to Miles, Aug. 28, 1886, Presidio of San Francisco, Calif., in Letters Received–AGO.

43. Miles to Mary Sherman Miles, Aug. 27, 1887, Wilcox, Ariz., in Johnson, *Unregimented General,* 243–44.

44. Miles, *Personal Recollections,* 501–4; Miles to AG, Sept. 18, 1886, Albuquerque, N.M., *SW Annual Report, 1886* 1:172; Parker, "The Geronimo Campaign," 32. The *Army and Navy Journal,* Sept. 11, 1886, 125, reprinted a story from the *San Francisco Report* claiming that with the removal Miles had "won the greatest victory in his life. An Army contractor in favor with the Department is a dangerous foe, and more difficult to frighten than the savage. The Army contractor was the dictator of Arizona until Miles took command." The article charges that "It was the Army contractor who kept the Indians at war and fought every measure for a permanent peace."

45. *Arizona Daily Star,* Aug. 31, 1886; Lyman W. V. Kennon, "The Case of the Chiricahuas," 252. One of the prisoners had escaped in Missouri. Worcester, *The Apaches: Eagles of the Southwest,* 308.

46. Col. Richard C. Drum to the President, Aug. 30, 1886, Washington, in Geronimo File, Lamont Papers, LC; *Arizona Daily Star,* Aug. 31, 1886.

47. Miles to AG, Sept. 18, 1886, Albuquerque, N.M., *SW Annual Report, 1886* 1:172; Charles B. Gatewood, "The Surrender of Geronimo," 49.

48. Gatewood to Miles, Oct. 15, 1886, Albuquerque, N.M., in Charles B. Gatewood Collection, Arizona Historical Society. Gatewood quotes Miles's terms in Gatewood, "The Surrender of Geronimo," 53.

49. Gatewood's background in Col. Charles B. Gatewood's introduction to his father's article, Gatewood, "The Surrender of Geronimo," 45–48.

50. Gatewood to Miles, Oct. 15, 1886, Albuquerque, N.M., in Gatewood Collection.

51. Ibid.; Miles to AG, Sept. 18, 1886, *SW Annual Report, 1886* 1:172.

52. Gatewood, "The Surrender of Geronimo," 53; Gatewood to his wife, Georgia McCulloch Gatewood, Aug. 26, 1886, camp on the Bavispe River, in Charles B. Gatewood, "Gatewood Reports to His Wife," 78.

53. Gatewood, "Gatewood Reports to His Wife," 78.

54. Gatewood to Miles, Oct. 15, 1886, Albuquerque, N.M., in Gatewood Collection; Gatewood, "The Surrender of Geronimo," 54.

55. Gatewood to Miles, Oct. 15, 1886, Albuquerque, N.M., in Gatewood Collection.

56. Wood's diary entry for Aug. 27, 1886, in Leonard Wood Papers, LC.

57. Ibid. Wood describes how Lawton's men turned back a large number of Mexican soldiers intent on capturing the Apaches themselves. Lawton rode ahead. Ibid., Aug. 30, 1886. Miles to Mary Sherman Miles, Aug. 29, 1886, Ft. Bowie, in Johnson, *Unregimented General,* 247.

58. Miles to Lawton, August 31, 1886, Ft. Bowie, in Lawton Papers.

59. Cleveland to Drum, Acting Sec. of War, Aug. 23, 1886, Prospect House, New York; Drum to Miles, telegram, Aug. 23, 1886, Washington, D.C., Ex. Doc. No. 117, 4–5; *Arizona Daily Star,* Sept. 14, 1886.

60. Debo, *Geronimo,* 290, 304; Miles, *Personal Recollections,* 520.

61. Miles, *Personal Recollections,* 521.

62. Gatewood, "The Surrender of Geronimo," 55; Miles to the asst. adj. gen., Pacific Div., Sept. 6, 1886, Ft. Bowie, in Howard to Drum, Oct. 2, 1886, Presidio of San Francisco, Calif., Ex. Doc. No. 117, 23.

63. Gatewood, "The Surrender of Geronimo," 59–60; Miles, *Personal Recollections,* 525.

64. Brig. Gen. David Stanley to Col. (Bvt. Brig. Gen.) Richard C. Drum, Sept. 30, 1886, San Antonio, Tex., Ex. Doc. No. 117, 22; Miles to AG, Sept. 18, 1886, *SW Annual Report, 1886* 1:173–74.

65. Miles, *Personal Recollections,* 526–27; Wood's diary entry, Sept. 5, 1886, Leonard Wood Papers.

66. Miles, *Personal Recollections,* 527; Miles to acting SW, Sept. 29, 1886, Albuquerque, N.M., Ex. Doc. No. 117, 21.

67. Miles, *Personal Recollections,* 527; Wood's diary entry, Sept. 8, 1886, Leonard Wood Papers; Miles to Mary Sherman Miles, Sept. 7, 8, 1886, Ft. Bowie, Ariz., in Johnson, *Unregimented General,* 250. On September 4, twenty-two warriors, fourteen women, and three children surrendered. Miles to asst. adj. gen., Pacific Div., Sept. 6, 1886, Ft. Bowie, Ex. Doc. No. 117, 23. On September 6 a child was born. When a mounted officer charged into Lawton's camp before daybreak on September 8, three warriors, three women, and a boy ran off.

9. Brigadier General Nelson A. Miles and the Aftermath of the Geronimo Campaign

1. Robert Utley, "Crook and Miles: Fighting and Feuding," 89; Worcester, *The Apaches, Eagles of the Southwest,* 307; *New York Herald,* Aug. 31, 1886. Endicott was away from Washington at least through September 29, 1886, as Drum signed correspondence as acting secretary of war through that day. Ex. Doc. No. 117, 21; *Daily Alta California,* Oct. 11, 1886; *New York Herald,* Sept. 28, 1886.

2. Howard to AG, Sept. 9, 1886, Presidio of San Francisco, Ex. Doc. No. 117, 12–13; Miles to Sheridan, Sept. 7, 1886, Ft. Bowie, Arizona, ibid., 10; Drum to Miles, Sept. 8, 1886, War Department, in ibid., 11.

3. Howard to AG, Sept. 9, 1886, Presidio of San Francisco, in ibid., 12–13.

4. Miles refers to Howard's dispatch of Nov. 2, 1886, when he explains why he did not receive the Sept. 8, 1886, order; Miles to Howard, Nov. 3, 1886, HQ Dept. of Arizona, Whipple Barracks, Prescott, Ariz., ibid., 30. Miles to Governor Ross, Nov. 1, 1886, Whipple Barracks, Ariz., in Edmund G. Ross Collection, Kansas State Historical Society. Howard first reprimanded Miles on September 9, 1886, in Howard to AG, Presidio of San Francisco, Ex. Doc. No. 117, 13. Although Miles may not have realized he had been reprimanded at the time, the *Army and Navy Journal,* Oct. 9, 1886, reported, "that General Miles' report [Miles to AG, Sept. 18, 1886] does not give satisfaction to all the authorities at Washington in obvious, . . . General Miles is considered to have departed from the letter of his instructions," and Miles more than likely read this story.

5. Wood diary entry, Sept. 8, 1886, Leonard Wood Papers.

6. Cleveland to Howard and Drum (who sent a copy to Endicott), Sept. 7, 1886, Prospect

House, New York, Ex. Doc. No. 117, 8–9; copy of Miles to asst. adj. gen., Pacific Div., Sept. 6, 1886, Ft. Bowie, in Howard to Drum, Oct. 2, 1886, Presidio of San Francisco, ibid., 23.

7. Howard to AG, U.S. Army, Sept. 7, 1886, Ft. Mason, San Francisco, ibid., 7; Howard to AG, Sept. 9, 1886, Presidio, ibid., 12.

8. Drum to Endicott, Sept. 23, 1886, Washington, D.C., Endicott Papers.

9. Howard to Drum, Oct. 2, 1886, Presidio of San Francisco, with a copy of Miles to asst. adj. gen., Pacific Div., Sept. 6, 1886, Ft. Bowie, Ex. Doc. No. 117, 23.

10. Howard's endorsement, Dec. 28, 1886, HQ Div. of the Pacific, to Miles to asst. adj. gen., Div. of the Pacific, Dec. 15, 1886, Washington, D.C., ibid., 31–32.

11. *Arizona* (Tucson) *Daily Star,* Oct. 5, 1886.

12. *Army and Navy Journal,* Oct. 9, 1886, 205.

13. Miles to Mary Sherman Miles, Oct. 14, 1886, Albuquerque, N.M., in Johnson, *Unregimented General,* 252–53.

14. Drum to Stanley in Drum to the president, Sept. 10, 1886, Washington, D.C., Ex. Doc. No. 117, 13; Endicott to Sheridan, Oct. 19, 1886, ibid., 26.

15. Utley, *Frontier Regulars,* 390–91, and Faulk, *The Geronimo Campaign,* 186–87.

16. *Army and Navy Journal,* Oct. 9, 1886, 215.

17. Ibid., Dec. 18, 1886, 408; Sherman to Miles, Oct. 22, 1886, New York, N.Y., in Miles-Cameron Family Papers.

18. Miles to Endicott, Oct. 9, 1886, Albuquerque, N.M., in Endicott Papers; *New York Times,* June 11, 1887. Apparently as a result of Miles's criticism, the quartermaster general obtained several new shoe patterns so that the secretary of war could select an army shoe to replace the style that fell apart in Mexico. *Army and Navy Journal,* Nov. 13, 1886, 305.

19. *Army and Navy Journal,* Nov. 13, 1886, 305.

20. Ibid., Jan. 8, 1887, 477; Miles to Grover Cleveland, Sept. 26, 1886, Albuquerque, N.M., and Drum to Miles, Sept. 29, 1886, Washington, D.C., Ex Doc. No. 117, 20.

21. Miles to Mary Sherman Miles, Oct. 4, 1886, Albuquerque, N.M., in Johnson, *Unregimented General,* 253.

22. Miles to Howard, May 12, 1887, Los Angeles, in Howard Papers. Although Miles protested personally to Howard by private letter, he never publicly revealed details of this disagreement.

23. Ibid. Miles to Howard, Apr. 16, 1887, Los Angeles, Howard Papers.

24. Ibid.

25. Ibid. McKeever had been promoted to colonel on Feb. 28, 1887.

26. Miles to AG (through HQ Div. of the Pacific), May 12, 1887, HQ Dept. of Arizona, in McKeever Personal File, RAGO, NA.

27. O. O. Howard, May 17, 1887, HQ Div. of the Pacific, San Francisco, and Col. Drum, May 25, 1887, office of the AG; by command of Lieutenant General Sheridan, June 3, 1887, War Dept., in McKeever Personal File, RAGO, NA.

28. *Washington* (D.C.) *Critic* quoted in *Army and Navy Journal,* Oct. 16, 1886, 238; *Arizona* (Tucson) *Daily Star,* Apr. 4, 1886.

29. *New York Herald,* Dec. 2, 1886. Miles remained in Washington through December, as reported in *New York Herald,* Dec. 30, 1886; and he was reported to be in Chicago on December 11 by the *Arizona* (Tucson) *Daily Star,* Dec. 12, 1886.

30. Miles to Mary Sherman Miles, Feb. 5, 1877, HQ Yellowstone Command, Mont., in Johnson, *Unregimented General,* 152.

31. Miles to Mary Sherman Miles, June 24, 1886, Deming, N.M., in ibid., 240.

32. *Lincoln* (Neb.) *Journal,* quoted in *Army and Navy Journal,* June 19, 1886, 965. Miles complained in letters to his wife about Crook but never criticized Crook in his public writings or remarks to the press.

33. *Daily Alta California,* Dec. 7, 1886; *Army and Navy Journal,* Dec. 18, 1886, 408.

34. *Army and Navy Journal,* Dec. 18, 1886, 408. As far as can be determined, Miles never revealed his opinion of Endicott.

35. *Arizona* (Tucson) *Daily Star,* Nov. 17, 1880; Sheridan to Miles, Apr. 3, 1886, Washington, D.C., in Miles to AG, Sept. 18, 1886, *SW Annual Report, 1886* 1:165.

36. Crook to Webb Hayes, Apr. 2, 1887, Omaha, Neb., in George Crook Papers, Rutherford B. Hayes Presidential Center, Fremont, Ohio.

37. *Daily Alta California* quoted in *Army and Navy Journal,* Oct. 9, 1886, 212.

38. Miles quoted by an *Albuquerque Democrat* reporter, reprinted in *Daily Alta California,* Oct. 6, 1886.

39. Parker, "The Geronimo Campaign," 43–44; and James Parker, *The Old Army,* 190.

40. *Arizona Daily Star,* Apr. 30, 1887; *New York Times,* Sept. 1, 1887.; Faulk, *The Geronimo Campaign,* 188, stated that "The fund [for the sword] was far undersubscribed; Miles did not want to lose the opportunity for public recognition, which was certain to be reported in Eastern newspapers, and quietly supplied the money needed to buy an extravagant blade." This is at least an exaggeration, since the fund lacked only two hundred dollars, a condition that is not "far undersubscribed." Furthermore, there was still time to raise the needed money, and there was an expectation of funds from the Prescott area.

41. *Arizona* (Tuscon) *Daily Star,* Apr. 30, 1887; Miles to Sherman, Dec. 7, 1887, Los Angeles, William T. Sherman Papers.

42. Miles to Sherman, Dec. 7, 1887, Los Angeles, William T. Sherman Papers; *New York Times,* Sept. 1, 1887; *Army and Navy Journal,* Nov. 12, Dec. 10, 1887; Don Schellie, "The Day Tucson Honored the 'Man Who Captured Geronimo.'" An *Arizona Daily Star,* July 31, 1887, editorial endorsed Miles for presidency.

43. *Arizona Daily Star,* Sept. 28, 1886; Schellie, "The 'Man Who Captured Geronimo,'" 39; Col. Charles B. Gatewood, "The Surrender of Geronimo," 31. Following service as the commanding officer of the Rough Riders in the Spanish-American War, Leonard Wood moved to the top rank of army officers and was named chief of staff in 1910. During the Civil War, Henry Ware Lawton rose to the rank of lieutenant colonel of the 30th Indiana Volunteer Infantry and earned the Medal of Honor for his conduct in the Battle of Atlanta. In 1899 Brigadier General Lawton was killed in the Philippines as he prepared his troops for a river crossing. Since Gatewood had only received his promotion to first lieutenant in 1885, the fact that he was not promoted after the campaign is not as surprising as his being denied a medal. Lawton had served as a first lieutenant for almost twelve years before being promoted to captain in 1879; however, in 1888 he entered the inspector general's department as a major. Wood remained an assistant surgeon until 1893, when he was transferred to Fort McPherson, Georgia, to serve as post surgeon; in 1895 he became assistant attending surgeon in Washington. Wood's first significant step up the ladder of command came on May 8, 1898, when he became colonel of the First Volunteer Cavalry Regiment. As for Miles, in 1888 President Cleveland overlooked him after Maj. Gen. Alfred H. Terry retired from command of the Division of the Missouri. Instead, Crook, who enjoyed seniority over his rival, received the appointment and the major general's stars that went with it. On March 21, 1890, General Crook died, and the following month Miles finally received the long-sought pro-

motion when President Benjamin Harrison nominated him to the vacant position.

44. Maj. Charles B. Gatewood to the editor of the *Saturday Evening Post,* Aug. 3, 1926, San Diego, Gatewood Collection.

45. *The Reader's Encyclopedia of the American West,* s.v. "Miles, Nelson Appleton."

46. Miles to AG, Sept. 18, 1886, *SW Annual Report, 1891* 1:172; *Washington* (D.C.) *Critic,* n.d., quoted in *Army and Navy Journal,* Oct. 16, 1886, 238.

47. William Baird to Gatewood, Sept. 21, 1886, Ft. Bayard, N.M., Gatewood Collection.

48. Miles to AG, U.S. Army, Dec. 28, 1886, Washington, D.C., Gatewood Collection.

49. Gatewood, "The Surrender of Geronimo," 31.

50. Notification of denial of Medal of Honor, Joseph B. Doe, acting secretary of war, June 26, 1895, Gatewood Collection.

51. Col. William C. Brown, ret., June 4, 1925, Washington, D.C., to E. A. Brininstool, Gatewood Collection. Although Miles consistently admired Gatewood's courage, a falling-out disturbed the relationship between the two officers. The ill will may have originated when the general used an ambulance to fetch the lieutenant from a bar in Prescott. H. W. Daly to Major General Gatewood, June 18, 1928, Washington, D.C., Gatewood Collection. Hostility between the two intensified when Gatewood was left behind, in charge of the Los Angeles headquarters, when Miles left for the sword presentation in Arizona. Although this is sometimes the duty of an aide, Gatewood's supporters have cause to resent Miles's failure to see that Gatewood also received his due; still, their partisan perspective can be misleading. Georgia McCulloch Gatewood to Major General, n.d., n.p., Gatewood Collection.

52. Thrapp, *The Conquest of Apacheria,* 364–65. That they would not care to live alone in Utley, *Frontier Regulars,* 390.

53. *New York Sun,* Feb. 16, 1890.

54. Gatewood to the editor, *The Army and Navy Register,* Washington, D.C., excerpted in Thrapp, *The Conquest of Apacheria,* 365.

55. As in this case, the *Army and Navy Journal* often does not identify those whose letters it publishes. *Army and Navy Journal,* May 29, 1886, 869.

56. Crook to Kennon, Mar. 7, 1890, n.p., in Crook, *Autobiography,* 300; Crook to Kennon, Feb. 18, 1890, Chicago, Ill., in Letters of General George Crook, Special Collection, University of Oregon Library.

57. *New York Sun,* Feb. 16, 1890.

58. Debo, *Geronimo,* 405; Report of Lt. Gatewood to Miles, Oct. 15, 1886, Albuquerque, N.M., Gatewood Collection.

59. Miles to AG, Sept. 18, 1886, *SW Annual Report, 1886* 1:173–74; Miles to Mary Sherman Miles, Oct. 14, 1886, Albuquerque, in Johnson, *Unregimented General,* 253.

60. *Arizona Daily Star,* Sept. 9, 1886; Utley, *Frontier Regulars,* 198–206.

61. *Arizona Daily Star,* Sept. 14, 1886.

62. Ibid., Oct. 5, 1886; Miles to asst. adj. gen., Div. of the Pacific, Oct. 2, 1886, Presidio of San Francisco, in Ex. Doc. No. 117, 23.

10. The "Messiah" Outbreak of 1890

1. John Sherman to Miles, Apr. 4, 17, 1888, Washington, D.C., Miles-Cameron Family Papers.

2. *New York Times,* Mar. 22, 1890; Miles to Dawes, Mar. 27, 1890, New York, in Henry L. Dawes Papers, LC.

3. John Sherman to Miles, Apr. 3, 1890, Washington, D.C., in Johnson, *Unregimented General,* 262.

4. Henry J. Sievers, *Benjamin Harrison, Hoosier Warrior, 1833–1865,* 253.

5. Matthew Josephson, *The Politicos, 1865–1896,* 437; Miles to Mary Sherman Miles, Apr. 5, 1890, Washington, D.C., in Johnson, *Unregimented General,* 262–63.

6. *New York Times,* July 4, 1890; ibid., Feb. 8, 1891.

7. *Washington* (D.C.) *Star,* Nov. 21, 1890; Miles to John M. Schofield, Nov. 26, 1890, Letters Received–AGO. Schofield became commanding general of the army at the death of Lt. Gen. Philip H. Sheridan on August 5, 1888. Schofield graduated seventh in his class from West Point in 1853, taught at West Point, and then took a leave of absence to teach physics at Washington University in St. Louis prior to the Civil War. John M. Schofield, *Forty-Six Years in the Army; DAB,* s.v. "John McAllister Schofield."

8. Miles to AG, Sept. 14, 1891, in *SW Annual Report, 1891* 1:133–4.

9. McLaughlin, a twenty-year veteran of the Indian Service, had spent fifteen years among the Sioux and was married to a mixed-blood Sioux woman. His self-proclaimed goals were to promote "the advancement, good government and ultimate civilization of Indians." McLaughlin to John T. Morgan, Feb. 4, 1891, Major James McLaughlin Papers, Assumption College Archives, Richardton, N.D. Background on McLaughlin is in Louis Pfaller, *Guide to the Microfilm Edition of Major James McLaughlin Papers;* and Flora W. Seymour, *Indian Agents of the Old Frontier,* 298–317.

10. *Deadwood Times,* Nov. 2, 1890. A slightly different version of the speech is in James McLaughlin, *My Friend the Indian,* 185–89.

11. E. B. Reynolds to commissioner of Indian affairs, Nov. 2, 1890, and Daniel F. Royer to commissioner of Indian affairs, Oct. 30, 1890, both quoted in Miles to AG, Sept. 14, 1891, *SW Annual Report, 1891* 1:140, 144.

12. Belt is quoted in Miles to SW, Sept. 14, 1891, *SW Annual Report, 1891* 1:144–45. For Brooke at Cold Harbor with Miles, see Humphreys, *The Virginia Campaign of '64 and '65.* During the Spanish-American War, Brooke's indifferent administration of Camp George H. Thomas, Georgia, contributed to unsanitary conditions at the training ground where 425 soldiers died. Graham A. Cosmos, *An Army for Empire: The United States Army in the Spanish-American War,* 173, 266; David F. Trask, *The War with Spain in 1898,* 160.

13. Miles to AG, Sept. 14, 1891, *SW Annual Report, 1891* 1:145. Miles to John R. Brooke, Nov. 18, 23, Dec. 7, 1890, Letters Received–AGO.

14. Miles to AG, Sept. 14, 1891, *SW Annual Report, 1891* 1:146. A Civil War veteran, lawyer, politician, and businessman, Proctor had been governor of Vermont and president of the Vermont Marble Company, the world's largest marble producer. He rose to national prominence in 1888 when he chaired the Vermont delegation, which seconded Benjamin Harrison's nomination for president. Charles R. Cummings, "Redfield Proctor, 1831–1908"; Jacob G. Ullery, comp., *Men of Vermont: An Illustrated Biographical History of Vermonters and Sons of Vermont,* 327–29; Josephson, *The Politicos, 1865–1896,* 440.

15. Secretary of War Proctor to Miles, Dec. 1, 1890, Washington, D.C., Redfield Proctor Papers, Proctor Public Library, Proctor, Vt.

16. *Deadwood Times,* Dec. 13, 1890, and Jan. 11, 1891; Miles to AG, Sept. 14, 1891, *SW Annual Report, 1891* 1:147–50.

17. Miles, *Serving the Republic,* 237–38. Tecumseh, a chief of the Shawnees, and his brother Tenskwatawa, the Prophet, who was known as a mystic, united thousands of western Indians in

1811. They unsuccessfully challenged settlers who, led by the governor of the Indian Territory, William Henry Harrison, destroyed their village in the Battle of Tippecanoe. *American Biography* (1974 ed.), s.v. "Tecumseh."

18. William F. Cody, *An Autobiography of Buffalo Bill,* 304–13; Miles to Schofield, Dec. 6, 1890, Chicago, Ill., in Schofield Papers, LC.

19. Schofield to Miles, Dec. 6, 1890, Washington, D.C., in ibid.

20. Merritt Barber, asst. adj. gen., Dept. of Dakota, to commanding officer, Ft. Yates, S.D., Dec. 12, 1890, St. Paul, Minn., in McLaughlin, *My Friend the Indian,* 214.

21. Vestal, *Sitting Bull, Champion of the Sioux,* 307. Details of the arrest in ibid., 300–315. Edward G. Fechet, "The True Story of the Death of Sitting Bull"; Alexander B. Adams, *Sitting Bull: An Epic of the Plains,* 357–64; James Mooney, *The Ghost Dance Religion and the Sioux Outbreak of 1890,* 855–64.

22. Cody, *Autobiography,* 311; Miles to AG, Sept. 14, 1891, *SW Annual Report, 1891* 1:146–47.

23. Miles to Mary Sherman Miles, Dec. 20, 1890, Rapid City, S.D., quoted in Johnson, *Unregimented General,* 282.

24. Miles to Schofield, Dec. 20, 1890, Rapid City, S.D., in Benjamin Harrison Papers, LC.

25. Utley, *Last Days of the Sioux Nation,* 200–204; Miles to AG, Sept. 14, 1891, *SW Annual Report, 1891* 1:147.

26. Mooney, "Ghost Dance Religion," 868–69; John C. Gresham, "The Story of Wounded Knee," 106.

27. Schofield to Miles, Dec. 30, 1890, Letters Received–AGO; Miles to Schofield and Schofield to Miles, Jan. 1, 1891, in James W. Forsyth to Daniel S. Lamont, Sept. 1, 1895, Manuscript and Archives Division, New York Public Library. Forsyth defends the actions of the Seventh Cavalry against the Sioux.

28. Miles to Mary Sherman Miles, Dec. 30, 1890, Rapid City, S.D., quoted in Johnson, *Unregimented General,* 288–89; Miles's order of Jan. 4, 1891, to Lamont, Sept. 1, 1895, Manuscripts and Archives, New York Public Library.

29. Miles to Mary Sherman Miles, Jan. 6, 1891, Pine Ridge, S.D., quoted in Johnson, *Unregimented General,* 289.

30. Schofield to Miles, Jan. 6, 1891, Washington, D.C., in *New York Tribune,* Jan. 7, 1891; findings of Maj. J. Ford Kent and Capt. Frank D. Baldwin, Pine Ridge, S.D., Jan. 13, 1891, are in Letters Received–AGO.

31. Findings of Kent and Baldwin, Jan. 18, 1891, Pine Ridge Agency, Letters Received–AGO; Forsyth to Lamont, Sept. 1, 1895, San Francisco, Manuscripts and Archives, New York Public Library.

32. Findings of Kent and Baldwin, Jan. 13, 1891, Letters Received–AGO; contractor's bill, enclosed in field quartermaster to asst. adj. gen., Div. of the Missouri, Jan. 5, 1891, Pine Ridge, S.D., both in Letters Received–AGO; Miles to Mary Sherman Miles, Jan. 30, 1891, Pine Ridge, S.D., quoted in Johnson, *Unregimented General,* 294; Robert M. Utley, *Frontier Regulars,* 412 n.17.

33. The *New York Times, New York Tribune,* and *New York Herald* for January 6, 1891, all contain identically worded stories. See also report from Pine Ridge in *New York Tribune,* Jan. 7, 1891.

34. Miles to Mary Sherman Miles, Jan. 15, 1891, Pine Ridge, S.D., in Johnson, *Unregimented General,* 294; Sherman to Mary Sherman Miles, Jan. 7, 1891, New York, N.Y., in Miles-Cameron Family Papers.

35. *Deadwood Times,* Jan. 21, 1891.

36. James H. McGregor, *The Wounded Knee Massacre from the Viewpoint of the Sioux.*

37. *Deadwood Times,* Dec. 31, 1890.

38. Schofield to SW, Feb. 4, 1891, Washington, D.C., and Proctor's endorsement, Feb. 12, 1891, Washington, D.C., both in Forsyth to Lamont, Sept. 1, 1895, Manuscripts and Archives, New York Public Library; Proctor to Henry R. Lemley, Feb. 24, 1891, Washington, D.C., in Redfield Proctor Papers.

39. *New York Times,* Jan. 22, Feb. 8, 1891; Chauncey McKeever to John C. Kelton, Jan. 17, 1891, in McKeever's personnel file, RAGO, NA. The file also contains a copy of McKeever's military record dated December 4, 1893. Proctor fired a War Department clerk who refused to name the officer who made the reports available to the press.

40. *New York Times,* Jan. 22, 1891. On January 22, 1891, the *New York Tribune* announced that McKeever "was relieved from the duty of attending to Army appointments, promotions and commissions, and the Office of Inspector of the Military Academy was revived for his detail."

41. Miles to AG, Sept. 14, 1891, Chicago, Ill., *SW Annual Reports, 1891* 1:151–52.

42. Ibid., 152; *Washington Evening Star,* Jan. 3, 1891; Mooney, "The Ghost Dance Religion," 882.

43. *Deadwood Times,* Jan. 13, 18, 1891. For additional details see *New York Tribune,* Jan. 16, 1891, and *New York Herald,* Jan. 15, 1891.

44. *New York Herald,* Jan. 16, 1891; *New York Tribune,* Jan. 16, 1891; Miles to AG, Sept. 14, 1891, Chicago, Ill., *SW Annual Report, 1891* 1:152.

45. Charles G. Seymour, "General Miles on the Campaign," 7, 1891; Sanford quoted in E. R. Hagemann, ed., *Experiences in the Army Life of Colonel George B. Sanford, 1861–1898,* 101. Mooney, "Ghost Dance Religion," 870, stated that at Wounded Knee "a number of men" were enlistees fresh from eastern recruiting stations. If Forsyth had not jeopardized the fragile peace by mixing inexperienced troops with nervous warriors, the new religion might have cloaked a bloodless revolution.

46. *Deadwood Times,* Jan. 25, 1891. As late as September 1891, however, Miles warned that even though "the 'volcano has cooled down' the fires of discord still remain." Miles to AG, Sept. 14, 1891, Chicago, Ill., *SW Annual Report, 1891* 1:154.

47. Seymour, "The Final Review," 106; Miles, *Serving the Republic,* 246; *DAB,* s.v."Eugene Asa Carr."

48. Forsyth's account of the Drexel Mission fight, in which one officer and one enlisted man were killed and five men were wounded, is in Forsyth to Lamont, Sept. 1, 1895, Forsyth statement, Manuscripts and Archives, New York Public Library. See also Guy V. Henry to Forsyth, Jan. 5, 1895, in ibid.; and Henry to Schofield, Jan. 5, 1891, in Schofield Papers. Miles had been particularly angered that at the Drexel Mission fight Forsyth had left one of his cavalrymen on the field with a broken leg after an officer and a sergeant volunteered to rescue the trooper. After the man's body was recovered, a surgeon concluded that the disabled soldier had "evidently been tortured, as some of his sockets had been disjointed." Miles found it shocking that Forsyth would abandon one of his men to the enemy, especially when there were "twelve troops of cavalry and five pieces of artillery, approximating six hundred men" facing only a "small number of Indians." Miles to Col. William Shafter, Nov. 19, 1891, Chicago, Ill., in William Shafter Papers, Stanford University Libraries.

49. Seymour, "The Final Review," 106; Johnson, *Unregimented General,* 110.

50. Seymour, "The Final Review," 106; *New York Tribune,* Jan. 23, 1891.

51. Miles to Mary Sherman Miles, Jan. 15, 1891, Pine Ridge, S.D., in Johnson, *Unregimented General,* 294; Miles to commissioner of Indian affairs, Mar. 13, 1917, quoted in Elaine Goodale Eastman, "The Ghost Dance War and Wounded Knee Massacre of 1890–91," 39.

52. "The Case of General Forsyth," *Army and Navy Journal,* Feb. 14, 1891, 425. The same argument was repeated in 1926, in Col. Peter E. Traub, "Sioux Campaign—Winter of 1890–1891," 63. Utley foreword to Miles, *Personal Recollections,* vii.

53. *New York Times,* Nov. 9, 1894.

54. Ibid., May 3, 1896; Wells, *United in Diversity,* 107–22; Charles Morris, *Heroes of the Army in America,* 336.

11. From Command in Chicago to Commanding General of the Army

1. *New York Times,* Oct. 18, 1891.

2. Ibid., Dec. 29, 1891. Of course, Miles had reported to Washington when no war threatened; but although the observation was an exaggeration, it indicated an awareness of the general's military ability.

3. *Chicago Daily News,* July 3, 1894; *Miles, Serving the Republic,* 253; Schofield, *Forty-Six Years in the Army,* 494; Allan Nevins, *Grover Cleveland: A Study in Courage,* 621; Almont Lindsey, *The Pullman Strike: The Story of a Unique Experiment and of a Great Labor Upheaval;* Gerald G. Eggert, *Railroad Labor Disputes.*

4. Nevins, *Cleveland,* 621, 618, 615; and Eggert, *Railroad Labor Disputes,* 166; Schofield, *Forty-Six Years in the Army,* 492. For a biography of the attorney general, see Henry James, *Richard Olney and His Public Service.*

5. Lindsey, *The Pullman Strike,* 172.

6. *Chicago Daily News,* July 3, 1894; *New York Times,* July 3, 1894. Eugene Debs, founder of the American Railway Union, and other ARU officers and "all persons combining and conspiring with them" were commanded and enjoined to desist and refrain "from in any way or manner interfering with, hindering, obstructing, or stopping any business" of any railroad line identified in the injunction. The order specified a broad range of interference that was to be prohibited. Eggert, *Railroad Labor Disputes,* 168.

7. *Chicago Daily News,* July 3, 1894.

8. Ibid.; Nevins, *Cleveland,* 620–21.

9. Schofield to Lt. Col. James P. Martin, asst. adj. gen., HQ Dept. of the Missouri, July 3, 1894, Washington, D.C., in Schofield, *Forty-Six Years in the Army,* 499.

10. Miles to AG, U.S. Army, July 4, 1894, Chicago, in ibid., 497; Lt. Col. James P. Martin, asst. adj. gen., Dept. of the Missouri, to AG, U.S. Army, July 4, 1894, Chicago, in ibid.; Schofield to commanding general, Dept. of the Missouri, July 2, 1894, Washington, D.C., in ibid., 496; Schofield's intentions in ibid., 494–95.

11. *Chicago Daily News,* July 5, 1894; *New York Times,* July 5, 1894.

12. *Chicago Daily News,* July 5, 1894.

13. Ibid.

14. Miles to AG, U.S. Army, July 5, 1894, Chicago, in Schofield, *Forty-Six Years in the Army,* 499–500.

15. Schofield to Miles, July 5, 1894, 10:15 P.M., Washington, D.C., in ibid., 500; Miles to AG, July 6, 1894, Chicago, in ibid., 500–501.

16. *Chicago Daily News,* July 6, 7, 1894.

17. Ibid.; Lindsey, *The Pullman Strike,* 174.

18. Frederic Remington, "Chicago under the Mob," 681.

19. Richard Olney to newsman A. H. Lewis, n.d., Washington, D.C., quoted in Eggert, *Railroad Labor Disputes,* 173.

20. Lindsey, *The Pullman Strike,* 207; *Chicago Daily News,* July 6, 1894; Miles to AG, U.S. Army, July 18, 1894, HQ Dept. of the Missouri, Chicago, Ill., RAGO, General Correspondence, 1890–1917, AGO, NA.

21. *New York Herald,* July 15, 1894.

22. Miles to AG, July 18, 1894, Chicago, Letters Received–AGO; Lindsey, *The Pullman Strike,* 208–14.

23. *Chicago Daily News,* July 7, 1894.

24. Miles to AG, July 18, 1894, HQ Dept. of the Missouri, Chicago, Ill., in AGO, NA.

25. *New York Herald,* July 9, 1894.

26. Ibid.

27. Ibid., July 13, 1894; *Chicago Daily News,* July 12, 1894.

28. *Chicago Daily News,* July 19, 1894; Miles, *Serving the Republic,* 258.

29. Patrick J. Dalton, master craftsman, Order of Knights of Labor, to Cleveland, July 10, 1894, Chicago, in Grover Cleveland Papers (microfilm), Graduate School, City University of New York; Miles to AG, Sept. 14, 1894, *SW Annual Report, 1894,* in Pohanka, *Nelson A. Miles,* 239; excerpt from *New York Evening Post* in *Army and Navy Journal,* July 14, 1894, 805; Roy Ginger, *The Bending Cross: A Biography of Eugene Victor Debs.*

30. *Lake County News,* July 12, 1894.

31. Ibid.

32. Ibid.; *Crown Point Register,* July 13, 1894; *Chicago Daily News,* July 8, 1894. For a brief history of the Pullman strike in Indiana, see Powell A. Moore, *The Calumet Region: Indiana's Last Frontier,* 494–96.

33. Alex Shields and Dr. T. E. Bell, July 8, 1894; Hammond to Gov. Claude E. Matthews; Governor Matthews to Shields and Bell, 9:30 P.M., July 8, 1894, Indianapolis, all in *Lake County News,* July 12, 1894. Number of militia regiments and troops in *Crown Point Register,* July 13, 1894.

34. *Chicago Daily News,* July 9, 1894.

35. Ibid., July 10, 1894.

36. Matilda Gresham, *Life of Walter Quintin Gresham, 1832–1895,* 1:418–19; Nelson A. Miles, "The Lessons of the Recent Strike."

37. Remington, "Chicago under the Mob," 680; Miles, "Lessons of the Recent Strike," 188.

38. Miles, "Lessons of the Recent Strike," 187–88.

39. *New York Times,* Nov. 9, 1894.

40. *New York Herald,* Nov. 22, 1894.

41. Carr quoted in James T. King, *War Eagle: A Life of General Eugene A. Carr,* 248.

42. Schofield to SW, Jan. 31, 1893, Washington, and Miles to Carr, Feb. 8, 1893, Chicago, in King, *War Eagle,* 249, 250.

43. Miles to AG, Mar. 25, 1893, Chicago, Ill., and Miles to Shafter, telegram, Oct. 16, 1896, Wichita, Kans., in William Shafter Papers.

44. *New York Times,* May 19, Apr. 28, 1895, Dec. 11, 1894.

45. *New York Times,* Mar. 19, 1895; Miles to AG, Aug. 31, 1895, *SW Annual Report, 1895* 1:64–68.

46. William Sherman to John Sherman, July 8, 1871, Washington, D.C., in Rachel Sherman

Thorndike, ed., *The Sherman Letters: Correspondence between General and Senator Sherman from 1837 to 1891,* 331; Edward Ranson, "Nelson A. Miles as Commanding General, 1895–1903."

47. Schofield, *Forty-Six Years in the Army,* 468–70.

48. *Army and Navy Journal,* Sept. 14, 1895, 25.

49. Ibid., Oct. 5, 1895, 73.

50. *New York Herald,* Oct. 1, 1895; *New York Times,* Sept. 30, 1895.

51. *New York Times,* Oct. 3, 1895; *Army and Navy Journal,* Oct. 5, 1895, 73.

52. *New York Herald,* Oct. 1, 1895. President Harrison's biographer, Harry J. Sievers, states that in the election campaign of 1892, "General Miles, for one, was active behind [John] Sherman." Sievers, *Benjamin Harrison: Hoosier President,* 224.

53. *New York Times,* June 19, 1896.

54. Ibid., Nov. 20, 1896; Miles to AG, Oct. 21, 1897, Washington, *SW Annual Report, 1897* 1:94.

55. Miles, *Serving the Republic,* 261.

56. Miles to AG, Nov. 15, 1895, Washington, *SW Annual Report, 1895* 1:64–68; *New York Times,* June 26, Sept. 13, 1896.

57. Policy of concentrating troops near cities in *New York Times,* Sept. 13, 1896.

58. Cosmos, *An Army for Empire,* 7, 15; *New York Times,* Jan. 22, 1898; Miles to SW, Jan. 20, 1898, Washington, D.C., and Brig. Gen. Daniel W. Flager to SW, Jan. 27, 1898, Washington, D.C., in Russell Alexander Alger Papers, William L. Clements Library, Ann Arbor, Michigan; Miles, *Annual Report, 1896,* 76; idem, *Annual Report,* 1897, 93.

59. *New York Times,* May 3, 5, 6, 1897.

60. Miles to Secretary of War Russell A. Alger: June 1, 1897, Athens, Greece; July 24, 1897, Carlsbad, Austria; and Sept. 27, 1897, London, England, in Miles personnel file in Military Archives Div., NA. Miles, *Serving the Republic,* 262–67.

61. *New York Times,* Apr. 14, 1896.

62. Ibid., Aug. 8, 1897.

63. Miles, *Serving the Republic,* 267.

12. The Spanish-American War: Girding for Battle

1. *New York Times,* Nov. 20, 1896.

2. Miles to AG, Nov. 5, 1898, in *SW Annual Report, 1898,* vol. 1, 2:4–5 (included is Miles to SW (Russell A. Alger), Apr. 9, 1898, Washington, 5); *New York Times,* Apr. 28, 1898.

3. Trask, *The War with Spain,* 155–58; Cosmos, *An Army for Empire,* 90–102; George J. A. O'Toole, *The Spanish War,* 196; T. Harry Williams, *The History of American Wars,* 323–24; Frank Freidel, *The Splendid Little War,* 33–34.

4. Miles, *Serving the Republic,* 270; Nelson A. Miles, "The War with Spain" 1:516.

5. Miles, "The War with Spain" 1:517.

6. Miles to SW (Alger), Apr. 26, 1898, HQ of the Army, Washington, D.C., in Alger Papers.

7. *New York Herald,* May 19, 1898.

8. Miles, *Annual Report, 1898,* 8; Trask, *The War with Spain,* 158–59; Cosmos, *An Army for Empire,* 137;. *New York Herald,* Apr. 6, 1898.

9. Miles to AG, Nov. 5, 1898, *SW Annual Report, 1898* 1:8; Trask, *The War with Spain,* 160.

10. Miles to SW, Apr. 18, 1898, Washington, D.C., Alger Papers.

11. Brig. Gen. Daniel W. Flager, chief of ordnance, to SW, May 2, 1898, Washington, D.C., in ibid.

12. Ibid.

13. Brig. Gen. A. R. Buffington, chief of ordnance, memorandum for the SW, Apr. 10, 1899, Washington, D.C., in ibid.

14. Flager to Alger, May 2, 1898, Washington, D.C., in ibid.

15. *Army and Navy Journal,* Dec. 31, 1898, 417. The *New York Herald,* July 10, 1898, also reported that the Mauser was "superior" to the Krag-Jorgensen in "some" respects. For example, the weapon and ammunition weighed less than the Krag.

16. *Army and Navy Journal,* June 10, 1899, 976.

17. Philip M. Shockley, *The Krag-Jorgensen Rifle in the Service,* 64.

18. Ibid., 7; Shockley quoted the "United States Magazine Rifle," in the *Scientific American Supplement* 46 (July 9, 1898); "New Sight and Wind Gauge," *Army and Navy Journal,* May 13, 1899, 871; ibid., Feb. 11, 1899, 550.

19. Miles to SW, Apr. 18, 1898, Washington, D.C., in Alger Papers; "Medical Statistics of the Spanish Army, 1896," 434–35; John M. Gibson, *Soldier in White: The Life of General George Miller Sternberg.* In 1899 Sternberg told a meeting of the American Medical Association that from May 1, 1898, to Apr. 30,1899, 5,438 soldiers had died of disease (213). *The New Orleans Medical and Surgical Journal* published two articles about yellow fever written by Sternberg: in July 1875 "An Inquiry into the Modus Operandi of the Yellow Fever Poison" and in March 1877 "A Study of the Natural History of Yellow Fever."

20. *New York Herald,* May 14, 1898.

21. Military service of Col. Arthur L. Wagner, General Staff, U.S. Army, in Brig. Gen. J. Franklin Bell to Lt. Gen. Adna R. Chaffee, chief of staff, War Dept., June 10, 1904, General Service and Staff College, Ft. Leavenworth, Kans. Brig. Gen. Arthur L. Wagner personal file, NA; Herman Hagedorn, *Leonard Wood: A Biography* 1:122. Wagner would die of consumption in Asheville, N.C., on June 17, 1905, the day he received his commission as brigadier general. *New York Times,* June 18, 1905.

22. Cosmos, *An Army for Empire,* 30–32.

23. Memorandum on operations in Cuba, prepared by Lt. Col. Arthur Wagner to the War Dept., office of the AG, Washington, Apr. 11, 1898, in Nelson A. Miles Collection, USAMHI.

24. *New York Herald,* June 5, 1898.

25. Ibid.; Lt. Gen. John M. Schofield, "General Schofield's Experiences in McKinley's Administration," 1, undated memoir, Schofield Papers.

26. Schofield, "General Schofield's Experiences in McKinley's Administration," 12–24. Schofield also asserted the need for a chief-of-staff appointed by the president "to aid him in the discharge of his duties. The President ought to have the power to retire such officer at any time with due regard for his rank and services, and to appoint another in the same manner." *Army and Navy Journal,* May 21, 1898, 755.

27. *DAB,* s.v. "Russell Alexander Alger"; see also Jasper B. Reid, Jr., "Russell A. Alger as Secretary of War," 227. Reid states that Alger cared for one sister (p. 225), while Cosmos, *An Army for Empire,* 55, wrote that he cared for "two younger children."

28. Alger to McKinley, May 26, 1898, Washington, D.C., in McKinley Papers. Here Alger explains that he did not agree with Miles's plan to land the regulars 480 miles east of Havana.

29. Alger to Miles, May 26, 1898, Washington, D.C., in Alger Papers.

30. Miles, *Serving the Republic,* 268–72.

31. *New York Herald,* May 31, 1898; *Tampa* (Fla.) *Morning Tribune,* June 2, 3, 1898.

32. *Tampa Morning Tribune,* June 3, 1898; Miles, *Serving the Republic,* 275–76.

33. John Black Atkins, *The War in Cuba: The Experiences of an Englishman in the U.S. Army,* 20; *Army and Navy Journal,* May 28, 1898, 763.

34. *Army and Navy Journal,* Apr. 23, 1898, 651; Trask, *The War with Spain,* 74–75, 183. The adjutant general of the army, Brig. Gen. Henry C. Corbin, provided more information about the choice of Tampa. According to Corbin, "Mr. [Henry B.] Plant, of the railroad system bearing his name [soon to become the Atlantic Coast Line], persuaded the Secretary of War that Tampa was the place [to organize the expedition] and that his railroad was competent to handle that army and all its supplies." The adjutant general further explained that "Secretary Alger had all confidence in his [Plant's] judgement and ability, and that was misplaced confidence, . . . When one had Alger's confidence he relied on him implicitly." Unpublished autobiography of Maj. Gen. Henry C. Corbin, p. 87, in Henry C. Corbin Papers, LC.

35. Memorandum, n.d., n.p., in Alger Papers; *New York Herald,* June 6, 1898.

36. Miles to Alger, June 4, 1898, Tampa, Fla., in *New York Herald,* June 6, 1898.

37. *Webster's American Biographies* (1974 ed.), s.v. "Bigelow, Poultney," "Bigelow, John"; Poultney Bigelow, *Seventy Summers.*

38. *New York Times,* June 4, 1898.

39. Ibid., June 7, 1898.

40. Bigelow, *Seventy Summers* 1:292–93.

41. *New York Times,* June 7, 1898. The expletives were deleted in the original *Times* story.

42. Ibid., June 10, 1898.

43. Undated "Topics of the Times" column quoted in Gibson, *Soldier in White,* 200; *New York Times,* June 11, 1898.

44. Russell Alexander Alger, *The Spanish-American War,* 69.

45. Miles to Alger, June 5, 1898, Tampa, Fla., in Alger Papers; Alger, *The Spanish-American War,* 69.

46. Nelson A. Miles, "The War with Spain" 1:528; Alger to Miles, June 15, 1898, Washington, D.C., and Miles to Alger, June 15, 1898, Tampa, Fla., in Alger Papers.

47. Miles to Alger, June 15, 1898, Tampa, Fla., in Alger Papers; *New York Times,* June 10, 1898; Miles to Lt. Gen. Calixto García,Cuban army, June 2, 1898, Tampa, Fla., in Alger Papers.

48. Miles, *Serving the Republic,* 276–77; Miles to Alger, June 2, 1898, Tampa, Fla., in Alger Papers.

49. Miles to Alger, June 9, 1898, Tampa, Fla., in ibid.

50. Miles to Alger, June 6, 1898, Tampa, Fla., in ibid.

51. Miles, *Serving the Republic,* 272–74.

52. Trask, *The War with Spain,* 340; Miles to Alger, Apr. 18, 1898, Washington, D.C., in Alger Papers.

53. Alger to Miles, June 6, 1898, War Dept., in Alger Papers.

54. Unpublished autobiography of Maj. Gen. Henry C. Corbin, 88–89, in Corbin Papers.

55. Two letters Miles to Shafter, June 11, 1898, Tampa, Fla., in Shafter Papers.

56. Unpublished autobiography of Maj. Gen. Henry C. Corbin, p. 89; and Shafter to Corbin, June 7, 1898, Tampa, Fla., in Corbin Papers.

57. "Confidential report of observations, made by Lt. Col. Marion P. Maus, inspector general, U.S.V[olunteers], and aide-de-camp, relating to operations during the Spanish-American War," p. 3, Maus to Miles, Sept. 18, 1898, Washington, D.C., in Miles Collection, USAMHI (hereafter cited as "Confidential report"); Miles, *Serving the Republic,* 175; Brig. Gen. Marion P. Maus personal file, Military Archives Division, NA. Maus (1850–1930) graduated from West Point in 1874,

won the Congressional Medal of Honor fighting the Apaches in January 1886, and retired from the army in 1913.

58. "Confidential report," 2, 4.

59. Ibid., 2; Frederic Remington, "With the Fifth Corps," in Douglas Allen, *Frederic Remington and the Spanish-American War,* 75; Remington, "A Gallant American Officer," in ibid., 131.

60. *New York Times,* June 18, 1898. In this interview, Miles placed some of the blame for delays in the delivery of supplies and equipment on the Post Office. When troops were concentrated in towns the size of Tampa or Chickamauga, the increased mail volume overwhelmed the local offices. Miles explained that "as a result the official communications to and from the War Department, on which depend the regularity of movement of many kinds of stores have been delayed."

61. *New York Herald,* June 17, 1898.

62. Ibid., June 14, 19, 1898. Admiral Manuel de la Cámara's fleet set sail for the Philippines rather than for the Caribbean.

63. Alger to Miles, June 26, 1898, Washington, D.C., in *SW Annual Report, 1898* 1:14.

64. *New York Times,* June 5, 18, 1898.

65. *Army and Navy Journal,* July 2, 1898, 881, 890; Shafter to Alger, July 3, 1898, Playa del Este, in Miles, *Serving the Republic,* 281–82.

66. Miles, *Serving the Republic,* 282; Shafter to AG, July 4, 1898, camp near San Juan River, in *SW Annual Report, 1898* 1:18.

67. Miles to Alger, July 5, 1898, Washington, D.C., in Alger, *The Spanish-American War,* 300–301.

68. *New York Herald,* June 24, 1898; *Tampa Morning Tribune,* July 6, 1898.

69. "Confidential report," 12.

70. *New York Times,* July 3, 1898; Corbin to Shafter, July 7, 1898, Washington, D.C., in *Army and Navy Journal,* Aug. 27, 1898, 1086; Miles, *Serving the Republic,* 294.

71. *New York Herald,* July 8, 1898. The blank space indicates a pause in the original account.

13. The Surrender at Santiago and the Puerto Rico Campaign

1. Miles, "The War with Spain" 2:755; Miles to Sampson, July 11, 1898, *USS Yale* off Siboney, Cuba, in Miles to AG, Nov. 5, 1898, Washington, D.C., *SW Annual Report, 1898* 1:19.

2. "Confidential report," 13–14.

3. Ibid., 20.

4. Miles to AG, Nov. 5, 1898, *SW Annual Report, 1898* 1:19.

5. Ibid. 1:20; Miles, "The War with Spain" 2:755; Alger to Miles, July 13, 1898, Washington, D.C., *SW Annual Report, 1898* 1:20.

6. Alger to Long, July 13, 1898, Washington, D.C., in Alger Papers; "Confidential report," 30.

7. "Confidential report," 27–30; Trask, *The War with Spain,* 299–305.

8. *New York Times,* July 15, 1898; Alger, *The Spanish-American War,* 198–215; Miles, *Serving the Republic,* 286–94. Alger referred to the tropical tree in the valley as a ceiba, which came to be known as the "Surrender Tree." Maus's term "Tree of Peace" appears to be a more appropriate designation. The tree has also been identified as a mango. "Confidential report," 31; *New York Times,* July 15, 1898.

9. "Confidential report," 31. According to the *New York Times* of July 15, 1898, "His [Toral's] brave words inspired a feeling of respect and admiration in the hearts of his adversaries."

10. "Confidential report," 32; *New York Times,* July 15, 1898; Trask, *The War With Spain,* 302.

Trask explained that the truce occurred before the navy had a chance to fire its heaviest guns, and Shafter limited the target areas to protect his troops.

11. Transcript of conference made by Ramón G. Mendoza, volunteer aide to Brig. Gen. Henry W. Lawton, in Alger, *The Spanish-American War,* 205–10.

12. *New York Times,* July 15, 1898.

13. Toral to general in chief of the American forces, [July] 14, [1898], Santiago, Cuba, in Alger, *The Spanish-American War,* 210. Maus contends in his report to Miles that this letter "was evidently intended for you, although it was appropriated by Captain [William H.] McKittrick." "Confidential report," 33.

14. Alger, *The Spanish-American War,* 211–13.

15. Ibid., 213. At the 9:30 P.M. conference, Toral "asked that the word 'capitulation' be substituted for 'surrender' in the tentative articles which had been drawn up." Shafter to Miles, July 15, 1898, Santiago, Cuba, in Shafter Papers.

16. Miles to Shafter, July 15, 1898, Daiquirí, in Shafter Papers; Miles to AG, Nov. 5, 1898, Washington, D.C., *SW Annual Report, 1898* 1:22.

17. *New York Times,* July 18, 1898.

18. *Army and Navy Journal,* July 23, 1898, 956. This account noted that Shafter's delegation included "Generals Wheeler, Lawton,[Jacob F.] Kent, [Adna R.] Chaffee, [Samuel B. M.] Young, [Samuel S.] Sumner, [Hamilton S.] Hawkins, [John C.] Bates . . . [and William] Ludlow."

19. Trask, *The War with Spain,* 321; "Confidential report," 33.

20. Miles to Shafter, July 17, 1898, Playa Del Este, and Shafter to Miles, July 17, 1898, Santiago, Cuba, in Shafter Papers.

21. Miles to Shafter, July 18, 1898, Playa Del Este, ibid.

22. *New York Times,* July 15, 1898; "Confidential report," 35–36.

23. "Confidential report," 36; Schofield, "General Schofield's Experiences in McKinley's Administration," 20–21.

24. *Army and Navy Journal,* Sept. 3, 1898, 17.

25. Miles to AG, Nov. 5, 1898, Washington, D.C., in *SW Annual Report, 1898* 1:29; *Army and Navy Journal,* July 30, 1898, 980; *New York Times,* July 20, 1898; Miles to Shafter, July 18, 1898, Playa Del Este, in Shafter Papers.

26. Alger, *The Spanish-American War,* 304–5, 308, 310; Miles to AG, Nov. 5, 1898, Washington, D.C., *SW Annual Report, 1898* 1:29; *Army and Navy Journal,* Nov. 12, 1898, 248.

27. Miles to Higginson, July 22, 1898, on board USS *Yale,* en route to Puerto Rico, in *SW Annual Report, 1898* 1:29.

28. *New York Times,* July 24, 1898.

29. *Army and Navy Journal,* Sept. 3, 1898, 5; *New York Times,* July 24, 1898; Miles, "The War with Spain" 3:129; Atkins, *The War in Cuba,* 247.

30. *Army and Navy Journal,* July 30, 1898, 980; Alger to Miles, July 23, 1898, Washington, D.C., in Miles Collection, USAMHI.

31. Miles, "The War with Spain" 3:129.

32. Ibid., 130; *New York Times,* July 27, 1898; Richard Harding Davis, "The Porto Rican Campaign," 517–18; Miles to AG, Nov. 5, 1898, Washington, D.C., *SW Annual Report, 1898* 1:31; *New York Times,* July 28, 1898. While the *New York Times,* July 27, 1898, mentioned that only thirty troops were ill, Miles reported "nearly a hundred" were sick. Miles to AG, Nov. 5, 1898, Washington, D.C., *SW Annual Report, 1898* 1:29.

33. *New York Times,* July 27, 1898.

34. Miles to AG, Nov. 5, 1898, Washington, D.C., *SW Annual Report, 1898* 1:31; Davis, "The Porto Rican Campaign," 518.

35. Miles, "The War with Spain" 3:131; Corbin to Miles, Aug. 4, 1898, Washington, D.C., and Miles to AG, Aug. 5, 1898, Ponce, in Alger Papers. Three majors and three captains of the 6th Massachusetts also resigned. See Corbin to Governor Roger Wolcott, Aug. 8, 1898, Washington, D.C., in Department of War, the Adjutant General's Office, *Correspondence Relating to the War with Spain and Conditions Growing Out of the Same, . . . between the Adjutant General of the Army and Military Commanders in the United States, Cuba, Puerto Rico, China, and the Philippine Islands, from April 15, 1898 to July 30, 1902* 1:376; *New York Times,* Aug. 6, 1898.

36. Alger, *The Spanish-American War,* 308–9; Miles, "The War with Spain" 3:131; French Ensor Chadwick, *The Relations of the United States to Spain: The Spanish-American War* 2:289. Miles had dispatched the cruiser *Columbia* to meet the fleet carrying Wilson, with word that the original expedition had landed at Guánica rather than at Fajardo. James H. Wilson, *Under the Old Flag: Recollections of Military Operations in the War for the Union, the Boxer Rebellion, etc.* 2:440.

37. Davis, "The Porto Rican Campaign," 519.

38. Chadwick, *The Spanish-American War* 2:293; Miles, "The War with Spain" 3:132.

39. Davis, "The Puerto Rican Campaign," 520.

40. Miles to the inhabitants of Puerto Rico, July 28, 1898, Ponce, in Alger Papers; Alger to Miles, July 23, 1898, Washington, D.C., in Miles Collection.

41. Miles to the inhabitants of Puerto Rico, July 28, 1898, Ponce, in Alger Papers; Stephen K. Hermann, *From Yauco to Las Marías,* 34.

42. Asst. Adj. Gen., Provisional Div., to Commanding Gen., 1st Brigade, Aug. 12, 1898, Adjuntas, P.R.; 2d endorsement, 6th Illinois Volunteer Infantry, Aug. 13, 1898, Adjuntas, P.R., RG 395, Records of U.S. Army Overseas Operations and Commands 1898–1942, Letters and Telegrams Received, August–September 1898, NA; AG, HQ Provisional Div., to Commanding Gen., 1st Brigade, Aug. 18, 1898, Utuado, P.R., in ibid.

43. Trask, *The War With Spain* , 365; Corbin to Miles, Aug. 14, 1898, Washington, D.C., and Gilmore to AG, Aug. 15, 1898, Ponce, both in Alger Papers; *New York Times,* Aug. 14, 1898.

44. Miles to AG, Nov. 5, 1898, Washington, D.C., *SW Annual Report, 1898* 1:31; *New York Times,* July 27, 1898.

45. Félix Matos Bernier, July 26, 1898, Ponce, P.R., in Miles, "The War with Spain" 3:132–33.

46. John C. Gilmore, Brig. Gen., USV, to Maj. Gen. James H. Wilson, USV, July 29, 1898, Port Ponce, P.R., in Miles to AG, Nov. 5, 1898, Washington, D.C., *SW Annual Report, 1898* 1:32–33.

47. Miles to SW, July 31, 1898, Ponce, P.R., in Alger Papers; Davis, "The Porto Rican Campaign," 520–21. One source of flags was the Lafayette Post of the GAR, which routinely supplied flags to New York City's public schools. Civil War veteran Daniel Butterfield offered to extend this policy to Puerto Rico's public schools. Subsequently, the War Department was notified that there were 546 public schools and 38 private ones on the island. Corbin to Miles, Aug. 6, 1898, Washington, D.C., and Gilmore to AG, Washington, D.C., Aug. 8, 1898, Ponce, P.R., both in Alger Papers.

48. Davis, "The Porto Rican Campaign," 523; "Confidential report."

49. "Confidential report"; Davis, "The Porto Rican Campaign," 527; Miles to Alger, July 30, 1898, Ponce, P.R., in Alger Papers.

50. John Black Atkins, *Incidents and Reflections,* 115.

51. Wilson, *Under the Old Flag* 2:441.

52. Miles to Alger, Aug. 2, 1898, Ponce, P.R., in Alger Papers; *New York Times,* Aug. 1, 1898.

53. "Confidential report." Wilson sent troops to arrest the leader of a band of revolutionaries who had robbed and then torched a village of Spanish sympathizers. Tried and found guilty by a military commission, he was sentenced to prison for fifteen years. Wilson believed that after island newspapers carried this story "the beneficial results were instantaneous." Wilson, *Under the Old Flag* 2:451.

54. *New York Times,* Aug. 1, 1898. Here the *Times* explained that because other volunteer infantry regiments in Cuba were "armed with Springfield rifles using black powder, they were kept in the background as far as possible." Carl Russell Fish, *The Path of Empire,* 166, states, "The Santiago campaign . . . was fought chiefly by regulars. The Rough Riders and the Seventy-first New York Regiment were the only volunteer units to take a heavy share."

55. The composition of the four commands of the First Corps in Alger, *The Spanish-American War,* 310–11; Atkins, *The War in Cuba,* 248.

56. Atkins, *The War in Cuba,* 248; *Army and Navy Journal,* Sept. 10, 1898, 26.

57. *New York Times,* Aug. 2, 6, 1898.

58. Ibid., Aug. 6, 1898; Wilson, *Under the Old Flag* 2:442. Wilson's command received the new rifles on August 3.

59. Wilson, *Under the Old Flag* 2:443; *New York Times,* Aug. 2, 6, 1898.

60. Wilson, *Under the Old Flag* 2:442.

61. Alger, *The Spanish-American War,* 311.

62. Miles to Alger, Aug. 6, 1898, Ponce, P.R., in Alger Papers; *New York Times,* Aug. 9, 1898. The *Scientific American Supplement* (46 [July 9, 1898]: 33) explained that "The Sims-Dudley pneumatic gun popularly but erroneously known as the 'dynamite gun'" is the weapon used at Guayama. Miles to SW, Aug. 10, 1898, Ponce, P.R., in Alger Papers; Chadwick, *The Spanish-American War* 2:309.

63. *New York Times,* Aug. 6, 1898.

64. Ibid., Aug. 7, 1905.

65. Ibid., Aug. 1, 2, 6, 1898.

66. Miles, "The War with Spain" 3:134; Davis, "The Porto Rican Campaign," 524; *New York Times,* Aug. 6, 1898.

67. Chadwick, *The Spanish-American War* 2:306; Brig. Gen. John C. Gilmore to Schwan, Aug. 6, 1898, Port Ponce, P.R., in ibid., 313–14; Miles, "The War with Spain" 3:134–35.

68. *New York Times,* Aug. 8, 1898.

69. Miles to SW, Aug. 10, 1898, Ponce, P.R., and Alger to Miles, Aug. 11, 1898, Washington, D.C., in Alger Papers. There is a possibility that the navy contemplated an independent action against San Juan. Trask, *The War with Spain,* 361.

70. Miles to AG, Nov. 5, 1898, Washington, D.C., in *SW Annual Report, 1898* 1:36; *New York Times,* Aug. 10, 1898.

71. *Lamb's Biographical Dictionary of the United States* (1900 ed.) "Schwan, Theodore."

72. Chadwick, *The Spanish-American War* 2:306–8; Miles to AG, Nov. 5, 1898, Washington, D.C., *SW Annual Report, 1898* 1:35; Alger, *The Spanish-American War,* 314–16; Miles to SW, Aug. 11, 1898, Ponce, P.R., and Miles to SW, Aug. 13, 1898, Ponce, P.R., both in Alger Papers; Miles, "The War with Spain" 3:136.

73. Miles, "The War with Spain" 3:136; Alger, *The Spanish-American War,* 316; Chadwick, *The Spanish-American War,* 308–9.

74. Atkins, *The War in Cuba,* 249; Alger, *The Spanish-American War,* 310; Miles to SW, Aug. 8, 1898, Ponce, P.R., in Alger Papers; *New York Times,* Aug. 19, 1898.

75. Henry to AG, HQ of the Army, Aug. 19, 1898, Ponce, P.R., in Miles Collection, USAMHI.

76. Atkins, *The War in Cuba,* 249; *New York Times,* Aug. 23, 1898.

77. *DAB,* s.v. "James Harrison Wilson."

78. *Lamb's Biographical Dictionary of the United States* (1900 ed.), s.v. "Ernst, Oswald Herbert."

79. Wilson, *Under the Old Flag* 2:443–44; Davis, "The Porto Rican Campaign," 524; Col. Willis J. Hulings, from Oil City, Pa., would become a brigadier general of volunteers in September 1898 and receive an honorable discharge on December 3, 1898. From 1907 to 1913 he commanded the Second Brigade of the Pennsylvania State Militia. Hulings would be elected to the Sixty-fifth Congress on the Progressive ticket, and to the Sixty-eighth Congress as a Republican. *New York Times,* Aug. 10, 1924.

80. Chadwick, *The Spanish-American War,* 2:301.

81. Wilson, *Under the Old Flag* 2:444.

82. Chadwick, *The Spanish-American War* 2:302–3. Besides providing the number of Spanish troops taken prisoner and those killed, this account estimated that between thirty and forty were wounded; apparently the wounded were not counted as prisoners. Thomas J. Steward, comp., *Record of Pennsylvania Volunteers in the Spanish-American War,* 657. In Wilson, *Under the Flag* 2:444–45, the general indicated that the blockhouse was set on fire at 8:00 A.M. Miles to SW, Aug. 9, 1898, Ponce, P.R., in Alger Papers; Davis, "The Porto Rican Campaign," 524.

83. Anthony Fiala, *Troop "C" in Service: An Account of the Part Played by Troop "C" of the New York Volunteer Cavalry in the Spanish-American War of 1898,* 68–76.

84. Wilson, *Under the Old Flag* 2:446–47. Interestingly, in this account Wilson makes no mention of the fight at Asomante.

85. Chadwick, *The Spanish-American War* 2:305; *New York Times,* Aug. 15, 1898; Davis, "The Porto Rican Campaign," 526.

86. Davis, "The Porto Rican Campaign," 526–27; *New York Times,* Aug. 15, 1898. Admiral Sir Albert Paget entered the English navy in 1865, becoming captain in 1896 and rear admiral in 1911; he was knighted in 1911 and received the Distinguished Service Order in 1917. *New York Times,* June 19, 1918.

87. Davis, "The Porto Rican Campaign," 527; *New York Times,* Aug. 15, 1898; Chadwick, *The Spanish American War* 2:305–6. Chadwick (p. 305) names two soldiers from the 3d Wisconsin who were killed and three infantrymen and an officer from the same regiment who were wounded, as was the lieutenant from the Third Artillery. J. Stanley Dietz, comp., *The Battle Flags and Wisconsin Troops in the Civil War and the War with Spain,* states that only two men from the 3d Wisconsin were wounded.

88. SW to Miles, 4:23 P.M., Aug. 12, 1898, Washington, D.C., in Alger Papers; *New York Times,* Aug. 15, 1898.

89. Atkins, *The War in Cuba,* 251. By August 21, 1898, Miles realized, and admitted, that four men had been killed in action. Miles to Mrs. E. W. Heintzelman, Aug. 21, 1898, Ponce, P.R., in Nelson A. Miles, Miscellaneous Manuscripts, Rutherford B. Hayes Presidential Center, Fremont, Ohio.

14. Following the Spanish-American War: Scandals and Military Pettiness

1. Proctor to Miles, Aug. 29, 1898, Redfield Proctor Papers.

2. Alger, *The Spanish-American War,* 317.

3. Davis, "The Porto Rican Campaign," 515–17.

4. Wilson, *Under the Old Flag* 2:449–50. In Brig. Gen. Henry C. Corbin's annual report, dated November 1, 1898, the adjutant general disclosed that 427 Americans died in Cuba "not including killed or died of wounds," compared to 137 in Puerto Rico. Also, "in Cuba 23 officers and 237 men were killed, 99 officers and 1,332 were wounded; in Puerto Rico 3 enlisted men killed, 4 officers and 36 men wounded." Reported in *Army and Navy Journal,* Nov. 12, 1898. Actually, four Americans were killed in action in Puerto Rico, two at Hormigueros and two at Asomante. Alger, *The Spanish-American War,* 313, 315. A more recent account supports these figures. Cosmos, *An Army for Empire,* 236.

5. *DAB,* s.v. "Nicholas Senn."

6. Senn to Greenleaf, n.d., n.p., in Miles to SW, Aug. 12, 1898, Ponce, P.R., in Adjutant General's Office, *Correspondence Relating to the War with Spain* 1:385.

7. *New York Times,* Aug. 22, 1898.

8. Henry to AG, HQ of the Army, Aug. 19, 1898, Ponce, P.R., in Miles Collection, USAMHI.

9. Miles to President William McKinley, Apr. 11, 1899, Washington, D.C., in McKinley Papers; *New York Times,* Aug. 17, 1898; *Army and Navy Journal,* Dec. 2, 1899, 316, and Jan. 13, 1900, 454. Reber became a colonel in 1916, and from 1914 to 1916 he was chief of the Army Aviation Section. During World War I, after serving with the Twenty-eighth Division, he became deputy chief of staff of the Second Army. At the time of his death on April 16, 1933, he was a vice president of the Radio Corporation of America. At that time, one son, 1st Lt. Miles Reber of the Army Engineer Corps, was stationed at West Point, and the other, Samuel Reber, Jr., was a diplomatic officer with the State Department. *New York Times,* Apr. 18, 1933.

10. Miles to Emily M. Heintzelman, Aug. 15, 1898, Ponce, P.R., in Miles Manuscripts, Rutherford B. Hayes Presidential Center; Capt. Charles Stewart Heintzelman, Veterans Records, Pension File, General Reference Branch, NA; *Kansas City Star,* Aug. 23, 1898.

11. *Kansas City Star,* Aug. 23, 25, 1898.

12. Ibid., Aug. 25, 1898.

13. *New York Times,* Aug. 25, 1898.

14. Ibid., Aug. 31, 1898.

15. *New York World,* Aug. 25, 1898.

16. *Army and Navy Journal,* Aug. 27, 1898, 1089.

17. *New York Times,* Aug. 28, 1898.

18. *Kansas City Star,* Aug. 25, 1898.

19. "Henry Clark Corbin, Lieutenant General United States Army," *Army and Navy Life and the United Services,* Sept. 1906, 8; *DAB,* s.v. "Henry Clark Corbin."

20. Henry C. Corbin, "Autobiography of Major General Henry C. Corbin," Jan. 29, 1906, Corbin Papers.

21. *New York Times,* Sept. 1, 1898.

22. Ibid., Sept. 2, 1898.

23. Ibid., Sept. 2, 4, 1898; Wilson, *Under Two Flags* 2:459.

24. *New York Times,* Sept. 8, 1898; Miles to Alger, Sept. 7, 1898, Staten Island, New York, in Alger Papers.

25. *New York World,* Sept. 8, 1898.

26. *New York Times,* Sept. 8, 1898; Shafter to Corbin, Sept. 26, 1898, HQ Fifth Army Corps, Camp Wikoff, L.I., in Corbin Papers.

27. *New York Times,* Sept. 9, 1898.

28. Ibid., Sept. 10, 1898; *New York World,* Oct. 1, 1898.

29. *New York Times,* Sept. 21, 1898.

30. *Army and Navy Journal,* Nov. 12, 1898, 249.

31. Miles to AG, Nov. 5, 1898, Washington, D.C.; *SW Annual Report, 1898* 1:37–38.

32. *New York Times,* Sept. 16, 1898.

33. *New York World,* Oct. 13, 1898.

34. *New York Times,* Oct. 7, 1898.

35. Shafter to Corbin, Oct. 23, 1898, Governors Island, N.Y., in Corbin Papers.

36. *New York Times,* Dec. 7, 13, 1898; *Army and Navy Journal,* Dec. 10, 1898, 345–46.

37. *Army and Navy Journal,* Dec. 10, 1898, 344.

38. Cosmos, *An Army for Empire,* 296; William H. Carter, "Army Reformers," 553–54.

39. Philip C. Jessup, *Elihu Root* 1:260; *Army and Navy Journal,* Mar. 29, 1902, 757. One instance of German admiration for the U.S. Army is related by Adjutant General Corbin. He wrote that Count Waldersee, a German general, told him that the American troops in China during the Boxer Rebellion had evidently been "selected men. They must have been, because they were all of that splendid spirit and intelligence that it was seldom that we were able to detect any difference between your men and your officers." Corbin, *Autobiography,* 110.

40. *New York Times,* Mar. 21, 1902; Carter, "Army Reformers," 554.

41. *New York Times,* Dec. 22, 1898.

42. *Report of the Commission Appointed by the President to Investigate the Conduct of the War Department in the War with Spain* 7:3240–58; *New York Times,* Feb. 6, 1899.

43. Major and Chief Surgeon William H. Daly to the Asst. Adj. Gen., Sept. 21, 1898, Washington, D.C., in *Report of the Commission . . . to Investigate the Conduct of the War Department* 7:3258–63. Daly had attended Jefferson Medical College in Philadelphia from 1863 to 1864, then served as a medical cadet for the duration of the Civil War before completing his medical studies at the University of Michigan in 1866. When he committed suicide in Pittsburgh on June 9, 1901, Miles attributed it to his "great personal bereavement" (Daly was a recent widower living alone) and the "undermining of his health . . . last winter." *New York Times,* June 10, 1901.

44. *Report of the Commission . . . to Investigate the Conduct of the War Department* 7:3259–62.

45. Dr. Nicholas Senn to Asst. Surgeon General Charles R. Greenleaf, in Miles to SW, Aug. 12, 1898, Port Ponce, P.R., in ibid. 7:3262.

46. Ibid. 7:3263–64; *New York Times,* Dec. 22, 1898.

47. Theodore Roosevelt to George Breckenridge Davis, recorder ofthe Army court of inquiry, Feb. 28, 1899, Albany, N.Y., in Theodore Roosevelt, *The Letters of Theodore Roosevelt* 2:952–54. For other views of the beef controversy, see Margaret Leech, *In the Days of McKinley,* 314–22; and Cosmos, *An Army for Empire,* 287–94.

48. Theodore Roosevelt to Miles, Jan. 14, 1899, Albany, N.Y., in reel 412, Theodore Roosevelt Papers. In the draft version of the letter, Roosevelt crossed out "General Wood's" (presumably Leonard Wood) and substituted "the report of many officers." See also Theodore Roosevelt to William H. H. Llewellyn, captain in the Rough Riders, Jan. 9, 1899, Albany, in Roosevelt, *Letters* 2:902–3, 912.

49. Corbin, *Autobiography,* 97.

50. Ibid., 85; *Lamb's Biographical Dictionary of the United States,* s.v. "Eagan, Charles Patrick."

51. *New York Times,* Jan. 13, 1899. For a full text of Eagan's testimony, see *Army and Navy Journal,* Jan. 14, 1899, 470–71. The *New York Times* refused to print "I wish to force the lie back into his throat, covered with the contents of a camp latrine." *Army and Navy Journal,* Jan. 14, 1899, 470.

52. "Answer to Ex-Secretary Alger's article in Jan., 1900," *North American Review*," 1900, n.p., in Miles Collection. The information included in the memorandum is substantially the same as "Some Findings of Fact," determined by the Beef Court of Inquiry, in *Army and Navy Journal*, May 13, 1899, 886–87.

53. *New York Times*, Feb. 8, 1899.

54. *Army and Navy Journal*, Jan. 21, 1899; *New York Times*, Feb. 8,1899.

55. *New York Times*, Feb. 8, 1899.

56. Ibid., Feb. 13, 1899; Cosmos, *An Army for Empire*, 292.

57. *Army and Navy Journal*, Feb. 18, 1899, 575; W. H. Carter, Asst. Adj. Gen., to W. Clarke Marshall, Produce Exchange, Chicago, Ill., Oct. 10, 1897, Washington, D.C., endorsed by Maj. Gen. Nelson A. Miles, in *New York Times*, Feb. 13, 1899.

58. *New York Times*, Feb. 10, 13, 1899.

59. Ibid., Feb. 21, 1899.

60. Ibid., Feb. 1, 21, 1899.

61. Ibid., Feb. 21, 1899.

62. Ibid., Feb. 22, 1899.

63. *Army and Navy Journal*, May 13, 1899, 885–87.

64. *New York Times*, Feb. 1, 1899; Army and Navy Journal, Apr. 29, May 13, 1899, 824, 887

65. Ibid., Feb. 3, 1899.

66. Ibid., Feb. 4, 1899; J. B. Bishop, "The Beef Verdict," 348. An example of a critical view of Miles's motives for complaining about bad beef is "Politically ambitious but naive, he [Miles] hoped to ride his revelations into the White House." Cosmos, *An Army for Empire*, 289. *The War of 1898 and U.S. Interventions 1898–1934 an Encyclopedia*, s.v. "War Department Investigating Commission."

67. Theodore Roosevelt to Henry Cabot Lodge, Aug. 10, 1899, Oyster Bay, N.Y., in Roosevelt, *Letters* 2:1048.

68. Undated memorandum in Miles Collection, USAMHI.

69. Miles to George F. Washburn, Jan. 23, 1902, HQ of the Army, Washington, D.C., in *Army and Navy Journal*, Feb. 1, 1902; and in *New York Times*, Jan. 26, 1902.

70. *New York Times*, Mar. 24, 1899.

71. Ibid., May 5, 1899.

72. Ibid., Mar. 23, 1899; Charles Eliot to Nelson Miles, May 28, 1896, Cambridge, Mass., in Miles-Cameron Family Papers.

15. Miles Inspires White House Discipline

1. *New York Times*, June 20, 1899; Leech, *In the Days of McKinley*, 376.

2. Leech, *In the Days of McKinley*, 368–71; *Army and Navy Journal*, July 22, 1899, 1121.

3. *Army and Navy Journal*, July 22, 1899, 1121; Leech, *In the Days of McKinley*, 376–78; *New York Times*, Nov. 22, 1899.

4. Corbin, *Autobiography*, 98–99. Hay took credit for suggesting Root in Hay to Henry White, Aug. 11, 1899, in Jessup, *Elihu Root* 1:217.

5. *DAB*, s.v. "Root, Elihu."

6. Ibid.; Jessup, *Elihu Root* 1:215–407.

7. Jessup, *Elihu Root* 1:220–23.

8. *New York Times*, Aug. 9, 11, 12, 1899.

9. Miles to SW, Oct. 17, 1899, HQ of the Army, Washington, D.C., *SW Annual Report, 1899,* vol. 1, 3:3–7.

10. Miles's date of rank in AGO memorandum, Dec. 27, 1901, Washington, D.C., RAGO, RG 94, NA; *New York Times,* June 9, 1900.

11. Miles to SW, July 18 and 20, 1900, Washington, D.C., in Elihu Root Papers, LC; Miles to SW, July 26, 1900, Washington, D.C., in William McKinley Papers.

12. Root to President McKinley, July 26, 1900, War Department, in William McKinley Papers.

13. Richard O'Connor, *The Spirit Soldiers: A Historical Narrative of the Boxer Rebellion,* 217–20; *DAB,* s.v. "Adna Romanza Chaffee." On July 8, 1898, Chaffee had been promoted to major general of volunteers after his brigade helped to take the fortified post of El Caney in the Santiago campaign. In the postwar reduction of the army, he was reduced to brigadier general of volunteers on April 13, 1899. Corbin, *Autobiography,* 108–9.

14. Chaffee to AG, Washington, Aug. 15, 1900, Peking, in Corbin, *Autobiography,* 110–11.

15. Jessup, *Elihu Root* 1:244; Miles, *Annual Report, 1900,* in *Army and Navy Journal,* Nov. 17, 1900, 270.

16. Both quotations in Jessup, *Elihu Root* 1:244.

17. Ibid. 1:243–44.

18. *New York Times,* Sept. 9, 1898.

19. Miles, *Serving the Republic,* 309.

20. Roosevelt to William Conant Church, May 8, 1899, Albany, in Roosevelt, *Letters* 2:1003.

21. Roosevelt to Henry Cabot Lodge, Aug. 10, 1899, Oyster Bay, N.Y., in ibid. 2:1047–48.

22. Roosevelt to George Hinckley Lyman, June 18, 1901, Oyster Bay, N.Y., in ibid. 3:96. San Juan Hill was about four hundred yards from Kettle Hill; both were on San Juan Heights. Trask, *The War with Spain,* 231.

23. Roosevelt to Lyman, June 18 and June 22, 1901, Oyster Bay, N.Y., in Roosevelt, *Letters* 3:96–98.

24. Invitation, Roosevelt to Miles, Sept. 30, 1901, Washington, D.C., in Theodore Roosevelt Papers.

25. A copy of Miles's interview, dateline Cincinnati, Ohio, Dec. 16, 1901 [newspaper not named], in Elihu Root Papers; Edward L. Beach, *The United States Navy, 200 Years,* 352–68.

26. Root to Miles, Dec. 19, 1901, Washington, D.C., in Elihu Root Papers; Miles to Root, Dec. 20, 1901, Washington, D.C., in ibid.; *New York Times,* Dec. 22, 1901.

27. Miles to Root, Dec. 21, 1901, Washington, D.C., in Elihu Root Papers.

28. Postscript to Root to Miles, Dec. 21, 1901, Washington, D.C., in ibid.

29. Root to Miles, Dec. 21, 1901, in ibid.

30. Roosevelt to Lodge, Aug. 20, 1901, Oyster Bay, N.Y., in Roosevelt, *Letters* 3:128.

31. Samuel Leland Powers, *Portraits of a Half Century,* 170–71.

32. Jessup, *Elihu Root* 1:248. Roosevelt to Matthews, Dec. 31, 1901, Washington, D.C., in Roosevelt, *Letters* 3:213.

33. Finley Peter Dunne, *Observations by Dr. Dooley,* 59–60; *DAB,* s.v. "Dunne, Finley Peter"; Roosevelt to Dunne, Nov. 28, 1899, n.p., in Elmer Ellis, *Mr. Dooley's America: A Life of Finley Peter Dunne,* 145.

34. *Army and Navy Journal,* Dec. 28, 1901, 413; Watterson to Miles, Jan. 3, 1902, Louisville, Ky., in Miles-Cameron Family Papers.

35. Henry F. Pringle, *Theodore Roosevelt: A Biography,* 315–16.

36. *New York Times,* Dec. 22, 1901.

37. Ibid., Jan. 19, 1902, and an editorial on Dec. 24, 1901.

38. Miles to Root, Feb. 17, 1902, Washington, D.C., in Nelson A. Miles Personnel File, Navy and Old Army Branch, NA. For a study of American troops in the Philippines, see Richard E. Welch, Jr., "American Atrocities in the Philippines: The Indictment and the Response"; Oscar M. Alfonso, *Theodore Roosevelt and the Philippines, 1897–1909.*

39. Draft copy of Roosevelt to Miles, Feb. 17, 1902, White House, Washington, D.C., in Theodore Roosevelt Papers. That Roosevelt at least verbally gave Miles the message contained in the draft is confirmed in Roosevelt to Root, Feb. 18, 1902, Washington, D.C., in ibid.

40. Roosevelt to Root, Mar. 7, 1902, White House, Washington, D.C., in Elihu Root Papers; Roosevelt to Miles, Jan. 14, 1899, Albany, N.Y., in Miles-Cameron Family Papers.

41. Roosevelt to Root, Mar. 7, 1902, White House, Washington, D.C., in Elihu Root Papers; Roosevelt to Lodge, Aug. 10, 1899, Oyster Bay, N.Y., in Roosevelt, *Letters* 2:1048; Roosevelt to Miles, Mar. 6, 1899, Washington, D.C., in Theodore Roosevelt Papers.

42. Roosevelt to Root, Mar. 15, 1902, Washington, D.C., in Elihu Root Papers. The attached undated, anonymous newspaper column explains that Miles's request to bring a delegation of Filipinos to Washington was in a pigeon hole because what was "going on in the Philippines, which, if known to the people, would sweep the Republicans out of power."

43. Roosevelt to Root, Mar. 19, 1902, Washington, D.C., in ibid.

44. Miles's order of Jan. 4, 1891, in Forsyth to Lamont, Sept. 1, 1895, Manuscripts and Archives, New York Public Library; Maj. J. Ford Kent and Capt. Frank D. Baldwin, Jan. 13, 18, 1891, Pine Ridge, S.D., in Letters Received–AGO; Schofield to Proctor, Feb. 4, 1891, Washington, D.C., and Proctor's endorsement, Feb. 12, 1891, both in Forsyth to Lamont, Sept. 1, 1895, Manuscripts and Archives, New York Public Library.

45. Roosevelt to Root, Mar. 19, 1902, Washington, D.C., in Elihu Root Papers.

46. Roosevelt quoted in David H. Burton, *Theodore Roosevelt,* 110; Miles, *Serving the Republic,* 305, 308.

47. Third endorsement by Miles, Mar. 24, 1902, HQ of the Army, Washington, D.C.; endorsement by Root, Mar. 25, 1902, War Dept., Washington, D.C., to Miles to Root, Feb. 17, 1902, in Nelson A. Miles Personal File, Navy and Old Army Branch, NA. This is not the first revelation of correspondence being suppressed by the War Department during this period of history. Roosevelt wrote Miles that two reports that he had written, one on July 20, 1898, the other on September 15, 1898, "had been withdrawn from the files prior to the election, because the department did not desire that they should be used in the campaign, and by omission they had not been restored to the files since." Roosevelt to Miles, Mar. 6, 1899, Washington, D.C., in Theodore Roosevelt Papers.

48. *New York Times,* Mar. 21, 23, 1902; Roosevelt to Oswald Garrison Villard, Mar. 22, 1902, Washington, D.C., in Roosevelt, *Letters* 3:247; Maj. Gen. William Harding Carter, "Army Reformers," 553–54; James Hewes, "The United States Army General Staff, 1900–1917," 38; *Army and Navy Journal,* Mar. 29, 1902, 739.

49. *New York Times,* Mar. 24, 1902.

50. Roosevelt to Kohlsaat, Mar. 24, 1902, Washington, D.C., in Roosevelt, *Letters* 3:248.

51. Herman H. Kohlsaat, *From McKinley to Harding: Personal Recollections of Our Presidents,* 107–9.

52. Frederick S. Wood, *Roosevelt As We Knew Him: The Personal Recollections of One Hundred and Fifty of His Friends and Associates,* 132–33.

53. *Army and Navy Journal,* Sept. 13, 1902, 33.

54. Jessup, *Elihu Root* 1:331; Leon Wolf, *Little Brown Brother: How the United States Purchased and Pacified the Philippines at the Turn of the Century,* 334; Miles, *Serving the Republic,* 306–7.

55. Miles, *Serving the Republic,* 307.

56. Miles to SW, Feb. 19, 1903, in *Army and Navy Journal,* May 2, 1903, 360–63; Maus to Commanding General, Division of the Philippines, Nov. 28, 1902, Manila, P.I., in ibid. In a discussion explaining reports of cruelty to Filipinos by American soldiers, the *Army and Navy Journal* cited a report by Brig. Gen. J. Franklin Bell when it reported "that natives accepted office under the Americans for the purpose of furthering the insurrection; that they violated their paroles; that they assassinated friendly natives; that they boloed [a long, heavy, single-edged machete] wounded Americans, used American uniforms, employed poisoned arrows and set mantraps." Ibid., Jan. 3, 1903, 427.

57. Ibid., Jan. 3, 31, 1903, 418, 520.

58. Ibid., Feb. 21, 1903, 596; Miles, *Serving the Republic,* 309. Here Miles mistakenly wrote that he returned to Washington on February 1; he arrived in New York on February 15, 1903. *New York Times,* Feb. 16, 1903.

59. Jessup, *Elihu Root* 1:344; Taft to Roosevelt, Dec. 30, 1902, n.p., in ibid. 1:249; Roosevelt to Villard, Mar. 31, 1903, Washington, D.C., in Roosevelt, *Letters* 3:406.

60. *New York Times,* Apr. 28, 1903; Jessup, *Elihu Root* 1:249.

61. *Army and Navy Journal,* May 2, 1903, 870.

62. Welch, "American Atrocities in the Philippines," 250–53. In 1971, 1st Lt. William L. Calley, Jr., was convicted of the premeditated murder of at least twenty-two South Vietnamese civilians at Mylai. He had sought to justify his actions with the same defense: "If I have committed a crime, the only crime I've committed is in judgement of my values. Apparently I valued my troops lives more than I did that of the enemy." *New York Times,* Mar. 31, 1971. Stuart Creighton Miller, *Benevolent Assimilation: The American Conquest of the Philippines, 1899–1903,* 90, 192–93. On May 5, 1900, General Otis would be replaced by Maj. Gen. Arthur MacArthur. *DAB,* s.v. "Elwell S. Otis."

63. *Harper's Weekly,* May 9, 1903, 47

64. "General Miles's Report: Our Estimate," 99–100; Miles, *Serving the Republic,* 307.

65. *Army and Navy Journal,* Mar. 29, 1902, 739; Carter, "Army Reformers," 552. For a history of the General Staff from 1900 to 1917, see James Hewes, "The United States Army General Staff, 1900–1917"; Russell F. Weigley, "The Elihu Root Reforms and the Progressive Era," 22.

66. Johnson, *The Unregimented General,* 357; *Army and Navy Journal,* July 18, 1903, 1161. Another account of Miles's ride appeared in *Army and Navy Journal* a week later, July 25, 1903, 1180. Here the military weekly reprinted a despatch first published in the *New York World,* dateline Fort Sill, Oklahoma, July 18, signed by Capt. Farrand Sayre, Eighth Cavalry. The captain, who had accompanied Miles, wrote that they left Fort Sill at 3:35 A.M. and arrived at Fort Reno at 2:20 P.M. Since the July 18 story quoted Miles when he dismounted, the reporter might have the more accurate time. The captain's story mentions that eight miles from Fort Sill the general bruised his left arm and leg when his horse fell, and that he did not use a whip or spurs during the ride.

67. Roosevelt to Cortelyou, July 14, 1903, Oyster Bay, N.Y., in Roosevelt, *Letters* 3:586.

68. *New York Herald,* Aug. 9 and 10, 1903.

69. *Army and Navy Journal,* Aug. 29, 1903, 1308; *Harper's Weekly,* Aug. 22, 1903, 1359.

70. *Army and Navy Journal,* Aug. 8, 1903.

71. *New York Times,* Aug. 9, 1903.

72. *New York Sun,* Aug. 8, 1903.

73. Roosevelt to Root, Aug. 11, 1903, White House, Washington, D.C., in Elihu Root Papers.

74. Root to Roosevelt, Aug. 19, 1903, Washington, D.C., in ibid.; Roosevelt to Root, Aug. 20, 1903, Oyster Bay, N.Y., and Roosevelt to Davis, Aug. 20, 1903, Oyster Bay, N.Y., both in Roosevelt, *Letters* 3:567; Miles, *Serving the Republic,* 312.

75. Miles, *Serving the Republic,* 313.

76. Trask, *The War with Spain,* 336.

77. *Historical Dictionary of the Spanish American War* (1996 ed.), s.v. "Beef Controversy"; Cosmos, *An Army for Empire,* 294.

78. *Harper's Weekly,* Aug. 22, 1903, 1359. In another article in the same issue, *Harper's* used the "mortifying episode in the retirement of Lieutenant General Miles" to repeat an earlier criticism of President Roosevelt. Calling the treatment of Miles "the worst blunder yet,—so short-sighted, unnecessary and inexcusable as to be almost past comprehension," the article went on to say "that the President lacks what he needs most—the daily advice of a sagacious politician. No member of the cabinet satisfies these requirements. The Secretary of State is not sufficiently practical, the Secretary of War is far too aggressive by temperament, and lacks the experience essential to wise counsel" (p. 1355).

79. *Boston Herald,* May 24, 1925.

80. Joseph Mills Hanson, "A Khaki Kick," in Miles, *Documentary Biography,* 11–12.

Epilogue

1. *New York Herald,* Aug. 10, 1903; *New York Tribune,* Aug. 10, 1903.

2. *New York Times,* May 24, 1904.

3. Miles to Overmyer, Washington, D.C., June 18, 1904. The head of the Pennsylvania delegation was J. M. Guffey of Pittsburgh. For a biography of Overmeyer see Shannon R. Brown, "David Overmyer: A Political History." Both items in David Overmyer Collection, Kansas State Historical Society.

4. Miles to AG, Oct. 1, 1901, *SW Annual Reports, 1901* 1:9–11.

5. Miles to John G. Wooley, n.p., n.d., excerpt in *New York Times,* June 29, 1904. The Prohibition National Convention met at Indianapolis and nominated Silas C. Swallow for president and George W. Carroll for vice president.

6. "A Glowing Tribute," *Topeka Journal,* July 9, 1904; *New York Times,* July 10, 1904.

7. Lodge to Roosevelt, Aug. 23, 1903, Heidelberg, in Henry Cabot Lodge, *Reflections from the Correspondence of Theodore Roosevelt and Henry Cabot Lodge* 2:48.

8. *New York Times,* Aug. 2, 1904; Pohanka, *Nelson A. Miles,* 315; *Army and Navy Journal,* Aug. 6, 13, 1904, 1270. Sherman Miles graduated from the U.S. Military Academy in 1905. From 1914 to 1916 he was an observer with the Russian army. In 1918 he served as chief of intelligence for the First Corps in France. He was the acting chief of military intelligence in the War Department on December 7, 1941. In January 1942 he was promoted to major general (temporary), and a month later he received command of the First Corps Area at Boston. He remained there until he retired in 1945. Sherman Miles died on October 7, 1966. *New York Times,* Oct. 9, 1966; "Biographical Sketches of General Officers in World War II," West Point.

9. *New York Tribune,* Aug. 3, 1904.

10. Ibid.; *Army and Navy Journal,* Aug. 13, 1904; *Army and Navy Journal,* Aug. 6, 1904, 1270.

11. "Our Country: An Opinion from General Miles," in *The Campaign Text Book of the Democratic Party of the United States,* 183–84.

12. *New York Times,* Dec. 4, 1904.

13. Ibid., Jan. 26, 1905.

14. Ibid., Feb. 3, 1905; ibid., Jan. 26, 1905. In December 1904 Miles resigned "his adjutant general's position in favor of an unpaid job as state inspector general." Miles resigned as state inspector general in December 1905. Wooster, *Nelson A. Miles,* 253–54.

15. *Army and Navy Journal,* Nov. 27, 1909, 348. The couple had two children, Juanita (Mrs. Allen Richmond Wright) and Nelson. Yulee Nolde Miles died in February 1953 at the age of sixty-four. *New York Times,* Feb. 23, 1953. Sherman remarried in 1954 to Edith Lawrence Coolidge; he died on October 7, 1966. Ibid., Oct. 8, 1966.

16. *New York Times,* Nov. 19, 1911.

17. Ibid., Dec. 3, 1911.

18. *The Independent,* Nov. 30, 1911, 1206.

19. *New York Times,* Aug. 30, Oct. 4, 1910. Roosevelt objected to the decision in the New York bakeshops case and the Knight Sugar Trust case: *U.S. vs E.C. Knight Co.,* 1895, and *Lochner vs. NewYork,* 1905. In the Knight Sugar Trust case the government charged the Knight Company with having a near-monoply in sugar refining. The decision was 8-1 against the government. In the case of *Lochner vs. New York* (New York bakeshops), a bare majority of the court ruled a New York maximum-hours law for bakers invalid as unreasonable interference with the right of free contract and as an excessive use of the state's police power.

20. *New York Times,* Oct. 4, 1910; *New York Herald,* Oct. 7, 1910.

21. William H. Harbaugh, *Power and Responsibility: The Life and Times of Theodore Roosevelt,* 190.

22. *Fitchburg Sentinel,* Feb. 23, 1912.

23. Ibid., Sept. 20, 22, 27, 1913.

24. "Guardians of Liberty," 152; Michael Williams, *The Shadow of the Pope,* 114.

25. *New York Times,* Jan. 7, 1913; editorial, "A Plague of Senseless Hate," ibid., Nov. 19, 1914.

26. Paul L. Hedren, "Charles King," in Hutton, *Soldiers West,* 257; *Denver Post,* Oct. 21, 1913, quoted in Kevin Brownlow, *The War and the West and the Wilderness,* 232; Charles King to John Gregory, ed., *Evening* (Milwaukee) *Wisconsin,* n.d., n.p., in Harry H. Anderson, "General Charles King and Buffalo Bill's Silent Western Movies," 97.

27. *Gardner Journal,* Oct. 23, 1913.

28. Brownlow, *The War and the West and the Wilderness,* 232–33.

29. Miles to Baldwin, Jan. 26, 1914, n.p., Frank D. Baldwin Papers, Henry E. Huntington Library, San Marino, California.

30. Cody to Baldwin, Jan. 29, 1914, Chicago, in ibid.

31. Brownlow, *The War and the West and the Wilderness,* 233–35; Anderson, "General Charles King," 93; "'Buffalo Bill' Picture Shown," 1370; Cody to Baldwin, Feb. 28, 1914, Washington, D.C., in Baldwin Papers.

32. *New York Times,* June 10, July 23, 25, Aug. 7, 1913, Oct. 9, 1966. Sherman Miles apparently did his job in the Balkans so well that in 1914 he was promoted to the ranking attaché's post at Saint Petersburg, from which he observed the Russian army fight World War I until 1916. "Biographical Sketches of General Officers in World War II," West Point.

33. *New York Times,* Aug. 3, 1914.

34. Ibid.

35. Ibid., Aug. 9, 1915. For one of Henry Ford's ventures, see Barbara S. Kraft, *The Peace Ship: Henry Ford's Pacifist Adventure in the First World War.*

36. *New York Times,* Sept. 16, 1915.

37. Slayden, *Washington Wife,* 317.

38. *New York Times,* Feb. 1, 1916.

39. Ibid., Feb. 9, 1916. Miles could also have cited the draft riots in New York City.

40. Miles to Baker, Mar. 17, 1917, Washington, D.C., and Baker to Miles, Mar. 19, 1917, Washington, D.C., in Nelson A. Miles Personal File, Navy and Old Army Branch, NA.

41. *New York Times,* Mar. 28, 1917.

42. Ibid., Oct. 27, 1920.

43. Ibid., Oct. 28, 1920.

44. Ibid., Aug. 8, 1903.

45. Ibid., Mar. 3, 1925; *DAB,* s.v. "William Mitchell."

46. *Boston Herald,* May 24, 1925. In April 1910 Miles broke two ribs after he was thrown from a horse; in 1922 and again in 1924 he was ill with pneumonia. Wooster, *Nelson A. Miles,* 254, 263; *New York Times,* Apr. 27, 1922.

47. Miles quoted in *Time,* May 18, 1925. This article incorrectly stated that Miles "married a daughter of General Sherman."

48. *Fitchburg Sentinel,* May 16, 19, 1925; *Washington Post,* May 16, 1925.

49. *Washington Post,* May 16, 17, 1925; *New York Times,* May 24, 1925.

50. *Army and Navy Journal,* May 23, 1925, 2182.

51. Gen. John J. Pershing quoted in *Washington Post,* May 17, 1925; *DAB* (Supplement 4), s.v. "John J. Pershing."

52. *Washington Post,* May 19, 20, 1925.

Bibliography

Manuscript Collections

Arizona Historical Society, Tucson
  Charles B. Gatewood Collection
Assumption Archives, Richardton, North Dakota
  James McLaughlin Papers
Bowdoin College Library, Brunswick, Maine
  Oliver Otis Howard Collection
William L. Clements Library, Ann Arbor, Michigan
  Russell Alexander Alger Papers
Rutherford B. Hayes Presidential Center, Fremont, Ohio
  George Crook Papers
  Nelson A. Miles Miscellaneous Manuscripts
Henry E. Huntington Library, San Marino, California
  Frank D. Baldwin Papers
Kansas State Historical Society, Topeka
  David Overmyer Collection
  Edmund G. Ross Collection
Library of Congress, Manuscripts Division, Washington, D.C.
  William C. Church Papers
  Grover Cleveland Papers
  Henry C. Corbin Papers
  Henry L. Dawes Papers
  Benjamin Harrison Papers
  Daniel S. Lamont Papers
  Henry W. Lawton Papers
  Miles-Cameron Family Papers
  Theodore Roosevelt Papers

Elihu Root Papers
John M. Schofield Papers
Philip H. Sheridan Papers
William T. Sherman Papers
Leonard Wood Papers
Massachusetts Historical Society, Boston
William C. Endicott Papers
Montana Historical Society, Helena
Edwin M. Brown Diaries, 1876–77
Nelson A. Miles to Assistant Adjutant General, Department of Dakota, Dec. 27, 1877, Fort Keogh
Operations in the District of the Yellowstone in 1877
John L. Penwell, photocopy of a narrative diary and letter, dated 1876 and 1877, cantonment on Tongue River
Lt. Thomas M. Woodruff letter to his mother, October 15, 1877
National Archives and Record Service, Washington, D.C.
General Reference Branch
Capt. Charles Stewart Heintzelman, Veterans Records, Pension File
Navy and Old Army Branch
Case of Nelson A. Miles, Application for a Medal of Honor
George Crook Personal File
Letters Received, Adjutant General's Office, 1780s–1917 (Letters Received–AGO)
Letters Sent and Received, Department of the South
Marion P. Maus Personal File
Chauncey McKeever Personal File
Nelson A. Miles Personal File
Records of United States Army Overseas Operations and Commands, 1898–1942, RG 395
Records of United States Continental Commands, RG 393
Arthur L. Wagner Personal File
Nebraska State Historical Society, Lincoln
Paddy Starr Testimony, Eli S. Ricker Tablets
New York Historical Society, New York
Francis C. Barlow Letter
Miscellaneous Manuscripts
New York Public Library, Manuscript and Archives Division, New York
Brig. Gen. James W. Forsyth's statement in defense of the Seventh Cavalry while under his command against the Sioux Indians

Nelson A. Miles Correspondence
Proctor Public Library, Proctor, Vermont
Redfield Proctor Papers
Stanford University Libraries, Stanford, California
William Shafter Papers
United States Army Military History Institute, Carlisle Barracks, Carlisle, Pennsylvania
Nelson A. Miles Papers
University of Oregon Library, Eugene
Letters of George Crook

Government Documents and Publications

Department of War, Adjutant General's Office, *Correspondence Relating to the War with Spain and Conditions Growing Out of the Same, . . . between the Adjutant General of the Army and Military Commanders in the United States, Cuba, Porto Rico, China, and the Philippine Islands, from April 15, 1898 to July 30, 1902,* 2 vols. Washington, D.C.: GPO, 1902.

"Letter from the Secretary of War transmitting . . . Correspondence with Miles Relative to the Surrender of Geronimo." *Senate Ex. Doc. No. 117, 49th Cong., 2d Sess., U.S. Senate.*

Papers Relating to the Foreign Relations of the United States Transmitted to Congress with the Annual Message of the President, Dec. 2, 1878. Washington, D.C.: GPO, 1878.

Report of the Commission Appointed by the President to Investigate the Conduct of the War Department in the War With Spain. 8 vols. Washington, D.C.: GPO, 1899.

"State of New York under the Supervision of the New York Monuments Commission." *In Memorium, Francis Channing Barlow, 1836–1896.* Albany: J. B. Lyon Co., 1923.

U.S. Secretary of War, Annual Reports, 1868, 1877, 1878, 1879, 1886, 1887, 1891, 1895, 1897, 1898.

War of the Rebellion: A Compilation of the Official Records of the Union and Confederate Armies. 128 vols. Washington, D.C.: GPO, 1880–1901. (References are to series 1 unless otherwise noted.)

Newspapers and News Magazines

(Tucson) *Arizona Daily Star,* 1877–87
(Prescott) *Arizona Weekly Miner,* 1874

Army and Navy Journal, 1868–1925
Boston Herald, 1925
Cheyenne (Wyo.) *Daily Leader,* 1874–78
Chicago Daily News, 1894
Chicago Herald, 1890
Chicago Times, 1877
Chicago Tribune, 1877
Crown Point Register (Lake County, Ind.), 1894
Daily Alta California (San Francisco), 1886–87
Deadwood (S.D.) *Times,* 1890–91
Fitchburg (Mass.) *Sentinel,* 1912–25
Gardner (Mass.) *Journal,* 1913
Harper's Weekly, 1903
The Independent, 1911
Kansas City (Mo.) *Star,* 1898
Lake County News (Hammond, Ind.), 1894
Literary Digest, 1912
The Moving Picture World, 1914
New York Herald, 1868–1903
New York Sun, 1890
New York Times, 1866–1966
New York Tribune, 1865–1925
New York World, 1898–1903
The Outlook, 1903
Raleigh Daily Sentinel, 1867–69
Tampa Morning Tribune, 1898
Time, 1925
Topeka (Kans.) *Journal,* 1904
Washington (D.C.) *Evening Star,* 1886–1903
Washington (D.C.) *Post,* 1925

Published Books and Articles

Adams, Alexander B. *Sitting Bull: An Epic of the Plains.* New York: G. P. Putnam's Sons, 1973.

Alfonso, Oscar M. *Theodore Roosevelt and the Philippines, 1897–1909.* New York: Oriole Editions, 1970.

Alger, Russell Alexander. *The Spanish-American War.* New York: Harper and Bros., 1901. Reprint, Freeport, N.Y.: Books for Libraries, 1971.

Allen, Douglas. *Frederic Remington and the Spanish-American War.* New York: Crown Publishers, 1971.

The American Heritage Pictorial History of the Civil War. Ed. Richard K. Ketchum. New York: American Heritage/Bonanza Books, 1982.

Anderson, Harry H. "General Charles King and Buffalo Bill's Silent Western Movies." *Historical Messenger of the Milwaukee County Historical Society* 22 (Sept. 1966): 93–98.

———. "Indian Peace Talkers and the Conclusion of the Sioux War of 1876." *Nebraska History* 44 (December 1963): 233–54.

———. "Nelson A. Miles and the Sioux War of 1876–77." *Westerners Brand Book* (Chicago) 16 (June 1959):25–27, 32.

Athearn, Robert G. *Thomas Francis Meagher: An Irish Revolutionary in America.* Boulder: Univ. of Colorado Press, 1949. Reprint, New York: Arno Press, 1976.

———. *William Tecumseh Sherman and the Settlement of the West.* Norman: Univ. of Oklahoma Press, 1956.

———. "A Winter Campaign against the Sioux." *Mississippi Valley Historical Review* 35 (Sept. 1948): 272–84.

Atkins, John Black. *Incidents and Reflections.* London: Christopher, 1947.

———. *The War in Cuba: The Experiences of an Englishman in the U.S. Army.* London: Smith, Elder and Co., 1899.

Bailey, Ralph Edgar. *The Story of Nelson A. Miles, Indian Fighter.* New York: William Morrow and Co., 1965.

Baird, George W. "General Miles' Indian Campaigns." *Century Magazine* 42 (July 1891): 351–70.

Baldwin, Alice Blackwood, ed. *Memoirs of the Late Frank D. Baldwin, Major General, U.S.A.* Los Angeles: Wetzel Publishing Co., 1929.

Barlow, Francis. "The Capture of the Salient, May 12, 1864." *Papers of the Military Society of Massachusetts.* Boston: Military Society of Massachusetts, 1905.

Beach, Edward L. *The United States Navy, 200 Years.* New York: Henry Holt and Co., 1986.

Beal, Merrill D. *"I Will Fight No More Forever": Chief Joseph and the Nez Perce War.* Seattle: Univ. of Washington Press, 1963.

Beede, Benjamin R., ed. *The War of 1898 and U.S. Interventions 1898–1934: An Encyclopedia.* New York: Garland Publishing, 1994.

Beyer, W. F., and Keydel, O. F., eds. *Deeds of Valor.* 2 vols. Detroit: Perrien-Keydel Co., 1906.

Bigelow, John, Jr. *The Campaign of Chancellorsville.* New Haven: Yale Univ. Press, 1910.

Bigelow, Poultney. *Seventy Summers.* 2 vols. New York: Longmans, Green and Co., 1925.

Billings, John D. *Hardtack and Coffee, or the Unwritten Story of Army Life.* Boston: George M. Smith and Co., 1887.

Bishop, J. B. "The Beef Verdict." *The Nation* 67 (May 11, 1899).

Bloom, Lansing B. "Bourke on the Southwest." *New Mexico Historical Review* 8 (Jan. 1933): 1–30.

Bradford, James C., ed. *Admirals of the New Steel Navy: Makers of the American Naval Tradition, 1880–1930.* Annapolis: Naval Institute Press, 1990.

Brown, Dee. *Bury My Heart at Wounded Knee.* New York: Holt Rinehart and Winston, 1970.

Brown, Mark H. *Flight of the Nez Perce.* New York: G. P. Putnam's Sons, 1967.

Brownlow, Kevin. *The War and the West and the Wilderness.* New York: Alfred A. Knopf, 1979.

Burton, David H. *Theodore Roosevelt.* New York: Twayne, 1972.

Burton, Theodore E. *John Sherman.* Boston: Houghton, Mifflin, 1906.

Calhoun, Charles W. *Gilded Age Cato: The Life of Walter Q. Gresham.* Lexington: Univ. Press of Kentucky, 1988.

The Campaign Textbook of the Democratic Party of the United States. Issued by the authority of the Democratic National Committee. New York: 1904.

Carlson, Paul H. *"Pecos Bill": A Military Biography of William R. Shafter.* College Station: Texas A & M Univ. Press, 1989.

Carpenter, John A. *Sword and Olive Branch: Oliver Otis Howard.* Pittsburgh: Univ. of Pittsburgh Press, 1964.

Carriker, Robert C. *Fort Supply, Indian Territory: Frontier Outpost on the Plains.* Norman: Univ. of Oklahoma Press, 1970.

———, ed. "Thomas McFadden's Diary of an Indian Campaign, 1874." *Southwestern Historical Quarterly* 75 (1971): 198–232.

Carroll, John A. "A Commentary on the Crook-Miles Controversy." *Smoke Signal* (Tucson Westerners) no. 15 (Spring 1967): 114–15.

Carter, Robert G. *Four Brothers in Blue, or Sunshine and Shadows of the War of Rebellion.* Austin: Univ. of Texas Press, 1978.

Carter, William H. "Army Reformers." *North American Review* 208 (October 1918): 548–57.

Catton, Bruce. *Glory Road.* Vol. 2 of *The Army of the Potomac.* Garden City, N.Y.: Doubleday, 1954.

———. *Mr. Lincoln's Army.* Vol. 1 of *The Army of the Potomac.* Garden City, N.Y.: Doubleday, 1951.

———. *Reflections on the Civil War.* Garden City, N.Y.: Doubleday, 1981.

Chadwick, French Ensor. *The Relations of the United States to Spain: The Spanish-American War.* 2 vols. New York: Charles Scribner's Sons, 1911.

Clark, Walter, ed. *Histories of the Several Regiments and Battalions from North Carolina in the Great War, 1861–'65.* Written by members of the respective commands. 5 vols. Goldsboro, N.C.: Nash Brothers, 1901.

Cleaves, Freeman. *Meade of Gettysburg.* Norman: Univ. of Oklahoma Press, 1960.

Cody, William F. *An Autobiography of Buffalo Bill.* New York: Cosmopolitan Book Co., 1920.

Cooper, Jerry M. *The Army and Civil Disorder: Federal Military Intervention in Labor Disputes, 1877–1900.* Westport, Conn.: Greenwood Press, 1980.

Cosmos, Graham A. *An Army for Empire: The United States Army in the Spanish-American War.* Columbia: Univ. of Missouri Press, 1971.

Craven, John L. *Prison Life of Jefferson Davis.* New York: Carleton, 1866.

Crocchiola, Stanley F. L. *E. V. Sumner: Major General, United States Army, 1797–1863.* Borger, Tex.: J. Hess Printers, 1968.

Crook, George. *General George Crook: His Autobiography.* Edited by Martin F. Schmitt. 1949. Reprint, Norman: Univ. of Oklahoma Press, 1960.

Cummings, Charles R. "Redfield Proctor, 1831–1908." *The Vermonter* 13 (March 1908).

Davis, Britton. *The Truth about Geronimo.* Edited by Milo M. Quaife. Chicago: Lakeside Press, R. R. Donnelley and Sons, 1951.

Davis, Richard Harding. "The Porto Rican Campaign." *Scribner's Magazine* 24 (Nov. 1898): 515–27.

Dawson, Joseph G., III. *Dictionary of American Military Biography.* Westport, Conn.: Greenwood Press, 1984.

Debo, Angie. *Geronimo: The Man, His Time, His Place.* Norman: Univ. of Oklahoma Press, 1976.

Dietz, J. Stanley, comp. *The Battle Flags and Wisconsin Troops in the Civil War and the War with Spain.* Madison, Wis.: Democratic Printing Co., 1943.

Dixon, David. *Hero of Beecher Island: The Life and Military Career of George A. Forsyth.* Lincoln: Univ. of Nebraska Press, 1994.

DeMontravel, Peter R. "General Nelson A. Miles and the Wounded Knee Controversy." *Arizona and the West* 28 (Spring 1986): 23–44.

Dumas, Malone, et al., eds. *Dictionary of American Biography.* 29 vols. 1946–81.

Dunne, Finley Peter. *Observations by Dr. Dooley.* New York: R. H. Russell, 1906.

Dyil, Donald H., ed. *Historical Dictionary of the Spanish American War.* Westport, Conn.: Greenwood Press, 1996.

Eastman, Elaine Goodale. "The Ghost Dance War and Wounded Knee Massacre of 1890–91." *Nebraska History* 26 (Jan.–March 1945): 26–42.

Eaton, Clement. *Jefferson Davis.* New York: Free Press, 1977.

Eggert, Donald G. *Richard Olney: Evolution of a Statesman.* University Park: Penn State Univ. Press, 1974.

Eggert, Gerald. *Railroad Labor Disputes.* Ann Arbor: Univ. of Michigan Press, 1967.
Ellis, Elmer. *Mr. Dooley's America: A Life of Finley Peter Dunne.* New York: Alfred A. Knopf, 1941.
Ellis, Richard N. *General Pope and U.S. Indian Policy.* Albuquerque: Univ. of New Mexico Press, 1970.
———. "The Humanitarian Generals." *Western Historical Quarterly* 3 (1972): 169–78.
Encyclopedia of American Biography. 1974 ed.
Faulk, Odie B. *The Geronimo Campaign.* New York: Oxford Univ. Press, 1969.
Fechet, Edmond G. "The True Story of the Death of Sitting Bull." *Cosmopolitan* 20 (March 1896): 493–501.
Fee, Chester A. *Chief Joseph.* New York: Wilson-Erickson, 1936.
Fiala, Anthony. *Troop "C" in Service: An Account of the Part Played by Troop "C" of the New York Volunteer Cavalry in the Spanish-American War of 1898.* Brooklyn, N.Y.: Eagle Press, 1899.
Finerty, John C. *War Path and Bivouac, or the Conquest of the Sioux.* 1890. Reprint, Norman: Univ. of Oklahoma Press, 1961.
Fish, Carl Russell. *The Path of Empire.* New Haven: Yale Univ. Press, 1919.
Foote, Shelby. *The Civil War: A Narrative.* 3 vols. New York: Random House, 1958–1975.
Fox, William. *Regimental Losses in the American Civil War, 1861–65.* Albany, N.Y.: Albany Publishing, 1893.
Frassanito, William A. *Antietam: The Photographic Legacy of America's Bloodiest Day.* New York: Scribners, 1978.
Frazer, Robert W. *Forts of the West.* Norman: Univ. of Oklahoma Press, 1965.
Freeman, Douglas Southall. *R. E. Lee: A Biography.* 4 vols. NewYork: Charles Scribner's Sons, 1934–35.
Freidel, Frank. *The Splendid Little War.* Boston: Little Brown, 1958.
Fry, James B. *The History and Legal Effect of Brevets in the Armies of Great Britain and the United States from Their Origin in 1692 to the Present Time.* New York: D. Van Nostrand, 1877.
Fuller, Charles A. *Personal Recollections of the War of 1861, 61st Regiment New York Volunteer Infantry.* Sherburne, N.Y.: News Job Printing House, 1906.
Furgurson, Ernest B. *Chancellorsville 1863: The Souls of the Brave.* New York: Alfred A. Knopf, 1992.
Gatewood, Charles B. "Gatewood Reports to His Wife." Edited by Charles Byars. *Journal of Arizona History* 7 (Summer 1966): 78–80.
———. "Lieutenant Charles B. Gatewood." *Arizona Historical Review* 4 (April 1931):29–32.

———. "The Surrender of Geronimo." *Proceedings of the Annual Meeting & Dinner of the Order of Indian Wars of the United States,* 49–61. Washington, D.C.: 1929.

Gibson, John M. *Soldier in White: The Life of General George Miller Sternberg.* Durham, N.C.: Duke Univ. Press, 1958.

Ginger, Roy. *The Bending Cross: A Biography of Eugene Victor Debs.* New Brunswick, N.J.: Rutgers Univ. Press, 1949.

Goldberg, Joyce S. *The "Baltimore" Affair.* Lincoln: Univ. of Nebraska Press, 1986.

Gordon, John B. *Reminiscences of the Civil War.* New York: Charles Scribner's Sons, 1904.

Govan, Gilbert E., and Livingood, James W. *A Different Valor: The Story of Joseph E. Johnston, CSA.* Indianapolis: Bobbs-Merrill, 1956.

Gray, John S. "The Lame Deer Fight Ends the Sioux War." *The Westerners Brand Book* (Chicago) 31 (May 1974): 17–19, 23–24.

———. "What Made Johnnie Bruguier Run?" *Montana Western History.* 14 (April 1964): 34–39.

Greene, Jerome A. *Yellowstone Command: Colonel Nelson A. Miles and the Great Sioux War, 1876–1877.* Lincoln: Univ. of Nebraska Press, 1991.

Gresham, John C. "The Story of Wounded Knee." *Harper's Weekly* 35 (Feb. 7, 1891): 106–7.

Gresham, Matilda. *Life of Walter Quintin Gresham, 1832–1895.* 2 vols. Chicago: Rand McNally, 1919.

Guernsey, Alfred H., and Henry M. Alden. *Harper's Pictorial History of the Civil War.* Part 2. New York: Harper and Brothers, 1868. Reprint, New York: Fairfax Press, 1977.

Hagedorn, Herman. *Leonard Wood: A Biography.* 2 vols. New York: Harper and Brothers, 1931.

Hagemann, E. R., ed. *Experiences in the Army Life of Colonel George B. Sanford, 1861–1898.* Norman: Univ. of Oklahoma Press, 1969.

Haley, James L. *The Buffalo War: The History of the Red River Uprising of 1874.* Garden City, N.Y.: Doubleday, 1976.

Haley, John W. *The Rebel Yell and the Yankee Hurrah: The Civil War Journal of a Maine Volunteer.* Edited by Ruth L. Silliker. Camden, Me.: Down East Books, 1977.

Harbaugh, William H. *Power and Responsibility: The Life and Times of Theodore Roosevelt.* New York: Farrar, Straus and Cudahy, 1961.

Harper's Pictorial History of the War with Spain. Intro. Nelson A. Miles. New York: Harper and Brothers, 1899.

Harris, William C. *William Woods Holden: Firebrand of North Carolina.* Baton Rouge: Louisiana State Univ. Press, 1987.

Hassler, Warren W., Jr. *General George B. McClellan: Shield of the Union.* Baton Rouge: Louisiana State Univ. Press, 1957.

Heitman, Francis B., comp. *Historical Register and Dictionary of the United States Army.* 2 vols. Washington, D.C., 1903.

Herbert, Walter H. *Fighting Joe Hooker.* Indianapolis: Bobbs-Merrill Co., 1944.

Hermann, Stephen K. *From Yauco to Las Marías.* Boston: Richard G. Badger, 1900.

Hewes, James. "The United States Army General Staff, 1900–1917." *Military Affairs* 38 (April 1974): 67–72.

Heywood, William S. *History of Westminster, Massachusetts, 1728–1893.* Lowell, Mass.: Vox Populi Press, 1893.

Howard, Oliver O. *Autobiography of Oliver Otis Howard, Major General, United States Army.* 2 vols. New York: Baker and Taylor Co., 1908.

———. *My Life and Experiences Among Our Hostile Indians.* Hartford, Conn.: A. D. Worthington and Co., 1907.

———. *Nez Perce Joseph.* Boston: Lee and Shepard, 1881. Reprint, New York: Da Capo Press, 1972.

Hough, Alfred Lacey. "A Winter Campaign against the Sioux." Edited by Robert G. Athearn. *Mississippi Valley Historical Review.* 35 (September 1948): 272–84.

Humphreys, Andrew A. *The Virginia Campaign of '64 and '65: The Army of the Potomac and the Army of the James.* New York: Charles Scribner's Sons, 1883.

Huntington, Samuel P. *The Soldier and the State.* New York: Random House, Vintage Books, 1957.

Hutton, Paul Andrew. *Phil Sheridan and His Army.* Lincoln: Univ. of Nebraska Press, 1985.

———, ed. *Soldiers West: Biographies from the Military Frontier.* Lincoln: Univ. of Nebraska Press, 1987.

James, Henry. *Richard Olney and His Public Service.* Boston: Houghton Mifflin, 1923.

Jessup, Philip C. *Elihu Root.* 2 vols. New York: Dodd, Mead, 1938.

Johnson, Virginia. *The Unregimented General: A Biography of Nelson A. Miles.* Boston: Houghton Mifflin, 1962.

Jones, Paul. *The Irish Brigade.* Washington, D.C.: Robert B. Luce, Inc., 1969.

Jorden, David M. *Winfield Scott Hancock: A Soldier's Life.* Bloomington: Indiana Univ. Press, 1988.

Joseph, Chief. "An Indian's View of Indian Affairs." *North American Review* 128 (1879): 412–33.

Josephson, Matthew. *The Politicos, 1865–1896.* New York: Harcourt Brace, 1938.

Josephy, Alvin M. *The Nez Perce Indians and the Opening of the Northwest.* New Haven: Yale Univ. Press, 1965.

Keegan, Thomas. *Fields of Battle: The Wars for North America.* NewYork: Alfred A. Knopf, 1996.

Kelly, Luther S. *Memoirs of Luther S. Kelly.* Edited by Milo M. Quaife, New Haven: Yale Univ. Press, 1926.

Kelly, Roger E. "Talking Mirrors versus the Indians." *Frontier Times* 44 (Dec.–Jan. 1970): 20–21, 58–60.

Kennon, Lyman W. V. "The Case of the Chiricahuas." *North American Review* 151 (1890): 251–53.

King, James T. "George Crook, Indian Fighter and Humanitarian." *Arizona and the West* 9 (1967): 333–48.

———. "Needed: A Re-evaluation of General George Crook." *Nebraska History* 45 (1964): 223–35.

———. *War Eagle: A Life of General Eugene A. Carr.* Lincoln: Univ. of Nebraska Press, 1963.

Kohlsaat, Herman H. *From McKinley to Harding: Personal Recollections of Our Presidents.* New York: Charles Scribner's Sons, 1923.

Kraft, Barbara. *The Peace Ship: Henry Ford's Pacifist Adventure in the First World War.* New York: Macmillan, 1978.

Lamb's Biographical Dictionary of the United States. 1900.

Lavender, David. *Let Me Be Free: The Nez Perce Tragedy.* New York: Harper Collins, 1992.

Leech, Margaret. *In the Days of McKinley.* New York: Harper, 1959. Reprint, Westport, Conn.: Greenwood Press, 1975.

Lefler, Hugh T., and Albert R. Newsome. *The History of a Southern State: North Carolina.* 3d ed. Chapel Hill: Univ. of North Carolina Press, 1973.

Leonard, Thomas C. "The Reluctant Conquerors." *American Heritage* 27 (August 1976): 34–41.

Lindsey, Almont. *The Pullman Strike: The Story of a Unique Experiment and of a Great Labor Upheaval.* Chicago: Univ. of Chicago Press, 1942.

Lodge, Henry Cabot. *Selections from the Correspondence of Theodore Roosevelt and Henry Cabot Lodge.* 2 vols. New York: Charles Scribner's Sons, 1925.

Lummis, Charles F. *Charles Fletcher Lummis Reports on an Apache War.* Edited and annotated by Dan L. Thrapp. Norman: Univ. of Oklahoma Press, 1979.

McDonough, James L. *Schofield: Union General in the Civil War and Reconstruction.* Tallahassee: Florida State Univ. Press, 1972.

McElroy, Robert. *Jefferson Davis.* 2 vols. New York: Harper and Brothers, 1937.

McFeely, William. *Grant: A Biography.* New York: W. W. Norton, 1981.

McGregor, James H. *The Wounded Knee Massacre from the Viewpoint of the Sioux.* Baltimore: Wirth Brothers, 1940.

McLaughlin, James. *My Friend the Indian.* Boston: Houghton Mifflin Co., 1910.

McWhorter, Lucullus. *Hear Me, My Chief! Nez Perce History and Legend.* Edited by Ruth Bordin. Caldwell, Idaho: Claxton Printers, 1952.

———. *Yellow Wolf: His Own Story.* Caldwell, Idaho: Claxton Printers, 1940.

Madsen, Brigham D. *The Bannocks of Idaho.* Caldwell, Idaho: Claxton Printers, 1958.

Marshall, Samuel L. A. *Crimsoned Prairie.* New York: Charles Scribner's Sons, 1972.

"Medical Statistics of the Spanish Army, 1896." *Journal of the Military Service Institution of the United States* 25 (1899): 434–35.

Meredith, Grace. *Girl Captives of the Cheyennes.* Los Angeles: Gem Publishing, 1927.

Merrill, James M. *William Tecumseh Sherman.* Chicago: Rand McNally, 1971.

Miles, Mary Sherman Miles [Mrs. Nelson A.]. "What Shall the Soldier's Wife Do?" *Harper's Bazaar* 33 (Sept. 8, 1902): 1207.

Miles, Nelson A. "The Future of the Indian Question." *North American Review* 152 (Jan. 1891): 1–10.

———. "General Meade Anniversary Banquet." *Pennsylvania Magazine of History* 35 (Jan. 1911): 28–31.

———. "The Indian Problem: The Lessons of the Recent Strikes." *North American Review* 159 (Aug. 1894): 180–88.

———. "My Treatment of Jefferson Davis." *Independent* 58 (Feb. 23, 1905): 413–17.

———. *Personal Recollections and Observations of General Nelson A. Miles . . .* Chicago: Werner Co., 1896.

———. *Serving the Republic: Memoirs of the Civil and Military Life of Nelson A. Miles, Lieutenant General.* New York: Harper and Brothers, 1911.

———. "The War with Spain." Parts 1, 2, and 3. *North American Review* 168 (May 1899): 513–29; (June 1899): 749–60; and 169 (July 1899): 125–37.

Miller, Stuart Creighton. *Benevolent Assimilation: The American Conquest of the Philippines, 1899–1903.* New Haven: Yale Univ. Press, 1982.

Montgomery, Mrs. Frank C. "Fort Wallace and Its Relation to the Frontier." In *Collections of the Kansas State Historical Society, 1926–1928.* Edited by William E. Connelley, 189–238. Topeka: Kansas State Print Plant, 1928.

Mooney, James. *The Ghost Dance Religion and the Sioux Outbreak of 1890.* 14th Annual Report of the Bureau of Ethnology, 1892–93, pt. 2. Washington, 1896. Reprint, Glorietta, N.M.: Rio Grande Press, 1973.

Moore, John W. *History of North Carolina from the Earliest Discoveries to the Present Time.* Raleigh: Alfred William Co., 1880.

Moore, Powell A. *The Calumet Region: Indiana's Last Frontier.* N.p.: Indiana Historical Bureau, 1959.

Morris, Charles. *Heroes of the Army in America.* Philadelphia: J. B. Lippincott Co., 1919.

Mulford, Ami Frank. *In the Seventh United States Cavalry: Custer's Favorite Regiment.* Corning, N.Y.: P. L. Mulford, 1879. Reprint, Fairfield, Wash.: Ye Galleon Press, 1972.

Nevins, Allan. *Grover Cleveland: A Study in Courage.* New York: Dodd, Mead, 1933.

O'Connor, Richard. *The Spirit Soldiers: A Historical Narrative of the Boxer Rebellion.* New York: G. P. Putnam's Sons, 1973.

O'Toole, George J. A. *The Spanish War.* New York: W. W. Norton, 1984.

Palmer, John McCaley. *America in Arms: The Experiences of the United States with Military Organization.* New Haven: Yale Univ. Press, 1941.

Parker, James. "The Geronimo Campaign." In *Proceedings of the Meeting and Dinner of the Order of Indian Wars of the United States,* 32–44. Washington, D.C.: 1929.

Parker, John L. *History of the 22nd Massachusetts Infantry, 2nd Company Sharpshooters, and 3rd Light Battery in the War of the Rebellion.* Boston: Rand Avery Co., 1887.

———. *The Old Army.* Philadelphia: Dorrance and Co., 1929.

Pearson, Henry G. *The Life of John J. Andrews, Governor of Massachusetts, 1861–1865.* 2 vols. Boston: Houghton Mifflin, 1904.

Pfaller, Louis. *Guide to the Microfilm Edition of Major James McLaughlin Papers.* Richardton, N.D.: Assumption College, 1969.

Pierce, Richard D. *The Most Promising Young Officer: The Life of Ranald Slidell Mackenzie.* Norman: Univ. of Oklahoma Press, 1993.

Pohanka, Brian C., ed. *Nelson A. Miles: A Documentary Biography of His Military Career, 1861–1903.* Glendale, Calif.: Arthur H. Clark, 1985.

Pond, George E. "Major-General Nelson A. Miles." *McClure's Magazine* 5 (Nov. 1895): 562–74.

Porter, Joseph C. *Paper Medicine Man: John Gregory Bourke and His American West.* Norman: Univ. of Oklahoma Press, 1986.

Powers, Samuel Leland. *Portraits of a Half Century.* Boston: Little, Brown, 1925.

Pringle, Henry F. *Theodore Roosevelt: A Biography.* New York:Harcourt Brace, 1931. Reprint, San Diego: Harcourt Brace Jovanovich, 1956.

Pullen, John J. *A Shower of Stars: The Medal of Honor and the Twenty-Seventh Maine.* Philadelphia: J. B. Lippincott, 1966.

Ranson, Edward. "Nelson A. Miles as Commanding General, 1895–1903." *Military Affairs* 39 (Winter 1965–66): 179–200.

Rawley, James A. *Turning Points of the Civil War.* Lincoln: Univ. of Nebraska Press, 1966.

The Reader's Encyclopedia of the American West. 1977 ed.

Records of Living Officers of the United States Army. Philadelphia: L. R. Hamersly and Co., 1884.

Reid, Jasper B., Jr. "Russell A. Alger as Secretary of War." *Michigan History* 43 (June 1959): 225–39.

Remington, Frederic. "Chicago under the Mob." *Harper's Weekly,* July 21, 1894, 680–81.

———. *The Collected Writings of Frederic Remington.* Edited by Peggy and Harold Samuels. Garden City, N.Y.: Doubleday and Co., 1979.

Rister, Carl. *Border Command: General Philip Sheridan in the West.* Norman: Univ. of Oklahoma Press, 1944.

Rickey, Don, Jr. "Battle of Wolf Mountain." *Montana: The Magazine of Western History* 13 (April 1963): 44–54.

Robertson, Robert S. *From the Wilderness to Spottsylvania: A Paper Read before the Ohio Commandry of the Military Order of the Loyal Legion of the United States.* Cincinnati: Robert Clarke and Co., 1888.

Rolack, Bruno J. "General Miles' Mirrors: The Heliograph in the Geronimo Campaign of 1886." *Journal of Arizona History* 16 (Summer 1975): 145–60.

Romeyn, Henry. "The Capture of Chief Joseph and the Nez Perce Indians." *Collections of the Historical Society of Montana* 2 (1896): 283–91.

Roosevelt, Theodore. *The Letters of Theodore Roosevelt.* Edited by E. Elting Morison et al. 8 vols. Cambridge, Mass.: Harvard Univ. Press, 1951–54.

Roper, Horace W. *William H. Holden: North Carolina's Political Enigma.* Chapel Hill: Univ. of North Carolina Press, 1985.

Russell, Don. *The Lives and Legend of Buffalo Bill.* Norman: Univ. of Oklahoma Press, 1960.

Sandoz, Mari. *Crazy Horse: The Strong Man of the Oglalas.* 1942. Reprint ed. Lincoln: Univ. of Nebraska Press, 1961.

Schellie, Don. "The Day Tucson Honored the 'Man Who Captured Geronimo.'" *The Westerners Brand Book* (Tucson)22 (Fall 1970): 38–43.

Schofield, John M. *Forty-Six Years in the Army.* New York: Century, 1897.

Schurz, Carl. *The Reminiscences of Carl Schurz.* 3 vols. New York: McClure Co., 1908.

Schutz, Wallace J., and Walter N. Trenerry. *Abandoned by Lincoln: A Military Biography of General John Pope.* Urbana: Univ. of Illinois Press, 1990.

Sears, Stephen W. *Landscape Turned Red: The Battle of Antietam.* New Haven: Ticknor and Fields, 1983.

Sefton, James E. *The United States Army and Reconstruction,1867–1877.* Baton Rouge: Louisiana State Univ. Press, 1967.

Semsch, Philip L. "Elihu Root and the General Staff." *Military Affairs* 27 (Spring 1963): 16–27.

Seymour, Charles G. "General Miles on the Campaign" and "The Final Review." *Harper's Weekly* 35 (Feb. 7, 1891): 106.

Seymour, Flora W. *Indian Agents of the Old Frontier.* New York: Appleton, 1941.

Sherman, William, and Philip Henry Sheridan. *Travel Accounts of General William T. Sherman to Spokane Falls, Washington Territory, in the Summers of 1877 and 1883.* 1878. Fairfield, Wash.: Ye Galleon Press, 1984.

Shockley, Philip M. *The Krag-Jorgensen Rifle in the Service.* Aledo, Ill.: World-Wide Gun Report, 1960.

Sievers, Harry J. *Benjamin Harrison, Hoosier President.* Indianapolis: Bobbs-Merrill, 1968.

Slayden, Ellen M. *Washington Wife: Journal of Ellen Maury Slayden.* New York: Harper and Row, 1962.

Smythe, Donald. John J. *Pershing: General of the Armies.* Bloomington: Univ. of Indiana Press, 1989.

Stackpole, Edward J. *Chancellorsville, Lee's Greatest Battle.* Harrisburg, Pa.: Stackpole, 1958.

———. *Drama on the Rappahannock: The Fredericksburg Campaign.* Harrisburg, Pa.: Military Service Publishing Co., 1957.

Steinbach, Robert H. *A Long March: The Lives of Frank and Alice Baldwin.* Austin: Univ. of Texas Press, 1989.

Steward, Thomas J., comp. *Record of Pennsylvania Volunteers in the Spanish-American War.* N.p.: William Stanley Ray, State Printer of Pennsylvania, 1900.

Stewart, Robert L. *History of the One Hundred and Fortieth Regiment, Pennsylvania Volunteers.* Philadelphia: Franklin Bindery, 1912.

Stewart, Theophilus G. *Colored Regulars in the United States Army.* Philadelphia: A.M.E. Book Co., 1904

Strode, Hudson. *Jefferson Davis, Tragic Hero.* 3 vols. New York: Harcourt Brace and World, 1955–64.

Swinton, William. *Campaigns of the Army of the Potomac.* New York: Charles Scribner's Sons, 1882.

Taylor, Joe F., ed. "The Indian Campaign on the Staked Plains, 1874–1875: Military Correspondence from the War Department Adjutant General's Office File 1815–1874." Parts 1 and 2. *Panhandle Plains Historical Review* 34 (1961): 7–216; (1962): 220–368.

Thomas, Benjamin P., and Harold M. Hyman, *Stanton: The Life and Times of Lincoln's Secretary of War.* New York: Alfred A. Knopf, 1962.

Thorndike, Rachel Sherman, ed. *The Sherman Letters: Correspondence between General and Senator Sherman from 1837 to 1891.* New York: Charles Scribner's Sons, 1894.

Thrapp, Dan. L. *The Conquest of Apacheria.* Norman: Univ. of Oklahoma Press, 1967.

Tilton, Henry [Remsen]. "After the Nez Perces." *Forest and Stream and Rod and Gun* 9 (Dec. 27, 1877): 403–4.

Titus, Nelson C. "The Last Stand of the Nez Perces." *Washington Historical Quarterly* 6 (July 1915): 145–53.

Tolman, Newton F. *The Search for General Miles.* New York: G. P. Putnam's Sons, 1968.

Trask, David F. *The War with Spain in 1898.* New York: Macmillan, 1981.

Traub, Peter E. "Sioux Campaign—Winter of 1890–1891." In *Proceedings of the Annual Meeting and Dinner of the Indian Wars of the U.S.* Washington, D.C.: 1926.

Trelease, Allan W. "Republican Reconstruction in North Carolina: A Roll-Call Analysis of the State House of Representatives, 1868–1870." *Journal of Southern History* 42 (1976): 319–44.

Trimble. Marshall. *Arizona: A Panoramic History of a Frontier State.* Garden City, N.Y.: Doubleday, 1977.

Turner, John P. *The North-West Mounted Police, 1873–93.* 2 vols. Ottawa: Ed Cloutier, King's Printer and Controller of Stationery, 1950.

Ullery, Jacob G., comp. *Men of Vermont: An Illustrated Biographical History of Vermonters and Sons of Vermont.* Brattleboro, Vt.: Transcript Publishing Co., 1894.

"United States Magazine Rifle." *Scientific American Supplement* 46 (July 9, 1898): 44.

Utley, Robert M. "Crook and Miles: Fighting and Feuding on the Indian Frontier." *MHQ: The Quarterly Journal of Military History* 2 (Autumn 1989): 81–91.

———. *Frontier Regulars: The United States Army and the Indians, 1866–1891.* New York: Macmillan, 1973.

———. "Geronimo." *MHQ: The Quarterly Journal of Military History* 4 (Winter 1992): 42–51.

———. *The Lance and the Shield: The Life and Times of Sitting Bull.* New York: Henry Holt, 1993.

———. *The Last Days of the Sioux Nation.* New Haven: Yale Univ. Press, 1963.

———. "Nelson A. Miles." In *Soldiers West: Biographies from the Military Frontier,* ed. Paul Andrew Hutton. Lincoln: Univ. of Nebraska Press, 1987.

———. "Sitting Bull." *MHQ: The Quarterly Journal of Military History* 5 (Summer 1993): 48–59.

Vandiver, Frank E. *Black Jack: The Life and Times of John J. Pershing.* 2 vols. College Station: Texas A&M Univ. Press, 1977.

———. *The Mighty Stonewall.* New York: McGraw Hill, 1957.

Vestal, Stanley. *Sitting Bull, Champion of the Sioux.* Boston: Houghton Mifflin, 1932.

Vinton, Lawrence. "The Geronimo Campaign: As Told by a Trooper of 'B' Troop of the 4th U.S. Cavalry." *Journal of the West* 11 (Jan. 1972): 157–65.

Wagner, Arthur L. *Report of the Santiago Campaign, 1898.* Kansas City, Mo.: Franklin Hudson Publishing, 1908.

Walker, Francis A. *General Hancock.* New York: Appleton, 1894.

———. *History of the Second Army Corps in the Army of the Potomac.* New York: Charles A. Scribner's Sons, 1886.

Warner, Ezra T. *Generals in Blue: Lives of the Union Commanders.* Baton Rouge: Louisiana State Univ. Press, 1964.

Webster's American Biographies. Rev. ed., 1974.

Weigley, Russell F. "The Elihu Root Reforms and the Progressive Era." In *Command and Commanders in Modern Warfare: The Proceedings of the Second Military History Symposium, U.S. Air Force Academy, 2–3 May 1968,* edited by William Geffen. Office of Air Force History and U.S. Air Force Academy, 1971.

———. *History of the United States Army.* New York: Macmillan, 1967.

Weland, Gerald. *O. O. Howard, Union General.* Jefferson, N.C.: McFarland and Co., 1995.

Welch, Richard E., Jr. "American Atrocities in the Philippines: The Indictment and the Response." *Pacific Historical Review* 43 (May 1974): 233–53.

Wells, Mildred White. *United in Diversity.* Washington, D.C.: General Federation of Women's Clubs, 1975.

White, Lonnie J., ed. *The Miles Expedition of 1874–1875: An Eye Witness Account of the Red River War by Scout J. T. Marshall.* Austin: Encino Press, 1971.

Williams, Michael. *The Shadow of the Pope.* New York: McGraw Hill, 1932.

Williams, T. Harry. *The History of American Wars.* New York: Alfred A. Knopf, 1981.

———, ed. *Hayes: The Diary of a President, 1875–1881.* New York: David McKay, 1964.

Wilson, James H. *Under the Old Flag: Recollections of Military Operations in the War for the Union, the Boxer Rebellion, etc.* 2 vols. New York: Appleton, 1912.

Wolf, Leon. *Little Brown Brother: How the United States Purchased and Pacified the Philippines at the Turn of the Century.* Garden City, N.Y.: Doubleday, 1961.

Wood, Frederick S. *Roosevelt As We Knew Him: The Personal Recollections of One Hundred and Fifty of His Friends and Associates.* Philadelphia: John C. Winston, 1927.

Woodman, Harold D. "Sequel to Slavery: The New History Views the Postbellum South." *Journal of Southern History* 43 (1977): 523–54.

Wooster, Robert. *Nelson A. Miles and the Twilight of the Frontier Army.* Lincoln: Univ. of Nebraska Press, 1993.

———. "Nelson Miles and the Twilight of the Old Army." *New Mexico Historical Review* 66 (Jan. 1991): 33–47.

Worcester, Donald E. *The Apaches: Eagles of the Southwest.* Norman: Univ. of Oklahoma Press, 1979.

Wyllie, Robert E. *Orders, Decorations and Insignia.* New York: G. P. Putnam's Sons, 1921.

Zuber, Richard L. *Jonathan Worth: A Biography of a Southern Unionist.* Chapel Hill: Univ. of North Carolina Press, 1965.

Unpublished Works

"Biographical Sketches of General Officers in World War II." N.p., n.d. Archives, United States Military Academy, West Point, N.Y. (typewritten).

Kirkland, John R. "Federal Troops in the South Atlantic States during Reconstruction, 1865–1877." Ph.D. diss., Univ. of North Carolina, 1967.

Roper, Horace W. "William Woods Holden: A Political Biography." Ph.D. diss., Univ. of North Carolina, 1951.

Index

A HERO TO HIS FIGHTING MEN

was composed in 11/14 Adobe Garamond on a Power Macintosh using PageMaker 6.5

at The Kent State University Press;

printed by sheet-fed offset on 50-pound Lions Falls Turin Book Natural stock

(an acid-free, totally chlorine-free paper),

Smyth sewn and bound over binder's boards in ICG Kennett cloth,

and wrapped with dust jackets printed in three colors on

100-pound enamel stock by Thomson-Shore, Inc.;

designed by Diana Dickson;

and published by

THE KENT STATE UNIVERSITY PRESS

Kent, Ohio 44242